DIRECTORY OF U.S. LABOR
ORGANIZATIONS

DIRECTORY OF U.S. LABOR ORGANIZATIONS

2006 Edition

Court Gifford
Editor

The Bureau of National Affairs, Inc. Washington, D.C. 20037

Published by BNA Books
1231 25th St., NW, Washington, DC 20037

http://www.bnabooks.com

International Standard Serial Number: 0734-6786
International Standard Book Numbers: 1-57018-564-6; 978-1-57018-564-9

Printed in Canada

Preface

This 2006 edition of the directory captures a year of monumental change in the American labor movement. For the first time since the formation of the AFL-CIO in 1955, a half-dozen unions split away in 2005 to form a new labor alliance called Coalition to Win. Coalition leaders hope to ignite a period of significant growth in U.S. union membership, a goal that is shared by the AFL-CIO.

The directory provides a basic overview of organized labor's structure, composition, and leadership, including the leadership of the AFL-CIO and the Coalition. Approximately 30,000 local, intermediate, state, and national labor organizations, representing millions of workers in the private and public sectors, are also identified in this edition.

Membership figures for the national unions listed in Part II are taken directly from the annual financial reports filed by the unions with the U.S. Labor Department in accordance with the Labor-Management Reporting and Disclosure Act and the Civil Service Reform Act. Part III identifies unions at the state and local levels that are affiliated with national unions or are independent.

Local and intermediate union bodies identified in Part III are arranged alphabetically by state and by union within each state, the District of Columbia, and U.S. territories and possessions. The location shown for each union indicates the state (or other jurisdiction) and the city where that union operates.

Some independent unions that represent municipal or state public employees exclusively are not required to file reports with the federal government and, therefore, may not be included.

Union membership figures in the Introduction are estimates compiled annually by the U.S. Department of Labor's Bureau of Labor Statistics. The estimates are obtained from the Current Population Survey, which provides basic information on the labor force, employment, and unemployment. The survey is conducted monthly for the BLS by the U.S. Census Bureau from a scientifically selected national sample of about 60,000 households.

Union membership has been trending downward for several decades, but there are indications that American attitudes toward unions are improving. An analysis of elections supervised by the National Labor Relations Board in 2005 by the Bureau of National Affairs, Inc., shows that unions are winning more representation elections than in the past.

Unions are complex and diverse organizations that serve the interests of millions of American workers. Growth is necessary for their survival. While recruitment is primarily the responsibility of individual unions, the AFL-CIO and the Coalition can play a supporting role by helping to reshape organized labor's image in a way that will resonate with American workers.

Contents

Part I. Introduction

Union Membership and Earnings

Union membership in the United States in 2005 rose by 213,000 members to 15.7 million across the economy, but membership as a percentage of the wage and salary workforce remained at 12.5 percent, the same as in 2004.

The year was marked by turmoil within the leadership ranks of the AFL-CIO that resulted in the loss of six affiliated unions and the formation of the Coalition to Win, a new labor federation that set membership growth as its first priority.

The data compiled by the U.S. Bureau of Labor Statistics shows that union membership grew by more than 200,000 for the first time since 1999 when unions added 265,000 net members. But the boost did not change the percentage of the workforce that belonged to unions, despite the addition of 2.3 million new jobs to the economy. Union membership as a percentage of the workforce reached its highest point, 20.1 percent, in 1983, the first year BLS began compiling comparable data. The total number of employed wage and salary workers was 125,889,000 in 2005, compared to 88,290,000 in 1983. The figures are based on an annual household survey conducted by the U.S. Census Bureau.

Median weekly earnings of full-time wage and salary workers 16 years and older by selected characteristics, 2005

(Numbers in thousands)

Characteristic	Total	Union Members	Non-Union
Total	$651	$801	$622
Men	$722	$857	$692
Women	$585	$731	$559
White	$672	$830	$641
Black or African American	$520	$656	$500
Asian	$753	$809	$744
Hispanic or Latino ethnicity	$471	$673	$449

See Appendix A, Table 2 for full details

Source: U.S. Bureau of Labor Statistics

About 7.8 percent of private industry wage earners belonged to unions in 2005, slightly below the 7.9 percent figure for 2004. Private-sector transportation and utilities continued to have the highest union membership rate at 24 percent, down from 24.9 percent in 2004 and 26.2 percent in 2003. Employment in transportation and utilities overall increased by about 319,000.

Union membership rates among professional wage and salary workers rose slightly from 18.2 percent in 2004 to 18.4 percent in 2005. Workers in education, training, and library occupations were the most organized group within this category at 38.5 percent in 2005.

In the service sector, 37 percent of protective service workers belonged to unions in 2005. Union membership among the category that includes natural resources, construction, and maintenance occupations fell from 18.4 percent in 2004 to 16.5 percent in 2005.

Other private industry sectors with traditionally higher-than-average union membership rates also experienced declines. They include construction, which dropped from 14.7 percent in 2004 to 13.1 percent in 2005, and information, which fell from 14.2 percent to 13.6. After falling from 13.5 percent in 2003 to 12.9 percent in 2004, manufacturing

Union affiliation of employed wage and salary workers 16 years and over by selected characteristics, 2005

(Numbers in thousands)

Characteristic	Total Employed	Union Members	Percent of Employed
Total	125,889	15,685	12.5
Men	65,466	8,870	13.5
Women	60,423	6,815	11.3
White	102,967	12,520	12.2
Black or African American	14,459	2,178	15.1
Asian	5,479	614	11.2
Hispanic or Latino ethnicity	17,191	1,793	10.4
Full-time	103,560	14,207	13.7
Part-time	22,052	1,441	6.5

See Appendix A, Table 1 for full details

Source: U.S. Bureau of Labor Statistics

grew to 13.0 percent in 2005, while total manufacturing employment in the same year fell by 236,000.

At 36.5 percent in 2005, the organized sector of the public workforce remained essentially unchanged from a year earlier. Local government workers had the highest union membership rate, 41.9 percent. This group includes teachers, police officers, and fire fighters.

Union workers' pay continued to exceed that of nonunion workers in 2005. Full-time wage and salary workers who were union members had median usual weekly earnings of $801 in 2005, up from $781 in 2004 and $760 the previous year, compared with a median of $622 in 2005 for nonunion wage and salary workers, up from $612 the year before and $599 the year before that. The difference was due mainly to the coverage of union workers by collective bargaining agreements negotiated by their unions.

A breakdown of 2005 earnings shows that union members in the private sector earned a median weekly income of $757, while non-union members earned $615. In the public sector, union members had a median weekly income of $850, compared with $692 for non-union public employees.

Legal occupations covered by collective bargaining agreements had the highest median weekly earnings of $1,155, compared to $1,042 among non-union workers in this category. In service occupations, non-union workers earned $392 weekly, while union members earned $643 weekly. The service category includes healthcare, protective service, food preparation, cleaning and maintenance, and personal care occupations.

About 1.5 million workers were entitled to union benefits at their workplace in 2005, but were not dues-paying union members, down slightly from 1.6 million in 2004. More than half of them were employed by the government.

In 2005, union membership rates were 13.5 percent for men, 11.3 percent for women, 15.1 percent for blacks, 12.2 percent for whites, 11.2 percent for Asians, and 10.4 percent for Hispanics or Latinos. Among age groups, union membership rates were highest among workers 45 to 54 years old, 16.5 percent, and were lowest among ages 16 to 24 years old, 4.6 percent. Full-time workers were more than twice as likely as part-time workers to be union members, 13.7 percent and 6.5 percent respectively.

Union Membership by State

On a state-by-state basis, 19 states had union membership rates above the U.S. average of 12.5 percent, while 31 states and the District of Columbia had lower rates. Five states had union membership rates over 20 percent in 2005: New York, 26.1 percent; Hawaii, 25.8 percent; Alaska, 22.8 percent; Michigan and New Jersey, both 20.5 percent. All but New Jersey have had rates above 20 percent every year since data became regularly available in 1995, according to BLS.

North Carolina and South Carolina continued to report the lowest union membership rates, 2.9 percent and 2.3 percent, respectively. These two states have had the lowest union membership rates each year since the state series became available. Five states reported union membership rates below 5.0 percent in 2005. In addition to North Carolina and South Carolina, the states were Arkansas and Virginia, 4.8 percent each, followed by Utah, at 4.9 percent.

The states with more than 2 million union members in 2005 were California, 2.4 million, and New York, 2.1 million. About half (7.9 million) of the 15.7 million union members in the U.S. lived in six states (California, New York, Michigan, Illinois, New Jersey, and Ohio), although these states accounted for slightly less than one-third of wage and salary employment nationally, according to BLS.

Union affiliation of employed wage and salary workers by industry, 2005

(Numbers in thousands)

Industry	Total Employed	Union Members	Percent of Employed
Private sector	105,508	8,255	7.8
Public sector	20,381	7,430	36.5
Federal government	3,427	954	27.8
State government	5,874	1,838	31.3
Local government	11,080	4,638	41.9

See Appendix A, Table 3 for full details

Source: U.S. Bureau of Labor Statistics

All states in the Middle Atlantic and Pacific divisions had union membership rates above the national average, while all states in the East South Central and West South Central divisions continued to have rates below it. Over the year, 24 states and the District of Columbia reported declining membership rates, 23 states recorded higher rates, and 3 states had no change.

Largest Unions

With 2.7 million members, the National Education Association tops the list of largest unions, according to financial disclosure reports filed annually with the U.S. Department of Labor. NEA is one of five labor organizations that reported more than 1 million members in 2005.

Other unions with more than a million members in 2005 were the Service Employees International Union, 1.7 million; American Federation of State, County and Municipal Employees, 1.4 million; International Brotherhood of Teamsters, 1.4 million; and United Food and Commercial Workers International Union, 1.3 million.

With the withdrawal of six unions from the AFL-CIO announced in 2005, including the SEIU, IBT, UFCW, UNITE HERE, Laborers' International Union, and the United Farm Workers, membership in unions affiliated with the AFL-CIO sank by approximately 4 million members, and left AFSCME as the largest union within the federation. It was followed by the American Federation of Teachers, with 828,500 members.

Total membership of the unions affiliated with the AFL-CIO prior to the break-up was approximately 13 million. As of July 2006, that figure had dropped to approximately 9 million.

AFL-CIO

The majority of national and international unions in the U.S. are affiliated with the American Federation of Labor-Congress of Industrial Organizations, commonly referred to as the AFL-CIO. The federation serves as labor's lobbying representative before the U.S. Congress and state legislatures, reinforcing the lobbying activities of individual

Union Membership, Ranked by State, 2005

New York	26.1%
Hawaii	25.8%
Alaska	22.8%
Michigan	20.5%
New Jersey	20.5%
Washington	19.1%
Illinois	16.9%
California	16.5%
Wisconsin	16.1%
Ohio	16.0%
Connecticut	15.9%
Rhode Island	15.9%
Minnesota	15.7%
Oregon	14.5%
West Virginia	14.4%
Massachusetts	13.9%
Nevada	13.8%
Pennsylvania	13.8%
Maryland	13.3%
Indiana	12.4%
Maine	11.9%
Delaware	11.8%
Iowa	11.5%
Missouri	11.5%
District of Columbia	11.3%
Vermont	10.8%
Montana	10.7%
New Hampshire	10.4%
Alabama	10.2%
Kentucky	9.7%
Colorado	8.3%
Nebraska	8.3%
New Mexico	8.1%
Wyoming	7.9%
North Dakota	7.3%
Mississippi	7.1%
Kansas	7.0%
Louisiana	6.4%
Arizona	6.1%
South Dakota	5.9%
Florida	5.4%
Oklahoma	5.4%
Tennessee	5.4%
Texas	5.3%
Idaho	5.2%
Georgia	5.0%
Utah	4.9%
Arkansas	4.8%
Virginia	4.8%
North Carolina	2.9%
South Carolina	2.3%

Source: U.S. Bureau of Labor Statistics

Unions With 100,000 Members or More, 2005

2,731,419	National Education Association
1,702,639	Service Employees International Union
1,350,000	American Federation of State, County and Municipal Employees
1,350,000	International Brotherhood of Teamsters
1,338,625	United Food and Commercial Workers International Union
828,512	American Federation of Teachers
704,794	International Brotherhood of Electrical Workers
692,558	Laborers' International Union of North America
654,657	International Union, United Automobile, Aerospace and Agricultural Implement Workers of America
610,426	International Association of Machinists and Aerospace Workers
545,638	Communications Workers of America
535,461	United Steel, Paper and Forestry, Rubber, Manufacturing, Energy, Allied Industrial and Service Workers International Union
524,237	United Brotherhood of Carpenters and Joiners of America
441,276	UNITE HERE
388,804	International Union of Operating Engineers
357,000	National Postal Mail Handlers Union
324,043	United Association of Journeymen and Apprentices of the Plumbing and Pipe Fitting Industry of the United States and Canada
292,221	National Association of Letter Carriers
271,463	International Association of Fire Fighters
227,425	American Postal Workers Union
226,599	American Federation of Government Employees
180,598	Amalgamated Transit Union
148,799	United American Nurses
144,480	Sheet Metal Workers International Association
128,351	International Union of Painters and Allied Trades
125,437	International Association of Bridge, Structural, Ornamental and Reinforcing Iron Workers
125,398	Transport Workers Union of America
109,188	American Association of Classified School Employees
107,541	Screen Actors Guild
107,452	Bakery, Confectionery, Tobacco Workers and Grain Millers International Union
105,460	National Rural Letter Carriers' Association
105,180	International Alliance of Theatrical Stage Employes, Moving Picture Technicians, Artists and Allied Crafts of the United States and Canada
100,609	United Mine Workers of America

Source: U.S. Department of Labor

unions. It also acts as a watchdog over state and federal regulatory activities, and as American labor's representative in national and international forums. The federation also disseminates labor policy developed by leaders of its affiliated unions, assists in coordinating organizing among its affiliates, and provides research and other assistance through its various departments.

Some affiliated unions are called "international" unions because they have members in both the United States and Canada. But Canada has a labor federation of its own, the Canadian Labour Congress (CLC).

Unions affiliated with the AFL-CIO pay per capita dues to support its activities (see Appendix C). The AFL-CIO network (see Part IV) is composed of its national headquarters in Washington, D.C., and four regional divisions. Within the regions are 50 state federations and the Puerto Rico Federation of Labor that function in much the same manner as the national headquarters by lobbying for labor's interests in the state legislatures and serving as centers to coordinate activities of affiliates. There also are hundreds of central councils to coordinate activities at the local level.

AFL-CIO policy between conventions is set by the Executive Council. The responsibilities of the council include developing positions for labor on major national and international issues, supporting political candidates, proposing and evaluating legislation of interest to the labor movement, assisting unions in organizing and other activities, and resolving jurisdictional disputes among unions.

Another AFL-CIO policy-making body between conventions is the General Board. It consists of the members of the Executive Council and a principal officer of each affiliated international union and department. The General Board acts on matters referred to it by the executive officers or the Executive Council. It meets upon the call of the AFL-CIO president. Unlike members of the Executive Council, General Board members vote as representatives of their unions. Voting strength is based on union membership.

AFL-CIO President John J. Sweeney was first elected to office on October 25, 1995, at the federa-

tion's national convention in New York. Sweeney previously was president of the Service Employees International Union. Sweeney went to work for SEIU Local 32B in New York City in 1960 as a contract director. He later became president of the local and was elected president of the international union in 1980.

AFL-CIO Executive Vice President Linda Chavez-Thompson and Secretary-Treasurer Richard L. Trumka also were first elected to office at the federation's 1995 convention. Chavez-Thompson began working for the Laborers' International Union in Texas. She later worked for the American Federation of State, County and Municipal Employees in San Antonio and was elected international vice president in 1988. Trumka was elected secretary-treasurer while serving his third term as president of the United Mine Workers of America.

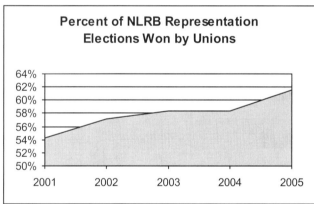

Source: BNA PLUS

Change to Win

Change to Win, a federation of seven unions representing approximately 4 million workers, was formed in 2005. It is made up of six AFL-CIO unions and one former AFL-CIO-affiliated union.

At its founding convention September 27, 2005, in St. Louis, delegates adopted a constitution stipulating that 75 percent of per capita tax paid by the participating unions will be spent on organizing new members.

One of the coalition's first actions was to create a Strategic Organizing Center to develop large-scale organizing campaigns directed at "the more than 50

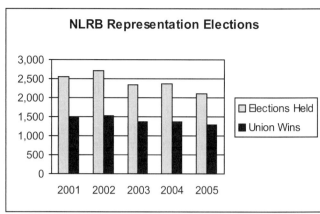

Source: BNA PLUS

million American workers who work in industries that cannot be outsourced or shipped overseas."

The coalition's Leadership Council elected Anna Burger, secretary-treasurer of the Service Employees International Union, as its first chairperson. Burger was elected to the SEIU post in 2001 following nearly 30 years of political and fieldwork for the union. Edgar Romney, an executive vice president of UNITE HERE since 1995, was chosen to serve as treasurer.

Union Elections

Unions prevailed in 61.5 percent of the representation elections certified by the National Labor Relations Board in 2005, up from 58.4 percent in 2004, according to an analysis of NLRB data by the Bureau of National Affairs, Inc. This marked the ninth consecutive year in which unions improved their win rate. Unions have won more than half of all representations elections in each of the past nine

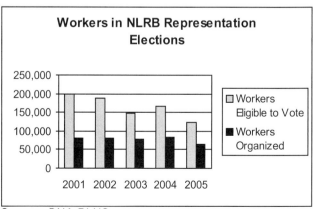

Source: BNA PLUS

years, according to the analysis conducted annually by BNA's research division, BNA PLUS. BNA also reported that 111 unions were decertified during the year, compared with 146 the previous year.

At the same time, the number of union elections certified by the board in 2005 decreased to 2,117 from 2,361 in 2004, continuing an annual decline since 1996. The actual number of elections won by unions also decreased to 1,302 in 2005, compared with 1,380 in 2004. Unions also organized fewer workers during the year through NLRB elections: 63,700, compared with 84,000 the previous year.

Of the 10 most active unions in 2005, the International Brotherhood of Teamsters led all other unions by participating in 555 representation elections, or approximately one-fourth of all NLRB representation elections. The Teamsters was involved in 592 elections in 2004. The win rate, however, rose from 47.1 percent in 2004 to 52.4 percent in 2005.

The other most active unions in terms of the number of elections were the Service Employees International Union, 196 elections; the United Food and Commercial Workers, 160 elections; International Brotherhood of Electrical Workers, 149 elections;

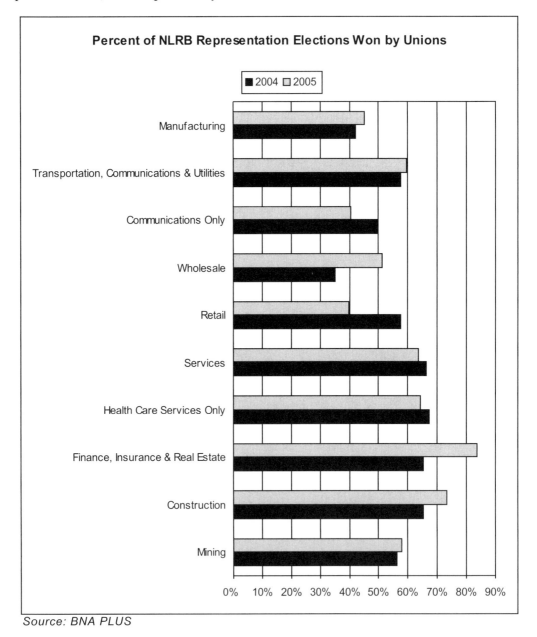

Source: BNA PLUS

Laborers' International Union, 129 elections; International Union of Operating Engineers, 113 elections; International Association of Machinists, 92 elections; United Steelworkers, 72 elections; United Auto Workers, 52 elections; and the Communications Workers of America, 37 elections.

The Laborers' International Union was the most successful of the top 10 unions, winning 72.1 percent of the NLRB-supervised elections in which it participated. SEIU ranked second, winning 69.4 percent of its elections, followed by IAM, 65.2 percent, IUOE, 61.1 percent, and UAW, 59.6 percent.

The NLRB statistics do not reflect the full extent of organizing being done by unions. Many unions organize largely through neutrality and card-check agreements and other methods.

Union Reporting Requirements

Under the Labor-Management Reporting and Disclosure Act of 1959, unions that represent workers in the private sector and the U.S. Postal Service are required to submit annual financial reports to the U.S. Department of Labor's Office of Labor-Management Standards (OLMS). Organizations that represent federal workers must file reports in accordance with the Civil Service Reform Act of 1978 (see Appendix D for the types of reports and requirements). Unions that exclusively represent public employees whose employers are states or political subdivisions of states such as counties or municipalities are not required to file reports with OLMS.

All reports, plus copies of the organization's constitution and bylaws, are public information and may be examined at most of the 33 OLMS field offices located in major U.S. cities or at the OLMS headquarters in Washington, D.C. Copies of reports for the year 2000 and subsequent years may be viewed at the following site:

http://www.union-reports.dol.gov.

Union Member Rights

The law guarantees certain rights to union members and imposes certain responsibilities on union officers. Title I of the Labor-Management Reporting and Disclosure Act (LMRDA) states that union members have equal rights to participate in union activities; freedom of speech and assembly; a voice in setting rates of dues, fees, and assessments; protection of the right to sue; and safeguards against improper discipline. Union members may enforce these rights through private suit in federal court.

Members also are guaranteed the right to receive or inspect copies of collective bargaining agreements, constitutions, bylaws, and financial reports; nominate candidates for union office, run for office, cast a secret ballot, and protest the conduct of an election; and remove an elected officer guilty of serious misconduct. Members also may not be threatened, fined, expelled, or otherwise disciplined for exercising any LMRDA right.

OLMS Field Offices

Staff is available to answer questions about the LMRDA at OLMS offices in the following cities:

City	Phone	City	Phone	City	Phone
Atlanta, GA	(404) 562-2083	Guaynabo, PR	(787) 277-1547	New Haven, CT	(203) 773-2130
Birmingham, AL	(205) 731-0239	Honolulu, HI	(808) 541-2705	New Orleans, LA	(504) 589-6174
Boston, MA	(617) 624-6690	Houston, TX	(713) 718-3755	New York, NY	(646) 264-3190
Buffalo, NY	(716) 842-2900	Indianapolis, IN	(317) 614-0013	Newark, NJ	(732) 750-5661
Chicago, IL	(312) 596-7160	Kansas City, MO	(816) 502-0290	Philadelphia, PA	(215) 861-4818
Cincinnati, OH	(513) 684-6840	Las Vegas, NV	(702) 388-6126	Pittsburgh, PA	(412) 395-6925
Cleveland, OH	(216) 357-5455	Los Angeles, CA	(213) 534-6405	St. Louis, MO	(314) 539-2667
Dallas, TX	(972) 850-2500	Miami, FL	(954) 356-6850	San Francisco, CA	(415) 848-6567
Denver, CO	(720) 264-3231	Milwaukee, WI	(414) 297-1501	Seattle, WA	(206) 398-8099
Detroit, MI	(313) 226-6200	Minneapolis, MN	(612) 370-3111	Tampa, FL	(813) 288-1314
Grand Rapids, MI	(616) 456-2335	Nashville, TN	(615) 736-5906	Washington, DC	(202) 513-7300

Union Member Rights and Officer Responsibilities Under the LMRDA

The Labor-Management Reporting and Disclosure Act (LMRDA) guarantees certain rights to union members and imposes certain responsibilities on union officers. The Office of Labor-Management Standards (OLMS) enforces many LMRDA provisions while other provisions, such as the bill of rights, may only be enforced by union members through private suit in federal court.

Union Member Rights

Bill of Rights   Union members have:
- equal rights to participate in union activities
- freedom of speech and assembly
- voice in setting rates of dues, fees, and assessments
- protection of the right to sue
- safeguards against improper discipline

Copies of Collective Bargaining Agreements   Union members and nonunion employees have the right to receive or inspect copies of collective bargaining agreements.

- Reports - Unions are required to file an initial information report (Form LM-1), copies of constitutions and bylaws, and an annual financial report (Form LM-2/3/4) with OLMS. Unions must make the reports available to members and permit members to examine supporting records for just cause. The reports are public information and copies are available from the OLMS Internet Public Disclosure Room at www.union-reports.dol.gov.

Officer Elections   Union members have the right to:
- nominate candidates for office
- run for office
- cast a secret ballot
- protest the conduct of an election

Officer Removal   Local union members have the right to an adequate procedure for the removal of an elected officer guilty of serious misconduct.

Trusteeships   Unions may only be placed in trusteeship by a parent body for the reasons specified in the LMRDA.

Prohibition Against Certain Discipline   A union or any of its officials may not fine, expel, or otherwise discipline a member for exercising any LMRDA right.

Prohibition Against Violence   No one may use or threaten to use force or violence to interfere with a union member in the exercise of LMRDA rights.

Union Officer Responsibilities

Financial Safeguards   Union officers have a duty to manage the funds and property of the union solely for the benefit of the union and its members in accordance with the union's constitution and bylaws. Union officers or employees who embezzle or steal union funds or other assets commit a Federal crime punishable by a fine and/or imprisonment.

Bonding   Union officers or employees who handle union funds or property must be bonded to provide protection against losses if their union has property and annual financial receipts which exceed $5,000.

Labor Organization Reports   Union officers must:
- file an initial information report (Form LM-1) and annual financial reports (Forms LM-2/3/4) with OLMS.
- retain the records necessary to verify the reports for at least five years.

Officer Reports   Union officers and employees must file reports concerning any loans and benefits received from, or certain financial interests in, employers whose employees their unions represent and businesses that deal with their unions.

Officer Elections   Unions must:
- hold elections of officers of local unions by secret ballot at least every three years

- conduct regular elections in accordance with their constitution and bylaws and preserve all records for one year
- mail a notice of election to every member at least 15 days prior to the election
- comply with a candidate's request to distribute campaign material
- not use union funds or resources to promote any candidate (nor may employer funds or resources be used)
- permit candidates to have election observers
- allow candidates to inspect the union's membership list once within 30 days prior to the election

Restrictions on Holding Office   A person convicted of certain crimes may not serve as a union officer, employee, or other representative of a union for up to 13 years.

Loans   A union may not have outstanding loans to any one officer or employee that in total exceed $2,000 at any time.

Fines   A union may not pay the fine of any officer or employee convicted of any willful violation of the LMRDA.

Source: U.S. Department of Labor

PART II. International, National, and State Unions

Union membership figures, where available, are from the latest Labor Organization Information Reports submitted by the unions to the U.S. Department of Labor's Office of Labor-Management Standards. Membership information was not available from state employee organizations, which are not covered by federal union reporting requirements.

Union acronyms are in brackets.

Actors and Artistes

Associated Actors and Artistes of America [AAAA]
165 W. 46th St., 16th Floor, New York, NY 10036
Phone: (212) 869-0358
Fax: (212) 869-1746
E-mail: actors1919@aol.com
Founded: 1919
Affiliation: AFL-CIO
Membership: 69,000
Note: AAAA is comprised of seven autonomous branches: The Actors' Equity Association (AEA); The American Federation of Television and Radio Artists (AFTRA); The American Guild of Musical Artists (AGMA); The American Guild of Variety Artists (AGVA); The Hebrew Actors' Union (HAU); The Screen Actors Guild (SAG); and The Guild of Italian American Actors (GIAA).
President: Theodore Bikel
Executive Secretary: Kim R. Hedgpath
Treasurer: Thomas Jamerson

Actors' Equity

Actors' Equity Association [AEA]
165 W. 46th St., 15th Floor, New York, NY 10036
Phone: (212) 869-8530
Fax: (212) 719-9815
E-mail: info@actorsequity.org
Web site: www.actorsequity.org
Founded: 1913
Affiliation: AAAA
Membership: 39,397
Publications: *Equity News* (9 times a year)
President: Patrick Quinn
Executive Director: Alan Eisenberg

Agricultural Employees

National Association of Agricultural Employees [NAAE]
P.O. Box 31143, Honolulu, HI 96820-1143
Phone: (808) 861-8449
Fax: (808) 861-8469
Web site: www.aginspectors.org
Founded: 1998
Affiliation: Independent
Membership: 846
National President: Michael Randall
National Vice President: Kathleen Richardson
National Secretary: Sarah Clore
National Treasurer: James Triebwasser

Air Traffic Controllers

National Air Traffic Controllers Association [NATCA]
1325 Massachusetts Ave., NW, Washington, DC 20005
Phone: (202) 628-5451
Fax: (202) 628-5767
E-mail: webstaff@natca.org
Web site: www.natca.org
Founded: 1987
Affiliation: AFL-CIO
Membership: 14,794
Publications: *The Air Traffic Controller* (monthly)
President: John S. Carr
Executive Vice President: Ruth E. Marlin
Regional Vice Presidents:
  Alaskan Region: Ricky Thompson
  Central Region: John Tune
  Eastern Region: Phil Barbarello
  Engineers and Architects: Jim D'Agati
  Great Lakes Region: Pat Forrey
  New England Region: Mike Blake
  Northwest Mountain Region: Carol Branaman
  Southern Region: Andy Cantwell
  Southwest Region: Darrell Meachum
  Western Pacific Region: Robert Marks

Air Traffic Specialists

National Association of Air Traffic Specialists [NAATS]
P.O. Box 2550, Landover Hills, MD 20784
Phone: (201) 459-5595
Fax: (201) 459-5597
E-mail: naatshq@aol.com
Web site: www.naats.org
Founded: 1959
Affiliation: Independent
Membership: 1,146
Publications: *NAATS News* (monthly)
President: Kate Breen
Regional Directors:
  Alaska Region: Phil Brown, III
  Central Region: Jerry Van Vacter
  Eastern Region: Ron Consalvo
  Great Lakes Region: Jack O'Connell
  New England Region: Mike Sheldon
  Northwest Mountain Region: Darrell Mounts
  Southern Region: Richard Anderson
  Southwest Region: Mark Jaffe
  Western Region: Mike Puffer

Aircraft Mechanics

Aircraft Mechanics Fraternal Association [AMFA]
67 Water St., Suite 208A, Laconia, NH 03246
Phone: (603) 527-9212
Toll-Free: (800) 520-2632
Fax: (603) 527-9151
E-mail: admin@amfanatl.org
Web site: www.amfanatl.org
Affiliation: Independent
Membership: 16,368
Director: O.V. Delle-Femine
Secretary: Steve Nowak
Treasurer: Doug Butz

Asbestos Workers

International Association of Heat and Frost Insulators and Asbestos Workers [HFIA]
9602 Martin Luther King, Jr. Hwy., Lanham, MD 20706
Phone: (301) 731-9101
Fax: (301) 731-5058
Web site: www.insulators.org
Founded: 1904
Affiliation: AFL-CIO
Membership: 21,961
Publications: *The Journal* (quarterly)
President: James A. Grogan
Secretary-Treasurer: James (Bud) McCourt

Athletes

Federation of Professional Athletes [FPA]
2021 L St., NW, Washington, DC 20036
Phone: (202) 463-2200
Affiliation: AFL-CIO
Membership: 1,700
President: Gene Upshaw
Secretary-Treasurer: Doug Allen

Atlantic Independent Union

Atlantic Independent Union [AIU]
520 Cinnaminson Ave., Palmyra, NJ 08065
Phone: (856) 303-0776
Toll-Free: (800) 346-4731
Fax: (856) 346-0803
Web site: www.aiuunion.com
Founded: 1937
Affiliation: Independent
Membership: 502
Publications: *A.I.U. News* (annually)
President: John W. Kerr
Vice President: Anthony J. Dellaratta
Secretary: Daniel Kalai
Treasurer: William Mehler

Automobile, Aerospace Workers

United Automobile, Aerospace and Agricultural Implement Workers of America [UAW]
8000 E. Jefferson Ave., Detroit, MI 48214
Phone: (313) 926-5000
Fax: (313) 823-6016
Web site: www.uaw.org
Founded: 1935
Affiliation: AFL-CIO
Membership: 654,657
Publications: *Solidarity* (monthly)
President: Ron Gettelfinger
Secretary-Treasurer: Elizabeth Bunn

Vice Presidents:
Gerald Bantom
Nate Gooden
Bob King
Cal Rapson
Richard Shoemaker

Bakery, Confectionery, Tobacco Workers and Grain Millers

Bakery, Confectionery, Tobacco Workers and Grain Millers International Union [BCTGM]
10401 Connecticut Ave., Kensington, MD 20895-3961
Phone: (301) 933-8600
Fax: (301) 946-8452
Web site: www.bctgm.org
Founded: 1886
Affiliation: AFL-CIO
Membership: 107,452
Publications: *BCTGM News* (bimonthly)
President: Frank Hurt
Secretary-Treasurer: David B. Durkee
International Executive Vice President: Joseph Thibodeau

Baseball Players

Major League Baseball Players Association [MLBPA]
12 E. 49th St., 24th Floor, New York, NY 10017
Phone: (212) 826-0808
Fax: (212) 752-4378
E-mail: feedback@mlbpa.org
Web site: www.mlbplayers.mlb.com
Founded: 1966
Affiliation: Independent
Membership: 1,524
Executive Director: Donald M. Fehr
Chief Operating Officer: Gene Orza
General Counsel: Michael Weiner

Baseball Umpires

World Umpires Association [WUA]
P.O. Box 394, Neenah, WI 54957
Web site: www.worldumpires.com
Founded: 2000
Affiliation: Independent
Membership: 64
President: John Hirschbeck
Vice President: Joe Brinkman
Secretary-Treasurer: Jeff Nelson

Basketball Players

National Basketball Players Association [NBPA]
2 Penn Plaza, Suite 2430, New York, NY 10121
Phone: (212) 655-0880
Fax: (212) 655-0881
E-mail: info@nbpa.com
Web site: www.nbpa.com
Founded: 1954
Affiliation: Independent
Membership: 428
Publications: *Time Out* (quarterly)
President: Antonio Davis
First Vice President: Derek Fisher
Vice Presidents:
P.J. Brown
Adonal Foyle
Juwan Howard
Shaquille O'Neal
Theo Ratliff
Eric Snow
Secretary-Treasurer: Pat Garrity
Executive Director: G. William Hunter

Boilermakers

International Brotherhood of Boilermakers, Iron Ship Builders, Blacksmiths, Forgers and Helpers [IBB]
753 State Ave., Suite 570, Kansas City, KS 66101
Phone: (913) 371-2640
Fax: (913) 281-8101
Web site: www.boilermakers.org
Founded: 1880
Affiliation: AFL-CIO
Membership: 67,173
Publications: *The Boilermaker Reporter* (6 times a year) and *The Boilermaker Bulletin for Local Lodge Editors* (bimonthly)
International President: Newton B. Jones
International Secretary-Treasurer: William T. Creeden
International Vice Presidents:
Central Region: George D. Rogers
CLGAW Division: James Hickenbotham
Eastern Canada: Edward Power
Great Lakes: Lawrence J. McManamon
Northeast Section: Sean Murphy
SFEAW Division: Othal Smith, Jr.
Southeast Section: Sam May
Western Canada: Joseph Maloney
Western States: Joe Stinger
Director: Carey Allen

Bricklayers
International Union of Bricklayers and Allied Craftworkers [BAC]
1776 Eye St., NW, Washington, DC 20006
Phone: (202) 783-3788
Toll-Free: (888) 880-8222
Fax: (202) 393-0219
E-mail: askbac@bacweb.org
Web site: www.bacweb.org
Founded: 1865
Affiliation: AFL-CIO
Membership: 99,892
Publications: *Journal* (monthly)
President: John J. Flynn
Secretary-Treasurer: James Boland
Executive Vice Presidents:
  Kenneth Lambert
  Gerald O'Malley
  Gerard Scarano

Broadcast Employees
National Association of Broadcast Employees and Technicians [NABET-CWA]
501 3rd St., NW, 8th Floor, Washington, DC 20001-2797
Phone: (202) 434-1100
Fax: (202) 434-1279
Web site: www.nabetcwa.org
Affiliation: CWA
President: John S. Clark
Vice Presidents:
  Region One: Richard Gelber
  Region Two: Fred W. Saburro
  Region Three: James Lee
  Region Four: Charles Braico
  Region Five: Keith Hendriks
  Region Six: William Wachenschwanz

California Nurses
California Nurses Association/National Nurses Organizing Committee [CNA/NNOC]
2000 Franklin St., Oakland, CA 94612
Phone: (510) 273-2200
Fax: (510) 663-1625
E-mail: execoffice@calnurses.org
Web site: www.calnurses.org
Founded: 1903
Affiliation: Independent
Membership: 50,241
Publications: *California Nurse* (10 times a year)
President: Deborah Burger, R.N.

California School Employees
California School Employees Association [CSEA]
2045 Lundy Ave., P.O. Box 640, San Jose, CA 95131
Phone: (408) 473-1000
Toll-Free: (800) 632-2128
Fax: (408) 954-0948
Web site: www.csea.com
Affiliation: AFL-CIO
Publications: *Focus Magazine*
President: Rod Feckner
Secretary: Lin Larson
First Vice President: Allan Clark
Second Vice President: Michael Bilbrey
Executive Director: Bud Dougherty

Carpenters
United Brotherhood of Carpenters and Joiners of America [UBC]
101 Constitution Ave., NW, Washington, DC 20001
Phone: (202) 546-6206
Fax: (202) 543-5724
Web site: www.carpenters.org
Founded: 1881
Affiliation: CTW
Membership: 524,237
Publications: *Carpenter* (bimonthly)
President: Douglas J. McCarron
Vice President: Doug Banes
Secretary-Treasurer: Andris J. Silins

Catholic School Teachers
National Association of Catholic School Teachers [NACST]
1700 Sansom St., Suite 903, Philadelphia, PA 19103
Phone: (800) 99-NACST
Fax: (215) 568-8270
E-mail: nacst.nacst@verizon.net
Web site: www.nacst.com
Founded: 1978
Affiliation: Independent
Membership: 5,434
Publications: *Newsworthy*
President: Rita C. Schwartz
Secretary-Treasurer: William Blumenstein
Executive Vice President: Michael A. Milz
Area Vice Presidents:
  Patrick Cassidy
  Stephen Lieb
  Catherine Sue Manzella
  George Rudolph

Christian Labor Association
Christian Labor Association [CLA]
405 Centerstone Ct., P.O. Box 65, Zeeland, MI 49464
Phone: (616) 772-9164
Fax: (616) 772-9830
E-mail: chrlabor@egl.net
Web site: www.cla-usa.com
Founded: 1931
Affiliation: Independent
Membership: 1,159
Publications: *Christian Labor Herald*
President: Doug Reese
Secretary-Treasurer: Jennifer Keegstra
Vice President: Ace Marquey

Civilian Technicians
Association of Civilian Technicians [ACT]
12620 Lake Ridge Dr., Lake Ridge, VA 22192
Phone: (703) 494-4845
Fax: (703) 494-0961
Web site: www.actnat.com
Founded: 1960
Affiliation: Independent
Local Affiliates: 105
Membership: 5,550
Publications: *The Technician* (monthly)
President: Thomas G. Bastas
Executive Vice President: Leon J. Cich
Secretary: Norman E. Smith
Treasurer: Michael Vasko
Vice Presidents:
  William Brown
  Julie Curtis
  Leslie Hackett
  Dwain Reynolds

Classified School Employees
American Association of Classified School Employees [AACSE]
7140 S.W. Childs Rd., Lake Oswego, OR 97035
Phone: (503) 620-5663
Fax: (503) 684-4597
Web site: www.aacse.org
Founded: 1958
Affiliation: Independent
Membership: 109,188
President: Gary A. Rychard
Vice President: Mike Campbell
Secretary: Jo Sheperd
Treasurer: Cindi Carlisle

Communications Workers

Communications Workers of America
[CWA]
501 Third St., NW, Washington, DC
20001
Phone: (202) 434-1100
Fax: (202) 434-1279
E-mail: cwaweb@cwa-union.org
Web site: www.cwa-union.org
Affiliation: AFL-CIO
Membership: 545,638
Publications: *CWA News*
Note: CWA-affiliated unions include
The Newspaper Guild (TNG-CWA),
International Union of Electronic,
Electrical, Salaried, Machine and
Furniture Workers (IUE-CWA), the
National Association of Broadcast
Employees and Technicians
(NABET-CWA), Association of
Flight Attendants (AFA-CWA), and
National Coalition of Public Safety
Officers (NCPSO-CWA).
President: Larry Cohen
Secretary-Treasurer: Barbara J. Easterling
Executive Vice President: Jeffrey A.
Rechenbach

Commuter Rail Employees

**Association of Commuter Rail
Employees** [ACRE]
420 Lexington Ave., Suite 215, New
York, NY 10017
Phone: (212) 599-5856
Fax: (212) 599-2029
Web site: www.goacre.com
Founded: 2000
Affiliation: Independent
Membership: 1,204
President: Michael Shaw
Secretary-Treasurer: Mark Amorello
Vice President: John Mancinelli

Directors Guild

Directors Guild of America [DGA]
7920 Sunset Blvd., Los Angeles, CA
90046
Phone: (310) 289-2000
Fax: (310) 289-2029
Web site: www.dga.org
Founded: 1936
Affiliation: Independent
Membership: 13,124
Publications: *DGA Magazine*
(bimonthly)
President: Michael Apted
National Vice President: Steven
Soderbergh
Secretary-Treasurer: Gilbert Cates
Vice Presidents:
Paris Barclay

William M. Brady
Gary Donatelli
Taylor Hackford
Ed Sherin
Betty Thomas

DuPont Workers

**International Brotherhood of DuPont
Workers** [IBDW]
P.O. Box 10, Waynesboro, VA 22980
Phone: (540) 942-4623
Fax: (540) 337-5442
Web site: www.dupontworkers.com
Affiliation: Independent
Membership: 3,035
Publications: *Voice of the IBDW*
(monthly)
President: Jim Flickinger
Secretary-Treasurer: Dave Gibson
Vice President, Communications: Donny
Irvin

Education

National Education Association [NEA]
1201 16th St., NW, Washington, DC
20036-3290
Phone: (202) 833-4000
Fax: (202) 822-7974
Web site: www.nea.org
Founded: 1857
Affiliation: Independent
Membership: 2,731,419
Publications: *NEA Focus*, *Works4Me*
(weekly), *NEA Announce*, *NEA
Member News* (bi-weekly)
President: Reg Weaver
Vice President: Dennis Van Roekel
Secretary-Treasurer: Lily Eskelsen
Executive Committee:
Mike Billirakis
Mark Cebulski
Carolyn Crowder
Michael Marks
Rebecca Pringle
Marsha Smith
Executive Director: John I. Wilson

Electrical Workers

**International Brotherhood of Electrical
Workers** [IBEW]
900 7th St., NW, Washington, DC
20001
Phone: (202) 833-7000
Fax: (202) 728-7676
Web site: www.ibew.org
Founded: 1891
Affiliation: AFL-CIO
Membership: 704,794
Publications: *IBEW Journal*
President: Edwin D. Hill

Vice Presidents:
Frank J. Carroll
Phillip Flemming
Jonathan B. Gardner
Ted C. Jensen
Robert P. Klein
Lindell K. Lee
Joseph F. Lohman
Michael S. Mowrey
John F. Schantzen
Donald C. Siegel
Paul J. Witte
Secretary-Treasurer: Jon F. Walters

Electrical, Radio and Machine Workers

**United Electrical, Radio and Machine
Workers of America** [UE]
One Gateway Center, Suite 1400,
Pittsburgh, PA 15222-1416
Phone: (412) 471-8919
Fax: (412) 471-8999
E-mail: ue@ranknfile-ue.org
Web site: www.ranknfile-ue.org
Washington, DC office: 1800 Diagonal
Rd., Suite 500, Alexandria, VA
22314
Phone: (703) 299-5120
Fax: (703) 299-5121
Founded: 1936
Affiliation: Independent
Membership: 35,000
Publications: *UE News* (monthly)
President: John H. Hovis, Jr.
Secretary-Treasurer: Bruce J. Klipple
Director of Organization: Robert B.
Kingsley

Electronic Workers

**CWA Industrial Division/International
Union of Electronic, Electrical,
Salaried, Machine and Furniture
Workers** [IUE-CWA]
501 3rd St., NW, Washington, DC
20001
Phone: (202) 434-1228
Fax: (202) 434-1343
Web site: www.iue-cwa.org
Founded: 1949
Affiliation: CWA
Publications: *IUE-CWA News* (five
times a year)
President: Jim Clark

Elevator Constructors

International Union of Elevator Constructors [IUEC]

7154 Columbia Gateway Dr., Columbia, MD 21046

Phone: (410) 953-6150

Fax: (410) 953-6169

E-mail: contact@iuec.org

Web site: www.iuec.org

Founded: 1901

Affiliation: AFL-CIO

Membership: 25,839

Publications: *Elevator Constructor* (monthly)

President: Dana A. Brigham

Secretary-Treasurer: Kevin P. Stringer

Vice Presidents:

Rick Baxter

Ernie Brown

Frank Christensen

Gerald Cluff

Raymond Hernandez

George Miller

Donald Mitchell

Thaddeus Tomei

Engineers

International Federation of Professional and Technical Engineers [IFPTE]

8630 Fenton St., Suite 400, Silver Spring, MD 20910

Phone: (301) 565-9016

Fax: (301) 565-0018

Web site: www.ifpte.org

Founded: 1918

Affiliation: AFL-CIO

Membership: 58,000

Publications: *The Outlook* (bimonthly)

President: Gregory J. Junemann

Secretary-Treasurer: Dolores A. Gorczyca

Farm Labor Committee

Farm Labor Organizing Committee [FLOC]

1221 Broadway, Toledo, OH 43609

Phone: (419) 243-3456

Fax: (419) 243-5655

E-mail: info@floc.com

Web site: www.floc.com

Founded: 1968

Affiliation: AFL-CIO

Membership: 8,366

Publications: *Nuestra Lucha*

President: Baldemar Velasquez

Secretary-Treasurer: Jerry Ceille

Farm Workers

United Farm Workers of America [UFW]

P.O. Box 62, 29700 Woodford-Tehachapi Rd., Keene, CA 93531

Phone: (661) 823-6250

Web site: www.ufw.org

Founded: 1962

Affiliation: CTW

Membership: 5,638

President: Arturo S. Rodriguez

Secretary-Treasurer: Tanis Ybarra

Vice Presidents:

Gustavo Aguirre

Efren Barajas

Irv Hershenbaum

Mary Mecartney

Evelia Menjivar

Federal Education Association

Federal Education Association [FEA]

1201 16th St., NW, Suite 117, Washington, DC 20036

Phone: (202) 822-7850

Fax: (202) 822-7867

E-mail: fea@feaonline.org

Web site: www.feaonline.org

Founded: 1956

Affiliation: NEA

Membership: 6,515

Publications: *FEA Journal* (bimonthly)

President: Sheridan Pearce

Vice President: Edward (Ted) Carlin

Executive Director: H.T. Nguyen

Federal Employees

National Federation of Federal Employees [NFFE]

1016 16th St., NW, Washington, DC 20036

Phone: (202) 862-4400

Fax: (202) 862-4432

Web site: www.nffe.org

Founded: 1917

Affiliation: IAMAW

Publications: *The Federal Employee* (monthly)

President: Richard N. Brown

Secretary-Treasurer: John Paolino

Vice Presidents:

Jozef Drozdowski

Patricia LaSala

Douglas Law

Kolleen McGrath

John R. Obst

Gloria Porter

Debbie Ransom

Fire Fighters

International Association of Fire Fighters [IAFF]

1750 New York Ave., NW, Washington, DC 20006

Phone: (202) 737-8484

Fax: (202) 737-8418

E-mail: pr@iaff.org

Web site: www.iaff.org

Founded: 1918

Affiliation: AFL-CIO

Membership: 271,463

Publications: *International Fire Fighter* (bimonthly)

President: Harold A. Schaitberger

Secretary-Treasurer: Vincent J. Bollon

Vice Presidents:

Dominick F. Barbera

Bruce Carpenter

Joseph M. Conway, Jr.

James A. Fennell

James T. Ferguson

Kevin Gallagher

James Johnson

Roy McGhee

Michael D. McNeill

Thomas H. Miller

Michael Mullane

William V. Taylor

Danny Todd

Ricky Walsh

Lorne West

Louie A. Wright

Flight Attendants

Association of Flight Attendants [AFA-CWA]

501 3rd St., NW, Washington, DC 20001

Phone: (202) 434-1300

E-mail: afatalk@afanet.org

Web site: www.afanet.org

Founded: 1973

Affiliation: CWA

Membership: 34,223

Publications: *Flightlog* (quarterly)

President: Patricia A. Friend

Secretary-Treasurer: Kevin Creighan

Vice President: George M. Donahue

Food and Commercial Workers

United Food and Commercial Workers International Union [UFCW]

1775 K St., NW, Washington, DC 20006

Phone: (202) 223-3111

Fax: (202) 466-1562

Web site: www.ufcw.org

Founded: 1979

Affiliation: CTW

Membership: 1,338,625

Publications: *Working America* (quarterly)

President: Joseph T. Hansen

Secretary-Treasurer: Anthony M. Perrone

Executive Vice Presidents:

Michael J. Fraser

William T. McDonough

Patrick J. O'Neill

Football Players

National Football League Players Association [NFLPA]

2021 L St., NW, Suite 600, Washington, DC 20036

Phone: (800) 372-2000

Fax: (202) 463-2200

E-mail: nflpaexecutivedept@ nflplayers.com

Web site: www.nflpa.org

Western Office: 423 Washington St., Suite 700, San Francisco, CA 94111

Phone: (800) 900-9404

Fax: (415) 385-3800

Founded: 1956

Affiliation: Independent

Publications: *Audible* (quarterly)

Executive Director: Gene Upshaw

President: Troy Vincent

Foreign Service Association

American Foreign Service Association [AFSA]

2101 E St., NW, Washington, DC 20037

Phone: (202) 338-4045

Toll-Free: (800) 704-AFSA

Fax: (202) 338-6820

E-mail: afsa@afsa.org

Web site: www.afsa.org

Founded: 1924

Affiliation: Independent

Membership: 12,852

Publications: *Foreign Service Journal* (monthly)

President: J. Anthony Holmes

Secretary: Tex Harris

Treasurer: Andrew Winter

Vice Presidents:

Donald Businger

Bill Carter

David E. Reuther

Laura Scandurra

Glass, Molders, Pottery and Plastics Workers

Glass, Molders, Pottery, Plastics and Allied Workers International Union [GMP]

608 E. Baltimore Pike, P.O. Box 1978, Media, PA 19063

Phone: (610) 565-5051

Fax: (610) 565-0983

E-mail: gmpiu@ix.netcom.com

Web site: www.gmpiu.org

Founded: 1842

Affiliation: AFL-CIO

Membership: 44,155

Publications: *Horizons* (monthly)

President: John P. Ryan

Secretary-Treasurer: Bruce R. Smith

Vice Presidents:

Ignacio de la Fuente

David Doyle

Government Employees

American Federation of Government Employees [AFGE]

80 F St., NW, Washington, DC 20001

Phone: (202) 737-8700

Fax: (202) 639-6441

E-mail: comments@afge.org

Web site: www.afge.org

Founded: 1932

Affiliation: AFL-CIO

Local Affiliates: 1,100

Membership: 226,599

Publications: *The Government Standard* (bimonthly)

President: John Gage

Secretary-Treasurer: Jim Davis

National Vice President for Women and Fair Practices: Andrea E. Brooks

Vice Presidents:

Dwight Bowman

Rogelio Flores

Charlotte Flowers

Joseph P. Flynn

Eugene Hudson, Jr.

Dorothy James

Michael C. Kelly

Jane Nygaard

Arnold R. Scott

Gerald D. Swanke

Derrick F. Thomas

Jeffery R. Williams

Government Employees Association

National Association of Government Employees [NAGE]

159 Burgin Pkwy., Quincy, MA 02169

Phone: (617) 376-0220

Fax: (617) 376-0285

Web site: www.nage.org

Founded: 1961

Affiliation: SEIU

Membership: 46,000

Publications: *Federal News Update*

Note: NAGE affiliates: International Brotherhood of Police Officers, International Brotherhood of Corrections Officers, National Association of Nurses, and International Association of EMTs and Paramedics.

President: David Holoway

Chief Financial Officer: Bernard Flynn

Executive Vice Presidents:

James Farley

Barbara Osgood

Vice Presidents:

Paul Birks

Jack Donegan

Deborah Ennis

Michael Eosco

Michael Lavin

Marc Lawson

Theresa McGoldrick

Charles Rambo

Greg Sorozan

Linda Spector

Government Security Officers

United Government Security Officers of America [UGSOA]

8620 Wolff Ct., Suite 210, Westminster, CO 80031

Phone: (303) 650-8515

Toll-Free: (800) 572-6103

Fax: (303) 650-8515

E-mail: admin@ugsoa.com

Web site: www.ugsoa.com

Founded: 1992

Affiliation: Independent

Local Affiliates: 125

Membership: 9,475

Publications: *UGSOA Newsletter*

President: James A. Vissar

Senior Vice President: James D. Carney

Vice Presidents:

Larry Ferris

Michael Hough

Donna Huff

Ron Smith

Graphic Artists

Graphic Artists Guild, Inc. [GAG]
90 John St., #403, New York, NY
10038
Phone: (212) 791-3400
Fax: (212) 791-0333
E-mail: execdir@gag.org
Web site: www.gag.org
Affiliation: UAW
Membership: 2,523
Publications: *Guild News* (bimonthly)
and *Handbook, Pricing & Ethical
Guidelines* (biannually)
President: John Schmelzer
Secretary: Lara Kisielowski
Treasurer: Susan Mathews

Graphic Communications

Graphic Communications Conference
[GCC/IBT]
1900 L St., NW, Washington, DC
20036
Phone: (202) 462-1400
Fax: (202) 721-0600
Web site: www.gciu.org
Founded: 1983
Affiliation: IBT
Membership: 62,261
Publications: *Graphic Communicator*
(8 times a year)
President: George Tedeschi
Secretary-Treasurer: Robert Lacey
Vice President: David A. Grabhorn

Hebrew Actors

Hebrew Actors' Union Inc. [HAU]
31 E. Seventh St., New York, NY
10003
Phone: (212) 674-1923
Affiliation: AAAA
Membership: 60
President: Ruth Ellin

Hockey Players

**National Hockey League Players
Association** [NHLPA]
777 Bay St., Suite 2400, Toronto, ON
M5G 2C8 Canada
Phone: (416) 313-2300
Fax: (416) 313-2301
Web site: www.nhlpa.com
Founded: 1967
Affiliation: Independent
President: Trevor Linden
Executive Director and General Counsel:
Ted Saskin
Vice Presidents:
Daniel Alfredsson
Bob Boughner
Vincent Demphouse

Bill Guerin
Arturs Irbe
Trent Klatt

Independent Unions

**National Federation of Independent
Unions** [NFIU]
1166 S. 11th St., Philadelphia, PA
19147
Phone: (215) 336-3300
Toll-Free: (888) 595-NFIU
Web site: www.nfiu.org
Founded: 1963
Affiliation: LIUNA
Membership: 5,532
Note: NFIU is comprised of 15
affiliates: Amalgamated Industrial
Workers Union, NFIU 61; Choice
Hospitality Independent Peoples
Union, NFIU 6; Hesston
Corporation Workers Association,
NFIU 228; Independent Employees
Union, NFIU 184; Litchfield
Independent Workers Union, NFIU
373; Local 22, NFIU 22;
Manchester Plastics Independent
Union, NFIU 595; National
Industrial Workers Union, NFIU
105; Sheridan Printing Employees
Association, NFIU 229; Stockton
Employees Independent Union,
NFIU 118; The Educational
Minnesota Professional
Organization, NFIU 270; United
Electro-Medical Workers Union,
NFIU 239; United Independent
Union, NFIU 4; United Services
Workers of America, NFIU 101;
Universal Employees' Union, NFIU
235; and Westfield Tanning
Employees Association, NFIU 269.
President: Francis J. Chiappardi
Secretary/Treasurer: Alonzo Wheeler
Vice Presidents:
Doug Bennett
Paul J. Diana
John Groves
Mark Iveson
John Romero

Industrial Trade Unions

**National Organization of Industrial
Trade Unions** [NOITU]
148-06 Hillside Ave., Jamaica, NY
11435
Phone: (718) 291-3434
Fax: (718) 526-2920
Web site: www.noitu.org
Affiliation: Independent
Membership: 3,916
Publications: *NOITU Reporter*
(quarterly)
President: Gerard Jones
Executive Vice President: Gerald Hustick,
Jr.
National President Emeritus Elect: Daniel
Lasky

Interns and Residents

Committee of Interns and Residents
[CIR]
520 Eighth Ave., Suite 1200, New
York, NY 10018
Phone: (212) 356-8100
Toll-Free: (800) 247-8877
Fax: (212) 356-8111
E-mail: info@cirseiu.org
Web site: www.cirseiu.org
Founded: 1957
Affiliation: SEIU
Publications: *CIR News Quarterly*
President: Simon Ahtaridis, M.D., M.P.H.
Executive Vice President: Christine
Dehlendorf, M.D.
Secretary-Treasurer: Rajani Surendar
Bhat, M.D.
Vice Presidents:
Maggie Bertisch, M.D.
Reuven Bromberg, M.D.
Ayodele Green, M.D.
Gina Jefferson, M.D.
Luella Toni Lewis, M.D.
Cristin McKenna, M.D.
Spencer Nabors, M.D.
James Rodriguez, M.D.
Paola Sequeira, M.D.
Nailah Thompson, D.O.
Hillary Tompkins, M.D.

Iron Workers

International Association of Bridge, Structural, Ornamental and Reinforcing Iron Workers
[BSORIW]
1750 New York Ave., NW, Suite 400, Washington, DC 20006
Phone: (202) 383-4800
Fax: (202) 638-4856
Web site: www.ironworkers.org
Founded: 1896
Affiliation: AFL-CIO
Membership: 125,437
Publications: *The Ironworker* (monthly)
President: Joseph J. Hunt
Secretary: Michael Fitzpatrick
Treasurer: Walter Wise

Italian Actors

The Guild of Italian American Actors
[GIAA]
Canal Street Station, P.O. Box 123, New York, NY 10013
Phone: (212) 420-6590
E-mail: info@giaa.us
Web site: www.giaa.us
Founded: 1937
Affiliation: AAAA
Membership: 250
President: Guy Palumbo
First Vice President: Carlo Fiorletta
Second Vice President: Rico Simonini
Secretary-Treasurer: Lea Serra

Jockeys

Jockeys' Guild, Inc. [JG]
P.O. Box 150, Monrovia, CA 91017
Phone: (866) 465-6257
Fax: (626) 305-5615
E-mail: info@jockeysguild.com
Web site: www.jockeysguild.com
Founded: 1940
Affiliation: Independent
Membership: 1,560
Note: Interim Board of Directors (National Election on July 1, 2006).
Chairman: John Velazquez
Vice Chairman: Mark Guidry
Secretary: Alex Solis
Treasurer: Jeff Johnson
At-Large Directors:
    G.R. Carter
    Jon Court
    Jerry LaSala
    Mike Luzzi
    Larry Reynolds

Journeymen and Allied Trades

International Union of Journeymen and Allied Trades [IUJAT]
93 Lake Ave., Suite 103, Danbury, CT 06810
Phone: (203) 205-0101
Fax: (203) 205-0006
E-mail: info@iujat.org
Web site: www.iujat.org
Founded: 1874
Affiliation: Independent
Membership: 42,292
President: Steven R. Elliott
Secretary-Treasurer: William Sweeney
Executive Vice President: Lori Ann Ames
Vice Presidents:
    Kevin Boyle
    Daniel Lasky
    Joseph M. Pecora

Laborers

Laborers' International Union of North America [LIUNA]
905 16th St., NW, Washington, DC 20006
Phone: (202) 737-8320
Fax: (202) 737-2754
Web site: www.liuna.org
Founded: 1903
Affiliation: CTW
Membership: 692,558
Publications: *The Laborer* (quarterly), *The LIUNA Leader* (quarterly) and *LIUNA Faxline* (biweekly)
President: Terence M. O'Sullivan
Secretary-Treasurer: Armand E. Sabitoni
Vice Presidents:
    Rocco Davis
    Mano Frey
    James C. Hale
    Vere O. Haynes
    Terrence M. Healy
    John Hegarty
    Joseph S. Mancinelli
    Dennis Martire
    Vincent Masino
    Jose Moreno
    Raymond M. Pocino
    Mike Quevedo, Jr.
    Robert Richardson
    Edward M. Smith

Letter Carriers

National Association of Letter Carriers [NALC]
100 Indiana Ave., NW, Washington, DC 20001-2144
Phone: (202) 393-4695
Fax: (202) 737-1540
E-mail: nalcinf@nalc.org
Web site: www.nalc.org
Founded: 1889
Affiliation: AFL-CIO
Membership: 292,221
Publications: *The Postal Record* (monthly), *NALC Activist* (quarterly), and *NALC Retiree* (quarterly)
President: William H. Young
Executive Vice President: Jim Williams
Vice President: Gary H. Mullins
Secretary-Treasurer: Jane E. Broendel

Locomotive Engineers

Brotherhood of Locomotive Engineers and Trainmen [BLET]
Standard Bldg., 1370 Ontario St., Cleveland, OH 44113-1702
Phone: (216) 241-2630
Fax: (216) 241-6516
Web site: www.ble-t.org
Founded: 1863
Affiliation: IBT
Membership: 51,318
Publications: *Locomotive Engineers Journal*
President: Don M. Hahs
First Vice President: Edward W. Rodzwicz
Secretary-Treasurer: William C. Walpert
Vice Presidents:
    Merle W. Geiger, Jr.
    Raymond Holmes
    Dale L. McPherson
    E. Lee Pruitt
    Rick Radek
    Paul T. Sorrow
    Stephen D. Speagle
    Paul L. Wingo, Jr.

Longshore and Warehouse
**International Longshore and
Warehouse Union** [ILWU]
1188 Franklin St., 4th Floor, San
Francisco, CA 94109
Phone: (415) 775-0533
Fax: (415) 775-1302
E-mail: ilwu@patriot.net
Web site: www.ilwu.org
Founded: 1937
Affiliation: AFL-CIO
Membership: 37,875
Publications: *The Dispatcher* (monthly)
President: James Spinosa
Vice Presidents:
Wesley Furtado
Robert McEllrath
Secretary-Treasurer: William E. Adams

Longshoremen
**International Longshoremen's
Association** [ILA]
17 Battery Pl., Suite 930, New York,
NY 10004
Phone: (212) 425-1200
Fax: (212) 425-2928
Web site: www.ilaunion.org
Founded: 1892
Affiliation: AFL-CIO
Membership: 59,000
Publications: *ILA Newsletter*
President: John M. Bowers
Secretary-Treasurer: Robert Gleason
General Vice President: Benny Holland,
Jr.
Vice Presidents:
Horace T. Alston
Jorge L. Aponte Fegueroa
Chauncey J. Baker
John D. Baker
John Bowers, Jr.
Edward L. Brown, Sr.
Capt. Timothy Brown
James A. Campbell
Ronald Capri
Charles Chillemi
Arthur Coffey
Raymond Desgagnes
Clyde Fitzgerald
Benjamin Flowers
Perry C. Harvey
Stephen Knott
John H. Mackey
James T. McCleland
William R. McNamara
James H. Paylor
Louis Pernice
Raymond Sierra
Harrison Tyler
Reuben Wheatley

Machine Printers and Engravers
**Machine Printers and Engravers
Association of the United States**
[MPEA]
2 Regency Plaza, Suite 7, Providence,
RI 02923
Phone: (401) 831-3309
Fax: (401) 831-3309
E-mail: mpea74@aol.com
Founded: 1874
Affiliation: Independent
Membership: 45
President: Albert A. Poitras
Secretary-Treasurer: William Aniszewski

Machinists
**International Association of Machinists
and Aerospace Workers** [IAM]
9000 Machinists Pl., Upper Marlboro,
MD 20772-2687
Phone: (301) 967-4500
Fax: (301) 967-4588
E-mail: websteward@goiam.org
Web site: www.goiam.org
Founded: 1888
Affiliation: AFL-CIO
Membership: 610,426
Publications: *IAM Journal* (quarterly)
President: R. Thomas Buffenbarger
Secretary-Treasurer: Warren Mart
Vice Presidents:
James E. Brown
Robert Martinez
Lee Pearson
Dave Ritchie
Robert Roach, Jr.
Robert V. Thayer
Lynn Tucker

Maintenance of Way Employes
**Brotherhood of Maintenance of Way
Employes** [BMWE]
20300 Civic Center Dr., Suite 320,
Southfield, MI 48076
Phone: (248) 948-1010
Fax: (248) 948-7150
Web site: www.bmwe.org
Founded: 1887
Affiliation: IBT
Membership: 34,367
Publications: *BMWE Journal*
(monthly)
President: Freddie N. Simpson
Secretary-Treasurer: Perry Geller
Vice Presidents:
J.R. Cook
Leon R. Fenhaus
E.R. Spears
Rick B. Wehrli
Henry W. Wise, Jr.

National Division Executive Board
Chairman: Bill R. Palmer

Marine Engineers
**Marine Engineers' Beneficial
Association** [MEBA]
444 North Capitol St., NW, Suite 800,
Washington, DC 20001
Phone: (202) 638-5355
Fax: (202) 638-5369
Web site: www.d1meba.org
Founded: 1875
Affiliation: AFL-CIO
Membership: 30,006
Publications: *The Marine Officer*
(bimonthly) and *The Telex Times*
(weekly)
President: Ron Davis
Secretary-Treasurer: Cecil A. McIntyre

Masters, Mates and Pilots
**International Organization of Masters,
Mates and Pilots** [MM&P]
700 Maritime Blvd., Linthicum
Heights, MD 21090-1941
Phone: (410) 850-8700
Fax: (410) 850-0973
Web site: www.bridgedeck.org
Founded: 1880
Affiliation: ILA
Membership: 6,542
Publications: *The Master, Mate & Pilot*
(bimonthly)
President: Timothy A. Brown
Secretary-Treasurer: Glen P. Banks
Vice President: George A. Quick

Mine Workers
United Mine Workers of America
[UMWA]
8315 Lee Hwy., Fairfax, VA 22031
Phone: (703) 208-7200
Fax: (703) 208-7227
Web site: www.umwa.org
Founded: 1890
Affiliation: AFL-CIO
Membership: 100,609
Publications: *UMWA Journal*
(bimonthly)
President: Cecil E. Roberts
Secretary-Treasurer: Daniel Kane
Vice Presidents:
Bill Brumfield
Joe Carter
Mike Dalpiaz
Daryl Dewberry
Rich Eddy
Ed Yankovich

Musical Artists
American Guild of Musical Artists
[AGMA]
1430 Broadway, 14th Floor, New
York, NY 10018
Phone: (212) 265-3687
Fax: (212) 262-9088
E-mail: agma@musicalartists.org
Web site: www.musicalartists.org
Founded: 1936
Affiliation: AAAA
Membership: 9,525
Publications: *AGMagazine* (quarterly)
President: Linda Mays
Vice Presidents:
John Coleman
Michael Geiger
Jimmy Odom
Gerald Otte
Colby Roberts
Secretary: Mitchell Sendrowitz
Treasurer: Lynn Lundgren
Executive Director: Alan S. Gordon

Musicians
American Federation of Musicians of
the United States and Canada
[AFM]
1501 Broadway, Suite 600, New York,
NY 10036
Phone: (212) 869-1330
Fax: (212) 764-6134
E-mail: info@afm.org
Web site: www.afm.org
Founded: 1896
Affiliation: AFL-CIO
Membership: 96,632
Publications: *International Musician*
(monthly) and *Officers Edge*
(usually quarterly)
President: Thomas Lee
Secretary-Treasurer: Sam Folio
Vice Presidents:
Harold Bradley
Bobby Herriot

National Staff Organization
National Staff Organization [NSO]
1216 Kendale Blvd., P.O. Box 2573,
East Lansing, MI 48826-2573
Phone: (989) 336-4024
Toll-Free: (800) 292-1934
Fax: (989) 723-3058
E-mail: cnso@aol.com
Web site: www.nationalstaff.org
Founded: 1969
Affiliation: Independent
Local Affiliates: 75
Membership: 5,037
Publications: *NSO Contact*
President: Chuck Agerstrand

Vice Presidents:
Lynn Adler
Marius Ambrose
Secretary: Mary Henson
Treasurer: Evelyn Smith

Newspaper Guild
The Newspaper Guild [TNG-CWA]
501 3rd St., NW, Suite 250,
Washington, DC 20001-2797
Phone: (202) 434-7177
Fax: (202) 434-1472
E-mail: guild@cwa-union.org
Web site: www.newsguild.org
Affiliation: CWA
President: Linda Foley
Secretary-Treasurer: Bernard Lunzer
Vice Presidents:
Karolynn DeLucca
Connie Knox
Donna Marks
Scott Stephens
Peter Szekely
Lucy Witeck

NLRB Professional Association
National Labor Relations Board
Professional Association [NLRBPA]
1099 14th St., NW, Suite 9120,
Washington, DC 20570
Phone: (202) 273-1749
Fax: (202) 273-4286
Web site: www.nlrb.gov
Founded: 1963
Affiliation: Independent
Membership: 875
President: Leslie Rossen
Vice President: Eric C. Marx
Secretary: Ruth Burdick
Treasurer: Tom Clark

Novelty and Production Workers
International Union of Allied Novelty
and Production Workers [NPW]
1950 W. Erie St., Chicago, IL 60622
Phone: (312) 738-0822
Fax: (312) 738-3553
Affiliation: AFL-CIO
Membership: 18,323
President: Mark Spano

Nurses
United American Nurses [UAN]
8515 Georgia Ave., Suite 400, Silver
Spring, MD 20910-3492
Phone: (301) 628-5118
Fax: (301) 628-5347
E-mail: uaninfo@uannurse.org
Web site: www.uannurse.org
Founded: 1999
Affiliation: AFL-CIO
Membership: 148,799
Publications: *UAN Activist*
President: Cheryl L. Johnson, R.N.
Vice President: Ann Converso, R.N.
Secretary-Treasurer: Jean Ross, R.N.
Directors-at-Large:
Sandra Falwell, R.N.
Carolyn Hietamaki, R.N.
Debbie Lund, R.N.
Marva Wade, R.N.
National Executive Director: Susan
Bianchi-Sand

Nurses Associations of California
United Nurses Associations of
California/Union of Health Care
Professionals [UNAC]
300 S. Park Ave., Suite 840, Pomona,
CA 91766
Phone: (909) 620-7749
Toll-Free: (800) 762-5874
Fax: (909) 620-9119
E-mail: info@unac-ca.org
Web site: www.unac-ca.org
Affiliation: AFSCME
Membership: 13,153
President: Kathy J. Sackman, R.N.
Executive Vice President: Sonia E.
Moseley, R.N.P.
Secretary: Barbara L. Blake, R.N.
Treasurer: Delima M. MacDonald, R.N.

Nurses, Professional
United Professional Nurses Association
[UPNA]
Bewley Bldg., Suite 318, Lockport, NY
14094
Phone: (716) 433-1477
Fax: (716) 433-1478
Affiliation: Independent
Membership: 171
Contact: Diane Flack

Office and Professional Employees

Office and Professional Employees International Union [OPEIU]

265 W. 14th St., 6th Floor, New York, NY 10011

Phone: (212) 675-3210

Toll-Free: (800) 346-7348

Fax: (212) 727-3466

E-mail: opeiu@opeiu.org

Web site: www.opeiu.org

Founded: 1945

Affiliation: AFL-CIO

Membership: 99,035

Publications: *White Collar* (quarterly)

President: Michael Goodwin

Secretary-Treasurer: Nancy Wohlforth

Operating Engineers

International Union of Operating Engineers [IUOE]

1125 17th St., NW, Washington, DC 20036

Phone: (202) 429-9100

Fax: (202) 778-2616

E-mail: iuoe@access.digex.net

Web site: www.iuoe.org

Founded: 1896

Affiliation: AFL-CIO

Membership: 388,804

Publications: *The International Operating Engineer* (bimonthly)

President: Vincent J. Giblin

Secretary-Treasurer: Christopher Hanley

Vice Presidents:

Vergil L. Belfi, Jr.

John Bonilla

Kenneth Campbell

Allan B. Darr

William Duffy

William E. Dugan

Gerald Ellis

John Hamilton

Brian E. Hickey

Jerry Kalamar

Gary W. Kroeker

James McLaughlin

Patrick Sink

William Waggoner

Painters

International Union of Painters and Allied Trades [IUPAT]

1750 New York Ave., NW, Washington, DC 20006

Phone: (202) 637-0700

Fax: (202) 637-0771

E-mail: webmaster@iupat.org

Web site: www.iupat.org

Founded: 1887

Affiliation: AFL-CIO

Membership: 128,351

President: James A. Williams

Secretary-Treasurer: George Galis

Executive Vice President: Kenneth E. Rigmaiden

Vice Presidents:

William D. Candelori, Jr.

Robert Kucheran

Raymond J. Price, III

Raymond Sesma

General President Emeritus: A.L. (Mike) Monroe

Petroleum and Industrial Workers

International Union of Petroleum and Industrial Workers [UPIW]

8131 E. Rosecrans Ave., Paramount, CA 90723

Phone: (562) 630-6232

Fax: (562) 408-1073

Affiliation: Independent

Membership: 2,068

President: George Beltz

Secretary-Treasurer: Pamela Barlow

Physicians and Dentists

Union of American Physicians and Dentists [UAPD]

1330 Broadway, Suite 730, Oakland, CA 94612

Phone: (510) 839-0193

Toll-Free: (800) 622-0909

Fax: (510) 763-8756

E-mail: uapd@uapd.com

Web site: www.uapd.com

Founded: 1972

Affiliation: AFSCME

Membership: 2,500

Publications: *The UAPD Report* (quarterly)

President: Robert L. Weinmann, M.D.

Secretary: Charles D. Goodman, M.D.

Treasurer: Peter A. Statti, M.D.

Vice Presidents:

Stuart A. Bussey, M.D., J.D.

Michael H. Lisiak, M.D.

Executive Director: Gary R. Robinson

Pilots, Air Line

Air Line Pilots Association International [ALPA]

535 Herndon Pkwy., P.O. Box 1169, Herndon, VA 20172

Phone: (703) 689-2270

Fax: (703) 689-4370

Web site: www.alpa.org

Founded: 1931

Affiliation: AFL-CIO

Membership: 50,811

Publications: *Air Line Pilot* (6 times a year) and *Point-to-Point* (4 times a year)

President: Capt. Duane Woerth

First Vice-President: Capt. Dennis J. Dolan

Vice President-Secretary: Capt. Paul Rice

Vice President-Treasurer: Capt. Chris Beebe

Pilots, Independent

Independent Pilots Association [IPA]

3607 Fern Valley Rd., Louisville, KY 40219-1916

Phone: (800) 285-4472

Fax: (502) 753-3252

Web site: www.ipapilot.org

Founded: 1990

Affiliation: Independent

Membership: 2,521

Publications: *Flight Times*

President: Capt. Tom Nicholson

Vice President: Capt. Chuck Patterson

Secretary: Capt. Herbert Hurst

Treasurer: F/O Dean Cibotti

At-Large Representative: Capt. Cindy Driscoll

Plant Protection

Plant Protection Association National Union [PPA]

302 N. Heron St., Ypsilanti, MI 48917-2947

Phone: (734) 487-5522

Fax: (734) 487-5588

Affiliation: Independent

Membership: 350

President: Larry Daniel

Secretary-Treasurer: Kenneth Pollack

Plasterers and Cement Masons

Operative Plasterers' and Cement Masons' International Association of the United States and Canada [OPCMIA]
14405 Laurel Pl., Suite 300, Laurel, MD 20707
Phone: (301) 470-4200
Fax: (301) 470-2502
Web site: www.opcmia.org
Founded: 1864
Affiliation: AFL-CIO
Membership: 40,035
Publications: *Plasterer and Cement Mason* (quarterly)
President: John J. Dougherty
Secretary-Treasurer: Patrick D. Finley
Executive Vice President: Ronald K. Bowser
Vice Presidents:
Mary Dougherty
Del French
Earl F. Hurd
Thomas Mora
Daniel Stepano

Plate Printers, Die Stampers and Engravers

International Plate Printers, Die Stampers and Engravers Union of North America [PPDSE]
14th and C Sts., SW, Room 213-5A, Washington, DC 20228
Phone: (202) 874-2554
Founded: 1893
Affiliation: AFL-CIO
Membership: 200
President: Ronald L. Payne
Secretary-Treasurer: James L. Kopernick

Plumbing and Pipe Fitting

United Association of Journeymen and Apprentices of the Plumbing and Pipe Fitting Industry of the United States and Canada [UA]
901 Massachusetts Ave., NW, Washington, DC 20001
Phone: (202) 628-5823
Fax: (202) 628-5024
Web site: www.ua.org
Founded: 1889
Affiliation: AFL-CIO
Membership: 324,043
Publications: *UA Journal* (monthly)
General President: William P. Hite
General Secretary-Treasurer: Patrick R. Perno
Assistant General President: Stephen Kelly

Police

National Fraternal Order of Police [FOP]
1410 Donelson Pike, Suite A-17, Nashville, TN 37217
Phone: (615) 399-0900
Fax: (615) 399-0400
E-mail: glfop@grandlodgefop.org
Web site: www.grandlodgefop.org
Founded: 1915
Affiliation: Independent
Publications: *FOP Journal*
President: Chuck Canterbury
Secretary: Patrick Yoes
Treasurer: Tom Penoza
Vice President: David Hiller

Police Associations

International Union of Police Associations [IUPA]
1549 Ringling Blvd., Suite 600, Sarasota, FL 34236
Phone: (941) 487-2560
Fax: (941) 487-2570
E-mail: iupa@iupa.org
Web site: www.iupa.org
Founded: 1954
Affiliation: AFL-CIO
Membership: 38,478
Publications: *Police Union News* (monthly)
President: Sam A. Cabral
Secretary-Treasurer: Timothy Scott
Vice President: Dennis J. Slocumb

Postal and Federal Employees

National Alliance of Postal and Federal Employees [NAPFE]
1628 11th St., NW, Washington, DC 20001
Phone: (202) 939-6325
Fax: (202) 939-6389
E-mail: headquarters@napfe.com
Web site: www.napfe.com
Founded: 1913
Affiliation: Independent
Membership: 10,564
Publications: *National Alliance* (monthly)
President: James M. McGee
Secretary: David A. Cage
Treasurer: Warren E. Powell
First Vice President: Charles J. Denson, Jr.
Second Vice President: Frederick D. Brown

Postal Mail Handlers

National Postal Mail Handlers Union [NPMHU]
1101 Connecticut Ave., NW, Suite 500, Washington, DC 20036
Phone: (202) 833-9095
Fax: (202) 833-0008
Web site: www.npmhu.org
Affiliation: LIUNA
Membership: 357,000
Publications: *Mail Handler Magazine*
President: John F. Hegarty
Secretary-Treasurer: Mark A. Gardner
Vice Presidents:
Samuel C. D'Ambrosio
Efraim Daniel
Paul Hogrogian
Bruce Miller
Hardy Williams

Postal Workers

American Postal Workers Union [APWU]
1300 L St., NW, Washington, DC 20005
Phone: (202) 842-4200
Fax: (202) 842-4297
Web site: www.apwu.org
Founded: 1971
Affiliation: AFL-CIO
Membership: 227,425
President: William Burrus
Executive Vice President: C.J. (Cliff) Guffey
Secretary-Treasurer: Terry R. Stapleton

Production Workers

National Production Workers Union [NPWU]
2210 Midwest Rd., Suite 310, Oak Brook, IL 60521
Phone: (630) 575-0560
Fax: (630) 575-0570
Affiliation: Independent
Membership: 625
President: Joseph Senese
Secretary-Treasurer: John Oliverio
Vice President: Susan Schreiner

Pulp and Paper Workers
Association of Western Pulp and Paper Workers [AWPPW]
  1430 S.W. Clay St., P.O. Box 4566, Portland, OR 97208-4566
  Phone: (503) 228-7486
  Fax: (503) 228-1346
  E-mail: info@awppw.org
  Web site: www.awppw.org
  Founded: 1964
  Affiliation: UBC
  Membership: 8,150
  Publications: *The Rebel* (monthly)
President: John Rhodes
Secretary-Treasurer: James L. Hassey
Vice President: Gregory Pallesen

Railroad Signalmen
Brotherhood of Railroad Signalmen [BRS]
  917 Shenandoah Shores Rd., Front Royal, VA 22630-6418
  Phone: (540) 622-6522
  Fax: (540) 622-6532
  E-mail: signalman@brs.org
  Web site: www.brs.org
  Founded: 1901
  Affiliation: AFL-CIO
  Membership: 8,842
President: W. Dan Pickett
Secretary-Treasurer: W.A. Barrows
Vice Presidents:
  J.C. Boles
  D.M. Boston
  G.E. Jones
  F.E. Mason
  J.L. Mattingly

Retail, Wholesale and Department Store
Retail, Wholesale and Department Store Union [RWDSU]
  30 E. 29th St., 4th Floor, New York, NY 10016
  Phone: (212) 684-5300
  Fax: (212) 779-2809
  Web site: www.rwdsu.org
  Founded: 1937
  Affiliation: UFCW
  Membership: 72,390
  Publications: *The Record* (bimonthly)
President: Stuart Appelbaum
Secretary-Treasurer: Jack Wurm

Roofers, Waterproofers and Allied Workers
United Union of Roofers, Waterproofers and Allied Workers [RWAW]
  1660 L St., NW, Suite 800, Washington, DC 20036-5646
  Phone: (202) 463-7663
  Fax: (202) 463-6906
  E-mail: roofers@unionroofers.com
  Web site: www.unionroofers.com
  Founded: 1919
  Affiliation: AFL-CIO
  Membership: 21,610
  Publications: *Journeyman Roofer and Waterproofer* (quarterly)
President: John C. Martini
Secretary-Treasurer: Kinsey M. Robinson
Vice Presidents:
  Paul F. Bickford
  Don Cardwell
  Robert J. Danley
  James A. Hadel
  Richard R. Mathis
  Donald A. O'Blenis
  Daniel O'Donnell
  Thomas Pedrick
  Robert Peterson
  Douglas Ziegler

Rural Letter Carriers
National Rural Letter Carriers' Association [NRLCA]
  1630 Duke St., 4th Floor, Alexandria, VA 22314-3465
  Phone: (703) 684-5545
  Fax: (703) 548-8735
  Web site: www.nrlca.org
  Founded: 1903
  Affiliation: Independent
  Membership: 105,460
  Publications: *The National Rural Letter Carrier*
President: Donnie Pitts
Vice President: Don Cantriel
Secretary-Treasurer: Clifford D. Dailing

School Administrators
American Federation of School Administrators [AFSA]
  1101 17th St., NW, Suite 408, Washington, DC 20036
  Phone: (202) 986-4209
  Fax: (202) 986-4211
  E-mail: afsa@admin.org
  Web site: www.admin.org
  Founded: 1971
  Affiliation: AFL-CIO
  Publications: *AFSA Newsletter* (10 times a year)
President: Baxter M. Atkinson

Executive Vice President: Jill Levy
Treasurer: Diann Woodard
Secretary: Roch Girard

Screen Actors
Screen Actors Guild [SAG]
  5757 Wilshire Blvd., Los Angeles, CA 90036-3600
  Phone: (323) 954-1600
  Fax: (323) 549-6603
  Web site: www.sag.org
  New York office: 360 Madison Ave., 12th Floor, New York, NY 10017
  Phone: (212) 944-1030
  Founded: 1933
  Affiliation: AAAA
  Membership: 107,541
  Publications: *Screen Actor Magazine* (quarterly)
President: Alan Rosenberg
Secretary-Treasurer: Connie Stevens
First Vice President: Anne-Marie Johnson
Second Vice President: Paul Christie
Third Vice President: Steve Fried

Seafarers
Seafarers International Union of North America [SIU]
  5201 Auth Way, Camp Springs, MD 20746
  Phone: (301) 899-0675
  Fax: (301) 899-7355
  Web site: www.seafarers.org
  Founded: 1938
  Affiliation: AFL-CIO
  Membership: 35,948
  Publications: *Seafarers Log* (monthly)
  Note: Seafarers' is a federation of 13 autonomous unions: American Maritime Officers; Fishermen's Union of America; Industrial, Professional, Technical Workers International Union; Marine Firemen's Union; Professional Security Officers Association; Sailors' Union of the Pacific; Seafarers Entertainment and Allied Trades Union; Seafarers International Union of North America-Atlantic, Gulf, Lakes and Inland Waters District/NMU; Seafarers International Union of Canada; SIU of Puerto Rico, Caribe and Latin America; Seafarers Maritime Union; Sugar Workers Union No. 1; and United Industrial, Service, Transportation, Professional and Government Workers of North America.
President: Michael Sacco

Executive Vice President: Augustin
  (Augie) Tellez
Secretary-Treasurer: David Heindel
Vice Presidents:
  Dean Corgey
  René Lioeanjie
  Kermett Mangram
  Nicholas J. Marrone
  Tom Orzechowski
  Joseph T. Soresi
  Charles Stewart
  George Tricker
National Director: John Spadaro

Security, Police and Fire Professionals

**International Union, Security, Police
  and Fire Professionals of America**
  [SPFPA]
  25510 Kelly Rd., Roseville, MI 48066
  Phone: (800) 228-7492
  Fax: (586) 772-9644
  E-mail: spfpa@aol.com
  Web site: www.spfpa.org
  Founded: 1948
  Affiliation: Independent
  Membership: 13,452
  Publications: *The Security Link*
    (semiannually)
President: David L. Hickey
Secretary-Treasurer: Dennis T. Eck
Vice Presidents:
  Mike Crawford
  Terry Fowler
  Bobby Jenkins
  Kerry Lacey
  Daniel Payne
  Mike Swartz

Service Employees

Service Employees International Union
  [SEIU]
  1313 L St., NW, Washington, DC
    20005
  Phone: (202) 898-3200
  Fax: (202) 898-3491
  E-mail: info@seiu.org
  Web site: www.seiu.org
  Founded: 1921
  Affiliation: CTW
  Membership: 1,702,639
  Publications: *SEIU Action* (bimonthly)
President: Andrew L. Stern
Executive Vice Presidents:
  Mary K. Henry
  Gerry Hudson
  Eliseo Medina
  Tom Woodruff
Secretary-Treasurer: Anna Burger

Sheet Metal Workers

**Sheet Metal Workers International
  Association** [SMW]
  United Unions Bldg., 1750 New York
    Ave., NW, Washington, DC
    20006
  Phone: (202) 783-5880
  Fax: (202) 662-0894
  E-mail: info@smwia.org
  Web site: www.smwia.org
  Founded: 1888
  Affiliation: AFL-CIO
  Membership: 144,480
  Publications: *The Journal* (bimonthly)
    and *Focus on Funds* (bimonthly)
President: Michael J. Sullivan
Secretary-Treasurer: Thomas J. Kelly
Vice Presidents:
  John D. Churuvia, Jr.
  John Harrington
  Timothy J. Hintze
  Stanley F. Karczynski
  Garry Kot
  Richard R. Lloyd
  Jay K. Potesta
  Roy Ringwood
  George B. Slater
  Gary Stevens
  Bruce W. Ward

Shoe and Allied Craftsmen

**Brotherhood of Shoe and Allied
  Craftsmen** [BSAC]
  P.O. Box 390, East Bridgewater, MA
    02333
  Phone: (508) 378-9300
  Fax: (508) 378-9800
  Founded: 1934
  Affiliation: Independent
President: Gerald Swimm
Vice President: Clinton Kimball

State, County and Municipal Employees

**American Federation of State, County
  and Municipal Employees**
  [AFSCME]
  1625 L St., NW, Washington, DC
    20036-5687
  Phone: (202) 429-1000
  Fax: (202) 429-1293
  E-mail: webmaster@afscme.org
  Web site: www.afscme.org
  Founded: 1936
  Affiliation: AFL-CIO
  Membership: 1,350,000
  Publications: *The Public Employee
    Magazine* (6 issues annually) and
    Leader
President: Gerald W. McEntee
Secretary-Treasurer: William Lucy

Vice Presidents:
  Ronald C. Alexander
  Ken Allen
  Henry L. Bayer
  Peter J. Benner
  George Boncoraglio
  Anthony Caso
  Jan Corderman
  Greg Devereux
  Danny Donohue
  David Fillman
  Mike Fox
  Albert Garrett
  Raglan George, Jr.
  Alice Goff
  Sherryl A. Gordon
  Ellie Ortiz López
  Salvatore Luciano
  Roberta Lynch
  Glenard S. Middleton
  Patricia Moss
  Michael D. Murphy
  Henry Nicholas
  Russell K. Okata
  George E. Popyack
  Greg Powell
  Joan Reed
  Eddie Rodriguez
  Joseph P. Rugola
  Kathy J. Sackman
  Mary Sullivan
  David Warrick
  Jeanette Wynn

Steelworkers

**United Steel, Paper and Forestry,
  Rubber, Manufacturing, Energy,
  Allied Industrial and Service
  Workers International Union** [USW]
  Five Gateway Ctr., Pittsburgh, PA
    15222
  Phone: (412) 562-2400
  Fax: (412) 562-2484
  E-mail: webmaster@
    steelworkers-usw.org
  Web site: www.usw.org
  Founded: 1942
  Affiliation: AFL-CIO
  Membership: 535,461
  Publications: *Steelabor* (four times
    yearly) and *PACE Setter*
President: Leo W. Gerard
Executive Vice President: Ron Hoover
Secretary-Treasurer: James D. English
International Vice Presidents:
  Thomas M. Conway
  Richard (Dick) LaCosse
Vice Presidents:
  James E. Pannell
  Lewis Peacock
  James K. Phillips

Teachers
American Federation of Teachers
[AFT]
555 New Jersey Ave., NW,
   Washington, DC 20001
Phone: (202) 879-4400
Fax: (202) 879-4545
E-mail: online@aft.org
Web site: www.aft.org
Founded: 1916
Affiliation: AFL-CIO
Membership: 828,512
Publications: *American Teacher*,
   American Educator, *PSRP*
   Reporter, *Healthwire*, *AFT On*
   Campus, *Public Employee*
   Advocate, and *American Academic*
President: Edward J. McElroy
Secretary-Treasurer: Nat LaCour
Executive Vice President: Antonia
   Cortese
Vice Presidents:
   Roger Benson
   Mary Bergan
   Barbara Bowen
   Kathy Chavez
   John Cole
   Paul F. Cole
   Edward Doherty
   Kathleen Donahue
   James Dougherty
   Andy Ford
   Janna Garrison
   David Gray
   David Hecker
   Thomas Hobart, Jr.
   Richard Ianuzzi
   Sandra Irons
   Lorretta Johnson
   Ted Kirsch
   Alan Lubin
   Herb Magidson
   Louis Malfaro
   James McGarvey
   Tom Mooney
   Maria Neira
   Ruby Newbold
   Candice Owley
   Maria Portalatin
   Marcia Reback
   Laura Rico
   Pat Santeramo
   Judy Schaubach
   William Scheuerman
   Sandra Schroeder
   Marilyn Stewart
   Louise Sundin
   Ivan Tiger
   Ann Twomey
   Adam Urbanski
   Randi Weingarten

Teamsters
International Brotherhood of
Teamsters [IBT]
25 Louisiana Ave., NW, Washington,
   DC 20001
Phone: (202) 624-6800
Fax: (202) 624-6918
E-mail: feedback@teamster.org
Web site: www.teamster.org
Founded: 1903
Affiliation: CTW
Membership: 1,350,000
Publications: *The Teamster* (monthly)
President: James P. Hoffa
General Secretary-Treasurer: C. Thomas
   Keegel
Vice Presidents:
   Randy Cammack
   Jack Cipriani
   Pat Flynn
   Tom Fraser
   Fred Gegare
   Richard K. Hall
   Carl E. Haynes
   Al Hobart
   Tyson Johnson
   Walt Lytle
   Chuck Mack
   Dotty W. Malinsky
   John Murphy
   Thomas R. O'Donnell
   Jim Santangelo
   Lester A. Singer
   Ralph J. Taurone
   Richard Volpe
   Ken Wood
   Phillip E. Young
   Garnet Zimmerman
President of Teamsters Canada: Robert
   Bouvier

Television and Radio Artists
American Federation of Television and
Radio Artists [AFTRA]
260 Madison Ave., New York, NY
   10016-2401
Phone: (212) 532-0800
Fax: (212) 532-2242
E-mail: info@aftra.com
Web site: www.aftra.org
Los Angeles office: 5757 Wilshire
   Blvd., 9th Floor, Los Angeles, CA
   90036-0800
Phone: (323) 634-8100
Fax: (323) 634-8194
Founded: 1937
Affiliation: AAAA
Membership: 57,452
Publications: *AFTRA Magazine* (3
   times a year)
President: John Connolly

Secretary: Matt Kimbrough
Treasurer: Mitch McGuire
Vice Presidents:
   Lainie Cooke
   Dave Corey
   Belva Davis
   Bob Edwards
   David Hartley-Margolin
   Dick Kay
   Ron Morgan
   Roberta Reardon
   Shelby Scott
Executive Director: Kim R. Hedgpath

Theatrical Stage Employees
International Alliance of Theatrical
Stage Employes, Moving Picture
Technicians, Artists and Allied
Crafts of the United States and
Canada [IATSE]
1430 Broadway, 20th Floor, New
   York, NY 10018
Phone: (212) 730-1770
Fax: (212) 730-7809
Web site: www.iatse-intl.org
West Coast office: 10045 Riverside
   Dr., Toluca Lake, CA 91602
Phone: (818) 980-3499
Fax: (818) 980-3496
Founded: 1893
Affiliation: AFL-CIO
Membership: 105,180
Publications: *The Official Bulletin*
   (quarterly)
International President: Thomas C. Short
Secretary-Treasurer: James B. Wood
Vice Presidents:
   Michael Barnes
   John T. Beckman
   J. Walter Cahill
   Thom Davis
   Anthony DePaulo
   Daniel DiTolla
   Brian J. Lawlor
   Matthew D. Loeb
   Timothy Magee
   Michael F. Miller
   Rudy N. Napoleone
   Damian Petti
   Mimi Wolch

Train Dispatchers

American Train Dispatchers Association [ATDA]

1370 Ontario St., Suite 1040, Cleveland, OH 44113

Phone: (216) 241-2770

Fax: (216) 241-6286

E-mail: atddble@aol.com

Web site: www.atdd.homestead.com

Founded: 1917

Affiliation: AFL-CIO

Membership: 2,508

Publications: *The Train Dispatcher* (quarterly)

President: F. Leo McCann

Secretary-Treasurer: Gary L. Melton

Vice Presidents:

C.L. Boggs

S.A. Hunnicutt

G.A. Pardlo

D.W. Volz

Transit Union

Amalgamated Transit Union [ATU]

5025 Wisconsin Ave., NW, Washington, DC 20016-4139

Phone: (202) 537-1645

Fax: (202) 244-7824

Web site: www.atu.org

Founded: 1892

Affiliation: AFL-CIO

Membership: 180,598

Publications: *In Transit* (bimonthly)

President: Warren S. George

Executive Vice President: Michael J. Siano

Secretary-Treasurer: Oscar Owens

Vice Presidents:

Robert H. Baker

Janis M. Borchardt

Paul Bowen

Charles Cook

Randy Graham

Lawrence J. Hanley

Donald T. Hansen

Ronald J. Heintzman

Bob M. Hykaway

Larry R. Kinnear

Kenneth Kirk

William G. McLean

Tommy Mullins

Richard M. Murphy

Javier Perez, Jr.

Rodney Richmond

Karen Simmons

Joseph Welch

Transport Workers

Transport Workers Union of America [TWU]

1700 Broadway, New York, NY 10019

Phone: (212) 259-4900

Fax: (212) 265-4537

E-mail: mailbox@twu.org

Web site: www.twu.org

Founded: 1934

Affiliation: AFL-CIO

Membership: 125,398

Publications: *TWU Express* (11 months a year)

President: Michael O'Brien

Executive Vice President: James Little

Secretary-Treasurer: John J. Kerrigan

Transportation Communications Union

Transportation Communications International Union/IAM [TCU/IAM]

3 Research Place, Rockville, MD 20850

Phone: (301) 948-4910

Fax: (301) 948-1872

Web site: www.tcunion.org

Founded: 1899

Affiliation: AFL-CIO

Membership: 61,578

Publications: *Interchange* (6 times annually) and *Telling It Like It Is* (6 times annually)

President: Robert A. Scardelletti

Secretary-Treasurer: Howard W. Randolph, Jr.

Vice Presidents:

Richard A. Arndt

Daniel L. Biggs

Joseph P. Condo

Robert F. Davis

Richard A. Johnson

Joel M. Parker

James L. Quilty

Transportation Union

United Transportation Union [UTU]

14600 Detroit Ave., Cleveland, OH 44107-4250

Phone: (216) 228-9400

Fax: (216) 228-5755

E-mail: utunews@utu.org

Web site: www.utu.org

Founded: 1969

Affiliation: AFL-CIO

Membership: 65,593

Publications: *UTU News* (monthly)

President: Paul C. Thompson

Secretary-Treasurer: Daniel E. Johnson, III

Vice Presidents:

Roy G. Arnold

James R. Cumby

David L. Hakey

Treasury Employees

National Treasury Employees Union [NTEU]

1750 H St., NW, Washington, DC 20006

Phone: (202) 572-5500

Fax: (202) 572-5640

E-mail: nteu-info@nteu.org

Web site: www.nteu.org

Founded: 1938

Affiliation: Independent

Membership: 77,234

Publications: *NTEU Bulletin* (monthly), *Steward Update* (monthly), and *Capital Report* (monthly)

President: Colleen M. Kelley

Executive Vice President: Frank D. Ferris

UNITE HERE

UNITE HERE [UNITE HERE]

275 7th Ave., New York, NY 10001-6708

Phone: (212) 265-7000

Fax: (212) 265-3415

Web site: www.unitehere.org

Founded: 1900

Affiliation: CTW

Membership: 441,276

Publications: *UNITE!*

President: Bruce S. Raynor

Executive Vice President: Edgar Romney

President, Hospitality Industry: John W. Wilhelm

University Professors

American Association of University Professors [AAUP]

1012 14th St., NW, Suite 500, Washington, DC 20005

Phone: (202) 737-5900

Fax: (202) 737-5526

E-mail: aaup@aaup.org

Web site: www.aaup.org

Founded: 1915

Affiliation: Independent

Membership: 43,977

Publications: *Academe* (6 issues annually)

President: Cary Nelson

First Vice President: Larry G. Gerber

Second Vice President: Estelle Gellman

Secretary-Treasurer: Jeffrey A. Butts

Utility Workers

Utility Workers Union of America
[UWUA]
815 16th St., NW, Washington, DC
20006
Phone: (202) 974-8200
Fax: (202) 974-8201
Web site: www.uwua.net
Founded: 1946
Affiliation: AFL-CIO
Membership: 48,892
Publications: *Light* (bimonthly)
President: Donald E. Wightman
Executive Vice President: D. Michael
Langford
Vice President: Gerald Waters
Secretary-Treasurer: Gary M. Ruffner

Variety Artists

American Guild of Variety Artists
[AGVA]
363 7th Ave., 17th Floor, New York,
NY 10001
Phone: (212) 675-1003
E-mail: agvany@aol.com
Affiliation: AAAA
Membership: 3,900
Executive President: Rod McKuen

Weather Service Employees

National Weather Service Employees
Organization [NWSEO]
601 Pennsylvania Ave., NW, Suite
900, Washington, DC 20004
Phone: (703) 293-9651
Fax: (703) 293-9653
Web site: www.nwseo.org
Founded: 1976
Affiliation: Independent
Membership: 1,300
Publications: *The Four Winds*
(monthly)
President: Dan Sobien
Secretary-Treasurer: Marguerite Matera
Vice President: William G. Hopkins

Westinghouse Salaried Employees

Association of Westinghouse Salaried
Employees [AWSE]
820 East Pittsburgh Plaza, Pittsburgh,
PA 15112
Phone: (412) 823-9333
Fax: (412) 823-9299
Founded: 1938
Affiliation: Independent
Membership: 1,700
Publications: *The A.W.S.E. Reporter*
President: Anthony Bozik

Writers

National Writers Union [NWU]
113 University Place, 6th Floor, New
York, NY 10003-1209
Phone: (212) 254-0279
Fax: (212) 254-0673
E-mail: nwu@nwu.org
Web site: www.nwu.org
Founded: 1981
Affiliation: UAW
Publications: *American Writer*
(quarterly)
President: Gerald Colby
Vice Presidents:
Jack Rasmus
Pamela Vossenas
Ken Wachsberger
Financial Secretary: Thomas J. Gradel

Writers, East

Writers Guild of America, East, Inc.
[WGAE]
555 W. 57th St., Suite 1230, New
York, NY 10019
Phone: (212) 767-7800
Fax: (212) 582-1909
Web site: www.wgaeast.org
Founded: 1954
Affiliation: AFL-CIO
Membership: 3,810
Publications: *WGAE Newsletter*
(bimonthly)
Note: Affiliated with Writers Guild of
America, West, Inc.
President: Chris Albers
Secretary-Treasurer: Gail Lee
Vice President: Tom Fontana
Executive Director: Mona Mangan

Writers, West

Writers Guild of America, West, Inc.
[WGAW]
7000 W. Third St., Los Angeles, CA
90048
Phone: (323) 951-4000
Toll-Free: (800) 548-4532
Fax: (323) 782-4800
Web site: www.wga.org
Founded: 1933
Affiliation: Independent
Membership: 7,627
Publications: *Written By*
Note: Affiliated with Writers Guild of
America, East, Inc.
President: Patric M. Verrone
Secretary-Treasurer: Elias Davis
Vice President: David N. Weiss
Executive Director: John McLean

PART III. Local, Intermediate, National, and Independent Unions by State and City

Union names and state and city locations are taken from the latest Labor Organization Reports submitted by the unions to the U.S. Department of Labor's Office of Labor-Management Standards.

The abbreviations used in Part III are shown below:

AREA	Area	LCH	Local Chapter
ASSN	Association	LDIV	Local Division
BCTC	Building and Construction Trades Council	LEC	Local Executive Council
		LG	Lodge
BD	Board	LJEB	Local Joint Executive Board
BR	Branch	LLG	Local Lodge
C	Council	LSC	Local Staff Council
CH	Chapter	LU	Local Union
COM	Committee	MEC	Master Executive Council
CONBD	Conference Board	MTC	Metal Trades Council
CONF	Conference	NC	National Council
D	District	NHQ	National Headquarters
DALU	Directly Affiliated Local Union	PC	Port Council
DC	District Council	R	Region
DIV	Division	RB	Regional Board
DJC	District Joint Council	RC	Regional Council
DLG	District Lodge	SA	State Association, State Affiliate
FASTC	Food and Allied Service Trade Council	SBA	System Board of Adjustment
FED	Federation	SC	System Council
GC	General Committee	SCOM	System Committee
GCA	General Committee of Adjustment	SD	System Division
IUDTC	Industrial Union Department Trades Council	SF	System Federation
		SFED	State Federation
JB	Joint Board	SLB	State Legislative Board
JC	Joint Council	SLG	Sub-Lodge, Subordinate Lodge
JCONF	Joint Conference	STC	State Council
JPB	Joint Protective Board	STCON	State Conference
LBR	Local Branch	ULSTC	Union Label Service Trades Council
LC	Local Council	UNIT	Unit

Alabama

AFL-CIO Trade and Industrial Departments

Building and Construction Trades Department
BCTC Alabama . . . . Mobile
BCTC Central Alabama . . . . Birmingham
BCTC Coosa Valley . . . . Gadsden
BCTC Mobile Alabama-Pensacola Florida . . . . Mobile
BCTC North Alabama . . . Sheffield
BCTC Shoals Area Central Labor Union . . . . Sheffield
BCTC Tuscaloosa . . . . Tuscaloosa

Maritime Trades Department
PC Mobile Area . . . . Mobile

Metal Trades Department
MTC Wiregrass Trades . Fort Rucker

Other Councils and Committees
C Northeast Alabama Labor Council . . . . Gadsden

AFL-CIO Directly Affiliated Locals

AFL-CIO
C Montgomery Central Labor . . . . Opelika

Affiliated Labor Organizations

Air Traffic Controllers
LU . . . . Dothan
LU BHM . . . . Birmingham
LU HSV . . . . Huntsville
LU MGM . . . . Hope Hull
LU MOB . . . . Mobile

Asbestos Workers
CONF 12 Southeastern States . . . . Birmingham
LU 55. . . . . Mobile
LU 78. . . . . Birmingham

Automobile, Aerospace Workers
LU 1155 . . . . Birmingham
LU 1413 . . . . Huntsville
LU 1639 . . . . Mobile
LU 1929 . . . . Huntsville
LU 1990 . . . . Hamilton
LU 2083 . . . . Tuscaloosa
LU 2195 . . . . Tanner
LU 2222 . . . . Birmingham
LU 2276 . . . . Huntsville

Bakery, Confectionery, Tobacco Workers and Grain Millers
LU 09-173-G . . . . Attalla

Boilermakers
LG 56-S . . . . Bridgeport
LG 79-D Cement Workers . . . . Demopolis
LG 108 . . . . Birmingham
LG 112 . . . . Mobile
LG 455 . . . . Muscle Shoals
LG 584 . . . . Moundville

Bricklayers
LU 1 . . . . Birmingham
LU 3 . . . . Montgomery
LU 4 . . . . Tuscaloosa
LU 6 . . . . Mobile
LU 8 . . . . Sheffield
LU 11. . . . . Arab
LU 15. . . . . Athens

Carpenters
LU 89. . . . . Mobile
LU 109 . . . . Sheffield
LU 127 . . . . Birmingham
LU 1192 . . . . Birmingham
LU 1274 . . . . Decatur
LU 2401 . . . . Birmingham
LU 4001 Alabama Carpenters Regional Council . . . . . Irondale

Civilian Technicians
CH 67 Northern Alabama . . Decatur
CH 68 Southern Alabama . . . . Fort Deposit
CH 123 Alabama Air . . Birmingham

Communications Workers
COM Alabama Political & Legislative . . . . Decatur
LU 3901 . . . . Anniston
LU 3902 . . . . Birmingham
LU 3903 . . . . Decatur
LU 3904 . . . . Gadsden
LU 3905 . . . . Huntsville
LU 3906 . . . . Jasper
LU 3907 . . . . Mobile
LU 3908 . . . . Montgomery
LU 3909. . . . . Sylacauga
LU 3910 . . . . Selma
LU 3911 . . . . Muscle Shoals
LU 3912 . . . . Tuscaloosa
LU 3950 . . . . Birmingham
LU 3971. . . . . Red Level
LU 3972 . . . . Dothan
LU 3974 . . . . Tallassee
LU 3990 . . . . Prattville
LU 14300. . . . . Birmingham
LU 14307. . . . . Birmingham
LU 83693 . . . . Selma
LU 83711. . . . . Gadsden
LU 83777 IUE . . . . Foley
LU 83783 . . . . Huntsville
LU 83793 . . . . Selma

Electrical Workers
LU 136 . . . . Birmingham
LU 253 . . . . Birmingham
LU 345 . . . . Mobile
LU 391 . . . . Sand Rock
LU 443 . . . . Montgomery
LU 505 . . . . Mobile
LU 558 . . . . Sheffield
LU 656. . . . . Pleasant Grove
LU 765 . . . . Sheffield
LU 780. . . . . Eufuala
LU 796 . . . . Columbia
LU 801 . . . . Tallassee
LU 833 . . . . Jasper
LU 841 . . . . Trussville
LU 904 . . . . Tallassee
LU 1053 . . . . Gallion
LU 1629. . . . . Sylacauga
LU 1642 . . . . Lineville
LU 1871 . . . . Birmingham
LU 1980. . . . . Ashford
LU 2040 . . . . Brewton
LU 2048 . . . . Pennington
LU 2077 . . . . Childersburg
LU 2129. . . . . Satsuma
LU 2152. . . . . Enterprise
LU 2251. . . . . Andalusia
LU 2298 . . . . Leroy
LU 2362. . . . . Selma
SC 19-U . . . . Birmingham

Elevator Constructors
LU 24. . . . . Birmingham
LU 124 . . . . Lillian

Engineers
LU 27 . . . . Huntsville
LU 561 . . . . Mobile

Federal Employees
LU 131 . . . . Tuscaloosa

Food and Commercial Workers
LU 88-T . . . . Decatur
LU 191-T. . . . . Trinity
LU 223-C . . . . Killen
LU 488-C. . . . . Saraland
LU 504-T . . . . Henagar
LU 683-T. . . . . Falkville
LU 1657 . . . . Birmingham

Glass, Molders, Pottery and Plastics Workers
LU 62. . . . . Birmingham
LU 65-B . . . . Boaz
LU 85-B. . . . . Ashville
LU 214 . . . . Madison
LU 248 . . . . Dearmanville
LU 256-B . . . . Tarrant
LU 324. . . . . Anniston
LU 413-A . . . . Piedmont

Government Employees
C 27 Alabama State . . Birmingham
C 67 Food Inspection Locals, Southern . . . . Deatsville
LU 110 VA . . . . Tuskegee
LU 131 VA . . . . Tuscaloosa
LU 503 . . . . Montgomery
LU 522 Montgomery . Montgomery
LU 997 DoD . . . . . Montgomery
LU 1815 DoD . . . . . . Fort Rucker
LU 1858 DoD . . . Redstone Arsenal
LU 1945 DoD . . . . Bynum
LU 2206 HHS . . . . . Birmingham
LU 2207 VA . . . . . . Birmingham
LU 2357 USDA . . . . Elmore
LU 3024 DoD . . . . . Birmingham
LU 3384 DoL . . . . Bessemer
LU 3434 NASA . . . Marshall Space Flight Center
LU 3438 HHS . . . . . Birmingham
LU 3844 . . . . Childersburg
LU 4058 CoP . . . . . Montgomery

Government Security Officers
LU 22 Browns Ferry Nuclear Plant . . . . Florence
LU 401 . . . . Fort Rucker

Graphic Communications
LU 100-C. . . . . Mobile
LU 121-C . . . . Vincent
LU 540-M . . . . Bessemer

Iron Workers
LU 92. . . . . Birmingham
LU 477 . . . . Sheffield
LU 798 . . . . Semmes

Laborers
LU 70. . . . . Mobile
LU 123 Public Employees . . . . . . Birmingham
LU 366 . . . . Sheffield
LU 559 . . . . Birmingham
LU 784 . . . . Ashford
LU 1317 Public Employees . . . . . . Birmingham

Letter Carriers
BR 106. . . . . Montgomery
BR 448. . . . . Anniston
BR 462 . . . . Huntsville
BR 469 . . . . Mobile
BR 530 . . . . Birmingham
BR 892 . . . . Florence
BR 937. . . . . Bessemer
BR 1047 . . . . Gadsden
BR 1096 . . . . Tuscaloosa
BR 1210. . . . . Talladega
BR 1314. . . . . Decatur
BR 1630 Wiregrass Letter Carriers . . . . Dothan
BR 2119. . . . . Andalusia
BR 2270 . . . . Hanceville
BR 3077. . . . . . . Alexander City
BR 3099. . . . . Jasper
BR 3122. . . . . Phenix City
BR 3135. . . . . Oneonta
BR 3266. . . . . Lanett
BR 3344 . . . . Jacksonville
BR 3359 . . . . Fort Payne
BR 3372. . . . . Heflin
BR 3386 . . . . Roanoke
BR 3457. . . . . Clanton
BR 3588. . . . . Eutaw
BR 3589 . . . . Marion
BR 3590. . . . . Montevallo
BR 3852 . . . . Haleyville
BR 4030. . . . . Luverne
BR 4309. . . . . Citronelle
BR 4352 . . . . Childersburg
BR 4626. . . . . Aliceville
BR 4671 . . . . Monroeville
BR 5007 . . . . Winfield
BR 5130 . . . . Valley
BR 6118 . . . . Foley
BR 6194 . . . . Moulton
BR 6375 . . . . Brundidge
BR 6494 . . . . Lafayette
SA Alabama . . . . Huntsville

Locomotive Engineers
DIV 73 . . . . Trussville
DIV 140 . . . . Mobile
DIV 150 . . . . Birmingham
DIV 156 . . . . Birmingham
DIV 223 . . . . Valley Grande
DIV 280 . . . . Sheffield
DIV 332. . . . . Deatsville
DIV 386 . . . . Empire
DIV 409. . . . . Phenix City
DIV 423 . . . . Muscle Shoals
DIV 495 . . . . Montgomery
DIV 684 . . . . Birmingham
DIV 899 . . . . Bessemer
SLB Alabama Legislative Board. . . . . Birmingham
SLB Georgia . . . . . Smiths Station

Longshoremen
LU 1410 . . . . Mobile
LU 1410-1 . . . . Mobile
LU 1459 . . . . Mobile
LU 1984 . . . . Mobile
LU 1985 . . . . Mobile

Machinists
DLG 75. . . . . Daleville
DLG 92. . . . . Sheffield
LG 7 . . . . Vincent
LG 65 . . . . Sheffield
LG 271 . . . . Birmingham
LG 291 International Association
  Machinists & Aerospace
  Workers . . . . Jacksonville
LG 359 . . . . Hueytown
LG 676 . . . . McKenzie
LG 985 . . . . Sylacauga
LG 1189 . . . . Sheffield
LG 1632 . . . . Dothan
LG 2003 . . . . Daleville
LG 2452 . . . . Leroy
LG 2766 . . . . Madison
LLG 44 . . . . Florence
STC . . . . Killen

Maintenance of Way Employes
LG 645 . . . . Glencoe
LG 682 . . . . Repton
SLG 529 . . . . . Valley Grande
SLG 536 . . . . Piedmont
SLG 585 . . . . Oxford
SLG 804. . . . . Phenix City
SLG 992 . . . . Hanceville
SLG 1857. . . . . . . Brundidge
SLG 2033 . . . . Aliceville
SLG 2154 . . . . Mobile

Mine Workers
LU 1288. . . . . Jasper
LU 1553 . . . . Holly Pond
LU 1554 . . . . Dora
LU 1867 . . . . Hueytown
LU 1876. . . . . Northport
LU 1881 . . . . Dora
LU 1926 . . . . Northport
LU 1928 . . . . Hueytown
LU 1947 . . . . Joppa
LU 1948 . . . . Cordova
LU 1987. . . . . Jasper
LU 2042 . . . . Jasper
LU 2133 . . . . Hueytown
LU 2245 . . . . Tuscaloosa
LU 2368 . . . . Brookwood
LU 2397 . . . . Brookwood
LU 2427 . . . . Adger
LU 5841 . . . . Winfield
LU 5986. . . . . Mulga
LU 6255 . . . . Empire
LU 6855 . . . . Nauvoo
LU 7154 . . . . . . Double Springs
LU 7813 . . . . Parrish
LU 7918 . . . . Adamsville
LU 7930 . . . . Jasper
LU 8460 . . . . West Blocton
LU 8982 . . . . Midfield
LU 9511 . . . . Jasper

Musicians
LU 256-733 Birmingham
  Musicians Protective
  Association. . . . . Birmingham

National Staff Organization
LU Staff Organization,
  Association, Alabama Education
  Association . . . . . Montgomery

LU Staff Organization, Professional,
  Alabama . . . . Mobile

Nurses
SA Alabama State Nurses
  Association . . . . Montgomery

Office and Professional Employees
LU 102 . . . . Daleville

Operating Engineers
LU 312 . . . . . Birmingham
LU 320 . . . . Florence
LU 653 . . . . Mobile

Painters
LU 57 . . . . Birmingham
LU 779 . . . . Mobile
LU 1293 Sheffield-Florence-
  Tuscumbia Local. . Muscle Shoals

Plumbing and Pipe Fitting
LU 52 . . . . . Montgomery
LU 91 . . . . Birmingham
LU 119 . . . . Mobile
LU 372 . . . . . . Tuscaloosa
LU 377 . . . . . . Huntsville
LU 498 . . . . Gadsden
LU 548 . . . . Anniston
LU 760 . . . . . . Muscle Shoals

Postal and Federal Employees
LU 402 . . . . Adamsville
LU 408 . . . . Eightmile

Postal Mail Handlers
LU 317 . . . . Birmingham

Postal Workers
LU 303 Birmingham . . Birmingham
LU 323 Montgomery
  Area . . . . Montgomery
LU 332 Dothan. . . . . . . Dothan
LU 359 North Alabama
  Area . . . . Huntsville
LU 399 West Alabama
  Area . . . . Tuscaloosa
LU 501 Jasper . . . . Jasper
LU 525 Anniston. . . . . Anniston
LU 537 Gadsden . . . . . Gadsden
LU 715 South Alabama
  Area . . . . Mobile
LU 805 Athens . . . . . . Athens
LU 810 Florence . . . . Florence
LU 895 Brewton . . . . . Brewton
LU 1105 Haleyville. . . Haleyville
LU 1515 Montevallo . . Montevallo
LU 1705 Guntersville. . Guntersville
LU 1800 Albertville . . . Albertville
LU 2634 Fayette . . . . . Fayette
LU 2635 Clanton . . . . . Clanton
LU 2660 Scottsboro . . . Scottsboro
LU 2675 Alexander
  City . . . . . . Alexander City
LU 2708 Enterprise . . . Enterprise
LU 2708 Enterprise . . . Enterprise
LU 2709 Opp . . . . Opp
LU 2827 Fort Payne . . . Fort Payne
LU 2870 Boaz . . . . Boaz
LU 3511 Pell City . . . . Pell City
LU 3513 Leeds . . . . . . Leeds
LU 5515 Hamilton. . . . . Hamilton
SA Alabama . . . . Saraland

Railroad Signalmen
GC 78 Southern Railway System
  Lines . . . . Ryland
LLG 137 . . . . Bay Minette

LLG 178 . . . . Pinson

**Retail, Wholesale and Department
Store**
JC 932 Alabama Mid-
  South . . . . Birmingham
LU 102-A. . . . . Birmingham
LU 105 . . . . Birmingham
LU 107 . . . . Birmingham
LU 201-A. . . . . Birmingham
LU 261 . . . . Birmingham
LU 405 . . . . Birmingham
LU 441 . . . . Birmingham
LU 451 . . . . Birmingham
LU 506 . . . . Gadsden
LU 555 . . . . Birmingham
LU 590 . . . . Birmingham
LU 615 . . . . Birmingham
LU 645 . . . . Birmingham
LU 928 Alabama ABC
  Employees . . . . . Birmingham
LU 1095 . . . . Birmingham

Rural Letter Carriers
SA Alabama . . . . . Guntersville

**Security, Police and Fire
Professionals**
LU 598 . . . . Athens
LU 599 . . . . Mobile
LU 600 . . . . Trinity
LU 601 . . . . Killen

Sheet Metal Workers
LU 48. . . . . Birmingham
LU 441 . . . . Mobile

Steelworkers
C Alabama . . . . Prattville
C Lehigh Joint Conference. . Moody
LU 125 . . . . Anniston
LU 3-267 . . . . . Hatchechubbee
LU 3-592 . . . . Mobile
LU 3-1535 . . . . Cherokee
LU 03-44 . . . . Ragland
LU 03-108 . . . . Leeds
LU 03-193 . . . . Courtland
LU 03-229 . . . . Mobile
LU 03-265 . . . . Fairhope
LU 03-297 . . . . . . Tuscaloosa
LU 03-300 . . . . . . Montgomery
LU 03-336 . . . . . . Grove Hill
LU 03-339 . . . . . . Thomasville
LU 03-361 . . . . Jackson
LU 03-462 . . . . Prattville
LU 03-488 . . . . Adger
LU 03-501 . . . . Huntsville
LU 03-516 . . . . Hollins
LU 03-524 Bayou La
  Batre Community
  Center. . . . . . Bayou La Batre
LU 03-537 . . . . Calera
LU 03-541 . . . . Mobile
LU 03-542 . . . . Leeds
LU 03-543 . . . . Birmingham
LU 03-546 . . . . . . Bay Minette
LU 03-562 . . . . McIntosh
LU 03-563 . . . . Calera
LU 03-593 . . . . Axis
LU 03-594 . . . . Northport
LU 03-675 . . . . Guin
LU 03-692 . . . . Childersburg
LU 03-719 . . . . Demopolis
LU 03-881 . . . . . . Meridianville
LU 03-888 . . . . Brewton
LU 03-906 . . . . Falkville
LU 03-923 . . . . . Pleasant Grove
LU 03-941 . . . . Brewton

LU 03-950 . . . . Linden
LU 03-952. . . . . Butler
LU 03-966 . . . . Linden
LU 03 971. . . . . Cottonton
LU 03-1083 . . . . Jackson
LU 03-1137 . . . . Courtland
LU 03-1161 . . . . Florence
LU 03-1286 . . . . Mobile
LU 03-1368 . . . . . Sweet Water
LU 03-1368 . . . . . Thomasville
LU 03-1394 . . . . Excel
LU 03-1406 . . . . . . Georgiana
LU 03-1421 . . . . . . Saraland
LU 03-1441 . . . . Selma
LU 03-1444 . . . . . Autaugaville
LU 03-1458 Prattville
  Maintenance . . . . . . Prattville
LU 03-1486. . . . . . Birmingham
LU 03-1514 . . . . . . Fort Payne
LU 03-1522 . . . . . . Talladega
LU 03-1575 . . . . . . Chickasaw
LU 03-1595 . . . . . . Sylacauga
LU 03-1684. . . . . . . Munford
LU 03-1704. . . . . . Birmingham
LU 03-1835 . . . . . . Demopolis
LU 03-1865 . . . . . . Columbia
LU 03-1873 . . . . . . Semmes
LU 03-1972 . . . . . Fort Mitchell
LU 03-1978 . . . . . . Prattville
LU 03-1995. . . . . . Grove Hill
LU 05-919. . . . . . . Flat Rock
LU 05-965. . . . . . . Flat Rock
LU 09-12-L . . . . Gadsden
LU 09-81-S . . . . . . Montevallo
LU 09-127-S . . . . . Huntsville
LU 09-200-ABG . . . Muscle Shoals
LU 09-203-A . . . . . . Decatur
LU 09-207-A . . . . . . Moulton
LU 09-217 . . . . Florence
LU 09-223 . . . . Leighton
LU 09-276. . . . . Jasper
LU 09-295 . . . . Winfield
LU 09-351-L . . . . . Tuscaloosa
LU 09-417 . . . . Cherokee
LU 09-481-G . . . . . . Florence
LU 09-553-S . . . . . . Bessemer
LU 09-753-L . . . . . . Opelika
LU 09-844-L . . . . . Birmingham
LU 09-896-L . . . . . . Lineville
LU 09-915-L . . . . . . Gadsden
LU 09-936-L . . . . . Scottsboro
LU 09-976-L . . . . . . Eutaw
LU 09-1013-S . . . . . Fairfield
LU 09-1057-S . . . . . Birmingham
LU 09-2122-S . . . Pleasant Grove
LU 09-2140-S . . . . . Bessemer
LU 09-2176-S . . . . . Gadsden
LU 09-2210-S . . . . . Fairfield
LU 09-2528-S . . . . . Bridgeport
LU 09-3768-S . . . . . Birmingham
LU 09-4754-S . . . . . Whistler
LU 09-4841-S . . . . . Bessemer
LU 09-7436-S . . . . . Pinson
LU 09-7468-S . . . . . Gadsden
LU 09-7700-S . . . . . Cullman
LU 09-7740-S . . . . . Warrior
LU 09-7750-S . . . . Montgomery
LU 09-8285-S . . . . . Birmingham
LU 09-8309-S . . . . . Centre
LU 09-8538-S . . . . . Pike Road
LU 09-8542-S . . . . . Moody
LU 09-8767-S . . . . Mount Vernon
LU 09-8855-S . . . . . Valley Head
LU 09-9201-S . . . . . Hueytown
LU 09-9226-S . . . . . Birmingham
LU 09-9282-S . . . . . Glencoe
LU 09-9287-S . . . . . Huntsville
LU 09-9361-S . . . . . Marion

LU 09-9506 . . . . Anniston
LU 09-12014-S . . . . . . Cordova
LU 09-12019-S . . . . . Dolomite
LU 09-12030-S . . . . . Birmingham
LU 09-12136-S . . . . . Warrior
LU 09-12768-S . . . . . Bessemer
LU 09-13140-S . . . . . Bessemer
LU 09-13350-S . . . . Montgomery
LU 09-13679-S . . . . Bryant
LU 09-14530-S . . . . . Cedar Bluff
LU 50-113 . . . . Mobile

Teamsters
LU 402 . . . . Muscle Shoals
LU 612 . . . . Birmingham
LU 991 . . . . Mobile

Theatrical Stage Employees
LU 78 . . . . Birmingham

LU 142 . . . . Mobile
LU 900 . . . . Huntsville

Transit Union
LDIV 725 . . . . Birmingham
LDIV 765 . . . . . . Montgomery

**Transportation Communications
Union**
D 376 . . . . Hanceville
D 1081 . . . . Saraland
D 1409 Southeastern System Board
96 . . . . Birmingham
LG 6060 Iron City . . . . Trussville
LG 6385 Birmingham . . . Quinton

Transportation Union
LU 598 . . . . Loxley
LU 622 . . . . Birmingham

LU 762 . . . . Coosada
LU 772 . . . . Leighton
LU 847 . . . . Hartselle
LU 1053 . . . . Jones
LU 1291 . . . . Birmingham
LU 1887 . . . . . . Sylvan Springs
SLB LO-1 Alabama . . Montgomery

Treasury Employees
CH 12 . . . . Birmingham
CH 220 . . . . McCalla

UNITE HERE
LU 719 . . . . Madison

Weather Service Employees
BR 02-12 . . . . Huntsville
BR 02-18 . . . . Alabaster
BR 02-29 . . . . Mobile

**Unaffiliated Labor
Organizations**
Alabama Organized Labor Awards
Foundation . . . . Decatur
Alabama Pipe Trades
Association . . . . . Birmingham
Alabama Plant Police Association
Birmingham LG 1 . . Birmingham
Association of Minor League
Umpires . . . . . . Birmingham
Court Security Officers Benevolent
Association . . . . Mobile
Representatives Union, International
Chemical Workers
Union . . . . Ohatchee
Workers Association
Independent . . . . . Birmingham

Alaska

AFL-CIO Trade and Industrial Departments

Building and Construction Trades Department
BCTC Juneau. . . . . Juneau
BCTC Ketchikan . . . . . Ketchikan
BCTC Western Alaska. . Anchorage

Other Councils and Committees
C Fairbanks Joint Crafts . Anchorage

Affiliated Labor Organizations

Agricultural Employees
BR 54. . . . . Anchorage

Air Traffic Controllers
LU A11. . . . . Anchorage
LU ANC . . . . Anchorage
LU FAI . . . . Fairbanks
LU JNU. . . . . Juneau
LU MRI . . . . Anchorage
LU NATCA FAY Local . Anchorage
LU ZAN . . . . Anchorage

Aircraft Mechanics
LU 34. . . . . Anchorage

Asbestos Workers
LU 97. . . . . Anchorage

Bricklayers
LU 1 . . . . Anchorage

Carpenters
C Alaska . . . . Anchorage
LU 1243 . . . . Fairbanks
LU 1281 . . . . Anchorage
LU 1501 Millwrights. . . Anchorage
LU 2247 . . . . Juneau
LU 2520 . . . . Anchorage

Civilian Technicians
CH 84 Alaska. . . . Fort Richardson

Electrical Workers
LU 1547 . . . . Anchorage

Food and Commercial Workers
LU 1496 . . . . Anchorage

Government Employees
LU 183 DoT . . . . . . Anchorage
LU 1101 Elmendorf
   AFB . . Elmendorf Air Force Base
LU 1668 DoD . . . . . Anchorage
LU 1712 DoD . . . Fort Richardson
LU 1834 . . . . . . Fort Wainwright
LU 1836 DoD . . . . . Eielson Air
                     Force Base
LU 1949 DoD . . . . Delta Junction
LU 3028 DoT . . . . . Anchorage

Government Security Officers
LU 46. . . . . Anchorage
LU 67. . . . . Anchorage

Graphic Communications
LU 327-C. . . . . Anchorage
LU 704-C . . . . Fairbanks

Iron Workers
LU 751 . . . . Anchorage

Laborers
DC Alaska . . . . Anchorage
LU 341 . . . . Anchorage
LU 942 . . . . Fairbanks

Letter Carriers
BR 4319 . . . . Anchorage
BR 4368. . . . . Ketchikan
BR 4491 . . . . Fairbanks
BR 4985 . . . . Juneau
BR 5275 . . . . Kodiak
BR 5893 . . . . Sitka

Longshore and Warehouse
LU 200 . . . . Juneau
LU 200 Alaska Division . . . Kodiak
LU 200 Dutch Harbor
   Unit . . . . Dutch Harbor
LU 200 Unit 16. . . . . . . Juneau
LU 200 Unit 60 . . . . . . Seward
LU 200 Unit 62 . . . . . Ketchikan
LU 200 Unit 62-B . . . . Klawock
LU 200 Unit 65. . . . . . Haines
LU 200 Unit 66. . . . . . Cordova
LU 200 Unit 87 . . . . . Wrangell
LU 200 Unit 222 . . . . . Kodiak

LU 200 Unit 223 . . . Dutch Harbor
LU 200 Unit 2201 . . . . . Juneau

Machinists
LG 601 . . . . Anchorage
LG 1735 . . . . Anchorage
LLG 1-1690 . . . . . . Anchorage
LLG FL-251 . . . . Sitka

Musicians
LU 650 . . . . Anchorage

National Staff Organization
LU Alaska . . . . Juneau

Nurses
SA Alaska . . . . Anchorage

Painters
LU 1140 . . . . Anchorage
LU 1555 . . . . Fairbanks

Plasterers and Cement Masons
LU 867 . . . . Anchorage

Plumbing and Pipe Fitting
LU 262 . . . . Juneau
LU 367 . . . . Anchorage
LU 375 . . . . Fairbanks
SA Alaska Pipe Trades . . Fairbanks

Postal Workers
LU 1416 Fairbanks . . . Fairbanks
LU 2756 Anchorage . . . Anchorage
LU 3323 Juneau. . . . . Auke Bay
LU 3667 Ketchikan. . . . Ketchikan
LU 6991 Sitka . . . . Sitka
SA Alaska. . . . . Auke Bay

Roofers, Waterproofers and Allied Workers
LU 190 . . . . Anchorage

Sheet Metal Workers
LU 23. . . . . Anchorage

Teachers
LU 5200 Alaska Public Employees
   Association. . . . . Juneau

Teamsters
LU 959 . . . . Anchorage

Theatrical Stage Employees
LU 918 . . . . Anchorage

Train Dispatchers
SCOM Alaska Railroad . Anchorage

Transportation Union
LU 1626 . . . . Anchorage

Treasury Employees
CH 69 . . . . Anchorage
CH 176 . . . . Anchorage

UNITE HERE
LU 878 . . . . Anchorage

Weather Service Employees
BR 05-8-A . . . . Anchorage
BR 05-9. . . . . Juneau
BR 05-10 . . . . Nome
BR 05-11 . . . . Fairbanks
BR 05-12 . . . . Yakutat
BR 05-13 . . . . Unalakleet
BR 05-14. . . . . . . Cold Bay
BR 05-15 . . . . Valdez
BR 05-16 . . . . Bethel
BR 05-17. . . . . Barrow
BR 05-20. . . . . . . King Salmon
BR 05-21. . . . . Kodiak
BR 05-23 . . . . . . St. Paul Island
BR 05-24. . . . . McGrath
BR 05-25 . . . . Kotzebue
BR 05-29 . . . . Anchorage
BR 05-30 . . . . Anchorage
BR 05-31 . . . . Anchorage
BR 05-32 . . . . Fairbanks
BR 05-33 . . . . Anchorage
BR 08-10 . . . . Juneau

Unaffiliated Labor Organizations

Alaska Independent Carpenters
   Millwrights LU 1 . . . . Fairbanks
Alaska Petroleum Joint Crafts
   Council. . . . . Anchorage
Anchorage Independent
   Longshoremen LU 1 . . Anchorage
Denali National Park Professional
   Drivers Association . . Anchorage
Fairbanks Building and Construction
   Trades Council . . . . . Fairbanks
Professional Labor Organization
   Alaska . . . . Juneau

American Samoa

Affiliated Labor
Organizations

Air Traffic Controllers
LU PPG. . . . . Pago Pago

Weather Service Employees
BR 07-4. . . . . Pago Pago

Arizona

AFL-CIO Trade and Industrial Departments

Building and Construction Trades Department
BCTC Phoenix . . . . Phoenix

Affiliated Labor Organizations

Air Traffic Controllers
LU DVT . . . . Phoenix
LU FFZ . . . . Mesa
LU GCN . . . . Grand Canyon
LU NATCA ZJX Local . . . Phoenix
LU PHX . . . . Phoenix
LU PRC . . . . Prescott
LU SDL . . . . Scottsdale
LU TUS . . . . Tucson
LU U90 . . . . Tucson

Aircraft Mechanics
LU 32 . . . . Tempe

Asbestos Workers
LU 73 . . . . Phoenix

Bakery, Confectionery, Tobacco Workers and Grain Millers
LU 232 . . . . Phoenix

Boilermakers
LG 4 . . . . Page
LG 361-D Cement
  Workers . . . . Kingman
LG 627 . . . . Phoenix

Bricklayers
LU 3 . . . . Phoenix

Carpenters
LU 408 . . . . Phoenix
LU 897 . . . . Bullhead City
LU 1914 . . . . Phoenix
LU 2093 . . . . Phoenix

Civilian Technicians
CH 61 Arizona Army . . . . Marana
CH 71 Phoenix Air . . . . . Phoenix

Communications Workers
LU 7019 . . . . Phoenix
LU 7026 . . . . Tucson
LU 7032 . . . . Yuma
LU 7050 . . . . Tempe
LU 7060 . . . . Phoenix
LU 7090 . . . . Tempe
LU 87124 . . . . Tucson
STC Arizona . . . . Phoenix

Electrical Workers
C GCC-1 Government
  Coordinating . . . . Phoenix
LU 266 . . . . Phoenix
LU 387 . . . . Phoenix
LU 518 . . . . Globe
LU 570 . . . . Tucson
LU 640 . . . . Phoenix
LU 769 . . . . Phoenix
LU 1116 . . . . Tucson

Elevator Constructors
LU 140 . . . . Phoenix

Federal Employees
LU 81 . . . . Tucson
LU 376 . . . . Tucson
LU 520 . . . . Sells
LU 1487 . . . . Yuma
LU 2094 . . . . Yuma
LU 2112 Coconino National
  Forest . . . . Tucson

Fire Fighters
LU 60-I United Emergency Medical
  Professionals . . . . . . Phoenix
LU 142-F . . . . Yuma
LU 3878-L United Maricopa County
  Firefighters . . . . Scottsdale

Food and Commercial Workers
LU 99-R . . . . Phoenix
LU 184-C . . . . Benson

Government Employees
C 159 Arizona State . . . . . Mesa
LU 376 . . . . Phoenix
LU 495 VA . . . . Tucson
LU 1207 . . . . Tucson
LU 1305 . . . . Grand Canyon
LU 1547 DoD . Luke Air Force Base
LU 1662 DoD . . . . Fort Huachuca
LU 2104 . . . . Yuma
LU 2313 DoJ . . . . Safford
LU 2382 VA . . . . Phoenix
LU 2401 VA . . . . Prescott
LU 2544 DoJ . . . . Tucson
LU 2595 DoJ . . . . Yuma
LU 2846 DoD . . . . Phoenix
LU 2859 DoJ . . . . . Arizona City
LU 2894 USDA . . . . Glendale
LU 2924 DoD . . . . Tucson
LU 3694 . . . . Phoenix
LU 3954 Federal Correctional
  Institution . . . . Glendale
LU 3955 . . . . Tucson
LU 3973 . . . . Tucson

Government Employees Association
LU 14-142 . . . . Yuma
LU 14-143 . . . . Yuma

Graphic Communications
LU 58-M . . . . Phoenix

Iron Workers
LU 75 . . . . Phoenix

Laborers
DC Souhwest Indian Health
  Service . . . . Phoenix
DC Southwest . . . . Phoenix
LU 383 . . . . Phoenix
LU 1376 . . . . Phoenix
LU 1386 SWNA Health Care
  Employees . . . . Phoenix

Letter Carriers
BR 576 . . . . Phoenix
BR 704 Carl J. Kennedy . . . Tucson
BR 859 . . . . Prescott
BR 1642 . . . . Yuma
BR 1902 . . . . Mesa
BR 2417 . . . . Tucson
BR 3238 . . . . Payson
BR 4761 . . . . Ajo
BR 5850 . . . . . Lake Havasu City
BR 6156 . . . . Sun City

BR 6320 . . . . Holbrook
SA Arizona . . . . Sun City

Locomotive Engineers
DIV 28 . . . . Tucson
DIV 123 . . . . Goodyear
DIV 134 . . . . Winslow
DIV 383 . . . . Fort Mohave
DIV 647 . . . . Phoenix
SLB Arizona . . . . Tucson

Machinists
LG 519 . . . . Phoenix
LG 933 . . . . Tucson
LG 2181 . . . . San Manuel
LG 2282 . . . . Yuma
LG 2559 . . . . Tempe
STC Arizona . . . . Goodyear

Maintenance of Way Employes
LG 508 . . . . Tucson
LG 2400 . . . . Houck
LG 2921 . . . . Indian Wells
SLG 2417 . . . . . Prescott Valley

Mine Workers
LU 1332 . . . . Window Rock
LU 1620 . . . . Kayenta
LU 1924 . . . . Kayenta
LU 2483 . . . . Kayenta

Musicians
LU 586 . . . . Phoenix

National Staff Organization
LU Staff Organization, Arizona
  Education Association . . . . Mesa

NLRB Professional Association
LU 28 . . . . Phoenix

Office and Professional Employees
LU 56 . . . . Phoenix
LU 319 . . . . Tucson

Operating Engineers
LU 428 . . . . Phoenix

Painters
LU 86 . . . . Phoenix

Plasterers and Cement Masons
LU 394 . . . . Phoenix

Plumbing and Pipe Fitting
LU 469 . . . . Phoenix
LU 741 . . . . Tucson

Postal and Federal Employees
LU 910 . . . . Phoenix

Postal Mail Handlers
LU 320 . . . . Tempe

Postal Workers
LU 93 Valley of the Sun . . Phoenix
LU 255 Tucson . . . . Tucson
LU 397 Globe . . . . Globe
LU 425 Douglas . . . . . . Douglas
LU 530 Yuma . . . . Yuma
LU 611 Kingman . . . . Kingman
LU 704 Holbrook . . . . Holbrook
LU 1459 Prescott . . . . . Prescott
LU 2367 Ajo . . . . Ajo

LU 6852 Lake Havasu
  City . . . . . . Lake Havasu City
LU 7001 Verde Valley
  Area . . . . Cottonwood
LU 7008 Show Low . . Show Low
LU 7071 Parker Local . . . Parker
LU 7083 Bullhead City
  Local . . . . Bullhead City
LU 7087 Sedona . . . . Cottonwood
SA Arizona . . . . Phoenix

Railroad Signalmen
LLG 126 . . . . Yuma
LLG 172 . . . . Williams

Roofers, Waterproofers and Allied Workers
LU 135 . . . . Phoenix

Rural Letter Carriers
D 1 Arizona . . . . Lake Havasu City
D 2 . . . . Flagstaff
D 3 Arizona . . . . Buckeye
D 5 . . . . Apache Junction
D 6 . . . . Yuma
SA Arizona . . . . Mesa

Security, Police and Fire Professionals
LU 820 . . . . Surprise

Sheet Metal Workers
LU 359 . . . . Phoenix

State, County and Municipal Employees
C 97 Arizona Public Employees
  Association . . . . Phoenix
LU 449 Tucson-Pima
  County . . . . Cortaro

Steelworkers
LU 9475 . . . . Bullhead City
LU 08-296 . . . . Tucson
LU 08-869 . . . . Snowflake
LU 08-968 . . . . Glendale
LU 08-978 . . . . Peoria
LU 12-470-S . . . . . . Douglas
LU 12-886-S . . . . . Winkelman
LU 12-915-S . . . . . . Kearny
LU 12-937-S . . . . . . Tucson
LU 12-3937-S . . . . . . Phoenix
LU 12-5252-S . . . . . . Kearny

Teachers
SFED 8002 Arizona . . . . Phoenix

Teamsters
LU 104 . . . . Phoenix
LU 752 Phoenix Mailers
  Union . . . . Phoenix

Television and Radio Artists
LU Phoenix . . . . Phoenix

Theatrical Stage Employees
LU 336 . . . . Phoenix
LU 415 . . . . Tucson
LU 485 . . . . Tucson
LU 748 . . . . Phoenix
LU 875 . . . . Mesa

Transit Union
LDIV 1433 . . . . Phoenix

Transport Workers
LU 580 . . . . Tempe

Transportation Union
LU 113 . . . . Winslow
LU 807 . . . . Tucson
LU 1081 . . . . Mesa
LU 1629 . . . . Mesa
LU 1800 . . . . Tucson

SLB LO-3 Arizona . . . . . Phoenix

Treasury Employees
CH 33 . . . . Phoenix
CH 116 . . . . Tucson

UNITE HERE
LU 631 . . . . Phoenix

Weather Service Employees
BR 04-15 . . . . Phoenix
BR 04-16 . . . . Tucson
BR 04-74 . . . . Bellemont

Unaffiliated Labor Organizations
Arizona Court Security Officers
    Association . . . . Flagstaff
D-M Training Association . . Tucson
Engineers & Associate Employees of
    KTVK . . . . Phoenix
International Employees Welfare
    Union . . . . Gold Canyon
International Guild of Symphony,
    Opera & Ballet Tucson Symphony
    Orchestra Musicians . . . . Tucson

Arkansas

AFL-CIO Trade and Industrial Departments

Building and Construction Trades Department
BCTC Arkansas . . . . . Little Rock
BCTC Central Arkansas . Little Rock
BCTC Northwestern
Arkansas . . . . Van Buren

Affiliated Labor Organizations

Air Traffic Controllers
LU FSM . . . . Fort Smith
LU LIT. . . . . Little Rock
LU TXK . . . . Texarkana

Asbestos Workers
LU 10 . . . . Little Rock

Automobile, Aerospace Workers
C Arkansas CAP . . . . . Fort Smith
LU 415 . . . . Malvern
LU 716 . . . . Fort Smith
LU 1000 . . . . Searcy
LU 1482 . . . . Melbourne
LU 1550 . . . . Marianna
LU 1762. . . . . Conway

Boilermakers
LG 66 . . . . Conway
LG 69 . . . . Little Rock
LG 397-D Cement
Workers . . . . Winthrop
LG 1510 . . . . Atkins

Carpenters
DC Arkansas/Southeast Missouri
4004 . . . . Russellville
LU 71 . . . . Fort Smith
LU 147 . . . . Conway
LU 216 . . . . Fort Smith
LU 497 . . . . Warren
LU 576 . . . . Little Rock
LU 690 . . . . Little Rock
LU 891 . . . . Hot Springs
LU 1225 . . . . Russellville
LU 1836 . . . . Russellville
LU 2019 . . . . Hope
LU 2186 . . . . Hot Springs
LU 2271 . . . . Stamps
LU 2345 . . . . Emerson
LU 2346. . . . . Huttig
LU 2661 . . . . Fordyce
LU 2697 . . . . Emerson
LU 2892 . . . . Rivervale

Civilian Technicians
CH 117 Arkansas Air National Guard
(Razorback) . . . . . Jacksonville

Communications Workers
C Arkansas State . . . . Little Rock
LU 6502 . . . . Charleston
LU 6503 . . . . Magnolia
LU 6505 . . . . Jonesboro
LU 6507 . . . . Little Rock
LU 6508 . . . . Little Rock
LU 86106 . . . . Forrest City
LU 86113 . . . . Little Rock
LU 86146 . . . . Baldknob
LU 86341 . . . . Walnut Ridge
LU 86747 . . . . Jonesboro

Electrical Workers
LU 295 . . . . Little Rock
LU 436 . . . . El Dorado
LU 647 . . . . Little Rock
LU 700 . . . . Fort Smith
LU 750 . . . . Pine Bluff
LU 807. . . . . Cabot
LU 1516. . . . . Jonesboro
LU 1658. . . . . Pine Bluff
LU 1703. . . . . El Dorado
LU 1758. . . . . Pine Bluff
LU 2022 . . . . Little Rock
LU 2033 . . . . Lonoke
LU 2219 . . . . Greenbrier
LU 2284. . . . . El Dorado

Elevator Constructors
LU 79 . . . . Little Rock

Federal Employees
LU 1079 . . . . Royal
LU 1669 . . . . Fort Smith
LU 2045. . . . . . North Little Rock

Fire Fighters
LU 99-F . . . . . North Little Rock

Food and Commercial Workers
LU 526-T . . . . Little Rock
LU 740-C . . . . Hoxie
LU 2008 . . . . Little Rock

Glass, Molders, Pottery and Plastics Workers
LU 131 . . . . Bay
LU 282 . . . . Turrell

Government Employees
LU 108 . . . . . . Mountain View
LU 922 . . . . Forrest City
LU 953 DoD . . . . . . Pine Bluff
LU 2054 VA . . . North Little Rock
LU 2066 DoD. . . . . . Jacksonville
LU 2201 VA . . . . . . Fayetteville
LU 2650 USDA . . . . . Hampton
LU 3253 USDA . . . . Bonnerdale
LU 3291 HHS . . . . . Jonesboro
LU 3963 Local Chapter . Little Rock

Graphic Communications
LU 502-M . . . . Little Rock
LU 527-M . . . . Jonesboro
LU 673-S . . . . Greenland

Iron Workers
LU 321 . . . . Little Rock

Laborers
LU 1282 . . . . Little Rock
LU 1671. . . . . Sherwood

Letter Carriers
BR 35 . . . . Little Rock
BR 240 . . . . Pine Bluff
BR 399 . . . . Fort Smith
BR 543 . . . . Hot Springs
BR 1004. . . . . Fayetteville
BR 1094 . . . . Helena
BR 1131. . . . . Jonesboro
BR 1293. . . . . Paragould
BR 1514 . . . . Rogers
BR 1592 . . . . Vilonia
BR 1684 . . . . Batesville
BR 1802. . . . . Warren
BR 1820. . . . . Forrest City

BR 1873. . . . . De Queen
BR 1922 . . . . Blytheville
BR 1946. . . . . Russellville
BR 2277 . . . . Harrison
BR 2353. . . . . Bentonville
BR 2357. . . . . Prescott
BR 2527 . . . . Wynne
BR 2642 . . . . Marianna
BR 2733 . . . . Harrisburg
BR 2755. . . . . Fordyce
BR 2756. . . . . Keiser
BR 2959 . . . . Eudora
BR 3191 . . . . Piggott
BR 3329 . . . . Pocahontas
BR 3360 . . . . McGehee
BR 3418 . . . . Booneville
BR 3612 . . . . Gurdon
BR 3642 . . . . Brinkley
BR 3671 . . . . Springdale
BR 3692 . . . . Clarksville
BR 3693 . . . . Ozark
BR 3706 . . . . Benton
BR 3719 . . . . Magnolia
BR 3730 . . . . Warren
BR 3733 . . . . Stamps
BR 3745. . . . . North Little Rock
BR 3754. . . . . Monticello
BR 3802. . . . . Nashville
BR 4189 . . . . West Memphis
BR 4294 . . . . Waldron
BR 4382. . . . . Corning
BR 4726 . . . . Lake Village
BR 4932 . . . . Heber Springs
BR 5141 . . . . Dumas
BR 5207 . . . . Hamburg
BR 5217. . . . . Dermott
BR 5383 . . . . De Witt
BR 5557 . . . . Ashdown
BR 5574. . . . . England
BR 5876 . . . . Marked Tree
BR 5877. . . . . Wilson
BR 6069 . . . . West Helena
BR 6075 . . . . Mountain Home
BR 6437 . . . . Clarendon
BR 6467 . . . . Smachover
BR 6478 . . . . Earle
BR 6522 . . . . Marion
SA Arkansas . . . . . Hot Springs

Locomotive Engineers
DIV 116 . . . . . Mountain Home
DIV 182. . . . . North Little Rock
DIV 278 . . . . Knoxville
DIV 496 . . . . Texarkana
DIV 524 . . . . Van Buren
DIV 585 . . . . Sherwood
DIV 858. . . . . Pine Bluff
GCA Union Pacific Railroad, Eastern
Region . . . . . North Little Rock
SLB Arkansas . . . . . Fort Smith

Machinists
CONF South Central
States . . . . Little Rock
DLG 156 . . . . Little Rock
LG 51 . . . . Pine Bluff
LG 224 . . . . El Dorado
LG 260 . . . . Van Buren
LG 325 . . . . Sherwood
LG 463 Hercules . . . . Jacksonville
LG 502 . . . . Little Rock
LG 911 . . . . Bay
LG 921 . . . . Little Rock
LG 1093 Ozark Lodge . . . Harrison
LG 1362 . . . . Crossett

LG 1948 . . . . Newport
LG 2248 . . . . Batesville
LLG W-15 Woodworkers. De Queen
LLG W-298
Woodworkers. . North Little Rock
LLG W-332 Woodworkers . Prescott
LLG W-475 Woodworkers . Crossett
LLG W-484 Woodworkers . Warren
STC Arkansas . . . . . Little Rock

Maintenance of Way Employes
LG 514 . . . . Colt
LG 1427 . . . . Cabot
LG 1549. . . . . Pine Bluff
LG 2729 . . . . Oil Trough
SLG 601 . . . North Little Rock
SLG 780 . . . . Searcy
SLG 1009 . . . . Cabot
SLG 1127 . . . . Arkadelphia
SLG 2717 . . . . Clarksville

National Staff Organization
LU Staff Organization,
Arkansas. . . . . Little Rock

Office and Professional Employees
LU 22 United
Healthcare . . . . . . Little Rock
LU 105 . . . . Little Rock
LU 420 . . . . Pine Bluff

Operating Engineers
LU 381 . . . . El Dorado

Painters
LU 424 . . . . Little Rock

Plumbing and Pipe Fitting
LU 29. . . . . Van Buren
LU 155 . . . . Little Rock
LU 706 . . . . El Dorado
SA Arkansas . . . . . . El Dorado

Postal and Federal Employees
D 9 . . . . Little Rock
LU 903 . . . . Little Rock
LU 907 . . . . Little Rock
LU 908 . . . . Little Rock
LU 909 . . . . Little Rock
LU 913 District IX. . . . Little Rock

Postal Workers
LU 122 Hot Springs. . . Hot Springs
LU 189 Central Arkansas
Area. . . . . . . North Little Rock
LU 217 Newport . . . . . Newport
LU 532 Arkadelphia . . Arkadelphia
LU 574 Blytheville . . . Blytheville
LU 632 Camden . . . . . Camden
LU 642 Pine Bluff . . . Pine Bluff
LU 660 Batesville . . . . Batesville
LU 667 Fayetteville . . Fayetteville
LU 1211 Western
Arkansas . . . . Fort Smith
LU 1415 Springdale . . Springdale
LU 1434 McGehee . . . McGehee
LU 1675 Benton . . . . . Benton
LU 1802 Mena. . . . . . . Mena
LU 1843 Jonesboro . . . Jonesboro
LU 2922 Marianna . . . Marianna
LU 2982 Magnolia . . . Magnolia
LU 3083 Stuttgart. . . . Stuttgart
LU 3187 Heber
Springs . . . . . . Heber Springs
LU 3688 El Dorado. . . El Dorado

LU 3727 Rogers . . . . Rogers
LU 3728 Bentonville. . . Bella Vista
LU 3915 Crossett . . . . . Crossett
LU 3930 Harrison Area . . Harrison
LU 4022 Monticello . . . Monticello
LU 5008 Mountain
 Home. . . . . . Mountain Home
LU 6003 Osceola . . . . . Osceola
SA Arkansas . . . . . . Pine Bluff

Railroad Signalmen
LLG 72 . . . . Jonesboro

Rural Letter Carriers
D 1 . . . . Forrest City
D 2. . . . . Eureka Springs
D 3 . . . . Dardanelle
D 4 . . . . Arkadelphia
D 5 Arkansas Rural Letter Carriers
 Association. . . . . Jacksonville
D 6. . . . . Wilmar
LU 91 Roughriders
 Association. . . . . . Texarkana
SA Arkansas . . . . . . Batesville

Security, Police and Fire
 Professionals
LU 726. . . . . Little Rock
LU 730 . . . . Alexander
LU 737 . . . . Clarksville
LU 739 . . . . Pine Bluff

Service Employees
LU 616 Firemen & Oilers . . . Rison
LU 718 Firemen & Oilers . . Benton

Sheet Metal Workers
LU 78 . . . . Conway
LU 428 . . . . Benton

State, County and Municipal
 Employees
C 38 Arkansas State . . . Little Rock
LU 966 Pine Bluff Municipal
 Employees. . . . . . . Atheimer

Steelworkers
LU 9452 . . . . Fort Smith
LU 5-90 . . . . Junction City
LU 05-368 . . . . Kingsland
LU 05-369. . . . . Crossett
LU 05-370 . . . . Fort Smith
LU 05-379 . . . . Little Rock
LU 05-434 . . . . El Dorado
LU 05-496 . . . . Fort Smith
LU 05-577 . . . . El Dorado
LU 05-589. . . . . Crossett
LU 05-619 . . . . Pine Bluff
LU 05-656 . . . . Fort Smith
LU 05-735 . . . . Grapevine
LU 05-796. . . . . Crossett
LU 05-833 . . . . White Hall
LU 05-844 . . . . White Hall
LU 05-898 . . . . Pine Bluff
LU 05-935 . . . . Pine Bluff
LU 05-936 . . . . White Hall
LU 05-1053 . . . . Rogers
LU 05-1253. . . . . . Jacksonville
LU 05-1288 United Paper
 Workers . . . . . . Little Rock
LU 05-1327 . . . . . . Ashdown

LU 05-1329 . . . . Ashdown
LU 05-1422 . . . . Little Rock
LU 05-1532 . . . . . . McGehee
LU 05-1533. . . . . . Arkansas City
LU 05-1671 Wire Workers. Star City
LU 05-1731. . . . . . . Pine Bluff
LU 05-1965 . . . . Morrilton
LU 12-74 . . . . Jonesboro
LU 12-230-A . . . . Benton
LU 12-558-L . . . . Benton
LU 12-602-B . . . . Malvern
LU 12-607-L. . . . . . . Magnolia
LU 12-752-L . . . . . . Texarkana
LU 12-769-L . . . . Calion
LU 12-883-L. . . . . . . Little Rock
LU 12-884-L . . . . . Russellville
LU 12-970-L. . . . . . . Delight
LU 12-4880-S . . . . . . Benton
LU 12-5073-S . . . . . Donaldson
LU 12-6433-S . . . . . . Benton
LU 12-6606-S. . . . . Forrest City
LU 12-6794-S. . . . . . Malvern
LU 12-6904-S . . . . . Mabelvale
LU 12-7366-S. . . . . . Malvern
LU 12-7612-S. . . . . . Malvern
LU 12-7893-S . . . . . Fort Smith
LU 12-7972-S. . . . . . Malvern
LU 12-9285-S . . . . . . Dumas
LU 12-9308-S . . . . . Texarkana
LU 12-9405 . . . . Benton
LU 50-929 . . . . . . West Helena

Teamsters
LU 373 . . . . Fort Smith
LU 878. . . . . Little Rock

Theatrical Stage Employees
LU 204 . . . . Mabelvale

Transit Union
LDIV 704 . . . . Little Rock

Transportation Communications
 Union
D 31 Southern Pacific . . Pine Bluff
D 5512 . . . . White Hall
LG 6007 TCU Lodge 6007. Sheridan
LG 6114 Harmony. . . . . Benton

Transportation Union
GCA GO-569 Missouri Pacific
 Railroad-P . . . North Little Rock
LU 221 . . . . . North Little Rock
LU 462 . . . . Pine Bluff
LU 507 . . . . Van Buren
LU 656 . . . . Sheridan
LU 1088 . . . . Cabot
SLB LO-4 Arkansas . . . Little Rock

Treasury Employees
CH 59 . . . . Little Rock

Weather Service Employees
BR 02-1. . . . . . North Little Rock

Unaffiliated Labor Organizations
Fordyce and Princeton Railroad
 Employees Union . . . . Hamburg
United Aluminum Workers of
 Arkansas . . . . Malvern

California

AFL-CIO Trade and Industrial Departments

Building and Construction Trades Department
BCTC. . . . . Stockton
BCTC Alameda County . . Oakland
BCTC California . . . . Sacramento
BCTC Contra Costa
County . . . . Martinez
BCTC Fresno-Madera-Kings-Tulare
Counties . . . . Fresno
BCTC Humboldt & Del Norte
Counties . . . . Eureka
BCTC Imperial County . . El Centro
BCTC Kern-Inyo & Mono
Counties . . . . Bakersfield
BCTC Los Angeles
County . . . . Los Angeles
BCTC Marin County. . . San Rafael
BCTC Mid-Valley . . . . Yuba City
BCTC Napa-Solano
Counties . . . . Fairfield
BCTC Northeastern
California. . . . . Redding
BCTC Sacramento-
Sierras. . . . . Sacramento
BCTC San Bernardino & Riverside
Counties . . . . Riverside
BCTC San Diego . . . . San Diego
BCTC San Francisco . San Francisco
BCTC San Mateo
County. . . . . Foster City
BCTC Santa Barbara-San Luis
Obispo Counties . . . . . Goleta
BCTC Santa Clara-San Benito-Santa
Cruz Counties . . . . . San Jose
BCTC Santa Cruz & Monterey
Counties . . . . Castroville
BCTC Sonoma & Mendocino
Counties . . . . Santa Rosa
BCTC Stanislaus-Merced-
Tuolumne . . . . Modesto
BCTC Ventura County . . . Oxnard

Maritime Trades Department
PC San Francisco . . . San Francisco
PC Southern California . Wilmington

Metal Trades Department
MTC Bay Cities . . . . . Oakland
MTC Indian Wells
Valley . . . . Ridgecrest
MTC Pacific Coast . . . . Oakland

Other Councils and Committees
COM Los Angeles-Orange Counties
Organizing . . . . . . Los Angeles

Affiliated Labor Organizations

Agricultural Employees
BR 23 . . . . San Francisco
BR 28 . . . . Los Angeles

Air Traffic Controllers
LU APC . . . . Napa
LU BFL . . . . Bakersfield
LU BWI. . . . . Burbank
LU CCR . . . . Concord
LU CMA . . . . Camarillo
LU CNO. . . . . Chino
LU CRW . . . . Carlsbad

LU E10 . . Edwards Air Force Base
LU EMT . . . . El Monte
LU ENM . . . . . Redondo Beach
LU FAT. . . . . Fresno
LU HWD. . . . . Hayward
LU LAX . . . . Los Angeles
LU LGB. . . . . Long Beach
LU LVK . . . . Livermore
LU MRY . . . . Monterey
LU MYF . . . . San Diego
LU NCT . . . . Mather
LU OAK . . . . Oakland
LU ONT . . . . Ontario
LU PBI. . . . . Palo Alto
LU POC . . . . La Verne
LU PSP . . . . . Palm Springs
LU RHV . . . . San Jose
LU SAN . . . . San Diego
LU SBA. . . . . Goleta
LU SCK . . . . Stockton
LU SCT. . . . . San Diego
LU SEE . . . . El Cajon
LU SFO . . . . . San Francisco
LU SJC . . . . Santa Clara
LU SMF. . . . . Sacramento
LU SMO . . . . . . Santa Monica
LU SNA . . . . Costa Mesa
LU STS . . . . Santa Rosa
LU TOA . . . . Torrance
LU VNY . . . . Van Nuys
LU ZLA . . . . Palmdale
LU ZOA . . . . Fremont

Aircraft Mechanics
LU 3 . . . . Los Angeles
LU 9 SFO . . . . San Bruno

Asbestos Workers
LU 5 . . . . Azusa
LU 16. . . . . Alameda

Automobile, Aerospace Workers
C Northern California. . . . Fremont
C Southern California
CAP. . . . . Pico Rivera
C 5 Region 5 Western States
CAP. . . . . Pico Rivera
LU 76 Emeryville-San Leandro
Local . . . . Fremont
LU 148 . . . . Lakewood
LU 179 . . . . . North Hollywood
LU 230. . . . . Ontario
LU 506 . . . . San Diego
LU 509 . . . . Pico Rivera
LU 805 . . . . Long Beach
LU 887 . . . . Paramount
LU 1519 . . . . Chatsworth
LU 1797 . . . . Badger
LU 2103. . . . . . . San Francisco
LU 2244. . . . . Fremont
LU 2350 Headquarters Staff
Organization . . . . . Sacramento
LU 6645 . . . . Rancho Cucamonga

Bakery, Confectionery, Tobacco Workers and Grain Millers
C Pacific Coast States . . . . Carson
LU 24. . . . . Redwood City
LU 31. . . . . Carson
LU 37. . . . . Commerce
LU 59-G . . . . Acampo
LU 83 . . . . Buena Park
LU 85 . . . . Sacramento
LU 102-G. . . . . . . Los Angeles
LU 125 . . . . San Leandro

LU 315 . . . . San Diego

Boilermakers
LG 6. . . . . Oakland
LG 46-D Cement
Workers . . . . Santa Cruz
LG 67-M . . . . Fontana
LG 92 . . . . Bloomington
LG 99-D. . . . . Dos Palos
LG 100-D Cement
Workers . . . . Greenwood
LG 106-S Stove Division . Littlerock
LG 125-S . . . . Huntington Park
LG 128-M. . . . . San Francisco
LG 228-S . . . . Huntington Beach
LG 232 . . . . Sylmar
LG 343 . . . . Ventura
LG 344 . . . . Ridgecrest
LG 549 . . . . Pittsburg
LG 583-D Cement Workers . Vallejo

Bricklayers
LU 3. . . . . Oakland
LU 4 Bricklayers & Allied
Craftworkers . . . . . Irwindale
LU 18 Tile, Marble &
Terrazzo. . . . . . Diamond Bar
STCON 99 California . . Bakersfield

California Nurses
SA. . . . . Oakland

Carpenters
C . . . . Oakland
CONF 46 Northern California
Counties . . . . Oakland
CONF California
Conference . . . . Oakland
CONF Eighth District
Organization & Educational
Program . . . . Los Angeles
DC Los Angeles County
4008 . . . . Los Angeles
LU 22 . . . . San Francisco
LU 25 . . . . Manteca
LU 34 . . . . Oakland
LU 35. . . . . San Rafael
LU 46 . . . . Sacramento
LU 68-L. . . . . Oakland
LU 83-L . . . . Fresno
LU 102 . . . . Livermore
LU 109-L . . . . . . Sacramento
LU 144-L. . . . . San Jose
LU 150 . . . . Camarillo
LU 152 . . . . Martinez
LU 180 . . . . Vallejo
LU 209 . . . . Sylmar
LU 214 Western Pulp and Paper
Workers . . . . Corona
LU 217. . . . . Foster City
LU 262 . . . . San Jose
LU 405 . . . . San Jose
LU 409 . . . . Los Angeles
LU 440-L . . . . Santa Ana
LU 505. . . . . Aptos
LU 547 . . . . San Diego
LU 605 . . . . Marina
LU 630 . . . . Long Beach
LU 701 . . . . Fresno
LU 713 . . . . Hayward
LU 721 . . . . Whittier
LU 743 . . . . Bakersfield
LU 751 . . . . Santa Rosa
LU 803 . . . . Orange
LU 944 . . . . . . San Bernardino

LU 1062. . . . . . . Santa Barbara
LU 1109 . . . . Visalia
LU 1240 . . . . Chico
LU 1496 . . . . Fresno
LU 1506 . . . . Los Angeles
LU 1553 . . . . Hawthorne
LU 1599 . . . . Redding
LU 1607 . . . . Los Angeles
LU 1607 Western Millwright
Conference. . . . . Los Angeles
LU 1618 . . . . Sacramento
LU 1789 . . . . South Lake Tahoe
LU 1800 . . . . . Arroyo Grande
LU 1861 . . . . . . Foster City
LU 2007 . . . . Orange
LU 2035 . . . . . . Kings Beach
LU 2236. . . . . Oakland
LU 2361 . . . . Orange
LU 2375 . . . . Wilmington
LU 2652 . . . . Standard
LU 2687 . . . . Marysville
LU 2749 . . . . Camino
LU 2927 . . . . . . Sutter Creek
LU 3074 . . . . Chester
LU 3088 . . . . Stockton

Christian Labor Association
LU 17 Dairy Employees
Union . . . . Ontario
LU 25 Poultry Workers
Union . . . . Ontario

Civilian Technicians
CH 105 Channel Islands . . . Oxnard
CH 109 Moffett Air . . Moffett Field
CH 118 Fresno Grizzlies . . . Fresno

Communications Workers
C Coastal Valley . . . . . Stockton
C Northern California-
Nevada. . . . . Foster City
C Southern California . . . Pasadena
LU 9000 . . . . . . Los Angeles
LU 9400 . . . . Paramount
LU 9401 . . . . Merced
LU 9404 . . . . San Rafael
LU 9408 . . . . Fresno
LU 9410. . . . . . San Francisco
LU 9412 . . . . Hayward
LU 9414 . . . . Chico
LU 9415. . . . . Oakland
LU 9416 . . . . Bakersfield
LU 9417 . . . . Stockton
LU 9419 . . . . Redding
LU 9421 . . . . Sacramento
LU 9423 . . . . San Jose
LU 9430 . . . . Foster City
LU 9431 . . . . Auburn
LU 9432. . . . . El Dorado
LU 9477 . . . . Taft
LU 9490 . . . . Salinas
LU 9503 . . . . . North Hollywood
LU 9504 . . . . Ventura
LU 9505 . . . . Pasadena
LU 9509 . . . . San Diego
LU 9510 . . . . Orange
LU 9511 . . . . Escondido
LU 9573 . . . . . San Bernardino
LU 9575 . . . . Camarillo
LU 9576 . . . . . . Santa Ynez
LU 9586 . . . . Norwalk
LU 9588 . . . . Colton
LU 9590 . . . . Alta Loma
LU 14903 . . . . Chico
LU 14904 . . . . . . Long Beach

LU 14908 . . . . Lodi
LU 14916 . . . . . . Ben Lomond
LU 39095 . . . . San Diego
LU 39098 . . . . San Jose
LU 39202 . . . . Bakersfield
LU 39521 San Francisco-
  Oakland. . . . . . . San Francisco
LU 59051 . . . . . . San Francisco
LU 59053 NABET Local
  53. . . . . Burbank
LU 59054 . . . . Chula Vista
LU 59057 NABET Local
  57. . . . . Burbank
LU 89111 . . . . Ontario
LU 89201 . . . . San Jose
LU 89262. . . . . San Leandro
LU 89850 . . . . Hesperia

Directors Guild of America Inc.
NHQ . . . . Los Angeles

Electrical Workers
C 4 Telephone Citizens
  Council . . . . Redding
LU 6. . . . . San Francisco
LU 11 . . . . Pasadena
LU 40 . . . . . North Hollywood
LU 45 . . . . Hollywood
LU 47 . . . . Diamond Bar
LU 100 . . . . Fresno
LU 180 . . . . Napa
LU 234 . . . . Castroville
LU 302 . . . . Martinez
LU 332 . . . . San Jose
LU 340 . . . . Sacramento
LU 360 . . . . Martinez
LU 413 . . . . Buellton
LU 428. . . . . Bakersfield
LU 440. . . . . Riverside
LU 441 . . . . Orange
LU 465 . . . . San Diego
LU 477 . . . . . . San Bernardino
LU 543 . . . . Victorville
LU 551 . . . . Santa Rosa
LU 569 . . . . San Diego
LU 595 . . . . Dublin
LU 617 . . . . San Mateo
LU 639 . . . . . San Luis Obispo
LU 684 . . . . Modesto
LU 800 . . . . Roseville
LU 889 . . . . . Redondo Beach
LU 946 . . . . . North Hollywood
LU 952 . . . . Ventura
LU 1023. . . . . Barstow
LU 1245 . . . . Vacaville
LU 1269 . . . . . San Francisco
LU 1682 . . . . Roseville
LU 1710 . . . . El Monte
LU 2131 . . . . Santa Clara
LU 2139. . . . . Santa Ana
LU 2295 . . . . El Monte

**Electrical, Radio and Machine
  Workers**
DC 10 . . . . Compton
LU 99 . . . . Sacramento
LU 1004 . . . . Valencia
LU 1009 . . . . Anaheim
LU 1010 . . . . Ontario
LU 1412. . . . . . . Walnut Creek
LU 1421 . . . . Compton

Elevator Constructors
LU 8. . . . . . . San Francisco
LU 18 . . . . Pasadena

Engineers
LU 16 NAPEP Council . . Coronado

LU 26 . . . . San Jose
LU 30 Ames Federal Employees
  Union . . . . . . Moffett Field
LU 32 . . . . San Diego
LU 49 . . . . San Francisco
LU 86 . . . . San Francisco
LU 103 California . . . . San Jose

Farm Workers
NHQ. . . . . Keene

Federal Employees
C Forest Service. . . . Mount Shasta
LU 1. . . . . San Francisco
LU 721 . . . . Strathmore
LU 777 . . . . Los Angeles
LU 919 . . . . . . Camp Pendleton
LU 951 . . . . Sacramento
LU 1263 . . . . Monterey
LU 1450 . . . . Berkeley
LU 1558 . . . . Mentone
LU 1650 . . . . Arcadia
LU 1690 . . . . Monterey
LU 1771 . . . . McCloud
LU 1781 . . . . Placerville
LU 1836 . . . . Alturas
LU 1865 . . . . Yreka
LU 1891. . . . Point Reyes Station
LU 1937 . . . . Eureka
LU 1979 . . . . San Dimas
LU 1981 . . . . Vallejo
LU 1995 . . . . Quincy
LU 2023. . . . . Santa Maria
LU 2035. . . . . Barstow
LU 2066 . . . . Placerville
LU 2081 . . . . Lone Pine
LU 2090 . . . . Sunnyvale
LU 2091 . . . . . . Crescent City
LU 2096 . . . . El Cajon
LU 2135 . . . . Kelseyville
LU 2152 . . . . Needles
LU 2153 . . . . Susanville
LU 2163 California National
  Guard . . . . Clovis
SFED California . . . . . Lompoc

Fire Fighters
LU 25-I . . . . Lancaster
LU 33-F . . . . San Diego
LU 53-F . . . . Edwards
LU 85-F Camp Pendleton
  Local . . . . Fallbrook
LU 102-F . . . . Lemoore
LU 116-F . . . . Santa Maria
LU 145 San Diego Fire Fighters
  Union . . . . San Diego
LU 166-F . . . . Monterey
LU 4403 Five Cities
  Firefighters . . . . . Pismo Beach

Food and Commercial Workers
C United Sugar Workers of
  California. . . . . Fresno
LU 1-C . . . . Norwalk
LU 25-C . . . . Pittsburg
LU 30-I . . . . Antioch
LU 45-D . . . . Fresno
LU 47-C . . . . Porterville
LU 78-C . . . . La Verne
LU 97-C . . . . Tranquility
LU 101 . . . . South San Francisco
LU 120 . . . . Oakland
LU 135 . . . . San Diego
LU 146-C . . . . Lompoc
LU 151-D . . . . Glendale
LU 174-D . . . . Brawley
LU 181-D. . . . . Stockton
LU 186-D. . . . . Modesto

LU 188-D . . . . Fresno
LU 193-I . . . . Fresno
LU 194-I . . . . Santa Cruz
LU 324. . . . . Buena Park
LU 350-C . . . . Rialto
LU 373-R . . . . Vallejo
LU 428 . . . . San Jose
LU 588-R . . . . Roseville
LU 648 . . . . San Francisco
LU 770 . . . . Los Angeles
LU 839 . . . . Salinas
LU 870 . . . . Hayward
LU 995-C . . . . Buena Park
LU 1036 . . . . Camarillo
LU 1096 . . . . Salinas
LU 1167 . . . . Bloomington
LU 1179 . . . . Martinez
LU 1288 . . . . Fresno
LU 1428 . . . . Claremont
LU 1442 . . . . Santa Monica
RC 8 . . . . Buena Park
RC 8 . . . . Buena Park

**Glass, Molders, Pottery and
  Plastics Workers**
LU 2 . . . . Livermore
LU 17 . . . . Modesto
LU 19 . . . . Los Angeles
LU 39 . . . . La Puente
LU 52 . . . . Santa Clara
LU 81 . . . . Orange
LU 137 . . . . Maywood
LU 141 . . . . Lanthrop
LU 142 . . . . Martinez
LU 164-B . . . . Oakland
LU 177 . . . . Oakley
LU 254 . . . . Madera
LU 279 . . . . Ione
LU 307-A . . . . Carson
LU 374-B . . . . Long Beach

Government Employees
C 31 Western Food Inspection
  Locals . . . . Merced
C 109 National SS Payment Center
  Locals. . . . . Oakland
C 170 Defense Contract Management
  Agency . . . . El Segundo
C 263 VA 12th District . Seal Beach
LU 51 DoD . . . . . San Francisco
LU 52 Independent . . . . Escondido
LU 490 VA . . . . . Los Angeles
LU 505 DoT . . . . . Los Angeles
LU 511 . . . . Diamond Bar
LU 926 USDA . . . . . Downey
LU 988 USDA. . . . . Tracy
LU 1061 VA . . . . . Los Angeles
LU 1122 HHS . . . . . Richmond
LU 1159 VA . . . . . . Oakland
LU 1200 . . . . . . Laguna Niguel
LU 1202. . . . . Oakland
LU 1203 VAMC. . . . . Seal Beach
LU 1206 Department of Veterans
  Affairs . . . . Martinez
LU 1216. . . . . . . San Francisco
LU 1217 CPL-33 . . . . Herlong
LU 1221 . . . . Torrance
LU 1222 . . . . Seaside
LU 1227 Defense Finance &
  Accounting
  Services . . . . . San Bernardino
LU 1233. . . . . . . San Francisco
LU 1242. . . . . Atwater
LU 1399 DoD . . . . . . Coronado
LU 1406 . . Edwards Air Force Base
LU 1482 . . . . Barstow
LU 1533 DoD . . . . . . Oakland
LU 1546 DoD . . . . . . Lathrop

LU 1613 DoJ . . . . . San Diego
LU 1616 DoJ . . . . . Sacramento
LU 1620 VA . . . . . Livermore
LU 1657 USDA . . . . . . Albany
LU 1680 DoJ . . . . . San Pedro
LU 1697 VA . . . . . North Hills
LU 1764 DoD. . . . . . Travis Air
  Force Base
LU 1808 DoD. . . . . . . Herlong
LU 1857 DoD . . . North Highlands
LU 1881 DoD. . . . . . San Diego
LU 1918 USDA . . . . . El Cajon
LU 2003 SSA . . . . . . Salinas
LU 2018 DoD . . Twentynine Palms
LU 2025 DoD. Beale Air Force Base
LU 2029 DoD . . . . . . Stockton
LU 2060 . . . . Canoga Park
LU 2110 VA . . . . . . Palo Alto
LU 2111 DoD . . . . . Lemoore
LU 2161 DoD . . . . Seal Beach
LU 2275 GSA . . . . San Francisco
LU 2297 VA . . . . . Los Angeles
LU 2391 DoL . . . . San Francisco
LU 2429 DoD . . . . . Hawthorne
LU 2433 DoD . . . . Mission Hills
LU 2452 HHS . . . . Hollywood
LU 2554 DoJ . . . . . El Centro
LU 2654 VA . . . . Fresno
LU 2723 DoD . . . . . Stockton
LU 2776 DoD. . . . . . March Air
  Force Base
LU 2805 DoJ . . . . . San Diego
LU 2879 . . . . San Diego
LU 2947 GSA . . . . Carson
LU 3048 DoJ . . . . . . Lompoc
LU 3172 HHS . . . . . . Pacifica
LU 3584 DoJ . . . . Dublin
LU 3619 DoJ . . . . . San Diego
LU 3723 DoD. . . . . . San Diego
LU 3854 ID . . . . . . March Air
  Reserve Base
LU 3899 DoE . . . . San Francisco
LU 3943 VA, Hospitals Professional
  Unit. . . . . Los Angeles
LU 3969 . . . . Adelanto
LU 4038 BoP, MDC, Los
  Angeles. . . . . . Los Angeles
LU 4048 BoP, FPC,
  Lompoc. . . . . Lompoc

**Government Employees
  Association**
LU 337 Police Officers . . . Ventura
LU 12-28 . . . . . Port Hueneme
LU 12-29 . . . . . Port Hueneme
LU 12-33 . . . . . Port Hueneme
LU 12-35 . . . . . National City
LU 12-40 . . . . . Port Hueneme
LU 12-44 . . . . . . Long Beach
LU 12-120 . . . North Highlands
LU 12-186 . . . . . . San Diego
LU 12-188 Army Air Technician
  Union . . . . . . Los Alamitos
LU 12-196 Federal Union of
  Scientists &
  Engineers. . . . . Port Hueneme
LU 12-198 Federal Union of
  Scientists &
  Engineers. . . . . Port Hueneme
LU 14-22 . . . . Ventura
LU R-12-90 Fort Hunter Liggett
  Labor Union . . . . Jolon

Government Security Officers
LU 52 . . . . San Diego
LU 57 . . . . Sacramento
LU 64 . . . . San Diego
LU 155 . . . . Fresno

LU 403. . . . . Moffett Field

Graphic Communications
DC 2 Southern California Printing
  Specialists . . . . Fullerton
LU 4-N . . . . San Francisco
LU 24-H . . . . . . San Francisco
LU 28-N . . . . Fullerton
LU 388-M . . . . Fullerton
LU 404-M . . . . Monrovia
LU 432-M . . . . San Diego
LU 468-S . . . . . . San Francisco
LU 541-S . . . . Fullerton
LU 583 . . . . San Francisco
LU 625-S . . . . Fullerton
LU 747-M . . . . Fullerton

Independent Unions
LU 2101 United Service
  Workers . . . . Colton

Iron Workers
DC California & Vicinity . . . Pinole
LU 118 . . . . Sacramento
LU 155 . . . . Fresno
LU 229 . . . . San Diego
LU 377 . . . . . San Francisco
LU 378 . . . . Benicia
LU 416 . . . . Norwalk
LU 433 . . . . . Los Angeles
LU 509 . . . . Norwalk
LU 624 . . . . Fresno
LU 627 . . . . San Diego
LU 790 . . . . Oakland
LU 844 Shoremen's Local . . Pinole

Jockeys Guild
NHQ . . . . Monrovia

Laborers
DC Northern California . Pleasanton
DC Southern California . . El Monte
LU 36 . . . . Daly City
LU 67 . . . . Oakland
LU 67 . . . . Salinas
LU 73 . . . . Stockton
LU 89 . . . . San Diego
LU 139 . . . . Santa Rosa
LU 166 . . . . Oakland
LU 185 . . . . Sacramento
LU 220 . . . . Bakersfield
LU 261 . . . . . San Francisco
LU 270 . . . . San Jose
LU 291 . . . . San Rafael
LU 294 . . . . Fresno
LU 300 . . . . . . Los Angeles
LU 304 . . . . Hayward
LU 324 . . . . Martinez
LU 326 . . . . Vallejo
LU 345 . . . . Burbank
LU 389 . . . . San Mateo
LU 507 . . . . Lakewood
LU 550 San Joaquin Valley Packing
  & Miscellaneous . . . . . Selma
LU 585 . . . . Ventura
LU 652 . . . . Santa Ana
LU 724 . . . . Hollywood
LU 783 Laborers . . San Bernardino
LU 792 United Public Employees of
  California . . . . Redding
LU 802 . . . . Wilmington
LU 886 . . . . Oakland
LU 1130 . . . . Modesto
LU 1141 National Parks & Public
  Employees . . . . . San Francisco
LU 1184 . . . . Riverside

Letter Carriers
BR 24 . . . . Los Angeles
BR 52 Central California
  Coast . . . . . . San Luis Obispo
BR 70 . . . . San Diego
BR 133 . . . . . North Highlands
BR 183 Northcoast . . . Santa Rosa
BR 193 . . . . San Jose
BR 213 . . . . Stockton
BR 214 . . . . . . San Francisco
BR 231 . . . . Fresno
BR 290 . . . . Goleta
BR 348 . . . . Eureka
BR 411 . . . . . San Bernardino
BR 627 . . . . Napa
BR 737 . . . . Santa Ana
BR 782 . . . . Bakersfield
BR 857 . . . . Watsonville
BR 866 . . . . Visalia
BR 1100 Garden
  Grove . . . . . . Garden Grove
BR 1111 . . . . Richmond
BR 1184 . . . . . . Pacific Grove
BR 1280 . . . . Burlingame
BR 1291 . . . . Modesto
BR 1310 . . . . Monterey
BR 1340 . . . . Merced
BR 1427 . . . . . Mountain View
BR 1432 . . . . Lodi
BR 1439 . . . . Ontario
BR 1469 . . . . Porterville
BR 1563 . . . . Ukiah
BR 1650 . . . . Culver City
BR 1707 . . . . Hayward
BR 1726 . . . . El Centro
BR 1742 . . . . Turlock
BR 1810 . . . . Tulare
BR 2009 . . . . Corning
BR 2086 . . . . Burbank
BR 2152 . . . . Exeter
BR 2168 . . . . Upland
BR 2200 . . . . Pasadena
BR 2207 . . . . Torrance
BR 2293 . . . . . . Beverly Hills
BR 2462 . . . . Van Nuys
BR 2472 . . . . Willows
BR 2525 . . . . Escondido
BR 2605 . . . . Calexico
BR 2608 . . . . Susanville
BR 2614 . . . . Hawthorne
BR 2704 Brawley Letter
  Carriers . . . . Brawley
BR 2757 . . . . Dunsmuir
BR 2854 . . . . Tracy
BR 2901 . . . . Hemet
BR 2902 . . . . Chatsworth
BR 3060 . . . . Auburn
BR 3217 . . . . . Crescent City
BR 3223 . . . . Yreka
BR 3275 . . . . Lemoore
BR 3347 . . . . La Mesa
BR 3656 . . . . Fort Bragg
BR 3768 . . . . Los Banos
BR 3982 . . . . Rialto
BR 4006 . . . . . . Canoga Park
BR 4114 . . . . Camarillo
BR 4149 . . . . . . Palm Springs
BR 4249 . . . . Manteca
BR 4430 . . . . Lancaster
BR 4494 . . . . . . Carmichael
BR 4625 . . . . Sonora
BR 4724 . . . . Rancho Cordova
BR 4735 . . . . Ripon
BR 4748 . . . . Atwater
BR 4850 . . . . Modesto
BR 4868 . . . . Oakdale
BR 4899 . . . . Cambria
BR 4941 . . . . . Santa Fe Springs

BR 5190 . . . . Cloverdale
BR 5502 . . . . Rio Vista
BR 5576 . . . . Gustine
BR 5583 . . . . Corcoran
BR 6201 . . . . Bishop
BR 6242 . . . . Firebaugh
BR 6264 . . . . Brisbane
BR 6354 . . . . . . Orange Cove
BR 6385 Marina . . . . . Marina
BR 6416 . . . . . . Farmersville
BR 6446 . . . . Newman
BR 6458 . . . . . . Mount Shasta
BR 6550 . . . . Winchester
BR 6667 . . . . Alturas
SA California State Association of
  Letter Carriers-Br . . . Sacramento

Locomotive Engineers
DIV 5 . . . . Diamond Bar
DIV 20 . . . . Oceanside
DIV 56 . . . . Yucaipa
DIV 65 San Jose . . . . . Berkeley
DIV 126 . . . . Bakersfield
DIV 144 . . . . Vacaville
DIV 214 . . . . Long Beach
DIV 283 . . . . Livermore
DIV 398 . . . . Helendale
DIV 415 . . . . Antelope
DIV 425 . . . . Dunsmuir
DIV 553 . . . . Clovis
DIV 660 . . . . . . Westminster
DIV 662 . . . . Ontario
DIV 664 . . . . Los Osos
DIV 692 . . . . Rocklin
DIV 739 . . . . Bakersfield
DIV 800 . . . . Portola
DIV 839 . . . . Glen Ellen

Longshore and Warehouse
DC Coast Pro Rata
  Committee . . . . . San Francisco
DC Northern
  California . . . . . San Francisco
DC Southern
  California . . . . . Los Angeles
LU 6 . . . . Oakland
LU 10 . . . . San Francisco
LU 13 . . . . Wilmington
LU 14 . . . . Eureka
LU 17 . . . . . . West Sacramento
LU 18 . . . . . . West Sacramento
LU 20-A . . . . Wilmington
LU 26 . . . . Los Angeles
LU 29 . . . . National City
LU 30 Mine Mineral & Processing
  Workers . . . . Boron
LU 34 . . . . San Francisco
LU 46 . . . . Port Hueneme
LU 54 . . . . Stockton
LU 56 Ship Scalers &
  Painters . . . . San Pedro
LU 63 Marine Clerks
  Association . . . . . . San Pedro
LU 63-OCU Office Clerical
  Unit . . . . Long Beach
LU 75 . . . . San Francisco
LU 91 . . . . Oakland
LU 94 . . . . San Pedro
NHQ . . . . San Francisco

Machinists
DLG 141 . . . . . . Redwood City
DLG 190 Automotive Trades
  Distributors . . . . Oakland
DLG 725 . . . . . Huntington Beach
DLG 947 . . . . Long Beach
LG 25 . . . . Ontario
LG 102 . . . . Long Beach

LG 201 Newspaper
  Lodge . . . . Los Angeles
LG 311 . . . . Bell
LG 389 . . . . San Diego
LG 536 . . . . Rocklin
LG 575 . . . . Ontario
LG 620 . . . . Los Angeles
LG 653 . . . . Fresno
LG 706 . . . . Barstow
LG 720-E . . . . Huntington Beach
LG 720-G . . . . Huntington Beach
LG 720-J . . . . Huntington Beach
LG 726 . . . . San Diego
LG 727-N . . . . Palmdale
LG 727-P . . . . Palmdale
LG 755 . . . . Chula Vista
LG 801 . . . . Oakland
LG 812 Security
  Lodge . . . . . Rancho Cordova
LG 821 . . . . Ontario
LG 906 . . . . Anaheim
LG 946 . . . . . Rancho Cordova
LG 964 . . . . Riverside
LG 1101 . . . . Santa Clara
LG 1125 . . . . San Diego
LG 1173 . . . . Concord
LG 1186 . . . . El Monte
LG 1209 . . . . Roseville
LG 1414 . . . . San Mateo
LG 1484 . . . . Wilmington
LG 1528 . . . . Modesto
LG 1546 . . . . Oakland
LG 1584 . . . . Oakland
LG 1596 . . . . Petaluma
LG 1781 . . . . . . Burlingame
LG 1782 Sierra Pacific Air
  Transport . . . . . San Francisco
LG 1910 . . . . Long Beach
LG 1932 Los Angeles Air
  Transport . . . . Hawthorne
LG 1980 . . . . Ontario
LG 2023 . . . . Hawthorne
LG 2024 . . . . Huntington Beach
LG 2182 . . . . Sacramento
LG 2228 . . . . Sunnyvale
LG 2230 . . . . Felton
LG 2231 . . . . Sunnyvale
LG 2765 . . . . San Diego
LG 2786 . . . . Santa Maria
LLG 93 . . . . San Jose
LLG 322 . . . . Valencia
LLG W-98 Woodworkers . Arcata
LU 1001 . . . . . Vandenberg Air
  Force Base
STC California . . . . . . Petaluma

Maintenance of Way Employes
FED Pacific . . . . . . Sacramento
LG 875 . . . . . Hacienda Heights
LG 914 . . . . Shasta
LG 922 . . . . Sacramento
LG 1246 . . . . Storrie
LG 2418 . . . . Los Angeles
SLG 134 . . . . Fontana
SLG 407 . . . . . . Suisun City
SLG 1002 . . . . Manteca
SLG 1096 . . . . Visalia
SLG 1196 . . . . Dunsmuir
SLG 2419 . . . . Clovis

Marine Engineers
ASSN Engineers & Scientists of
  California . . . . Oakland

Musicians
CONF California
  Conference . . . . San Francisco
CONF Western . . . San Francisco

LU 6 Musicians
Union . . . . San Francisco
LU 7. . . . . Santa Ana
LU 12 . . . . Sacramento
LU 47 . . . . Los Angeles
LU 153 . . . . San Jose
LU 189 . . . . Stockton
LU 292 . . . . Santa Rosa
LU 308 . . . . Santa Barbara
LU 325 . . . . San Diego
LU 353 . . . . Long Beach
LU 367 . . . . Vallejo
LU 424 . . . . Pinole
LU 581 . . . . Ventura

National Staff Organization
LU Staff Organization of California
Professionals. . . . . . . Anaheim
LU Staff Union, California Higher
Education. . . . . . Los Angeles

NLRB Professional Association
LU 20 . . . . San Francisco
LU 21 . . . . Los Angeles
LU 31 . . . . Los Angeles
LU 32 . . . . Oakland

Nurses Associations of California
LU Balboa Registered Nurses
Association . . . . Pomona
LU Garden Grove Registered Nurses
Association . . . . Pomona
LU Kaiser San Gabriel
Valley. . . . . Pomona
LU Kaiser Sunset Registered Nurses
Association . . . . Pomona
LU KPASCO . . . . Pomona
LU Registered Nurses Association
Kaiser Bellflower . . . . . Pomona
LU Registered Nurses Association
Kaiser Fontana . . . . . . Pomona
LU Registered Nurses Association
Kaiser San Diego . . . . Pomona
LU Registered Nurses Association
Kaiser West Los Angeles. Pomona
LU Registered Nurses Association St.
Francis . . . . Pomona
LU 40 LRNA . . . . Pomona
LU 41 Irvine Association of
Nurses. . . . . Pomona
LU 31-14 Registered Nurses
Association Kaiser
Woodland Hills . . . . . Pomona
LU 31-23 Kaiser Panorama
Registered Nurses
Association . . . . Pomona
LU 31-24 Kaiser Harbor County
Registered Nurses. . . . Pomona
LU 31-27 Pettis Memorial Registered
Nurses. . . . . Pomona
LU 31-32 Kaiser Riverside
Registered Nurses. . . . Pomona
LU 31-36 Bear Valley . . . Pomona
LU 31-39 Kaiser Orange County
Professionals Association. Pomona
NHQ. . . . . Pomona

Office and Professional Employees
LU 3 . . . . Daly City
LU 29 . . . . Oakland
LU 30 . . . . Ontario
LU 62 . . . . Walnut
LU 140 . . . . Burbank
LU 174 . . . . Burbank
LU 472 . . . . Tarzana
LU 537 . . . . Pasadena

Operating Engineers
CONF California-
Nevada . . . . Sacramento
CONF Western . . . . . Sacramento
LU 3 . . . . Alameda
LU 12 . . . . Pasadena
LU 39 . . . . San Francisco
LU 82 . . . . El Cajon
LU 501 . . . . Los Angeles

Painters
DC 16 . . . . Livermore
DC 36 . . . . Pasadena
LU 3 . . . . Oakland
LU 12 Carpet, Linoleum, Soft Tile
Workers . . . . San Jose
LU 52 . . . . Bakersfield
LU 83 . . . . Petaluma
LU 95 . . . . Downey
LU 169 . . . . Oakland
LU 256. . . . . Buena Park
LU 272 . . . . Watsonville
LU 294 . . . . Fresno
LU 333 . . . . San Diego
LU 376 . . . . Vallejo
LU 487 . . . . Sacramento
LU 507 . . . . San Jose
LU 510 . . . . San Francisco
LU 636 . . . . Pasadena
LU 718 . . . . San Francisco
LU 741 . . . . Martinez
LU 767 . . . . Sacramento
LU 775 . . . . Riverside
LU 831 Trade Show & Sign
Crafts . . . . El Monte
LU 913 . . . . Redwood City
LU 1053. . . . . Oakland
LU 1176. . . . . Oakland
LU 1237 . . . . Sacramento
LU 1247. . . . . Whittier
LU 1399 . . . . San Diego
LU 1595 . . . . Pasadena
LU 1621 . . . . San Jose
LU 2345 . . . . Inglewood

Petroleum and Industrial Workers
LCH 6 . . . . Paramount
LCH 9 . . . . Paramount
LCH 22 . . . . . . Point Richmond
LCH 25 . . . . Paramount
LU 12 . . . . Paramount
LU 13 . . . . Paramount
LU 34 . . . . Paramount
LU 35 . . . . Paramount
LU 36 . . . . Paramount
NHQ . . . . Paramount

Physicians and Dentists
NHQ California. . . . . . Oakland

Plasterers and Cement Masons
DC Northern California . San Mateo
DC Southern California. . Pomona
LU 66 . . . . San Francisco
LU 200 . . . . Pomona
LU 300 . . . . San Mateo
LU 400 . . . . Sacramento
LU 500 . . . . Santa Ana
LU 600 . . . . Bell Gardens
LU 755 . . . . Sherman Oaks
STCON California . . . San Mateo

Plumbing and Pipe Fitting
C California State Pipe
Trades. . . . . Sacramento
DC 16 . . . . Los Angeles
DC 36 Pipe Trades . . . . . Fresno
LU 38 . . . . San Francisco

LU 62. . . . . Castroville
LU 78 . . . . Los Angeles
LU 114 . . . . Buellton
LU 159 . . . . Martinez
LU 228 . . . . Yuba City
LU 230 Labor Hall
Association. . . . . . . San Diego
LU 246 . . . . Fresno
LU 250 . . . . Gardena
LU 342 . . . . Concord
LU 343 . . . . Vallejo
LU 345 . . . . Monrovia
LU 355 . . . . Vallejo
LU 389 Plumbers &
Steamfitters . . . . . . Ventura
LU 393 . . . . San Jose
LU 398 . . . . Montclair
LU 409 . . . . . . San Luis Obispo
LU 442 . . . . Stockton
LU 447 . . . . Sacramento
LU 467 . . . . Burlingame
LU 483 . . . . Hayward
LU 484 . . . . Ventura
LU 494 . . . . Long Beach
LU 582 . . . . Santa Ana
LU 709 . . . . Whittier
LU 761 . . . . Burbank

Police
LU 2 U.S.P.S. . . . . . Los Angeles

Postal and Federal Employees
D 10 . . . . Culver City
LU 1002 . . . . Culver City
LU 1003. . . . . . North Hollywood
LU 1004. . . . . Oakland
LU 1008. . . . . . . Culver City
LU 1014. . . . . Rialto
LU 1016 Glendale (Foothills)
Local . . . . Lancaster

Postal Mail Handlers
LU 302 . . . . Emeryville
LU 303 . . . . Los Angeles

Postal Workers
LU 2 San Francisco. . San Francisco
LU 47 East Bay Area . Walnut Creek
LU 64 Los Angeles. . Los Angeles
LU 66 Sacramento
Area . . . . Sacramento
LU 71 Bernard Skip Whalen
Area . . . . . . Mountain View
LU 73 San Jose . . . . . . San Jose
LU 78 Oakland Area . . . . Oakland
LU 115 Long Beach
Area. . . . . Long Beach
LU 159 Salmont Area . . . Monterey
LU 197 Area Local . . . San Diego
LU 211 Marysville . . . Marysville
LU 264 Santa Barbara . . . Goleta
LU 320 Stockton . . . . Stockton
LU 339 Fresno . . . . . . Fresno
LU 401 Calexico . . . . . Calexico
LU 423 Tri County
Area . . . . Palm Springs
LU 472 Bakersfield . . . Bakersfield
LU 589 Channel Islands
Area. . . . . Oxnard
LU 614 Visalia . . . . . . Visalia
LU 635 Modesto . . . . . Modesto
LU 731 Pasadena . . . . Pasadena
LU 885 Bishop . . . . . . Bishop
LU 891 Susanville . . . Susanville
LU 917 Southwest Coastal
Area . . . . Anaheim
LU 926 Wilmington . . Wilmington
LU 960 Redding . . . . . Redding

LU 1053 Tulare . . . . Tulare
LU 1056 Eureka . . . . . . Eureka
LU 1071 Merced. . . . . . Merced
LU 1099 Inglewood . . . Culver City
LU 1159 San Fernando Valley
Area . . . . Panorama City
LU 1174 Crescent
City . . . . Crescent City
LU 1199 Paso Robles. . Paso Robles
LU 1291 Redwood Empire
Area . . . . Petaluma
LU 1465 Sonora . . . . . Sonora
LU 1702 Fort Bragg . . . Fort Bragg
LU 1977 La Mesa . . . . . La Mesa
LU 2052 Alturas . . . . . . Alturas
LU 2587 Lancaster . . . . Lancaster
LU 2875 El Cajon . . . . El Cajon
LU 4604 Arcata. . . . . . Arcata
LU 4635 California Area . . Whittier
LU 5765 Lemoore . . . . . Lemoore
LU 5864 Chatsworth . . Chatsworth
LU 6074 High Desert Area . Mojave
LU 6135 South Lake
Tahoe. . . . . South Lake Tahoe
LU 6159 Daly City . . . . Daly City
LU 6212 Thousand
Oaks. . . . . . . Thousand Oaks
LU 6669 San Mateo Postal Data
Center . . . . San Mateo
LU 6792 Tahoe City . . . Tahoe City
LU 6916 Altadena . . . . . Altadena
LU 7060 Truckee . . . . . Truckee
SA California . . . . . Garden Grove

Pulp and Paper Workers
LU 49. . . . . Eureka
LU 83 . . . . Stockton
LU 249 . . . . Antioch
LU 657. . . . . Santa Clara
LU 672 . . . . Anaheim
LU 863 . . . . Ripon

Railroad Signalmen
LLG 19 . . . . Brea
LLG 92 . . . . Hayward
LLG 104 . . . . . . Grand Terrace
LLG 153 . . . . . . San Francisco
LLG 156 . . . . Hinkley
LLG 173 . . . . Wasco
LLG 229 . . . . Roseville
LLG 233 Arte. . . . . . Concord

**Roofers, Waterproofers and Allied
Workers**
DC California-Hawaii-Nevada
Roofers . . . . Oakland
LU 27 . . . . Fresno
LU 36 . . . . Los Angeles
LU 40 . . . . San Francisco
LU 45 . . . . San Diego
LU 81 . . . . Oakland
LU 95 . . . . Santa Clara
LU 220 . . . . Orange

Rural Letter Carriers
LU California Unit 15 . . . . Winton
LU California Unit 18. Crescent City
LU Fresno-Madera Counties . Clovis
LU Riverside-San Bernardino
Counties . . . . Ontario
LU San Joaquin County Unit
01. . . . . Stockton
LU Unit 02 . . . . . . Sacramento
LU Unit 04. . . . . . . El Centro
LU Unit 05. . . . . . Bakersfield
LU Unit 06 . . . . Encino
LU Unit 08 . . . . Anderson
LU Unit 09 . . . . Petaluma

LU Unit 11 . . . . Ramona
LU Unit 16 . . . . Porterville
LU Unit 17 . . . . . Santa Paula
LU 13 San Luis Obispo
  County . . . . Nipomo
LU 14 California . . . . . San Jose
LU 20 California . . . . . . Jamul
LU 22 California. . . . . Winchester
SA California . . . . Chino
UNIT 7 California . . . . Yuba City
UNIT 12 California . . . . Martinez

Screen Actors
LBR Arizona . . . . . Los Angeles
LBR Atlanta . . . . . Los Angeles
LBR Boston . . . . . Los Angeles
LBR Chicago. . . . . Los Angeles
LBR Colorado . . . . Los Angeles
LBR Dallas . . . . . Los Angeles
LBR Detroit . . . . . Los Angeles
LBR Florida . . . . . Los Angeles
LBR Hawaii . . . . . Los Angeles
LBR Houston Branch . Los Angeles
LBR Nashville . . . . Los Angeles
LBR Nevada . . . . . Los Angeles
LBR New Mexico . . . Los Angeles
LBR New York . . . . Los Angeles
LBR Philadelphia. . . Los Angeles
LBR San Diego. . . . Los Angeles
LBR San Francisco. . . Los Angeles
LBR Seattle. . . . . . Los Angeles
LBR Utah . . . . . . Los Angeles
LBR Washington DC. . Los Angeles
NHQ . . . . Los Angeles

Seafarers
LU Fishermen's Union Pacific &
  Carib . . . . San Diego
LU Industrial Professional &
  Technical Workers . . . . Downey
LU Marine Firemen's
  Union . . . . San Francisco
LU Mortuary Employees'
  Union . . . . South San Francisco
LU Sailors' Union of the
  Pacific . . . . . . San Francisco
LU 1 Industrial, Professional &
  Technical Workers . . . . Downey
LU 1 Sugar Workers
  Union . . . . Crockett
LU 2 Industrial, Professional &
  Technical Workers . . . . Downey

**Security, Police and Fire
  Professionals**
LU 158 . . . . Oceanside
LU 159 . . . . . . Garden Grove
LU 160 . . . . Los Angeles
LU 165. . . . . El Centro

Service Employees
C California State . . . . Sacramento
LU 24-7. . . . . Oakland
LU 87 . . . . San Francisco
LU 99 . . . . Oakland
LU 121 SEIU Nurse Alliance,
  Southern California . . Commerce
LU 250 Health Care Workers
  Union . . . . Oakland
LU 265 . . . . San Bruno
LU 280 . . . . Duarte
LU 399 . . . . Los Angeles
LU 415 . . . . Santa Cruz
LU 434-B . . . . . . Los Angeles
LU 504 Firemen & Oilers . Riverside
LU 535 . . . . Oakland
LU 616 United Services
  Employees . . . . . . Oakland

LU 660 Los Angeles
  County Employees
  Association. . . . . Los Angeles
LU 707 Sonoma County
  Public/Private
  Employees. . . . . . Santa Rosa
LU 715 . . . . San Jose
LU 758 Firemen &
  Oilers . . . . . . San Bernardino
LU 782 Firemen & Oilers . Foresthill
LU 790 . . . . Oakland
LU 817 . . . . Salinas
LU 949 Marin Association of Public
  Employees . . . . . . San Rafael
LU 998 . . . . Ventura
LU 1186 Firemen & Oilers . Barstow
LU 1280 Solano Association of
  Government Employees . Fairfield
LU 1292. . . . . Redding
LU 1401 Firemen &
  Oilers . . . . Granite Bay
LU 1877 . . . . Los Angeles
LU 1997 . . . . Riverside
LU 2005 United Healthcare
  Workers-West . . . . . Oakland
LU 2028 San Diego County
  Service . . . . San Diego
LU 4988 . . . . Jackson

Sheet Metal Workers
LU 104. . . . . San Ramon
LU 105 . . . . Glendora
LU 162 . . . . Sacramento
LU 170 . . . . Pico Rivera
LU 206 . . . . San Diego
LU 273 . . . . Goleta
LU 376 . . . . Pasadena
LU 434 . . . . . Rancho Cucamonga
LU 461 . . . . Walnut
LU 476 . . . . Barstow

**State, County and Municipal
  Employees**
DC 36. . . . . Los Angeles
DC 57 Northern California . Oakland
LU 31-037 Sharp Professional Nurses
  Network. . . . . Pomona
LU 35 Fountain Valley Professional
  Association . . . . . . Pomona
LU 101 . . . . San Jose
LU 800 Community & Social Agency
  Employees . . . . . . Los Angeles
LU 829 San Mateo County
  Workers . . . South San Francisco
LU 1108 Social Service Agency
  Employees . . . . . Los Angeles

Steelworkers
C Tesoro Nationwide
  Council. . . . . Martinez
C Tosco Nationwide . Arroyo Grande
DC 1 . . . . Bakersfield
LU 2801. . . . . Long Beach
LU 9440 . . . . Helm
LU 9518 . . . . Maywood
LU 8-326 . . . . Rodeo
LU 08-5 . . . . Martinez
LU 08-6 . . . . Taft
LU 08-49 . . . . Victorville
LU 08-52. . . . . Mojave
LU 08-192. . . . . . . Oro Grande
LU 08-208 . . . . Downey
LU 08-219 Kern River Coalinga
  Avenal. . . . . Bakersfield
LU 08-307. . . . . Bell
LU 08-427 . . . . . . Shasta Lake
LU 08-471 . . . . Bakersfield
LU 08-534 . . . . . Arroyo Grande

LU 08-535 . . . . Newberry Springs
LU 08-675 . . . . Carson
LU 08-682 . . . . Oxnard
LU 08-810 . . . . . Grand Terrace
LU 08-819. . . . . . . Sacramento
LU 08-846 . . . . Seal Beach
LU 08-854. . . . . Turlock
LU 08-961 . . . . Ontario
LU 08-1876 . . . . Red Bluff
LU 08-1979 . . Rancho Cucamonga
LU 08-7601 . . . . El Monte
LU 12-18 . . . . Oakdale
LU 12-19-T . . . . Madera
LU 12-44-L . . . . . . Los Angeles
LU 12-139-T . . . . . . San Dimas
LU 12-171-L . . . . Covina
LU 12-418. . . . . Lathrop
LU 12-458-L . . . . . El Segundo
LU 12-474-G . . . . Fresno
LU 12-515-U . . . . . . Maywood
LU 12-555 . . . . Fresno
LU 12-560-L . . . . . Los Alamitos
LU 12-565-S . . . . . Sacramento
LU 12-703-L . . . . Selma
LU 12-766-L . . . . . . La Puente
LU 12-843-B . . . . . . Riverside
LU 12-1304-S . . . . . San Leandro
LU 12-1440-S . . . . . Pittsburg
LU 12-1981-S . . . . . . Covina
LU 12-2018-S . . . . . Maywood
LU 12-2571-S . . . . . Pittsburg
LU 12-4997-S . . . . . Maywood
LU 12-5632-S . . . . . . Fontana
LU 12-6703-S . . . . . Riverside
LU 12-7600-S . . . . . . Fontana
LU 12-8049-S . . . . Selma
LU 12-8065-S . Rancho Cucamonga
LU 12-8433-S . . . . . Simi Valley
LU 12-8599-S . . . . . . Fontana
LU 12-8844 . . . . Fontana
LU 12-8957-S . . . . . Maywood
LU 30-89 . . . . Yucaipa
LU 39-6966-S . . . . . . Stockton

Teachers
LU 1475 Early Childhood
  Federation . . . . . . Burbank
LU 4128 Oakwood . . . . Burbank
LU 4163 Buckley Faculty
  Association . . . . . . Burbank
LU 4269 University of San
  Francisco Faculty
  Association . . . . . San Francisco
LU 4886 Westridge . . Granada Hills
LU 4986 Sacramento Job
  Corps . . . . Sacramento
SFED California . . . . . Burbank

Teamsters
C California Cannery & Food
  Processing Unions . . . . Visalia
JC 7 . . . . San Francisco
JC 38 . . . . Modesto
JC 42 . . . . Covina
LU 15 Northern California Mailers
  Union . . . . Union City
LU 36 . . . . San Diego
LU 63. . . . . Covina
LU 70 . . . . Oakland
LU 78 . . . . Hayward
LU 85 . . . . San Francisco
LU 87 . . . . Bakersfield
LU 94. . . . . Visalia
LU 137 . . . . Redding
LU 150 . . . . Sacramento
LU 166. . . . . Bloomington
LU 186 . . . . Ventura
LU 228 . . . . Sacramento

LU 278 . . . . San Francisco
LU 287 . . . . San Jose
LU 315 . . . . Martinez
LU 350 Sanitary Truck Drivers &
  Helpers Union. . . . . Daly City
LU 381 . . . . Santa Maria
LU 386 . . . . Modesto
LU 396 . . . . Covina
LU 399 Studio Transportation
  Drivers Local . . North Hollywood
LU 431 . . . . Fresno
LU 439 . . . . Stockton
LU 481 . . . . San Diego
LU 490 . . . . Vallejo
LU 495 . . . . Pico Rivera
LU 517 . . . . Visalia
LU 542 . . . . San Diego
LU 572 . . . . Carson
LU 578 . . . . Orange
LU 601 . . . . Stockton
LU 624 . . . . Santa Rosa
LU 630 . . . . Los Angeles
LU 665 . . . . Daly City
LU 683 . . . . San Diego
LU 848 . . . . Covina
LU 853 . . . . San Leandro
LU 856 . . . . San Bruno
LU 890 . . . . Salinas
LU 896 . . . . Los Angeles
LU 911 . . . . Long Beach
LU 912 . . . . Watsonville
LU 952 General Truck Drivers Office
  Food . . . . Orange
LU 986 . . . . . . South El Monte

Television and Radio Artists
LU Los Angeles . . . . Los Angeles
LU San Diego. . . . . . San Diego
LU San Francisco. . . San Francisco
LU 224 Sacramento-
  Stockton. . . . . . . Sacramento

Theatrical Stage Employees
ASSN District 2 Locals . Bakersfield
LU 16 . . . . San Francisco
LU 18-B. . . . . San Francisco
LU 33 . . . . Burbank
LU 44 . . . . . North Hollywood
LU 50 . . . . Sacramento
LU 66-B . . . . Sacramento
LU 80 IATSE. . . . . . . Burbank
LU 107 International Alliance of
  Theatrical Stage . . . . . Oakland
LU 119 BAFA/IA119 . . San Carlos
LU 122 . . . . San Diego
LU 134 . . . . San Jose
LU 150 . . . . Culver City
LU 158 . . . . Fresno
LU 166 . . . . Rohnert Park
LU 169 . . . . Oakland
LU 192-B . . . . . North Hollywood
LU 215 . . . . Bakersfield
LU 297 . . . . La Mesa
LU 442 . . . . Santa Barbara
LU 504 . . . . Anaheim
LU 521 . . . . Long Beach
LU 564 . . . . Merced
LU 600 . . . . Los Angeles
LU 611 . . . . Santa Cruz
LU 614 . . . . San Bernardino
LU 683 . . . . Burbank
LU 695 . . . . . North Hollywood
LU 700 Motion Picture Editors
  Guild . . . . Los Angeles
LU 705 Motion Picture
  Costumers . . . . . Valley Village
LU 706 . . . . Burbank
LU 707 . . . . Palm Desert

LU 728 . . . . Panorama City
LU 729 . . . . Burbank
LU 767 . . . . Burbank
LU 768 Theatrical Wardrobe
  Union . . . . . . Sherman Oaks
LU 784 . . . . San Francisco
LU 790 Illustrators & Matte
  Artists . . . . . . Sherman Oaks
LU 795 Television Broadcast Studio
  Employees . . . . La Mesa
LU 839 . . . . . North Hollywood
LU 847 Set Designers & Model
  Makers . . . . . Sherman Oaks
LU 857 Treasures and Ticket
  Sellers . . . . . Sherman Oaks
LU 871 . . . . . North Hollywood
LU 874 . . . . Sacramento
LU 876 . . . . Studio City
LU 884 . . . . Los Angeles
LU 892 . . . . . . Sherman Oaks
LU 905 . . . . San Diego
LU 916 . . . . Los Angeles
LU 923 . . . . Anaheim

Transit Union
LDIV 1225 . . . . Marina
LDIV 1309 . . . . San Diego
LU 192 . . . . Oakland
LU 256 . . . . Sacramento
LU 1027 . . . . Fresno
LU 1574 . . . . Foster City
LU 1605 . . . . Martinez

Transport Workers
LU 250-A . . . . . San Francisco
LU 502 . . . . El Segundo
LU 505 . . . . Burlingame
LU 564 . . . . El Segundo

**Transportation Communications
Union**
D 666 Santa Fe . . . . Valley Springs
D 674 Union Pacific-Eastern Lines
  SB 106 . . . . Tustin
D 802 Southern Pacific . . . Arcadia
D 2507 . . . . Long Beach
D 2508 . . . . Compton
D 2511 . . . . Riverside
D 5504 WRSA . . . . Lincoln
D 5514 . . . . Fontana
LG 2506 . . . . Richmond
LG 5050 Southern Pacific . . Covina
LG 6357 Streamline . . . . Covina
LG 6510 Woodbridge . . . Roseville
LG 6601 Los Angeles . . . . Fontana
LG 6713 Barstow . . . . . Barstow
LG 6721 Mission
  Bay . . . . San Francisco

Transportation Union
GCA GO-17 . . . . Chino
GCA GO-20 Atchison Topeka Santa
  Fe-Coast . . . . Rosemead
GCA GO-887 Southern Pacific
  Trans Company-Western Lines
  Railroad . . . . Santa Cruz
GCA GO-888 Southern Pacific
  Trans Company-Western Lines
  Railroad . . . . Aptos
LU 23 . . . . Santa Cruz
LU 31 . . . . Fremont
LU 32 . . . . Arcadia
LU 84 . . . . San Diego
LU 98 . . . . . . San Luis Obispo
LU 100 . . . . Pleasant Hill
LU 239 . . . . Davis
LU 240 . . . . Alta Loma
LU 492 . . . . Rocklin

LU 694 . . . . Dunsmuir
LU 771 . . . . Needles
LU 811 . . . . . . San Bernardino
LU 835 . . . . Bakersfield
LU 1200 . . . . Portola
LU 1201 . . . . Acampo
LU 1241 . . . . Antioch
LU 1252 . . . . Fresno
LU 1422 . . . . Anaheim
LU 1544 . . . . Whittier
LU 1570 . . . . Roseville
LU 1581 . . . . Bakersfield
LU 1674 . . . . Alta Loma
LU 1694 . . . . Barstow
LU 1730 . . . . Fairfield
LU 1732 . . . . Hayward
LU 1741 . . . . San Francisco
LU 1770 . . . . Los Angeles
LU 1801 . . . . Pleasant Hill
LU 1813 . . . . Colton
LU 1846 . . . . Victorville
SLB LO-5 California . . Sacramento

Treasury Employees
CH 15 . . . . Los Angeles
CH 20 . . . . Oakland
CH 81 . . . . Walnut Creek
CH 92 . . . . San Diego
CH 97 . . . . Fresno
CH 103 . . . . Long Beach
CH 105 . . . . San Ysidro
CH 107 . . . . El Monte
CH 108 . . . . Laguna Niguel
CH 111 . . . . Los Angeles
CH 117 . . . . Long Beach
CH 118 . . . . Bakersfield
CH 123 . . . . Calexico
CH 165 . . . . San Francisco
CH 198 . . . . El Segundo
CH 212 . . . . San Francisco
CH 227 . . . . San Francisco
CH 233 . . . . Van Nuys
CH 234 . . . . Riverside
CH 238 . . . . San Jose
CH 239 . . . . Sacramento
CH 267 . . . . Los Angeles
CH 283 . . . . Venice
CH 295 . . . . San Francisco

UNITE HERE
JB Western Regional . . Los Angeles
LU 2 . . . . San Francisco
LU 3-LDC . . . . . . San Leandro
LU 11 . . . . Los Angeles
LU 14-T . . . . Los Angeles
LU 14-Y . . . . Los Angeles
LU 19 . . . . San Jose
LU 30 . . . . San Diego
LU 44 . . . . Los Angeles
LU 49 . . . . Sacramento
LU 50 . . . . Lakewood
LU 52-LDC . . . . . . Los Angeles
LU 55-D . . . . Los Angeles
LU 71-JT . . . . Los Angeles
LU 74-JT . . . . Los Angeles
LU 75 . . . . Sacramento
LU 99-A . . . . Los Angeles
LU 101 . . . . Los Angeles
LU 107 . . . . Los Angeles
LU 142 . . . . Los Angeles
LU 188-T . . . . Los Angeles
LU 214 . . . . Los Angeles
LU 215-I . . . . Los Angeles
LU 277 . . . . Los Angeles
LU 289 . . . . Los Angeles
LU 294 . . . . Los Angeles
LU 309 . . . . Los Angeles
LU 311 . . . . Los Angeles

LU 482-I . . . . Los Angeles
LU 483 . . . Pacific Grove
LU 512-I . . . . Los Angeles
LU 535 . . . . . . San Bernardino
LU 681 . . . . Garden Grove
LU 711 . . . . Los Angeles
LU 818-A . . . . Los Angeles
LU 1007 . . . . Culver City
LU 1089 . . . . Los Angeles
LU 1108-T . . . . . . Los Angeles
LU 1291 . . . . Los Angeles
LU 2732 Western States Regional
  Joint Board . . . . . . Los Angeles
LU 2850 . . . . Oakland
STC California . . . . Sacramento

Utility Workers
C California Water Utility . Stockton
LU 132 . . . . Whittier
LU 160 . . . . Stockton
LU 160-C . . . . Sunnyvale
LU 160-D . . . . Oroville
LU 170 . . . . Bakersfield
LU 205 . . . . Bakersfield
LU 246 . . . . Los Alamitos
LU 259 . . . . San Jose
LU 283 . . . . San Gabriel
LU 483 . . . . Palmdale
LU 484 . . . . San Pedro
LU 508-A . . . . . . Newbury Park
LU 511 . . . . Pacific Grove
LU 522 . . . . Los Angeles

Weather Service Employees
BR 04-17 . . . . Sacramento
BR 04-29 . . . . Fremont
BR 04-35 . . . . Hanford
BR 04-36 . . . . Oxnard
BR 04-37 . . . . Palmdale
BR 04-45 . . . . Eureka
BR 04-61 . . . . San Diego
BR 04-80 . . . . Monterey
BR 08-8 . . . . Long Beach

Writers, West
NHQ . . . . Los Angeles

Unaffiliated Labor Organizations

Aerospace Professional Staff
  Association . . . . . Hawthorne
Allied Service Workers Union
  of the Thirteen Western States
  LU 1 . . . . Grand Terrace
Amalgamated Industrial Workers
  Union . . . . Colton
American Federation of Guards
  LU 1 . . . . Los Angeles
APW Union of Southern
  California . . . . Cudahy
Association Employees
  Union . . . . San Jose
Association of Building Trades
  Instructors LU 1 . . . . Pleasanton
Association of Contract Employees
  National Union . . . . . Norwalk
Atlantic Maritime Employees
  Independent . . . . . Wilmington
Atlantic Maritime Officers
  Association
  Independent . . . . . Long Beach
Bet Tzedek Legal Services
  Union . . . . Los Angeles
California Associate Staff . . Ventura
California Licensed Vocational
  Nurses Association
  Inc . . . . . . West Sacramento

California Log Scalers
  Association . . . . Trinidad
California Security Officers
  Union . . . . San Jose
Canyon Manor Employees
  Association . . . . Novato
Caregivers and Healthcare
  Employees Union . . . . Oakland
Coca Cola Bottlers Employees
  Union . . . . Sacramento
Committee for Recognition of
  Nursing Achievement-Stanford
  University . . . . Redwood City
Community Workers Union
  California . . . . Salinas
Court Security Officers Union-
  CDC . . . . Los Angeles
Dameron Hospital Employees
  Association . . . . Stockton
Department of Defense Police
  Officers Association
  (IBPO) . . . . San Diego
Douglas Association of Security
  Officers Independent . . . Torrance
Engineering Technicians & Technical
  Inspectors . . . . . Sacramento
Engineers & Architects Association
  Independent General Dynamics
  Electronics Technical
  Division . . . . Vista
Engineers & Architects Association
  Independent Technical Engineering
  Division . . . . San Diego
Engineers & Scientists Guild
  Lockheed Section . . . . Palmdale
Exxon Employees Federation
  Western Division . . . . . Goleta
Federation of Agents and
  International
  Representatives . . . . Sacramento
Field Representatives Union,
  California Federation of
  Teachers . . . . Oakland
Friedman Brothers Employees
  Association . . . . . Rohnert Park
Grocery Employees Association
  Independent . . . . Valley Springs
Independent Employees of Merced
  County . . . . Merced
Independent Employees Service
  Association . . . . Anaheim
Independent Oil & Chemical
  Workers . . . . Sacramento
Independent Pharmacists
  Association . . . Rancho Cordova
Independent Staff Union . . Oakland
International Association of EMTs
  Paramedics AFL-CIO LU
  R12-187 . . . . Covina
International Union of Industrial and
  Independent Workers . Paramount
Kaiser Permanente Nurse
  Anesthetists Association of
  Southern California . . . . Orange
Labor Workers Union . . . Berkeley
Latin-American Musicians
  Union . . . . South Gate
Law Professors of the University of
  San Francisco School of Law,
  Associated . . . . San Francisco
Local 399 Staff Union . Los Angeles
Lumber & Moulding Handlers
  Union . . . . Orangevale
Marin Medical Laboratories
  Employees Association . Petaluma
Motion Picture Industry Basic
  Crafts . . . . . North Hollywood

National Association of Aeronautical Examiners LU 5 . . . . San Diego
National Electronics Systems Technicians' Union . . . San Jose
National Emergency Medical Services Association . Sacramento
National Independent Industrial Workers Union LU 3333. . Colton
National Union of Labor Investigators . . . . . Los Angeles
Nor-Cal Beverage Company Employees Union . . . . . West Sacramento
Pepsi People Employees Association . . . . Redding
Physical Therapists-United California State Federation . . . . Berkeley
Pipe Trades Association . . . Vallejo
Private Duty Security Officers Association . . . . . Sacramento
Professional Pharmacists Guild . . . . . . Woodland Hills

Professional Resource Federation Nurses . . . . San Jose
Public & Industrial Workers LU 1 . . . . Paramount
Public & Industrial Workers International Union . . Paramount
Representatives of Los Angeles United Union. . . . . Los Angeles
Royal Service Warehouse Employees Association . . . . . Sacramento
Salinas Auto Employees Association . . . . Salinas
Security Officers Association . . . . . Long Beach
Security Police Employees Service Union . . . . Long Beach
Shipyard Workers Union . . . . National City
Sport Air Traffic Controllers Organization SATCO. . Helendale
Staff and Office Employees Union International Federation . Ventura

Staff Nurses Association of Santa Rosa Memorial Hospital . . . . Santa Rosa
Stanford Deputy Sheriffs Association. . . . . . . Stanford
Studio Security & Fire Association Warner Bros. . . . . Burbank
Tile Setters & Finishers Union of Northern California . . Sacramento
Trainers & Recruiters Unity Council . . . . Orangevale
Turlock Emergency Medical Service Association . . . . Turlock
United Domestic Workers of America . . . . San Diego
United Nurses of Children's Hospital LU 33-0887911 . . . . San Diego
United Packinghouse Workers LU 5183. . . . . Coachella
United Police & Security Association . . . . Tracy

United Screeners Association Local Chapter-Association LU 1 . . . . San Francisco
United Service Workers for Democracy . . . . . San Francisco
United Wholesalers and Retailers Union . . . . Hickman
University of San Francisco Public Safety Officers Association. . . . . . San Bruno
Utility Business Representatives LU 1 . . . . Cloverdale
Valley Truck Drivers Association . . . . . . Clements
West Coast Employees Union . . . . Bakersfield
Western Region Wildlife Specialist Association. . . . . Penn Valley
Western States Independent National Union . . . . Corona
Western States Pipe Trades Council . . . . San Jose
Yuba City Plant Employees Association . . . . Oroville

Colorado

AFL-CIO Trade and Industrial Departments

Building and Construction Trades Department
BCTC Colorado . . . . . Lakewood

Food and Allied Service Trades Department
C Colorado Food & Beverage
Trades . . . . Denver

Metal Trades Department
MTC Western Slope . Grand Junction

Affiliated Labor Organizations

Air Traffic Controllers
LU APA . . . . Englewood
LU ASE . . . . Aspen
LU BJC . . . . Broomfield
LU D-01 . . . . Denver
LU DEN . . . . Denver
LU NATCA Local
P50 . . . . . . Colorado Springs
LU PUB . . . . Pueblo
LU ZDV . . . . Longmont

Aircraft Mechanics
LU 8 . . . . Elizabeth

Asbestos Workers
LU 28 . . . . Denver

Automobile, Aerospace Workers
C Colorado . . . . Strasburg
LU 186 . . . . Thornton
LU 431 . . . . Aurora
LU 766 . . . . Englewood
LU 1415 . . . . Denver

Bakery, Confectionery, Tobacco Workers and Grain Millers
LU 26 . . . . Denver

Boilermakers
LG 101 . . . . Denver

Bricklayers
LU 7 Colorado . . . . Denver

Carpenters
LU 244 . . . . Denver
LU 510 . . . . Denver
LU 515 . . . . . . Colorado Springs
LU 1068 . . . . Denver
LU 2834 . . . . Denver

Civilian Technicians
CH 48 Mile High Chapter . . Aurora
CH 130 . . . . Sedalia

Communications Workers
C Colorado State . Colorado Springs
LU 7702 . . . . Pueblo
LU 7707 . . . . Fort Collins
LU 7708 . . . . . . Colorado Springs
LU 7716 . . . . . . Pagosa Springs
LU 7717 . . . . Boulder
LU 7743 . . . . . . Grand Junction
LU 7750 . . . . Denver
LU 7774 . . . . Pueblo
LU 7777 . . . . Englewood

LU 7781 United Professional Ski
Patrols of America . . . Gunnison
LU 7790 . . . . Thornton
LU 14705 . . . . Denver
LU 14708 . . . . . Colorado Springs
LU 37074 . . . . Denver
LU 37174 Pueblo Newspaper
Guild . . . . Pueblo
LU 57052 . . . . Denver
LU 87020 . . . . Denver

Electrical Workers
LU 12 . . . . Pueblo
LU 68 . . . . Denver
LU 111 . . . . Denver
LU 113 . . . . . . Colorado Springs
LU 667 . . . . Pueblo
LU 708 . . . . Denver
LU 969 . . . . Clifton
LU 2159 . . . . Montrose

Elevator Constructors
LU 25 . . . . Lakewood

Engineers
LU 128 . . . . Lakewood

Federal Employees
LU 1945 . . . . Littleton
LU 1950 . . . . Fort Collins
LU 2004 . . . . Monte Vista
SFED Colorado . . . . . Lakewood

Food and Commercial Workers
LU 7-R . . . . Wheat Ridge

Government Employees
C 236 National GSA Locals . Denver
LU 695 ID . . . . Denver
LU 709 DoJ . . . . Littleton
LU 898 DoL . . . . Commerce City
LU 925 USDA . . . . Brush
LU 1105 . . . . Lakewood
LU 1301 . . . . Florence
LU 1302 DoJ . . . . Florence
LU 1303 Council of Prisons . Aurora
LU 1345 DoD . . . . . Fort Carson
LU 1557 VA . . . . Lakewood
LU 1802 HHS . . . . Denver
LU 1867 DoD . . . Colorado Springs
LU 2040 DoD . . . . Denver
LU 2074 . . . . Fort Collins
LU 2186 DoC . . . . . . Boulder
LU 2197 DoD . . . . Commerce City
LU 2241 VA . . . . Denver
LU 2430 VA . . . . Swink
LU 2477 DoD . . . . Pueblo
LU 3230 EEOC . . . . . . Denver
LU 3275 GSA . . . . Denver
LU 3373 USDA . . . . . . Greeley
LU 3392 GPO . . . . Pueblo
LU 3416 DoL . . . . Arvada
LU 3499 USDA . . . . Pueblo West
LU 3540 DoD . . . Colorado Springs
LU 3607 EPA . . . . Denver
LU 3806 ID . . . . Denver
LU 3824 DoE . . . . . . Loveland
LU 3898 DoE . . . . Denver
LU 3942 . . . . Denver
LU 3972 HUD . . . . Denver

Government Employees Association
LU 14-5 . . . . Pueblo
LU 14-77 . . . . . . Grand Junction

Government Security Officers
LU 1 . . . . Arvada
LU 21 . . . . Westminster
LU 43 . . . . Westminster
LU 50 . . . . Louisville
LU 53 . . . . Denver
NHQ . . . . Westminster

Graphic Communications
LU 22-N . . . . Denver
LU 440-M . . . . Denver

Iron Workers
DC Rocky Mountain
Area . . . . Englewood
LU 24 . . . . Denver

Laborers
DC Colorado . . . . Denver
LU 578 . . . . . . Colorado Springs
LU 720 . . . . Denver

Letter Carriers
BR 47 . . . . Denver
BR 179 . . . . Trinidad
BR 204 . . . . . Colorado Springs
BR 229 . . . . Pueblo
BR 324 . . . . Greeley
BR 642 . . . . Boulder
BR 792 . . . . Durango
BR 849 . . . . Fort Collins
BR 913 . . . . Grand Junction
BR 1105 . . . . Longmont
BR 1178 . . . . Pueblo
BR 1207 . . . . Loveland
BR 1426 . . . . Delta
BR 1511 . . . . Sterling
BR 1517 . . . . Montrose
BR 1861 . . . . Las Animas
BR 1960 . . . . Brush
BR 2139 . . . . Walsenburg
BR 3631 . . . . Eckley
BR 3681 . . . . Fowler
BR 4259 . . . . Wheat Ridge
BR 4405 . . . . Arvada
BR 4459 . . . . Springfield
BR 5225 . . . . Cortez
BR 5236 . . . . Craig
BR 5301 . . . . Gunnison
BR 5996 . . . . Denver
BR 6202 . . . . Aspen
SA Colorado . . . . Greeley

Locomotive Engineers
DIV 29 . . . . Pueblo
DIV 47 . . . . Lakewood
DIV 133 . . . . Lakewood
DIV 186 . . . . Aurora
DIV 215 . . . . Whitewater
DIV 256 . . . . Brighton
DIV 430 . . . . Trinidad
DIV 488 . . . . . . Grand Junction
DIV 505 . . . . La Junta
DIV 727 . . . . Sterling
DIV 940 . . . . Centennial
GCA C&S, FWD & JTD BNSF
Railway . . . . Hoehne
GCA Santa Fe Railroad . . La Junta
SLB Colorado SLB . . . Centennial

Machinists
LG 13 . . . . Arvada
LG 47 . . . . Commerce City
LG 606 . . . . Thornton
LG 1338 . . . . Arvada

LG 1886 . . . . . . Commerce City
LG 1910-FL . . . . Frederick
LLG FL-185 Florida . . . . . Aurora
STC Colorado . . . . . Fort Lupton
STC Montana . . . . Arvada

Maintenance of Way Employes
FED Mountain &
Plains . . . . . Colorado Springs
LG 1351 . . . . Longmont
LG 1517 . . . . Pueblo
SLG 14 . . . . Lakewood
SLG 204 . . . . Trinidad
SLG 833 . . . . Pueblo
SLG 925 . . . . Pueblo West
SLG 941 . . . . Lakewood
SLG 1501 . . . . . . Walsenburg
SLG 1516 . . . . Phippsburg

Mine Workers
LU 1281 . . . . Nucla
LU 1385 . . . . Hayden
LU 1799 . . . . Craig
LU 1984 . . . . Rangely
LU 6417 . . . . Somerset
LU 6778 . . . . Oak Creek
LU 8431 . . . . Denver
LU 8935 . . . . Trinidad
LU 9856 . . . . Trinidad

Musicians
LU 20-623 . . . . Denver
LU 154 . . . . . Colorado Springs

National Staff Organization
LU Staff Organization, Colorado
Education Association . . . Denver

NLRB Professional Association
LU 27 . . . . Denver

Nurses
SA Colorado . . . . Denver

Office and Professional Employees
LU 5 . . . . Denver

Operating Engineers
LU 1 . . . . Northglenn
LU 9 . . . . Denver

Painters
DC 1 . . . . Denver
LU 79 . . . . Denver
LU 419 . . . . Denver
LU 930 . . . . Denver

Plasterers and Cement Masons
LU 577 . . . . Denver
STCON Rocky Mountain
Multi-States Operation
CMIA . . . . Denver

Plumbing and Pipe Fitting
LU 3 . . . . Aurora
LU 58 . . . . Colorado Springs
LU 145 . . . . . . Grand Junction
LU 208 . . . . Denver
SA Colorado Pipe
Trades . . . . . Colorado Springs

Postal Mail Handlers
LU 321 . . . . Denver

Postal Workers

LU 229 Denver. . . . . Aurora
LU 247 Colorado Springs
 Area. . . . . . . Colorado Springs
LU 382 Loveland . . . . . Loveland
LU 436 Pueblo . . . . Pueblo
LU 441 Fort Morgan . . Fort Morgan
LU 539 Fort Collins. . . Fort Collins
LU 600 Western Colorado
 Area . . . . Grand Junction
LU 706 Alamosa . . . . . Alamosa
LU 918 Sterling . . . . . . Sterling
LU 1337 Steamboat
 Springs. . . . Steamboat Springs
LU 3477 Littleton. . . . . Littleton
LU 6315 Aurora . . . . . . Aurora
LU 7029 Denver Bulk Mail
 Center . . . . Denver
SA Colorado . . . . Eastlake

Roofers, Waterproofers and Allied Workers

DC Southwest Roofers. . . Denver
LU 41 . . . . Denver
LU 58 . . . . . . Colorado Springs

Rural Letter Carriers

D 1 . . . . Evans
D 2 . . . . Merino
D 3 . . . . Denver
D 4 . . . . Fowler
D 5 . . . . Pueblo
D 6 . . . . Bayfield
D 7 . . . . Ridgway
SA Colorado . . . . Loveland

Security, Police and Fire Professionals

LU 265 . . . . Littleton

Service Employees

LU 105 . . . . Denver
LU 607 Firemen & Oilers . . Aurora

Sheet Metal Workers

LU 9 . . . . Lakewood
LU 253. . . . . . . Grand Junction

State, County and Municipal Employees

C 76 Colorado . . . . Pueblo
LU 1572 University of Denver
 Employees . . . . Denver

Steelworkers

LU 05-477 . . . . Arvada
LU 05-594 . . . . Canon City
LU 05-655 . . . . . Grand Junction
LU 05-710 . . . . Brighton
LU 05-844 . . . . Canon City
LU 05-920 . . . . Centennial
LU 05-1960 . . . . Commerce City
LU 08-742 . . . . Lakewood
LU 12-2102-S . . . . Pueblo
LU 12-3267-S . . . . Pueblo
LU 12-3405-S . . . . Pueblo
LU 12-8031-S . . . . Golden
LU 12-14457-S . . . Grand Junction
LU 12-14482-S . . . . . . Florence

Teachers

LU 5016 Denver Federation of
 Nurses and Health . . . . . Denver

SFED Colorado . . . . . . Denver

Teamsters

JC 3 . . . . Denver
LU 17 . . . . Denver
LU 267. . . . . Laporte
LU 435 . . . . Denver
LU 537 . . . . Denver
LU 961 Line Drivers . . . . Denver

Television and Radio Artists

LU 208 Denver. . . . . . . Denver

Theatrical Stage Employees

LU 7 . . . . Denver
LU 7-B . . . . Denver
LU 30-B . . . . Denver
LU 47 . . . . Pueblo
LU 62 . . . . . . Colorado Springs
LU 229 . . . . Fort Collins
LU 719 . . . . Edgewater

Transit Union

LDIV 19. . . . . Colorado Springs
LU 1755 . . . . Westminster

Transportation Communications Union

D 934. . . . . Arvada
D 5516 WRSA . . . Grand Junction
LG 270 . . . . Denver
LG 6146 Main Line . . . . . Arvada

Transportation Union

GCA GO-245 Burlington
 Northern . . . . Arvada
GCA GO-306 . . . . . . Lakewood

LU 49 . . . . Pueblo
LU 201 . . . . Trinidad
LU 202 . . . . Brighton
LU 204 . . . . Pueblo
LU 500 . . . . Clifton
LU 945 . . . . La Junta
LU 1136 . . . . Sterling
SLB LO-7 Colorado . . . Lakewood

Treasury Employees

CH 32 . . . . Denver
CH 235 . . . . Denver
CH 301 . . . . Aurora

University Professors

CH Regis College . . . . . Denver

Weather Service Employees

BR 03-16 . . . . Boulder
BR 03-56 . . . . . Grand Junction
BR 03-95 . . . . Pueblo

Unaffiliated Labor Organizations

Frontier Airline Pilots
 Association. . . . . Aurora
International Guards Union of
 America LU 65 . . Grand Junction
International Guards Union of
 America LU 66 . . Commerce City
International Guards Union of
 America RC
 Sixth . . . . . . Commerce City
Ski Patrol Association, Aspen
 Professional. . . . . Aspen
Steamboat Professional Ski Patrol
 Association . . Steamboat Springs
United Local Seven Staff
 Union . . . . Wheat Ridge

Connecticut

AFL-CIO Trade and Industrial Departments

Building and Construction Trades Department

BCTC Connecticut State . Harwinton
BCTC District Council . . . . Berlin
BCTC Fairfield County, Greenwich & Vicinity . . . . . North Haven
BCTC Hartford & Vicinity . . . . Rocky Hill
BCTC New Haven & Vicinity . . . . Hamden
BCTC New London-Norwich . . . . . . East Hartford

Metal Trades Department

MTC New London County . . Groton

Affiliated Labor Organizations

Air Traffic Controllers

LU BDL . . . . Windsor Locks
LU Y90 . . . . East Granby

Asbestos Workers

LU 33 . . . . Wallingford

Automobile, Aerospace Workers

C Connecticut UAW CAP Council . . . . . . Farmington
C Main State Community Action Program . . . . . . Farmington
C Maine UAW CAP Council . . . . . . Farmington
C Massachusetts UAW CAP Council . . . . . . Farmington
C New Hampshire UAW CAP Council . . . . . . Farmington
C Puerto Rico UAW CAP Council . . . . . . Farmington
C Region 9A New York UAW CAP Council . . . . . . Farmington
C Rhode Island UAW CAP Council . . . . . . Farmington
C Vermont UAW CAP Council . . . . . . Farmington
LU 376 Elmwood-Hartford Local . . . . Newington
LU 379 . . . . Hartford
LU 405 . . . . . West Hartford
LU 571 . . . . Groton
LU 712 . . . . Bristol
LU 1645 . . . . Torrington
LU 1699 . . . . Torrington
LU 2232 . . . . . . Farmington
LU 8868 . . . . . South Windsor

Boilermakers

LG 237 . . . . East Hartford
LG 558 . . . . East Windsor
LG 614 . . . . Groton

Bricklayers

LU 1 Connecticut . . . . Wallingford

Carpenters

LU 24 . . . . Yalesville
LU 43 . . . . Hartford
LU 210 . . . . Fairfield
LU 1302 . . . . Groton

Catholic School Teachers

LU Greater Hartford. . . Manchester

Civilian Technicians

CH 97 Flying Yankees . East Granby
CH 98 Connecticut Army . . Groton

Communications Workers

LU 1290 . . . . Rocky Hill
LU 1298 Connecticut Union of Telephone Workers. . . . Hamden
LU 14101 Bridgeport Typographical Union. . . . . Stratford
LU 14102 . . . . . Marlborough
LU 14105 . . . . . . North Haven
LU 14106 . . . . Quaker Hill
LU 14109 . . . . Darien
LU 51014 . . . . . . North Haven
LU 51017 NABET Local 17 . . . . Newington
LU 81143 . . . . Stevenson
LU 81203 . . . . Bridgeport
LU 81215 . . . . Newington
LU 81237 . . . . Trumbull
LU 81238 . . . . Bridgeport
LU 81244 . . . . Westport
LU 81247 . . . . Torrington
LU 81266 . . . . Newington
LU 81281 . . . . Bloomfield
LU 81295 . . . . Elmwood

Commuter Rail Employees

LDIV 166 . . . . Branford

Electrical Workers

LU 35 . . . . Hartford
LU 42 . . . . Manchester
LU 90 . . . . Wallingford
LU 208 . . . . Norwalk
LU 261 . . . . Groton
LU 420 . . . . Waterbury
LU 457 . . . . Meriden
LU 488 . . . . Monroe
LU 747 . . . . Hamden
LU 859 . . . . Stamford
LU 1040 . . . . Hartford
LU 2015 . . . . Danbury
SA Connecticut State Association. . . . . Groton

Electrical, Radio and Machine Workers

LU 211 . . . . Milford
LU 243 . . . . New Haven
LU 275 . . . . New Britain

Elevator Constructors

LU 91 . . . . North Haven

Fire Fighters

LU 68-I . . . . Stratford

Food and Commercial Workers

LU 197-B . . . . Stratford
LU 315-C . . . . Newtown
LU 371 . . . . Westport
LU 436-C . . . . . . Wallingford
LU 919 . . . . Farmington

Glass, Molders, Pottery and Plastics Workers

LU 39-B . . . . Bethel

Government Employees

C 137 Food Inspection Locals, Northeast . . . . Windsor
C 163 New England DCAA Locals . . . . South Windsor
LU 1661 DoJ . . . . New Fairfield
LU 1674 VA . . . . . West Haven
LU 2105 DoD . . . . . . Groton
LU 2138 . . . . . . West Haven
LU 2538 DoJ . . . . . Hartford
LU 2749 USDA . . . Torrington
LU 3237 DoD. . . . . Guilford
LU 3244 DCAA . . . . East Hartford
LU 3655 DoT . . . New London

Government Employees Association

LU 01-100 . . . . Groton
LU 01-109 . . . . . . Newington
LU 01-143 . . . . . New Haven
LU 01-145 . . . . . New London
LU 01-181 . . . . Stratford

Government Security Officers

LU 19 Millstone . . . . . . Oakdale

Graphic Communications

LU 74-M . . . . . . North Haven
LU 488-S . . . . South Windsor

Iron Workers

LU 15 . . . . Hartford
LU 424 . . . . . . North Haven
LU 832 . . . . Newington

Laborers

DC Connecticut. . . . . . Hartford
LU 146 . . . . Norwalk
LU 230 . . . . Hartford
LU 390 . . . . Waterbury
LU 455 . . . . East Haven
LU 547 . . . . Groton
LU 611 . . . . New Britain
LU 665 . . . . Bridgeport
LU 675 . . . . Danbury
LU 1224 . . . . Hartford

Letter Carriers

BR 19 . . . . North Haven
BR 20 . . . . Meriden
BR 32 . . . . Stratford
BR 60 . . . . Stamford
BR 86 . . . . East Hartford
BR 109 . . . . Derby
BR 147 . . . . Norwalk
BR 363 . . . . Danbury
BR 746 . . . . Naugatuck
BR 759 . . . . Greenwich
BR 2313 . . . . Fairfield
BR 5016 . . . . Essex
BR 5427 . . . . Plainfield
BR 6374 . . . . Moosup
BR 6582 . . . . Madison
SA Connecticut . . . . North Haven

Locomotive Engineers

DIV 77 Brotherhood of Locomotive Engineers . . . . . . Middletown

Longshoremen

LU 1398 . . . . New Haven
LU 1411 . . . . . . Gales Ferry

Machinists

CONF New England . . . Higganum

DLG 26 . . . . Kensington
LG 354 . . . . . . East Hartford
LG 609 . . . . New Haven
LG 700 Canel . . . . . Middletown
LG 743 . . . . . . Windsor Locks
LG 782 . . . . Middletown
LG 983 . . . . Oakville
LG 1112 . . . . . . East Haven
LG 1137 . . . . . . Kensington
LG 1249 . . . . Plainville
LG 1396 . . . . Branford
LG 1433 . . . . . . Kensington
LG 1746 Industrial Aircraft Lodge . . . . . . East Hartford
LG 1746-A . . . . . . Marion
LG 1871 . . . . Groton
STC Connecticut . . . Kensington

Maintenance of Way Employes

LG 90 . . . . Groton
SLG 1718 . . . . . . West Haven

Musicians

LU 52-626 . . . . . . Norwalk
LU 87 . . . . Danbury
LU 186 . . . . Waterbury
LU 234-486 . . . . . . Hamden
LU 285 . . . . Gales Ferry
LU 400 . . . . Rocky Hill
LU 499 . . . . Middletown
LU 514 . . . . Torrington
STCON Connecticut . . . Litchfield

National Staff Organization

LU Staff Organization, Association, Connecticut Education Association . . . . Hartford
LU Staff Organization, Professional, Connecticut Education Association . . . . . . Trumbull

NLRB Professional Association

LU 34 . . . . Hartford

Office and Professional Employees

LU 106 . . . . Groton
LU 376 . . . . . . North Haven

Operating Engineers

LU 478 . . . . Hamden

Painters

DC 11 . . . . Berlin
LU 186 . . . . New Haven
LU 481 . . . . Windsor
LU 1122 . . . . . . New London
LU 1274 . . . . . . West Haven
LU 1719 . . . . Berlin

Plumbing and Pipe Fitting

LU 676 . . . . Newington
LU 777 . . . . Meriden

Police Associations

LU 1178 Waterbury Emergency Services Union . . . . . Prospect

Postal and Federal Employees

LU 808 . . . . Bridgeport
LU 811 . . . . New Haven
LU 815 Stamford, Connecticut . . . . . . Stamford

Postal Workers

LU 147 Hartford. . . . East Hartford

LU 237 Greater Connecticut
   Area . . . . North Haven
LU 240 Stamford . . . . Stamford
LU 549 Bridgeport . . . . Bridgeport
LU 832 Willimantic . . Willimantic
LU 1097 Fairfield . . . . . Fairfield
LU 2921 Waterbury . . . Waterbury
LU 3093 Norwalk . . . . Norwalk
LU 3151 Meriden . . . . Meriden
LU 4865 West Conn Area . Danbury
SA Connecticut . . . . . Bridgeport

Railroad Signalmen
GC 56 Southern New
   England . . . . Guilford
LLG 5 . . . . Guilford
LLG 62 . . . . Danielson

Roofers, Waterproofers and Allied
   Workers
LU 9 . . . . Rocky Hill
LU 12 . . . . North Haven

Rural Letter Carriers
BR 29 . . . . Thomaston
LU 1 Litchfield
   County . . . . Washington Depot
LU 2 Hartford County . . East Berlin
LU 3 Tolland County . . . Vernon
LU 4 Windham County . . Brooklyn
LU 5 Fairfield County . . . Norwalk
LU 6 New Haven
   County . . . . Waterbury
LU 7 Middlesex County . Old Lyme
LU 29-8 New London
   County . . . . Jewett City

Security, Police and Fire
   Professionals
LU 538 . . . . . . Middle Haddam
LU 690 . . . . Stratford
LU 691 . . . . Milford

Service Employees
D 1199 New England Health Care
   Employees Union . . . . Hartford
LU 760 . . . . Hartford
LU 760 Conn Service
   Council . . . . New Britain
LU 2001 Connecticut State
   Employees . . . . Hartford

Sheet Metal Workers
DC SMWIA NE District
   Council . . . . Rocky Hill
LU 40 . . . . Rocky Hill
LU 328 . . . . New Haven

State, County and Municipal
   Employees
C 4 . . . . Berlin
D 1199 NUHHCE,
   CHCA . . . . Wallingford
DC 4 Connecticut & Special District
   Employees . . . . . New Britain
LU 184 Hartford, Connecticut, Metro
   District Employees . West Hartford

LU 1026 . . . . Coventry
LU 1303 . . . . New Britain
LU 1522 . . . . Bridgeport
LU 3145 Red Cross
   Employees . . . . . . Farmington
UNIT 10 NUHHCE, CHCA,
   Waterbury Hospital Registered
   Nurses . . . . Waterbury
UNIT 23 Connecticut Health Care
   Associates . . . . Norwalk
UNIT 45-46 NUHHCE, CHCA,
   Wallingford Hospital . Wallingford
UNIT 53 Connecticut Health Care
   Associates . . . . . . Wallingford
UNIT 61 NUHHCE, CHCA, Bradley
   Memorial Hospital . . Southington
UNIT 75 NUHHCE, CHCA, Milford
   Hospital Nurses . . . . . Oxford

Steelworkers
LU 01-46 . . . . Rogers
LU 01-457 . . . . Hamden
LU 01-655 . . . . Sprague
LU 01-745 . . . . Middletown
LU 01-753 . . . . Meriden
LU 01-845 . . . . Danbury
LU 01-859 . . . . Rocky Hill
LU 01-902 . . . . Southbury
LU 01-1554 . . . . . . Manchester
LU 01-1840 . . . . Versailles
LU 01-5370 . . . . . . Wallingford
LU 04-134-L . . . . Orange
LU 04-837-L . . . . Stratford
LU 04-895-L . . . . . . Waterbury
LU 04-2242-S . . . . . Wallingford
LU 04-6445-S . . . . . . Ansonia
LU 04-9411-S . . . . . Colchester
LU 04-12000-S . . . . . Shelton
LU 04-12160-S . . . . . Hamden
LU 04-14323-A . . . . . . Baltic
LU 04-15536-S . . . South Norwalk

Teachers
LU 933 New Haven Federation of
   Teachers . . . . . . New Haven
LU 3249 Mitchell College Faculty
   Federation . . . . . New London
LU 3394 Quinnipiac Faculty
   Federation . . . . . . Hamden
LU 3949 West Hartford Dormitory
   Supervisors . . . . West Hartford
LU 4230 American School for the
   Deaf . . . . West Hartford
LU 5041 Windham Hospital
   Registered Nurses . . . Canterbury
LU 5046 Johnson Memorial
   Registered Nurses . . . . Enfield
LU 5047 Danbury Hospital
   Professional Nurses
   Association . . . . . . Danbury
LU 5048 Nurses Association,
   Visiting, Professional
   Nurses . . . . Fairfield
LU 5049 Lawrence & Memorial
   Hospitals Registered
   Nurses . . . . New London

LU 5051 Lawrence & Memorial
   Hospitals LPN &
   Technicians . . . . . New London
LU 5052 Natchaug Federation
   of Registered
   Nurses . . . . . Mansfield Center
LU 5055 Manchester Memorial
   Hospital Professional
   Nurse . . . . Tolland
LU 5099 Windham Community
   Memorial Hospital
   Employees . . . . . Willimantic
LU 5101 New Milford Hospital
   Federation of Registered
   Nurses . . . . . . New Milford
LU 5121 SSMEU . . . . Manchester
LU 5123 L & M Healthcare Workers
   Union . . . . New London
SFED Connecticut State . Rocky Hill

Teamsters
LU 145 . . . . Stratford
LU 191 . . . . Bridgeport
LU 443 . . . . New Haven
LU 493 . . . . Uncasville
LU 559 . . . . South Windsor
LU 671 . . . . Bloomfield
LU 677 . . . . Waterbury
LU 1035 . . . . South Windsor
LU 1150 . . . . Stratford

Theatrical Stage Employees
LU 74 . . . . East Haven
LU 84 . . . . West Hartford
LU 109 . . . . Stratford
LU 133 . . . . Stamford
LU 486 . . . . Hartford
LU 538 . . . . Danielson

Transit Union
CONBD Connecticut . East Hartford
LDIV 281 . . . . New Haven
LU 425 . . . . East Hartford
LU 1336 . . . . Bridgeport
LU 1348 . . . . Norwich
LU 1588 . . . . . . South Windsor
LU 1734 . . . . Milford

Transport Workers
LU 2055 . . . . New Haven

Transportation Communications
   Union
D 227 Conrail . . . . . East Haven
D 1402 . . . . Killingworth

Transportation Union
GCA GO-663 Conrail-PC-NHR-
   NYNH&H . . . . . . Woodbridge
LU 277 . . . . Prospect
LU 328 . . . . North Branford
LU 352 . . . . Enfield
SLB LO-8 Connecticut . Woodbridge

Treasury Employees
CH 18 . . . . Broad Brook
CH 124 . . . . Beacon Falls

UNITE HERE
LU 34 . . . . New Haven
LU 35 . . . . New Haven
LU 217 . . . . New Haven

University Professors
CH Post College Faculty
   Association . . . . . . Waterbury

Utility Workers
LU 380 . . . . Sandy Hook
LU 384 . . . . Danbury
LU 470-001 . . . . . North Haven

Unaffiliated Labor
Organizations
Association of Court
   Security Officers-
   Connecticut . . . . North Branford
Clerks Secretaries & Bookkeepers
   Unlimited LG 1 . . . Old Saybrook
Connecticut Independent Utility
   Workers LU 12924 . . . . Hartford
Environmental Workers
   Association . . . . . . Bridgeport
Graduate Employees & Students
   Organization . . . . . New Haven
Greater Hartford Emergency Medical
   Technicians Association . . Enfield
Hamilton Standard Independent
   Security Officers
   Association . . . . Windsor Locks
New Milford Employees
   Association . . . . . New Milford
Plant Protection Employees
   Independent Union of, General
   Electric Company . . . Bridgeport
Regional Emergency
   Medical Technician
   Association . . . . . North Haven
Saint Bernard Education
   Association . . . . . . Uncasville
Staff Union of Connecticut
   Independent . . . . . Rocky Hill
Stamford Paramedic
   Association . . . . . . Stamford
United Technologies Corporation
   Fire & Security Officers
   Association LU East
   Hartford . . . . . . East Hartford
United Technologies Corporation
   Fire & Security Officers
   Association LU
   Middletown . . . . . Middletown
United Technologies Corporation
   Fire & Security Officers
   Association LU
   Southington . . . . . . Waterbury
United Technologies Corporation
   Fire & Security Officers
   Association NHQ . . East Hartford
Yale Police Benevolent
   Association . . . . . Killingworth

Delaware

AFL-CIO Trade and Industrial Departments

Building and Construction Trades Department
BCTC Delaware . . . . Wilmington

Affiliated Labor Organizations

Air Traffic Controllers
LU ILG . . . . New Castle

Asbestos Workers
LU 42 . . . . Wilmington

Automobile, Aerospace Workers
LU 435 . . . . Wilmington
LU 498. . . . . Smyrna
LU 1183 . . . . Newark
LU 1212. . . . . Bear
LU 1516. . . . . Middletown
LU 1542. . . . . Wilmington

Carpenters
LU 626. . . . . New Castle
LU 1545 . . . . New Castle
LU 2001 Milford Manor. . . Milford
LU 2006 Rehabilitation & Retirement
Center. . . . . Laurel
LU 2012. . . . . Seaford

Civilian Technicians
CH 24 Delaware . . . . Wilmington

Communications Workers
LU 13100 Diamond State Telephone
Commercial. . . . . Wilmington
LU 13101 United Telephone Workers
of Delaware . . . . Newark
LU 14801 . . . . Hockessin

Electrical Workers
LU 313. . . . . New Castle

LU 1238 . . . . New Castle
LU 2201 . . . . Georgetown
LU 2270. . . . . Wilmington

Fire Fighters
LU 135-F . . . Dover Air Force Base

Food and Commercial Workers
LU 987-C . . . . Georgetown

Government Employees
LU 1709 DoD . . . . Dover

Iron Workers
LU 451 . . . . Wilmington

Laborers
LU 199 . . . . Wilmington
LU 1029 Delaware State Employees
Union. . . . . Georgetown

Letter Carriers
BR 191 . . . . Wilmington
BR 906 . . . . Dover
BR 1977 . . . . Newark
BR 3846. . . . . Lewes
BR 4015 . . . . New Castle
SA Delaware . . . . . Wilmington

Locomotive Engineers
DIV 484 . . . . Magnolia

Longshoremen
LU 1694. . . . . Wilmington
LU 1694-001 . . . . . Wilmington
LU 1883 Clerks &
Checkers . . . . . . Wilmington
LU 1884. . . . . Wilmington

Machinists
LG 1284 . . . . Smyrna

Maintenance of Way Employes
SLG 3052 . . . . New Castle
SLG 3077 . . . . Felton

Marine Engineers
LG 3095 . . . . Newark

Musicians
LU 21 . . . . Wilmington

National Staff Organization
LU Staff Organization, Delaware
State Education
Association . . . . Dover

Nurses
LU 709 PSEA Crozer Chester
Medical Center. . . . . . Milton

Painters
LU 100 . . . . Wilmington

Plumbing and Pipe Fitting
LU 74 . . . . New Castle
LU 782. . . . . Seaford

Postal Workers
LU 152 Wilmington, Delaware/MTS
Area . . . . New Castle
LU 1742 Newark Delaware Local,
APWU . . . . Newark
LU 5885 Dover . . . . Dover
SA Delaware State
Branch . . . . Wilmington

Rural Letter Carriers
SA Delaware . . . . . . Hockessin

Sheet Metal Workers
LU 526 . . . . Wilmington

State, County and Municipal Employees
C 81 Delaware Public
Employees. . . . . . New Castle
LU 3898 Kent
Convalescent . . . . . . Smyrna

Steelworkers
LU 02-770 . . . . . . Marshallton
LU 02-786 . . . . Edgemoor
LU 02-898. . . . . Newark
LU 02-1134 . . . . . . New Castle
LU 04-6628-S . . . . . New Castle
LU 04-8184-S . . . . . Wilmington
LU 04-13028-S . . . . . Wilmington

Teamsters
LU 326. . . . . New Castle

Theatrical Stage Employees
LU 284 . . . . Wilmington

Transport Workers
LU 2015. . . . . Wilmington

Transportation Communications Union
D 584 . . . . Bear
LG 5087 Amtrak . . . . Wilmington
SBA 86 Conrail. . . . . Wilmington

Transportation Union
GCA GO-743 National Railroad
Passenger Corporation . . . Felton
LU 1378 . . . . Seaford
SLB LO-9 Delaware. . . New Castle

Treasury Employees
CH 56 . . . . Wilmington

Utility Workers
LU 584 . . . . Wilmington

Unaffiliated Labor Organizations

Dupont Employees Philadelphia
Works Union . . . . Wilmington
Dupont Systems Unions Independent
Seaford Nylon Employees
Council . . . . Seaford
Texaco Employees Association South
Jersey Employees . . . New Castle
Veterans Administration Nurses
Association . . . . . . Wilmington

District of Columbia

AFL-CIO Trade and Industrial Departments

Building and Construction Trades Department
NHQ . . . . Washington

Food and Allied Service Trades Department
FASTC Food & Allied
　Services. . . . . . . Washington
NHQ . . . . Washington

Maritime Trades Department
NHQ . . . . Washington

Metal Trades Department
MTC Washington DC
　Area. . . . . Washington
NHQ . . . . Washington

Union Label and Service Trades Department
NHQ . . . . Washington

AFL-CIO Directly Affiliated Locals

AFL-CIO
NHQ . . . . Washington

Affiliated Labor Organizations

Agricultural Employees
BR 30 . . . . Washington

Air Traffic Controllers
LU DCA . . . . Washington
LU IAD . . . . Washington
NHQ . . . . Washington

Athletes
FED NFL Players
　Association . . . . . . Washington
NHQ . . . . Washington

Bricklayers
NHQ . . . . Washington

Carpenters
NHQ . . . . Washington

Communications Workers
LU 2336. . . . . Washington
LU 2382. . . . . Washington
LU 2385 Federation of National
　Representatives. . . . Washington
LU 14200 . . . . Washington
LU 21005-AFA United
　Airlines. . . . . . . Washington
LU 21006-AFA United
　Airlines. . . . . . . Washington
LU 21007-AFA United
　Airlines. . . . . . . Washington
LU 21020-AFA United
　Airlines. . . . . . . Washington
LU 21024-AFA United
　Airlines. . . . . . . Washington
LU 21027-AFA United
　Airlines. . . . . . . Washington
LU 21032-AFA American Trans
　Air . . . . Washington

LU 21055-AFA American Eagle
　Airlines. . . . . . . Washington
LU 21055-AFA Mesa. . Washington
LU 21058-AFA Flagship
　Airlines. . . . . . . Washington
LU 21068-AFA Panam . Washington
LU 21069-AFA US
　Airways. . . . . . . Washington
LU 21082-AFA US
　Airways. . . . . . . Washington
LU 22021-AFA United
　Airlines. . . . . . . Washington
LU 22041-AFA USAir . Washington
LU 22050-AFA Atlantic Coast
　Airlines. . . . . . . Washington
LU 22061-AFA Piedmont
　Airlines. . . . . . . Washington
LU 23049-AFA Executive
　Airlines. . . . . . . Washington
LU 23057-AFA Air
　Tran. . . . . Washington
LU 23059-AFA Flagship
　Airlines. . . . . . . Washington
LU 23060-AFA Southeast
　Airlines. . . . . . . Washington
LU 23078-AFA Spirit
　Airlines. . . . . . . Washington
LU 23089-AFA US
　Airways. . . . . . . Washington
LU 24008-AFA United
　Airlines. . . . . . . Washington
LU 24028-AFA Air
　Wisconsin. . . . . . Washington
LU 24033-AFA American Trans
　Air . . . . Washington
LU 24035-AFA American Trans
　Air . . . . Washington
LU 24044-AFA Midwest Express
　Airlines. . . . . . . Washington
LU 24045-AFA Mesaba
　Airlines. . . . . . . Washington
LU 24046-AFA Mesaba
　Airlines. . . . . . . Washington
LU 24051-AFA Simmons
　Airlines. . . . . . . Washington
LU 24076-AFA PSA . . Washington
LU 24076-AFA Spirit
　Airlines. . . . . . . Washington
LU 26052-AFA Simmons
　Airlines. . . . . . . Washington
LU 27009-AFA United
　Airlines. . . . . . . Washington
LU 27010-AFA United
　Airlines. . . . . . . Washington
LU 27017-AFA Horizon
　Airlines. . . . . . . Washington
LU 27019-AFA Alaska
　Airlines. . . . . . . Washington
LU 27029-AFA Air
　Wisconsin. . . . . . Washington
LU 27039-AFA Alaska
　Airlines. . . . . . . Washington
LU 27039-AFA US
　Airways. . . . . . . Washington
LU 27048-AFA Mesaba
　Airlines. . . . . . . Washington
LU 27066-AFA America
　West . . . . Washington
LU 28023-AFA United
　Airlines. . . . . . . Washington
LU 28065-AFA
　Allegheny. . . . . . Washington
LU 28070-AFA US
　Airways. . . . . . . Washington

LU 29011-AFA United
　Airlines. . . . . . . Washington
LU 29012-AFA United
　Airlines. . . . . . . Washington
LU 29014-AFA United
　Airlines. . . . . . . Washington
LU 29018-AFA Alaska
　Airlines. . . . . . . Washington
LU 29025-AFA United
　Airlines. . . . . . . Washington
LU 29026-AFA United
　Airlines. . . . . . . Washington
LU 29037-AFA American Trans
　Air . . . . Washington
LU 29038-AFA United
　Airlines. . . . . . . Washington
LU 29043-AFA Hawaiian
　Airlines. . . . . . . Washington
LU 29047-AFA Hawaiian
　Airlines. . . . . . . Washington
LU 29053-AFA Wings West
　Airlines . . . . . . Washington
LU 29054-AFA Aloha
　Airlines. . . . . . . Washington
LU 32035 Washington-
　Baltimore . . . . . . Washington
NHQ . . . . Washington

Education
NHQ . . . . Washington
SA Federal Education
　Association . . . . . Washington

Electrical Workers
LU 26 . . . . Washington
NHQ . . . . Washington

Engineers
LU 9. . . . . Washington
LU 75 Congressional
　Research Employees
　Association . . . . . Washington

Federal Employees
LU 2. . . . . Washington
LU 1461. . . . . Washington
LU 1919. . . . . Washington
LU 2008. . . . . Washington
LU 2015. . . . . Washington
LU 2080. . . . . Washington

Fire Fighters
LU 151-F Walter Reed
　AMC . . . . Washington
NHQ . . . . Washington

Flight Attendants
LEC 15 United Airlines. Washington
LEC 16 United Airlines. Washington
LEC 22 United Airlines. Washington
LEC 31 American Trans
　Air . . . . Washington
LEC 34 American Trans
　Air . . . . Washington
LEC 36 American Trans
　Air . . . . Washington
LEC 42 Pro Air . . . Washington
LEC 62 CC Air . . . . Washington
LEC 63 Midway
　Airlines . . . . . . Washington
LEC 71 Tower Airlines . Washington
LEC 73 Atlantic Coast
　Airlines . . . . . . Washington
LEC 74 Spirit Airlines . Washington
LEC 77 Iberia Airlines . Washington

LEC 87 USAir . . . . Washington
MEC Air Wisconsin . . Washington
MEC Alaska Airlines . . Washington
MEC Aloha Airlines . . Washington
MEC America West . . Washington
MEC American Eagle
　Airlines. . . . . . . Washington
MEC American Trans
　Air . . . . Washington
MEC Eastern Region . . Washington
MEC Hawaiian
　Airlines . . . . . . Washington
MEC Mesaba Airlines . Washington
MEC Midwest Express
　Airlines . . . . . . Washington
MEC Spirit Airlines. . . Washington
MEC Tower Airlines . . Washington
MEC United Airlines . . Washington
MEC US Airways. . . . Washington
MEC Western Region. . Washington
NHQ . . . . Washington

Food and Commercial Workers
NHQ . . . . Washington

Foreign Service Association
NHQ . . . . Washington

Government Employees
C 252 Department of Education
　Locals. . . . . Washington
JC Printing Crafts U.S. Government
　Printing Office . . . . Washington
LU 12 DoL . . . . . . Washington
LU 17 VA, Central
　Office . . . . Washington
LU 25 VA. . . . . . . Washington
LU 32 MSPB-OPM . . . Washington
LU 421 DoE . . . . . . Washington
LU 476 HUD . . . . . Washington
LU 1041 DoD . . . . . Washington
LU 1118 DoT . . . . . Washington
LU 1534 DoS . . . . . Washington
LU 1733 GSA. . . . . . Washington
LU 1812 USIA . . . . . Washington
LU 1831 NGA . . . . . Washington
LU 1935. . . . . Washington
LU 2151 GSA. . . . . . Washington
LU 2211 USITC . . . . Washington
LU 2272 DoJ . . . . . . Washington
LU 2303 DoT . . . . . Washington
LU 2463 SI . . . . . . Washington
LU 2532. . . . . Washington
LU 2607 DoE . . . . . Washington
LU 2667 EEOC . . . . Washington
LU 2798 VA . . . . . . Washington
LU 2876 GPO. . . . . . Washington
LU 3295 FHLBB . . . . Washington
LU 3313 DoT . . . . . Washington
LU 3331 EPA . . . . . Washington
LU 3546 BoP, Headquarters Office
　Staff. . . . . Washington
LU 3653 DoT . . . . . Washington
LU 3810 DoC . . . . . Washington
LU 4060. . . . . Washington
NHQ . . . . Washington

Government Employees Association
LU 3-77-R . . . . . . Washington

Government Security Officers
LU 21 . . . . Washington
LU 80 . . . . Washington

Graphic Communications
CONF Commercial
  Unions . . . . Washington
LU 285-M . . . . Washington
LU 449-S . . . . Washington
LU 713-S . . . . Washington
NHQ . . . . Washington

Iron Workers
LU 201 . . . . Washington
LU 846 . . . . Washington
NHQ . . . . Washington

Laborers
NHQ . . . . Washington

Letter Carriers
BR 142 Capitol . . . . Washington
NHQ . . . . Washington

Locomotive Engineers
SLB District of Columbia
  SLB . . . . Washington

Machinists
DLG 1 NFFE FD 1 . . . Washington
LG 174 Columbia
  Lodge . . . . Washington
LLG 1-1 National Professional
  Employees . . . . . Washington
LLG NP-2 . . . . Washington

Marine Engineers
D 1 Pacific Coast
  District . . . . Washington
D 6 Professional Airways Systems
  Specialists . . . . . Washington
NHQ . . . . Washington

Musicians
CONF Pennsylvania
  Maryland Delaware & DC
  Areas . . . . Washington
LU 161-710 . . . . . . Washington

National Staff Organization
ASSN NEA Staff
  Organization . . . . Washington
LU NEA Association of Field Service
  Employees . . . . . Washington

Nurses
SA DC Nurses
  Association . . . . . Washington

Office and Professional Employees
NHQ . . . . Washington

Operating Engineers
LU 99 . . . . Washington
LU 560 . . . . Washington
NHQ . . . . Washington

Painters
LU 1997 . . . . Washington
NHQ . . . . Washington

Plasterers and Cement Masons
LU 891 . . . . Washington

Plate Printers, Die Stampers and Engravers
LU 32 . . . . Washington

Plumbing and Pipe Fitting
NHQ . . . . Washington

Police
LG 1 BEP Police Labor
  Committee . . . . . Washington
LG 1 Defense Protective Labor
  Committee . . . . . Washington
LG 1 Library of Congress Labor
  Committee . . . . . Washington
LG 1 U.S. Capitol Police Labor
  Committee . . . . . Washington
LG 1-F WRAM/DoD Police Labor
  Committee . . . . . Washington
LU DC 1 . . . . Washington

Police Associations
LU 1991 . . . . Washington

Postal and Federal Employees
LU 209 Washington,
  D.C. . . . . Washington
NHQ . . . . Washington

Postal Mail Handlers
NHQ . . . . Washington

Postal Workers
LU 140 Nation's Capital Southern
  Maryland . . . . . . Washington
LU 7002 Washington Mail
  Equipment Shops . . . Washington
NHQ . . . . Washington

Roofers, Waterproofers and Allied Workers
NHQ . . . . Washington

Security, Police and Fire Professionals
LU 291 . . . . Washington

Service Employees
CONF National Conference of
  Firemen & Oilers . . . Washington
LU 64 Firemen &
  Oilers . . . . Washington
LU 82 . . . . Washington
LU 722 . . . . Washington
LU 1199 NUHHCE D 1199 Strategic
  & Defense Fund . . . Washington
NHQ . . . . Washington

Sheet Metal Workers
NHQ . . . . Washington

State, County and Municipal Employees
C 20 District of
  Columbia . . . . . . Washington
C 26 Capital Area . . . . Washington
D 1199 Hospital and Healthcare
  Employees . . . . . Washington
LU 1418 . . . . Washington
LU 2477 Library of Congress
  Employees . . . . . Washington

LU 2478 Commission on Civil Rights
  Employees . . . . . Washington
LU 2830 . . . . Washington
LU 2910 . . . . Washington
LU 3300 . . . . Washington
LU 3548 . . . . Washington
NHQ . . . . Washington

Teachers
LU Staff Union . . . . Washington
LU 6 Washington Teachers
  Union . . . . Washington
NHQ . . . . Washington

Teamsters
CONF Brewery & Soft Drink
  Workers . . . . Washington
JC 55 . . . . Washington
LU 67 . . . . Washington
LU 96 Public Utility
  Workers . . . . Washington
LU 639 . . . . Washington
LU 730 . . . . Washington
LU 922 Automotive, Petroleum, Etc.
  Local Union . . . . Washington
NHQ . . . . Washington

Theatrical Stage Employees
LU 224 . . . . Washington
LU 815 . . . . Washington
LU 819 . . . . Washington
LU 868 . . . . Washington
LU 868-B . . . . Washington

Transit Union
NHQ . . . . Washington

Treasury Employees
CH 65 . . . . Washington
CH 83 . . . . Washington
CH 86 . . . . Washington
CH 101 . . . . Washington
CH 128 . . . . Washington
CH 159 . . . . Washington
CH 201 . . . . Washington
CH 204 . . . . Washington
CH 209 . . . . Washington
CH 213 . . . . Washington
CH 229 . . . . Washington
CH 250 . . . . Washington
CH 251 . . . . Washington
CH 280 . . . . Washington
CH 293 . . . . Washington
CH 297 . . . . Washington
NHQ . . . . Washington

UNITE HERE
LU 25 . . . . Washington
LU 2000 . . . . Washington

University Professors
NHQ . . . . Washington

Utility Workers
NHQ . . . . Washington

Weather Service Employees
BR 01-74 . . . . Washington
BR 01-88 . . . . Washington
BR 08-1 . . . . Washington
NHQ . . . . Washington

Unaffiliated Labor Organizations

Alliance for Economic
  Justice . . . . Washington
Arena Football League Players
  Association AFLPA . Washington
Coalition of Kaiser Permanente
  Union . . . . Washington
Communications Workers of
  America Guild . . . . Washington
CWA Guild . . . . Washington
Detective Benevolent Association of
  Police National Association of
  Police Detectives . . . Washington
English Language Institute Faculty
  Association . . . . . . Washington
Executive Staff Association of B'nai
  B'rith/Jewish Women
  International . . . . . Washington
Federation Professional & Technical
  Engineers LU 70 . . . Washington
House Staff Association, Childrens
  Hospital National Medical
  Center . . . . Washington
IBT & HERE Employee
  Representatives
  Council . . . . Washington
Interstate Commerce
  Commission Professional
  Association . . . . . . Washington
Joint Council of Unions Government
  Printing Office . . . . Washington
LIUNA Women's Caucus
  Association . . . . . . Washington
Major League Soccer Players
  Union . . . . Washington
Mechanical Allied
  Crafts . . . . Washington
National Association of Special
  Police and Security
  Officers . . . . Washington
National Union of Law Enforcement
  Associations . . . . . Washington
National Union of Protective Services
  Associations . . . . . Washington
Organized NATCA Employees
  Union . . . . Washington
Police Association of
  DC . . . . Washington
Professional Association, Merit
  Systems Protection
  Board . . . . Washington
Professional Association,
  National Labor Relations
  Board . . . . Washington
Rail Conference United States of
  America . . . . Washington
Staff Unions of Congress
  International . . . . . Washington
UMWA Welfare & Retirement Fund
  Employees Union . . Washington
Union of Staff Emplyees
  National . . . . Washington
United Staff Union . . . Washington
United States National Soccer Team
  Players Association . . Washington
Washington International School
  Staff Association . . . Washington

Florida

AFL-CIO Trade and Industrial Departments

Building and Construction Trades Department
BCTC Central Florida. . . . Orlando
BCTC Florida Big
   Bend . . . . Jacksonville
BCTC Florida State . . . Tallahassee
BCTC Northeastern
   Florida . . . . Jacksonville
BCTC Palm
   Coast . . . . . . West Palm Beach
BCTC Tampa Area. . . . . Mango

Maritime Trades Department
PC Greater South
   Florida . . . . Dania Beach
PC South Atlantic Area. Jacksonville

Other Councils and Committees
C Brevard County Central
   Labor . . . . Cocoa
C Service Trades . . . . . . Orlando

Affiliated Labor Organizations

Agricultural Employees
BR 8 . . . . Miami
BR 26 . . . . Fort Lauderdale
BR 29 . . . . Jacksonville
BR 36 . . . . Orlando

Air Traffic Controllers
LU DAB . . . . . . Daytona Beach
LU FLO . . . . . Fort Lauderdale
LU FPR . . . . Fort Pierce
LU FXE . . . . . . Fort Lauderdale
LU JAX . . . . Jacksonville
LU MCO . . . . Orlando
LU MIA. . . . . Miami
LU MLB . . . . Melbourne
LU NATCA-MHT. . . . . Hilliard
LU ORL . . . . Orlando
LU P31 . . . . Pensacola
LU PBI . . . . West Palm Beach
LU PIE . . . . Clearwater
LU PMP . . . . . Pompano Beach
LU PNS . . . . Pensacola
LU RSW . . . . Fort Myers
LU SFB . . . . Sanford
LU SRQ. . . . . Bradenton
LU TLH . . . . Tallahassee
LU TMB . . . . Miami
LU TPA . . . . Tampa
LU VRB . . . . Vero Beach
LU ZMA . . . . Miami

Asbestos Workers
LU 13 . . . . Jacksonville
LU 60 . . . . Opa Locka
LU 67 . . . . Tampa

Automobile, Aerospace Workers
LU 298 . . . . Clearwater
LU 323 . . . . Jacksonville
LU 788 . . . . Orlando
LU 1124. . . . . St. Petersburg
LU 1522 . . . . Kissimmee
LU 1649 . . . . Orlando
LU 1707. . . . . Orlando
LU 1821 . . . . Ocala
LU 2405 . . . . Tampa

LU 3043 . . . . Jacksonville
LU 6520 . . . . Jacksonville

Bakery, Confectionery, Tobacco Workers and Grain Millers
LU 103 . . . . Orlando
LU 482 . . . . Jacksonville

Boilermakers
LG 199 . . . . Jacksonville
LG 433 . . . . Tampa

Bricklayers
LU 1 . . . . Pembroke Park

Carpenters
C Florida Industrial & Public
   Employees. . . . . Winter Garden
LU 72 DALU . . . . Hialeah
LU 75 . . . . Gainesville
LU 79 . . . . . . Fort Lauderdale
LU 140 . . . . Tampa
LU 627 . . . . Jacksonville
LU 1000 . . . . Tampa
LU 1026 . . . . Hallandale
LU 1765 . . . . Orlando
LU 1820 . . . . . . Winter Garden
LU 2357. . . . . Old Town
LU 2411 . . . . Jacksonville
LU 4254 Florida Regional
   Council . . . . Hialeah

Civilian Technicians
CH 86 Florida Air . . . Jacksonville
CH 87 Florida Army . . Jacksonville

Communications Workers
LU 3101 . . . . Cocoa
LU 3102 . . . . Port Orange
LU 3103 . . . . Chipley
LU 3104 . . . . . . Pompano Beach
LU 3105 . . . . Gainesville
LU 3106 . . . . Jacksonville
LU 3108 . . . . Orlando
LU 3109 . . . . Pensacola
LU 3110 . . . . . . St. Augustine
LU 3111 . . . . Fort Pierce
LU 3112. . . . . . West Palm Beach
LU 3113 . . . . Deltona
LU 3114 . . . . Panama City
LU 3115 . . . . Brooksville
LU 3120 . . . . Hollywood
LU 3121 . . . . Hialeah
LU 3122 . . . . Miami
LU 3140 . . . . Orlando
LU 3151 . . . . Jacksonville
LU 3171 . . . . Wewahitchka
LU 3174 . . . . Wellborn
LU 3175 . . . . Miami
LU 3176 . . . . Ocala
LU 3177 . . . . Marathon
LU 3190 . . . . Sunrise
LU 14309 . . . New Smyrna Beach
LU 14310 . . . . Lakeland
LU 14315 . . . . Tampa
LU 53033 . . . . Hollywood
LU 83712 . . . . . . Lake Worth
LU 83736 . . . . . Pembroke Pines
LU 83740 . . . . . . Jacksonville
LU 83751 . . . . . . Jacksonville
STC Florida State . . . . Chipley

Education
LU United Faculty of
   Florida. . . . . Tallahassee

SA . . . . Tallahassee

Electrical Workers
LU 108 . . . . Tampa
LU 177 . . . . Jacksonville
LU 199 . . . . Fort Myers
LU 222 . . . . Reddick
LU 349 . . . . Miami
LU 359 . . . . Miami
LU 433 . . . . Crystal River
LU 606 . . . . Orlando
LU 622 . . . . Sanderson
LU 624 . . . . Panama City
LU 626 . . . . Winter Haven
LU 627 . . . . Port St. Lucie
LU 641 . . . . Fort Myers
LU 676 . . . . Pensacola
LU 682 . . . . St. Petersburg
LU 728 . . . . . . Fort Lauderdale
LU 756 . . . . . . Daytona Beach
LU 759 . . . . . . Pompano Beach
LU 820 . . . . Ellenton
LU 824 . . . . Tampa
LU 862 . . . . Jacksonville
LU 915 . . . . Tampa
LU 1042 . . . . Lake Monroe
LU 1055 . . . . Pensacola
LU 1066 . . . . Port Orange
LU 1191 . . . . . West Palm Beach
LU 1205 . . . . Gainesville
LU 1263 . . . . Pomona Park
LU 1346 . . . . . . Pembroke Pines
LU 1412 . . . . Clermont
LU 1491 . . . . Deland
LU 1496 . . . . Fort Walton Beach
LU 1583 . . . . Palatka
LU 1908 . . . . Titusville
LU 1924 . . . . Fernandina Beach
LU 1933 . . . . North Fort Myers
LU 1937 . . . . Molino
LU 2000 . . . . Orlando
LU 2072 . . . . Eustis
LU 2088 . . . . . . Merritt Island
SC U-4 Florida Power &
   Light . . . . Bradenton
SC 8-U . . . . Crystal River

Elevator Constructors
LU 49 . . . . Jacksonville
LU 71 . . . . Miami
LU 74. . . . . Tampa
LU 139 . . . . Orlando

Engineers
LU 22 NAPEP Council . Jacksonville

Federal Employees
C Veterans Administration
   Locals. . . . . . . Coral Springs
LU 153 . . . MacDill Air Force Base
LU 1608 . . . . Miami
LU 2154 . . . . Orange Park

Food and Commercial Workers
LU 35-C . . . . Mulberry
LU 39-C . . . . Mulberry
LU 328-C . . . . Panama City
LU 359-C . . . . Orlando
LU 377-C . . . . Fort Meade
LU 428-C . . Palm Beach Gardens
LU 439-C . . . . Gibsonton
LU 573-C . . . . Lakeland
LU 753-C . . . . Lakeland
LU 784-C . . . . . . White Springs
LU 814-C . . . . . . Bowling Green

LU 836-C . . . . Port St. Joe
LU 1038-C. . . . . Lakeland
LU 1625 . . . . Lakeland

Glass, Molders, Pottery and Plastics Workers
LU 91 . . . . Jacksonville
LU 208 . . . . Palmetto
LU 211 . . . . Eustis
LU 310 . . . . Plant City

Government Employees
C 41 Florida State . . . . Gainesville
LU 192 ID . . . . Jacksonville
LU 501 FBoP . . . . Miami
LU 506 FCC Coleman . Sumterville
LU 507 . . . . Riviera Beach
LU 508 DFAS. . . . . . Orlando
LU 513 . . . Kennedy Space Center
LU 515 Miami VAMC . . . . Miami
LU 547 VA . . . . Tampa
LU 548 . . . . Bay Pines
LU 696 DoD . . . . . . Jacksonville
LU 1113. . . . . Parker
LU 1167 . . . . Homestead
LU 1380 . . . . Panama City
LU 1458 DoJ . . . . Miami
LU 1566 DoD . . . . . Key West
LU 1570 DoJ . . . . . Tallahassee
LU 1594 WCFB . . St. Petersburg
LU 1897 DoD . Eglin Air Force Base
LU 1942 . . . . Eglin Air Force Base
LU 1943 . . . . Jacksonville
LU 1960 DoD . . . . . . Pensacola
LU 1976 VA . . . . . . Lake City
LU 2010 DoD . . . . Mayport Naval
   Station
LU 2014 DoD . . . . . . Margate
LU 2113 . . . . Orlando
LU 2447 DoD. . . . . . . Miami
LU 2453 DoD. . . . . . Jacksonville
LU 2568 DoD . . . . . Patrick Air
   Force Base
LU 2779 VA . . . . . . Gainesville
LU 2875 DoC. . . . . . . Miami
LU 3168 USDA . . . . . Sunrise
LU 3240 DoD . . . . . Tyndall Air
   Force Base
LU 3412 DoJ . . . . . Jacksonville
LU 3690 DoJ . . . . Miami
LU 3725 DoJ . . . . . Jacksonville
LU 3953 DLA, Florida
   Employees . . . . . . Melbourne
LU 4035 BoP, FPC, Eglin
   AFB . . . . . Eglin Air Force Base
LU 4036 FCI. . . . . . . Marianna
LU 4037 FPCP . . . . . Pensacola
LU 4056 SSA . . . . Valrico

Government Employees Association
LU 05-45 . . . . . St. Petersburg
LU 05-82. . . . . . Atlantic Beach
LU 05-95 . . . . . . Gulf Breeze

Government Security Officers
LU 125 . . . . Jacksonville
LU 131 . . . . Palm Beach
LU 132 . . . . Tampa
LU 166 . . . . Tallahassee
LU 236 . . . . Tampa

Graphic Communications
LU 61-N . . . . . West Palm Beach
LU 180-C . . . . . . St. Petersburg

LU 193-C . . . . Quincy	DIV 49 . . . . . . Pembroke Pines	SLG 2057. . . . . Greenville	LU 323 . . . . Pensacola
LU 444-C . . . . . Ormond Beach	DIV 92 . . . . Lakeland	SLG 2162 . . . . Lawtey	LU 327 . . . . Tampa
LU 628-S . . . . Miramar	DIV 216 . . . . Valrico		LU 329 . . . . Lake Mary
	DIV 275. . . . . Cantonment	**Marine Engineers**	LU 334 . . . . Fort Lauderdale
Iron Workers	DIV 309 . . . . Orange Park	D 1 Federation of Private Employees,	
DC Southeastern States. Jacksonville	DIV 769 . . . . Sanford	Division of NFOPAE. . Plantation	**Postal Mail Handlers**
LU 272 . . . . . Fort Lauderdale	GCA CSX Transportation . Chuluota	D 1 National Federation of Public &	LU 318 . . . . Orlando
LU 397 . . . . Mango	GCA CSXT Northern Railroad	Private Employees . . . Plantation	
LU 402 . . . . Riviera Beach	Lines . . . . Ponte Vedra Beach	D 2-A Transportation & Service	**Postal Workers**
LU 597 . . . . Jacksonville	GCA CSXT Western Railroad	Employees . . . . . Dania Beach	LU 138 Northeast Florida
LU 698 . . . . Jacksonville	Lines . . . . Jacksonville		Area . . . . Jacksonville
LU 808 . . . . Orlando	SLB Florida . . . . Deland	**Musicians**	LU 172 Miami Area . . . . Miami
		LU 283 . . . . Pensacola	LU 259 Tampa Area . . . . . Tampa
Laborers	**Longshoremen**	LU 389 . . . . Orlando	LU 551 Pensacola . . Pensacola
LU 478 . . . . Miami	C Southeastern Dock &	LU 427-721 . . . . . . Clearwater	LU 620 Florida Keys
LU 517 . . . . Orlando	Marine . . . . Jacksonville	LU 444 . . . . Jacksonville	Area . . . . Key West
LU 630 . . . . Jacksonville	LU 1359 . . . . Fort Pierce	LU 655 . . . . Hollywood	LU 749 Palm Beach
LU 767 . . . . . West Palm Beach	LU 1402 . . . . Tampa	STCON Florida	Area . . . . . . Lake Worth
LU 1652. . . . . West Palm Beach	LU 1408 . . . . Jacksonville	Georgia . . . . . Jacksonville	LU 1073 Sarasota. . . . Sarasota
	LU 1416 . . . . Miami		LU 1201 Broward County
Letter Carriers	LU 1526 . . . Fort Lauderdale	**National Staff Organization**	Area. . . . . Plantation
BR 53 . . . . Jacksonville	LU 1569 . . . . Tampa	LU Staff Organization,	LU 1209 Melbourne
BR 321 . . . . Pensacola	LU 1593 . . . . Jacksonville	Florida . . . . Orange Park	Area . . . . Melbourne
BR 599 . . . . Tampa	LU 1691 . . . . Tampa		LU 1228 Suncoast
BR 689 . . . . . . St. Augustine	LU 1713 . . . . Port St. Joe	**NLRB Professional Association**	Area. . . . . . Pinellas Park
BR 818 . . . . Key West	LU 1759 . . . . Tampa	LU 12 . . . . Tampa	LU 1279 Fort Myers . . . Fort Myers
BR 1025 . . . . . . Gainesville	LU 1922 . . . . Miami	NHQ . . . . Tampa	LU 1414 . . . . . Panama City
BR 1071 . . . . Miami	LU 1922-1 . . . . Miami		LU 1462 Central Florida
BR 1091. . . . . Orlando	LU 1988 . . . . Pensacola	**Nurses**	Area. . . . . Orlando
BR 1103 . . . . Ocala	LU 2062 . . . . Miami	LU Florida Nurses Association of	LU 1519 Tallahassee . . Tallahassee
BR 1172 . . . . Tallahassee		Shands Hospital. . . . Orlando	LU 1672 Daytona
BR 1477 . . . . Pinellas Park	**Machinists**	LU Florida Nurses, Wuesthoff	Beach . . . . . Daytona Beach
BR 1690. . . . . West Palm Beach	DLG 112 . . . . Jacksonville	Unit . . . . Orlando	LU 1684 New Smyrna
BR 1753 . . . . Bradenton	DLG 166 . . . . . Cape Canaveral	SA Florida Nurses	Beach. . . . . New Smyrna Beach
BR 1779 . . . . Lakeland	LG 20 . . . . Niceville	Association . . . . . . Orlando	LU 2502 Titusville . . . . Titusville
BR 2008 Springtime	LG 40 Island. . . . . Yulee		LU 2503 Madison . . . Madison
City . . . . Clearwater	LG 57 . . . . Clewiston	**Office and Professional Employees**	LU 2510 Perry . . . . Perry
BR 2072 . . . . . . Fort Myers	LG 192 . . . . Pensacola	LU 46 . . . . . . Apollo Beach	LU 2664 Cocoa . . . . Cocoa Beach
BR 2088. . . . . Winter Haven	LG 257 . . . . Jacksonville	LU 73 . . . . Jacksonville	LU 3057 Manatee Area. . Bradenton
BR 2148. . . . . . . Sarasota	LG 368 . . . . . Miami Springs	LU 80. . . . . . . Panama City	LU 3399 Clearwater . . . Clearwater
BR 2325 . . . . . . MacClenny	LG 449 . . . . Callaway	LU 337 . . . . Palatka	LU 3450 Vero Beach . . Vero Beach
BR 2550 . . . . Sunrise	LG 458-FL . . . . . . Tallahassee		LU 3525 Gainesville. . . Gainesville
BR 2591 . . . . Deland	LG 501. . . . . . . Daytona Beach	**Operating Engineers**	LU 3537 Plant City . . . . Plant City
BR 2689 . . . . . . Melbourne	LG 610 . . . . . Cape Canaveral	LU 487 . . . . Miami	LU 3732 Marianna . . . . Marianna
BR 2744 . . . . Sebring	LG 731 . . . . Jacksonville	LU 673-ABC . . . . Jacksonville	LU 3796 St. Cloud. . . . St. Cloud
BR 2750. . . . . . Lake Wales	LG 759 . . . . Jacksonville	LU 925 . . . . Mango	LU 3799 Citrus Center
BR 2776 . . . . Quincy	LG 773. . . . . Titusville		Area . . . . Lakeland
BR 2796 . . . . Madison	LG 815 . . . . . . Merritt Island	**Painters**	LU 3803 Venice . . . . . Venice
BR 2889 . . . . Perry	LG 971 . . . . Jupiter	DC 78 . . . . Orlando	LU 3804 Jasper . . . . . Jasper
BR 3018 . . . . Williston	LG 1003 . . . . Jacksonville	LU 88 . . . . Tampa	LU 3858 Bonifay . . . . Bonifay
BR 3129 . . . New Smyrna Beach	LG 1098 . . . . Hollister	LU 164 . . . . Jacksonville	LU 3936 Crestview . . . Crestview
BR 3367 . . . . . Panama City	LG 1106 . . . . . Panama City	LU 365 . . . . . Pompano Beach	LU 4158 DeLand . . . . DeLand
BR 3641 . . . . . . Monticello	LG 1163. . . . . Cape Canaveral	LU 452 . . . . . Pompano Beach	LU 4613 Dunnellon . . . Dunnellon
BR 3663 . . . . . Apalachicola	LG 1453 NFFE . . . Coral Springs	LU 1010. . . . . Orlando	LU 5643 Play Ground Area
BR 3667 . . . . Chipley	LG 1852 . . . . . Fort Lauderdale	LU 1175 . . . . Pompano Beach	Local . . . . Gulf Breeze
BR 3761 . . . . Cocoa	LG 2061 Banana River . . . . Cocoa		LU 5661 Orange City . . Deltona
BR 4000 . . . . Avon Park	LG 2152 . . . . South Bay	**Plate Printers, Die Stampers and**	LU 6676 Lake Placid . . Lake Placid
BR 4559 . . . Fort Walton Beach	LG 2319 . . . . Seminole	**Engravers**	LU 7041 Jacksonville Bulk Mail
BR 4669 . . . . . Chattahoochee	LG 2460 . . . . Pensacola	NHQ . . . . . Sun City Center	Center . . . . . . Jacksonville
BR 4716 . . . . Naples	LG 2508 . . . . Orlando		LU 7136 . . . . Tallevast
BR 4997 . . . . Frostproof	LG 2777 . . . . Milton	**Plumbing and Pipe Fitting**	LU 7138 APWU Mid-
BR 5002 . . . Fort Walton Beach	LG 2902 . . . . Milton	DC Florida Pipe Trades . Opa Locka	Florida . . . . . . Lake Mary
BR 5192 . . . . Apopka	LG 2915 . . . . Valrico	LU 123 . . . . Tampa	LU 8002 First Coast
BR 5201 . . . . Overstreet	STC Florida State Council of	LU 234 . . . . Jacksonville	Local . . . . . . Jacksonville
BR 5480 . . . . Venice	Machinists . . . . . Melbourne	LU 295 . . . . . Daytona Beach	SA Florida . . . . . . Tallahassee
BR 5561 . . . . Casselberry		LU 366 . . . . Pensacola	
BR 5951 . . . . Edgewater	**Maintenance of Way Employes**	LU 519. . . . . . . Miami Lakes	**Railroad Signalmen**
BR 5955 . . . . Altamonte Springs	FED Seaboard . . . . Jacksonville	LU 592 . . . . Tallahassee	GC 3690 Seaboard Coastline
BR 5957 . . . . Lake Hamilton	LG 540 . . . . Kissimmee	LU 630 . . . . . West Palm Beach	Railroad . . . . . Jacksonville
BR 6013 . . . . Inverness	LG 2655. . . . . Dover	LU 719 . . . . . Fort Lauderdale	LLG 16 . . . . . . Jacksonville
BR 6200 . . . . . . Blountstown	LG 2912 . . . . Sebring	LU 725 . . . . Opa Locka	
BR 6491 . . . Crystal River	LG 2914 . . . . St. Augustine	LU 803 . . . . Orlando	**Retail, Wholesale and Department**
BR 6551 . . . . Havana	LG 2915 . . . . . Fort Pierce	LU 821. . . . . Ocala	**Store**
BR 8008. . . . . St. Petersburg	LG 2916 . . . . . Opa Locka		LU 43 . . . . Dade City
SA Florida . . . . Sarasota	SLG 539 . . . . . Jacksonville	**Postal and Federal Employees**	LU 531 . . . . Jacksonville
	SLG 547 . . . . Lakeland	LU 302 . . . . Havana	
Locomotive Engineers	SLG 702. . . . . . . Century	LU 320 . . . . Jacksonville	
DIV 35 . . . . . Jacksonville	SLG 739 . . . . . . Avon Park	LU 322 . . . . . . Carol City	

Roofers, Waterproofers and Allied Workers
LU 103 . . . . . . West Palm Beach
LU 181 . . . . Jacksonville

Rural Letter Carriers
D 1 . . . . Port St. Lucie
D 2 . . . . Naples
D 3 . . . . Kissimmee
D 4 . . . . Lutz
D 5 . . . . Citra
D 6 . . . . Gainesville
D 7 . . . . Leesburg
D 8 . . . . Live Oak
D 9 . . . . Lynn Haven
D 10. . . . . Cantonment
D 11. . . . . Jacksonville
D 12 . . . . Lake Wales
D 13 . . . . St. Augustine
D 14 Florida. . . . . . . Florida City
D 15 Florida . . . . North Port
D 16 Florida . . . . Titusville
D 17 Florida . . . . Bradenton
D 18 Florida . . . . Spring Hill
SA Florida . . . . Floral City

Security, Police and Fire Professionals
LU 127 . . . . Merritt Island
LU 129 . . . . Port St. Lucie
LU 603 . . . . . . Lake Buena Vista
LU 604. . . . . Beverly Hills
LU 607 . . . . Orlando
LU 610 . . . . Homestead
LU 611 . . . . Miramar

Service Employees
LU 8 . . . . Orlando
LU 11 Provisional Organizing . . . . Miami
LU 125 United Service Workers . . . . Tequesta
LU 1199 . . . . Miami
LU 1991 . . . . Miami

Sheet Metal Workers
DC Southeast . . . . Tampa
LU 15 . . . . Tampa
LU 32. . . . . . North Miami Beach
LU 435 . . . . Jacksonville
LU 490 . . . . Deltona

State, County and Municipal Employees
C 79 Florida Public Employees . . . . . . Tallahassee
LU 1781 University Medical Center Employees . . . . . . Jacksonville
LU 2897 Shands Teaching Hospital & Clinics Employees . Tallahassee

Steelworkers
ASSN Southern Pulp & Paper Industry . . . . Interlachen
LU 991-003. . . . . Oldsmar
LU 3-585 . . . . Perry
LU 3-985 . . . . Wimauma

LU 03-30 . . . . Palatka
LU 03-392 . . . . Miami
LU 03-395 . . . Fernandina Beach
LU 03-415 . . . Fernandina Beach
LU 03-426 . . . . Jacksonville
LU 03-444. . . . . Pensacola
LU 03-447 . . . . Cantonment
LU 03-450 . . . Fernandina Beach
LU 03-458 . . . . Plant City
LU 03-475 . . . . . Winter Haven
LU 03-530 . . . . Palatka
LU 03-547 . . . . Cantonment
LU 03-606 . . . . Riverview
LU 03-622 . . . . . . Winter Haven
LU 03-720 . . . . Riverview
LU 03-766 . . . Fernandina Beach
LU 03-802 . . . Fernandina Beach
LU 03-834 . . . . Orlando
LU 03-835 . . . . Polk City
LU 03-874 . . . . Yulee
LU 03-984 . . . . Brandon
LU 03-1138 . . . . . . Lake Placid
LU 03-1192 . . . . Perry
LU 03-1342 . . . . . Panama City
LU 03-1466 . . . . Starke
LU 03-1561 . . . . . . Cantonment
LU 03-1649 . . . . . . Jacksonville
LU 03-1717 . . . . Palatka
LU 05-130 . . . . . . Thonotosassa
LU 09-38 . . . . Jacksonville
LU 09-174-S . . . . Havana
LU 09-775-L. . . . . . Gainesville
LU 09-4987-S . . . . . Jacksonville
LU 09-7609-S. . . . . Miami
LU 09-7752-S . . . . . . Wildwood
LU 09-7858-S. . . . . . Plant City
LU 09-8461-S . . . . . Jacksonville
LU 09-9292-S . . . . . Jacksonville
LU 09-12130-S . . . . . Pensacola
LU 09-14963-S . . . . . Port St. Joe
LU 09-15431-S . . . . Jacksonville

Teachers
LU 3842 De Soto County Teachers Association . . . . Arcadia

Teamsters
CONF Georgia-Florida. . . . Tampa
LU 79 . . . . Tampa
LU 173 . . . . Bradenton
LU 385 . . . . Orlando
LU 390 . . . . North Miami
LU 512 . . . . Jacksonville
LU 769 . . . . Miami
LU 947 . . . . Jacksonville

Television and Radio Artists
LU Miami . . . . Hollywood

Theatrical Stage Employees
D 14. . . . . Jacksonville
LU 60 . . . . Pensacola
LU 115 . . . . Jacksonville
LU 321 . . . . Tampa
LU 412 . . . . Tallevast
LU 477 . . . . Miami
LU 500 South Florida . Oakland Park
LU 558 . . . . Daytona Beach

LU 631 . . . . Orlando
LU 647 . . . . Estero
LU 835 Exhibition Employees . . . . Orlando
LU 843 . . . . Orlando
LU 937 . . . . Oakland Park
LU 938-AE . . . . . Jacksonville

Train Dispatchers
SCOM CSX. . . . . . Jacksonville
SCOM Duluth Missabe & Iron Range . . . . Ponte Vedra Beach

Transit Union
LDIV . . . . Tampa
LDIV 1197 . . . . . . Jacksonville
LDIV 1395 . . . . . . Pensacola
LDIV 1593 . . . . Tampa

Transport Workers
LU 500 . . . . Miami Springs
LU 525 . . . . Cocoa Beach
LU 561 . . . . Miami
LU 568 . . . . Miami
LU 570 . . . . Miami Springs

Transportation Communications Union
D 697 . . . . Jacksonville
D 724 . . . . Switzerland
D 1220. . . . . . . Thonotosassa
D 1523 . . . . Jacksonville
D 1908 Allied Services Division . . . . . Winter Garden
D 2502 System Division 250 . . . . Dade City
LG 5093 Amtrak. . . . . . Seminole
LG 6046 Carmen Division. . Debary
LG 6633 Lakeland . . . . Lakeland
LG 6649 Sun Queen. . Delray Beach
SBA 3 SCL-L&N Southeastern . . . . Jacksonville

Transportation Union
GCA GO-49 . . . . . Jacksonville
GCA GO-513 Louisville & Nashville Railroad . . . . Jacksonville
GCA GO-851 Seaboard Coast Line Railroad . . . . Jacksonville
LU 903 . . . . Jacksonville
LU 1035 . . . . Lakeland
LU 1138 . . . . North Miami
LU 1221 . . . . Brandon
LU 1312. . . . . Pace
LU 1502 . . . . Clermont
LU 1900 . . . . Miami
SLB LO-11 Florida . . . . Hialeah

Treasury Employees
CH 16 . . . . Jacksonville
CH 77. . . . . Miami
CH 84 . . . . Maitland
CH 87. . . . . Tampa
CH 93 . . . . Plantation
CH 137 . . . . Miami
CH 171 . . . . Jacksonville
CH 174 . . . . Tampa
CH 249 . . . . Fort Myers

UNITE HERE
LU 10 . . . . Fort Lauderdale
LU 55 . . . . Orlando
LU 355 . . . . Miami
LU 362 . . . . Orlando
LU 737 . . . . Orlando

University Professors
CH Edward Waters College . . Ocala

Utility Workers
LU 551 . . . . Palatka

Weather Service Employees
BR 02-19 . . . . Tallahassee
BR 02-21 . . . . Jacksonville
BR 02-25 . . . . Key West
BR 02-62 . . . . Ruskin
BR 02-65 . . . . Miami
BR 02-72 . . . . Melbourne
BR 02-77 . . . . Hilliard
BR 02-84 . . . . Miami
BR 08-7. . . . . . . St. Petersburg

Unaffiliated Labor Organizations

American Longshoremens Association of West Florida LU 1482 . . . . Panama City
American Maritime Officers . . . . Dania Beach
Florida Rural Legal Services Workers Union . . . . Fort Pierce
Florida Staff Union . . . Jacksonville
Hospitality Workers Union LU 10 . . . . Fort Lauderdale
Jacksonville Symphony Players Association. . . . . . Jacksonville
National Association of Aeronautical Examiners LU 3 . . . Orange Park
National Association of Aeronautical Examiners NHQ . . . Middleburg
National Association of Basketball Referees. . . . . Ocoee
National Association of Government Inspectors UNIT 1 . . Jacksonville
National Federation of Licensed Practical Nurses SA Licensed Practical Nurses Association of Florida . . . . . . St. Petersburg
Pari-Mutuel Employees Florida Independent Association . . Miami
Professional Association of Golf Officials . . . . Cantonment
Restaurant Hotel Motel Nightclub. . . . . Fort Lauderdale
Seabulk Seamens Association . . . West Palm Beach
Security Enforcement Workers Union LU 1 . . . . . . Winter Springs
The South Florida Building and Trades Council . . . . North Miami Beach
United Government Security of America LU 202 . . . . . . Miami
United Health Care Association . . . . . . Cantonment

Georgia

AFL-CIO Trade and Industrial Departments

Building and Construction Trades Department
BCTC Augusta . . . . . . Augusta
BCTC North Georgia . . . Atlanta
BCTC Savannah . . . . . Savannah

Metal Trades Department
MTC Columbus . . . . Fort Benning

AFL-CIO Directly Affiliated Locals

AFL-CIO
DALU 461 . . . . Macon

Affiliated Labor Organizations

Agricultural Employees
BR 37 . . . . Atlanta
LU 25 . . . . Savannah

Air Traffic Controllers
LU ABY . . . . Albany
LU AGS . . . . Augusta
LU ATL . . . . Hapeville
LU ATL . . . . . Peachtree City
LU CSG . . . . Columbus
LU DEN . . . . Chamblee
LU ESO . . . . . . College Park
LU MCN . . . . Macon
LU SAV . . . . Savannah
LU ZTL . . . . Hampton

Asbestos Workers
LU 48 . . . . Atlanta
LU 96 . . . . Pooler

Automobile, Aerospace Workers
C Georgia . . . . Smyrna
LU 10 . . . . Doraville
LU 472 . . . . Covington
LU 868 . . . . Morrow
LU 882 . . . . Hapeville
LU 1103 . . . . Armuchee
LU 1726 . . . . Covington
LU 2188 . . . . Chula
LU 2378 . . . . Suwanee

Bakery, Confectionery, Tobacco Workers and Grain Millers
LU 42 . . . . Atlanta
LU 362-T . . . . Macon

Boilermakers
LG 23-D Cement Workers . . . . . . Hawkinsville
LG 26 . . . . Savannah
LG 100-M . . . . Albany
LG 425 . . . . Waycross
LG 523-D Cement Workers . . . . . . Milledgeville
LG 545-D Cement Workers . . . . . . Montrose

Bricklayers
LU 3 . . . . Forest Park
LU 7 . . . . Athens
LU 22 . . . . Jesup

LU 33 Georgia/North Carolina/South Carolina . . . . Atlanta

Carpenters
LU Eastern Millwrights Conference . . . . . . Kennesaw
LU 144 . . . . Macon
LU 225 . . . . Atlanta
LU 256 . . . . Savannah
LU 283 . . . . Augusta
LU 1263 . . . . Kennesaw
LU 1723 . . . . Columbus
LU 2268 . . . . Gray
LU 3078 . . . . Watkinsville
LU 4043 Southeastern . . . Augusta

Civilian Technicians
CH 36 Aaron B. Roberts . Robins Air Force Base
CH 38 Savannah Act . . . . Rincon
CH 55 North Georgia Armact . . . . Atlanta
CH 56 South Georgia . . . Hinesville
STC Georgia . . . . . McDonough

Communications Workers
C Georgia Political Council . Macon
LU 3201 . . . . Albany
LU 3203 . . . . Athens
LU 3204 . . . . Atlanta
LU 3205 . . . . Covington
LU 3207 . . . . Martinez
LU 3209 . . . . Brunswick
LU 3212 . . . . Columbus
LU 3215 . . . . Griffin
LU 3217 . . . . Macon
LU 3218 . . . . Marietta
LU 3220 . . . . Savannah
LU 3250 . . . . Norcross
LU 3263 . . . . Norcross
LU 3290 . . . . Canton
LU 14320 . . . . Atlanta
LU 14322 . . . . Atlanta
LU 83190 . . . . Lindale
LU 83295 . . . . Atlanta

Electrical Workers
LU 84 . . . . Smyrna
LU 508 . . . . Savannah
LU 613 . . . . Atlanta
LU 632 . . . . . . Locust Grove
LU 1132 . . . . Cochran
LU 1193 . . . . Conyers
LU 1208 . . . . Savannah
LU 1316 . . . . Macon
LU 1391 . . . . Savannah
LU 1531 . . . . Albany
LU 1545 . . . . Jesup
LU 1579 . . . . Augusta
LU 1947 . . . . Valdosta
LU 1984 . . . . Waycross
LU 2064 . . . . Valdosta
LU 2109 . . . . Athens
LU 2127 . . . . Lithonia
LU 2194 . . . . Americus
SC 6 Railroad . . . . Cumming

Elevator Constructors
LU 32 . . . . Atlanta

Federal Employees
LU 122 . . . . Atlanta
LU 460 . . . . Kingsland
LU 1329 . . . . Gainesville
LU 1766 . . . . Atlanta

LU 2047 . . . . Atlanta
LU 2102 . . . . Atlanta

Fire Fighters
LU 107-F Robins Air Force Base . . . . . . Warner Robins
LU 118-F Moody AFB Local . . . . Valdosta
LU 152-F Dobbins AFB Local . . . . Woodstock

Food and Commercial Workers
LU 90-T . . . . Rockmart
LU 218 . . . . Atlanta
LU 354 . . . . Cedartown
LU 609-C . . . . Albany
LU 722-C . . . . Atlanta
LU 736-C . . . . Brunswick
LU 832-C . . . . Woodbine
LU 1016-C . . . . Hinesville
LU 1996 . . . . Suwanee
LU 2600 . . . . Union City
RC 3 . . . . Suwanee

Glass, Molders, Pottery and Plastics Workers
LU 25 . . . . Griffin
LU 63 . . . . Newnan
LU 98 . . . . Midland
LU 101 . . . . Snellville
LU 204 . . . . Austell
LU 234 . . . . . . Warner Robins
LU 236 . . . . Palmetto
LU 251 . . . . Austell
LU 260 . . . . Athens
LU 377-A . . . . Winder
LU 393-A . . . . Greensboro
LU 395 . . . . . . Social Circle

Government Employees
C 19 Fifth District . . . . Riverdale
C 39 Georgia State . . Warner Robins
LU 54 DoD . . . . . Fort Benning
LU 81 DoD . . . . Stone Mountain
LU 217 VA . . . . Augusta
LU 500 Council of Prisons 33 . . . . Glynco
LU 504 . . . . . . Fort Benning
LU 517 . . . . Atlanta
LU 518 . . . . Atlanta
LU 987 DoD . . . . Warner Robins
LU 1011 USDA . . . . Cartersville
LU 1106 OGC/USDA . . . . Atlanta
LU 1145 DoJ . . . . Atlanta
LU 1568 DoC . . . . . . Atlanta
LU 1759 DoD . . . . . . Atlanta
LU 1845 DoD . . . . . Kings Bay
LU 1922 DoD . . . . Fort Stewart
LU 1985 VA . . . . . . Dublin
LU 2002 HHS . . . . . Glynco
LU 2017 DoD . . . . Fort Gordon
LU 2069 DoD . . . . . Marietta
LU 2252 USDA . . . . Gainesville
LU 2317 DoD . . . . . . Albany
LU 2778 VA . . . . . . Decatur
LU 2883 DoD . . . . . Decatur
LU 3123 INS . . . . . . Atlanta
LU 3152 USDA . . . . . Vienna
LU 3627 HHS . . . . . Guyton
LU 3836 FEMA . . . Riverdale
LU 3855 CPSC . . . . . Atlanta
LU 3887 DE . . . . . . Atlanta
LU 3981 FCI . . . . Jesup

Government Employees Association
LU 5-120-R Army & Air Force Exchange Service . . . . . Smyrna

Government Security Officers
LU 62 . . . . Fayetteville
LU 135 . . . . Augusta

Graphic Communications
CONF Southern . . . . . . Fairburn
DC 7-S Southeastern Printing Specialists . . . . Mableton
LU 8-M . . . . Atlanta
LU 96-B . . . . Smyrna
LU 465-S . . . . Mableton
LU 527-S . . . . Mableton

Iron Workers
LU 387 . . . . Atlanta
LU 709 . . . . . Port Wentworth

Letter Carriers
BR 73 . . . . Decatur
BR 263 . . . . Martinez
BR 270 . . . . Macon
BR 313 . . . . Brunswick
BR 420 . . . . Leesburg
BR 536 . . . . Rome
BR 546 . . . . Columbus
BR 578 . . . . Savannah
BR 588 . . . . Athens
BR 958 . . . . Waycross
BR 972 . . . . Cordele
BR 998 . . . . Valdosta
BR 1026 . . . . . . Thomasville
BR 1068 . . . . Dublin
BR 1119 . . . . Marietta
BR 1150 . . . . Tifton
BR 1200 . . . . . . Bainbridge
BR 1230 . . . . Griffin
BR 1269 . . . . . Milledgeville
BR 1342 . . . . . . Lagrange
BR 1393 . . . . . . Fitzgerald
BR 1421 . . . . Newnan
BR 1441 . . . . . . Gainesville
BR 1478 . . . . . . Quitman
BR 1537 . . . . Lilburn
BR 1565 . . . . . . Carrollton
BR 1585 . . . . . . Moultrie
BR 1751 . . . . . . Statesboro
BR 1833 . . . . Dalton
BR 1919 . . . . . West Point
BR 2225 . . . . Decatur
BR 2389 . . . . . . Eastman
BR 2390 . . . . . . Thomson
BR 2476 . . . . Vienna
BR 2480 . . . . Dawson
BR 2567 . . . . Ashburn
BR 2584 . . . . . Clarkesville
BR 2660 . . . . . . Cedartown
BR 2758 . . . . . . Cuthbert
BR 2761 . . . . . . Tallapoosa
BR 2808 . . . . . . Cohutta
BR 2809 . . . . . . Concord
BR 2853 . . . . Canton
BR 2882 . . . . Vidalia
BR 2894 . . . . . Sandersville
BR 2987 . . . . . . Lafayette
BR 3006 . . . . Baxley
BR 3025 . . . . Trion
BR 3070 . . . . . . Abbeville
BR 3076 . . . . Ocilla
BR 3091 . . . . . . Hogansville
BR 3203 . . . . . . Commerce

BR 3224 . . . . Thomson
BR 3227. . . . . Louisville
BR 3245 . . . . Glennville
BR 3248. . . . . Sparta
BR 3249 . . . . Hawkinsville
BR 3254 . . . . Waynesboro
BR 3261 . . . . Blakely
BR 3269 . . . . Pelham
BR 3299 . . . . Sylvania
BR 3353 . . . . Barnesville
BR 3354 . . . . Manchester
BR 3361 . . . . Tennille
BR 3364 . . . . Douglas
BR 3365 . . . . McRae
BR 3369 . . . . Lyons
BR 3370 . . . . Swainsboro
BR 3371 . . . . Warrenton
BR 3445 . . . . Forsyth
BR 3458 . . . . Monroe
BR 3504 . . . . Cochran
BR 3511 . . . . Rockmart
BR 3514 . . . . Jesup
BR 3539 . . . . Metter
BR 3547. . . . . . . Donalsonville
BR 3578 . . . . Monticello
BR 3580 . . . . Adel
BR 3581 . . . . Blackshear
BR 3582 . . . . Cairo
BR 3583 . . . . Camilla
BR 3584 . . . . Hartwell
BR 3585 . . . . Millen
BR 3598 . . . . Lavonia
BR 3637 . . . . Alma
BR 3654 . . . . Greensboro
BR 3722 . . . . Claxton
BR 3723 . . . . Wrightsville
BR 3793 . . . . Buford
BR 3960 . . . . Juniper
BR 4040 . . . . Leesburg
BR 4057 . . . . Warner Robins
BR 4060 . . . . Lyerly
BR 4135 . . . . Bremen
BR 4191 . . . . Hazlehurst
BR 4557 . . . . Eatonton
BR 4558 . . . . Cornelia
BR 4568 . . . . Forest Park
BR 4572 . . . . Montezuma
BR 4831 . . . . Union Point
BR 4847 . . . . Colquitt
BR 4854 . . . . Homerville
BR 4862 . . . . Roswell
BR 4871 . . . . Jackson
BR 4944 . . . . Hinesville
BR 4946 . . . . Perry
BR 5020 . . . . Lakeland
BR 5177 . . . . Ellijay
BR 5756 . . . . Soperton
BR 5795 . . . . St. Marys
BR 5891 . . . . Royston
BR 6030 . . . . Scottdale
BR 6070 . . . . Tucker
BR 6275 . . . . Cumming
BR 6277 . . . . . . Powder Springs
BR 6278 . . . . Villa Rica
BR 6425 . . . . Folkston
BR 6578 . . . . Chatsworth
SA Georgia . . . . Savannah

Locomotive Engineers
DIV 30 . . . . Dallas
DIV 59 . . . . Valdosta
DIV 210 . . . . Macon
DIV 316 . . . . Franklin
DIV 323 . . . . Evans
DIV 328 . . . . . . Powder Springs
DIV 503 . . . . Buford
DIV 646 . . . . Statesboro
DIV 648 . . . . Waycross

DIV 696 Currahee . . . . . Suwanee
DIV 706 . . . . Fitzgerald
DIV 779 . . . . Midland
DIV 786 . . . . Macon
DIV 803 . . . . Richmond Hill

Longshoremen
LU 1414 . . . . Savannah
LU 1423 . . . . Brunswick
LU 1475 . . . . Savannah
LU 1863 . . . . Brunswick
LU 2046 . . . . Garden City

Machinists
DLG 96 . . . . Savannah
DLG 131 . . . . Albany
LG 1 . . . . Conyers
LG 2 . . . . Palmetto
LG 23 . . . . Savannah
LG 272 . . . . Ludowici
LG 414 . . . . Rome
LG 458 . . . Moody Air Force Base
LG 611 . . . . Marietta
LG 615 Plant Protection . . Marietta
LG 625 . . . . Hoboken
LG 650 . . . . Savannah
LG 709 . . . . Marietta
LG 713 . . . . Evans
LG 1034 . . . . Macon
LG 1141 . . . . Hampton
LG 2204 . . . . Waycross
LG 2590 . . . . Warner Robins
LG 2665 . . . . College Park
LG 2699 . . . . Albany
LG 2731 . . . . Griffin
LG 2772 Kings Bay . . . St. Marys
LG 2783 . . . . St. Marys
LG 2789 . . . . Grovetown
LG 2901 . . . . Conley
LLG W-356 Woodworkers . . . Adel
STC Georgia . . . . Savannah

Maintenance of Way Employes
LG 806 . . . . Jesup
LG 808 . . . . Warner Robins
LG 1643 . . . . Manchester
SLG 56 . . . . Cherry Log
SLG 619 . . . . Lake Park
SLG 621 . . . . Winterville
SLG 627 . . . . Warthen
SLG 665 . . . . Adairsville
SLG 673 . . . . Mount Airy
SLG 2060 . . . . Americus
SLG 2067 . . . . Pembroke
SLG 2163 . . . . Blackshear
SLG 2167 . . . . Tybee Island

Musicians
CONF International Symphony &
  Opera . . . . Atlanta
LU 148-462 . . . . Atlanta
LU 447-704 . . . . Savannah

National Staff Organization
LU Georgia Staff . . . . . . Tucker

NLRB Professional Association
LU 10 . . . . Atlanta

Nurses
SA Georgia Nurses
  Association . . . . Atlanta

Office and Professional Employees
LU 179 . . . . Rossville
LU 455 . . . . Eden
LU 4873 . . . . Savannah

Operating Engineers
LU 329 . . . . Columbus
LU 474 . . . . Pooler
LU 926 . . . . Atlanta

Painters
DC 77 . . . . Forest Park
LU 193 . . . . Forest Park
LU 1169 . . . . Brunswick
LU 1940 . . . . Forest Park
LU 1961 . . . . Forest Park

Plant Protection
LU 109 Atlanta Unit . . College Park

Plasterers and Cement Masons
LU 15 . . . . Savannah
LU 62 . . . . Atlanta
LU 148 . . . . Atlanta

Plumbing and Pipe Fitting
C Georgia Pipe Trades . . . . Atlanta
LU 72 . . . . Atlanta
LU 150 . . . . Augusta
LU 177 . . . . Brunswick
LU 188 . . . . Savannah
LU 473 . . . . Jesup

Postal and Federal Employees
D 3 . . . . Atlanta
LU 301 . . . . Albany
LU 303 . . . . Atlanta
LU 305 . . . . Atlanta
LU 306 . . . . Decatur
LU 307 . . . . Augusta
LU 310 . . . . Atlanta
LU 314 . . . . Columbus
LU 315 . . . . Atlanta
LU 321 . . . . Marietta
LU 333 . . . . Atlanta

Postal Mail Handlers
LU 310 . . . . Atlanta

Postal Workers
LU 12 Athens . . . . Athens
LU 29 Savannah . . . . . . Savannah
LU 32 Atlanta Metro Area . . Atlanta
LU 35 Americus . . . . . . Americus
LU 118 Columbus . . . . Columbus
LU 124 Brunswick . . . . Brunswick
LU 290 Augusta . . . . . . Augusta
LU 322 Valdosta . . . . . Valdosta
LU 538 Thomasville . . Thomasville
LU 569 Waycross . . . . Waycross
LU 717 Rome . . . . Rome
LU 979 Gainesville . . Gainesville
LU 1002 Dalton . . . . . . Dalton
LU 1054 Bainbridge . . . Bainbridge
LU 1061 LaGrange . . . . LaGrange
LU 1075 Cordele . . . . . Cordele
LU 1090 Washington . . Washington
LU 1338 Dublin . . . . . . Dublin
LU 1340 Macon . . . . Macon
LU 1346 Newnan . . . . . Newnan
LU 1377 Albany . . . . . . Albany
LU 1586 Elberton . . . . . Elberton
LU 1676 Marietta . . . . . Marietta
LU 1687 Winder . . . . . . Winder
LU 1689 Statesboro . . . Statesboro
LU 2074 McRae . . . . . . McRae
LU 2314 Swainsboro . . Swainsboro
LU 2319 Cedartown . . . Cedartown
LU 2427 Vidalia . . . . . . Vidalia
LU 2472 Baxley . . . . . . Baxley
LU 2534 Fitzgerald . . . Fitzgerald
LU 2535 Toccoa . . . . . . Toccoa
LU 2637 Buford . . . . . . Buford

LU 2678 Griffin . . . . . . Griffin
LU 2694 Cornelia . . . . . Cornelia
LU 2695 Calhoun . . . . . Calhoun
LU 2997 Eastman . . . . . Eastman
LU 3434 Decatur . . . . . Decatur
LU 3499 Hinesville . . . Allenhurst
LU 3655 Dallas . . . . . . Dallas
LU 3684 Warner
  Robins . . . . . Warner Robins
LU 3908 Bremen . . . . . Bremen
LU 3927 Dahlonega . . . Dahlonega
LU 4349 Moultrie . . . . . Moultrie
LU 5215 Hampton . . . . Hampton
LU 5281 Cartersville . . Cartersville
LU 5923 Forest Park . . Forest Park
LU 6088 Adairsville . . . Adairsville
LU 6089 Norcross . . . . Norcross
LU 6221 Hartwell . . . . Hartwell
LU 6394 Conyers . . . . Conyers
LU 7063 Cleveland . . . . Cleveland
LU 7131 Powder
  Springs . . . . . Powder Springs
LU 7161 Suwanee . . . . . Suwanee
SA Georgia . . . . Thomasville

Railroad Signalmen
GC 44 Louisville &
  Nashville . . . . . . Silver Creek
LLG 11 . . . . Macon
LLG 208 . . . . Jonesboro

Retail, Wholesale and Department Store
C Southeast Council . . . . . Atlanta
LU 315 . . . . Atlanta
LU 586 . . . . Atlanta
LU 595 . . . . Atlanta

Roofers, Waterproofers and Allied Workers
LU 136 . . . . Atlanta

Rural Letter Carriers
D 1 . . . . Midway
D 2 . . . . Moultrie
D 3 . . . . Box Springs
D 4 . . . . Gainesville
D 5 . . . . Douglasville
D 6 . . . . Forsyth
D 7 . . . . Ellisay
D 8 . . . . Denton
D 9 . . . . Royston
D 10 . . . . Waynesboro
SA Georgia . . . . Moultrie

Security, Police and Fire Professionals
LU 570 . . . . Fayetteville
LU 572 . . . . Austell
LU 574 . . . . Kingsland
LU 575 . . . . . . Stone Mountain
LU 576 . . . . Vidalia

Service Employees
LU 413 Firemen & Oilers . Waycross
LU 679 Firemen &
  Oilers . . . . College Park
LU 1985 Georgia State . . . Atlanta

Sheet Metal Workers
LU 85 . . . . Atlanta
LU 422 . . . . Waycross

State, County and Municipal Employees
LU 1644 Atlanta Georgia Public
  Employees . . . . Atlanta

Steelworkers
DC 5 . . . . Cartersville
LU 03-232 . . . . Macon
LU 03-233 . . . . Gordon
LU 03-238 . . . . Oconee
LU 03-346 . . . . Savannah
LU 03-400 . . . . Brunswick
LU 03-518 . . . . Rome
LU 03-527 . . . . Brunswick
LU 03-531 . . . . . . Jeffersonville
LU 03-572 . . . . Macon
LU 03-613 . . . . Trenton
LU 03-643 . . . . Savannah
LU 03-646 . . . . Lake Park
LU 03-673 . . . . Rincon
LU 03-700 . . . . . Lawrenceville
LU 03-703 . . . . Conley
LU 03-734 . . . . Savannah
LU 03-777 . . . . Lake Park
LU 03-787 . . . . Screven
LU 03-794 . . . . Colbert
LU 03-804 . . . . Rome
LU 03-816 . . . . Augusta
LU 03-838 . . . . Coosa
LU 03-958 Georgia State . Kingsland
LU 03-983 . . . . Augusta
LU 03-1086 . . . . Riceboro
LU 03-1087 . . . . Riceboro
LU 03-1354 . . . . Midway
LU 03-1465 . . . . . . Blackshear
LU 03-1471 . . . . Columbus
LU 03-1496 . . . . Eden
LU 03-1504 . . . . Martinez
LU 03-1648 . . . . Valdosta
LU 03-1703 . . . . . Cedar Springs
LU 03-1755 . . . . . . Jonesboro
LU 03-1762 . . . . Albany
LU 03-1803 . . . . Martinez
LU 03-1864 . . . . . Donalsonville
LU 03-1958 . . . . Augusta
LU 03-1993 . . . . Savannah
LU 03-1994 . . . . . . Monticello
LU 05-219 . . . . . . Chickamauga
LU 05-237 . . . . McIntyre
LU 09-3-T . . . . Perry
LU 09-6 . . . . Newnan
LU 09-170-S . . . . . . Attapulgus
LU 09-190-A . . . . . Savannah
LU 09-254 . . . . Snellville
LU 09-486 . . . . Winder
LU 09-871-L . . . . Athens
LU 09-2401-S . . . . . . Mableton
LU 09-2948-S . . . . . Columbus
LU 09-3944-S . . . . . . Jackson
LU 09-5812-S . . . . . Waycross
LU 09-7834-S . . . . . . Tifton
LU 09-8074-S . . . . . Tallapoosa
LU 09-9326-S . . . Milledgeville
LU 09-14087-S . . . . Flintstone
LU 09-14102-S . . . . . Newnan
LU 09-14981-S . . . . . Americus
LU 09-15329-S . . . . . Ringgold
LU 30-795 . . . . Savannah
LU 50-26 Southern Regional Joint
   Board . . . . Union City

Teamsters
LU 528 . . . . Atlanta
LU 728 . . . . Atlanta

LU 1129 . . . . Cartersville

Television and Radio Artists
LU Atlanta . . . . Atlanta

Theatrical Stage Employees
LU 320 Savannah Mixed
   Local . . . . Savannah
LU 479 . . . . Conyers
LU 629 . . . . Augusta
LU 824 . . . . Athens
LU 834 . . . . Atlanta
LU 837 Charlotte Exhibition &
   Display Employees . . . . Atlanta
LU 859 . . . . Douglasville
LU 927 . . . . Atlanta

Transit Union
LDIV 732 . . . . Decatur
LDIV 898 . . . . Macon
LDIV 1324 . . . . Savannah

Transport Workers
LU 269 . . . . College Park
LU 526 . . . . St. Marys
LU 527 . . . . Grovetown

**Transportation Communications
   Union**
D 146 . . . . Macon
D 892 . . . . Villa Rica
D 943 Southeastern System Board
   96 . . . . College Park
D 1295 . . . . Marietta
JPB 410 Seaboard Coast Line-
   Georgia Railroad . . . Woodstock
LG 6045 Georgia . . . . Adairsville
LG 6354 Atlanta . . . . . Jonesboro
LG 6508 Waycross . . . . Patterson

Transportation Union
GCA GO-25 Atlanta & West Point
   Railway . . . . Dallas
GCA GO-169 Central of Georgia
   Railroad . . . . Gordon
LU 30 . . . . Folkston
LU 511 . . . . Kennesaw
LU 535 . . . . Lizella
LU 674 . . . . Augusta
LU 941 . . . . Columbus
LU 998 . . . . Waycross
LU 1031 . . . . Savannah
LU 1033 . . . . Douglasville
LU 1245 . . . . Snellville
LU 1261 . . . . Lithonia
LU 1263 . . . . Valdosta
LU 1598 . . . . Senoia
LU 1790 . . . . Fitzgerald
LU 1910 . . . . Gordon
SLB LO-12 Georgia . . . . Snellville

Treasury Employees
CH 26 . . . . Atlanta
CH 70 . . . . Chamblee
CH 104 . . . . Atlanta
CH 150 . . . . Tybee Island
CH 177 . . . . Atlanta
CH 210 . . . . Atlanta
CH 268 . . . . Atlanta

CH 281 EPA Region 4 . . . . Atlanta
CH 284 . . . . Atlanta

UNITE HERE
JB Southern Regional . . Union City
LU 5-012 . . . . Union City
LU 5-029 . . . . Union City
LU 5-032 . . . . Union City
LU 14-L . . . . Union City
LU 50-11 . . . . Union City
LU 50-13 . . . . Union City
LU 50-14 . . . . Union City
LU 50-15 . . . . Union City
LU 50-16 . . . . Union City
LU 50-17 . . . . Union City
LU 50-18 . . . . Union City
LU 50-19 . . . . Union City
LU 50-20 . . . . Union City
LU 50-21 . . . . Union City
LU 50-22 . . . . Union City
LU 50-23 . . . . Union City
LU 50-24 . . . . Union City
LU 50-25 . . . . Union City
LU 50-27 . . . . Union City
LU 50-28 . . . . Union City
LU 50-30 . . . . Union City
LU 95 . . . . Union City
LU 104 . . . . Union City
LU 116 . . . . Union City
LU 121 . . . . Union City
LU 122 . . . . Union City
LU 147-G . . . . Union City
LU 151 . . . . Union City
LU 302 . . . . Union City
LU 310 . . . . Union City
LU 358 . . . . Union City
LU 360 . . . . Union City
LU 362 . . . . Union City
LU 364 . . . . Union City
LU 365 . . . . Union City
LU 369 . . . . Union City
LU 415-475 . . . . . . Union City
LU 457 . . . . Union City
LU 479-I . . . . Union City
LU 515 . . . . Union City
LU 516 . . . . Union City
LU 550-LDC . . . . . . Union City
LU 551-I . . . . Union City
LU 565 . . . . Union City
LU 570-I . . . . Union City
LU 574-I . . . . Union City
LU 576-I . . . . Union City
LU 586 . . . . Union City
LU 588-I . . . . Union City
LU 804 . . . . Columbus
LU 829-A . . . . Union City
LU 903-A . . . . Union City
LU 963-A . . . . Union City
LU 1021-C . . . . . . Union City
LU 1504 . . . . Union City
LU 1633 . . . . Union City
LU 1716 . . . . Union City
LU 1752 . . . . Union City
LU 1781 . . . . Union City
LU 1807 . . . . Union City
LU 1833 . . . . Union City
LU 1836 . . . . Union City
LU 1876 . . . . Union City
LU 1882 . . . . Union City

LU 1922 . . . . Union City
LU 1997 . . . . Union City
LU 2000 . . . . Union City
LU 2031 . . . . Union City
LU 2295 . . . . Union City
LU 2341 . . . . Union City
LU 2351 . . . . Union City
LU 2376 . . . . Union City
LU 2386 . . . . Union City
LU 2420 . . . . Union City
LU 2423 . . . . Union City
LU 2448 . . . . Union City
LU 2490 . . . . Union City
LU 2496 . . . . Union City
LU 2500 . . . . Union City
LU 2524 . . . . Union City
LU 2534 . . . . Union City
LU 2535 . . . . Union City
LU 2554 . . . . Union City
LU 2558 . . . . Union City
LU 2566 . . . . Union City
LU 2570 . . . . Union City
LU 2589 . . . . Union City
LU 2603 . . . . Union City
LU 2609 . . . . Union City
LU 2610 . . . . Union City
LU 2618 . . . . Union City
LU 2620 . . . . Union City
LU 2625 . . . . Union City
LU 2648 . . . . Union City
LU 2653 . . . . Union City
LU 2679 . . . . Union City
LU 2690 . . . . Union City
LU 2691 . . . . Union City
LU 2692 . . . . Union City
LU 2695 . . . . Union City
LU 2696 . . . . Union City

Utility Workers
LU 121 . . . . Ringgold

Weather Service Employees
BR 02-46 . . . . . . Peachtree City
BR 02-64 . . . . Atlanta
BR 02-71 . . . . Hampton

Westinghouse Salaried Employees
ASSN Athens Employee's . . Athens

**Unaffiliated Labor
Organizations**
Dixie Pipeline Union Oil
   Industry . . . . Acworth
National Basketball Trainers
   Association . . . . Atlanta
National Pilots Association . Atlanta
Professional Airline Flight Control
   Association . . . . Atlanta
Professional Airline Flight Control
   Association Local
   (PAFCA-Delta) . . . . . Atlanta
Professional Airline Flight Control
   Association Local
   PAFCA-ASA . . . . . . Atlanta
Truck Drivers Association
   Inc. . . . . Riverdale
Wholesale Sales Representatives,
   Bureau of . . . . Atlanta

Guam

Affiliated Labor Organizations

Air Traffic Controllers
LU ZUA . . . . Yigo

Fire Fighters
LU 150-F . . . . Barrigada

Government Employees
LU 1689 DoD . . . . Hagatna

Government Security Officers
LU 159 . . . . Hagatna

Letter Carriers
BR 4093 . . . . Barrigada

Machinists
LLG G-2339 Guam . . . . . Dededo

Postal Workers
LU 6255 Agana . . . . . . Barrigada

Weather Service Employees
BR 07-2 . . . . Barrigada

Hawaii

AFL-CIO Trade and Industrial Departments

Building and Construction Trades Department
BCTC Honolulu . . . . . . Honolulu

Maritime Trades Department
PC Honolulu . . . . Honolulu

Metal Trades Department
MTC Hawaii . . . . Aiea

Affiliated Labor Organizations

Agricultural Employees
BR 11 . . . . Honolulu
NHQ . . . . Honolulu

Air Traffic Controllers
LU HCF . . . . Honolulu
LU ITO . . . . Hilo
LU JRK . . . . Kapolei
LU OGG . . . . Puunene

Asbestos Workers
LU 132. . . . . Honolulu

Boilermakers
LG 90 . . . . Aiea

Bricklayers
LU 1 . . . . Honolulu

Carpenters
LU 745. . . . . Honolulu

Communications Workers
LU 14921 . . . . Honolulu
LU 39117 Hawaii . . . . Honolulu

Electrical Workers
C Citizens Utilities Coordinating. . . . . . Honolulu
LU 1186 . . . . Honolulu
LU 1260 . . . . Honolulu
LU 1357 . . . . Honolulu

Elevator Constructors
LU 126. . . . . Honolulu

Engineers
LU 121 . . . . Aiea

Fire Fighters
LU 263-F . . . . Pearl City

Food and Commercial Workers
LU 480. . . . . Honolulu

Government Employees
LU 1209 . . . . Kailua
LU 1213 . . . . Honolulu
LU 1229. . . . . Aiea
LU 2886 DoJ. . . . . . Honolulu

Government Employees Association
LU R-6002 Kauai Paramedics Association . . . . Lihue
LU 12-556 International Association of EMTs and Paramedics . . . . . Honolulu

Government Security Officers
LU 81 . . . . Honolulu

Graphic Communications
LU 413-N . . . . Honolulu
LU 501-M . . . . Honolulu

Iron Workers
LU 625 . . . . Waipahu
LU 742. . . . . Honolulu
LU 803 . . . . Waipahu

Laborers
LU 368. . . . . Honolulu
LU 368. . . . . Honolulu

Letter Carriers
BR 860. . . . . Honolulu
BR 2932. . . . . Hilo
BR 4372 . . . . Wailuku
BR 4454 . . . . Kailua
BR 4644. . . . . Kahului
BR 4682 Aiea-Pearl City . Pearl City
BR 4683 . . . . Waipahu
BR 4836 . . . . Kaneohe
BR 4837. . . . . Mililani
BR 5206 . . . . Ewa Beach
BR 5306 . . . . Lahaina
BR 5316 . . . . Waimanalo
BR 5516 . . . . . . Kailua Kona
BR 5579 . . . . Waianae
BR 6241. . . . . Kapaa
BR 6254. . . . . Kapaa
BR 6312. . . . . Haleiwa
SA Hawaii . . . . Honolulu

Longshore and Warehouse
LU 142. . . . . Honolulu
LU 142 2420 . . . . . . Wailuku
LU 142 2507 . . . . . . Wailuku
LU 142 3405. . . . . . . Lihue
LU 142 4428. . . . . . Honolulu
LU 142 4521 . . . . . . Honolulu
LU 142 Unit 1201. . . . . . Hilo
LU 142 Unit 1401. . . . . . Hilo
LU 142 Unit 1402. . . . . . Hilo
LU 142 Unit 1403. . . . . . Hilo
LU 142 Unit 1409. . . . . . Hilo
LU 142 Unit 1410. . . . . . Hilo
LU 142 Unit 1412. . . . . . Hilo
LU 142 Unit 1413. . . . . . Hilo
LU 142 Unit 1414. . . . . . Hilo
LU 142 Unit 1416. . . . . . Hilo
LU 142 Unit 1417. . . . . . Hilo
LU 142 Unit 1418. . . . . . Hilo
LU 142 Unit 1419. . . . . . Hilo
LU 142 Unit 1421. . . . . . Hilo
LU 142 Unit 1426. . . . . . Hilo
LU 142 Unit 1501. . . . . . Hilo
LU 142 Unit 1503. . . . . . Hilo
LU 142 Unit 1505. . . . . . Hilo
LU 142 Unit 1510. . . . . . Hilo
LU 142 Unit 1513. . . . . . Hilo
LU 142 Unit 1515. . . . . . Hilo
LU 142 Unit 1516. . . . . . Hilo
LU 142 Unit 1517. . . . . . Hilo
LU 142 Unit 1518. . . . . . Hilo
LU 142 Unit 1519. . . . . . Hilo
LU 142 Unit 2101 . . . . Wailuku
LU 142 Unit 2107 . . . . Wailuku
LU 142 Unit 2201 . . . . Wailuku
LU 142 Unit 2305 . . . . Wailuku
LU 142 Unit 2306 . . . . Wailuku
LU 142 Unit 2307 . . . . Wailuku
LU 142 Unit 2401 . . . . Wailuku

LU 142 Unit 2403 . . . . Wailuku
LU 142 Unit 2404 . . . . Wailuku
LU 142 Unit 2405 . . . . Wailuku
LU 142 Unit 2406 . . . . Wailuku
LU 142 Unit 2408 . . . . Wailuku
LU 142 Unit 2409 . . . . Wailuku
LU 142 Unit 2411 . . . . Wailuku
LU 142 Unit 2417 . . . . Wailuku
LU 142 Unit 2419 . . . . Wailuku
LU 142 Unit 2501 . . . . Wailuku
LU 142 Unit 2502 . . . . Wailuku
LU 142 Unit 2505 . . . . Wailuku
LU 142 Unit 2506 . . . . Wailuku
LU 142 Unit 2508 . . . . Wailuku
LU 142 Unit 2509 . . . . Wailuku
LU 142 Unit 2511 . . . . Wailuku
LU 142 Unit 2512 . . . . Wailuku
LU 142 Unit 2514 . . . . Wailuku
LU 142 Unit 2515 . . . . Wailuku
LU 142 Unit 2516 . . . . Wailuku
LU 142 Unit 2518 . . . . Wailuku
LU 142 Unit 2520 . . . . Wailuku
LU 142 Unit 2522 . . . . Wailuku
LU 142 Unit 2523 . . . . Wailuku
LU 142 Unit 2525 . . . . Wailuku
LU 142 Unit 2526 . . . . Wailuku
LU 142 Unit 3105 . . . . . Lihue
LU 142 Unit 3201 . . . . . Lihue
LU 142 Unit 3401 . . . . . Lihue
LU 142 Unit 3402 . . . . . Lihue
LU 142 Unit 3403 . . . . . Lihue
LU 142 Unit 3404 . . . . . Lihue
LU 142 Unit 3406 . . . . . Lihue
LU 142 Unit 3407 . . . . . Lihue
LU 142 Unit 3408 . . . . . Lihue
LU 142 Unit 3409 . . . . . Lihue
LU 142 Unit 3410 . . . . . Lihue
LU 142 Unit 3411 . . . . . Lihue
LU 142 Unit 3503 . . . . . Lihue
LU 142 Unit 3504 . . . . . Lihue
LU 142 Unit 3505 . . . . . Lihue
LU 142 Unit 3510 . . . . . Lihue
LU 142 Unit 3511 . . . . . Lihue
LU 142 Unit 3514 . . . . . Lihue
LU 142 Unit 4106 . . . . Honolulu
LU 142 Unit 4201 . . . . Honolulu
LU 142 Unit 4202 . . . . Honolulu
LU 142 Unit 4203 . . . . Honolulu
LU 142 Unit 4204 . . . . Honolulu
LU 142 Unit 4207 . . . . Honolulu
LU 142 Unit 4209 . . . . Honolulu
LU 142 Unit 4301 . . . . Honolulu
LU 142 Unit 4303 . . . . Honolulu
LU 142 Unit 4304 . . . . Honolulu
LU 142 Unit 4305 . . . . Honolulu
LU 142 Unit 4306 . . . . Honolulu
LU 142 Unit 4402 . . . . Honolulu
LU 142 Unit 4403 . . . . Honolulu
LU 142 Unit 4404 . . . . Honolulu
LU 142 Unit 4405 . . . . Honolulu
LU 142 Unit 4406 . . . . Honolulu
LU 142 Unit 4407 . . . . Honolulu
LU 142 Unit 4408 . . . . Honolulu
LU 142 Unit 4409 . . . . Honolulu
LU 142 Unit 4410 . . . . Honolulu
LU 142 Unit 4411 . . . . Honolulu
LU 142 Unit 4412 . . . . Honolulu
LU 142 Unit 4414 . . . . Honolulu
LU 142 Unit 4415 . . . . Honolulu
LU 142 Unit 4419 . . . . Honolulu
LU 142 Unit 4420 . . . . Honolulu
LU 142 Unit 4421 . . . . Honolulu
LU 142 Unit 4422 . . . . Honolulu
LU 142 Unit 4427 . . . . Honolulu
LU 142 Unit 4436 . . . . Honolulu

LU 142 Unit 4524 . . . . Honolulu
LU 160. . . . . Honolulu

Machinists
LG 1245 . . . . Honolulu
LG 1979 . . . . Honolulu
LG 1998 . . . . Honolulu
STC Hawaii . . . . Honolulu

Musicians
LU 677. . . . . Honolulu

National Staff Organization
LU Hawaii State Teachers Staff Organization. . . . . . Honolulu

Nurses
SA Hawaii Nurses Association . . . . . . Honolulu

Painters
DC 50 . . . . Honolulu
LU 1791 . . . . Honolulu
LU 1889 . . . . Honolulu
LU 1903 . . . . Honolulu
LU 1926 . . . . Honolulu
LU 1944 . . . . Honolulu

Plasterers and Cement Masons
LU 630. . . . . Honolulu

Plumbing and Pipe Fitting
LU 675. . . . . Honolulu
LU 811 . . . . Kailua

Postal Mail Handlers
LU 299. . . . . Honolulu

Postal Workers
LU 162 Honolulu . . . . . Honolulu
LU 664 Big Island Area. Kealakekua
LU 5434 Kauai Area . . . . . Lihue
LU 5528 Maui Area . . . . . Kihei
LU 5918 Windward Area. . . Kailua
LU 6044 Wahiawa . . . . . Mililani
LU 6069 Leeward Oahu Area. . . . . Pearl City
SA Hawaii. . . . . Mililani

Roofers, Waterproofers and Allied Workers
LU 221. . . . . Honolulu

Security, Police and Fire Professionals
LU 650. . . . . Honolulu
LU 652. . . . . Honolulu

Service Employees
LU 50 International Association of Government EMTs & Paramedics . . . . Honolulu

Sheet Metal Workers
LU 293. . . . . Honolulu

State, County and Municipal Employees
LU 646. . . . . Honolulu
LU 646 Division 075 Hospital Workers . . . . Honolulu
LU 646 UPW 527 Kuakini Geriatric Care . . . . Honolulu
LU 646 UPW Unit 503 Nuuanu Hale . . . . Honolulu

LU 646 UPW Unit 504 Kuakini
  Hospital . . . . Honolulu
LU 646 UPW Unit 505 Molokai
  Hospital . . . . Honolulu
LU 646 UPW Unit 509 Wahiawa
  Hospital . . . . Honolulu
LU 646 UPW Unit 512, Convalescent
  Center . . . . Honolulu
LU 646 UPW Unit 513, Beverly
  Manor . . . . Honolulu
LU 646 UPW Unit 516, Hale
  Makua . . . . Honolulu
LU 646 UPW Unit 520,
  Rehabilitation Center . . Honolulu
LU 646 UPW Unit 522, Lunalilo
  Home . . . . Honolulu
LU 646 UPW Unit 523 Kapiolani
  Medical Center . . . . . Honolulu

LU 646 UPW Unit 531
  Intercontinental . . . . Honolulu
LU 646 UPW Unit 532 Aloha United
  Way . . . . Honolulu
LU 928 East West Center . Honolulu

Teamsters
LU 681 . . . . Honolulu
LU 996 . . . . Honolulu

Treasury Employees
CH 35 . . . . Honolulu
CH 151 . . . . Honolulu

UNITE HERE
LU 5 . . . . Honolulu

Weather Service Employees
BR 07-1 . . . . Lihue
BR 07-5 . . . . Honolulu
BR 07-6 . . . . Hilo
BR 07-7 . . . . Honolulu
BR 07-8 . . . . Kahului
BR 07-9 . . . . Ewa Beach

Unaffiliated Labor Organizations

Allied Crafts & Employees LU
  1 . . . . Kaneohe
Clerical, Professional, & Technical
  Employees Bargaining
  Committee . . . . Honolulu
Handivan Drivers
  Association . . . . Waipahu

Hawaii Association of Security
  Officers . . . . Waianae
Hawaii Association of Union
  Agents . . . . Honolulu
Hawaii Council of Defense
  Commissary Unions . . . Honolulu
Hawaii Hospital and Health Care
  Workers Union . . . . . Honolulu
Hawaii Office Workers
  Union . . . . Honolulu
Hawaii United Independent Workers
  Union . . . . Honolulu
Kamehameha Schools Faculty
  Association . . . . Honolulu
Maui County Paramedics
  Association . . . . Puunene
Mid-Pacific Teachers
  Association . . . . Honolulu
Security Officers Union International
  LU 1 . . . . Kamuela

Idaho

AFL-CIO Trade and Industrial Departments

Building and Construction Trades Department
BCTC Idaho . . . . Pocatello
BCTC Southwest Idaho, Southeast Oregon. . . . . Boise

Metal Trades Department
MTC Eastern Idaho . . . . . Shelley

Affiliated Labor Organizations

Air Traffic Controllers
LU BOI . . . . Boise
LU SUN . . . . Hailey
LU TWF . . . . Twin Falls

Bakery, Confectionery, Tobacco Workers and Grain Millers
LU 282-G . . . . Burley
LU 283-G . . . . Twin Falls
LU 284-G . . . . Caldwell
LU 290-G . . . . . . New Plymouth

Boilermakers
LG 234-D Cement Workers . Inkom

Carpenters
LU 313 . . . . Moscow
LU 635. . . . . Boise
LU 808 . . . . Idaho Falls
LU 1691 . . . . . . Coeur d'Alene
LU 2816 . . . . Emmett

Communications Workers
C Idaho State. . . . . Boise
LU 7603 . . . . Boise
LU 7610 . . . . Twin Falls
LU 7621 . . . . Pocatello
LU 7670 . . . . . . Coeur d'Alene

Electrical Workers
LU 283 . . . . Rupert
LU 291. . . . . Boise
LU 449 . . . . Pocatello

Engineers
LU 94 . . . . Idaho Falls

Federal Employees
LU 1436 . . . . Grangeville

Food and Commercial Workers
LU 368-A . . . . Boise

Government Employees
LU 1273 VA . . . . Boise
LU 2233 USDA . . . . Eagle
LU 3006 DoD . . . . Boise
LU 3872 USAF. . . Mountain Home Air Force Base
LU 3923 INS. . . . . Boise

Government Security Officers
LU 118 . . . . Coeur d'Alene
LU 164 . . . . Moscow

Graphic Communications
LU 278-C . . . . Chubbuck

Iron Workers
LU 732 . . . . Pocatello

Laborers
LU 155 . . . . Idaho Falls

Letter Carriers
BR 331 . . . . Boise
BR 927 . . . . Pocatello
BR 1039 . . . . Wallace
BR 1192 . . . . Lewiston
BR 1260 . . . . . . Coeur d'Alene
BR 1296 . . . . Moscow
BR 1364 . . . . Idaho Falls
BR 1386 . . . . Caldwell
BR 1392 . . . . Twin Falls
BR 1409 . . . . Nampa
BR 1411 . . . . Blackfoot
BR 1481 . . . . Moscow
BR 1602 . . . . Sandpoint
BR 1703 . . . . Weiser
BR 1837 . . . . St. Maries
BR 1857 . . . . Burley
BR 1979 . . . . Payette
BR 2095 . . . . Rexburg
BR 2097 . . . . Rupert
BR 2208 . . . . Kellogg
BR 2616 . . . . Preston
BR 2777 . . . . . . American Falls
BR 3011 . . . . St. Anthony
BR 3277 . . . . Grangeville
BR 3838 . . . . Emmett
BR 4420 . . . . Gooding
BR 4745 . . . . Meridian
BR 4822 . . . . . Mountain Home
BR 5297 . . . . Montpelier
BR 5580 . . . . Malad City
BR 5581 . . . . Jerome
SA Idaho . . . . Pocatello

Locomotive Engineers
DIV 113 . . . . Heyburn
DIV 228 . . . . Pocatello
DIV 443 . . . . Rathdrum
DIV 676 . . . . Nampa

GCA Union Pacific Western
Region . . . . Pocatello
SLB Idaho 5051 . . . . . Pocatello

Machinists
LG 364-W . . . . Lewiston
LG 1295 . . . . St. Maries
LG 1753 . . . . . Coeur d'Alene
LG 1933 . . . . Pocatello
LG 2052-FL . . . . . . Meridian
STC . . . . Lewiston

Maintenance of Way Employes
SLG 1402 . . . . Pocatello

National Staff Organization
LU Staff Organization, Idaho Education Association . . . . Coeur d'Alene

Nurses
SA Idaho Nurses Association . Boise

Painters
LU 477 . . . . Boise
LU 764 . . . . Pocatello

Plasterers and Cement Masons
LU 219 . . . . Meridian
LU 629 . . . . Pocatello

Plumbing and Pipe Fitting
LU 296 . . . . Meridian
LU 648 . . . . Pocatello
SA Idaho . . . . Pocatello

Postal Mail Handlers
LU 330 . . . . Boise

Postal Workers
LU Idaho Panhandle Area . Post Falls
LU 129 Nampa . . . . Nampa
LU 179 Twin Falls . . . Twin Falls
LU 479 Caldwell . . . . . Caldwell
LU 627 Burley . . . . . . Burley
LU 650 Boise . . . . Boise
LU 703 Pocatello . . . . Pocatello
LU 1001 Lewiston . . . . Lewiston
LU 1104 Idaho Falls . . Idaho Falls
LU 1262 Moscow. . . . . Moscow
LU 1327 Blackfoot . . . Blackfoot
SA Idaho . . . . Boise

Pulp and Paper Workers
LU 747 . . . . Nampa

Railroad Signalmen
LLG 111 . . . . Pocatello

Roofers, Waterproofers and Allied Workers
LU 200 . . . . Pocatello

Rural Letter Carriers
D 1 . . . . Midvale
D 2 . . . . Twin Falls
D 3 . . . . Blackfoot
D 5 North Idaho . . . Coeur d'Alene
SA Idaho . . . . Fruitland

Security, Police and Fire Professionals
LU 3 . . . . Idaho Falls
LU 6 . . . . Boise
LU 14 . . . . Boise

Service Employees
LU 276 Firemen & Oilers . Rathdrum

Sheet Metal Workers
LU 60 . . . . Pocatello
LU 213 . . . . Boise

Steelworkers
C Atomic Energy Workers Council . . . . Rexburg
LU 02-632 . . . . Chubbuck
LU 08-608 . . . . Lewiston
LU 08-652 . . . . Idaho Falls
LU 11-5114-S . . . . Osburn

Teachers
SFED Idaho Federation of Teachers . . . . Moscow

Teamsters
LU 483 . . . . Boise
LU 983 . . . . Pocatello

Transit Union
LDIV 398 . . . . Boise
LDIV 1517 . . . . Idaho Falls

Transportation Union
LU 78 . . . . Bloomington
LU 265 . . . . Pocatello
LU 1058 . . . . Nampa
SLB LO-15 Idaho . . . . Pocatello

Treasury Employees
CH 5 . . . . Boise

Weather Service Employees
BR 04-23 . . . . Boise
BR 04-38 . . . . Pocatello

Unaffiliated Labor Organizations
Heavy & Highway Committee Five Basic Crafts AREA 1 . . Pocatello

Illinois

AFL-CIO Trade and Industrial Departments

Building and Construction Trades Department

BCTC Central Illinois . . Springfield
BCTC Chicago & Cook
  County . . . . Chicago
BCTC Danville . . . . . . Danville
BCTC De Kalb County . . . DeKalb
BCTC Decatur. . . . . Decatur
BCTC Du Page County . Warrenville
BCTC East Central
  Illinois. . . . . Champaign
BCTC Egyptian . . . West Frankfort
BCTC Fox Valley . . . . . Aurora
BCTC Illinois Valley . . . . Utica
BCTC Kankakee . . . . Kankakee
BCTC Lake County . . . . . Volo
BCTC Livingston-McLean
  Counties . . . . . . Bloomington
BCTC McHenry
  County . . . . Crystal Lake
BCTC Northwestern
  Illinois. . . . . Rockford
BCTC Southwestern
  Illinois. . . . . Collinsville
BCTC Tri-City . . . . Rock Island
BCTC West Central Illinois . Peoria
BCTC Will & Grundy
  Counties . . . . Joliet

Maritime Trades Department

PC Greater Chicago Area . . . Joliet

Other Councils and Committees

C Western Employees . . East Alton

Affiliated Labor Organizations

Agricultural Employees

BR 17 . . . . Villa Park

Air Traffic Controllers

LU ALN . . . . East Alton
LU ARR . . . . Somonauk
LU CID. . . . . Elgin
LU CMI . . . . Savoy
LU CPS . . . . Cahokia
LU DPA . . . . West Chicago
LU EGL . . . . Rosemont
LU MDW . . . . Chicago
LU MLI . . . . Milan
LU MWA . . . . Marion
LU ORD . . . . Chicago
LU PIA . . . . Peoria
LU PWK. . . . . Wheeling
LU RFD . . . . Rockford
LU SPI . . . . Springfield
LU ZAU . . . . Aurora

Aircraft Mechanics

LU 4 . . . . Arlington Heights

Asbestos Workers

LU 17 . . . . Chicago
LU 56. . . . . Jerseyville

Automobile, Aerospace Workers

C Central Illinois CAP. . East Peoria
C Chicago Area CAP . . Des Plaines
C Fox River Valley . . Montgomery
C Illinois State CAP. . . Des Plaines
C Iowa State CAP
  Council . . . . Des Plaines
C Quad Cities Area . . . East Moline
C R.L. Kelly/Downstate Illinois
  CAP . . . . Granville
C Wisconsin CAP . . . . Des Plaines
LU 6 . . . . Stone Park
LU 79 . . . . East Moline
LU 145 . . . . Montgomery
LU 152. . . . . Plano
LU 285 . . . . La Salle
LU 419 . . . . Dolton
LU 434 . . . . East Moline
LU 477 . . . . Des Plaines
LU 543 . . . . Fairfield
LU 551 . . . . Chicago
LU 565 . . . . Pekin
LU 579 . . . . Danville
LU 588 . . . . . Chicago Heights
LU 592 . . . . Rockford
LU 622 . . . . Rockford
LU 694 Chicago-La Grange
  Local . . . . Brookfield
LU 718 . . . . Rockford
LU 719 La Grange-Chicago
  Local . . . . Countryside
LU 751 . . . . Decatur
LU 803 . . . . Loves Park
LU 844 . . . . Vermont
LU 865 . . . . East Moline
LU 890 . . . . Morton Grove
LU 904 . . . . Sublette
LU 974 . . . . East Peoria
LU 1023 . . . . Rockford
LU 1066 . . . . Chicago
LU 1088 . . . . Mendota
LU 1178 . . . . Sugar Grove
LU 1235 . . . . Springfield
LU 1268 . . . . Belvidere
LU 1271 . . . . Georgetown
LU 1277 . . . . Moline
LU 1304 . . . . East Moline
LU 1414 . . . . Rock Island
LU 1576 . . . . Rockford
LU 1615 . . . . Aurora
LU 1720 . . . . Forreston
LU 1761 . . . . Rockford
LU 1948 . . . . Rock Island
LU 2030 . . . . Havana
LU 2056 . . . . Rockford
LU 2059. . . . . . Spring Valley
LU 2096 . . . . Pontiac
LU 2114 . . . . Bolingbrook
LU 2127 . . . . Freeport
LU 2128 . . . . Danville
LU 2152 . . . . Batavia
LU 2201 . . . . Freeport
LU 2282 . . . . Rock Island
LU 2293 . . . . Stone Park
LU 2323 . . . . Ottawa
LU 2343 . . . . Paris
LU 2419 . . . . Danville
LU 2488 . . . . Bloomington
LU 2840 . . . . Rockford
LU 3206 . . . . Granite City

Bakery, Confectionery, Tobacco Workers and Grain Millers

C Biscuit . . . . Chicago
LU 1 . . . . Lyons
LU 7-G . . . . Hamilton
LU 40-G . . . . Galesburg
LU 69-G . . . . Chicago
LU 103-G . . . . Decatur
LU 115-G. . . . . Paris
LU 300 . . . . Chicago
LU 303-G . . . . Normal
LU 316-G . . . . Geneva
LU 325-G . . . . Gibson City
LU 342 . . . . Bloomington
LU 343-G . . . . Eola
LU 347-G . . . . Danville

Boilermakers

C Great Lakes Area
  Industrial . . . . . . Hoffman Estates
C Southern Illinois
  Industrial . . . . . . East Alton
LG 1 . . . . Chicago
LG 3-S . . . . Quincy
LG 4-S . . . . Belleville
LG 6-M Metal Polishers . . Chicago
LG 7-S . . . . East Alton
LG 8-S Willow Lake
  Mine . . . . Harrisburg
LG 12-D Cement Workers. Granville
LG 16-S . . . . Belleville
LG 60 . . . . Morton
LG 60-S . . . . Belleville
LG 81-D Cement Workers . . Dixon
LG 105-S. . . . . Dieterich
LG 158 . . . . Peoria
LG 185-S. . . . . . . East Alton
LG 363. . . . . Belleville
LG 480 . . . . Murrayville
LG 482 . . . . East Alton
LG 483 . . . . East Alton
LG 484 . . . . Meredosia
LG 486 . . . . East Alton
LG 1234 . . . . Waukegan
LG 1247. . . . . Chicago
LG 1255 . . . . . . Spring Grove
LG 1600 . . . . Aurora
LG 1626. . . . . St. Joseph
LG 1993-S . . . . Harrisburg

Bricklayers

DC 1 Illinois . . . . Chicago
LU 6 . . . . Rockford
LU 8 Bricklayers & Allied
  Craftworkers . . . . . Champaign
LU 20 . . . . Waukegan
LU 21 . . . . Chicago
LU 27 . . . . Elgin
LU 52 . . . . Chicago
LU 56 . . . . Winfield
LU 67 . . . . Chicago
LU 74 . . . . Westmont

Carpenters

DC Chicago & Northeast
  Illinois . . . . Chicago
DC Mid-Central Illinois
  4281 . . . . Springfield
LU 1 . . . . Chicago
LU 10 . . . . Bridgeview
LU 13 . . . . Chicago
LU 16 . . . . Springfield
LU 44 . . . . Champaign
LU 54 . . . . Bridgeview
LU 58 . . . . Chicago
LU 62 . . . . Chicago Heights
LU 63 . . . . Bloomington
LU 74-L . . . . Hinsdale
LU 80 . . . . Elmwood Park
LU 141 . . . . Bridgeview
LU 166 . . . . Rock Island
LU 169 . . . . Belleville
LU 174 . . . . Joliet
LU 181 . . . . Elmwood Park
LU 183 . . . . East Peoria
LU 189 . . . . Quincy
LU 195 . . . . Ottawa
LU 250 . . . . Waukegan
LU 269 . . . . Westville
LU 272 . . . . . . Chicago Heights
LU 295 . . . . Wood River
LU 347 . . . . Mattoon
LU 363 . . . . St. Charles
LU 377 . . . . Wood River
LU 433 . . . . Belleville
LU 434 . . . . . Chicago Heights
LU 480 . . . . Belleville
LU 496 . . . . Kankakee
LU 558 . . . . Glen Ellyn
LU 578 . . . . Hinsdale
LU 633 . . . . Belleville
LU 634 . . . . Salem
LU 636 . . . . . . Mount Vernon
LU 638 . . . . Marion
LU 640 . . . . Metropolis
LU 644 . . . . Pekin
LU 725 . . . . Litchfield
LU 742 . . . . Decatur
LU 790 . . . . Rock Falls
LU 792 . . . . Rockford
LU 839 . . . . . . Hoffman Estates
LU 904 . . . . . . Jacksonville
LU 916 . . . . St. Charles
LU 1027 . . . . . . Burr Ridge
LU 1051 . . . . Lincoln
LU 1185 . . . . Hinsdale
LU 1186 . . . . Brighton
LU 1307 . . . . . . Warrenville
LU 1361 . . . . Chester
LU 1535 . . . . . . Wood River
LU 1539 . . . . . . Des Plaines
LU 1693 . . . . Hinsdale
LU 1889 . . . . . . Warrenville
LU 1997 . . . . Columbia
LU 2087 . . . . . . St. Charles

Civilian Technicians

CH 34 Illinois Air . . . Bartonville
CH 106 Springfield Air . Springfield
CH 111 Windy City . . . . . Troy
CH 120 Land of Lincoln. . . Auburn

Communications Workers

LU 906 . . . . Benton
LU 4202 . . . . Rantoul
LU 4214 . . . . . . Peoria Heights
LU 4215 . . . . Danville
LU 4216 . . . . Chicago
LU 4217 . . . . Belleville
LU 4250 . . . . Chicago
LU 4252 . . . . Marseilles
LU 4260 . . . . . . Warrenville
LU 4270 . . . . Rantoul
LU 4290 . . . . Lemont
LU 4711 . . . . . Lawrenceville
LU 14405 . . . . . Carlinville
LU 14406 Central Illinois
  Typographical . . . Springfield
LU 14407 . . . . Savoy
LU 14408 . . . . Chicago
LU 14411 . . . . . . Highland
LU 14413 Jacksonville
  Typographical . . . . . Virginia
LU 14420 Mascoutah Typographical
  Union . . . . . New Baden
LU 14423
  Murphysboro . . . Murphysboro
LU 14424 Pana Typographical
  Union . . . . Pana

LU 14426 . . . . Peoria
LU 14427 . . . . Rockford
LU 14430 Chicago Mailers
   Union. . . . . Hinsdale
LU 14431 Peoria Mailers
   Union . . . . Peoria
LU 14434 . . . . Springfield
LU 34071 Chicago Newspaper
   Guild . . . . Chicago
LU 34086 . . . . Peoria
LU 54041 . . . . Chicago
LU 84060 . . . . Danville
LU 84078 . . . . Lombard
LU 84081 . . . . DeKalb
LU 84840 . . . . Highland
LU 84865 . . . . Martinsville

Education
SA Illinois Education
   Association . . . . . . Springfield

Electrical Workers
C Central Illinois
   Coordinating . . . . . . Decatur
LU 9 . . . . Hillside
LU 15 . . . . Naperville
LU 19 . . . . Aurora
LU 21 . . . . Downers Grove
LU 34 . . . . Peoria
LU 51 . . . . Springfield
LU 109 . . . . East Moline
LU 117 . . . . Crystal Lake
LU 134 . . . . Chicago
LU 145 . . . . Moline
LU 146 . . . . Decatur
LU 150 . . . . Libertyville
LU 176 . . . . Joliet
LU 193 . . . . Springfield
LU 196 . . . . Elgin
LU 197 . . . . Bloomington
LU 214 . . . . Romeoville
LU 309 . . . . Collinsville
LU 364 . . . . Rockford
LU 461 . . . . Aurora
LU 513 . . . . Decatur
LU 533 . . . . Brookfield
LU 538 . . . . Danville
LU 601 . . . . Champaign
LU 633 . . . . Belleville
LU 649 . . . . Alton
LU 701 . . . . Warrenville
LU 702 . . . . . West Frankfort
LU 794 . . . . Chicago
LU 963 . . . . Kankakee
LU 1031 . . . . Warrenville
LU 1220 . . . . Chicago
LU 1306 . . . . Decatur
LU 1475 . . . . Walnut Hill
LU 2285 . . . . Waukegan
SC . . . . Chicago
STCON Illinois . . . . . Springfield

Electrical, Radio and Machine
  Workers
DC 11 . . . . Chicago
LU 151 . . . . Chicago
LU 189 . . . . Hodgkins
LU 1114 . . . . Chicago
LU 1160 . . . . Rock Island
LU 1166 . . . . Chicago
LU 1174 . . . . Moline

Elevator Constructors
LU 2 . . . . Chicago
LU 55 . . . . Peoria

Engineers
C Central States . . . . . . Chicago

LU 81 . . . . Melrose Park
LU 777 . . . . Chicago

Federal Employees
LU 739 . . . . Chicago
LU 1840 . . . . Golconda
LU 2119 . . . . Moline
LU 2144 Shawnee National
   Forest . . . . Murphysboro

Fire Fighters
LU 21-I . . . . Batavia
LU 37-F . . . . Great Lakes
LU 292-F Rock Island
   Arsenal . . . . Moline
LU 1889 Mehlville . . . . Mascoutah

Food and Commercial Workers
LU 4-D . . . . Pekin
LU 5-C . . . . Lansing
LU 6-C . . . . Brighton
LU 12-C . . . . Collinsville
LU 16-C . . . . Marion
LU 50-C . . . . Granite City
LU 68-C . . . . East Alton
LU 79-C . . . . Ladd
LU 79-I . . . . Carbon Cliff
LU 200-T . . . . Glendale Heights
LU 203-C . . . . Peru
LU 498-C . . . . Bradley
LU 524-C . . . . Joliet
LU 534 . . . . Belleville
LU 536 . . . . Peoria
LU 580-T . . . . Chicago
LU 617-C . . . . Oakwood
LU 686 . . . . Oakwood
LU 758-C . . . . Dixon
LU 763-C . . . . Plainfield
LU 764-C . . . . Bethalto
LU 872-C . . . . . . Bourbonnais
LU 881 . . . . Rosemont
LU 894-C . . . . Morris
LU 1009-C . . . . Sherrard
LU 1015-C . . . . Streator
LU 1281-P . . . . . . Bourbonnais
LU 1546 . . . . Chicago
RC 6 . . . . Itasca

Glass, Molders, Pottery and
  Plastics Workers
LU 3 . . . . Streator
LU 70 . . . . Park Forest
LU 71 . . . . Beason
LU 117 . . . . Lincoln
LU 138 . . . . Chicago
LU 140 . . . . Toluca
LU 174 . . . . Grand Ridge
LU 182-B . . . . Belleville
LU 221 . . . . Chicago
LU 233-B . . . . Berkeley
LU 263-B . . . . . East Dubuque
LU 267 . . . . Dix
LU 468 . . . . Kewanee

Government Employees
C 57 Railroad Retirement
   Board . . . . Chicago
C 59 VA, Seventh District . . Ozark
C 224 National SS Field Assessment
   Locals . . . . Chicago
LU 15 . . . . Rock Island
LU 44 USDA . . . . . Schaumburg
LU 57 . . . . Chicago
LU 375 RRB . . . . Chicago
LU 584 . . . . Rushville
LU 603 . . . . Chicago
LU 648 DoL . . . . . Countryside
LU 701 . . . . Pekin

LU 704 . . . . Chicago
LU 739 USDA . . . . . Granite City
LU 741 USDA . . . . Beardstown
LU 808 RRB . . . . Chicago
LU 911 HUD . . . . . . Chicago
LU 1304 Council of Prisons
   C-33 . . . . Greenville
LU 1395 HHS . . . . . . Chicago
LU 1765 VA . . . . Chicago
LU 1963 VA . . . . Danville
LU 2075 GSA . . . . . . Chicago
LU 2086 DoI . . . . Creal Springs
LU 2107 VA . . . . North Chicago
LU 2121 DoD . . Arlington Heights
LU 2326 DoD . . . . . Great Lakes
LU 2343 DoJ . . . . Herrin
LU 2461 . . . . Benton
LU 2483 VA . . . . Marion
LU 2718 . . . . Chicago
LU 3247 USDA . . . . . . Peoria
LU 3356 USDA . . . Lawrenceville
LU 3415 . . . . . Fairview Heights
LU 3504 EEOC . . . . . Chicago
LU 3531 DLA . . . . . . Chicago
LU 3652 DoJ . . . . . . Chicago
LU 3896 DoE . . . . . . Chicago

Government Employees
  Association
LU 07-23 . . . Scott Air Force Base
LU 07-51 . . . . . North Chicago
LU 07-68 . . . . . . Rock Island
LU 07-72 . . . . . . Belleville
LU 14-116 . . . . . . Waterloo

Government Security Officers
LU 63 . . . . Collinsville
LU 79 . . . . Chicago
LU 112 . . . . Urbana
LU 117 . . . . Peoria
LU 150 . . . . Rock Island
LU 152 . . . . Rock Island

Graphic Communications
C Mount Morris Allied Printing
   Trades . . . . . . Mount Morris
CONF Specialty Unions . . Chicago
LU 7-N . . . . Chicago
LU 8-IW . . . . Hazel Crest
LU 32-M . . . . Springfield
LU 65-B . . . . . . Mount Morris
LU 68-C . . . . Princeville
LU 91-P . . . . Leaf River
LU 98-C . . . . East Moline
LU 111-C Joliet Graphic
   Communications . . . . . Joliet
LU 124-C . . . . . Mount Morris
LU 171-C . . . . Quincy
LU 219-M . . . . Decatur
LU 415-S . . . . Chicago
LU 418-C . . . . . . Murphysboro
LU 458-3M . . . . . Carol Stream
LU 467-S . . . . . Mount Morris
LU 471-M . . . . Joliet
LU 680-S . . . . Marseilles

Iron Workers
DC Ironworkers District Council of
   Chicago . . . . La Salle
LU 1 . . . . Forest Park
LU 46 . . . . Springfield
LU 63 . . . . Broadview
LU 111 . . . . Rock Island
LU 112 . . . . East Peoria
LU 136 . . . . River Grove
LU 380 . . . . Urbana
LU 392 . . . . . . East St. Louis
LU 393 . . . . Aurora

LU 444 . . . . Joliet
LU 473 . . . . Berkeley
LU 498 . . . . Rockford
LU 590 . . . . Naperville

Laborers
DC Chicago . . . . . . Burr Ridge
DC Southern Illinois . . . . Marion
DC The Great Plains . . . . Peoria
DC 8 Southwestern
   Illinois . . . . Collinsville
LU Great Lakes Region Organizing
   Committee . . . . . . Chicago
LU Midwest Region Organizing
   Committee . . . . . Springfield
LU 1 . . . . Franklin Park
LU 2 . . . . Brookfield
LU 4 . . . . Chicago
LU 5 . . . . Chicago Heights
LU 6 . . . . Chicago
LU 25 . . . . Westchester
LU 32 . . . . Rockford
LU 44 . . . . Collinsville
LU 75 . . . . Joliet
LU 76 . . . . Chicago
LU 96 . . . . Glen Ellyn
LU 100 . . . . Caseyville
LU 118 . . . . . . Mount Prospect
LU 149 . . . . Aurora
LU 152 . . . . . . Highland Park
LU 159 . . . . Decatur
LU 165 . . . . Peoria
LU 196 . . . . Waterloo
LU 218 . . . . Godfrey
LU 225 . . . . Des Plaines
LU 231 . . . . Pekin
LU 269 . . . . Chicago
LU 288 . . . . Westmont
LU 309 . . . . Rock Island
LU 338 . . . . Wood River
LU 362 . . . . Bloomington
LU 393 . . . . Marseilles
LU 397 . . . . Edwardsville
LU 459 . . . . Belleville
LU 477 . . . . Springfield
LU 505 . . . . Burr Ridge
LU 538 . . . . Wataga
LU 581 . . . . Carlyle
LU 582 . . . . Elgin
LU 622 . . . . Greenville
LU 670 . . . . O'Fallon
LU 677 . . . . Pocahontas
LU 681 . . . . Westmont
LU 703 . . . . Urbana
LU 727 . . . . Dixon
LU 742 . . . . Mascoutah
LU 751 . . . . Kankakee
LU 773 . . . . Marion
LU 996 . . . . Roanoke
LU 1035 . . . . Marengo
LU 1084 . . . . Hillsboro
LU 1197 . . . . . . McLeansboro
LU 1655 . . . . . . North Riverside

Letter Carriers
BR 11 Charles D. Duffy . . Chicago
BR 31 . . . . Peoria
BR 80 . . . . Springfield
BR 88 . . . . Galesburg
BR 155 . . . . Belleville
BR 206 . . . . Sterling
BR 209 . . . . Delavan
BR 216 . . . . Clayton
BR 219 . . . . Leland
BR 223 . . . . Freeport
BR 245 . . . . Kingston
BR 287 . . . . Streator
BR 292 . . . . Rock Island

BR 305 . . . . Joliet	BR 3592 . . . . . Morton Grove	**Longshoremen**	SLG 41 . . . . Chrisman
BR 309 . . . . Alton	BR 3652 . . . . . . Moweaqua	LU 19 . . . . Chicago	SLG 42 . . . . Chicago
BR 311 . . . . Danville	BR 3736 . . . . Barry	LU 101 . . . . Chicago	SLG 46 . . . . Atwood
BR 316 . . . . Ottawa	BR 3770 . . . . Aledo	LU 1427 . . . . Peoria	SLG 97 . . . . Thompsonville
BR 317 . . . . Decatur	BR 3980 . . . . Morton	LU 1652 . . . . . . Wood River	SLG 212 . . . . . . Steeleville
BR 318 . . . . Moline	BR 4007 . . . . . . Glenview		SLG 226 . . . . Decatur
BR 319 . . . . . . East St. Louis	BR 4016 . . . . . . Flossmoor	**Machinists**	SLG 358 . . . . . Tinley Park
BR 384 . . . . Mattoon	BR 4073 . . . . Mount Carroll	CONF Tool & Die . . . Westchester	SLG 436 . . . . Cicero
BR 406 . . . . La Salle	BR 4099 . . . . Mount Prospect	DLG 8 . . . . Forest Park	SLG 469 . . . . . New Lenox
BR 407 . . . . Kankakee	BR 4180 . . . . . . Wilmington	DLG 55 . . . . Joliet	SLG 505 . . . . Marshall
BR 522 . . . . . . Bloomington	BR 4268 . . . . Palatine	DLG 111 International Association of	SLG 510 . . . . . Milledgeville
BR 561 . . . . Dixon	BR 4364 . . . . . . Mundelein	Machinists . . . . Herrin	SLG 565 . . . . McLeansboro
BR 608 . . . . Oak Park	BR 4380 . . . . Minonk	LG 48 . . . . . . Hickory Hills	SLG 694 . . . . Bradley
BR 658 . . . . Macomb	BR 4739 . . . . . . Deerfield	LG 49 . . . . Crete	SLG 788 . . . . Virginia
BR 671 . . . . Champaign	BR 4741 . . . . Mount Olive	LG 124 . . . . Joliet	SLG 798 . . . . . . Galesburg
BR 688 . . . . Toulon	BR 4799 . . . . Arcola	LG 126 . . . . Hinsdale	SLG 965 . . . . . . Nashville
BR 706 . . . . DeKalb	BR 4955 . . . . Red Bud	LG 213 . . . . Galesburg	SLG 1003 . . . . Texico
BR 738 . . . . Centralia	BR 4958 . . . . Warsaw	LG 266 . . . . Centralia	SLG 1046 . . . . Elburn
BR 784 . . . . Urbana	BR 4961 . . . . . . Hamilton	LG 308 . . . . Belleville	SLG 1069 . . . . . Champaign
BR 825 . . . . Elmhurst	BR 4962 . . . . Benld	LG 313 . . . . . . Caseyville	SLG 1152 . . . . Lyndon
BR 843 . . . . Wheaton	BR 5143 . . . . . . Wyoming	LG 360 . . . . Peoria	SLG 1162 . . . . Breese
BR 861 . . . . Clinton	BR 5168 . . . . Rockton	LG 478 A.J. Hayes . . . . Chicago	SLG 1302 . . . . Streator
BR 942 . . . . Mendota	BR 5369 . . . . Genoa	LG 492 . . . . . . Midlothian	SLG 1599 . . . . Chapin
BR 953 . . . . Princeton	BR 5783 . . . . Milan	LG 524 . . . . . . Countryside	SLG 1867 . . . . Ottawa
BR 977 . . . . Hoopeston	BR 5933 . . . . Hartford	LG 554 . . . . Herrin	SLG 1983 . . . . Lerna
BR 1063 . . . . Sycamore	BR 6237 . . . . . East Dubuque	LG 628 . . . . Springfield	SLG 2401 . . . . Cicero
BR 1107 . . . . Wilmette	SA Illinois . . . . Chicago	LG 660 Bluff City . . . . East Alton	SLG 2677 . . . . Clinton
BR 1132 . . . . . Granite City		LG 701 . . . . . . Countryside	SLG 2703 . . . . Fithian
BR 1151 . . . . . . Naperville	**Locomotive Engineers**	LG 710 Vermilion . . . . Danville	SLG 2834 . . . . Mason
BR 1197 . . . . . Murphysboro	DIV 10 . . . . Plainfield	LG 742 . . . . Argonne	SLG 3060 . . . . . . Dennison
BR 1235 . . . . . . Shelbyville	DIV 24 . . . . Salem	LG 746 . . . . . . Westchester	
BR 1316 . . . . La Salle	DIV 32 . . . . Oswego	LG 822 . . . . Quincy	**Mine Workers**
BR 1396 . . . . . . Monticello	DIV 40 . . . . Grayslake	LG 833 . . . . . . Lovington	LU 12 . . . . Hillsboro
BR 1496 . . . . Galva	DIV 45 . . . . Ava	LG 851 . . . . . . Channahon	LU 15 District 12 . . . . . Tamaroa
BR 1498 . . . . . . Winnetka	DIV 96 . . . . Lombard	LG 1000 . . . . . Bloomington	LU 1131 . . . . . . Galesburg
BR 1499 . . . . Morrison	DIV 109 . . . . Troy	LG 1052 . . . . Dixon	LU 1148 . . . . Freeburg
BR 1505 . . . . Sullivan	DIV 118 . . . . . . Edwardsville	LG 1165 . . . . Lincoln	LU 1392 . . . . Pinckneyville
BR 1516 . . . . Geneseo	DIV 131 Brotherhood of Locomotive	LG 1191 . . . . Silvis	LU 1393 . . . . . . Hillsboro
BR 1539 . . . . . . Du Quoin	Engineers . . . . . Oak Forest	LG 1197 . . . . . South Beloit	LU 1458 . . . . Red Bud
BR 1555 . . . . Tuscola	DIV 135 . . . . . Jacksonville	LG 1202 . . . . Aurora	LU 1474 . . . . Marion
BR 1649 . . . . Dundee	DIV 155 . . . . Decatur	LG 1239 . . . . Streator	LU 1487 . . . . . Christopher
BR 1672 . . . . Carthage	DIV 184 . . . . Gilberts	LG 1242 . . . . . Carbondale	LU 1523 . . . . Fairview
BR 1762 . . . . . Spring Valley	DIV 200 . . . . Silvis	LG 1487 . . . . . Des Plaines	LU 1545 . . . . Herrin
BR 1830 . . . . Rock Falls	DIV 251 . . . . . . St. Joseph	LG 1553 . . . . . . Belvidere	LU 1602 . . . . . . Ridgway
BR 1859 . . . . Abingdon	DIV 266 . . . . Savanna	LG 1557 . . . . Huntley	LU 1613 . . . . . . Gillespie
BR 1870 . . . . Downers Grove	DIV 294 . . . . . . Algonquin	LG 1613 . . . . . . Vandalia	LU 1820 . . . . Baldwin
BR 2076 . . . . . Des Plaines	DIV 302 . . . . Plainfield	LG 1623 . . . . . . Morrison	LU 1825 . . . . Tamaroa
BR 2083 . . . . Virden	DIV 315 . . . . . . Monticello	LG 1815 . . . . . Springfield	LU 1969 . . . . . . Carlinville
BR 2093 . . . . . . Gibson City	DIV 354 . . . . . Bourbonnais	LG 1832 . . . . . . Marengo	LU 2117 . . . . Pittsburg
BR 2107 . . . . Nokomis	DIV 394 General Committee of	LG 1880 . . . . Streator	LU 2161 . . . . . Coulterville
BR 2131 . . . . . Assumption	Adj . . . . Chicago	LG 2068 . . . . Rockford	LU 2216 . . . . . Vergennes
BR 2183 . . . . . Melrose Park	DIV 404 . . . . Aurora	LG 2125 . . . . . . Wheeling	LU 2295 . . . . . Germantown
BR 2210 . . . . . . Roodhouse	DIV 444 . . . . . Glen Carbon	LG 2293 Lincoln Trail . . . Robinson	LU 2412 . . . . Marissa
BR 2340 . . . . Pittsfield	DIV 458 . . . . Chicago	LG 2421 . . . . Justice	LU 2414 . . . . . . Woodlawn
BR 2392 . . . . . . Greenfield	DIV 512 . . . . . Edwardsville	LG 2458 . . . . . . Shorewood	LU 2420 . . . . . Johnston City
BR 2411 . . . . . . Farmer City	DIV 551 . . . . . . New Lenox	LG 2600 . . . . . . Oak Forest	LU 2463 . . . . . . Metropolis
BR 2439 . . . . . Mount Sterling	DIV 575 . . . . Fox Lake	STC Illinois . . . . Herrin	LU 2488 . . . . . . Rushville
BR 2517 . . . . Rantoul	DIV 577 . . . . Trilla		LU 5134 . . . . . Du Quoin
BR 2603 . . . . . . Carrollton	DIV 582 . . . . . Orland Park	**Maintenance of Way Employes**	LU 7031 . . . . Omaha
BR 2624 . . . . . Winchester	DIV 602 BLET . . . . Monticello	LG 122 . . . . Pittsfield	LU 7110 . . . . . Lewistown
BR 2790 . . . . Girard	DIV 644 . . . . East Galesburg	LG 377 . . . . . . Lombard	LU 7333 . . . . . Du Quoin
BR 2799 . . . . Fulton	DIV 665 . . . . . . Centralia	LG 409 . . . . Chicago	LU 8317 . . . . West Frankfort
BR 2810 . . . Arlington Heights	DIV 724 . . . . Salem	LG 507 . . . . Chicago	LU 9111 . . . . West Frankfort
BR 3071 . . . . Skokie	DIV 790 . . . . . West Chicago	LG 591 . . . . Chicago	LU 9746 . . . . . Farmersville
BR 3072 . . . . Stockton	DIV 815 . . . . . Calumet Park	LG 783 . . . . . . Colchester	LU 9819 . . . . . Taylorville
BR 3092 . . . . Lockport	DIV 848 . . . . Manito	LG 1063 . . . . . Bridgeport	LU 9878 . . . . West Frankfort
BR 3107 . . . . Lebanon	GCA Burlington	LG 1081 . . . . O'Fallon	LU 9905 . . . . . Du Quoin
BR 3148 . . . . Amboy	Northern . . . . . Galesburg	LG 1107 . . . . Butler	LU 9939 . . . . . Stonefort
BR 3172 . . . . . . Sandwich	GCA Canadian Central-Illinois	LG 1259 . . . . . Kankakee	
BR 3232 . . . . Chenoa	Central . . . . Salem	LG 1514 . . . . . New Lenox	**Musicians**
BR 3350 . . . . . . Lexington	GCA Norfolk & Western	LG 2853 . . . . Arlington Heights	LU 10-208 . . . . . . Chicago
BR 3352 . . . . . . Windsor	Railway . . . . Decatur	LG 2854 . . . . Creve Coeur	LU 26 . . . . Peoria
BR 3398 . . . . Bement	GCA Terminal Railroad . . Waterloo	LG 3086 . . . . Chicago	LU 29 . . . . . . Collinsville
BR 3470 . . . . . . Highwood	GCA The Belt Railway Company of	SD Chicago & Eastern	LU 37 . . . . Plainfield
BR 3536 . . . . Prophetstown	Chicago . . . . Chicago	Illinois . . . . Salem	LU 48 . . . . . Schaumburg
BR 3542 . . . . . . Knoxville	GCA WC . . . . . . St. Charles	SF Chicago &	LU 88 . . . . Benld
BR 3555 . . . . Palestine	SLB Illinois . . . . Fairview Heights	Northwestern . . . . . Rock Falls	LU 98 . . . . . Edwardsville
BR 3558 . . . . Oglesby		SLG 17 . . . . Marion	LU 100 Kewanee . . . Kewanee

LU 175 . . . . Highland
LU 196 . . . . Champaign
LU 240 . . . . Rockford
LU 265 Quincy . . . . Quincy
LU 301 . . . . Morton
LU 307 . . . . Spring Valley
LU 717 . . . . Granite City
LU 759 . . . . Streator
LU 798 . . . . Taylorville
STCON Illinois . . . . . Schaumburg

National Staff Organization
LU Staff Organization, Illinois
   Education Association . Springfield

NLRB Professional Association
LU 13 . . . . Chicago
LU 33 . . . . Peoria

Novelty and Production Workers
JB Central States . . . . . . Chicago
LU 12 Production Workers . Chicago
LU 16 Metal Processors . . . Chicago
LU 18 Plastic Workers . . . Chicago
LU 24 Toy & Novelty
   Workers . . . . Chicago
LU 30 Chemical & Production
   Workers Union . . . . . . Chicago
NHQ . . . . Chicago

Nurses
LU Hines VA INA . . . . Chicago
LU Illinois . . . . Harvey
LU North Chicago VA
   INA . . . . Chicago
LU St. Joseph Hospital Nurses
   Association . . . . Joliet
LU Union Health Service
   Unit . . . . Chicago
SA Illinois Nurses
   Association . . . . Chicago
UNIT INA University of Chicago
   Local . . . . Chicago

Office and Professional Employees
LU 28 . . . . Chicago
LU 391 . . . . Chicago
LU 444 . . . . Abingdon

Operating Engineers
C Illinois State Council . Springfield
LU 148 . . . . Maryville
LU 150 . . . . Countryside
LU 318 . . . . Marion
LU 399 . . . . Chicago
LU 520 . . . . Granite City
LU 649 . . . . Peoria
LU 965 . . . . Springfield

Painters
CONF Central Region
   Conference . . . . . . St. Charles
DC 14 . . . . Chicago
DC 30 . . . . St. Charles
DC 58 . . . . Collinsville
LU 27 . . . . Lyons
LU 32 . . . . Carterville
LU 33 . . . . Joliet
LU 85 . . . . Mascoutah
LU 90 . . . . Springfield
LU 97 . . . . St. Charles
LU 120 . . . . Granite City
LU 124 . . . . Collinsville
LU 147 . . . . Chicago
LU 154 . . . . Elgin
LU 157 . . . . Peoria
LU 180 . . . . Darien
LU 184 . . . . Chicago Ridge

LU 191 . . . . Oak Forest
LU 194 . . . . Chicago
LU 209 . . . . Bloomington
LU 265 . . . . Crestwood
LU 273 . . . . Palos Hills
LU 275 . . . . Round Lake
LU 288 . . . . Decatur
LU 363 . . . . Champaign
LU 448 . . . . Aurora
LU 467 . . . . Clifton
LU 471 . . . . Wood River
LU 502 . . . . Rock Island
LU 521 . . . . Buffalo Grove
LU 581 . . . . Rock Island
LU 607 . . . . Rockford
LU 830 . . . . Hickory Hills
LU 849 . . . . Belleville
LU 863 . . . . Crystal Lake
LU 910 . . . . Hillsboro
LU 1168 . . . . Springfield
LU 1285 . . . . St. Charles
LU 1299 . . . . Caseyville
LU 1332 . . . . Chicago
LU 1705 . . . . Robinson
LU 1850 . . . . Collinsville
LU 2007 . . . . Jacksonville

Plant Protection
LU 522 Ford Motor
   Company . . . . Chicago

Plasterers and Cement Masons
DC Northern Illinois . . . Villa Park
LU 5 . . . . Alsip
LU 11 . . . . McHenry
LU 18 . . . . Peoria
LU 90 . . . . Troy
LU 143 . . . . Champaign
LU 502 . . . . Bellwood
LU 803 . . . . Villa Park
STCON Illinois . . . . Troy

Plumbing and Pipe Fitting
DC 34 Pipe Trades . . . . . Peoria
LU 23 . . . . Rockford
LU 25 . . . . Rock Island
LU 63 . . . . East Peoria
LU 65 . . . . Decatur
LU 93 . . . . Volo
LU 99 . . . . Bloomington
LU 101 . . . . Belleville
LU 130 . . . . Chicago
LU 137 . . . . Springfield
LU 149 . . . . Savoy
LU 160 . . . . Murphysboro
LU 281 . . . . Alsip
LU 353 . . . . Peoria
LU 360 . . . . Collinsville
LU 422 . . . . Joliet
LU 439 . . . . East St. Louis
LU 501 . . . . Chicago
LU 551 . . . . West Frankfort
LU 553 . . . . East Alton
LU 597 . . . . Chicago
LU 649 . . . . East St. Louis
LU 653 . . . . Centralia
SA Illinois Pipe Trades . . . Chicago

Police
LG 1-F Federal Police Officers,
   Illinois . . . . Chicago

Postal and Federal Employees
D 7 . . . . Chicago
LU 701 Chicago Illinois . . Chicago
LU 702 . . . . Chicago
LU 703 . . . . Chicago
LU 704 Evanston . . . . . Chicago

LU 706 . . . . Chicago
LU 709 . . . . Chicago

Postal Mail Handlers
LU 306 . . . . Chicago

Postal Workers
LU 1 Chicago . . . . Chicago
LU 39 Matton . . . . Mattoon
LU 74 East St. Louis . East St. Louis
LU 77 Quincy Area . . . . . Quincy
LU 79 Rockford . . . . . . Rockford
LU 97 Lake Country
   Area . . . . Waukegan
LU 105 Ottawa . . . . Ottawa
LU 109 Bi-State Area . . Rock Island
LU 117 Freeport . . . . . . Freeport
LU 182 Gem Area . . . . . . Alton
LU 228 Bloomington . Bloomington
LU 239 Lincoln Land
   Area . . . . Springfield
LU 243 Danville . . . . . Danville
LU 279 Streator Local . . . Streator
LU 324 Robert J. Govoni . . . Joliet
LU 337 Mount
   Carmel . . . . . . Mount Carmel
LU 351 Aurora . . . . . . Aurora
LU 407 Belleville . . . . . Belleville
LU 563 Elgin Local . . . . . Elgin
LU 594 Blue Island . . . Blue Island
LU 604-605 . . . . . . Countryside
LU 671 Galesburg . . . . Galesburg
LU 686 Jacksonville . . Jacksonville
LU 692 Champaign . . . Champaign
LU 734 Olney . . . . Olney
LU 854 Heart of Illinois
   Area . . . . Peoria
LU 920 Oak Park . . . . . Oak Park
LU 944 . . . . Carbondale
LU 1021 Illinois Valley . . . Pontiac
LU 1050 Cairo . . . . Cairo
LU 1051 Metropolis . . . Metropolis
LU 1152 Marion . . . . . . Marion
LU 1208 Rantoul . . . . . Rantoul
LU 1222 Effingham . . . Effingham
LU 1224 Evanston . . . . Evanston
LU 1258 De Kalb . . . . . Dekalb
LU 1306 Harvey . . . . . . Harvey
LU 1343 Elmhurst . . . . Elmhurst
LU 1621 Salem . . . . Salem
LU 1679 West
   Frankfort . . . . . West Frankfort
LU 1701 . . . . Peru
LU 1730 Des Plaines . . Des Plaines
LU 1788 Park Ridge . . . Park Ridge
LU 1879 Crystal Lake . East Dundee
LU 1884 Flora . . . . Flora
LU 2072 Benton . . . . . . Benton
LU 2250 Macomb . . . . Macomb
LU 2257 Marengo . . . . Marengo
LU 2536 Paris . . . . Paris
LU 2583 Harrisburg . . Harrisburg
LU 3090 Sparta . . . . . . Sparta
LU 3092 O'Fallon . . . . . O'Fallon
LU 3226 Belvidere . . . Belvidere
LU 3417 Urbana . . . . . Urbana
LU 3455 Centralia . . . Centralia
LU 3558 Grayslake . . . . Grayslake
LU 3987 Sandwich . . . Sandwich
LU 4248 . . . . Romeoville
LU 4319 Skokie . . . . Skokie
LU 4545 Arlington
   Heights . . . . . Arlington Heights
LU 4726 Decatur . . . . . Decatur
LU 4733 Bellwood . . . . Bellwood
LU 4779 Kewanee . . . . Kewanee
LU 4803 Morton
   Grove . . . . Morton Grove

LU 4871 Schaumburg . Schaumburg
LU 5007 Kankakee . . . . Kankakee
LU 5154 Mendota . . . . . Mendota
LU 5924 Charleston . . . Charleston
LU 6111 Carlinville . . . Carlinville
LU 6479 Monmouth . . . . Macomb
LU 6591 South Suburban
   Facility . . . . Bedford Park
LU 6993 Wheeling . . . . Wheeling
LU 7011 O'Hare-Midway
   Terminals . . . . Chicago
LU 7033 Chicago Bulk Mail
   Center . . . . Forest Park
LU 7081 . . . . Bartlett
LU 7139 Fox Valley . . . . . Aurora
LU 7140 Northwest Illinois
   Area . . . . Elmhurst
SA Illinois . . . . Westchester

Production Workers
LU 142 Chicago . . . . Chicago
LU 707 Chicago &
   Vicinity . . . . Oak Brook
LU 707 Cleveland and
   Vicinity . . . . Oak Brook
LU 707 Professional Technical &
   Clerical Employees . . Oak Brook
LU 707 Truck Drivers Chauffeurs
   Warehousemen . . . . Oak Brook
NHQ . . . . Oak Brook

Railroad Signalmen
GC 12 Burlington
   Northern . . . . Galesburg
LLG 3 . . . . Chicago
LLG 20 . . . . Dahinda
LLG 25 Brotherhood of Railroad
   Signalmen . . . . . Mount Carmel
LLG 29 . . . . Lena
LLG 81 . . . . Tuscola
LLG 85 . . . . Carlinville
LLG 97 . . . . Joliet
LLG 103 Aurora-Galesburg
   Local . . . . Knoxville
LLG 108 . . . . Rock Falls
LLG 130 . . . . Gilberts
LLG 132 . . . . Collinsville
LLG 143 . . . . Oak Forest
LLG 174 . . . . Mount Vernon
LLG 183 . . . . Manteno
LLG 191 . . . . Pinckneyville
NHQ . . . . Mount Prospect

Retail, Wholesale and Department Store
JB Chicago . . . . Chicago
LU 15 . . . . Chicago
LU 17 . . . . Peru
LU 20 . . . . Chicago
LU 200 Cook County Pharmacy
   Association . . . . Chicago
LU 239 . . . . Chicago
LU 291 . . . . Chicago
LU 317 . . . . Chicago
LU 578 . . . . Rochelle
LU 853 . . . . Chicago

Roofers, Waterproofers and Allied Workers
DC Illinois Roofers . . . Westchester
LU 11 . . . . Westchester
LU 32 . . . . Rock Island
LU 69 . . . . Peoria
LU 92 . . . . Decatur
LU 97 . . . . Champaign
LU 112 . . . . Springfield

Rural Letter Carriers

D 16 Cumberland County . . Toledo
D 17 De Kalb County . . Somonauk
D 46 Lawrence
County. . . . . West Liberty
LU Bond County . . . . Smithboro
LU Champaign County. . . Sidney
LU Clinton County . . . Addieville
LU Edgar County. . . . . . . Paris
LU Effingham County . . . . Toledo
LU Gallatin County . . . . . Omaha
LU Iroquois County. . . Martinton
LU Jo Daviess County . Orangeville
LU Kane, Du Page, & Northern Cook
Counties. . . . . Woodridge
LU Kankakee County . . Herscher
LU Kendall County . . . . . Plano
LU Knox County . . . . Galesburg
LU Livingston-Ford
Counties. . . . . Strawn
LU Macon County. . . . . Decatur
LU Madison County . . Granite City
LU McLean County . . Bloomington
LU Mercer County. . . . Little York
LU Montgomery County . Litchfield
LU Peoria County . . . . Hopedale
LU Perry-Jackson County. Du Quoin
LU Piatt County . . . . White Heath
LU Rock Island County . . . Milan
LU Sangamon County . Springfield
LU Stark County . . . . . Bradford
LU Vermilion County. . . . Catlin
LU Whiteside County . . Rock Falls
LU 1 Adams-Brown-Pike
County. . . . . Quincy
LU 4 Boone-Winnebago
Counties. . . . . Belvidere
LU 6 Bureau-Putnam
Counties. . . . . Putnam
LU 8 Carroll County . Mount Carroll
LU 11 Christian County . . . . Pana
LU 11 Clark County . . Martinsville
LU 21 Edwards County . . . Albion
LU 23 Fayette County . . . . Farina
LU 25 Franklin
County. . . . . . West Frankfort
LU 26 Fulton County . . . . . Avon
LU 44 Lake County . . . . . Russell
LU 45 LaSalle County . . . Oglesby
LU 52 Crawford County . Flat Rock
LU 53 Jersey-Macoupin
Counties. . . . . Otterville
LU 55 Marion County . . . . . Odin
LU 56 Mason-Logan-Menard
Counties. . . . . . . Mason City
LU 60 Monroe County . . Columbia
LU 62 Morgan-Scott-Cass-Green
Counties. . . . . . . Jacksonville
LU 63 Moultrie County. . . Sullivan
LU 64 Ogle County . . . . . Dixon
LU 70 Randolph County. . Waterloo
LU 73 St. Clair County . . Belleville
LU 74 Saline County . . . . Galatia
LU 77 Shelby County . . . . Findlay
LU 83 Washington County . Venedy
LU 84 Wayne County . . . Fairfield
LU 87 Will-South Cook
Counties. . . . . Plainfield
SA Illinois . . . . Illiopolis

Security, Police and Fire Professionals

LU 200 . . . . Berwyn
LU 228 . . . . Gardner
LU 237 . . . . Byron
LU 238 . . . . Hillsdale

Service Employees

C Illinois State Council . . . Chicago
JC 28 . . . . Caseyville
LU 1. . . . . Chicago
LU 4. . . . . Chicago
LU 7 Firemen & Oilers . . Chicago
LU 8 Firemen & Oilers . . . . Peoria
LU 15. . . . . Chatham
LU 19 Firemen & Oilers . Springfield
LU 20 . . . . Chicago
LU 73 . . . . Chicago
LU 116. . . . . Belleville
LU 342 Metal
Engravers . . . . . . Spring Grove
LU 352 . . . . Pinckneyville
LU 398 Firemen & Oilers . . . Joliet
LU 570 Firemen & Oilers. . Chicago
LU 660 Firemen &
Oilers. . . . . . . North Riverside
LU 728 Firemen &
Oilers . . . . Taylorville
LU 865 Firemen &
Oilers. . . . . Galesburg
LU 944 Firemen &
Oilers . . . . East Hazel Crest

Sheet Metal Workers

LU 1 . . . . Peoria Heights
LU 73 . . . . Hillside
LU 91 . . . . Rock Island
LU 218 . . . . Springfield
LU 219 . . . . Rockford
LU 256 . . . . Bourbonnais
LU 265 . . . . Carol Stream
LU 268 . . . . Caseyville
LU 367 . . . . Chicago
LU 450 . . . . Kankakee
LU 484 . . . . Orland Hills
STC Illinois . . . . . Peoria Heights

State, County and Municipal Employees

C 31 Illinois Public
Employees. . . . . . . Springfield
LU . . . . Anna
LU 46 Illinois Department
Corrections Rock Island
County . . . . Matherville
LU 203 Illinois Department of
Corrections Employees
Center . . . . Centralia
LU 486 . . . . Broadview
LU 494 Pontiac Correctional
Center . . . . Pontiac
LU 501 Lincoln Correctional
Center. . . . . Hartsburg
LU 817 . . . . Dixon
LU 993 Vandalia, Illinois State Penal
Farm . . . . Vandalia
LU 1133 Illinois Reformatory for
Women, Dwight. . . . Streator
LU 1175 . . . . Chester
LU 1274 Hill Correctional
Center. . . . . Galesburg
LU 1514 Aurora Area Public
Employees . . . . Aurora
LU 1753 Illinois Youth Center Joliet
Employees . . . . Joliet
LU 1831 St. Clair Association
Vocational Enterprise . Collinsville
LU 2052 Danville Correctional
Center Employees. . . . Westville
LU 2073 Illinois Department of
Corrections/Log/Center . . Lincoln
LU 2335 Southern Illinois
Corrections
Employees . . . . . Murphysboro

LU 2481 The Hope School
Employees. . . . . . . Springfield
LU 3017 Peoria Association for
Retarded Citizens . Peoria Heights
LU 3237 United Cerebral Palsy of
Will County . . . . Romeoville
LU 3280 Anna Veterans' Home
Employees . . . . Ullin
LU 3436 . . . . Hazel Crest
LU 3464 City of Peoria Municipal
Employees . . . . Peoria
LU 3513 Family Counseling
Center . . . . Golconda
LU 3534 Glenkirk Association
Employees . . . . Waukegan
LU 3653 . . . . Taylorville
LU 3663 Big Muddy Correctional
Center . . . . Centralia
LU 3784 Beverly Farm Foundation
Inc. . . . . Bethalto
LU 3863 Orchard Village
Employees . . . . Chicago

Steelworkers

C Corn. . . . . Summit
C Illinois Council of
Locals. . . . . West Peoria
LU 923 . . . . Freeport
LU 1345 . . . . Plainfield
LU 2-19-G . . . . Ottawa
LU 7-122-T. . . . Elk Grove Village
LU 7-1899 . . . . Granite City
LU 01-7999-S . . . . Plainfield
LU 05-1538 . . . . Cairo
LU 06-91 . . . . Westchester
LU 06-188 . . . . Delavan
LU 06-189 . . . . Illiopolis
LU 06-194. . . . . Peoria
LU 06-268 . . . . Chicago
LU 06-325 . . . . Dolton
LU 06-347 . . . . Waterloo
LU 06-429. . . . . Kankakee
LU 06-455 . . . . Argonne
LU 06-507 . . . . Summit
LU 06-517 . . . . Oak Lawn
LU 06-626 . . . . Morris
LU 06-643 . . . . Abingdon
LU 06-647 . . . . Capentersville
LU 06-657 . . . . Peru
LU 06-662 . . . . Green Valley
LU 06-717 . . . . Burbank
LU 06-728 . . . . Decatur
LU 06-765 . . . . . . Chicago Heights
LU 06-807 . . . . Tremont
LU 06-837 . . . . Decatur
LU 06-838 . . . . Decatur
LU 06-839 . . . . Decatur
LU 06-865 . . . . Bolingbrook
LU 06-876 . . . . Decatur
LU 06-904 . . . . Joliet
LU 06-960. . . . . Peoria
LU 06-972 . . . . Georgetown
LU 06-975 . . . . Fairmount
LU 06-1085 . . . . Frankfort
LU 06-1195 . . . . Peotone
LU 06-1210 . . . . . . Downers Grove
LU 06-1211 . . . . Plainfield
LU 06-1215 . . . . Highland
LU 06-1216 . . . . Worth
LU 07-17-U . . . . Chicago
LU 07-31-G . . . . Ottawa
LU 07-63-S . . . . Sterling
LU 07-68-S . . . . . . Granite City
LU 07-85 . . . . Streator
LU 07-87-T . . . . . Richton Park
LU 07-89 . . . . South Holland
LU 07-96-T . . . . Lincoln
LU 07-193-S . . . . . . Mount Zion

LU 07-215-L . . . . . . Rock Island
LU 07-436-S . . . . . . Granville
LU 07-685-L . . . . . . Galesburg
LU 07-704-L . . . . . . Shabbona
LU 07-706-A . . . . . Georgetown
LU 07-745-L . . . . . . Freeport
LU 07-787-L. . . . . . . Normal
LU 07-960-L . . . . . South Beloit
LU 07-1053-S . . . . . Bridgeview
LU 07-1063-S . . . . . Granite City
LU 07-1201 . . . . . . Beach Park
LU 07-1636-S . . . . . . Aurora
LU 07-1651 . . . . . . Morrison
LU 07-1744-S . . . . . Hainesville
LU 07-2154-S. . . . . . Chicago
LU 07-3510-S . . . . . Bardolph
LU 07-3643-S . . . . . . Alton
LU 07-4268-S. . . . . . . Peru
LU 07-4294-S . . . . . Cahokia
LU 07-4804-S . . . . . Granite City
LU 07-5109-S . . . . Mount Olive
LU 07-6063-S . . . . Edwardsville
LU 07-6496-S . . . . . O'Fallon
LU 07-7234-S . . . . . Harvey
LU 07-7252-S. . . . . Pinckneyville
LU 07-7367-S . . . . . Hennepin
LU 07-7495-S . . . . South Elgin
LU 07-7773-S . . . . . Chicago
LU 07-9189-S. . . . Wood River
LU 07-9777 . . . . . Bridgeview
LU 07-13605-S. . . . . Tamaroa
LU 07-13748-S . . . . . Pekin
LU 07-13881-S . . . . . Burbank
LU 07-14676-S . . . . Carterville
LU 07-14728-S. . . . Bourbonnais
LU 07-15009-S. . . . . Pittsburg
LU 34-8390 . . . . . . Charleston

Teachers

LU 2063 Faculty-University of
Chicago Lab Schools . . . Chicago
SFED 310 Illinois. . . . . . Westmont

Teamsters

CONF Illinois Conference of
Teamsters . . . . Springfield
JC 25 . . . . Chicago
JC 65 . . . . Springfield
LU 26 . . . . Danville
LU 50 . . . . Belleville
LU 179 . . . . Joliet
LU 279 . . . . Decatur
LU 301 . . . . Waukegan
LU 325 . . . . Rockford
LU 330 . . . . Elgin
LU 347 . . . . West Frankfort
LU 371 . . . . Rock Island
LU 525 . . . . Alton
LU 627 . . . . Peoria
LU 673 . . . . West Chicago
LU 703 . . . . Chicago
LU 705 . . . . Chicago
LU 706 . . . . Chicago
LU 710 . . . . Chicago
LU 714 . . . . Berwyn
LU 722 . . . . La Salle
LU 727 . . . . Chicago
LU 731 . . . . Burr Ridge
LU 734 . . . . Chicago
LU 743 Health Care, Professional,
Technical . . . . Chicago
LU 744 . . . . Chicago
LU 754 . . . . Elmhurst
LU 777 . . . . Brookfield
LU 781 . . . . Des Plaines
LU 786 . . . . Chicago
LU 916 . . . . Springfield

Television and Radio Artists
LU Chicago . . . . Chicago
LU 1080 218 Peoria . . . . . Peoria

Theatrical Stage Employees
CONF Illinois State . . . . Sidney
D 9 Wisconsin-Iowa-Illinois-
   Missouri-Minnesota-North
   Dakota-South Dakota-Nebraska-
   Kansas . . . . Sidney
LU 2 . . . . Chicago
LU 46-B . . . . Chicago
LU 110 . . . . Chicago
LU 124 . . . . Joliet
LU 138 . . . . Springfield
LU 193 . . . . Bloomington
LU 217 . . . . Rockford
LU 374 . . . . Bradley
LU 421 . . . . Metropolis
LU 433 . . . . East Moline
LU 476 Motion Picture Studio
   Mechanics . . . . Chicago
LU 482 . . . . Urbana
LU 750 Treasurers &
   Ticketsellers . . . La Grange Park
LU 769 . . . . . Hoffman Estates
LU 780 . . . . Chicago

Train Dispatchers
SCOM Belt Railroad of
   Chicago . . . . Tinley Park
SCOM Norfolk & Western
   Railway . . . . Mount Zion
SCOM Northeast Illinois Regional
   Commute . . . . Chicago
SCOM Terminal Railroad
   Association of St.
   Louis . . . . Caseyville

Transit Union
LDIV 313 . . . . Rock Island
LDIV 416 . . . . Glasford
LDIV 752 . . . . Bloomington
LDIV 859 . . . . Decatur
LDIV 1333 . . . . Rockford
LU 1028 . . . . . Elk Grove Village
LU 1702 . . . . Richton Park

Transport Workers
LU 512 . . . . . Elk Grove Village
LU 540 . . . . Palatine
LU 563 . . . . Des Plaines
LU 571 . . . . Chicago
LU 572 . . . . Skokie
LU 2014 . . . . Chicago
LU 2037 . . . . Alhambra

Transportation Communications Union
D 245 Great Lakes System Board
   118 . . . . New Lenox
D 439 . . . . Decatur
D 521 Southeastern System Board
   96 . . . . Alton
D 781 . . . . Downers Grove
D 782 . . . . Hometown
D 829 Allied Services
   Division . . . . Arlington Heights
D 867 College City . . . . Galesburg
D 1068 . . . . Dewey
D 1505 Great Lakes System Board
   118 . . . . Claredon Hills
D 1960 . . . . . Arlington Heights
D 2500 . . . . . Country Club Hills
D 2503 . . . . Springfield
JPB 600 Chicago Milwaukee St. Paul
   & Pacific . . . . Chicago
LG 574 . . . . Troy

LG 695 . . . . Crestwood
LG 6100 Fellowship . . . . Manteno
LG 6176 Proviso . . . . . . Chicago
LG 6266 Cook County . . . Palatine
LG 6277 Decatur . . . . . . Decatur
LG 6560 Stony Island . . . . Lansing
LG 6591 Purple . . . . Chicago
LG 6608 Chesterfield . . . . Steger
LG 6738 Morton Park . . . . Plano
LG 6787 Galesburg . . . . Wataga
LG 6861 Beacon . . . . . . Bluford
SBA 155 Allied Services
   Division . . . . Arlington Heights

Transportation Union
GCA GO-65 Belt Railroad of
   Chicago . . . . Palos Heights
GCA GO-209 Chicago & Eastern
   Railway . . . . Grant Park
GCA GO-330 Elgin Joliet Eastern
   Railway . . . . Elwood
GCA GO-401 SPCSL-GWWR-IC
   Railroad . . . . Mokena
GCA GO-449 Indiana Harbor Belt
   Railroad . . . . Matteson
GCA GO-919 Terminal
   Railroad Association-St.
   Louis . . . . Granite City
LU 168 . . . . Frankfort
LU 171 . . . . Aurora
LU 195 . . . . Galesburg
LU 196 . . . . Beardstown
LU 198 . . . . Rome
LU 234 . . . . Lincoln
LU 281 . . . . Spring Grove
LU 432 . . . . Urbana
LU 453 . . . . Clinton
LU 469 . . . . Granite City
LU 490 . . . . Mount Carmel
LU 528 . . . . Chicago
LU 565 . . . . Odin
LU 577 . . . . Elmwood Park
LU 597 . . . . Carol Stream
LU 620 . . . . . Country Club Hills
LU 653 . . . . Tinley Park
LU 740 . . . . Joliet
LU 768 . . . . Decatur
LU 979 . . . . Salem
LU 1003 . . . . Bourbonnais
LU 1083 . . . . Villa Grove
LU 1258 . . . . Schaumburg
LU 1290 . . . . Chicago
LU 1299 . . . . Burbank
LU 1358 . . . . Danville
LU 1402 . . . . Millstadt
LU 1405 . . . . Glen Carbon
LU 1421 . . . . Tinley Park
LU 1423 . . . . Cameron
LU 1433 . . . . Elmhurst
LU 1534 . . . . Plainfield
LU 1538 . . . . Beecher
LU 1597 . . . . Midlothian
LU 1895 . . . . Midlothian
LU 1929 . . . . Belleville
SLB LO-16 Illinois . . . . Chicago

Treasury Employees
CH 10 . . . . Chicago
CH 43 . . . . Champaign
CH 172 . . . . Carol Stream
CH 237 . . . . Chicago
CH 242 . . . . Dunlap
CH 300 OCC . . . . . . Chicago

UNITE HERE
JB Chicago & Central
   States . . . . Chicago
JB Cincinnati . . . . Chicago

JB Kentuckiana . . . . . . Chicago
LJEB Chicago . . . . Chicago
LU 1 . . . . Chicago
LU 5 . . . . Chicago
LU 5-H . . . . Chicago
LU 14-M . . . . Chicago
LU 16 . . . . Peoria
LU 17-T . . . . Chicago
LU 36-A . . . . Chicago
LU 39-C . . . . Chicago
LU 43 . . . . Chicago
LU 48 . . . . Chicago
LU 50-010 . . . . Chicago
LU 56 . . . . Chicago
LU 56-ASW . . . . Chicago
LU 61 . . . . Chicago
LU 62 . . . . Chicago
LU 63-H . . . . Chicago
LU 73-A . . . . Chicago
LU 76 . . . . Chicago
LU 81-R . . . . Chicago
LU 86-C . . . . Chicago
LU 90-I . . . . Chicago
LU 91 . . . . Chicago
LU 99-H . . . . Chicago
LU 104 . . . . Chicago
LU 108 . . . . Chicago
LU 108-A . . . . Chicago
LU 112 . . . . Chicago
LU 114 . . . . Chicago
LU 120 . . . . Chicago
LU 144-JTU . . . . Chicago
LU 150 . . . . Chicago
LU 168-AC . . . . Chicago
LU 171 . . . . Chicago
LU 183 . . . . Chicago
LU 188-I . . . . Chicago
LU 189-T . . . . Chicago
LU 199 . . . . Chicago
LU 208-A . . . . Chicago
LU 210-T . . . . Chicago
LU 224-T . . . . Chicago
LU 225-A . . . . Chicago
LU 229-LDC . . . . Chicago
LU 254-C . . . . Chicago
LU 255 . . . . Chicago
LU 261 . . . . Chicago
LU 270-A . . . . Chicago
LU 272-A . . . . Chicago
LU 284-SW . . . . Chicago
LU 295-C . . . . Chicago
LU 304 . . . . Chicago
LU 310 . . . . East Moline
LU 319-C . . . . Chicago
LU 322 . . . . Chicago
LU 323 . . . . Chicago
LU 335-T . . . . Chicago
LU 379 . . . . Chicago
LU 393-T . . . . Chicago
LU 398 . . . . Chicago
LU 399 . . . . Chicago
LU 428-A . . . . Chicago
LU 428-I . . . . Chicago
LU 450 . . . . Forest Park
LU 463 . . . . Chicago
LU 465-C . . . . Chicago
LU 479-A . . . . Chicago
LU 488-I . . . . Chicago
LU 496-A . . . . Chicago
LU 501-A . . . . Chicago
LU 504-A . . . . Chicago
LU 512-A . . . . Chicago
LU 517 . . . . Chicago
LU 529-I . . . . Chicago
LU 546-I . . . . Chicago
LU 562-A . . . . Chicago
LU 594 . . . . Chicago
LU 617 . . . . Chicago

LU 777-I . . . . Chicago
LU 782-A . . . . Chicago
LU 839-A . . . . Chicago
LU 840-A . . . . Chicago
LU 851-T . . . . Chicago
LU 871-A . . . . Chicago
LU 872-A . . . . Chicago
LU 874-A . . . . Chicago
LU 920-A . . . . Chicago
LU 950 . . . . Chicago
LU 958-A . . . . Chicago
LU 969-A . . . . Chicago
LU 978-A . . . . Chicago
LU 981-A . . . . Chicago
LU 1050 . . . . Chicago
LU 1051 . . . . Chicago
LU 1094-T . . . . Chicago
LU 1106 . . . . Chicago
LU 1107 . . . . Chicago
LU 1110 . . . . Chicago
LU 1164 . . . . Chicago
LU 1170 . . . . Chicago
LU 1385 . . . . Chicago
LU 1406 . . . . Chicago
LU 1422 . . . . Chicago
LU 1426 . . . . Chicago
LU 1448 . . . . Chicago
LU 1481 . . . . Chicago
LU 1490 . . . . Chicago
LU 1525-T . . . . Chicago
LU 1538 . . . . Chicago
LU 1557 . . . . Chicago
LU 1558 . . . . Chicago
LU 1749 . . . . Chicago
LU 1755-56H . . . . Chicago
LU 1758 . . . . Chicago
LU 1812 . . . . Chicago
LU 1818 . . . . Chicago
LU 1820 . . . . Chicago
LU 1871 . . . . Chicago
LU 1872 . . . . Chicago
LU 1899 . . . . Chicago
LU 1902 . . . . Chicago
LU 2299 . . . . Chicago
LU 2302 . . . . Chicago
LU 2375 . . . . Chicago
LU 2378 . . . . Chicago
LU 2403 . . . . Chicago
LU 2405 . . . . Chicago
LU 2430 . . . . Chicago
LU 2458 . . . . Chicago
LU 2483 . . . . Chicago
LU 2484 . . . . Chicago
LU 2497 . . . . Chicago
LU 2512 . . . . Chicago
LU 2543 . . . . Chicago
LU 2565 . . . . Chicago
LU 2568 . . . . Chicago
LU 2573 . . . . Chicago
LU 2577 . . . . Chicago
LU 2580 . . . . Chicago
LU 2590 . . . . Chicago
LU 2615 . . . . Chicago
LU 2616 . . . . Chicago
LU 2635 . . . . Chicago
LU 2636 . . . . Chicago
LU 2646 . . . . Chicago
LU 2656 . . . . Chicago
LU 2668 . . . . Chicago
LU 2675 . . . . Chicago
LU 2685 . . . . Chicago
LU 2686 . . . . Chicago
LU 2702 . . . . Chicago
LU 2722 . . . . Chicago
LU 3008-LDC . . . . Chicago

Utility Workers
LU 405 . . . . Belleville

LU 467 . . . . Bourbonnais
LU 500 . . . . Urbana
LU 18007 . . . . Chicago

Weather Service Employees
BR 03-44 . . . . Romeoville
BR 03-46 . . . . Chicago
BR 03-84 . . . . Aurora
BR 03-94 . . . . Lincoln

Unaffiliated Labor Organizations

Amalgamated Workers Union
    Independent LU
    711 . . . . Franklin Park
American Allied Workers
    Information Technology &
    Engineering LU 16 . Richton Park
American Allied Workers Laborers
    International Union LU
    101 . . . . Chicago
American Allied Workers Laborers
    Union LU 120 . . . . . Chicago
Chicago Barbers Hairdressers
    Cosmetologists Union LU
    939 . . . . Chicago
Congress of Independent Unions
    NHQ . . . . Alton
Contract Mail Drivers Association
    Independent . . . . Franklin Park
Elgin Trades Council
    AFL-CIO . . . . Elgin

Faculty Association Francis W.
    Parker School. . . . . . Chicago
Faculty Association of DeVry
    Chicago Inc. . . . . . . Chicago
Food Clerks Union
    Independent . . . . Highland Park
Guards & Watchmen of America
    Independent. . . . . . . Chicago
Highlands Supply Corporation
    Workers Union . . . . . Highland
Hospital Employees Labor
    Program. . . . . Chicago
Illinois Central Train Dispatchers
    Association . . . . Matteson
Illinois Department of Corrections
    Employees, Lawrenceville . Cisne
Illinois State Security Service
    Association . . . . Chicago
Independent Installation Workers
    Union . . . . Romeoville
Independent Union of Professionals
    & Associates LU 7 . . . . Chicago
Industrial Construction Equipment
    Builders Union Employees
    Association of Kewanee. Kewanee
International Brotherhood of General
    Workers NHQ . . . . . Chicago
International Federation of
    Independent Labor Unions . Sidell
Lift Truck Builders
    Independent . . . . . . Danville
Lincolnshire Local . . . Lincolnshire

Liquor & Wine Sales Representatives
    Tire Plastic & Allied Workers LU
    3. . . . . Chicago
Marine & Machinists Association
    Independent Johnson Division
    Outboard Marine
    Corporation . . . . . Waukegan
Medical Staff of the Union Health
    Service of Chicago . . . . Chicago
Modern Metal Products Employee
    Benefit Association . . Loves Park
Mosstype Employees Association
    Illinois . . . . . Elk Grove Village
MPC Employees Representative
    Union . . . . Niles
National Alliance of Business
    and Professionals LU
    100 . . . . Palos Heights
National Allied Workers
    Union. . . . . Cicero
National Allied Workers Union LU
    831 . . . . Cicero
National Association of Bus
    Drivers. . . . . . . Vernon Hills
National Federation of Licensed
    Practical Nurses DIV 1 Licensed
    Practical Nurses Association of
    Illinois . . . . Chicago
National Federation of Licensed
    Practical Nurses SA Licensed
    Practical Nurses Association of
    Illinois . . . . Springfield

National Organization of Workers
    National Inside Union. Des Plaines
National Pharmacists
    Association. . . . . . Naperville
Oil & Chemical Workers
    Independent Procter &
    Gamble-Texas. . . . . Waterloo
Private Sector Police Benevolent
    Labor Council . . . . Springfield
Procter & Gamble Employees
    Association St. Louis
    Plant. . . . . New Douglas
Production & Maintenance Union LU
    101 . . . . Chicago
Professional Airline Flight Control
    Association (PAFCA-
    United). . . . . Elk Grove Village
Roosevelt Adjunct Faculty
    Organization (RAFO) . . Oak Park
Steel Workers Alliance
    Independent . . . . . Bartonville
Stockton Employees Independent
    Union. . . . . Stockton
The United Independent Workers
    International Union. . . . Chicago
United Professional Workers and
    Affiliates LU 267 . . . . Elmhurst
United Security Services
    Union . . . . Oregon
Weatherstrip Workers Union,
    Independent. . . . . . . Lansing
Western Illinois Correctional
    Center Employees, Mount
    Sterling . . . . . Mount Sterling
Workers Security League Union
    League. . . . . Blue Island

Indiana

AFL-CIO Trade and Industrial Departments

Building and Construction Trades Department
BCTC Central Indiana . Indianapolis
BCTC Central Wabash
  Valley . . . . Terre Haute
BCTC Dearborn & Ripley
  Counties . . . . . . Lawrenceburg
BCTC Floyd & Clark
  Counties . . . . Charlestown
BCTC Indiana State . . Indianapolis
BCTC La Porte-Satarke-Pulaski
  Counties . . . . La Porte
BCTC Lower Ohio
  Valley . . . . Evansville
BCTC North Central . . . . Kokomo
BCTC Northeastern
  Indiana . . . . Fort Wayne
BCTC Northwest
  Indiana . . . . Hammond
BCTC South Central
  Indiana . . . . Indianapolis
BCTC St. Joseph
  Valley . . . . South Bend
BCTC Tippecanoe
  County . . . . Lafayette
BCTC United East Central . Muncie

Other Councils and Committees
C Council of Industrial
  Organizers . . . . . . Newburgh

AFL-CIO Directly Affiliated Locals

AFL-CIO
JC Wabash Valley Central
  Labor . . . . Terre Haute

Affiliated Labor Organizations

Air Traffic Controllers
LU EVV . . . . Evansville
LU FWA . . . . Fort Wayne
LU HUF . . . . Terre Haute
LU IND . . . . Indianapolis
LU LAF . . . . . . West Lafayette
LU SBN . . . . South Bend
LU ZID . . . . Indianapolis

Asbestos Workers
CONF Central States . . Fort Wayne
LU 18 . . . . Indianapolis
LU 37 . . . . Evansville
LU 41 . . . . Fort Wayne
LU 75 . . . . South Bend

Automobile, Aerospace Workers
C Adams Allen Wells Joint
  CAP . . . . Fort Wayne
C Bartholomew Decatur Rush-
  Shelby . . . . Indianapolis
C Cass-Carroll-Fulton-
  Pulaski . . . . Winamac
C Clark-Floyd-Harrison-Jennings-
  Scott . . . . Sellersburg
C Clinton Tippecanoe County
  CAP . . . . Lafayette
C Elkhart County . . . . . Osceola

C Fayette Union-Franklin
  Counties . . . . . . Connersville
C Grant-Wabash Counties . . Marion
C Greater Marion
  County . . . . Indianapolis
C Henry CAP . . . . . New Castle
C Howard County . . . . Kokomo
C Huntington-Noble-
  Whitley . . . . Marion
C Lagrange-Steuben . . . . Angola
C Lawrence-Orange-
  Washington . . . . Bedford
C Madison-Hamilton
  Counties . . . . Anderson
C Region 3 CAP . . . Indianapolis
C Region 3 Lake-Porter County
  CAP . . . . Gary
C St. Joseph County . . . South Bend
C Starke-Marshall-
  Kosciusko . . . . Warsaw
C Vanderburch County UAW CAP
  Council . . . . Evansville
C Wayne-Randolph . . . Richmond
LU 5 . . . . South Bend
LU 9 . . . . South Bend
LU 23 . . . . Indianapolis
LU 52 . . . . Argos
LU 98 . . . . Indianapolis
LU 151 . . . . Connersville
LU 164 . . . . Auburn
LU 194 . . . . North Liberty
LU 226 . . . . Indianapolis
LU 287 . . . . Muncie
LU 292 . . . . Kokomo
LU 295 . . . . Elkhart
LU 321 . . . . Muncie
LU 358 . . . . . North Manchester
LU 364 . . . . Elkhart
LU 371 . . . . New Castle
LU 428 . . . . Osceola
LU 440 . . . . Bedford
LU 494 . . . . Union City
LU 499 . . . . Muncie
LU 499 Delawre County
  CAP . . . . Muncie
LU 531 . . . . Attica
LU 550 . . . . Indianapolis
LU 607 . . . . Plymouth
LU 661 . . . . Greenfield
LU 662 . . . . Anderson
LU 663 . . . . Anderson
LU 685 . . . . Kokomo
LU 729 . . . . New Castle
LU 761 . . . . Anderson
LU 871 UAW . . . . . . Rome City
LU 933 . . . . Indianapolis
LU 941 . . . . Elkhart
LU 947 . . . . Rochester
LU 957 . . . . Yorktown
LU 977 . . . . Marion
LU 1073 . . . . Richmond
LU 1101 . . . . Ossian
LU 1111 . . . . Indianapolis
LU 1118 . . . . Connersville
LU 1123 . . . . Bedford
LU 1166 . . . . Kokomo
LU 1168 . . . . Greensburg
LU 1244 . . . . Richmond
LU 1302 . . . . Kokomo
LU 1317 . . . . Butler
LU 1368 . . . . Bremen
LU 1373 . . . . Kendallville
LU 1389 . . . . Ossian
LU 1405 . . . . Leesburg
LU 1417 . . . . . . South Milford

LU 1448 . . . . Kewanna
LU 1457 . . . . Connersville
LU 1497 . . . . Mulberry
LU 1518 . . . . Connersville
LU 1571 . . . . Anderson
LU 1763 . . . . Greencastle
LU 1888 . . . . Uniondale
LU 1904 . . . . Connersville
LU 1949 . . . . Frankfort
LU 1954 . . . . Logansport
LU 1963 . . . . Anderson
LU 1969 . . . . Waterloo
LU 1983 . . . . Fishers
LU 2046 . . . . Noblesville
LU 2049 . . . . Columbia City
LU 2050 . . . . Brookville
LU 2052 . . . . Rushville
LU 2140 . . . . Shirley
LU 2158 . . . . Bedford
LU 2209 . . . . Roanoke
LU 2242 . . . . Albion
LU 2274 . . . . Indianapolis
LU 2277 . . . . Angola
LU 2289 . . . . Corydon
LU 2317 . . . . Lafayette
LU 2335 . . . . Hammond
LU 2339 . . . . Rushville
LU 2345 . . . . Kendallville
LU 2357 . . . . Fort Wayne
LU 2371 . . . . Gas City
LU 2374 . . . . Richmond
LU 2382 . . . . Greencastle
LU 2401 . . . . Edinburgh
LU 2414 . . . . Charlottesville
LU 2911 Society of Engineer
  Employees . . . . . Fort Wayne
LU 3042 . . . . Ossian
LU 3044 . . . . Rockport
LU 3048 . . . . Evansville
LU 3050 . . . . Richmond
LU 3053 . . . . Terre Haute
LU 6291 . . . . Valparaiso

Bakery, Confectionery, Tobacco Workers and Grain Millers
LU 33-G . . . . New Albany
LU 102-G . . . . Oxford
LU 104-G . . . . Frankfort
LU 132 . . . . Columbus
LU 280 . . . . Evansville
LU 315-G . . . . . . Mount Vernon
LU 372-A . . . . Indianapolis
LU 372-B . . . . Indianapolis

Boilermakers
C Indiana State . . . . . Connersville
LG 24-M . . . . Kokomo
LG 39-D Cement
  Workers . . . . Greencastle
LG 51 . . . . Indianapolis
LG 209-D Cement
  Workers . . . . Sellersburg
LG 300-M . . . . Aurora
LG 357 . . . . Peru
LG 374 . . . . Hammond
LG 524 . . . . Hammond
LG 999 National Cement
  Lodge . . . . Cloverdale
LG 1240 . . . . Wabash
LG 1620 . . . . Portland

Bricklayers
LU 4 Indiana and
  Kentucky . . . . Anderson

Carpenters
DC State of Indiana . . . Indianapolis
LU 60 . . . . Indianapolis
LU 90 . . . . Evansville
LU 133 . . . . Terre Haute
LU 193 . . . . Indianapolis
LU 215 . . . . Lafayette
LU 232 . . . . Fort Wayne
LU 364 . . . . Indianapolis
LU 413 . . . . South Bend
LU 546 . . . . Vincennes
LU 599 . . . . Hammond
LU 615 . . . . Warsaw
LU 631 . . . . Charlestown
LU 758 . . . . Indianapolis
LU 859 . . . . Greencastle
LU 912 . . . . Richmond
LU 1003 . . . . Indianapolis
LU 1005 . . . . Hobart
LU 1016 . . . . Muncie
LU 1029 . . . . Warsaw
LU 1043 . . . . Hobart
LU 1142 . . . . Lawrenceburg
LU 1155 . . . . Columbus
LU 1406 . . . . Hobart
LU 1481 Great Lakes Regional
  Industrial . . . . . . South Bend
LU 1485 . . . . La Porte
LU 1664 . . . . Bloomington
LU 1775 . . . . Columbus
LU 1788 . . . . Hartford City
LU 2133 . . . . Corydon
LU 2177 . . . . Martinsville
LU 2489 . . . . Salem
LU 2577 . . . . Salem
LU 2930 . . . . Jasper
LU 3056 . . . . La Porte
LU 8093-T . . . . Williams

Civilian Technicians
CH 72 Fort Wayne . . . Fort Wayne

Communications Workers
C Indiana State . . . . . Indianapolis
LU 855 . . . . Rosedale
LU 999 IUE-CWA Industrial
  Division . . . . Fort Wayne
LU 4700 . . . . Evansville
LU 4703 . . . . Clarksville
LU 4770 . . . . Connersville
LU 4773 . . . . La Porte
LU 4780 . . . . Richmond
LU 4800 . . . . Fishers
LU 4802 . . . . South Bend
LU 4818 . . . . Bloomington
LU 4900 . . . . Indianapolis
LU 4998 . . . . Indianapolis
LU 14438 . . . . Michigan City
LU 14441 La Porte Typographical
  Union . . . . La Porte
LU 14442 . . . . Linton
LU 14446 Terre Haute Typographical
  Union . . . . Terre Haute
LU 14448 Evansville Mailers
  Union . . . . Evansville
LU 14449 Indianapolis Mailers
  Union . . . . Terre Haute
LU 34014 . . . . Gary
LU 34046 Terre Haute Newspaper
  Guild . . . . Terre Haute
LU 34070 . . . . Indianapolis
LU 84001 . . . . Clayton
LU 84302 . . . . Indianapolis
LU 84303 . . . . Rensselaer
LU 84802 . . . . Bluffton

LU 84805 . . . . Tell City
LU 84807 . . . . Jeffersonville
LU 84808 . . . . Evansville
LU 84809 . . . . South Bend
LU 84826 . . . . Bloomington
LU 84845 . . . . Evansville
LU 84848 . . . . Evansville
LU 84859 . . . . Evansville
LU 84863 . . . . Auburn
LU 84888 . . . . Fremont
LU 84901 . . . . Fort Wayne
LU 84903 . . . . Auburn
LU 84907 . . . . Mitchell
LU 84911 . . . . South Bend
LU 84913 . . . . South Bend
LU 84919 . . . . Connersville
LU 84924 . . . . Fort Wayne
LU 84950 . . . . Attica
LU 84963 . . . . Fort Wayne
LU 84998 . . . . Fort Wayne

Electrical Workers
CONF Indiana State . . Indianapolis
LU 16 . . . . Evansville
LU 153 . . . . South Bend
LU 186 . . . . Wheatfield
LU 281 . . . . Anderson
LU 305 . . . . Fort Wayne
LU 473 . . . . Moores Hill
LU 481 . . . . Indianapolis
LU 531 . . . . La Porte
LU 668 . . . . Lafayette
LU 697 . . . . Hammond
LU 723 . . . . Fort Wayne
LU 725 . . . . Terre Haute
LU 757 . . . . Crown Point
LU 784 . . . . Shirley
LU 855 . . . . Muncie
LU 873 . . . . Kokomo
LU 983 . . . . Huntington
LU 1000 . . . . Marion
LU 1048 . . . . Indianapolis
LU 1109 . . . . Goshen
LU 1160 . . . . Marion
LU 1225 . . . . Indianapolis
LU 1392 . . . . South Bend
LU 1393 . . . . Indianapolis
LU 1395 . . . . Indianapolis
LU 1400 . . . . Indianapolis
LU 1424 . . . . Columbus
LU 1865 . . . . Elkhart
LU 1976 . . . . Argos
LU 2043 . . . . Richmond
LU 2249 . . . . Bloomington
LU 2344 . . . . Lafayette
LU 2355 . . . . Michigan City
SC EM-4 BICC/General
   Cable . . . . Gas City

**Electrical, Radio and Machine
Workers**
LU 770 . . . . Kendallville
LU 1177 . . . . Merrillville

Elevator Constructors
LU 34 . . . . Indianapolis

Engineers
LU 137 . . . . Fort Wayne

Food and Commercial Workers
C Indiana-Kentucky
   State . . . . Indianapolis
LU 13-D . . . . Lawrenceburg
LU 15-C . . . . Clarksville
LU 157-C . . . . Whiting
LU 493-C . . . . La Porte
LU 557-T . . . . Goshen

LU 692-C . . . . . . Jeffersonville
LU 700 . . . . Indianapolis
LU 833-C . . . . Evansville
LU 988-C . . . . Charlestown

**Glass, Molders, Pottery and
Plastics Workers**
CONF Indiana Educational . Muncie
LU 14 . . . . Muncie
LU 32 . . . . Shelbyville
LU 37 . . . . Fairmount
LU 38 . . . . Marion
LU 42 . . . . Lawrenceburg
LU 65 . . . . Winchester
LU 66 . . . . Sullivan
LU 96 . . . . Dunkirk
LU 121 . . . . Dunkirk
LU 127-B . . . . Terre Haute
LU 166 . . . . Griffith
LU 207 . . . . Lapel
LU 229 . . . . Ligonier
LU 238 . . . . Kokomo
LU 242 . . . . Winchester
LU 262 . . . . La Grange
LU 285 . . . . Fort Wayne
LU 316-B . . . . La Porte
LU 322 . . . . Fort Wayne
LU 447 . . . . La Grange

Government Employees
C 3 Sixth District . . . . New Albany
C 175 Food Inspection Locals, North
   Central . . . . . . North Vernon
LU 128 GSA . . . . . Indianapolis
LU 516 USDA . . . . . Rochester
LU 609 . . . . Indianapolis
LU 720 DoJ . . . . . Terre Haute
LU 1016 . . . . Indianapolis
LU 1020 AFGE Local 1020, VA
   Medical Center Marion . . Marion
LU 1384 VA . . . . . Fort Wayne
LU 1415 DoD . . . . Crane
LU 1438 . . . . Jeffersonville
LU 1744 DoD . . . . Indianapolis
LU 2150 USDA . . . New Salisbury
LU 3098 DoD . . . . Terre Haute
LU 3254 DoD . . . . Bunker Hill
LU 3571 HHS . . . . . Greenwood
LU 3956 HUD . . . . Indianapolis

Government Security Officers
LU 113 . . . . South Bend

Graphic Communications
LU 17-M . . . . Indianapolis
LU 19-M . . . . Fort Wayne
LU 128-N Midwest Newspaper
   Printing Pressmen . Indianapolis
LU 303-M . . . . Indianapolis
LU 411-M . . . . Huntington
LU 571-M . . . . Evansville

Independent Unions
LU 235 Universal Employees
   Union . . . . Butler

Iron Workers
LU 22 . . . . Indianapolis
LU 103 . . . . Evansville
LU 147 . . . . Fort Wayne
LU 292 . . . . South Bend
LU 379 . . . . Lafayette
LU 395 . . . . Hammond
LU 439 . . . . Terre Haute
LU 529 . . . . Muncie
LU 585 . . . . Vincennes
LU 726 . . . . Fort Wayne
LU 730 . . . . Elkhart

LU 799 . . . . Lafayette

Laborers
DC 57 Indiana . . . . . Terre Haute
LU 41 . . . . Hammond
LU 81 . . . . Valparaiso
LU 120 . . . . Indianapolis
LU 204 . . . . Terre Haute
LU 213 . . . . Fort Wayne
LU 274 . . . . Lafayette
LU 561 . . . . Evansville
LU 645 . . . . South Bend
LU 741 . . . . Bloomington
LU 795 . . . . New Albany
LU 1047 . . . . Richmond
LU 1112 . . . . Muncie
LU 1325 . . . . Rushville

Letter Carriers
BR 39 . . . . Indianapolis
BR 98 . . . . Muncie
BR 116 . . . . Fort Wayne
BR 160 . . . . Columbus
BR 198 . . . . Crawfordsville
BR 200 . . . . La Porte
BR 239 . . . . Connersville
BR 271 . . . . Richmond
BR 323 Bridge City . . . Logansport
BR 330 . . . . South Bend
BR 367 . . . . New Albany
BR 368 . . . . Frankfort
BR 377 . . . . Evansville
BR 378 . . . . Marion
BR 428 . . . . Huntington
BR 455 . . . . Michigan City
BR 466 . . . . Lafayette
BR 472 . . . . Madison
BR 479 . . . . Terre Haute
BR 489 . . . . Anderson
BR 533 . . . . Kokomo
BR 547 . . . . Elkhart
BR 553 . . . . Jeffersonville
BR 580 . . . . Hammond
BR 670 . . . . Brazil
BR 748 . . . . Attica
BR 753 . . . . Valparaiso
BR 789 . . . . Seymour
BR 790 . . . . North Vernon
BR 799 . . . . Winchester
BR 801 . . . . Greensburg
BR 814 . . . . New Castle
BR 820 . . . . Mishawaka
BR 828 South Central
   Indiana . . . . . . Bloomington
BR 867 . . . . Hartford City
BR 868 . . . . Portland
BR 877 . . . . Warsaw
BR 878 . . . . Rushville
BR 882 . . . . Greencastle
BR 888 . . . . Carmel
BR 918 . . . . Franklin
BR 952 . . . . Kendallville
BR 1011 . . . . Union City
BR 1054 . . . . Columbia City
BR 1060 . . . . Decatur
BR 1288 . . . . Rochester
BR 1319 . . . . Tipton
BR 1326 . . . . Lake Station
BR 1395 . . . . Lawrenceburg
BR 1399 . . . . East Chicago
BR 1405 . . . . Sullivan
BR 1472 . . . . . . North Manchester
BR 1584 . . . . Ligonier
BR 1624 . . . . Crown Point
BR 1689 . . . . Whiting
BR 1816 . . . . French Lick
BR 1834 . . . . Aurora
BR 1835 . . . . Nappanee

BR 1868 . . . . Boonville
BR 1899 . . . . Delphi
BR 1974 . . . . Rensselaer
BR 2132 . . . . Monticello
BR 2240 . . . . Petersburg
BR 2256 . . . . Brookville
BR 2298 . . . . Butler
BR 2374 . . . . Liberty
BR 2421 . . . . Greenwood
BR 2448 . . . . La Grange
BR 2658 . . . . Hagerstown
BR 2717 . . . . Salem
BR 2724 . . . . Argos
BR 2802 . . . . Dunkirk
BR 2919 . . . . Loogootee
BR 2968 . . . . Winamac
BR 3032 . . . . Hobart
BR 3146 . . . . Cannelton
BR 3153 . . . . Berne
BR 3293 . . . . Batesville
BR 3323 . . . . Edinburg
BR 3333 . . . . Clay City
BR 3394 . . . . Montpelier
BR 3416 . . . . Veedersburg
BR 3447 . . . . Bremen
BR 3448 . . . . Thorntown
BR 3519 . . . . Paoli
BR 3532 . . . . Williamsport
BR 3546 . . . . Covington
BR 3571 . . . . Vevay
BR 3608 . . . . Orleans
BR 3646 . . . . Kentland
BR 3661 . . . . Crothersville
BR 3708 . . . . Ridgeville
BR 4260 . . . . Charlestown
BR 4426 . . . . Fowler
BR 4649 . . . . Walkerton
BR 4800 . . . . Chesterton
BR 5251 . . . . Sellersburg
BR 5276 . . . . Austin
BR 5568 . . . . Brownsburg
BR 5652 . . . . Flora
BR 5684 . . . . Odon
BR 5706 . . . . Albany
BR 5967 . . . . Winona Lake
BR 6318 . . . . Churubusco
BR 6473 . . . . Brownstown
BR 6492 . . . . Yorktown
SA Indiana . . . . . Beech Grove

Locomotive Engineers
DIV 7 . . . . Lebanon
DIV 25 . . . . Terre Haute
DIV 100 . . . . Covington
DIV 106 . . . . New Haven
DIV 121 . . . . Mooresville
DIV 153 . . . . Auburn
DIV 154 . . . . Evansville
DIV 165 . . . . New Albany
DIV 204 . . . . Linton
DIV 246 . . . . Evansville
DIV 270 . . . . Wheatland
DIV 289 . . . . Washington
DIV 343 . . . . Princeton
DIV 348 . . . . Goshen
DIV 474 . . . . Walkerton
DIV 520 . . . . Gary
DIV 537 . . . . Fort Wayne
DIV 545 . . . . Valparaiso
DIV 548 . . . . Peru
DIV 597 . . . . Plainfield
DIV 613 . . . . Dyer
DIV 682 . . . . Schererville
DIV 683 . . . . Schererville
DIV 722 . . . . Camby
DIV 754 . . . . Terre Haute
GCA Elgin Joliet & Eastern
   Railroad . . . . Gary

SLB Indiana . . . . Angola

Longshoremen
DIV Conrail Division 12/Amtrak and
CSX-T . . . . Kendallville
LU 1803 . . . . Whiting
LU 1969 . . . . Portage
LU 2038 . . . . Portage
LU 2058 . . . . Portage

Machinists
DLG 90 . . . . Indianapolis
DLG 153 . . . . Evansville
LG 70 . . . . Fort Wayne
LG 161 . . . . Indianapolis
LG 162 . . . . Sunman
LG 229 . . . . Goshen
LG 327 . . . . Hammond
LG 450 . . . . Logansport
LG 498 . . . . Hammond
LG 511 . . . . Rockville
LG 1109 . . . . Lexington
LG 1118 . . . . Elkhart
LG 1227 IAM & AW
Valparaiso . . . . . . Valparaiso
LG 1315 . . . . Elkhart
LG 1391 . . . . . . Lawrenceburg
LG 1541 . . . . . . Kendallville
LG 1595 . . . . Portland
LG 1621 . . . . Fort Wayne
LG 2034 . . . . Churubusco
LG 2069 . . . . Peru
LG 2294 Hoosier Air
Transport . . . . . . Indianapolis
LG 2410 Unity . . . . . . Madison
LG 2520 . . . . Fort Wayne
LG 2532 Richmond . . . . Richmond
LG 2543 . . . . La Porte
LG 2569 . . . . Fort Wayne
LG 2574 . . . . Huntington
LG 2584 . . . . Fremont
LG 2723 . . . . Underwood
LG 2819-PM . . . . . . Speedway
LG 2903 . . . . Westville
LLG 1270 . . . . Columbus
LLG W-197
Woodworkers . . . . Indianapolis
STC Indiana . . . . . Indianapolis

Maintenance of Way Employes
LG 74 . . . . Carlisle
LG 302 . . . . Floyds Knob
LG 466 . . . . Nappanee
LG 696 . . . . Oaktown
LG 1056 . . . . Kendallville
LG 1355 . . . . Bloomington
LG 1362 . . . . Muncie
LG 1532 . . . . Hobart
LG 1806 . . . . Union Mills
LG 1903 . . . . La Porte
LG 2856 . . . . Logansport
LG 3025 . . . . Fort Wayne
SD Elgin Joliet & Eastern
Railroad . . . . Hobart
SLG 34 . . . . Dale
SLG 63 . . . . Lowell
SLG 287 . . . . Fort Wayne
SLG 463 . . . . Lake Village
SLG 498 . . . . Medaryville
SLG 542 . . . . Elizabeth
SLG 991 . . . . Elkhart
SLG 1035 . . . . Evansville
SLG 1060 . . . . Mitchell
SLG 1155 . . . . New Albany
SLG 1297 . . . . Merrillville
SLG 1363 . . . . Columbia City
SLG 1649 . . . . Liberty
SLG 1916 . . . . Bedford

SLG 1980 . . . . Whiteland
SLG 1984 . . . . Alexandria
SLG 3043 . . . . Logansport
SLG 3097 . . . . Greensburg

Mine Workers
LU 11 . . . . Evansville
LU 352 . . . . Winslow
LU 1038 . . . . Boonville
LU 1189 . . . . Boonville
LU 1216 . . . . Staunton
LU 1410 . . . . Linton
LU 1423 . . . . Linton
LU 1791 . . . . Princeton
LU 1851 . . . . Lynnville
LU 1907 . . . . Boonville
LU 4011 . . . . Francisco
LU 4343 . . . . Petersburg
LU 5179 . . . . Oakland City
LU 8682 . . . . Terre Haute
LU 9926 . . . . Boonville

Musicians
LU 3 . . . . Indianapolis
LU 25 . . . . Clinton
LU 58 . . . . Fort Wayne
LU 203 . . . . Hammond
LU 232 . . . . South Bend
LU 245 . . . . Muncie
LU 278 . . . . South Bend

National Staff Organization
ASSN Indiana Professional Staff
Teacher . . . . Noblesville
ASSN Indiana State
Teachers . . . . Bicknell

NLRB Professional Association
LU 25 . . . . Indianapolis

Nurses
SA Indiana State Nurses
Association . . . . . Indianapolis

Office and Professional Employees
LU 1 . . . . Bunker Hill
LU 476 . . . . Flat Rock
LU 509 . . . . Elkhart

Operating Engineers
BR Indiana State
Branch . . . . Terre Haute
LU 103 . . . . Fort Wayne
LU 841 . . . . Terre Haute

Painters
DC 91 . . . . Evansville
LU 13 . . . . Lawrenceburg
LU 47 . . . . Indianapolis
LU 80 . . . . Lafayette
LU 156 . . . . Evansville
LU 197 . . . . Terre Haute
LU 460 . . . . Merrillville
LU 469 . . . . Fort Wayne
LU 669 . . . . Chesterfield
LU 1118 . . . . South Bend
LU 1165 . . . . Indianapolis

Plant Protection
LU 123 Visteon Steering
Systems . . . . Camby

Plasterers and Cement Masons
LU 692 . . . . Indianapolis

Plumbing and Pipe Fitting
LU 136 . . . . Evansville
LU 157 . . . . Terre Haute

LU 166 . . . . Fort Wayne
LU 172 . . . . South Bend
LU 210 . . . . Merrillville
LU 440 . . . . Indianapolis
LU 661 . . . . Muncie
SA Indiana State Pipe
Trades . . . . Fort Wayne

Postal and Federal Employees
D 6 . . . . Indianapolis
LU 608 . . . . Indianapolis
LU 612 . . . . Indianapolis

Postal Workers
LU New Albany . . . New Albany
LU 130 Indianapolis . . Indianapolis
LU 210 Northern Indiana Unified
Area . . . . South Bend
LU 224 La Porte . . . . . La Porte
LU 266 Gary . . . . Gary
LU 278 Mishawaka . . . Mishawaka
LU 280 Hammond . . . . Hammond
LU 286 Fort Wayne Indiana
Area . . . . Fort Wayne
LU 347 Evansville Area . Evansville
LU 398 Whiting . . . . . Whiting
LU 618 Terre Haute
Area . . . . Terre Haute
LU 753 Jeffersonville . Jeffersonville
LU 774 Vincennes . . . . Vincennes
LU 839 Lafayette . . . . Lafayette
LU 914 . . . . East Chicago
LU 1014 Kokomo Area . . Kokomo
LU 1077 Marion . . . . . Marion
LU 1524 Crown Point . Crown Point
LU 1921 Aurora . . . . . Aurora
LU 2122 Bloomington . Bloomington
LU 2432 Muncie . . . . . Muncie
LU 2514 Valparaiso . . . Valparaiso
LU 2658 . . . . Frankfort
LU 2668 Noblesville . . Noblesville
LU 2724 Richmond . . . Richmond
LU 2769 Washington . . Washington
LU 2889
Crawfordsville . . . Crawfordsville
LU 3223 Dunes Area . Michigan City
LU 3740 Columbus . . . . Columbus
LU 3980 North
Manchester . . . North Manchester
LU 4166 Bedford . . . . . Bedford
SA Indiana . . . . . . Fort Wayne

Railroad Signalmen
LLG 42 . . . . Mooresville
LLG 45 . . . . Anderson
LLG 68 . . . . Hammond
LLG 71 . . . . Evansville
LLG 91 . . . . Crawfordsville
LLG 228 . . . . Tipton

**Retail, Wholesale and Department
Store**
JB Indiana . . . . . . Fort Wayne
LU 29 John Sexton &
Company . . . . . . Indianapolis
LU 202 . . . . Fort Wayne
LU 357 . . . . Chesterfield
LU 512 . . . . Indianapolis
LU 810 . . . . New Haven
LU 835 . . . . Fort Wayne
LU 1096 . . . . Indianapolis
LU 1976 . . . . Indianapolis
UNIT D-Indiana Joint
Board . . . . Fairmount

**Roofers, Waterproofers and Allied
Workers**
LU 23 . . . . South Bend

LU 26 . . . . Merrillville
LU 106 . . . . Evansville
LU 119 . . . . Indianapolis
LU 150 . . . . Terre Haute
LU 205 . . . . Chesterfield

Rural Letter Carriers
BR 34 . . . . Tipton
LU Bartholomew-Brown
Counties . . . . Columbus
LU Boone County . . . . Lebanon
LU Cass County . . . Logansport
LU Dubois-Martin-Pike
Counties . . . . Jasper
LU Fountain-Warren
Counties . . . . Attica
LU Grant County . . . . Fairmount
LU Greene County . . . . Lyons
LU Hendricks County . Martinsville
LU Jennings County . North Vernon
LU Johnson County . . . Shelbyville
LU Lagrange County . . Wolcottville
LU Lawrence Orange County
Chapter . . . . Bedford
LU Marshall-St. Joseph-Starke
Counties . . . . Osceola
LU Monroe County . Bloomington
LU Montgomery
County . . . . . . Crawfordsville
LU Morgan County Unit
55 . . . . Martinsville
LU Owen County . . . . Spencer
LU Perry-Spencer
Counties . . . . . . St. Meinrad
LU Porter County . . . Cedar Lake
LU Putnam County . . . Greencastle
LU Southeastern Indiana . Rising Sun
LU Steuben-De Kalb
Counties . . . . Angola
LU Sullivan County . . . . Sullivan
LU Tippecanoe County . Monticello
LU Vanderburg-Warrick
Counties . . . . Evansville
LU Wabash County . . . . Roann
LU Whitley County . . . Huntington
LU 7 Fayette-Henry-Rush-Union-
Wayne County . . Cambridge City
LU 18 Delaware Jay
Blackford . . . . Muncie
LU 48 Madison County . . . Kirklin
LU 49 Marion County . Indianapolis
LU 72-88 Southern
Indiana . . . . Scottsburg
LU 84 Vigo County . . . Terre Haute
LU 603 Elkhart County . Middlebury
SA Allen County . . . . Huntington
SA Indiana . . . . Galveston

**Security, Police and Fire
Professionals**
LU 7 . . . . Osceola
LU 8 . . . . Clinton
LU 19 . . . . Kokomo
LU 21 . . . . Gas City
LU 23 . . . . Anderson
LU 24 . . . . Mishawaka
LU 123 . . . . Muncie
LU 133 . . . . New Castle
LU 134 . . . . Fort Wayne
LU 202 . . . . Indianapolis
LU 205 . . . . Connersville
LU 227 . . . . Highland

Service Employees
LU 131 Firemen &
Oilers . . . . Indianapolis
LU 431 Firemen &
Oilers . . . . Indianapolis

LU 551 . . . . Indianapolis
LU 571 Firemen &
  Oilers . . . . Schererville

Sheet Metal Workers
LU 20 . . . . Indianapolis
LU 179 . . . . Beech Grove
LU 204 . . . . Huntington
LU 237 . . . . Fort Wayne

State, County and Municipal
  Employees
C 62 Indiana State . . . Indianapolis
LU 531 . . . . Frankfort
LU 725 . . . . Indianapolis
LU 1000 CSEA Region III,
  Southern . . . . Bicknell
LU 2077 Headstart . . . . Richmond
LU 2502 . . . . Merrillville
LU 2539 . . . . Portage

Steelworkers
LU 304-007 . . . . . . Fort Wayne
LU 2003 . . . . Gary
LU 5133 . . . . Gary
LU 7703 . . . . Shelbyville
LU 9463 . . . . Hudson
LU 9497 . . . . Lawrenceburg
LU 2-201-B . . . . Covington
LU 6-30 . . . . Mitchell
LU 6-696 W.R. Grace . . Hammond
LU 6-899 . . . . North Manchester
LU 6-945 . . . . Arcadia
LU 7-9481 . . . . St. John
LU 05-53 . . . . Mexico
LU 05-814 . . . . Brookville
LU 05-848 . . . . New Salisbury
LU 05-1261 . . . . Tell City
LU 06-1 . . . . Whiting
LU 06-7 . . . . Logansport
LU 06-69 . . . . Carthage
LU 06-103 . . . . Camden
LU 06-113 . . . . Marion
LU 06-154 . . . . Mooresville
LU 06-164 . . . . . Crawfordsville
LU 06-168 . . . . Indianapolis
LU 06-182 . . . . . Hartford City
LU 06-184 . . . . Fort Wayne
LU 06-186 . . . . Dunkirk
LU 06-210 . . . . Whiting
LU 06-248 Tulox Plastics . Gas City
LU 06-254 . . . . Fort Wayne
LU 06-285 . . . . Wabash
LU 06-307 . . . . Andrews
LU 06-320 . . . . Marion
LU 06-336 . . . . . . Crown Point
LU 06-354 . . . . Shoals
LU 06-472 . . . . Logansport
LU 06-509 . . . . Bruceville
LU 06-518 . . . . Logansport
LU 06-521 . . . . Hammond
LU 06-555 . . . . Vincennes
LU 06-596 . . . . Gary
LU 06-613 . . . . Terre Haute
LU 06-645 . . . . Hammond
LU 06-652 . . . . Peru
LU 06-706 . . . . Indianapolis
LU 06-729 . . . . Fort Wayne
LU 06-809 . . . . Warsaw
LU 06-822 . . . . Seymour
LU 06-903 . . . . Fort Wayne
LU 06-1043 . . . . Flat Rock

LU 06-1046 . . . . Princeton
LU 06-1047 . . . . . . Indianapolis
LU 06-1052 . . . . Elkhart
LU 06-1055 . . . . . . Fort Wayne
LU 06-1056 . . . . Elkhart
LU 06-1106 . . . . Eaton
LU 06-1109 . . . . Freetown
LU 06-1135 . . . . . . Terre Haute
LU 07-14-S . . . . . . Logansport
LU 07-70 . . . . Portage
LU 07-81-T . . . . Lapel
LU 07-93-G . . . . Muncie
LU 07-103-S . . . . . . Terre Haute
LU 07-104-S . . . . Newburgh
LU 07-104-T . . . . . . Winchester
LU 07-106-T . . . . . . Winchester
LU 07-112 . . . . Winchester
LU 07-112-A . . . . . . Boonville
LU 07-115 . . . . Lafayette
LU 07-115-T . . . . . . Winchester
LU 07-118-A . . . . Kentland
LU 07-119-A . . . . Mitchell
LU 07-138 . . . . Milan
LU 07-138-L . . . . . . Noblesville
LU 07-188-S . . . . Wanatah
LU 07-331-U . . . . . Huntingburg
LU 07-466-L . . . . Marion
LU 07-501-T . . . . Dunkirk
LU 07-513 . . . . . . Hartford City
LU 07-518-T . . . . Modoc
LU 07-525-U . . . . Batesville
LU 07-607 . . . . Rochester
LU 07-614 . . . . Etna Green
LU 07-626-L . . . . Wabash
LU 07-634-L . . . . Auburn
LU 07-650-L . . . . Milford
LU 07-715-L . . . . . . Woodburn
LU 07-726 . . . . Albany
LU 07-798-L . . . . Plymouth
LU 07-1010-S . . . . East Chicago
LU 07-1011-S . . . . East Chicago
LU 07-1014-S . . . . Gary
LU 07-1015-L . . . . Angola
LU 07-1066-S . . . . Gary
LU 07-1191-S . . . . . Mishawaka
LU 07-1999-S . . . . . Indianapolis
LU 07-2695-S . . . . Gary
LU 07-2818-S . . . . . . Evansville
LU 07-2958-S . . . . Kokomo
LU 07-3261-S . . . . . . Rockfield
LU 07-3875-S . . . . Cicero
LU 07-4863-S . . . . . Logansport
LU 07-5163-S . . . . . . Richmond
LU 07-5840-S . . . . . . Rochester
LU 07-6103-S . . . . Portage
LU 07-6743-S . . . . . Indianapolis
LU 07-6787-S . . . . . Chesterton
LU 07-6805-S . . . . Warsaw
LU 07-6982-S . . . . . Rensselaer
LU 07-7441-S . . . . . Terre Haute
LU 07-8535-S . . . . . New Castle
LU 07-8985-S . . . . . Valparaiso
LU 07-9231-S . . . . New Carlisle
LU 07-12213 . . . . Muncie
LU 07-12273-S . . . . Osceola
LU 07-12502-S . . . . Dyer
LU 07-12775-S . . . . Portage
LU 07-13584-S . . . . . Valparaiso
LU 07-13796-S . . . . . . La Porte
LU 07-15173-S . . . . Decatur

Teamsters
JC 69 . . . . Indianapolis
LU 135 . . . . Indianapolis
LU 142 . . . . Gary
LU 215 . . . . Evansville
LU 364 . . . . South Bend
LU 414 . . . . Fort Wayne
LU 716 . . . . Indianapolis
LU 1070 . . . . Lafayette
LU 2001 Indiana Mailers
Union . . . . Mooresville

Theatrical Stage Employees
D 8 Michigan-Indiana-Ohio-
  Kentucky . . . . Demotte
LU 30 . . . . Greenwood
LU 30 . . . . Indianapolis
LU 49 . . . . Terre Haute
LU 102 . . . . Evansville
LU 125 . . . . Demotte
LU 146 . . . . Fort Wayne
LU 163 . . . . Clarksville
LU 174 . . . . Lafayette
LU 187 . . . . South Bend
LU 194 . . . . Greenwood
LU 194-B . . . . Greenwood
LU 373 . . . . Terre Haute
LU 618 . . . . Bloomington
LU 836 . . . . Indianapolis
LU 893 . . . . Indianapolis
LU 897 Theatrical Wardrobe
Union . . . . Jeffersonville

Train Dispatchers
SCOM Chicago South Shore-South
  Bend . . . . Michigan City
SCOM Indiana Harbor Belt Railroad
  System Commission . . Demotte
SCOM Indiana Harbor Belt
  Railway . . . . Hammond
SCOM New York Chicago & St.
  Louis Railroad . . . . Fort Wayne

Transit Union
LDIV 517 . . . . Gary
LDIV 996 . . . . Osceola
LDIV 1070 . . . . . . Indianapolis
LDIV 1474 . . . . Richmond

Transport Workers
LU 2003 . . . . Indianapolis
LU 2053 . . . . Mishawaka

Transportation Communications
  Union
D 357 Conrail . . . . . . Hammond
D 464 . . . . North Liberty
D 905 . . . . Hobart
LG 5001 Chicago &
  Northwestern . . . . . . Portage
LG 5088 Amtrak . . . Indianapolis
LG 6011 . . . . Griffith
LG 6295 South Shore . . . La Porte
LG 6760 Fort Wayne . . New Haven

Transportation Union
GCA GO-329 Elgin Joliet Eastern
  Railway . . . . Portage
GCA GO-623 Conrail-PC-ILL-DIV-
  NYC-IHB . . . . . . Schererville
LLG 1973 . . . . La Porte
LU 6 . . . . New Palestine

LU 206 . . . . Bunker Hill
LU 298 . . . . Auburn
LU 333 . . . . Vincennes
LU 383 . . . . Lanesville
LU 744 . . . . Lafayette
LU 904 . . . . Evansville
LU 1202 . . . . Craigville
LU 1328 . . . . Georgetown
LU 1381 . . . . Dyer
LU 1383 . . . . Portage
LU 1399 . . . . Plainfield
LU 1494 . . . . Highland
LU 1518 . . . . Lafayette
LU 1526 . . . . Trail Creek
LU 1548 . . . . Greenfield
LU 1663 . . . . Greencastle
LU 1883 . . . . Dyer
SLB LO-17 Indiana . . . Indianapolis

Treasury Employees
CH 49 . . . . Indianapolis
CH 246 . . . . Indianapolis

Utility Workers
LU 418 . . . . Lawrenceburg

Weather Service Employees
BR 03-1 . . . . Indianapolis
BR 03-98 . . . . Syracuse

Unaffiliated Labor
Organizations

American Allied Workers Laborers
  International Union Skill
  Trademens LU 103 . . . . . Gary
American Federation of
  Professional . . . . . Crown Point
Bertrand Employees LU
  7701 . . . . South Bend
Diesel Workers Union
  Independent . . . . Columbus
Employees Protective Association
  Circulation Department-
  Indianapolis
  Newspapers . . . . . Indianapolis
Fort Wayne Patrolman's Benevolent
  Association Inc. . . . . Fort Wayne
Independent Employees Union of
  Northwest Indiana Markets
  Inc. . . . . Hobart
Indiana Council Employees Union
  Council 62 Employees Union LU
  10 . . . . Indianapolis
International Guards Union of
  America LU 26 . . . Lawrenceburg
Lift Workers of Greensburg
  United . . . . Greensburg
Lincoln Land Building &
  Construction Trades
  Council . . . . Terre Haute
Midstates Independent
  Union . . . . Schererville
Office Committee Union of Cummins
  Engine Company Inc. . Columbus
Professional Salesmen American
  Federation . . . . Granger
Steel Workers Progressive Union of
  Hammond . . . . . . Hammond
Stonecutters Association of Indiana,
  Journeymen . . . . Norman
Ultra-Cast Inc. Employee
  Committee . . . . Peru

Iowa

AFL-CIO Trade and Industrial Departments

Building and Construction Trades Department

BCTC Cedar Rapids. . Cedar Rapids
BCTC Central Iowa. . . Des Moines
BCTC Dubuque . . . . . . Dubuque
BCTC Iowa. . . . . Bettendorf
BCTC South Central Iowa. Ottumwa
BCTC Southeastern
  Iowa . . . . Burlington
BCTC Waterloo . . . . . . Waterloo

Metal Trades Department

MTC Dubuque . . . . . . Dubuque

Affiliated Labor Organizations

Air Traffic Controllers

LU ALO . . . . Waterloo
LU CID . . . . Cedar Rapids
LU DSM . . . . Des Moines
LU SUX . . . . Sioux City

Asbestos Workers

LU 57. . . . . Sioux City
LU 74 . . . . Des Moines
LU 81 . . . . Cedar Rapids

Automobile, Aerospace Workers

C Iowa-UAW North Central CAP
  Council. . . . . Dubuque
C Southeast Iowa UAW CAP
  Council . . . . Ottumwa
C West Central CAP . . . . Newton
LU 13 . . . . Dubuque
LU 74 . . . . Ottumwa
LU 94 . . . . Dubuque
LU 120 . . . . Creslo
LU 242 . . . . Cedar Rapids
LU 270 . . . . Des Moines
LU 281 . . . . Davenport
LU 411 . . . . Waverly
LU 442. . . . . Webster City
LU 450 . . . . Des Moines
LU 616 . . . . Cedar Rapids
LU 807 . . . . Burlington
LU 838 . . . . Waterloo
LU 893 . . . . Marshalltown
LU 997 . . . . Newton
LU 1024 . . . . Cedar Rapids
LU 1201. . . . . Grinnell
LU 1237 . . . . Burlington
LU 1349. . . . . Cedar Rapids
LU 1391 . . . . Dubuque
LU 1540 . . . . Jefferson
LU 1551 . . . . Fort Madison
LU 1613 . . . . Monticello
LU 1672 . . . . Des Moines
LU 1896 . . . . Davenport
LU 1946 . . . . Creston
LU 1982 . . . . Dyersville
LU 2310 . . . . Bloomfield

Bakery, Confectionery, Tobacco Workers and Grain Millers

LU 10-G . . . . Cedar Rapids
LU 36. . . . . Davenport
LU 48-G . . . . Keokuk
LU 49-G . . . . Iowa Falls
LU 100-G . . . . Cedar Rapids
LU 269-G . . . . Mason City
LU 349-G . . . . Atlantic
LU 389-G . . . . Indianola

Boilermakers

LG 6-D Cement Workers . . Buffalo
LG 66-D Cement
  Workers . . . . Fort Dodge
LG 106-D Cement
  Workers . . . . Mason City
LG 584-D . . . . Davenport

Bricklayers

LU 3 Iowa . . . . Des Moines

Carpenters

LU 4 . . . . Davenport
LU 106 . . . . Des Moines
LU 308 . . . . Cedar Rapids
LU 678 . . . . Dubuque
LU 772 . . . . Clinton
LU 948 . . . . Sioux City
LU 1039 . . . . Marson
LU 1260 . . . . Iowa City
LU 2158 . . . . Bettendorf
LU 2704 . . . . Epworth
LU 2831 . . . . Decorah

Civilian Technicians

CH 75 Hawkeye . . . Sergeant Bluff
CH 101 Heartland . . . . Johnston

Communications Workers

C State of Iowa. . . . . . Waterloo
LU 7101 . . . . Marion
LU 7102 . . . . Des Moines
LU 7103 . . . . Sioux City
LU 7107 . . . . Humboldt
LU 7108 . . . . Waterloo
LU 7109 . . . . Oelwein
LU 7110 . . . . Dubuque
LU 7113 . . . . Council Bluffs
LU 7115 . . . . Ottumwa
LU 7171 . . . . Fort Dodge
LU 7172 . . . . Tama
LU 7175 . . . . Waterloo
LU 7181 . . . . Burlington
LU 14712. . . . . Burlington
LU 14719 . . . . Cedar Falls
LU 37123. . . . . Sioux City
LU 84110. . . . . Bettendorf

Electrical Workers

LU 13 . . . . Burlington
LU 55 . . . . Des Moines
LU 204 . . . . Cedar Rapids
LU 231 . . . . Sioux City
LU 288 . . . . Waterloo
LU 347 . . . . Des Moines
LU 405 . . . . Cedar Rapids
LU 452 . . . . West Burlington
LU 499 . . . . Clive
LU 618 . . . . Missouri Valley
LU 704 . . . . Dubuque
LU 825 . . . . Davenport
LU 1362 . . . . Cedar Rapids
LU 1379 . . . . Bettendorf
LU 1429 . . . . Cedar Rapids
LU 1634 . . . . North Liberty
SC 2 Railroad . . . . . . Mondamin

Electrical, Radio and Machine Workers

LU 793 . . . . Tama
LU 811 . . . . Lawton

Elevator Constructors

LU 33 . . . . Des Moines

Fire Fighters

LU 1672 . . . . Muscatine
SA Iowa Professional Fire Fighters
  A-00-14. . . . . West Des Moines

Food and Commercial Workers

LU 79. . . . . Estherville
LU 86-D . . . . Muscatine
LU 179 . . . . Cherokee
LU 222 . . . . Sioux City
LU 230 . . . . Ottumwa
LU 431 . . . . Davenport
LU 440 . . . . Denison
LU 617 . . . . Fort Madison
LU 1142 . . . . Sioux City
LU 1149 . . . . Perry

Glass, Molders, Pottery and Plastics Workers

CONBD Iowa Area . . . . Newton
LU 9-B . . . . Keokuk
LU 17-B . . . . Creston
LU 74-B . . . . Newton
LU 359 . . . . Batavia
LU 388-A . . . . Ottumwa
LU 459 . . . . Waterloo

Government Employees

C 45 Food Inspection Councils
  National Joint. . . . . . . Sibley
C 202 Food Inspection Locals, Mid
  West . . . . Lone Tree
LU 744 USDA . . . . New Vienna
LU 766 USDA . . . . Storm Lake
LU 769 USDA . . . . . Sioux City
LU 836 . . . . Des Moines
LU 1226 VA . . . . . . Knoxville
LU 1228 VA . . . . . Des Moines
LU 2071 USDA . . . . . Waukee
LU 2315 USDA . . . . . . Ames
LU 2323 USDA. . . . . Denison
LU 2547 VA . . . . . . Iowa City
LU 2752 DoD . . . . . Hiawatha
LU 2773 USDA. . . . Washington
LU 2814 DoT . . . . Council Bluffs
LU 2826 DoD. . . . . Middletown
LU 2925 USDA . . . . Bettendorf
LU 2955 DoD . . . . Des Moines
LU 3390 USDA . . . . Storm Lake
LU 3452 HUD . . . . Des Moines
LU 3722 HHS . . . . . Dubuque
LU 3738 HHS . . . . . Davenport
LU 3886 SSA . . . . Cedar Rapids

Government Security Officers

LU 161 . . . . New Virginia

Graphic Communications

LU 157-M . . . . Des Moines
LU 518-M . . . . Davenport
LU 727-S . . . . Des Moines

Iron Workers

LU 67 . . . . Des Moines
LU 89 . . . . Cedar Rapids
LU 184 . . . . Sioux City
LU 493 . . . . Des Moines
LU 577 . . . . West Burlington
LU 691 . . . . Clinton

Laborers

LU 43 . . . . Cedar Rapids

LU 177 . . . . Des Moines
LU 205 . . . . Des Moines
LU 353 . . . . Des Moines

Letter Carriers

BR 69. . . . . Sioux City
BR 126 . . . . Clinton
BR 222 . . . . Burlington
BR 257 . . . . Dubuque
BR 314 . . . . Council Bluffs
BR 352 . . . . Des Moines
BR 371 . . . . Keokuk
BR 373 . . . . Cedar Rapids
BR 403 . . . . West Point
BR 445 . . . . Decorah
BR 447 . . . . Ottumwa
BR 471 . . . . Mason City
BR 483 . . . . Iowa City
BR 506 . . . . Davenport
BR 512 . . . . Waterloo
BR 611 . . . . Ogden
BR 644 . . . . Muscatine
BR 645 . . . . Fort Dodge
BR 655 . . . . Webster City
BR 660 . . . . Mount Pleasant
BR 665 . . . . Grinnell
BR 719 . . . . Waterloo
BR 726 . . . . Fairfield
BR 741 . . . . Independence
BR 805 . . . . Charles City
BR 851 . . . . Shenandoah
BR 925 . . . . Centerville
BR 1010 . . . . Estherville
BR 1036 . . . . Iowa Falls
BR 1040. . . . . Le Mars
BR 1070 . . . . Cherokee
BR 1075 . . . . Sheldon
BR 1081 . . . . Ames
BR 1268 . . . . Albia
BR 1284 . . . . Chariton
BR 1312 . . . . Indianola
BR 1318 . . . . Clarinda
BR 1373 . . . . Waverly
BR 1534 . . . . Hampton
BR 1559 . . . . Eagle Grove
BR 1626 . . . . Storm Lake
BR 1686 . . . . Jefferson
BR 1704 . . . . Harlan
BR 1791 . . . . Cresco
BR 1805 . . . . Eldora
BR 1808 . . . . Emmetsburg
BR 1839 . . . . Lamoni
BR 1920 . . . . Pella
BR 1931 . . . . New Hampton
BR 2034 . . . . Nevada
BR 2035 . . . . Rockwell City
BR 2192 . . . . Bloomfield
BR 2193 . . . . Corning
BR 2195 . . . . Murray
BR 2196 . . . . Seymour
BR 2197. . . . . Sigourney
BR 2198 . . . . Woodbine
BR 2227 . . . . Belle Plaine
BR 2231 . . . . Forest City
BR 2243 . . . . Manchester
BR 2334 . . . . Ida Grove
BR 2409 . . . . Waukon
BR 2413 . . . . Audubon
BR 2483 . . . . Clarion
BR 2507 . . . . Manning
BR 2508 . . . . Moulton
BR 2513 . . . . Hamburg
BR 2634 . . . . Rock Rapids
BR 2725 . . . . Dunlap
BR 2903 . . . . Greenfield

BR 2953. . . . . West Union
BR 2989 . . . . Villisca
BR 3043 . . . . Monticello
BR 3054. . . . . Sibley
BR 3142 . . . . Logan
BR 3149 . . . . Onawa
BR 3181 . . . . Tipton
BR 3429 . . . . Belmond
BR 3463 . . . . Spirit Lake
BR 3803 . . . . Rolfe
BR 3811 . . . . Bettendorf
BR 4140 . . . . Bellevue
BR 4196 . . . . Rock Valley
BR 4375 . . . . Garner
BR 4643 . . . . . . Orange City
BR 5026 . . . . Columbus Junction
BR 5028. . . . . Lake City
BR 5181 . . . . Lake Mills
BR 5182 . . . . Ackley
BR 5218 . . . . Laurens
BR 5221. . . . . Britt
BR 5222 . . . . Pocahontas
BR 5258 . . . . Sumner
BR 5341 . . . . Milford
BR 5392 . . . . Reinbeck
BR 5603 . . . . Traer
BR 5636. . . . . Wapello
BR 5667 . . . . Lenox
BR 5669 . . . . Mount Ayr
BR 5670. . . . . Story City
BR 5975 . . . . . . Underwood
BR 6004 . . . . Rockwell
BR 6265 . . . . Norwalk
BR 6294 . . . . Coon Rapids
SA Iowa . . . . Dubuque

Locomotive Engineers
DIV 6 . . . . Boone
DIV 114 . . . . Cedar Falls
DIV 125 . . . . Clinton
DIV 391 . . . . . . Fort Madison
DIV 642 . . . . Creston
DIV 656 . . . . Rockwell
DIV 687 . . . . . . Sergeant Bluff
DIV 778 . . . . Grimes
SLB Iowa . . . . Boone

Machinists
DLG 6 . . . . Des Moines
LG 254 . . . . Des Moines
LG 388 Tri City . . . . . Davenport
LG 831 . . . . Cedar Rapids
LG 1010 . . . . Fort Madison
LG 1045 . . . . Algona
LG 1238 . . . . Dubuque
LG 1293 . . . . Stockport
LG 1300 . . . . Clarinda
LG 1426 . . . . Sioux City
LG 1498 . . . . Eddyville
LG 1499 . . . . Muscatine
LG 1526 . . . . Amana
LG 1728 . . . . Waterloo
LLG W-2908 Woodworkers . . Elgin
STC Iowa . . . . . . Des Moines

Maintenance of Way Employes
LG 36 . . . . Wilton
LG 67 . . . . Cedar Rapids
LG 342 . . . . Des Moines
LG 381 . . . . Marshalltown
LG 437 . . . . Ogden
LG 626 . . . . Clare
LG 1148 . . . . Indianola
LG 1393 . . . . . . Fort Dodge
LG 1533 . . . . Burlington
LG 1757 . . . . Swaledale
LG 1935 . . . . Oelwein
LG 2920 . . . . Stuart

SLG 692. . . . . Deloit
SLG 1788 . . . . . Council Bluffs
SLG 1832 . . . . . Mount Pleasant
SLG 1847 . . . . . Cedar Rapids
SLG 1888 . . . . Creston

Musicians
LU 67 . . . . Davenport
LU 75 . . . . Des Moines
LU 137 . . . . . . Mount Vernon
LU 450 . . . . Iowa City

National Staff Organization
LU Staff Association, Support,
   Iowa Education
   Association . . . . . Des Moines
LU Staff Union, NSO,
   Iowa . . . . Sioux City

Nurses
LSC United Nurses
   Caring . . . . Le Grand
LU Professional Security Unit
   JEMH . . . . Persia
SA Iowa Nurses
   Association . . . West Des Moines
UNIT IANA-Des Moines
   VA . . . . Des Moines

Operating Engineers
LU 234 . . . . Des Moines
LU 275 . . . . Cedar Rapids
LU 758 . . . . Dubuque

Painters
DC 81 . . . . Ankeny
LU 214 . . . . Sioux City
LU 246 . . . . Des Moines
LU 447 . . . . Cedar Rapids
LU 676 . . . . Davenport
LU 1075 Glaziers and Glass
   Workers . . . . Ankeny
LU 2003 . . . . Alburnett

Plasterers and Cement Masons
LU 21 . . . . Des Moines
LU 561 . . . . Robins

Plumbing and Pipe Fitting
LU 33 . . . . Des Moines
LU 125 . . . . Cedar Rapids

Postal Mail Handlers
LU 333 . . . . . West Des Moines

Postal Workers
LU Iowa. . . . . Des Moines
LU 38 Keokuk. . . . . . . Keokuk
LU 44 Des Moines . . . Des Moines
LU 91 Davenport . . . Davenport
LU 153 Marshalltown
   Area. . . . . Marshalltown
LU 166 Rapid Area . . Cedar Rapids
LU 186 Sioux City . . . Sioux City
LU 213 Iowa Falls . . . Iowa Falls
LU 306 Mason City . . Mason City
LU 317 Fort Dodge . . . Fort Dodge
LU 383 Red Oak . . . Red Oak
LU 394 Mount
   Pleasant . . . . Mount Pleasant
LU 411 Burlington . . Burlington
LU 426 Carroll . . . . . . Carroll
LU 451 Waterloo . . . . Waterloo
LU 510 Council
   Bluffs . . . . Council Bluffs
LU 528 Hawkeye . . . . Iowa City
LU 725 Clinton . . . . . Clinton
LU 758 Maquoketa . . . Maquoketa

LU 813 Creston . . . . . . Creston
LU 881 Ottumwa . . . . Ottumwa
LU 904 Sheldon. . . . . . Sheldon
LU 1023 Centerville . . . Centerville
LU 1445 Fort
   Madison . . . . . Fort Madison
LU 1949 Grinnell . . . . . Grinnell
LU 1997 Muscatine. . . Muscatine
LU 2166 Oelwein. . . . . Oelwein
LU 2339 Dubuque . . . Dubuque
LU 3121 Ames . . . . . . Ames
LU 3962 Decorah. . . . . Decorah
LU 4082 Boone. . . . . . Boone
LU 4122 Cedar Falls . . Cedar Falls
LU 4266 Oskaloosa. . . Oskaloosa
LU 7027 Des Moines Bulk Mail
   Center. . . . . . Des Moines

Railroad Signalmen
GC 88 Union Pacific. . . . Rockford
LLG 43 . . . . Lake View
LLG 98 . . . . Norwalk

Retail, Wholesale and Department Store
LU 110 . . . . Cedar Rapids

Roofers, Waterproofers and Allied Workers
LU 142 . . . . Des Moines
LU 182 . . . . Marion

Rural Letter Carriers
D North Central Iowa . . . . Aredale
D Northeast Iowa . . . . . Peosta
D Southeast Iowa . . . . . Preston
D 63 South Central . . . . . Collins
D 65 Southwest Iowa . . . . Lenox
D 97 Northwest Iowa . . . Dickens
LU Benton County . . Mount Auburn
LU Bremer County . . . . Waverly
LU Butler County . . . . . Allison
LU Calhoun County . Rockwell City
LU Cass County . . . . . Griswold
LU Clayton County . . . Guttenberg
LU Clinton County . . . Charlotte
LU Crawford County. . . Manning
LU Jasper County . . . . . Newton
LU Marshall County . . . . Laurel
LU Muscatine County . . Muscatine
LU Palo Alto County . . . Havelock
LU Plymouth County . . . . Akron
LU Story County. . . . . . Huxley
LU Tama County . . . . Gladbrook
LU Wayne County . . . Allerton
LU 10 Buchanan County. . Hazleton
LU 14 Carroll County . Coon Rapids
LU 16 Cedar County . . . Clarence
LU 30 Hancock County . . . Keokuk
LU 66 Mitchell County . . . Osage
LU 83 Shelby County . . . Harlan
LU 96 Winneshiek
   County . . . . . . Fort Atkinson
SA Iowa . . . . Boyden

Security, Police and Fire Professionals
LU 214 . . . . Palo
LU 215 . . . . Newton
LU 218 . . . . Dubuque
LU 777 . . . . Council Bluffs

Service Employees
LU 199 . . . . Coralville

Sheet Metal Workers
DC Great Plains. . . . Des Moines
LU 45 . . . . Des Moines

LU 263 . . . . Cedar Rapids

State, County and Municipal Employees
C 61 . . . . Des Moines
C 2051 Prairie Meadows Racetrack &
   Casino. . . . . Des Moines
LU 1547 University of Osteo
   Medicine & Health
   Sciences . . . . . . Des Moines
LU 3420 Alliance of Chiropractic
   Educators . . . . Davenport
LU 3538 Heritage 53 Employees
   Council 31 . . . . . . Davenport
LU 3746 Iowa Council
   61 . . . . Marshalltown

Steelworkers
LU 07-249 . . . . Keokuk
LU 07-436 . . . . Center Point
LU 07-502 . . . . Fort Dodge
LU 07-503 . . . . Fort Dodge
LU 07-604 . . . . Mason City
LU 07-709 . . . . Waterloo
LU 07-743 . . . . Tama
LU 07-761 . . . . Clinton
LU 07-795 . . . . Council Bluffs
LU 07-827 . . . . Waterloo
LU 07-1257. . . . . . . Sioux City
LU 07-1774. . . . . . Marshalltown
LU 11-105-A . . . . . . Bettendorf
LU 11-164-L . . . . . . Des Moines
LU 11-310-L . . . . . . Des Moines
LU 11-444-L . . . . Keokuk
LU 11-932-L . . . . Argyle
LU 11-1149-L . . . . . Farmington
LU 11-1861-U . . . . . . Dubuque
LU 11-3141-S . . . . Council Bluffs
LU 11-3311-S . . . . Keokuk
LU 11-8581-S . . . . Wilton
LU 11-9310-S . . . . . Mason City
LU 11-9317-S . . . . . Mason City

Teamsters
LU 90 . . . . Des Moines
LU 238 . . . . Cedar Rapids
LU 421 . . . . Dubuque

Theatrical Stage Employees
LU 67 . . . . Bondurant
LU 85 . . . . Davenport
LU 690 . . . . Iowa City

Transit Union
LDIV 1192 . . . . Waterloo

Transportation Communications Union
LG 512 . . . . Council Bluffs
LG 713 . . . . Fort Madison
LG 763 . . . . Council Bluffs
LG 6069 Trans United . . Oelwein
LG 6091 Hawkeye. . . . Cedar Falls

Transportation Union
LU 17 . . . . Marshalltown
LU 199 . . . . Creston
LU 228 . . . . Hiawatha
LU 258 . . . . Davenport
LU 306 . . . . Eagle Grove
LU 316 . . . . Clinton
LU 329 . . . . Boone
LU 493 . . . . Waterloo
LU 643 . . . . West Point
LU 646 . . . . Council Bluffs
LU 867 . . . . Ames
LU 872 . . . . Council Bluffs
SLB LO-18 Iowa . . . Des Moines

Treasury Employees
CH 4 . . . . Des Moines

UNITE HERE
LU 146 . . . . Hudson
LU 180-LDC . . . . Dubuque
LU 497 . . . . Cedar Rapids

Utility Workers
LU 525 . . . . Davenport
LU 526 . . . . Clinton

Weather Service Employees
BR 03-49 . . . . Johnston
BR 03-96 . . . . Davenport

Unaffiliated Labor Organizations
Drug Products Employees
    Association Iowa City . . Riverside
Employee's Committee of Le Mars
    and Omaha . . . . George
Industrial Workers Union LU
    860 . . . . Des Moines

International Association of Tool
    Craftsmen LU 1 . . . . Bettendorf
International Guards Union of
    America LU 22 . . . Fort Madison
International Guards Union of
    America RC Third . . . Burlington
Transparent Film Workers
    Inc . . . . Clinton
Umthun Trucking Employees
    Association . . . . . Eagle Grove
United Staff Union of
    Iowa . . . . Des Moines

Kansas

AFL-CIO Trade and Industrial Departments

Building and Construction Trades Department
BCTC Central & Western Kansas . . . . Wichita
BCTC Kansas . . . . Topeka
BCTC Northeast Kansas . . . Topeka
BCTC Southeast Kansas . . Parsons

Metal Trades Department
MTC Coffeyville . . . . Coffeyville

Affiliated Labor Organizations

Air Traffic Controllers
LU ICT . . . . Wichita
LU ZKC . . . . Olathe

Asbestos Workers
LU 1 Production Workers . . . . Kansas City

Automobile, Aerospace Workers
LU 31 . . . . Kansas City
LU 31 Kansas State Community Action Program . . . Kansas City
LU 1021 . . . . Olathe
LU 2366 . . . . Coffeyville

Bakery, Confectionery, Tobacco Workers and Grain Millers
LU 57-G . . . . Topeka
LU 73-G . . . . Lawrence
LU 99-G . . . . Wichita
LU 107-G . . . . Salina
LU 158-G . . . . Dodge City
LU 200-G . . . . Newton
LU 218-A . . . . Overland Park
LU 245 . . . . Wichita
LU 335-G . . . . Leavenworth
LU 402-G . . . . Atchison

Boilermakers
LG 34 . . . . Topeka
LG 75-D Cement Workers . Fredonia
LG 76-D Cement Workers . Sun City
LG 84 . . . . Paola
LG 93-D Cement Workers . . . . Humboldt
LG 109-D Cement Workers . . . . Independence
LG 194-D Cement Workers . . . . Chanute
LG 1101 Quality Control . . . . Kansas City
NHQ . . . . Kansas City

Carpenters
LU 168 . . . . Kansas City
LU 201 . . . . Wichita
LU 714 . . . . Olathe
LU 918 . . . . Manhattan
LU 1445 . . . . Topeka

Civilian Technicians
CH 74 Wichita Air Capitol . Wichita
CH 104 Jayhawk . . . . . . Topeka
CH 129 Kansas Coyotes . . . Lyndon

Communications Workers
LU 6401 . . . . Topeka

LU 6402 . . . . Wichita
LU 6406 . . . . Colby
LU 6407 . . . . Lawrence
LU 6409 . . . . Basehor
LU 6410 . . . . Pittsburg
LU 6411 . . . . Abilene
LU 6412 . . . . Liberal
LU 14607 . . . . Peck
LU 86004 . . . . . . Arkansas City

Electrical Workers
LU 226 . . . . Topeka
LU 271 . . . . Wichita
LU 304 . . . . Topeka
LU 661 . . . . Hutchinson
LU 959 . . . . Horton
LU 1523 . . . . Wichita

Federal Employees
LU 1765 . . . . Leavenworth
LU 1807 . . . . Topeka

Food and Commercial Workers
LU 74-D . . . . Atchison
LU 188-C . . . . Hutchinson
LU 278-C . . . . Chase
LU 409-G . . . . . . Baxter Springs
LU 431-G . . . . Tonganoxie
LU 509-G . . . . Fontana
LU 605-C . . . . Lawrence

Glass, Molders, Pottery and Plastics Workers
LU 198 . . . . Buffalo
LU 233 . . . . Olathe

Government Employees
C 131 Ninth District . . . . Mission
LU 9 At-Large . . . . Erie
LU 85 VA . . . . . . Leavenworth
LU 477 VA . . . . Wichita
LU 482 USDA . . . . . Emporia
LU 738 DoD . . . Fort Leavenworth
LU 834 USDA . . . . . Derby
LU 919 DoJ . . . . . Leavenworth
LU 1737 DoD . . . . . . Wichita
LU 1939 Topeka . . . . . . Topeka
LU 2324 DoD . . . . . Fort Riley
LU 3629 EEOC . . . . Kansas City
LU 3960 HUD . . . . Kansas City

Government Employees Association
LU 14-8 . . . . Topeka

Government Security Officers
LU 154 . . . . Topeka

Graphic Communications
LU 49-C . . . . Tecumseh
LU 147-C . . . . Wichita
LU 560-S . . . . Topeka
LU 575-M . . . . Wichita

Independent Unions
LU 228 Hesston Corporation Workers Association . . . Hesston

Iron Workers
LU 606 . . . . Wichita

Laborers
LU 142 . . . . Topeka

Letter Carriers
BR 10 Capital City Letter Carriers . . . . Topeka
BR 104 . . . . Lawrence
BR 141 . . . . Atchison
BR 185 . . . . Emporia
BR 194 . . . . . . Arkansas City
BR 201 . . . . Wichita
BR 412 . . . . Winfield
BR 477 . . . . Erie
BR 485 . . . . Hutchinson
BR 486 . . . . Salina
BR 499 . . . . Kansas City
BR 582 . . . . Ottawa
BR 695 . . . . Pittsburg
BR 766 . . . . Edna
BR 834 . . . . Iola
BR 1018 . . . . Manhattan
BR 1035 . . . . . . Independence
BR 1055 . . . . Chanute
BR 1122 . . . . . . Great Bend
BR 1171 . . . . . . McPherson
BR 1190 . . . . Girard
BR 1205 . . . . Beloit
BR 1344 . . . . Fredonia
BR 1412 . . . . . . Garden City
BR 1560 . . . . . . Columbus
BR 1573 . . . . Anthony
BR 1579 . . . . . . Dodge City
BR 1679 . . . . Pratt
BR 2046 . . . . Lyons
BR 2115 . . . . Liberal
BR 2161 . . . . Hays
BR 2275 . . . . . . Goodland
BR 2276 . . . . Norton
BR 2338 . . . . . . Osborne
BR 2451 . . . . Horton
BR 2519 . . . . . . Sterling
BR 2630 . . . . Marion
BR 2774 . . . . Seneca
BR 2787 . . . . . . Washington
BR 2895 . . . . . . Baxter Springs
BR 3197 . . . . . . Frankfort
BR 3313 . . . . . . Oswego
BR 4036 . . . . . . Oberlin
BR 4170 . . . . . . Hillsboro
BR 4288 . . . . . . Mankato
BR 4289 . . . . . . Ellinwood
BR 4306 . . . . Kiowa
BR 4341 . . . . . . Scott City
BR 4635 . . . . Colby
BR 4720 . . . . . . Haysville
BR 4727 . . . . . . Peabody
BR 4746 . . . . . . Plainville
BR 4824 . . . . . . Valley Center
BR 4832 . . . . . . Oakley
BR 4840 . . . . . . Ness City
BR 4983 . . . . . . Halstead
BR 5034 . . . . . . Harper
BR 5035 . . . . . . Wakefield
BR 5336 . . . . . . Hill City
BR 5418 . . . . . . St. Marys
BR 5521 . . . . . . Prairie Villiage
BR 5587 . . . . . . Wakeeney
BR 5884 . . . . . . Atwood
BR 6031 . . . . . . Greensburg
SA Kansas . . . . Colby

Locomotive Engineers
DIV 64 . . . . Douglass
DIV 90 . . . . . . Council Grove
DIV 130 . . . . Lenexa
DIV 179 . . . . Altamont
DIV 224 . . . . . . Marysville
DIV 237 . . . . . . Fort Scott

DIV 261 . . . . Herington
DIV 344 . . . . . . Wellington
DIV 364 . . . . Wichita
DIV 462 . . . . . . Arkansas City
DIV 527 . . . . . . Pittsburg
DIV 587 . . . . Salina
DIV 740 . . . . Iuka
SLB Kansas . . . . . Hoisington

Machinists
DLG 70 . . . . Wichita
LG 293 . . . . Altamont
LG 356 . . . . Olathe
LG 378 . . . . . . Silver Lake
LG 639 . . . . Wichita
LG 693 . . . . . . Cherryvale
LG 708 . . . . Wichita
LG 733 . . . . Wichita
LG 774 . . . . Wichita
LG 834 . . . . Wichita
LG 839 . . . . Wichita
LG 1989 . . . . . . Wichita
LG 1992 . . . . . . Wichita
LG 1994 . . . . . . Wichita
LG 2328 . . . . . . Wichita
LG 2799 . . . . . . Wichita
STC Kansas . . . . . Wichita

Maintenance of Way Employes
FED Southwestern . . . . Coffeyville
LG 455 . . . . . . Fort Scott
LG 1333 . . . . . . Hoisington
LG 1659 . . . . . . Lenexa
LG 2404 . . . . . . Ottawa
LG 2407 . . . . . . Hutchinson
SF Atchison Topeka & Santa Fe . . . . . . Newton
SLG 345 . . . . Erie
SLG 376 . . . . . . Herington
SLG 487 . . . . . . Atchison
SLG 518 . . . . . . Cherokee
SLG 688 . . . . . . Hiawatha
SLG 934 . . . . . . Marion
SLG 1175 . . . . . Wellington
SLG 1216 . . . . . Topeka
SLG 2405 . . . . . Topeka
SLG 2406 . . . . . Newton
SLG 2412 . . . . . Newton

Mine Workers
LU 14 . . . . Pittsburg

Musicians
CONF Regional Orchestra Players' Association . . . . . Wichita
LU 169 Manhattan . . . . Manhattan
LU 297 . . . . Wichita

National Staff Organization
LU Local Union Staff Organization, Kansas . . . . Topeka

NLRB Professional Association
LU 17 . . . . Overland Park

Nurses
SA Kansas State Nurses Association . . . . . . Topeka

Operating Engineers
LU 119 . . . . Wichita
LU 123 . . . . Coffeyville
LU 126 . . . . Parsons
LU 418 . . . . Russell
LU 647 . . . . Allen

Painters
LU 76 . . . . Wichita
LU 96 . . . . Topeka
LU 229 . . . . Kansas City
LU 1594. . . . . Kansas City

Plumbing and Pipe Fitting
LU 441 . . . . Wichita

Postal Workers
LU 194 Dodge City . . . Dodge City
LU 238 Kansas Kaw Valley
   Area. . . . . Kansas City
LU 265 Pittsburg . . . . . . Pittsburg
LU 393 Lawrence . . . . Lawrence
LU 439 Hutchinson . . . Hutchinson
LU 447 Coffeyville . . . Coffeyville
LU 506 Atchison . . . . . . Atchison
LU 576 Parsons . . . . . . Parsons
LU 582 Arkansas
   City . . . . Arkansas City
LU 588 Manhattan . . . . Manhattan
LU 617 Chanute . . . . . . Chanute
LU 639 Great Bend . . . Great Bend
LU 670 Topeka . . . . . . Topeka
LU 735 Wichita . . . . . . Wichita
LU 743 Fort Scott . . . . Fort Scott
LU 886 Salina . . . . Salina
LU 890 Olathe . . . . Olathe
LU 1145 Garden City . . Garden City
LU 1274 Leavenworth . Leavenworth
LU 2009 Northwest Kansas
   Area . . . . Hays
LU 2021 Liberal . . . . . . Liberal
LU 2665 Colby . . . . Colby
LU 4117 Ottawa . . . . . . Ottawa
LU 4458 Junction City . . Fort Riley
LU 5706 Paola . . . . Paola
LU 6862 Western Area Supply
   Center . . . . Topeka
SA Kansas . . . . Topeka

Railroad Signalmen
LLG 21 . . . . Kansas City
LLG 33 . . . . Emporia

LLG 157 . . . . Herington

Retail, Wholesale and Department Store
LU 184-L . . . . Kansas City

Rural Letter Carriers
D 1 . . . . Tonganoxie
D 2 . . . . Emporia
D 3 . . . . Beloit
D 4 . . . . Great Bend
LU Clay County . . . . . Clay Center
LU Cowley County . . . . Burden
LU Marshall County . . . . Beatie
LU 21 Brown County . . . Seneca
LU 23 Cloud County . . . . Clyde
LU 52 Chase County . . Strong City
LU 113 Mitchell County . Glen Elder
LU 133 Osborne County . Natoma
LU 141 Pottowatomie
   County . . . . Onaga
LU 181 Washington
   County . . . . Washington
LU 203 Saline County . . . Salina
SA Kansas . . . . McPherson

Security, Police and Fire Professionals
LU 252 . . . . Burlington
LU 253 . . . . Galesburg
LU 255 . . . . Derby

Service Employees
LU 513 . . . . Wichita
LU 1086 Firemen & Oilers . Topeka
LU 1099 Firemen & Oilers . Newton

Sheet Metal Workers
LU 29 . . . . Wichita
LU 77 . . . . Topeka
LU 165 . . . . Mission
LU 472. . . . . St. Marys

Steelworkers
DC 5 . . . . El Dorado

LU 05-114. . . . . . . Tonganoxie
LU 05-241 . . . . El Dorado
LU 05-348 . . . . . . Kansas City
LU 05-495 . . . . Pittsburg
LU 05-508. . . . . Oswego
LU 05-558. . . . . . . McPherson
LU 05-571 . . . . Marysville
LU 05-765 . . . . . . Kansas City
LU 05-813 . . . . . . Edwardsville
LU 05-1146 . . . . . . Shawnee
LU 05-1350 . . . . . . Hutchinson
LU 11-307-L . . . . . . Topeka
LU 11-3092-S . . . . . . Atchison
LU 11-6943-S . . . . . . Atchison
LU 11-12561-S . . . . Kansas City
LU 11-12606-S . . . . Hutchinson
LU 11-12788-S . . . . . Ellsworth
LU 11-13417-S . . . . . Wichita
LU 11-15312-S . . . . . Neodesha

Teamsters
LU 696. . . . . Topeka
LU 795 . . . . Wichita

Theatrical Stage Employees
LU 190 . . . . Wichita
LU 464 . . . . Salina
SA Kansas . . . . Benton

Transportation Communications Union
LG 427 . . . . Topeka
LG 843 . . . . Topeka
LG 6026 Berwind . . . Independence
LG 6054 Coffeyville . . . . Wichita
LG 6762 Armstrong . . Kansas City
LG 6850 Argentine . . . Kansas City
LG 6887 Shawnee . . . . . Topeka

Transportation Union
GCA GO-953 Union Pacific Railroad
   Eastern. . . . . Topeka
LU 44 . . . . Agra
LU 94 . . . . Kansas City
LU 445 . . . . Overland Park

LU 464 . . . . Arkansas City
LU 477 . . . . Emporia
LU 495 . . . . Salina
LU 506 . . . . Herington
LU 527 . . . . Coffeyville
LU 533 . . . . Osawatomie
LU 707 . . . . Marysville
LU 763 . . . . Frontenac
LU 774 . . . . Leavenworth
LU 1126. . . . . Pratt
LU 1227 . . . . Wichita
LU 1409 . . . . Shawnee
LU 1532. . . . . Kansas City
LU 1780 . . . . Merriam
SLB LO-19 Kansas. . . Osawatomie

Treasury Employees
CH 51 . . . . Mission
CH 254 . . . . Lenexa
CH 294 . . . . Kansas City

UNITE HERE
LU 803. . . . . Junction City

Weather Service Employees
BR 03-12. . . . . Topeka
BR 03-17 . . . . Wichita
BR 03-55 . . . . Goodland
BR 03-61 . . . . Olathe
BR 03-91 . . . . . . Dodge City

Unaffiliated Labor Organizations
Contech Construction Products,
   Topeka Shop Committee . Topeka
Dillons Employees
   Association . . . . . Hutchinson
Kansas State Union Label & Service
   Trades Council of the Kansas
   AFL-CIO . . . . Topeka
Office Employees Committee
   International
   Brotherhood . . . . . Kansas City
Quality Control Council of the United
   States Joint Council . Kansas City

Kentucky

AFL-CIO Trade and Industrial Departments

Building and Construction Trades Department
BCTC Central Kentucky . Lexington
BCTC Greater Louisville . Louisville
BCTC Kentucky. . . . . . Frankfort
BCTC Owensboro . . . . . Owensboro
BCTC Tri-State . . . . . . Ashland
BCTC Western Kentucky. . Paducah

AFL-CIO Directly Affiliated Locals

AFL-CIO
DALU 3039 Billposters &
  Billers . . . . Florence

Affiliated Labor Organizations

Air Traffic Controllers
LU CKB . . . . Erlanger
LU LEX. . . . . Lexington
LU LOU. . . . . Louisville
LU OWB . . . . Owensboro
LU SDF . . . . Louisville

Asbestos Workers
LU 51 . . . . Louisville

Automobile, Aerospace Workers
C 5th & 6th Districts of
  Kentucky. . . . . Livingston
C Kentucky-First Area . . . Kuttawa
C South Central
  Kentucky . . . . Bowling Green
C Third & Fourth Areas-
  Kentucky . . . . Louisville
LU 43 . . . . Louisville
LU 523 . . . . Calvert City
LU 862 . . . . Louisville
LU 912. . . . . Nicholasville
LU 1584 . . . . Milton
LU 1608 . . . . Winchester
LU 1772 . . . . Versailles
LU 1813 . . . . Milton
LU 1937. . . . . Cynthiana
LU 2012 . . . . Buffalo
LU 2164 . . . . . . Bowling Green
LU 2302 . . . . Bardstown
LU 2306 . . . . Burkesville
LU 2309. . . . . Fairdale
LU 2370. . . . . Franklin
LU 2383 . . . . Frankfort
LU 2386 . . . . Nebo
LU 2407. . . . . Russellville
LU 2926 . . . . Shelbyville
LU 3047. . . . . Vine Grove

Bakery, Confectionery, Tobacco Workers and Grain Millers
LU 16-T. . . . . Louisville
LU 196-T . . . . Owensboro
LU 201-T . . . . Louisville
LU 365-T. . . . . Mayfield
LU 531. . . . . London

Boilermakers
LG 3-P Professional EMTs and
  Paramedics . . . . . Owensboro
LG 20-S . . . . Louisville

LG 40. . . . . Elizabethtown
LG 595-D . . . . . . Brandenburg
LG 726. . . . . Owensboro
LG 727. . . . . Whitesville
LG 1633 . . . . Greenup

Bricklayers
LU 17. . . . . Lexington

Carpenters
LU 64 . . . . Louisville
LU 96-T . . . . Frankfort
LU 357 . . . . Paducah
LU 472 . . . . Ashland
LU 549. . . . . Owensboro
LU 1031. . . . . Louisville
LU 1080 . . . . Owensboro
LU 1299 . . . . Covington
LU 1650. . . . . Lexington
LU 2501. . . . . Louisville
LU 3191 . . . . Beaver Dam
LU 3223 . . . . . . Elizabethtown

Civilian Technicians
CH 69 Bluegrass . . . . . Louisville
CH 83 Kentucky Longrifle
  Chapter . . . . Magnolia

Communications Workers
LU 229 . . . . Lexington
LU 3301 . . . . . Bowling Green
LU 3304 . . . . Danville
LU 3305 . . . . Shelbyville
LU 3309 . . . . Hopkinsville
LU 3310. . . . . Louisville
LU 3312 . . . . Madisonville
LU 3313 . . . . Pineville
LU 3314 . . . . Owensboro
LU 3315. . . . . Paducah
LU 3317 . . . . Pikeville
LU 3321 . . . . Winchester
LU 3371 . . . . Flatwoods
LU 3372. . . . . Lexington
LU 54044. . . . . Newport
LU 83697. . . . . . . Lebanon
LU 83701 . . . . . . Madisonville
LU 83743. . . . . Leitchfield
LU 83761 . . . . Louisville
LU 83766. . . . . . Elizabethtown
LU 83767 . . . . Somerset
LU 84795. . . . . . . Taylormill

Electrical Workers
LU 369 . . . . Louisville
LU 463. . . . . Campbellsville
LU 816 . . . . Paducah
LU 940 . . . . Worthington
LU 1353 . . . . London
LU 1625 . . . . Corbin
LU 1627. . . . . Lexington
LU 1701 . . . . Owensboro
LU 2100. . . . . Louisville
LU 2220. . . . . Lexington
LU 2246 . . . . . Mount Sterling
LU 2356 . . . . Richmond
SC 9 Railroad . . . . . London

Elevator Constructors
LU 20 . . . . Louisville

Engineers
LU 852 . . . . Louisville

Federal Employees
LU 466. . . . . Whitley City

LU 1579. . . . . Louisville

Fire Fighters
LU 45 Newport. . . . . . . Newport
LU 291-F Lexington Blue Grass
  Army Depot . . . . . Richmond
LU 927. . . . . . . Bowling Green

Food and Commercial Workers
LU 10-D . . . . Lawrenceburg
LU 23-D . . . . Bardstown
LU 24-D . . . . Frankfort
LU 28-D . . . . Guston
LU 31-D . . . . Owensboro
LU 38-D . . . . Frankfort
LU 72-D. . . . . Louisville
LU 111-D. . . . . Bardstown
LU 227 . . . . Louisville
LU 342-C . . . . Covington
LU 663-C . . . . Louisville
LU 664-C . . . . Elsmere
LU 970-C . . . . . . Elizabethtown
RC 4 . . . . Florence

Glass, Molders, Pottery and Plastics Workers
LU 176 . . . . Sparta
LU 334-A . . . . Somerset

Government Employees
C 73 National Field Labor
  Locals . . . . Pikeville
LU 608 . . . . Fort Knox
LU 817 HHS . . . . . . Lexington
LU 1123 USDA. . . . . . Louisville
LU 1133 VA . . . . . . Louisville
LU 1160 DoL . . . . . Louisville
LU 1286 DoJ . . . . . . Ashland
LU 1411 DoD. . . . . . Louisville
LU 2022 DoD . . . . Fort Campbell
LU 2302 DoD. . . . . . Fort Knox
LU 3228 USDA. . . . . . Paducah
LU 3431 DoL . . . . . Middlesboro
LU 3984 . . . . Frankfort
LU 4051 . . . . Manchester
LU 12-612 CPL-33 . . . Debord

Government Employees Association
LU 05-184 . . . . Lexington

Government Security Officers
LU 143. . . . . Owensboro

Graphic Communications
LU 619-M. . . . . Louisville

Iron Workers
LU 70 . . . . Louisville
LU 769 . . . . Ashland
LU 782 . . . . Paducah

Laborers
DC 210 Kentucky . . Lawrenceburg
LU 189 . . . . Lexington
LU 576 . . . . Louisville
LU 1214. . . . . Paducah
LU 1392 . . . . Owensboro
LU 1445. . . . . Catlettsburg

Letter Carriers
BR 14 . . . . Louisville
BR 234. . . . . Owensboro
BR 361 . . . . Lexington
BR 374 . . . . . Highland Heights

BR 383 . . . . Paducah
BR 410 . . . . Henderson
BR 468. . . . . . . Bowling Green
BR 745 . . . . Ashland
BR 836. . . . . Hopkinsville
BR 1106 . . . . Mayfield
BR 1265 . . . . . . Mount Sterling
BR 1408 . . . . Madisonville
BR 1616 . . . . Middlesboro
BR 1701 . . . . Shelbyville
BR 1827. . . . . Fulton
BR 1909 . . . . Lebanon
BR 1988. . . . . Russellville
BR 2010 . . . . Morganfield
BR 2014 . . . . . Dawson Springs
BR 2039 . . . . Somerset
BR 2156 . . . . Murray
BR 2188 . . . . Princeton
BR 2226 . . . . Pineville
BR 2242 . . . . London
BR 2306 . . . . Providence
BR 2444 . . . . Earlington
BR 2648 . . . . Carlisle
BR 2668 . . . . Harlan
BR 2773 . . . . . . Campbellsville
BR 2856 . . . . . . Barbourville
BR 2883. . . . . Carrollton
BR 2891 . . . . Clinton
BR 2892 . . . . Pikeville
BR 2933 . . . . Hickman
BR 2973 . . . . Paintsville
BR 3308 . . . . Marion
BR 3438 . . . . La Grange
BR 3484. . . . . Franklin
BR 3494. . . . . . . Flemingsburg
BR 3515 . . . . . . Elizabethtown
BR 3554 . . . . . . Williamstown
BR 3569 . . . . Irvine
BR 3623. . . . . Augusta
BR 3624 . . . . . . Lawrenceburg
BR 3640 . . . . Sturgis
BR 3660 . . . . Walton
BR 3666 . . . . Morehead
BR 3753 . . . . Bardstown
BR 3857 . . . . Hazard
BR 4391 . . . . Prestonsburg
BR 5355 . . . . Columbia
BR 5492 . . . . Scottsville
BR 5799 . . . . Leitchfield
BR 5883 . . . . . . Tompkinsville
BR 6067 . . . . Springfield
BR 6094 . . . . Greensburg
BR 6288 . . . . Manchester
BR 6531 . . . . Brandenburg
BR 6537 . . . . Cumberland
BR 6538 . . . . West Liberty
BR 6547 . . . . West Point
BR 6609 . . . . Whitesburg
SA Kentucky . . . . . . Lexington

Locomotive Engineers
DIV 39 . . . . Fort Thomas
DIV 78 . . . . Shepherdsville
DIV 110 . . . . Edgewood
DIV 199 . . . . . . Mount Vernon
DIV 211 . . . . Cold Spring
DIV 271. . . . . Flatwoods
DIV 365 Adair
  Division . . . . . Shepherdsville
DIV 463 Corbin . . . . . Corbin
DIV 489 . . . . Edgewood
DIV 698 . . . . Pikeville
DIV 742 . . . . Hanson
DIV 804 . . . . Covington
DIV 829 . . . . Irvine

DIV 830 . . . . Sassafras

Machinists
DLG 19 . . . . Paducah
DLG 27 . . . . Louisville
DLG 154 . . . . Calvert City
LG 123 . . . . Paducah
LG 249 . . . . Worthington
LG 376 . . . . Erlanger
LG 619 . . . . Winchester
LG 681 . . . . Louisville
LG 804 . . . . Florence
LG 830 . . . . Louisville
LG 859 . . . . Richmond
LG 1073 . . . . Corbin
LG 1157 . . . . . . West Paducah
LG 1294 . . . . Boaz
LG 1404 . . . . Lexington
LG 1441 . . . . Russellville
LG 1720 . . . . Calvert City
LG 1969 . . . . Gilbertsville
LG 2244 . . . . Graham
LG 2396 . . . . Crofton
LG 2409 . . . . Louisville
LG 2507 . . . . Fredonia
LG 2781 . . . . Eddyville
LLG W-366
  Woodworkers . . . Bradfordsville
STC Kentucky State Council of
  Machinists . . . . . . Calvert City

Maintenance of Way Employes
FED Illinois Central Gulf . Mayfield
LG 8 . . . . Vanceburg
LG 225 . . . . Prestonsburg
LG 1038. . . . . Argillite
LG 1210 . . . . Princeton
LG 2388 . . . . . Mammoth Cave
LG 2619 . . . . Walton
SF Affiliated System
  Federation . . . . . Catlettsburg
SLG 139 . . . . London
SLG 613 . . . . South Williamson
SLG 636 . . . . Erlanger
SLG 671 . . . . Brodhead
SLG 818 . . . . Henderson
SLG 1464 . . . . Louisa
SLG 1674 . . . . Irvine
SLG 1745 . . . . Jackson

Mine Workers
LU 30 . . . . Pikeville
LU 105 . . . . Pikeville
LU 621 District 17 . . . . . Phelps
LU 1092 . . . . Central City
LU 1178 . . . . Central City
LU 1464 . . . . Powderly
LU 1468 . . . . Pikeville
LU 1511 . . . . Phelps
LU 1569 . . . . Middlesboro
LU 1605 . . . . Central City
LU 1623 . . . . . Dawson Springs
LU 1740 . . . . Uniontown
LU 1741 . . . . Wayland
LU 1793 . . . . Morganfield
LU 1802 . . . . Sturgis
LU 1812 . . . . Whitesburg
LU 1830 . . . . Madisonville
LU 1905 . . . . Uniontown
LU 2001 School Employees . Evarts
LU 2264 . . . . Pikeville
LU 2305 . . . . Sturgis
LU 2360 . . . . Lewisburg
LU 2390 Moorman Surface
  Mines. . . . . Greenville
LU 2395 . . . . Greenville
LU 2470 . . . . Morganfield
LU 3000 . . . . Beaver Dam

LU 5138 . . . . Princeton
LU 5737 . . . . Pinsonfork
LU 5741 . . . . Jenkins
LU 5899 . . . . Bevinsville
LU 5967 . . . . Hi Hat
LU 6492 . . . . Beaver Dam
LU 7093 . . . . Lovely
LU 7425 . . . . Cumberland
LU 8198 . . . . Benton
LU 8588 . . . . Elkhorn City
LU 8790 . . . . Beechmont
LU 8941 . . . . Caneyville
LU 9653 . . . . Madisonville
LU 9800 . . . . Hartford
LU 9845 . . . . Langley

Musicians
LU 11-637. . . . . Louisville
LU 554-635 . . . . Lexington

National Staff Organization
LU Staff Organization,
  Kentucky Education
  Association. . . . . Elizabethtown

Nurses
LSC Hazard ARH Unit, KNA Local
  Union 104 . . . . Hazard
LSC McDowell ARH-KNA-Unit
  Local Union 112 . . . . Langley
LSC Middlesboro ARH KNA Unit
  Local Union 106 . . . Middlesboro
LSC Whiteburg-ARH Unit KNA
  Local Union 111 . . . . . . Eolia
LU 102 Kentucky. . . . . Lexington
LU 103 Williamson Appalachian
  Regional . . . . Mouthcard
LU 114 Harlan ARH-KNA Unit
  114 . . . . Cawood
SA Kentucky Nurses
  Association . . . . Louisville

Office and Professional Employees
LU 172 . . . . Paducah

Operating Engineers
LU 181 . . . . Henderson

Painters
LU 118 . . . . Louisville
LU 238 . . . . Alexandria
LU 500 . . . . Paducah

Pilots, Independent
NHQ. . . . . Louisville

Plant Protection
LU 115 Ford Motor Company
  Unit. . . . . Bellevue

Plasterers and Cement Masons
LU 135 . . . . Murray

Plumbing and Pipe Fitting
LU 184 . . . . Paducah
LU 248 . . . . Ashland
LU 452 . . . . Lexington
LU 502 Pipe Fitter's . . . Louisville
LU 633. . . . . Owensboro

Postal Workers
LU 4 Louisville . . . . . Louisville
LU 343 Russellville . . . Russellville
LU 350 Owensboro . . . Owensboro
LU 453 Bowling Green
  Area . . . . Bowling Green
LU 1318 Lebanon . . . . Lebanon
LU 1370 Covington . . . Covington

LU 1552 Madisonville. Madisonville
LU 2275
  Elizabethtown . . . Elizabethtown
LU 2307 Central Kentucky
  Area. . . . . Lexington
LU 2324 Pikeville . . . . Pikeville
LU 2325 Somerset . . . . . Somerset
LU 2500 Paducah . . . . Paducah
LU 2608 Southeastern Kentucky
  Area . . . . London
LU 3298 La Grange . . . La Grange
LU 3332 Whitesburg . . Whitesburg
LU 4551 Louisa. . . . . Catlettsburg
LU 4741 Grayson. . . . Catlettsburg
LU 5529 Maysville . . . . Maysville
LU 5546 Fort Knox. . . . Fort Knox
LU 6593 Campton . . . . . Campton
LU 6605 Salyersville . . Salyersville
LU 6662 Radcliff . . . . . Radcliff
LU 6696
  Shepherdsville. . . Shepherdsville
SA Kentucky . . . . . . Louisville

Railroad Signalmen
LLG 13 . . . . Louisville
LLG 46 . . . . Beaver Dam
LLG 51 . . . . Princeton
LLG 176 . . . . Walton
LLG 215 . . . . Irvine
LLG 234 Safetran. . . . Taylorsville

Roofers, Waterproofers and Allied Workers
LU 147 . . . . Louisville

Rural Letter Carriers
D 1 . . . . Louisa
D 1 District A . . . . Kevil
D 2 District B . . . . . Leitchfield
D 3 District C . . . . Bowling Green
D 4 District D. . . . . Hodgenville
D 5 District E . . . . . . Louisville
D 6 District F. . . . . . . Walton
D 7 District G. . . . . Georgetown
D 8 District H . . . . . Monticello
LU Obion-Lake Counties . Hickman
LU Warren County . Bowling Green
SA Kentucky . . . . . . Louisville

Security, Police and Fire Professionals
LU 110 . . . . Louisville
LU 111 . . . . Paducah

Service Employees
LU 5 National Conference of
  Firemen & Oilers. . . . . Grayson
LU 77 Firemen & Oilers. . . Berea
LU 320 Firemen & Oilers. Louisville
LU 362 Firemen & Oilers . . Corbin
LU 541 Racetrack Employees
  Union . . . . Louisville
LU 578 Firemen & Oilers . . Walton
LU 593 Firemen &
  Oilers. . . . . Worthington
LU 637 Firemen & Oilers. Ashland
LU 754 Firemen & Oilers . Greenup

Sheet Metal Workers
LU 110 . . . . Louisville
LU 226 . . . . Erlanger
LU 261 . . . . Flatwoods
LU 354. . . . . London
LU 433. . . . . Bowling Green

State, County and Municipal Employees
LU 3911 Nurses
  Professional. . . . . . . Louisville

Steelworkers
ASSN Mid-Valley Pipeline
  Group. . . . . . . Elizabethtown
LU 5-518 . . . . Florence
LU 01-14340-S . . . . . Edgewood
LU 02-512. . . . . . . Salyersville
LU 05-214 . . . . Ashland
LU 05-367 . . . . . . Brandenburg
LU 05-372 . . . . . . Prestonsburg
LU 05-505 . . . . Ashland
LU 05-511 . . . . Dayton
LU 05-523 . . . . Wurtland
LU 05-550 . . . . Paducah
LU 05-556 . . . . Benton
LU 05-680 . . . . Mayfield
LU 05-727 . . . . . . Calvert City
LU 05-744 . . . . Martin
LU 05-775 . . . . Wickliffe
LU 05-783 . . . . Owensboro
LU 05-805 . . . . Elsmere
LU 05-832 . . . . Florence
LU 05-879 . . . . Murray
LU 05-931 . . . . Alexandria
LU 05-1048 . . . . Louisville
LU 05-1241 . . . . Fairfield
LU 05-1737 . . . . Louisville
LU 06-669 . . . . Paducah
LU 07-532 . . . . . . Lawrenceburg
LU 08-133-S . . . South Shore
LU 08-152-S . . . Clarkson
LU 08-153. . . . . Upton
LU 08-155. . . . . Louisville
LU 08-665-L . . . . Mayfield
LU 08-857-G . . . . Olive Hill
LU 08-1009. . . . . Stanford
LU 08-1016-T . . . . Harrodsburg
LU 08-1693-S. . . . Louisville
LU 08-1865-S. . . . Ashland
LU 08-1870-S. . . Highland Heights
LU 08-7054-S. . . . Ashland
LU 08-7153-S. . . . Catlettsburg
LU 08-7173 . . . . Hopkinsville
LU 08-7461-S . . . Tompkinsville
LU 08-7926-S . . . . Van Lear
LU 08-8158-S. . . . . Dover
LU 08-8411-S . . . Barbourville
LU 08-9120-S. . . . East Point
LU 08-9148-S . . . West Liberty
LU 08-9345-S . . . . Kimper
LU 08-9423 . . . . Lewisport
LU 08-9443 . . . . Robards
LU 08-9447 . . . . Eddyville
LU 08-12593-S. . . . Dana
LU 08-13675-S. . . . Greenville
LU 08-14002-S . . . Nicholasville
LU 08-14269-S . . . Grand Rivers
LU 08-14300-S . . . Hinkle
LU 08-14398-S. . . . Toler
LU 08-14491-S . . . . Cumberland
LU 08-14558-S. . . . Whitesburg
LU 08-14581-S . . . Elkhorn City
LU 08-14628-S . . . Middlesboro
LU 08-14636-S . . . McDowell
LU 08-14637-S . . . Bulan
LU 08-14746-S . . . . Central City

Teamsters
CONF Kentucky-West
  Virginia Conference of
  Teamsters . . . . Louisville
JC 94 . . . . Louisville
LU 89 . . . . Louisville
LU 236 . . . . Paducah

LU 513 . . . . Florence
LU 651 . . . . Lexington
LU 783 . . . . Louisville
LU 2727. . . . . Louisville

Theatrical Stage Employees
LU 17 . . . . Louisville
LU 38-B . . . . Ludlow
LU 346 . . . . Lexington

Transportation Communications Union
D 359. . . . . Vanceburg
LG 6088 Southwind. . . . Louisville
LG 6344 Raceland . . . . Flatwoods
LG 6401 Cincinnati . . . . . Hebron

Transportation Union
GCA GO-347 UTU . . . Henderson
LU 376 . . . . Crestwood
LU 496 . . . . South Shore
LU 573 . . . . . . Kings Mountain
LU 630 . . . . Ashland
LU 785 . . . . Hickory

LU 1062 . . . . Flatwoods
LU 1190 . . . . Ludlow
LU 1310 . . . . Williamsburg
LU 1315 . . . . Independence
LU 1316 . . . . Irvine
LU 1377. . . . . Ashland
LU 1389. . . . . Ashland
LU 1517 . . . . Florence
LU 1567 . . . . Corbin
LU 1869. . . . . . . Turkey Creek
LU 1917. . . . . Park Hills
LU 1963 . . . . Henderson
SLB LO-20 Kentucky . . . Stanford

Treasury Employees
CH 25 . . . . Louisville
CH 73 . . . . Covington

UNITE HERE
LU 181 . . . . Louisville
LU 350 . . . . Hopkinsville

Weather Service Employees
BR 03-4 . . . . Louisville

BR 03-7 . . . . Jackson
BR 03-63 . . . . . . West Paducah

Unaffiliated Labor Organizations

Allied Mechanical Workers
    Independent 714 . . Independence
American Sign & Marketing Services
    Inc. Independent Union . Florence
Diocese of Owensboro Catholic
    Educators, Inc. . . . . Owensboro
Falcon Coal Company Employees
    Association . . . . Jackson
Florence Steelworkers LU
    1 . . . . Florence
Independent Factory Workers
    Union . . . . Louisville
International Guards Union of
    America LU 8 . . . . . . Florence
International Guards Union of
    America LU 15 . . . Brandenburg
International Guards Union of
    America LU 78 . . . . . Lexington

International Guards Union of
    America LU 143 . . . . Louisville
International Guards Union of
    America RC
    Seventh . . . . . . Brandenburg
Kentucky Nurses Association
    Morgan County Appalachian
    Region Hospital Center LU
    115 . . . . Campton
Kentucky State Pipe Trades
    Association . . . . Ashland
Neoprene Clerical Workers
    Independent. . . . . . . Louisville
Neoprene Craftsmen Union
    Independent LU
    05-2002 . . . . Louisville
Plant Protection Association,
    National Ford's Louisville
    Assembly Plant LU
    118 . . . . Louisville
Scotia Employee
    Utilities Union
    Independent . . . . Newport
Vending Machine Seviceman's
    Union . . . . Melbourne

Louisiana

AFL-CIO Trade and Industrial Departments

Building and Construction Trades Department
BCTC Baton Rouge . . Baton Rouge
BCTC Lafayette . . . . Lake Charles
BCTC Louisiana . . . . . Metairie
BCTC Shreveport . . . Shreveport
BCTC Southeast
  Louisiana . . . . . New Orleans
BCTC Southwest
  Louisiana . . . . . Lake Charles

Maritime Trades Department
PC New Orleans Area . . . . Harvey

Metal Trades Department
MTC Lake Charles . . Lake Charles
MTC New Orleans . . . Bridge City

Affiliated Labor Organizations

Agricultural Employees
BR 3 . . . . New Orleans

Air Traffic Controllers
LU BTR . . . . Baton Rouge
LU LCH . . . . Lake Charles
LU LFT . . . . Lafayette
LU MLU. . . . . Monroe
LU MSY . . . . New Orleans
LU NEW . . . . New Orleans
LU SHV . Barksdale Air Force Base

Asbestos Workers
CONF Southwestern States . Kenner
LU 53 . . . . Kenner
LU 112. . . . . Lake Charles

Automobile, Aerospace Workers
C Louisiana State . . . . Shreveport
LU 1532 . . . . Shreveport
LU 1805 . . . . New Orleans
LU 1921 . . . . New Orleans
LU 1977. . . . . Monroe
LU 2166 . . . . Shreveport
LU 2297 . . . . Shreveport

Boilermakers
DLG 5 . . . . Baton Rouge
LG 37 . . . . Slidell
LG 582. . . . . Baton Rouge
LG 1814. . . . . Bridge City

Carpenters
DC Louisiana . . . . . . Chalmette
LU 720 . . . . Baton Rouge
LU 764 . . . . Shreveport
LU 953. . . . . . . Lake Charles
LU 1098 . . . . Baton Rouge
LU 1846 . . . . New Orleans
LU 1897 . . . . Lafayette
LU 1931 . . . . New Orleans
LU 2091. . . . . Jonesboro
LU 3094 . . . . Florien
LU 3101. . . . . Oakdale
LU 3172. . . . . Jonesboro

Communications Workers
LU 1105 IUE-CWA . . . . Meraux
LU 3402 . . . . Alexandria
LU 3403 . . . . Baton Rouge

LU 3404 . . . . Covington
LU 3406 . . . . Lafayette
LU 3407 . . . . . . Lake Charles
LU 3410 . . . . . . New Orleans
LU 3411 . . . . Shreveport
LU 3412 . . . . Houma
LU 3414 . . . . Monroe
LU 3513 . . . . Vidalia

Electrical Workers
LU 130 . . . . Metairie
LU 194 . . . . Shreveport
LU 329 . . . . Shreveport
LU 446 . . . . Monroe
LU 576 . . . . Alexandria
LU 767 . . . . Baton Rouge
LU 861 . . . . Lake Charles
LU 895. . . . . Bastrop
LU 995. . . . . . . Baton Rouge
LU 1077 . . . . Bogalusa
LU 1139 . . . . New Orleans
LU 1700 . . . . Westwego
LU 1829 . . . . Bossier City
LU 2149 . . . . New Orleans

Elevator Constructors
LU 16. . . . . Metairie

Federal Employees
LU 95 . . . . New Orleans
LU 1124 . . . . New Orleans
LU 1593. . . . . Slidell
LU 1707 . . . . Belle Chasse
LU 1708 . . . . Fort Polk
LU 1737. . . . . Natalbany
LU 1904 . . . . New Orleans
LU 1953 . Barksdale Air Force Base
LU 1956 . . . . Shreveport

Fire Fighters
LU 189-F Naval Air Station
  Local. . . . . . . New Orleans

Food and Commercial Workers
LU 27-C . . . . Avery Island
LU 29-C . . . . New Iberia
LU 88-C . . . . Bastrop
LU 187-C . . . . Dubach
LU 273-C . . . . Ville Platte
LU 458-C . . . . Lydia
LU 483-C . . . . Franklin
LU 496 . . . . Metairie
LU 638-C . . . . Franklin
LU 883-C . . . . Lafayette
LU 1101 . . . . Arabi
LU 1167-P. . . . . Gramercy

Glass, Molders, Pottery and Plastics Workers
LU 253. . . . . Simsboro

Government Employees
C 237 Federal Grain Inspection
  Locals . . . . La Place
LU 1034 . . . . Pollock
LU 1972 VA. . . . . Tioga
LU 2000 DoD. . . . . Barksdale Air
             Force Base
LU 2038 DoJ . . . . . . Oakdale
LU 2062 VA . . . . . New Orleans
LU 2139 DoL . . . . . . Lafayette
LU 2341 USDA . . . . New Orleans
LU 2525 VA . . . . . . Shreveport
LU 2528 . . . . Pineville
LU 2867 SBA . . . . . New Orleans

LU 2873 USDA . . . . . Spearsville
LU 3157 USDA . . . . . La Place
LU 3457 DoI. . . . . New Orleans
LU 3475 HUD . . . . New Orleans
LU 3501 USDA . . . . . Hammond
LU 3553 VA . . . . . New Orleans
LU 3957 BoP, FDC,
  Oakdale . . . . Oberlin

Government Employees Association
LU 05-87. . . . . . . New Orleans
LU 05-168 . . . . Fort Polk
LU 05-169 . . . . Fort Polk
LU 05-190 . . . . . . New Orleans

Government Security Officers
LU 109 . . . . Chatham
LU 110 . . . . Baton Rouge
LU 111 . . . . New Orleans

Graphic Communications
LU 260-C . . . . . . Lake Charles
LU 537-M . . . . Marrero

Iron Workers
DC Mid South . . . Denham Springs
LU 58 . . . . New Orleans
LU 591 . . . . Shreveport
LU 623 . . . . Baton Rouge
LU 710 . . . . Monroe

Laborers
LU 207 . . . . Lake Charles
LU 689 . . . . New Orleans
LU 692 . . . . Baton Rouge
LU 762. . . . . Lafayette
LU 1177 . . . . Baton Rouge

Letter Carriers
BR 124. . . . . . . New Orleans
BR 129. . . . . . . Baton Rouge
BR 136 . . . . Monroe
BR 197 Queen City . . . Shreveport
BR 914. . . . . . . Lake Charles
BR 932. . . . . Alexandria
BR 988. . . . . New Iberia
BR 1659 . . . . Bogalusa
BR 1760 . . . . Lafayette
BR 2223 . . . . Hammond
BR 2464 Houma-
  Thibodaux . . . . . . Thibodaux
BR 2730 . . . . Gretna
BR 3063 . . . . Bunkie
BR 3295. . . . . Rayne
BR 3632 . . . . Arabi
BR 3696 . . . . Donaldsonville
BR 3713 . . . . Beville
BR 3769 . . . . St. Martinville
BR 3815 . . . . Morgan City
BR 3861 Westwego . . . Westwego
BR 3868 . . . . Harvey
BR 3940. . . . . Tallulah
BR 4218 . . . . Homer
BR 4323 . . . . Marrero
BR 4342 . . . . Kenner
BR 4413. . . . . Slidell
BR 4489 . . . . Ponchatoula
BR 4521. . . . . Amite
BR 4591. . . . . Rayville
BR 4617 . . . . Bossier City
BR 5318 . . . . Eunice
BR 5604 . . . . Ville Platte
BR 5605 . . . . New Roads
BR 5607 . . . . Norco

BR 5608 . . . . . . Golden Meadow
BR 5609 . . . . . . Breaux Bridge
BR 5611. . . . . Berwick
BR 5614 . . . . Many
BR 5856 . . . . Church Point
BR 6102 . . . . Erath
BR 6119. . . . . Metairie
BR 6160 . . . . . . Lake Providence
BR 6268 . . . . Kentwood
BR 6377 . . . . Mandeville
BR 6379 . . . . Vidalia
BR 6461 . . . . Delcambre
BR 6462 . . . . Jonesville
BR 6601. . . . . Ferriday
SA Louisiana State Association of
  Letter Carriers . . . . . Metairie

Locomotive Engineers
DIV 18 . . . . New Orleans
DIV 193 . . . . Kenner
DIV 219 . . . . Greenwood
DIV 326 . . . . Bossier City
DIV 426 . . . . Baton Rouge
DIV 531 . . . . Baton Rouge
DIV 599 . . . . Vivian
DIV 632. . . . . Heflin
DIV 755 . . . . Dequincy
DIV 765 . . . . Monroe
DIV 914 . . . . Baton Rouge
DIV 915 . . . . Pineville
SLB Louisiana. . . . . Greenwood

Longshoremen
D East Gulf Dock & Marine
  Council . . . . Metairie
LU 1349 . . . . . . Lake Charles
LU 1497 . . . . . . New Orleans
LU 1998 . . . . Sulphur
LU 2036 . . . . New Orleans
LU 2047 . . . . . . Lake Charles
LU 3000 . . . . . . New Orleans
LU 3033. . . . . Port Allen

Machinists
DLG 161 . . . . . . Lake Charles
LG 37 . . . . Gretna
LG 69 . . . . Breaux Bridge
LG 281 . . Barksdale Air Force Base
LG 470. . . . . . . Lake Charles
LG 1317 . . . . . . Lake Charles
LG 1366 . . . . . . Baton Rouge
LG 1905. . . . . Metairie
LG 2518 . . . . Tioga
STC Louisiana . . . . . . Tullos

Maintenance of Way Employes
LG 564 . . . . Shreveport
LG 944 . . . . Winnsboro
LG 1048 . . . . Carencro
LG 1176 . . . . Opelousas
LG 1193 . . . . Shreveport
SLG 655 . . . . Bridge City
SLG 1100 . . . . Marrero
SLG 1165 . . . . Reserve
SLG 1404 . . . . Plaquemine
SLG 1630 . . . . Harvey

Marine Engineers
ASSN American Radio Association
  Local Union 2057 . . . . Metairie

Musicians
CONF Southern . . . . Shreveport
LU 116 . . . . Shreveport
LU 174-496 . . . . . New Orleans

National Staff Organization
LU Staff Organization, Louisiana
   State . . . . Baton Rouge

NLRB Professional Association
LU 15 . . . . New Orleans

Office and Professional Employees
LU 87 . . . . Sulphur
LU 89 . . . . Bogalusa
LU 107 . . . . New Iberia
LU 108 . . . . New Iberia
LU 383 . . . . Baton Rouge
LU 411 . . . . Springhill
LU 428 . . . . Baton Rouge
LU 465 . . . . Alexandria

Operating Engineers
LU 216 . . . . Baton Rouge
LU 406 . . . . New Orleans
LU 407 . . . . Lake Charles

Painters
DC 80 . . . . Kenner
LU 728 . . . . Baton Rouge
LU 1244 . . . . Kenner
LU 2350 . . . . Kenner

Plasterers and Cement Masons
LU 487 . . . . Lake Charles
LU 567 . . . . New Orleans
LU 812 . . . . Baton Rouge

Plumbing and Pipe Fitting
LU 60 . . . . Metairie
LU 106 . . . . Lake Charles
LU 141 . . . . Shreveport
LU 198 . . . . Baton Rouge
LU 247 . . . . Alexandria
LU 659 . . . . Monroe
SA Louisiana . . . . . . Alexandria
SA Tri-States Pipe
   Trades . . . . Alexandria

Postal and Federal Employees
D 1 . . . . New Orleans
LU 102 . . . . Baton Rouge
LU 110 . . . . New Orleans

Postal Mail Handlers
LU 312 . . . . New Orleans

Postal Workers
LU Covington . . . . . Covington
LU 83 New Orleans . . New Orleans
LU 174 Baton Rouge . Baton Rouge
LU 205 Alexandria . . . Alexandria
LU 223 Southwest Louisiana
   Area . . . . Lake Charles
LU 418 Northwest Louisiana
   Area . . . . Shreveport
LU 792 Monroe . . . . . Monroe
LU 1171 Plaquemine . . Plaquemine
LU 1182 Winnfield . . . Winnfield
LU 1278 Hammond . . . Hammond
LU 1430 Rayville . . . . . Rayville
LU 2102 Houma . . . . . . Houma
LU 2103 Thibodaux . . . Thibodaux
LU 2106 Morgan City . Morgan City
LU 2803 Lafayette Local . Lafayette

LU 2848 Leesville . . . . . Leesville
LU 2871 Tri-Parish Area . . . Gretna
LU 3036 Ville Platte . . . Ville Platte
LU 3037 Springhill . . . . Springhill
LU 3049 Bogalusa . . . . Bogalusa
LU 3067 New Iberia . . . New Iberia
LU 3234 Many . . . . Many
LU 3815 Jena . . . . Jena
LU 3900 Lockport . . . . Lockport
LU 3902 Slidell . . . . Slidell
LU 4300 Denham
   Springs . . . . . Denham Springs
LU 4653 Opelousas . . . . Opelousas
LU 5283
   Napoleonville . . . . Napoleonville
LU 5903 Gonzales . . . . . Gonzales
LU 5959 Metairie Area . . . Metairie
LU 6101 Vidalia . . . . Vidalia
LU 6190 Mandeville . . Mandeville
LU 6347 Chalmette . . . . Chalmette
LU 6598 Baker . . . . Baker
LU 6665 St.
   Francisville . . . . St. Francisville
SA Louisiana . . . . . . Lafayette

Roofers, Waterproofers and Allied
  Workers
DC Southern Roofers . Baton Rouge
LU 317 . . . . Baton Rouge

Rural Letter Carriers
D 1 Deep South . . . . . Destrehan
D 4 . . . . Greenwood
D 5 . . . . Sterlington
D 6 Southeast . . . Denham Springs
D 7 Southwest District . . New Iberia
D 8 Central District . . . . Pineville
SA Louisiana . . . . Noble

Security, Police and Fire
  Professionals
LU 700 . . . . Lake Charles
LU 704 . . . . New Orleans
LU 706 . . . . Shreveport
LU 707 . . . . . St. Francisville
LU 709 . . . . Edgard
LU 710 . . . . Avondale

Service Employees
LU 100 . . . . New Orleans
LU 880 . . . . New Orleans

Sheet Metal Workers
LU 11 . . . . Metairie
LU 21 . . . . Baton Rouge
LU 361 . . . . Shreveport

State, County and Municipal
  Employees
C 17 Louisiana Public
   Employees . . . . . Baton Rouge

Steelworkers
C . . . . Norco
DC 4 . . . . Dequincy
LU 3-584 . . . . . Denham Springs
LU 4-500 Citgo Nationwide
   Council . . . . Sulphur

LU 04-189 Recovery
   Local . . . . Bogalusa
LU 04-245 . . . . . Shreveport
LU 04-272 . . . . Bastrop
LU 04-335 . . . . Zachary
LU 04-351 Red River
   Local . . . . Pineville
LU 04-360 . . . . Bastrop
LU 04-364 . . . . . West Monroe
LU 04-382 . . . . Bastrop
LU 04-398 . . . . Cullen
LU 04-447 . . . . Westwego
LU 04-500 . . . . Sulphur
LU 04-522 . . . . Chalmette
LU 04-554 . . . . Springhill
LU 04-555 . . . . Sulphur
LU 04-618 . . . . Tallulah
LU 04-620 . . . . Gonzales
LU 04-654 . . . . . West Monroe
LU 04-677 . . . . Minden
LU 04-725 . . . . Deridder
LU 04-750 . . . . Norco
LU 04-752 . . . . Zachary
LU 04-786 . . . . . . Sterlington
LU 04-836 . . . . Starks
LU 04-928 . . . . Zachary
LU 04-1081 . . . . . . Simsboro
LU 04-1226 . . . . Deridder
LU 04-1331 . . . . Campti
LU 04-1334 . . . . Zachary
LU 04-1362 . . . . . . Bogalusa
LU 04-1505 . . . . Hodge
LU 04-1685 . . . . . Shreveport
LU 09-70-T . . . . Ruston
LU 09-211-A . . . . Lake Charles
LU 09-275-A . . . Denham Springs
LU 09-711-T . . . . . Shreveport
LU 09-832-L . . . . . Baton Rouge
LU 09-5651 . . . . Kenner
LU 09-5702-S . . . . . . Vacherie
LU 09-6296-S . . . . . . Zachary
LU 09-8363-S . . . New Orleans
LU 09-8373-S . . . Belle Chasse
LU 09-8394-S . . . . . Zachary
LU 09-9059-S . . . . . . Oscar
LU 09-9121-S . . . . . La Place
LU 09-13000-S . . . . . Chalmette
LU 09-13841-S . . . Ville Platte
LU 09-14425-S . . . . Loreauville
LU 09-14465-S . . . . Gonzales

Teamsters
LU 5 . . . . Baton Rouge
LU 270 . . . . New Orleans
LU 568 . . . . Shreveport

Theatrical Stage Employees
LU 39 . . . . New Orleans
LU 260 . . . . Lake Charles
LU 298 . . . . Shreveport
LU 478 Studio
   Mechanics . . . . New Orleans
LU 540 . . . . Baton Rouge
LU 668 . . . . West Monroe
LU 840 . . . . Hammond

Train Dispatchers
SCOM Louisiana & Arkansas
   Railroad . . . . Benton

Transit Union
CONBD Louisiana
   Legislative . . . . . New Orleans
LDIV 558 . . . . Shreveport
LDIV 1400 . . . . Gretna
LDIV 1546 . . . . . Baton Rouge
LDIV 1560 . . . . . New Orleans
LU 1535 . . . . New Orleans

Transportation Communications
  Union
D 1461 Southwestern . . Shreveport
LG 6136 True Blue . . White Castle
LG 6461 Crescent . . . . . Avondale
LG 6825 Red Stick . . . St. Amant
LG 6872 New Orleans . . . Geismar

Transportation Union
GCA GO-460 Kansas City Southern
   Railway . . . . Vivian
LU 659 . . . . Sulphur
LU 781 . . . . Mooringsport
LU 976 . . . . Stonewall
LU 1066 . . . . New Orleans
LU 1337 . . . . Port Allen
LU 1501 . . . . Denham Springs
LU 1545 . . . . Bastrop
LU 1678 . . . . Shreveport
LU 1836 . . . . Belle Chasse
LU 1947 . . . . . . Lake Charles
SLB LO-21 . . . . . . Baton Rouge

Treasury Employees
CH 6 . . . . New Orleans
CH 168 . . . . New Orleans

UNITE HERE
LU 166 . . . . New Orleans

Weather Service Employees
BR 02-7 . . . . Lake Charles
BR 02-10 . . . . Shreveport
BR 02-15 . . . . Slidell
BR 02-81 . . . . Slidell

Unaffiliated Labor
Organizations
Allied Oil Workers Union of Baton
   Rouge, Louisiana . . . . Fordoche
American Federation of Unions LU
   102 . . . . Prairieville
Baton Rouge Oil & Chemical
   Workers Union . . . Baton Rouge
Exxon Employees Federation
   Southeastern Division . . . Morse
Independent Coca Cola Employees
   Union LU 1060 . . . Lake Charles
Industrial Guards Association
   Independent . . . . . Baton Rouge
International Guards Union of
   America LU 81 . . . . . Haughton
Louisiana Electrical Workers
   Association . . . . . Baton Rouge
Southern Association of Nurse
   Anesthetists . . . . Metairie
Southern Pipe Liners Union-
   Exxon . . . . Broussard
Texas Gulf Federation Shell Pipe
   Line . . . . Donaldsonville
United Security Workers of America
   Local National . . . . New Orleans

Maine

AFL-CIO Trade and Industrial Departments

Building and Construction Trades Department
BCTC Maine . . . . Clinton

Affiliated Labor Organizations

Air Traffic Controllers
LU BGR . . . . Bangor
LU PWM . . . . Portland

Asbestos Workers
LU 134 . . . . South Berwick

Automobile, Aerospace Workers
LU 3999 . . . . Bath

Bakery, Confectionery, Tobacco Workers and Grain Millers
LU 334 . . . . Portland

Carpenters
LU 658 . . . . Lincoln
LU 1612 . . . . . East Millinocket
LU 1996 . . . . Augusta
LU 2400 . . . . Baileyville
LU 3196 . . . . South Portland

Civilian Technicians
CH 79 Pine Tree . . . . . Montville
CH 128 Maine Acts . . . . Bangor

Communications Workers
LU 14112 . . . . Bangor
LU 14113 . . . . Gorham
LU 14115 International Typographical Union . . Winslow
LU 14116 . . . . Brewer
LU 31128 . . . . Portland

Education
SA Maine Education Association . . . . Augusta

Electrical Workers
LU 567 . . . . Lewiston
LU 1057 . . . . Baileyville
LU 1253 . . . . Augusta
LU 1750 . . . . Clinton
LU 1768 . . . . Hinkley
LU 1777 . . . . Sorrento
LU 1837 . . . . Manchester
LU 2071 . . . . Eliot
LU 2144 . . . . Mexico
LU 2233 . . . . Buxton
LU 2327 . . . . Augusta
SC T-6 New England Telephone Company . . . . Augusta

Fire Fighters
LU 123-F . . . . Kittery

Food and Commercial Workers
LU 650-C . . . . Knox

Government Employees
LU 294 . . . . Limestone
LU 2610 VA . . . . Augusta
LU 2635 DoD . . . . Cutler
LU 2711 DoJ . . . . Bangor
LU 2906 DoD . . . . Bath

LU 3728 USDA . . . . . Lewiston

Government Employees Association
LU 01-77 . . . . Brunswick

Graphic Communications
LU 22-C . . . . Windham
LU 558-C . . . . Orrington

Iron Workers
LU 496 . . . . Clinton
LU 807 . . . . Smithfield

Laborers
LU 327 . . . . Augusta
LU 1377 . . . . Bangor

Letter Carriers
BR 92 . . . . Westbrook
BR 241 . . . . Lewiston
BR 345 . . . . Auburn
BR 391 Trans-Maine Merged . . . . Hampden
BR 774 . . . . Litchfield
BR 1448 . . . . Sanford
BR 2394 . . . . Presque Isle
BR 5484 . . . . . . East Holden
BR 6115 . . . . . Chebeague Island
SA Maine . . . . Westbrook

Locomotive Engineers
DIV 72 . . . . Clinton
DIV 191 . . . . Raymond
DIV 274 . . . . Auburn

Longshoremen
LU 861 . . . . Portland
LU 1519 . . . . Swanville

Machinists
DLG 4 . . . . Topsham
LG 5 Mid Coast United Health Care Employees . . . . Dresden
LG 6-S . . . . Bath
LG 7-S . . . . Bath
LG 362 . . . . . East Millinocket
LG 409 . . . . Waterville
LG 559 . . . . Madison
LG 836 . . . . Sanford
LG 1490 Border . . . . . Alexander
LG 1821 . . . . Holden
LG 2287 . . . . Scarborough
LG 2740 . . . . Fairfield

Maintenance of Way Employes
LG 602 . . . . Saco
LG 633 . . . . Benton
LG 1159 . . . . Houlton
LG 1318 . . . . Caribou
SLG 32 . . . . Oxford

National Staff Organization
LU Staff Organization of the Maine Teachers Association . . . Auburn

Nurses
LU 1 Maine State Nurses Association . . . . Augusta
LU 116 Maine State Nurses Association . . . . Augusta
LU 124 Maine State Nurses Association . . . . Augusta
LU 188 Maine State Nurses Association . . . . Augusta

LU 210 Maine State . . . . . Augusta
LU 296 Maine State Nurses Association . . . . Augusta
LU 384 Maine State Nurses Association . . . . Augusta
LU 911 Maine State Nurses . Augusta
LU 982 Maine State Nurses . Augusta
LU 1082 Maine State Nurses . . . . Augusta
LU 5050 Maine State . . . . . Augusta
LU 7631 Aroostook Medical Center . . . . Augusta
SA Maine State Nurses Association . . . . Augusta

Office and Professional Employees
LU 192 . . . . Millinocket
LU 232 . . . . Madawaska
LU 295 . . . . Baileyville
LU 442 . . . . . Livermore Falls
LU 555 . . . . Bucksport

Painters
LU 1468 . . . . Oakland
LU 1915 . . . . Kennebunk

Plumbing and Pipe Fitting
LU 485 . . . . Millinocket
LU 716 . . . . Augusta

Postal Workers
LU 289 Biddeford . . . . . Biddeford
LU 458 Portland . . . . . Portland
LU 461 Augusta . . . . . Augusta
LU 536 Bangor . . . . . . Bangor
LU 2767 Caribou . . . . . Caribou
LU 3185 Calais . . . . . . Calais
LU 3437 Gardiner . . . . . Gardiner
LU 4910 Houlton . . . . . Houlton
LU 5435 Ellsworth . . . . Ellsworth
LU 5622 Armand Rowe Area Local . . . . Auburn
LU 5729 Waterville Area . . . . Waterville
LU 5998 Presque Isle . . Presque Isle
LU 6484 Freeport . . . . . Freeport
SA Maine . . . . . Cape Elizabeth

Rural Letter Carriers
LU Aroostook County . . . Houlton
LU Cumberland County . Westbrook
LU Hancock County . . . . Lamoine
LU Kennebec County . Farmingdale
LU Mid-Coast Association . . . . . . Newcastle
LU Oxford-Androscoggin-Franklin Counties . . . . Kingfield
LU Penobscot County . . Brownville
LU Somerset County . . Cambridge
LU Washington County . . Milbridge
LU York County . . . . . . Lyman
SA Maine . . . . Limerick

Security, Police and Fire Professionals
LU 549 . . . . Millinocket
LU 550 . . . . Waterville

Service Employees
LU 247 Firemen & Oilers . . . . Jay
LU 398 Green Valley . . . . Patten
LU 1030 Firemen & Oilers . Gorham
LU 1989 B.A. Green Maine State Employees Association 697 . . . . Bangor

LU 1989 Maine State Employees Association . . . . Augusta

Steelworkers
LU 01-9 . . . . Skowhegan
LU 01-11 . . . . Fayette
LU 01-12 . . . . Millinocket
LU 01-14 . . . . Jay
LU 01-27 . . . . Calais
LU 01-36 . . . . Madison
LU 01-37 . . . . . East Millinocket
LU 01-80 . . . . Old Town
LU 01-152 . . . . Medway
LU 01-261 . . . . Bucksport
LU 01-291 . . . . Madawaska
LU 01-365 . . . . Madawaska
LU 01-396 . . . . Lincoln
LU 01-449 . . . . Waterville
LU 01-900 . . . . Rumford
LU 01-1069 . . . . Westbrook
LU 01-1188 . . . . Bucksport
LU 01-1247 . . . . Madawaska
LU 01-1310 . . . . Ashland
LU 01-1363 . . . . Stacyville
LU 01-1367 . . . . Pembroke
LU 01-1977 . . . . Madawaska

Teachers
LU 5059 Health Professionals, Lubec Federation of . . . . Lubec
LU 5073 Health Care Professionals, Downeast Federation of . Jonesport

Teamsters
LU 340 . . . . South Portland

Theatrical Stage Employees
LU 114 . . . . Portland
LU 926 IATSE TBSE . . . . Auburn

Transportation Communications Union
LG 6923 Kennebec . . China Village

Transportation Union
LU 663 . . . . Orrington
LU 1400 . . . . . . South Portland

Treasury Employees
CH 7 . . . . South Portland
CH 141 . . . . Madawaska

Utility Workers
LU 341 . . . . . Old Orchard Beach
LU 497 . . . . Wiscasset

Weather Service Employees
BR 01-24 . . . . Caribou
BR 01-37 . . . . Grey

Unaffiliated Labor Organizations
Consolidated Railway Supervisors Association . . . . Freeport
Independent Guards Association . . . . Bath
Plant Protection Quarantine Office Support Employees . . Winterport
Professional Fire Fighters of Maine . . . . Bangor
SAPPI Council . . . . . Skowhegan
Staff Organization of Maine State Employees Association . . Augusta

Maryland

AFL-CIO Trade and Industrial Departments

Building and Construction Trades Department
BCTC Baltimore Building & Construction Trades Company . . . . Baltimore
BCTC Maryland State & District of Columbia . . . . Baltimore
BCTC Washington DC . . . . Camp Springs
BCTC Western Maryland . . . . . . Cumberland

Maritime Trades Department
PC None . . . . Cockeysville

Metal Trades Department
MTC Baltimore Area . . . Baltimore
MTC East Coast . . . . . . Crofton

Affiliated Labor Organizations

Agricultural Employees
BR 6 . . . . Baltimore

Air Traffic Controllers
LU ABA . . . . . . Fort Washington
LU ADW . . . . . . Camp Springs
LU BWI . . . . Baltimore

Air Traffic Specialists
NHQ . . . . Wheaton

Asbestos Workers
LU 24 . . . . Laurel
NHQ . . . . Lanham

Automobile, Aerospace Workers
LU 66 . . . . Baltimore
LU 171 . . . . Hagerstown
LU 239 . . . . Baltimore
LU 404 . . . . Port Deposit
LU 738 . . . . Baltimore
LU 1247 . . . . Maugansville
LU 1338 . . . . . Havre de Grace
LU 1590 . . . . . . Williamsport
LU 1748 . . . . Baltimore
LU 2301 . . . . Elkridge
LU 2372 . . . . Baltimore

Bakery, Confectionery, Tobacco Workers and Grain Millers
LU 68 . . . . Baltimore
LU 118 . . . . Lanham
NHQ . . . . Kensington

Boilermakers
LG 50-S . . . . Baltimore
LG 193 . . . . Baltimore
LG 533-D Cement Workers . . . . Hagerstown

Bricklayers
LU 1 Maryland Virginia & District Columbia . . . . . Camp Springs

Carpenters
C Mid-Atlantic Regional . Forestville
LU 101 . . . . Baltimore
LU 132 . . . . Forestville
LU 340 . . . . Hagerstown

LU 491 . . . . Baltimore
LU 1024 . . . . Cumberland
LU 1145 . . . . Glen Burnie
LU 1548 . . . . Baltimore
LU 1590 . . . . Harwood
LU 1694 . . . . Dunkirk
LU 2311 . . . . Forestville

Civilian Technicians
CH Chesapeake 122 . . . . . Joppa
CH 125 Chesapeake Air . Baltimore
CH 132 Chesapeake Army Chapter . . . . . Havre de Grace

Communications Workers
LU 2100 . . . . Chase
LU 2101 . . . . Baltimore
LU 2105 . . . . Williamsport
LU 2106 . . . . Salisbury
LU 2107 . . . . Annapolis
LU 2108 . . . . Landover
LU 2109 . . . . Cumberland
LU 2300 . . . . College Park
LU 14201 . . . . . Upper Marlboro
LU 14203 . . . . . . Cumberland
LU 32100 The Translators Guild . . . . Silver Spring
LU 52031 NABET Local 31 . . . . Silver Spring
LU 82075 . . . . Baltimore
LU 82109 . . . . Baltimore
LU 82130 . . . . Baltimore
LU 82472 . . . . Hagerstown
STC Maryland . . . . . . Landover

Electrical Workers
LU 24 . . . . Baltimore
LU 70 . . . . Forestville
LU 307 . . . . Cumberland
LU 362 . . . . Glen Burnie
LU 865 . . . . Severn
LU 870 . . . . Cumberland
LU 1200 . . . . . . Upper Marlboro
LU 1307 . . . . Delmar
LU 1383 . . . . Baltimore
LU 1501 . . . . Cockeysville
LU 1653 . . . . Cumberland
LU 1718 . . . . Hughesville
LU 1805 . . . . Glen Burnie
LU 1900 . . . . Largo

Electrical, Radio and Machine Workers
LU 120 . . . . Baltimore
LU 121 . . . . Baltimore

Elevator Constructors
LU 7 . . . . Baltimore
LU 10 . . . . Lanham
NHQ . . . . Columbia

Engineers
LU 29 Goddard Scientists . Greenbelt
NHQ . . . . Silver Spring

Federal Employees
LU 178 . . . . Gunpowder
LU 639 . . . . Baltimore
LU 1153 . . . . Cascade
LU 1705 . . . . Temple Hills
LU 2058 . . . . Edgewood

Fire Fighters
LU 121-F . . . . Indian Head

LU 121-F National Capital Federal Firefighters . . . . . . Annapolis
LU 254-F U.S. Naval Academy . . . . . . Annapolis
LU 267-F . . . . Conowingo
LU 271-F NIH Professional Firefighters . . . . Germantown
LU 297-F . . . . Suitland

Food and Commercial Workers
C Mid-Atlantic Regional . Landover
LU 27 . . . . Baltimore
LU 34-D . . . . Baltimore
LU 217-C . . . . Baltimore
LU 261-C . . . . Cumberland
LU 266-T . . . . North East
LU 392 . . . . Baltimore
LU 400 . . . . Landover
LU 976-C . . . . Baltimore
LU 1994 Montgomery County Government Employees Organization . . . . . Gaithersburg

Glass, Molders, Pottery and Plastics Workers
LU 19-B . . . . Baltimore
LU 113 . . . . Baltimore
LU 218 . . . . Baltimore

Government Employees
C 143 Food Inspection Locals, Midatlantic . . . . . Chestertown
C 220 National SSA Field Operations Local . . . . Towson
C 260 NARA . . . . . College Park
LU 331 VA . . . . . . Perry Point
LU 361 DoD . . . . . . Bethesda
LU 896 DoD . . . . . . Annapolis
LU 902 DoD . . . Chesapeake City
LU 966 USDA . . . . . Manchester
LU 1092 DoD . . . . . . Wharton
LU 1401 . . Andrews Air Force Base
LU 1603 DoD . . . Patuxent River
LU 1622 DoD . . . . . . Odenton
LU 1923 HHS . . . . . . Baltimore
LU 1983 . . . . Emmitsburg
LU 2117 DoD . . . . . . Baltimore
LU 2146 VA . . . . Baltimore
LU 2371 USCG . . . . Glen Burnie
LU 2419 HHS . . . . . Bethesda
LU 2422 USDA . . . . . Quantico
LU 2484 DoD . . . . . . Frederick
LU 2578 GSA . . . . College Park
LU 2594 . . . . Cambridge
LU 2640 DoC . . . . . Greenbelt
LU 2756 INS . . . . . Salisbury
LU 2782 DoC . . . . . Suitland
LU 3090 DoD . . . Mount Rainier
LU 3122 HUD . . . . . Baltimore
LU 3147 USDA . . . . Beltsville
LU 3176 DoD . . . . . Bel Air
LU 3302 HHS . . . . . Baltimore
LU 3407 DoD . . . . Glen Echo
LU 3579 CPSC . . . . Bethesda
LU 3614 EEOC . . . Davidsonville
LU 4010 . . . . . . Cumberland

Government Employees Association
LU 03-84 . . . . . . Camp Springs
LU 03-112 . . . . Baltimore
LU 04-93 Arlington National Cemetery . . . . Suitland
LU 04-102 . . . . . Camp Springs

Government Security Officers
LU 34 U.S. Department of Agriculture . . . . Upper Marlboro
LU 44 . . . . Clinton

Graphic Communications
LU 1-C . . . . Temple Hills
LU 31-N . . . . Baltimore
LU 72-C . . . . Riverdale
LU 98-L . . . . Boyds
LU 144-B . . . . Greenbelt
LU 481-S . . . . Baltimore
LU 582-M . . . . Baltimore
LU 754-S . . . . Cumberland

Iron Workers
LU 5 . . . . Upper Marlboro
LU 16 . . . . Baltimore
LU 568 . . . . Cumberland

Laborers
DC Baltimore County . . . . Towson
LU 194 . . . . Baltimore
LU 481 Production Employee . . . . Baltimore
LU 516 . . . . Baltimore
LU 616 . . . . Cumberland
LU 912 Material Yard & Residential Construction . . . . . Baltimore
LU 1231 Amalgamated Municipal Employees . . . . Towson
LU 1273 . . . . Towson
LU 1396 . . . . Rockville

Letter Carriers
BR 176 Oriole Branch . . Baltimore
BR 638 . . . . Cumberland
BR 651 . . . . Annapolis
BR 664 . . . . Frederick
BR 902 . . . . Salisbury
BR 1050 . . . . East New Market
BR 1052 . . . . Easton
BR 1718 . . . . Crisfield
BR 1749 . . . . . Havre de Grace
BR 1869 . . . . Chestertown
BR 2069 . . . . Elkton
BR 2611 . . . . Mount Airy
BR 2820 . . . . Federalsburg
BR 2961 . . . . Mount Lake
BR 3325 . . . . Snow Hill
BR 3338 . . . . Denton
BR 3755 . . . . Laurel
BR 3825 . . . . Rockville
BR 3939 . . . . . . Gaithersburg
BR 4266 . . . . Kensington
BR 4422 . . . . . . Glen Burnie
BR 4444 . . . . . . Indian Head
BR 5203 . . . . Hancock
BR 5394 . . . . Centreville
BR 6076 . . . . North East
BR 6079 . . . . . Lexington Park
BR 6080 . . . . . Patuxent River
BR 6273 . . . . Damascus
BR 6545 . . . . . Upper Marlboro
SA Maryland-District of Columbia . . . . . . Cumberland

Locomotive Engineers
DIV 97 . . . . Ellicott City
DIV 181 . . . . Brunswick
DIV 482 . . . . . . Charlotte Hall
DIV 934 . . . . Cumberland

Longshoremen
DC Baltimore . . . . . . Baltimore

LU 333 . . . . Baltimore
LU 921 . . . . Baltimore
LU 953 . . . . Baltimore
LU 1429 . . . . Baltimore
LU 2066 . . . . Arnold

Machinists
LG 43-S . . . . Baltimore
LG 186 . . . . Baltimore
LG 193 . . . . Waldorf
LG 486 . . . . Perry Hall
LG 846 . . . . Baltimore
LG 1299 . . . . Pasadena
LG 1486 . . . . . Chesapeake Beach
LG 1784 . . . . Baltimore
LG 2135 . . . . Lanham
LG 2424 . . . . Aberdeen
LG 2795 . . . . Salisbury
LLG 24 . . . . Mechanicsville
LLG fl-2181 . . . . Suitland
NHQ . . . . Upper Marlboro
STC Maryland/DC State
    Council . . . . Baltimore

Maintenance of Way Employes
LG 3041 . . . . Owings Mills
SLG 695 . . . . Baltimore
SLG 711 . . . . Hagerstown
SLG 993 . . . . Frederick
SLG 1028 . . . . Bloomington
SLG 3005 . . . . Colora
SLG 3028 . . . . Brentwood
SLG 3075 . . . . Baltimore

Masters, Mates and Pilots
NHQ . . . . Linthicum

Musicians
LU 40-543 . . . . Baltimore
LU 770 . . . . Hagerstown

National Staff Organization
ASSN Tabco Staff
    Association . . . . Towson
LU Staff Organization,
    Maryland State Teachers
    Association . . . . . . Annapolis

NLRB Professional Association
LU 5 . . . . Baltimore

Nurses
NHQ . . . . Silver Spring

Office and Professional Employees
LU 2 . . . . Silver Spring

Operating Engineers
LU 37 . . . . Baltimore
LU 77 . . . . Suitland

Painters
DC 51 . . . . Suitland
LU 1 . . . . Baltimore
LU 368 . . . . Suitland
LU 963 . . . . Suitland
LU 1773 Montgomery County
    Local . . . . St. Leonard
LU 1937 . . . . . . Upper Marlboro

Plasterers and Cement Masons
NHQ . . . . Laurel

**Plate Printers, Die Stampers and
    Engravers**
LU 2 . . . . Baltimore
LU 24 Electrolytic Plate Makers
    Washington DC . . . College Park

Plumbing and Pipe Fitting
C Multistate Pipe Trades . Baltimore
LU 5 . . . . Camp Springs
LU 486 . . . . Baltimore
LU 489 . . . . Cumberland
LU 536 . . . . Baltimore
LU 602 . . . . . . Capitol Heights
LU 669 . . . . Columbia
SA Maryland Pipe Trades . Landover

Police
LG 1 NIH Police LC
    Committee . . . . Bethesda
LG 116-F Aberdeen Proving
    Ground . Aberdeen Proving Ground

Postal and Federal Employees
LU 202 . . . . Baltimore

Postal Workers
LU 181 Baltimore Francis 'Stu
    Filbey' Area . . . . . . Baltimore
LU 512 Southwest Maryland Bay
    Area . . . . Cockeysville
LU 513 Cumberland . . Cumberland
LU 2315 Frederick . . . Frederick
LU 2574 Hagerstown . Hagerstown
LU 3630 Silver Spring . Gaithersburg
LU 4321 Salisbury . . . . Salisbury
LU 5744 Patuxent
    River . . . . . Lexington Park
LU 5932 Lexington
    Park . . . . . . Lexington Park
LU 6743 Germantown . Germantown
SA Maryland-District of
    Columbia . . . . . . Cumberland

Railroad Signalmen
LLG 31 . . . . Cresaptown
LLG 48 . . . . Rising Sun
LLG 65 . . . . Baltimore
LLG 114 . . . . Baltimore
LLG 238 . . . . Bel Air

Rural Letter Carriers
LU Delaware-Maryland-Virginia
    Association . . . . . . Berlin
LU Mid-Shore Group . . Centreville
LU Mid-State Group . . Jarrettsville
LU Southern Maryland County
    Association . . . . . . Waldorf
SA 27 Maryland . . . . . . Joppa

Seafarers
D Atlantic Gulf Lakes & Inland
    Waters . . . . . . Camp Springs
LU Entertainment & Allied Trades
    Union . . . . Camp Springs
LU Seafarers Maritime
    Union . . . . Camp Springs
NHQ . . . . Camp Springs

**Security, Police and Fire
    Professionals**
LU 270 . . . . Baltimore
LU 275 . . . . Glen Dale
LU 293 . . . . Clinton
LU 410 . . . . Chestertown

Service Employees
D 1199 District 1199E-
    DC . . . . Baltimore
JC 54 . . . . Baltimore
LU 439 Firemen &
    Oilers . . . . Cumberland
LU 500 . . . . Gaithersburg
LU 1998 PSNA of
    Maryland . . . . . . Columbia

Sheet Metal Workers
LU 100 . . . . Suitland
LU 363 . . . . Lothian

**State, County and Municipal
    Employees**
C 67 Maryland . . . . . Baltimore
C 92 Maryland State
    Employees . . . . . . Baltimore
LU 1509 . . . . Odenton
LU 2751 . . . . Baltimore
LU 3097 DoJ . . . . Bowie
LU 3374 John's Hopkins Bay View
    Medical Center . . . Baltimore

Steelworkers
LU 9477 . . . . Baltimore
LU 02-20 . . . . Nottingham
LU 02-31 . . . . Frederick
LU 02-33 . . . . Hagerstown
LU 02-111 . . . . Baltimore
LU 02-388 . . . . Thurmont
LU 02-482 . . . . Thurmont
LU 02-676 . . . . Westernport
LU 02-741 . . . . Freeland
LU 02-798 . . . . Baltimore
LU 02-822 . . . . Baltimore
LU 02-1038 . . . . Baltimore
LU 02-1165 . . . . Baltimore
LU 04-13788-S . . . . . . Elkton
LU 08-679-L . . . . . . Baltimore
LU 08-6221-S . . . . . . Baltimore
LU 08-6967-S . . . . . . Baltimore
LU 08-7886-S . . . . . Hagerstown
LU 08-8034-S . . . . . . Dundalk
LU 08-8094-S . . . . . . Arnold
LU 08-8678-S . . . . . Cambridge
LU 08-9386-S . . . . . Hagerstown
LU 08-12200-S . . . . . Baltimore
LU 08-12328-S . . . . . Hyattsville
LU 08-12517-S . . . . . Baltimore
LU 08-12978-S . . . . . Baltimore
LU 08-12993-S . . . . . Baltimore
LU 08-14019-S . . . . . Baltimore

Teamsters
JC 62 . . . . Glen Burnie
LU 311 . . . . Baltimore
LU 355 . . . . Baltimore
LU 453 . . . . Cumberland
LU 570 . . . . Baltimore
LU 888 Baltimore Mailers
    Union . . . . Baltimore
LU 992 . . . . Hagerstown

Television and Radio Artists
LU Washington . . . . . Bethesda

Theatrical Stage Employees
LU 19 . . . . Baltimore
LU 22 . . . . Silver Spring
LU 181 IATSE . . . . Baltimore
LU 487 Mid Atlantic Studio
    Mechanic . . . . . . Baltimore
LU 591 . . . . Damascus
LU 772 . . . . Cheverly
LU 833 . . . . Timonium
LU 913 . . . . Catonsville

Transit Union
LU 1708 . . . . Forestville

Transport Workers
LU 2025 . . . . Baltimore

**Transportation Communications
    Union**
D 511 . . . . Baltimore

D 514 Conrail . . . . . . Pasadena
D 570 . . . . Cheltenham
D 1097 . . . . Germantown
D 2512 . . . . Sunderland
LG 5058 Washington Terminal
    Company . . . . . . Ellicott City
LG 5092 Amtrak . . . . Fallston
LG 6195 Silver Star . . . Pasadena
LG 6364 Capitol . . . . Riverdale
LG 6656 Maryland . . . Cumberland
NHQ . . . . Rockville
SBA 250 Amtrak . . . . Rockville

Transportation Union
LU 454 . . . . Perryville
LU 600 . . . . Frostburg
LU 610 . . . . Arbutus
LU 1361 . . . . Odenton
LU 1470 . . . . Catonsville
LU 1881 . . . . Hanover
SLB LO-23 Maryland . . . Frostburg

Treasury Employees
CH 62 . . . . Baltimore
CH 132 . . . . Baltimore
CH 202 . . . . Hyattsville
CH 208 . . . . Rockville
CH 228 . . . . Germantown
CH 282 . . . . College Park
CH 286 Chapter 286 . . . Columbia
CH 287 . . . . Hyattsville

UNITE HERE
JB Mid Atlantic Regional . Baltimore
LU 4-I . . . . Baltimore
LU 7 . . . . Baltimore
LU 9 . . . . Baltimore
LU 14-R . . . . Baltimore
LU 15 . . . . Baltimore
LU 27 Parking & Service
    Workers . . . . Baltimore
LU 50 . . . . Baltimore
LU 50-7 . . . . Baltimore
LU 50-9 . . . . Baltimore
LU 51 . . . . Baltimore
LU 70 . . . . Baltimore
LU 86 . . . . Baltimore
LU 118-C . . . . Baltimore
LU 128-C . . . . Baltimore
LU 131 . . . . Baltimore
LU 131-A . . . . Baltimore
LU 132 . . . . Baltimore
LU 133-A . . . . Baltimore
LU 137 . . . . Baltimore
LU 138-C . . . . Baltimore
LU 141-LDC . . . . Baltimore
LU 188-A . . . . Baltimore
LU 208-C . . . . Baltimore
LU 224 . . . . Baltimore
LU 239-I . . . . Baltimore
LU 262 . . . . Baltimore
LU 317-C . . . . Baltimore
LU 371-T . . . . Baltimore
LU 393-C . . . . Baltimore
LU 402 . . . . Baltimore
LU 402-C . . . . Baltimore
LU 426-A . . . . Baltimore
LU 427-A . . . . Baltimore
LU 429 . . . . Baltimore
LU 464 . . . . Baltimore
LU 528-A . . . . Baltimore
LU 584-A . . . . Baltimore
LU 604-A . . . . Baltimore
LU 622-A . . . . Baltimore
LU 658-T . . . . Baltimore
LU 673-A . . . . Baltimore
LU 730-T . . . . Baltimore
LU 806-A . . . . Baltimore

LU 844-T . . . . Baltimore
LU 879-A . . . . Baltimore
LU 976-C . . . . Baltimore
LU 998-T . . . . Baltimore
LU 1099 . . . . Baltimore
LU 1118 . . . . Baltimore
LU 1335 . . . . Baltimore
LU 1403 . . . . Baltimore
LU 1436 . . . . Baltimore
LU 1493 . . . . Baltimore
LU 1566 . . . . Baltimore
LU 1598 . . . . Baltimore
LU 1607 . . . . Baltimore
LU 1678 . . . . Baltimore
LU 1701 . . . . Baltimore
LU 1706 . . . . Baltimore
LU 1710 . . . . Baltimore
LU 1739 . . . . Baltimore
LU 1785 . . . . Baltimore
LU 1808 . . . . Baltimore
LU 1853-T . . . . Baltimore
LU 1934 . . . . Baltimore
LU 2247 . . . . Baltimore
LU 2278 . . . . Baltimore

LU 2304 . . . . Baltimore
LU 2326 . . . . Baltimore
LU 2331 . . . . Baltimore
LU 2567 . . . . Baltimore

Utility Workers
LU 102-Q Frederick . . . . Jefferson
LU 102-S . . . . Sharpsburg
LU 419 . . . . Lavale
LU 459 . . . . Port Deposit

Weather Service Employees
BR 01-73 . . . . Suitland
BR 01-76 . . . . . . Silver Spring
BR 01-77 . . . . . . Silver Spring
BR 01-78 . . . . . . Silver Spring
BR 01-80 . . . . . . Silver Spring
BR 01-84 . . . . . . Silver Spring
BR 08-2 . . . . Silver Spring
BR 08-3 . . . . Silver Spring
BR 08-4 . . . . Silver Spring
BR 08-5 . . . . Silver Spring

Westinghouse Salaried Employees
ASSN Baltimore Division . Hanover

Unaffiliated Labor Organizations

Aluminum Racing Plate Workers Union . . . . Middle River
Certified Registered Nurses Anesthetists, Washington Hospital Center . . . . Burtonsville
Certified Registered Nurses Association of Fairfax (CRNA) . . . . Bethesda
Exxon Employees Association of Pennsylvania . . . . Elkton
Faculty Association of the French International School . . Bethesda
French International School of Washington Association of Administrative & Maintenance Personnel . . . . Bethesda
German School-Washington DC Employees Association . Potomac

IAM Representatives Association Independent . . . . Owings
Maryland Professional Staff Association Staff Organization, Professional, Maryland State Teachers . . . . Kensington
National Postal Professional Nurses . . . . Temple Hills
Nurses United of the National Capital Region . . . . Silver Spring
Petroleum Transport Workers . . . . Severn
Security Police & Guards Union Independent LU 1852 . . Baltimore
Staff Union Independent, Communications Workers of America, AFL-CIO . . . Washington Grove
United American Nurses American Nurses Association . Silver Spring
United Industrial, Service, Transportation, Professional and Government Workers of North America NHQ . . . Camp Springs
United Union of Security Guards . . . . Baltimore

Massachusetts

AFL-CIO Trade and Industrial Departments

Building and Construction Trades Department

BCTC Boston . . . . Boston
BCTC Brockton . . . . . Lakeville
BCTC Framingham-
  Newton. . . . . Dorchester
BCTC Merrimack
  Valley . . . . Dorchester
BCTC North Shore . . . . Medway
BCTC Pioneer Valley . . Springfield
BCTC Quincy-South Shore-
  Norfolk . . . . Quincy
BCTC Southeast
  Massachusetts. . . . . Fairhaven
BCTC Worcester . . . . Worcester

Maritime Trades Department

PC Boston-New England
  Area . . . . Boston

Affiliated Labor Organizations

Air Traffic Controllers

LU BFI . . . . Bedford
LU BOS . . . . Boston
LU K90 . . . . . Otis Air National
  Guard Base
LU NATCA Engineers
  Architects . . . . . . Burlington
LU NATCA Local COS . Nantucket
LU NEW . . . . Dennis

Aircraft Mechanics

LU 2 . . . . East Boston

Asbestos Workers

LU 6 . . . . Boston

Automobile, Aerospace Workers

LU 422 . . . . Framingham
LU 470. . . . . Avon
LU 1596. . . . . Dedham
LU 2322 . . . . Holyoke
LU 2324 Boston
  University-Technical
  Office Professionals . . . . Boston

Bakery, Confectionery, Tobacco Workers and Grain Millers

LU 45 . . . . Stoughton
LU 348 . . . . Framingham

Boilermakers

LG 29 . . . . North Quincy
LG 132-D Cement Workers . Dalton
LG 651 . . . . Medford
LG 725 . . . . Springfield
LG 748 . . . . Oxford
LG 1851 . . . . Chicopee

Bricklayers

LU 1 Massachusetts . . . Springfield
LU 3 Eastern
  Massachusetts . . . . Charlestown

Carpenters

C New England Regional . . Boston
LU 26 . . . . Wilmington
LU 33 . . . . South Boston
LU 40 . . . . Cambridge

LU 51. . . . . Dorchester
LU 56. . . . . Boston
LU 67. . . . . Dorchester
LU 107 . . . . Worcester
LU 108 . . . . Springfield
LU 111 . . . . Methuen
LU 218 . . . . Medford
LU 275 . . . . Newton
LU 424 . . . . Randolph
LU 475 . . . . Ashland
LU 535 . . . . Randolph
LU 624 . . . . Randolph
LU 723 . . . . Boston
LU 1121 . . . . Allston
LU 1305 . . . . Fall River
LU 2168 . . . . Dorchester

Catholic School Teachers

LU Boston Archdiocesan Teachers
  Association . . . . . Watertown

Civilian Technicians

CH 39 Western
  Massachusetts. . . . . Westfield

Communications Workers

LU 261 . . . . Lynn
LU 1051. . . . . Fairhaven
LU 1171 . . . . East Boston
LU 1301 . . . . Cambridge
LU 1302 . . . . Lynn
LU 1365 . . . . . North Andover
LU 1395. . . . . Fayville
LU 14117 ITU Local Union
  13 . . . . South Boston
LU 14122 Lawrence Typographical
  Union . . . . . North Andover
LU 14173 . . . . Somerset
LU 31027 . . . . Whitman
LU 31032. . . . . Boston
LU 31055. . . . . Lynn
LU 31245. . . . . Boston
LU 51018 . . . . Swampscott
LU 51019 . . . . Chicopee
LU 81154 . . . . Gardner
LU 81201. . . . . Lynn
LU 81204 . . . . Dracut
LU 81206 . . . . Chicopee
LU 81214 . . . . Marblehead
LU 81216 . . . . Hyannis
LU 81225. . . . . Pittsfield
LU 81228 Moore Drop Forging
  Employees. . . . . Ludlow
LU 81231 . . . . Clarksburg
LU 81232. . . . . Boston
LU 81246 . . . . . . South Hadley
LU 81250 . . . . Warren
LU 81251 . . . . Wilmington
LU 81254. . . . . Pittsfield
LU 81255. . . . . Pittsfield
LU 81274 . . . . Waltham
LU 81284 . . . . . . Indian Orchard
LU 81288 . . . . . . Indian Orchard
LU 81298. . . . . Lynn

Education

LU Endicott College Faculty
  Association . . . . Beverly
LU Laboure College Staff
  Association. . . . . Boston

Electrical Workers

C TCC-1 National Bell
  Coordinating. . . . . . . Quincy
LU 7 . . . . Springfield

LU 96 . . . . Worcester
LU 103 . . . . Dorchester
LU 104 . . . . Walpole
LU 123 . . . . Waltham
LU 223 . . . . Lakeville
LU 326 . . . . Lawrence
LU 455 . . . . Hadley
LU 486 . . . . Worcester
LU 674 . . . . Melrose
LU 791 . . . . Somerville
LU 1014 . . . . Medford
LU 1228 . . . . Newton Highlands
LU 1386 . . . . Newburyport
LU 1465 . . . . Fall River
LU 1499 . . . . Fall River
LU 1505 . . . . Woburn
LU 2222 . . . . Quincy
LU 2313 . . . . Hanover
LU 2321 . . . . . . North Andover
LU 2322 . . . . Middleboro
LU 2324 . . . . Springfield
LU 2325 . . . . Northborough

Electrical, Radio and Machine Workers

DC 2. . . . . Taunton
LU 204 . . . . Taunton
LU 226 . . . . Taunton
LU 240 Looseleaf Book Binder
  Workers Union . . . . Somerset
LU 248 . . . . Fairhaven
LU 262 . . . . South Boston
LU 264 . . . . Ware
LU 269 . . . . Phillipston
LU 270 . . . . Holyoke
LU 271 . . . . South Hamilton
LU 274 . . . . Greenfield
LU 279 . . . . Salem
LU 299 . . . . Taunton

Elevator Constructors

LU 4 . . . . Dorchester
LU 41 . . . . Sterling

Engineers

C General Electric
  Locals. . . . . Wilmington
LU 15 . . . . Boston
LU 101 . . . . Adams
LU 140 . . . . Pittsfield
LU 142 . . . . Lynn
LU 149 . . . . Lynn

Federal Employees

LU 1164 . . . . Concord
LU 1384 . . . . . New Bedford
LU 1884 . . . . Boston

Fire Fighters

LU 78-F Hanscom Air Force Base
  Fire Department . . . . Bedford
LU 264-F Otis Air National
  Guard. . . . . . East Falmouth

Food and Commercial Workers

LU 8-D . . . . Boston
LU 414-C . . . . Belchertown
LU 791 Warehouse Employees
  Union . . . . South Easton
LU 1445. . . . . Dedham
LU 1459 . . . . Springfield

Glass, Molders, Pottery and Plastics Workers

LU 95 . . . . Westfield

LU 169 . . . . Milford
LU 399 . . . . Hanover

Government Employees

C 258 Veteran Affairs
  Department. . . . . . . Boston
LU 38 INS . . . . . . East Boston
LU 221 Boston VA Medical
  Center . . . . Boston
LU 829 USDA. . . . . . . Beverly
LU 948 DoL . . . Swampscott
LU 1164 HHS . . . . . Gloucester
LU 1900 DoD . . . Roslindale
LU 1906 DoD . . . . . . Norton
LU 2143 VA. . . . . . . Brockton
LU 2264 GSA . . . . Boston
LU 2682 DoD. . . . Buzzards Bay
LU 2772 VA . . . . Boston
LU 3004 DoD . . . Otis Air National
  Guard Base
LU 3033 USDA . . . . . . Holden
LU 3258 HUD . . . . . . Boston
LU 3428 EPA . . . . . . Boston
LU 3707 DoD . . . . . Chicopee
LU 3760 HHS . . . . . . Boston
LU 3789 DoI . . . . South Wellfleet
LU 3830 DoD . . . . Pittsfield
LU 3893 DE . . . . Boston

Government Employees Association

LU 1 EMT & Paramedics . . Quincy
LU 556 Police Officers . Springfield
LU 01-4 . . . . Devens
LU 01-8 . . . . Bedford
LU 01-9 . . . . Boston
LU 01-25 . . . . Brockton
LU 01-32 . . . . Woburn
LU 01-34 . . . . Natick
LU 01-54 . . . Otis Air National
  Guard Base
LU 01-86 . . . . . West Roxbury
LU 01-127 . . . . Bourne
LU 01-132 . . . . Pepperell
LU 01-154 . . . . Natick
LU 01-187 . . . . Brockton
LU 01-195 . . . . . . Cambridge
LU 01-274 . . . . Leeds
LU 01-529 . . . . Boston
LU LU-347 IBPO Boston University
  Police Patrolman. . . . . Boston
LU O1-112 General Electric
  Company. . . . . Lynn
LU R1-107. . . . . Leeds
NHQ . . . . Quincy

Government Security Officers

LU 15. . . . . Greenfield

Graphic Communications

CONF Newspaper . . . . Quincy
LU 3-N . . . . Quincy
LU 264-M Springfield-Hartford
  Local. . . . . Belchertown
LU 600-48M . . . . Revere

Iron Workers

DC New England
  States . . . . South Boston
LU 7 . . . . South Boston
LU 501 . . . . Braintree

Journeymen and Allied Trades

LU 15 . . . . East Boston

Laborers

DC Massachusetts . . . . Hopkinton
LU 14 . . . . Salem
LU 22 . . . . Malden
LU 39 . . . . Fitchburg
LU 88 Compressed Air
  Workers . . . . Quincy
LU 133 . . . . Quincy
LU 138 . . . . Norwood
LU 151 . . . . Cambridge
LU 175 . . . . Methuen
LU 223 . . . . Dorchester
LU 243 . . . . Auburn
LU 367 . . . . Scituate
LU 380 . . . . Cambridge
LU 381 . . . . Burlington
LU 385 . . . . Fairhaven
LU 429 . . . . Lowell
LU 473 . . . . Pittsfield
LU 560 . . . . Waltham
LU 596 . . . . Holyoke
LU 609 . . . . Framingham
LU 610 Construction . . . Fall River
LU 721 . . . . . East Bridgewater
LU 876 . . . . Taunton
LU 999 . . . . . East Longmeadow
LU 1144 . . . . Taunton
LU 1162 . . . . Brockton
LU 1249 . . . . Falmouth
LU 1285 . . . . Beverly
LU 1421 Building Wreckers . Boston

Letter Carriers

BR 7 . . . . Revere
BR 12 . . . . Worcester
BR 25 . . . . Tewksbury
BR 33 . . . . Beverly
BR 34 . . . . South Boston
BR 46 . . . . Springfield
BR 51 . . . . Somerset
BR 64 . . . . Northampton
BR 71 . . . . Taunton
BR 156 . . . . Middleboro
BR 212 . . . . Lawrence
BR 286 . . . . Pittsfield
BR 308 . . . . Milford
BR 334 . . . . Framingham
BR 362 . . . . Natick
BR 539 . . . . . . North Attleboro
BR 742 . . . . Norwood
BR 764 . . . . Dedham
BR 1614 . . . . Turners Falls
BR 1661 . . . . Nantucket
BR 1708 . . . . Fairhaven
BR 1798 . . . . Shelburne Falls
BR 1800 . . . . Walpole
BR 1978 . . . . . West Springfield
BR 2124 . . . . Ayer
BR 2512 . . . . Brockton
BR 3240 . . . . Merrimac
BR 4497 . . . . East Walpole
BR 5525 . . . . Seekonk
SA Massachusetts . . . . . Brockton

Locomotive Engineers

DIV 57 . . . . Boston
DIV 63 . . . . West Springfield
DIV 312 . . . . . North Weymouth
LU 112 BLE-T . . . . . Greenfield
SLB Massachusetts . . . . . Oakham

Longshoremen

DC New England Dock &
  Marine . . . . Braintree
LU 799 . . . . Boston
LU 800 . . . . Dorchester
LU 805 . . . . Rockland
LU 809 . . . . Boston

LU 1066 . . . . Raynham
LU 1413 . . . . New Bedford
LU 1572-2 . . . . Malden
LU 1604 . . . . Stoneham
LU 1749 . . . . New Bedford
LU 1908 . . . . Everett

Machinists

LG 25-S . . . . Winthrop
LG 264 . . . . Quincy
LG 318 . . . . Foxboro
LG 481 . . . . Erving
LG 587 . . . . Fall River
LG 1271 . . . . Methuen
LG 1420 Hassett . . . . Chicopee
LG 1726 . . . . East Boston
LG 2654 . . . . Gloucester
STC Massachusetts . . . . . Norton

Maintenance of Way Employes

LG 160 . . . . Phillipston
LG 347 . . . . Greenfield
LG 987 . . . . Danvers
SLG 201 . . . . Beverly
SLG 612 . . . . Granby

Musicians

CONF New England . . . . Taunton
LU 9-535 . . . . Belmont
LU 126 . . . . Amesbury
LU 138 . . . . Holbrook
LU 143 . . . . Worcester
LU 171 . . . . Springfield
LU 173 . . . . Lunenburg
LU 216 . . . . Fall River
LU 231 . . . . Taunton
LU 281 . . . . Kingston
LU 300 . . . . Lowell
LU 302 . . . . Haverhill
LU 393 Framingham-
  Marlboro . . . . Maynard

National Staff Organization

LU Field Services
  Organization . . . . Auburn
LU Staff Association, Massachusetts
  Teachers Association . . Raynham
LU Teacher Attorneys,
  Massachusetts Association
of . . . . Boston

NLRB Professional Association

LU 1 . . . . Boston

Nurses

D 2 Massachusetts Nurses
  Association . . . . Fiskdale
D 3 Massachusetts . . . . Edgartown
D 4 Massachusetts . . . . . Peabody
D 5 Massachusetts . . . . . Canton
SA Massachusetts Nurses
  Association . . . . Canton

Office and Professional Employees

LU 6 . . . . Quincy
LU 453 . . . . South Boston
LU 1021 . . . . Peabody
LU 1295 . . . . Woburn

Operating Engineers

LU 4 . . . . Medway
LU 98 . . . . . East Longmeadow
LU 877 . . . . Norwood

Painters

DC 35 . . . . Roslindale
LU 48 . . . . Worcester
LU 257 . . . . Springfield

LU 391 . . . . Roslindale
LU 402 . . . . East Boston
LU 577 . . . . Roslindale
LU 691 . . . . New Bedford
LU 939 . . . . Dorchester
LU 1044 . . . . Roslindale
LU 1138 . . . . Dorchester
LU 1280 . . . . Sutton
LU 1333 . . . . . . North Dartmouth

Plasterers and Cement Masons

LU 534 . . . . Boston

Plumbing and Pipe Fitting

LU 4 . . . . Worcester
LU 12 . . . . Boston
LU 104 . . . . Chicopee
LU 138 . . . . Danvers
LU 537 . . . . Allston
LU 550 . . . . Boston

Police Associations

LU 364 Police Officers . Springfield

Postal Mail Handlers

LU 301 . . . . Natick

Postal Workers

LU 100 Boston . . . . Boston
LU 219 North
  Attleboro . . . . . North Attleboro
LU 366 Northeast Area . Tewksbury
LU 485 Peabody . . . . . Peabody
LU 497 Springfield . . . Springfield
LU 511 Fall River . . . . . Fall River
LU 638 North Adams . North Adams
LU 755 Western Mass
  Area . . . . East Hampton
LU 756 Framingham . . Framingham
LU 2461 Lynn . . . . Lynn
LU 3451 Pittsfield . . . . . Pittsfield
LU 3844 South Shore
  Area . . . . Brockton
LU 4553 Central Massachusetts
  Area . . . . Worcester
LU 4631
  Williamstown . . . Williamstown
LU 4692 Attleboro . . . . Attleboro
LU 4930 Hyannis
  Area . . . . South Dennis
LU 4952 Randolph . . . . Randolph
LU 5045 Taunton . . . . . Taunton
LU 5345 Whitinsville . . Whitinsville
LU 6005 Cape Cod
  Area . . . . West Wareham
LU 6021 Athol . . . . Athol
LU 6492 Gloucester . . . Rockport
LU 6592 Whitman . . . . Whitman
LU 6758 Sharon . . . . . Sharon
SA Massachusetts . . . South Hadley

Railroad Signalmen

LLG 120 . . . . Woburn
LLG 213 . . . . . West Brookfield

Retail, Wholesale and Department Store

JB New England Joint
  Board . . . . Leominster
LU 60 . . . . Leominster
LU 173 New England Joint
  Board . . . . Leominster
LU 224 . . . . Leominster
LU 444 . . . . Leominster
LU 513 . . . . Leominster
LU 515 . . . . Leominster
LU 566 . . . . Leominster
LU 584 . . . . Leominster

LU 588 . . . . Leominster
LU 593 . . . . Leominster
LU 599 . . . . Leominster
LU 875 . . . . Leominster
LU 965 . . . . Leominster

Roofers, Waterproofers and Allied Workers

LU 33 . . . . Stoughton
LU 248 . . . . Chicopee

Rural Letter Carriers

D 1 . . . . Granby
D 2 . . . . Middleboro
D 3 . . . . Shirley
D 4 . . . . Westborough
SA Massachusetts . . . . . Boston

Security, Police and Fire Professionals

LU 540 . . . . Manomet
LU 541 . . . . Centerville
LU 543 . . . . Leicester
LU 547 . . . . Saugus

Service Employees

C Massachusetts State
  Council . . . . Boston
LU Committee of Interns &
  Residents . . . . Boston
LU 3 Firemen & Oilers . Charlestown
LU 9 . . . . Boston
LU 46 . . . . Chicopee
LU 143 Firemen &
  Oilers . . . . Northampton
LU 211 . . . . Holyoke
LU 263 Smith College
  Emloyees . . . . Florence
LU 509 . . . . Watertown
LU 615 . . . . Boston
LU 888 . . . . Charlestown
LU 2020 . . . . Roxbury
LU 2020 . . . . Roxbury

Sheet Metal Workers

LU 17 . . . . Dorchester
LU 63 . . . . Springfield
LU 139 . . . . Hyde Park
LU 377 . . . . Lowell

Shoe and Allied Craftsmen

LU Cutters . . . . . East Bridgewater
LU Dressers &
  Packers . . . . . East Bridgewater
LU Edgetrimmers . East Bridgewater
LU Finishers . . . . East Bridgewater
LU Goodyear
  Operators . . . . East Bridgewater
LU Heelers . . . . East Bridgewater
LU Lasters . . . . . East Bridgewater
LU Mixed Local . . . . Middleboro
LU Stitchers . . . . East Bridgewater
LU Treers . . . . Brockton
LU Vampers . . . . East Bridgewater
NHQ . . . . East Bridgewater

State, County and Municipal Employees

C 93 AFSCME . . . . Boston
LU 683 Salem Hospital
  RN's . . . . Boston
LU 851 Southern Bristol
  County Municipal
  Employees . . . . . New Bedford
LU 2511 . . . . Boston
LU 2824 . . . . Plymouth
LU 3650 Harvard Clerical &
  Technical Workers . . . Cambridge

Steelworkers
LU 9431 . . . . Rockland
LU 7-9432 . . . . Medford
LU 01-3 . . . . Lawrence
LU 01-78. . . . . Lee
LU 01-197. . . . . Westfield
LU 01-204 . . . . Haverhill
LU 01-366. . . . . Stoneham
LU 01-383 . . . . Thorndike
LU 01-453 . . . . Attleboro
LU 01-513 . . . . Holyoke
LU 01-516 . . . . Hudson
LU 01-521 . . . . Baldwinville
LU 01-579. . . . . Longmeadow
LU 01-594 . . . . Orange
LU 01-599 . . . . Norwood
LU 01-708 . . . . Warren
LU 01-818. . . . . Gardner
LU 01-836 . . . . Worcester
LU 01-880 . . . . West Groton
LU 01-905 . . . . Somerville
LU 01-916 . . . . Wareham
LU 01-917. . . . . Athol
LU 01-1102. . . . . . . Westminster
LU 01-1395 . . . . Monson
LU 01-1409 . . . . . . South Boston
LU 01-1702 . . . . . . Marlborough
LU 01-1772 . . . . Lowell
LU 01-1889 . . . . Brockton
LU 04-94 . . . . Milford
LU 04-421-U. . . . . Brockton
LU 04-506-L . . . . Templeton
LU 04-562-L. . . . . Brockton
LU 04-2285-S . . . . Auburn
LU 04-2431-S . . . . Medford
LU 04-2782-S . . . . Somerset
LU 04-2936-S . . . . Auburn
LU 04-7896-S . . . . Fitchburg
LU 04-7912-S . . . . Chicopee
LU 04-8672-S . . . . . . Sturbridge
LU 04-8751-S . . . . . . Roslindale
LU 04-9358-S . . . . Charlestown
LU 04-9360-S . . . . Charlestown
LU 04-12003-s . . . . . Dorchester
LU 04-12004-S . . . . . . Hudson
LU 04-12012-s . . . . . . Peabody
LU 04-12026-S . . . . Springfield
LU 04-12266-S . . . . Georgetown
LU 04-12282-S . . . . . . Dracut
LU 04-12325-S. . . . . . . Pittsfield
LU 04-13492-S . . . . . . Norwell
LU 04-13507-S . . . . . . Pocasset
LU 04-13585-S . . . . . . Dedham
LU 23-1357 . . . . North Dartmouth

Teachers
LU 2403 Wentworth Faculty
　Federation . . . . Boston
LU 3359 Becker Junior College
　Federation of Teachers . Worcester
LU 4412 Berklee Federation of
　Teachers . . . . Boston
LU 5023 Nurses & Health
　Professionals, Fairview. Mill River
SFED Massachusetts . . . . Boston

Teamsters
JC 10 . . . . Charlestown
LU 1 Boston Mailers Union . Quincy
LU 25. . . . . Charlestown
LU 42. . . . . Lynn
LU 49. . . . . Dracut
LU 59 . . . . New Bedford
LU 82 . . . . South Boston
LU 122 Metro Boston Auto Salesman
　Union. . . . . Boston
LU 170 . . . . Worcester
LU 259 . . . . South Boston

LU 379 . . . . Charlestown
LU 404. . . . . Springfield
LU 653 International Brotherhood of
　Teamsters . . . . . South Easton

Television and Radio Artists
LU Boston . . . . Boston

Theatrical Stage Employees
D 3 Maine-New Hampshire-
　Vermont-Massachusetts-Rhode
　Island-Connecticut. . . . . Boston
LU 4-B . . . . Boston
LU 11. . . . . Boston
LU 53 . . . . Springfield
LU 83 . . . . North Adams
LU 96 . . . . Hubbardston
LU 182 IATSE. . . . . . Cambridge
LU 186. . . . . Ludlow
LU 232 . . . . Amherst
LU 437. . . . . Abington
LU 481 . . . . Woburn
LU 753 Treasures and Ticket
　Sellers . . . . Boston
LU 775. . . . . Plymouth
LU 792. . . . . Plymouth
LU 935-B Arena
　Employees . . . . Charlton

Train Dispatchers
SCOM Amtrak . . . . . . Franklin
SCOM SCOM MBCR . . . Dedham

Transit Union
LDIV 22 . . . . Worcester
LDIV 690 . . . . Fitchburg
LDIV 1037 . . . . . New Bedford
LDIV 1363 . . . . Swansea
LDIV 1547. . . . . Brockton
LDIV 1548 . . . . Plymouth
LU 448. . . . . Springfield
LU 1512 . . . . Springfield

Transport Workers
LU 507. . . . . Winthrop
LU 2054 . . . . Attleboro

**Transportation Communications
　Union**
D 812 . . . . Shrewsbury
D 1089 . . . . Hanover
D 1374 Conrail. . . . . . . Lynn
LG 6315 Prospect . . . Tewksbury

Transportation Union
GCA GO-81 . . . . . Framingham
LU 262. . . . . Plymouth
LU 587. . . . . Gill
LU 1462 . . . . Weymouth
LU 1473 . . . . Framingham
SLB LO-24 . . . . Natick

Treasury Employees
CH 23. . . . . Boston
CH 68. . . . . Andover
CH 102 BATF . . . . . . Boston
CH 133 . . . . Boston
CH 236 . . . . Boston
CH 241 . . . . Lexington
CH 253 . . . . Boston
CH 288 FDA
　Massachusetts . . . . Winchester

UNITE HERE
JB New England . . . . . . Boston
LU 1 . . . . . . North Dartmouth
LU 12. . . . . Boston
LU 12-ASW. . . . North Dartmouth

LU 24. . . . . Boston
LU 26. . . . . Boston
LU 31 . . . . . . North Dartmouth
LU 33-I. . . . . Boston
LU 73-I. . . . . Boston
LU 75. . . . . Boston
LU 80-I. . . . . Boston
LU 88 . . . . . . North Dartmouth
LU 110-A . . . . North Dartmouth
LU 121-H . . . . North Dartmouth
LU 141 . . . . Boston
LU 151-I . . . . Boston
LU 164 . . . . Boston
LU 177 . . . . . North Dartmouth
LU 178 . . . . Boston
LU 187-A . . . . North Dartmouth
LU 223 . . . . Boston
LU 226 . . . . Boston
LU 229 . . . . Boston
LU 242 . . . . Boston
LU 257 . . . . Boston
LU 281 . . . . Boston
LU 301 . . . . Boston
LU 305-T . . . . North Dartmouth
LU 311 . . . . Boston
LU 313 . . . . Boston
LU 324 . . . . Boston
LU 341 . . . . Boston
LU 359-I . . . . Boston
LU 361 . . . . Boston
LU 377-C . . . . North Dartmouth
LU 400-A . . . . North Dartmouth
LU 406-A . . . . North Dartmouth
LU 431-T . . . . North Dartmouth
LU 438 . . . . . North Dartmouth
LU 469-A . . . . North Dartmouth
LU 471-A . . . . North Dartmouth
LU 477-A . . . . North Dartmouth
LU 484-I . . . . Boston
LU 486-C . . . . North Dartmouth
LU 513 . . . . Boston
LU 533-I . . . . Boston
LU 554-I . . . . Boston
LU 580 . . . . Boston
LU 616-T . . . . North Dartmouth
LU 624 . . . . Boston
LU 652-T . . . . North Dartmouth
LU 687-T . . . . North Dartmouth
LU 808-A . . . . North Dartmouth
LU 911 . . . . . North Dartmouth
LU 939-A . . . . North Dartmouth
LU 1016-A . . . . North Dartmouth
LU 1036-T. . . . North Dartmouth
LU 1156-T. . . . North Dartmouth
LU 1198-T. . . . North Dartmouth
LU 1208-T. . . . North Dartmouth
LU 1226 . . . . . North Dartmouth
LU 1296 . . . . . North Dartmouth
LU 1321 . . . . . North Dartmouth
LU 1362 . . . . . North Dartmouth
LU 1371 . . . . . North Dartmouth
LU 1460 . . . . . North Dartmouth
LU 1468-T. . . . North Dartmouth
LU 1483 . . . . . North Dartmouth
LU 1554-T. . . . North Dartmouth
LU 1560 . . . . . North Dartmouth
LU 1569 . . . . . North Dartmouth
LU 1723 . . . . . North Dartmouth
LU 1751 . . . . . North Dartmouth
LU 1832 . . . . . North Dartmouth
LU 1834-T. . . . North Dartmouth
LU 1856 . . . . . North Dartmouth
LU 1999 . . . . Boston
LU 2001 . . . . Boston
LU 2370-T. . . . North Dartmouth
LU 2527 . . . . . North Dartmouth
LU 2624 . . . . . North Dartmouth
LU 2661 . . . . . North Dartmouth

LU 2687-T. . . . North Dartmouth
LU 2688-T. . . . North Dartmouth

University Professors
CH Curry College . . . Milton
CH Emerson College. . . . . Boston

Utility Workers
LU 273 . . . . Norton
LU 362 . . . . Nantucket
LU 369. . . . . Braintree
LU 396. . . . . Somerset
LU 431 . . . . Swansea
LU 464. . . . . Somerset
LU 472 . . . . . . South Attleboro
LU 480 . . . . Sandwich
LU 590. . . . . Manomet
LU 654. . . . . Malden

Weather Service Employees
BR 01-11 . . . . Taunton
BR 01-62 . . . . Taunton
BR 08-6 . . . . Gloucester

Unaffiliated Labor
Organizations
American General Workers Union
　LU 86. . . . . Walpole
Berkshire Transportation Association
　LU 2 . . . . Pittsfield
Boston College Police
　Association Union of Campus
　Police . . . . Chestnut Hill
Brandeis University Police
　Association . . . . Waltham
Court Security Officers
　Association. . . . . Boston
Diocesan Educators Lay Teacher
　Association National Association
　of Catholic School
　Teachers . . . . Worcester
Educational Foundation Employees
　Association . . . . . Cambridge
Exxon Workers Union Inc. . Billerica
Harvard University Police
　Association . . . . . . Whitman
Harvard University Security, Parking,
　and Museum Guards
　Union . . . . Cambridge
Independent Union of Plant
　Protection Employees LU 2 . Lynn
Jewish Family & Children
　Service Employees
　Association . . . . Newton Centre
Ken's Food's Employee
　Union . . . . Marlborough
Laundry Workers Union Independent
　LU 66-L . . . . North Dartmouth
Maintenance & Service Employees
　Union of America. . . . Wellesley
Massachusetts Building Trade
　Council Inc. . . . . . Dorchester
Massachusetts Institute of
　Technology Campus
　Police Association
　Independent . . . . . . Cambridge
Massachusetts Nurses Association
　New England Nurses
　Association . . . . Canton
Museum of Fine Arts Independent
　Security Union (MISU) . . Boston
Northeastern University Police
　Association (NUPA) . . Boston
Patriot Ledger Associates . Kingston
Petroleum Workers Association
　Middlesex . . . . Arlington

Professional Chapter St. Elizabeth Hospital Local . . . . Quincy

Raytheon Guards Association . . . . Foxboro

Raytheon Guards Association LU 2 . . . . Haverhill

Research Development & Technical Employees Union . . . . Arlington

Security & Guard Association of Rhode Island . . . . . . Seekonk

Security & Watchmens Amalgamated Union. . . . . Boston

Service Maintenance & Mechanics Association Inc. . . . . . . Revere

Springfield Newspapers Employees Association Inc. . . . . Springfield

Staff Association of AJCC Greater Boston. . . . . Newton

Suffolk University Police Association. . . . . Boston

Tanker Officers American Association . . . Great Barrington

The Guild of Massachusetts Nurses Association Employees . . Canton

Union Employees, American Federation, Independent . . Holden

Union of Campus Police Wellesley College Campus Police . Wellesley

Union Workers Union Staff Union of SEIU LU 285. . . . . . . Roxbury

Utility Workers Council LU 317 . . . . Beverly

Utility Workers Council LU 318 . . . . Beverly

Utility Workers Council LU 322 . . . . Monson

Utility Workers Council LU 329. . . . . . West Boylston

Utility Workers Council LU 330 . . . . Worcester

Utility Workers Council LU 340 . . . . Fitchburg

Utility Workers Council LU 343. . . . . Dudley

Utility Workers Council LU 345 . . . . Westborough

Utility Workers Council LU 350 . . . . Leominster

Utility Workers Council LU 355 . . . . Berlin

Waltham Drivers Association . . . . . . Waltham

Michigan

AFL-CIO Trade and Industrial Departments

Building and Construction Trades Department

BCTC Detroit-Wayne County . . . . Detroit
BCTC Flint-Genesee-Shiawassee & Lapeer . . . . Flint
BCTC Michigan. . . . . . . Lansing
BCTC Northern Michigan . . . . . . Traverse City
BCTC Southeastern Michigan . . . . Jackson
BCTC Southwestern Michigan . . . . Galesburg
BCTC Tri-County . . . . . Bay City
BCTC Upper Peninsula. . . . . . Iron Mountain
BCTC Washtenaw County . . . . Ann Arbor
BCTC Washtenaw County Skilled Building & Construction Trades . . . . Ann Arbor

Maritime Trades Department

PC Michigan . . . . Algonac

AFL-CIO Directly Affiliated Locals

AFL-CIO

DALU 3064 Billposters & Billers . . . . Warren
DALU 23409 Protection Employees . . . . . . Muskegon

Affiliated Labor Organizations

Agricultural Employees

BR 20 . . . . Willis

Air Traffic Controllers

LU ARB . . . . Ann Arbor
LU AZO . . . . Portage
LU D21. . . . . Detroit
LU DTW . . . . Detroit
LU FNT. . . . . Flint
LU GRR. . . . . . . Grand Rapids
LU LAN. . . . . Lansing
LU MBS . . . . Freeland
LU MKG . . . . Muskegon
LU PTK . . . . Waterford
LU TVC . . . . Traverse City
LU YIP . . . . Belleville

Aircraft Mechanics

LU 5 . . . . Romulus

Asbestos Workers

LU 25 . . . . Southfield
LU 47 . . . . Saginaw
LU 207 . . . . Taylor

Automobile, Aerospace Workers

C Barry County . . . . Grand Rapids
C Bay County. . . . . . Saginaw
C Berrien-Cass-Van Buren . . . . . . Three Rivers
C Central U.P. UAW CAP Council . . . . . . Escanaba
C Dekalb County . . . . . Coldwater
C Ionia-Montcalm Counties. . . . . . Grand Rapids
C Kalamazoo/St. Joseph County CAP Council . . . . . . Three Rivers
C Kent County CAP . . Grand Rapids
C Menominee County . . . Escanaba
C Michigan CAP . . . . . . Detroit
C Muskegon County . Grand Rapids
C National CAP . . . . . . Detroit
C Northern Michigan . Traverse City
C Quad County CAP . . . Saginaw
C Region 1 CAP . . . . . . Detroit
C Region 1-A CAP. . . . . Detroit
C Region 1-C CAP. . . . . Detroit
C Region 1-D CAP. . . . . Detroit
C Region 1-D CAP . . Grand Rapids
C Saginaw County CAP . . Saginaw
C Wexford-Osceola Counties. . . . . . Traverse City
LU 1 . . . . Watervliet
LU 4 . . . . Ionia
LU 7 . . . . Warren
LU 8. . . . . Sparta
LU 19 . . . . Wyoming
LU 21 . . . . Traverse City
LU 22. . . . . Detroit
LU 36 . . . . Wixom
LU 38. . . . . Ann Arbor
LU 44 . . . . Port Huron
LU 51 . . . . Detroit
LU 62 . . . . Jackson
LU 67 . . . . Alma
LU 113 . . . . Muskegon
LU 135 . . . . Grand Rapids
LU 137 . . . . Greenville
LU 138 . . . . Hastings
LU 140. . . . . Warren
LU 155 Warren-Detroit Local. . . . . Warren
LU 160. . . . . Warren
LU 163 . . . . Detroit
LU 167 . . . . Wyoming
LU 174 New West Side . . Romulus
LU 182. . . . . Livonia
LU 212 . . . . . Sterling Heights
LU 220 . . . . Marshall
LU 228 . . . . . Sterling Heights
LU 235 . . . . Hamtramck
LU 245 . . . . Dearborn
LU 246 . . . . Detroit
LU 247 . . . . . Sterling Heights
LU 262 . . . . Hamtramck
LU 284 . . . . Holland
LU 306 . . . . Detroit
LU 308 . . . . Grand Rapids
LU 318 . . . . Alpena
LU 330 . . . . Wyoming
LU 334 . . . . Blissfield
LU 362 . . . . Bay City
LU 369 . . . . . . St. Clair Shores
LU 372 . . . . Trenton
LU 375 St. Clair . . . . Marysville
LU 383 . . . . Benton Harbor
LU 387 . . . . Flat Rock
LU 388 . . . . Gaylord
LU 389 . . . . Big Rapids
LU 400 Mount Clemens-Highland Park Local . . . . Utica
LU 412 . . . . Warren
LU 437 . . . . Chelsea
LU 455 . . . . Saginaw
LU 467 . . . . Saginaw
LU 475 . . . . Jackson
LU 496 . . . . Bay City
LU 503 . . . . Mendon
LU 504 . . . . Michigan Center
LU 524 Fenton-Holly Local . . Flint
LU 537 . . . . Saginaw
LU 539 . . . . Muskegon
LU 566 . . . . Menominee
LU 594 . . . . Pontiac
LU 598 . . . . Flint
LU 599 . . . . Flint
LU 600 . . . . Dearborn
LU 602 . . . . Lansing
LU 637 . . . . Muskegon
LU 649 . . . . Watervliet
LU 651 . . . . Flint
LU 652 . . . . Lansing
LU 653 Pontiac Local . . . . Pontiac
LU 659 . . . . Flint
LU 660 . . . . Jackson
LU 668 . . . . Saginaw
LU 670 . . . . Litchfield
LU 699 . . . . Saginaw
LU 704 . . . . Galesburg
LU 708 Corunna-Flint Local . Burton
LU 723 . . . . Monroe
LU 724 . . . . Lansing
LU 730 . . . . Grand Rapids
LU 735 . . . . Canton
LU 743 . . . . Owosso
LU 771 Warren-Detroit Local . Troy
LU 783 . . . . Scottville
LU 811 . . . . Ludington
LU 812 . . . . Minden City
LU 822 . . . . Bronson
LU 828 . . . . Grandville
LU 845 . . . . Canton
LU 849 . . . . Ypsilanti
LU 869 . . . . Warren
LU 878 . . . . Monroe
LU 889 Detroit-Warren Local. . . . . Warren
LU 892 . . . . Saline
LU 898 . . . . Ypsilanti
LU 900 . . . . Wayne
LU 909 . . . . Warren
LU 925 . . . . St. Johns
LU 931 . . . . Dearborn
LU 961 . . . . Detroit
LU 963 . . . . Adrian
LU 1002 . . . . Middleville
LU 1009 . . . . Battle Creek
LU 1134 . . . . Pinconning
LU 1135 . . . . Freeland
LU 1149 . . . . Marysville
LU 1158 . . . . Greenville
LU 1176 . . . . Albion
LU 1210 . . . . South Haven
LU 1218 . . . . Dowagiac
LU 1223 . . . . Bronson
LU 1231 . . . . . . Comstock Park
LU 1243 . . . . Whitehall
LU 1248 Allen Park-Warren Local. . . . . Warren
LU 1264 . . . . . Sterling Heights
LU 1279 . . . . Muskegon
LU 1284 . . . . Chelsea
LU 1292 . . . . Grand Blanc
LU 1294 . . . . Homer
LU 1313 . . . . Plymouth
LU 1320 . . . . . . Byron Center
LU 1348 . . . . Petersburg
LU 1374 . . . . Detroit
LU 1386 . . . . Coldwater
LU 1395 . . . . Bronson
LU 1402 . . . . Holland
LU 1403 . . . . Boyne City
LU 1433 . . . . Cadillac
LU 1436 . . . . Edmore
LU 1440 . . . . Plymouth
LU 1464 . . . . Ludington
LU 1485. . . . . . . Grand Rapids
LU 1488 . . . . Lansing
LU 1511 . . . . Mancelona
LU 1554 . . . . Greenville
LU 1586. . . . . Reed City
LU 1618 . . . . Lansing
LU 1637 . . . . West Branch
LU 1660 . . . . Elsie
LU 1666 . . . . Kalamazoo
LU 1669 . . . . Petoskey
LU 1700 . . . . Detroit
LU 1703 . . . . Muskegon
LU 1753 . . . . Lansing
LU 1781 . . . . Southfield
LU 1811 . . . . . . Swartz Creek
LU 1819 . . . . . . Roscommon
LU 1869 . . . . Ira
LU 1966 . . . . Munith
LU 1970 . . . . Dearborn
LU 1972 . . . . . . Benton Harbor
LU 1996 . . . . Watervliet
LU 2017 . . . . Greenville
LU 2031 . . . . Adrian
LU 2064 . . . . Allegan
LU 2076 . . . . . . New Buffalo
LU 2093 . . . . . . Three Rivers
LU 2101 . . . . Manton
LU 2122 . . . . Dowagiac
LU 2145 . . . . Grand Rapids
LU 2151 . . . . Coopersville
LU 2214 . . . . . . Roscommon
LU 2228 . . . . Portage
LU 2256 . . . . Lansing
LU 2270 . . . . Evart
LU 2275 . . . . Pinconning
LU 2280 . . . . Utica
LU 2304 . . . . . . Byron Center
LU 2331 . . . . Hudson
LU 2344 . . . . . . Byron Center
LU 2363 Mesa . . . . Adrian
LU 2392 . . . . Grand Rapids
LU 2393 . . . . Zeeland
LU 2403 . . . . . . Traverse City
LU 2416 . . . . Hillsdale
LU 2417 . . . . Big Rapids
LU 2500 . . . . Detroit
LU 2600 . . . . Wyoming
LU 3000. . . . . Woodhaven
LU 3032 . . . . Mesick
LU 3037 . . . . Watervliet
LU 3803 . . . . . Sault Ste. Marie
LU 3911 . . . . Pontiac
LU 4077 . . . . Howell
LU 4911 . . . . Lansing
LU 5110 . . . . Kingsley
LU 5960 . . . . Lake Orion
LU 6911 Pontiac General Hospital Nurses . . . . Pontiac
LU 7777 . . . . Detroit
LU 9699. . . . . Marlette
NHQ . . . . Detroit

Bakery, Confectionery, Tobacco Workers and Grain Millers

LU 3-G . . . . Battle Creek
LU 66-G . . . . Dowling
LU 70 . . . . Grand Rapids
LU 81 . . . . Traverse City
LU 259-G . . . . Chesaning
LU 260-G . . . . Cass City
LU 261-G . . . . Sebewaing
LU 262-G . . . . Croswell

LU 263-G . . . . Essexville
LU 326 . . . . Allen Park
LU 365-G . . . . Battle Creek

Boilermakers
LG 7-M . . . . Saranac
LG 169 . . . . Dearborn
LG 335-D Cement
  Workers . . . . Essexville
LG 351-D Cement Workers . Alpena
LG 408-D Cement
  Workers . . . . Petersburg
LG 472-D Cement Workers . . Posen
LG 480-D Cement
  Workers . . . . Charlevoix
LG 500-D Cement Workers . Hawks
LG 699 . . . . Menominee

Bricklayers
LU 1 Michigan . . . . Warren
LU 6 Michigan . . . . . Marquette
LU 9 . . . . Lansing

Carpenters
C Michigan Regional 4085 . . Detroit
LU 100 . . . . Coopersville
LU 202 . . . . Bay City
LU 525 . . . . Kalamazoo
LU 687 . . . . Detroit
LU 706 . . . . Saginaw
LU 1004 . . . . Lansing
LU 1045 . . . . Warren
LU 1102 . . . . Warren
LU 1234 . . . . Warren
LU 1510 . . . . Escanaba
LU 1615 . . . . Alto
LU 1701 . . . . Kentwood
LU 2776 . . . . Kalamazoo

Christian Labor Association
LU 10 United Construction
  Workers . . . . Zeeland
LU 12 Service Employees . Zeeland
LU 18 United Construction
  Workers . . . . Zeeland
LU 55 United Metal
  Workers . . . . Zeeland
NHQ . . . . Zeeland

Civilian Technicians
CH 13 Detroit Area . . Selfridge Air
  National Guard Base
CH 15 Battle Creek . . . Battle Creek
STC State . . . . Selfridge Air
  National Guard Base

Communications Workers
C Metro Area . . . . Southfield
JB Unified Council of
  Michigan . . . . Lansing
LU 4004 . . . . Detroit
LU 4008 . . . . . Mount Clemens
LU 4009 . . . . Southfield
LU 4011 . . . . Ann Arbor
LU 4013 . . . . Pontiac
LU 4017 . . . . Wayne
LU 4018 . . . . Wyandotte
LU 4024 . . . . Chassell
LU 4025 . . . . Ishpeming
LU 4032 . . . . Coloma
LU 4034 . . . . Wyoming
LU 4035 . . . . Holland
LU 4039 . . . . Kalamazoo
LU 4040 . . . . Lansing
LU 4050 . . . . Detroit
LU 4070 . . . . Warren
LU 4090 . . . . Detroit
LU 4100 . . . . Detroit

LU 4101 . . . . Bay City
LU 4103 . . . . Flint
LU 4107 . . . . Port Huron
LU 4108 . . . . Saginaw
LU 14501 . . . . Alpena
LU 14503 . . . . Detroit
LU 14504 . . . . Escanaba
LU 14508 . . . . Lake Ann
LU 34022 . . . . Detroit
LU 54043 NABET Local
  43 . . . . Southfield
LU 54046 . . . . Flint
LU 54048 . . . . Bay City
LU 54412 . . . . . Mount Pleasant
LU 84415 . . . . . Grand Rapids
LU 84419 . . . . Petoskey
LU 84422 . . . . Flint
LU 84436 . . . . Ionia
LU 84438 . . . . Greenville
LU 84444 . . . . Ionia
LU 84932 . . . . . . Garden City
LU 84981 . . . . . Grand Rapids

Education
ASSN Detroit College Business
  Faculty . . . . Dearborn
LU Adrian College Association of
  Professors . . . . Adrian
LU Baker College Education
  Association . . . . Flint
LU University of Detroit Professors'
  Union . . . . Birmingham
LU University of Detroit Support
  Staff . . . . Detroit
SA Michigan Education
  Association . . . . . East Lansing

Electrical Workers
LU 17 . . . . Southfield
LU 58 . . . . Detroit
LU 131 . . . . Galesburg
LU 205 . . . . Southgate
LU 219 . . . . Iron Mountain
LU 252 . . . . Ann Arbor
LU 275 . . . . Coopersville
LU 352 . . . . Lansing
LU 445 . . . . Battle Creek
LU 498 . . . . Traverse City
LU 510 . . . . Marquette
LU 557 . . . . Saginaw
LU 665 . . . . Lansing
LU 692 . . . . Bay City
LU 876 . . . . . . Comstock Park
LU 948 . . . . Flint
LU 979 . . . . Escanaba
LU 1070 . . . . Marquette
LU 1106 . . . . Lansing
LU 1672 . . . . . . Benton Harbor

Elevator Constructors
LU 36 . . . . Detroit
LU 85 . . . . Lansing

Federal Employees
LU 1804 . . . . Detroit
LU 1928 . . . . . . Bruce Crossing
LU 2083 . . . . Gladstone
LU 2086 . . . . Cadillac

Food and Commercial Workers
C United Local
  Unions . . . . . Madison Heights
LU 16 . . . . Saginaw
LU 70-C . . . . Muskegon
LU 132-C . . . . Zeeland
LU 169-B . . . . Kalamazoo
LU 232 . . . . Battle Creek
LU 600-A . . . . Rockford

LU 689 . . . . Ann Arbor
LU 799-C . . . . . Sault Ste. Marie
LU 867-C . . . . . . Smiths Creek
LU 876 . . . . . Madison Heights
LU 951 . . . . . . Grand Rapids
LU 1039-C . . . . . . Roscommon
LU 1044-C . . . . . . Tawas City

**Glass, Molders, Pottery and
  Plastics Workers**
CONBD Michigan L
  Vicinity . . . . Quincy
LU 120-B . . . . Quincy
LU 202 . . . . Grand Ledge
LU 265 . . . . Constantine
LU 412 . . . . Kalamazoo
LU 421 . . . . Cedar Springs

Government Employees
C 117 National INS . . Birmingham
LU 46 DoJ . . . . Dearborn
LU 138 VA . . . . Southfield
LU 722 USDA . . . . Detroit
LU 723 . . . . Ann Arbor
LU 830 DoD . . . . Sault Ste. Marie
LU 933 VA . . . . Detroit
LU 1626 DoD . . . . Battle Creek
LU 1629 VA . . . . . Battle Creek
LU 1658 DoD . . . . . . Warren
LU 1741 DoJ . . . . Inkster
LU 2077 DoD . . . . Selfridge Air
  National Guard Base
LU 2092 VA . . . . . . Ann Arbor
LU 2130 DoD . . . . . . Detroit
LU 2274 VA . . . . . . Saginaw
LU 2280 VA . . . . Iron Mountain
LU 2499 INS, Border
  Patrol . . . . . . Chesterfield
LU 2795 DoD . . . . Center Line
LU 3239 HHS . . . . . Dearborn
LU 3265 USDA . . . . . Athens
LU 3272 HHS . . . . Grand Rapids
LU 3604 HHS . . . . . Marquette
LU 3907 EPA . . . . . Ann Arbor
LU 3908 DoC . . . . . Ann Arbor

Graphic Communications
LU 13-N . . . . Canton
LU 27-N . . . . Blissfield
LU 135-C . . . . . . Battle Creek
LU 507-S . . . . Kalamazoo
LU 514-M . . . . Niles
LU 555-S . . . . Wyoming
LU 705-S . . . . . . Battle Creek

Independent Unions
LU 373 Litchfield Independent
  Workers Union . . . . . Litchfield

Industrial Trade Unions
LU 614 . . . . Pontiac

Iron Workers
DC Great Lakes and
  Vicinity . . . . Brighton
LU 25 . . . . Novi
LU 340 . . . . Battle Creek
LU 499 . . . . Temperance
LU 508 . . . . Wayne
LU 831 . . . . Garden City

Laborers
DC Michigan . . . . Lansing
LU 334 . . . . Detroit
LU 355 . . . . Battle Creek
LU 465 . . . . Monroe
LU 959 . . . . Ann Arbor
LU 998 . . . . Lansing

LU 1075 . . . . Flint
LU 1076 . . . . Pontiac
LU 1098 . . . . Saginaw
LU 1191 . . . . Detroit
LU 1329 . . . . . . Iron Mountain
LU 2132 . . . . Grand Ledge

Letter Carriers
BR 1 . . . . Detroit
BR 13 . . . . Muskegon
BR 49 . . . . Manistee
BR 56 . . . . Grand Rapids
BR 74 . . . . Saginaw
BR 83 . . . . Albion
BR 95 . . . . Marquette
BR 122 . . . . Lansing
BR 187 . . . . Bay City
BR 232 . . . . Jackson
BR 249 . . . . Menominee
BR 256 . . . . Flint
BR 259 . . . . Alpena
BR 262 . . . . Battle Creek
BR 320 North Oakland
  County . . . . Waterford
BR 386 . . . . Ishpeming
BR 395 . . . . . . Iron Mountain
BR 434 . . . . Ann Arbor
BR 437 . . . . Ironwood
BR 438 . . . . Escanaba
BR 523 . . . . Petoskey
BR 529 . . . . Kimball
BR 560 . . . . . . Benton Harbor
BR 568 . . . . Laurium
BR 579 . . . . Adrian
BR 601 . . . . Holland
BR 618 . . . . Traverse City
BR 653 . . . . St. Joseph
BR 654 . . . . . . Mount Clemens
BR 669 . . . . Ludington
BR 672 . . . . Big Rapids
BR 707 . . . . . . Sault Ste. Marie
BR 750 . . . . Newport
BR 758 Wyandotte . . . Wyandotte
BR 775 . . . . Niles
BR 788 . . . . Charlotte
BR 794 . . . . Cadillac
BR 919 . . . . Hancock
BR 1056 . . . . . Mount Pleasant
BR 1147 . . . . . Grand Haven
BR 1282 . . . . Caro
BR 1466 . . . . Belding
BR 1580 . . . . Alma
BR 1691 . . . . Gladstone
BR 1817 . . . . Bad Axe
BR 2006 . . . . Negaunee
BR 2178 . . . . Zeeland
BR 2184 Western Wayne County,
  Michigan . . . . Taylor
BR 2317 . . . . Midland
BR 2347 . . . . Otsego
BR 2469 . . . . Quincy
BR 2555 . . . . . . East Lansing
BR 2672 . . . . Crystal Falls
BR 2701 . . . . St. Louis
BR 2768 . . . . Lowell
BR 2845 . . . . Munising
BR 2846 . . . . Iron River
BR 2952 . . . . Hart
BR 2958 . . . . Cassopolis
BR 2975 . . . . . . Harbor Beach
BR 3023 . . . . Reed City
BR 3126 . . . . . Madison Heights
BR 3476 . . . . Homer
BR 3477 . . . . Bronson
BR 3478 . . . . Constantine
BR 3479 . . . . Dundee
BR 3480 . . . . Croswell
BR 3481 . . . . Hart

BR 3785 . . . . Newberry
BR 3786 . . . . . West Branch
BR 3804 . . . . Vassar
BR 3810 . . . . Bessemer
BR 3860 . . . . Iron Mountain
BR 3876 . . . . Bangor
BR 3908 . . . . . Lake Odessa
BR 4227 . . . . Milford
BR 4314 . . . . Wakefield
BR 4345 . . . . L'Anse
BR 4366 . . . . Ithaca
BR 4374 . . . . Roseville
BR 4417 . . . . Grandville
BR 4439 . . . . . Lake Linden
BR 4547 . . . . Gaylord
BR 4642 . . . . Stevensville
BR 4772 . . . . . . East Tawas
BR 4779 . . . . . . Allen Park
BR 4851 . . . . Marlette
BR 4926 . . . . Sandusky
BR 5041 . . . . Ontonagon
BR 5145 . . . . Fruitport
BR 5175 . . . . St. Charles
BR 5179 . . . . . . Spring Lake
BR 5233 . . . . Cass City
BR 5239 . . . . Union City
BR 5270 . . . . Hudsonville
BR 5284 . . . . Montague
BR 5380 . . . . Rockford
BR 5530 . . . . St. Ignace
BR 5591 . . . . Richmond
BR 5764 . . . . Conklin
BR 5785 . . . . Houghton
BR 6002 . . . . Oscoda
BR 6530 . . . . Sebewaing
BR 11246 . . . . Kalamazoo
SA Michigan . . . . Detroit

Locomotive Engineers
DIV 1 . . . . Petersburg
DIV 2 . . . . Portland
DIV 19 . . . . . Clinton Township
DIV 33 . . . . Athens
DIV 122 . . . . Port Huron
DIV 185 . . . . Gladstone
DIV 286 . . . . Grand Rapids
DIV 304 . . . . Saginaw
DIV 385 . . . . Adrian
DIV 542 . . . . Plymouth
DIV 650 . . . . Owosso
DIV 812 . . . . Eastpointe
DIV 831 . . . . Brownstown
DIV 850 BLET . . . . . . Trenton
DIV 920 . . . . Holly
GCA Grand Trunk Western
   Railroad . . . . . . Battle Creek
SLB BLE Michigan State Legislative
   Board 33-996-077 . . Battle Creek

Machinists
DLG 60 . . . . Southgate
LG 46 . . . . Battle Creek
LG 46-S . . . . Taylor
LG 82 . . . . Southgate
LG 110-DS . . . . . St. Clair Shores
LG 117 . . . . Marysville
LG 141 . . . . Romulus
LG 194 . . . . Marquette
LG 218 . . . . Burtchville
LG 435 . . . . Jackson
LG 475 . . . . Coopersville
LG 600 . . . . Bridgman
LG 698 . . . . Southgate
LG 1418 . . . . Holland
LG 1813 . . . . Muskegon
LG 1918 . . . . . . Benton Harbor
LG 2184 . . . . Okemos
LG 2259 . . . . Marine City

LG 2597 . . . . Muskegon
LG 2839-PM . . . . Saginaw
LG 2848-PM . . . . Warren
LLG W-166 Woodworkers . Gaylord
LLG W-260
   Woodworkers . . . . . Ossineke
LLG W-268
   Woodworkers . . . . . . Houghton
LLG W-283 Woodworkers . L'Anse
LLG W-303
   Woodworkers . . . . Manistique
STC Michigan . . . . . . Lansing

Maintenance of Way Employes
LG 25 . . . . Millington
LG 109 . . . . Gaines
LG 367 . . . . Southfield
LG 427 . . . . Detroit
LG 721 . . . . Escanaba
LG 1629 . . . . Mattawan
LG 1834 . . . . Southfield
LG 2225 . . . . Niles
LG 2627 . . . . Southfield
LG 2725 . . . . . . Lincoln Park
LG 2926 . . . . Escanaba
NHQ . . . . Rock
SLG 28 . . . . Gowen
SLG 166 . . . . . . Battle Creek
SLG 176 . . . . Detroit
SLG 460 . . . . Wyoming
SLG 583 . . . . Bridgman
SLG 1349 . . . . Southfield
SLG 1388 . . . . Baldwin
SLG 1489 . . . . Marquette
SLG 1504 . . . . Munith

Musicians
CONF Tri-State . . . . Grand Rapids
LU 5 . . . . Southfield
LU 56 . . . . Grand Rapids
LU 57 . . . . Pinckney
LU 228 . . . . Kalamazoo
LU 387 . . . . Jackson
LU 542 . . . . Flushing
LU 625 . . . . Ann Arbor
LU 784 Pontiac Federation of
   Musicians . . . . Bloomfield Hills

National Staff Organization
LU Financial Service Marketing
   Representatives Michigan
   Education Association . . Jackson
LU Staff Association Michigan
   Educators Financial Service
   Association . . . . . East Lansing
LU Staff Organization, Association,
   Michigan Education
   Association . . . . . East Lansing
LU Staff Organization, Professional,
   Michigan Education
   Association . . . . . East Lansing
LU Staff Organization, Professional,
   Michigan Education
   Association . . . . . East Lansing
LU Staff Organization, Professional,
   Michigan Education Specialists
   Service . . . . Owosso
NHQ . . . . Grand Junction
STC Staff Organization/NSO, United,
   (Michigan) . . . . . East Lansing

NLRB Professional Association
LU 7 . . . . Detroit

Nurses
C Borgess Medical Center
   Staff . . . . Nazareth
C Staff Council . . . . Port Huron

LSC Borgess Pipp Health
   Center . . . . Plainwell
LSC Lansing Community Health
   Nurses . . . . Fowlerville
LSC Professional Nurses
   Association, Bixby . . . . . Adrian
LSC Professional Nurses, Portage
   View Hospital . . . . Dollar Bay
LSC Registered Nurses, Allegan
   General Hospital . . . . . Gobles
LSC Registered Nurses, Community
   Memorial Hospital . . Cheboygan
LSC Registered Nurses, Marquette
   General Hospital . . . . Marquette
LSC Sparrow Hospital Professional
   Employees . . . . Lansing
LSC Visiting Nurse Association of
   Metro Detroit . . . . . Northville
LSC Visiting Nurse
   Services . . . . . . Grand Rapids
SA Michigan Nurses
   Association . . . . Okemos

Office and Professional Employees
LU 40 . . . . Chesterfield
LU 42 . . . . St. Clair Shores
LU 393 . . . . Flint
LU 459 . . . . Lansing
LU 494 . . . . Warren
LU 512 . . . . Lansing

Operating Engineers
CONF North Central States . Livonia
LU 324 . . . . Livonia
LU 547 . . . . Detroit

Painters
DC 22 . . . . Warren
DC 26 . . . . Flint
LU 37 . . . . Warren
LU 42 . . . . Brighton
LU 213 . . . . . Macomb Township
LU 312 . . . . Portage
LU 357 . . . . Warren
LU 514 . . . . Belleville
LU 591 . . . . Warren
LU 675 . . . . Temperance
LU 826 . . . . Grand Blanc
LU 845 . . . . Lansing
LU 1011 . . . . Escanaba
LU 1052 . . . . Flint
LU 1396 . . . . . . Benton Harbor
LU 1401 . . . . Warren
LU 1474 . . . . Port Huron
LU 1803 . . . . Freeland

Plant Protection
LU 100 Rouge Unit . . . . Detroit
LU 101 Wayne Plant Unit . Dearborn
LU 103 World Headquarters
   Unit . . . . Taylor
LU 104 Branch Plant Unit . . Monroe
LU 105 Automotive Assembly Plant
   Unit . . . . Rockwood
LU 106 Detroit Parts Unit . . Detroit
NHQ . . . . Ypsilanti

Plasterers and Cement Masons
LU 16 . . . . Lansing
LU 67 . . . . . . Madison Heights
LU 514 . . . . Detroit
STCON Michigan . . . . . Lansing

Plumbing and Pipe Fitting
LU 85 . . . . Saginaw
LU 98 . . . . . . Madison Heights
LU 174 West
   Michigan . . . . . . Coopersville

LU 190 . . . . Ann Arbor
LU 333 . . . . Lansing
LU 357 Kalamazoo Pipefitters &
   HVAC Service . . . . Schoolcraft
LU 370 . . . . Flushing
LU 506 . . . . Escanaba
LU 636 . . . . . . Farmington Hills
LU 671 . . . . Monroe
LU 704 . . . . Farmington
SA Michigan . . . . . . Ann Arbor

Postal and Federal Employees
LU 711 . . . . Saginaw

Postal Mail Handlers
LU 307 . . . . Detroit

Postal Workers
LU 143 Greater Southwestern
   Area . . . . Kalamazoo
LU 235 Battle Creek . . Battle Creek
LU 271 Flint Michigan Area . . Flint
LU 273 Jackson . . . . . Jackson
LU 281 Western Michigan
   Area . . . . Grand Rapids
LU 282 Saginaw 486/487
   Area . . . . Saginaw
LU 293 Charlotte . . . . Charlotte
LU 295 Detroit Area . . . . Detroit
LU 307 Cheboygan . . . Cheboygan
LU 329 Manistee . . . . . Manistee
LU 424 Muskegon . . . Muskegon
LU 467 Hillsdale . . . . Hillsdale
LU 480-481 . . . . Ferndale
LU 488-489 Central Michigan
   Area . . . . Lansing
LU 498-499 Iron
   Mountain . . . . . Iron Mountain
LU 519 Petoskey . . . . . Petoskey
LU 531 Traverse City . Traverse City
LU 1304 Twin City
   Area . . . . Menominee
LU 1766 Pontiac Area . . . Pontiac
LU 3307 St. Ignace . . . St. Ignace
LU 3466 Ludington . . . Ludington
LU 3529 Fenton . . . . . Fenton
LU 3971 Sault Ste.
   Marie . . . . . . Sault Ste. Marie
LU 4752 Rogers City . . Rogers City
LU 4881 Gaylord . . . . Gaylord
LU 5024 Alpena . . . . . Alpena
LU 5858
   Farmington . . . Farmington Hills
LU 6178 Stevensville . . Stevensville
LU 6723 Troy . . . . . . Troy
LU 6818 Tecumseh . . . Tecumseh
SA Michigan . . . . Flint

Railroad Signalmen
LLG 14 . . . . Durand
LLG 28 . . . . Pleasant Lake
LLG 123 . . . . Bay City

Retail, Wholesale and Department Store
C 30 United Distributive
   Workers . . . . Warren
LU 83 . . . . Southfield
LU 86 . . . . Ovid
LU 87 . . . . Saginaw
LU 93 . . . . Lansing
LU 374 United Cereal Bakery &
   Food Workers . . . . Battle Creek
LU 383 . . . . Burton
LU 386 . . . . Grand Rapids
LU 530 . . . . Fremont
LU 602 . . . . Burton
LU 665 . . . . Marquette

LU 705 . . . . Holland
LU 822 . . . . Grand Rapids
LU 825. . . . . Lawton
LU 1064 . . . . Southfield

Roofers, Waterproofers and Allied Workers
LU 70 . . . . Howell
LU 149 . . . . Detroit

Rural Letter Carriers
LU 1 Allegan County . . . . . Dorr
LU 2 Barry County . . . Nashville
LU 4 Berrien County. . . . . Niles
LU 5 Branch County . . . Bronson
LU 6 Calhoun County . . . Bellevue
LU 7 Cass-St. Joseph
  Counties . . . . . . Edwardsburg
LU 8 Clare-Gladwin-Isabella
  Counties . . . . Rosebush
LU 9 Clinton-Shiawassee
  Counties . . . . . . St. Johns
LU 11 Genesee
  County . . . . . . Swartz Creek
LU 12 Northwest
  Michigan . . . . . . Fife Lake
LU 13 Gratiot County . . . . Ashley
LU 14 Hillsdale County . . Clarklake
LU 15 Huron County . . Owendale
LU 16 Ingham-Livingston
  Counties . . . . Jackson
LU 17 Ionia County . . . . Pewamo
LU 19 Jackson County . . . Jackson
LU 20 Kalamazoo
  County . . . . Vicksburg
LU 21 Kent County. . . . . . Dorr
LU 22 Lake-Osceola
  Counties . . . . Hersey
LU 23 Lenawee County . . . Clinton
LU 24 Lapeer County . North Branch
LU 26 Mason County. . . Ludington
LU 27 Mecosta County . . . Mecosta
LU 29 Monroe County . Ottawa Lake
LU 30 Montcalm County . . Stanton
LU 31 Marinette
  County . . . . . . Menominee
LU 31 Muskegon County . Whitehall
LU 32 Newaygo County. . . . Grant
LU 33 Northeastern Area . Rose City
LU 34 Oakland County . . . Milford
LU 36 Ottawa County . Hudsonville
LU 37 Tri-County
  Association . . . . . . Alpena
LU 38 Saginaw-Bay-Midland
  Counties . . . . . . Chesaning
LU 39 Macomb-St. Clair
  Counties . . . . . Marine City
LU 42 Top-O-Michigan
  RLCA . . . . Oden
LU 43 Tuscola-Sanilac
  Counties . . . . . . Gagetown
LU 44 Upper Peninsula
  Association . . . . . Bark River
LU 45 Van Buren County. . Pullman
LU 46 Washtenaw
  County . . . . . . Ann Arbor
LU 47 Wayne County . . . Belleville
SA Michigan . . . . . . Bark River

Security, Police and Fire Professionals
LU . . . . Roseville
LU 1 . . . . Roseville
LU 20 . . . . Roseville
LU 32. . . . . Topinabee
LU 35 . . . . Manchester
LU 40 . . . . Coloma
LU 100. . . . . Roseville

LU 113. . . . . Clarkston
LU 116 . . . . Swartz Creek
LU 117 . . . . Flint
LU 118 . . . . Flint
LU 119 . . . . Detroit
LU 121 . . . . Port Huron
LU 128. . . . . Westland
LU 146. . . . . Roseville
LU 149 . . . . Lansing
LU 151 . . . . Roseville
LU 167 . . . . Roseville
LU 168 . . . . Saginaw
LU 235. . . . . Roseville
LU 349. . . . . Boyne City
LU 415 . . . . Chase
LU 418 . . . . Roseville
LU 525 . . . . Tecumseh
LU 564 . . . . Republic
LU 794. . . . . Roseville
LU 823 . . . . Roseville
LU 1111 . . . . Detroit
LU 1212 . . . . Detroit
LU 1227 . . . . Roseville
NHQ . . . . Roseville

Service Employees
JC 35 . . . . Detroit
LU 79. . . . . Detroit
LU 79 Hackley Hospital . Muskegon
LU 79 Professional Registered
  Nurses . . . . Bay City
LU 517 Michigan Public
  Employees . . . . . . Lansing
LU 1219 Firemen & Oilers . Corunna

Sheet Metal Workers
C Michigan/Indiana States . . . Troy
LU 7. . . . . Lansing
LU 80 . . . . Southfield
LU 292 . . . . Troy

State, County and Municipal Employees
C 25 Michigan. . . . . . . Lansing
LU 139 Jackson Medical Center
  Employees . . . . Jackson
LU 140 Hospital & Nursing Home
  Employees . . . . Detroit
LU 181 Detroit Receiving
  Hospital . . . . Detroit
LU 226 Houghton County Public
  Employees Union . . . Hancock
LU 249 Lenawee County Hospital &
  Medical Care. . . . . . Adrian
LU 825 Hurley Medical Center
  LPN . . . . Flint
LU 867 Kelsey Memorial
  Hospital . . . . . . Lakeview
LU 875 McLaren Registered
  Nurses . . . . Flint
LU 992 Gogebic County Public
  Employees. . . . . . Ironwood
LU 1106 Olivet College
  Employees . . . . Olivet
LU 1511 Gratiot County Public &
  Hospital Employees . . Elm Hall
LU 1640 Community Social Agency
  Employees . . . . Detroit
LU 1820 St. Joseph Mercy Hospital
  Employees Union . . . . Pontiac
LU 1855 Public & Hospital
  Employees, 3 Counties . Shepherd
LU 1923 Ontonagon County Public
  Employees Union . . . Ontonagon
LU 2372 Greenery Nursing Home
  Employees . . . . Howell
LU 2568 Oakwood
  Employees. . . . . Lincoln Park

LU 2569 Mount Clemens General
  Hospital Employees . . . Warren
LU 2642 Hills & Dales General
  Hospital Employees. . . Cass City
LU 2650. . . . . Flint
LU 2653 St. Francis Hospital
  Employees. . . . . . Escanaba
LU 2793 Oakland County Private
  Sector Employees . . . . Detroit
LU 2818 McLaren Health Care
  Skilled Maintenance . . . . Flint
LU 3069 Michigan Legal Services
  Plan Attorneys . . . . . Saginaw
LU 3082 Metropolitan Hospital
  Employees . . . . . . Hamtramck
LU 3110 Genesee County Michigan
  Convalescent. . . . . Grand Blanc
LU 3518 Grmc Health Park. Davison
LU 3579 Bay Medical
  Center . . . . Bay City
LU 3582 Grand Valley
  State University Food
  Service . . . . Allendale
LU 3695 . . . . Detroit

Steelworkers
LU 6-4. . . . . Kenockee
LU 6-6. . . . . Three Oaks
LU 6-513. . . . . Ypsilanti
LU 6-762 . . . . Corunna
LU 6-814 . . . . Weidman
LU 6-921. . . . . . . Grand Ledge
LU 6-2000 . . . . Paw Paw
LU 02-49-L . . . . Grand Rapids
LU 02-84-S . . . . Owosso
LU 02-110-T . . . . . . Charlotte
LU 02-139-S . . . . Hubbard Lake
LU 02-182-S . . . . . . Pickford
LU 02-199-S . . . . . . Alpena
LU 02-204-S . . . . . . Alpena
LU 02-206-A . . . . . . Alpena
LU 02-207-S . . . . . . Alpena
LU 02-209-S . . . . . . Alpena
LU 02-210-L . . . . Benton Harbor
LU 02-211-SA . . . . . . Alpena
LU 02-431-L . . . . . . Hartford
LU 02-609-L . . . . . . Kalamazoo
LU 02-690-L . . . . . . Pontiac
LU 02-882-L . . . . . Deckerville
LU 02-1018-L . . . . . . Caro
LU 02-1279-S . . . . . . Macomb
LU 02-1299-S . . . . River Rouge
LU 02-1358-S. . . . . . Southfield
LU 02-1900-S . . . . South Lyon
LU 02-2167-S . . . . . Plainwell
LU 02-2395 . . . . . . Tecumseh
LU 02-2511-S . . . . . Monroe
LU 02-2659-S . . . . . Southgate
LU 02-3056-S . . . . . . Niles
LU 02-3135-S. . . . . . Marquette
LU 02-4933-S. . . . Chesterfield
LU 02-4950-S . . . . . Ishpeming
LU 02-4974-S. . . . . Marquette
LU 02-5024-S . . . . . White Pine
LU 02-5187-S . . . . . Bay City
LU 02-5965-S . . . . . Hastings
LU 02-6119-S . . . . . Augusta
LU 02-6222-S . . . . . . Caro
LU 02-6265-S . . . . . . Delton
LU 02-6277-S . . . . . . Delton
LU 02-7237-S . . . . . . Adrian
LU 02-7380-S . . . . . Bay City
LU 02-7489-S . . . Orion Township
LU 02-7720-S . . . . . Macomb
LU 02-7798-S . . . . South Range
LU 02-7948-S . . . . Rogers City
LU 02-8058-S . . . . . Charlotte
LU 02-8140-S . . . . . . Kinross

LU 02-8287-S . . . . . Mancelona
LU 02-8293-S . . . . . Ishpeming
LU 02-8339-S . . . . . . Jackson
LU 02-8384-S. . . . . . Brutus
LU 02-8410-S . . . . . . Saginaw
LU 02-8422-S . . . . . Bay City
LU 02-8569-S . . . . West Branch
LU 02-8874-S . . . . . . Britton
LU 02-8986-S . . . . . Hesperia
LU 02-9036-S . . . . . Saginaw
LU 02-9162-S . . . . . . Berkley
LU 02-9264-S . . . . River Rouge
LU 02-9491. . . . . . Brighton
LU 02-12075-S . . . . . Midland
LU 02-12295-S . . . . . Bridgman
LU 02-12585-S. . . . . . Manistee
LU 02-12773-S . . . . Ludington
LU 02-12934-S . . . . . Midland
LU 02-13569-S . . . Sault Ste. Marie
LU 02-13635-S . . . Sault Ste. Marie
LU 02-13685-S . . . . . Brimley
LU 02-13702-A . . . New Baltimore
LU 02-13729-S. . . . . . Niles
LU 02-14009-S . . . . . Sanford
LU 02-14178-S . . . . . Coldwater
LU 02-14317-S . . . . . . Boon
LU 02-14449-S . . . . . . Boon
LU 02-14450-S . . . . . Manistee
LU 02-14540-S . . . . . . Mio
LU 02-14557-S . . . Thompsonville
LU 02-14723-S . . . . . Adrian
LU 02-14758-S. . . . . . Manistee
LU 02-14965-S . . . . . Essexville
LU 02-15095-S . . . . West Branch
LU 02-15100-S. . . . . . Coleman
LU 02-15157-S . . . . . Bay City
LU 02-15301-S . . . . . Essexville
LU 02-15528-S . . . . West Branch
LU 02-16201-S. . . . . . Niles
LU 03-9998 . . . . . Cheboygan
LU 06-51 . . . . . . North Street
LU 06-100 . . . . Onaway
LU 06-111 . . . . . . Unionville
LU 06-126. . . . . . North Branch
LU 06-127. . . . . . . Jackson
LU 06-196. . . . . . . Trenton
LU 06-220 . . . . Portage
LU 06-239 . . . . . . East Tawas
LU 06-252. . . . . . . Whitehall
LU 06-255. . . . . Hart
LU 06-278 . . . . . Grand Haven
LU 06-286 . . . . . . Muskegon
LU 06-314 . . . . Detroit
LU 06-323 . . . . . . Vicksburg
LU 06-332 . . . . . Battle Creek
LU 06-358 . . . . Vassar
LU 06-363 . . . . . . Dowagiac
LU 06-389 . . . . . River Rouge
LU 06-402 . . . . Dorr
LU 06-403 . . . . Auburn
LU 06-410 . . . . . Grand Haven
LU 06-414. . . . . . . Lansing
LU 06-416 . . . . . . Kalamazoo
LU 06-421 . . . . Flint
LU 06-430 . . . . Niles
LU 06-431 . . . . . . Brighton
LU 06-433 . . . . Freeland
LU 06-479 . . . . . . Galesburg
LU 06-495 . . . . Warren
LU 06-502 . . . . . Pleasant Lake
LU 06-540 . . . . Alma
LU 06-544 . . . . . Grand Haven
LU 06-561 . . . . . . Bellevue
LU 06-564 . . . . Reese
LU 06-568 . . . . . . Roseville
LU 06-569 . . . . . Grand Haven
LU 06-585 . . . . . . Rosebush
LU 06-591. . . . . . . Southgate

LU 06-628 . . . . Bad Axe
LU 06-636 . . . . Boyne City
LU 06-639 . . . . Detroit
LU 06-644 . . . . Muskegon
LU 06-667 . . . . Manistee
LU 06-668 . . . . Ludington
LU 06-670 . . . . Jackson
LU 06-672 . . . . Twin Lake
LU 06-677 . . . . Grand Haven
LU 06-682 . . . . Kalamazoo
LU 06-720 . . . . Hart
LU 06-816 . . . . Union Pier
LU 06-824 . . . . Muskegon Heights
LU 06-825 . . . . Flat Rock
LU 06-829 . . . . Corunna
LU 06-842 . . . . Detroit
LU 06-946 . . . . Kalamazoo
LU 06-987 . . . . Twin Lake
LU 06-1005 . . . . Plymouth
LU 06-1007 . . . . Lansing
LU 06-1008 . . . . White Pigeon
LU 06-1010 . . . . Kalamazoo
LU 06-1012 . . . . Niles
LU 06-1015 . . . . Fruitport
LU 06-1017 . . . . Fargo
LU 06-1019 . . . . Portage
LU 06-1021 . . . . Battle Creek
LU 06-1026 . . . . Adrian
LU 06-1029 . . . . Coloma
LU 06-1033 . . . . . Three Rivers
LU 06-1034 . . . . . White Pigeon
LU 06-1035 . . . . Wayne
LU 06-1044 . . . . La Salle
LU 06-1050 . . . . Wyoming
LU 06-1063 . . . . Clare
LU 06-1077 . . . . Monroe
LU 06-1082 . . . . Belleville
LU 06-1117 . . . . Buchanan
LU 07-21 . . . . Perkins
LU 07-44 . . . . Manistique
LU 07-87 . . . . Munising
LU 07-96 . . . . Au Train
LU 07-172 . . . . Menominee
LU 07-176 . . . . Rochester
LU 07-354 . . . . Ontonagon
LU 07-979 . . . . St. Louis
LU 11-13547-S . . . Sault Ste. Marie

Teachers
LU 1899 Hebrew Teachers
  Association, Shaarez
  Zedek . . . . . . West Bloomfield
LU 1899 Hillel Day School Teachers
  Association . . . West Bloomfield
LU 4437 Federation of Credit Union
  Employees . . . . Taylor
SFED Michigan . . . . . . Detroit

Teamsters
JC 43 . . . . Detroit
LU 7 . . . . Kalamazoo
LU 51 . . . . Detroit
LU 164 . . . . Jackson
LU 243 . . . . Plymouth
LU 247 . . . . Detroit
LU 283 . . . . Wyandotte
LU 299 . . . . Detroit
LU 328 . . . . Escanaba
LU 332 . . . . Flint
LU 337 . . . . Detroit
LU 339 . . . . Port Huron
LU 372 . . . . Detroit
LU 406 . . . . Grand Rapids
LU 486 . . . . Saginaw
LU 580 . . . . Lansing
LU 614 . . . . Pontiac
LU 1038 . . . . Detroit
LU 1620 . . . . Canton

LU 2040 Detroit Mailers
  Union . . . . Detroit

Television and Radio Artists
LU 202 Detroit . . . . . Southfield

Theatrical Stage Employees
LU 26 . . . . Grand Rapids
LU 38 . . . . Detroit
LU 179-B . . . . Warren
LU 199 . . . . Hazel Park
LU 201 . . . . Flint
LU 395 . . . . Ann Arbor
LU 472 . . . . Burton
LU 757 . . . . . St. Clair Shores
LU 786 . . . . . . Sterling Heights
LU 812 . . . . Detroit
LU M-274 Lansing . . . . . Lansing
SA Michigan
  Alliance . . . . . St. Clair Shores

Train Dispatchers
SCOM Grand Trunk Western
  Railroad . . . . Waterford

Transit Union
LU 1564 . . . . . Madison Heights
LU 1639 . . . . . . Kalamazoo

Transport Workers
LU 521 . . . . Romulus
LU 574 . . . . Ishpeming
LU 2011 . . . . Erie
LU 2051 . . . . Allen Park

**Transportation Communications
Union**
D 493 . . . . Newport
LG 187 . . . . Palmer
LG 6318 Pontiac . . . . . Marysville
LG 6327 Flint . . . . . . Auburn
LG 6334 Detroit . . . . . Woodhaven

Transportation Union
GCA GO-377 Grand Trunk Western
  Railroad . . . . . . Battle Creek
GCA GO-627 Conrail-PC-ND-
  NYC . . . . Brownstown
LU 72 . . . . Marshall
LU 194 . . . . Edwardsburg
LU 278 . . . . Perry
LU 313 . . . . Wyoming
LU 320 . . . . Saginaw
LU 734 . . . . Battle Creek
LU 881 . . . . Milan
LU 886 . . . . Marquette
LU 927 . . . . Warren
LU 1075 . . . . Lambertville
LU 1183 . . . . Fort Gratiot
LU 1438 . . . . Melvindale
LU 1477 . . . . Carleton
LU 1549 . . . . Temperance
LU 1620 . . . . Buchanan
LU 1709 . . . . White Lake
LU 1736 . . . . Davison
LU 1760 . . . . Livonia
LU 1765 . . . . . . Grand Rapids
SLB LO-25 Michigan . . . . Lansing

Treasury Employees
CH 24 . . . . Detroit
CH 78 . . . . Detroit
CH 152 . . . . Port Huron
CH 173 . . . . Detroit
CH 187 . . . . . . Sault Ste. Marie
CH 230 . . . . Detroit

UNITE HERE
LU 24 . . . . Detroit
LU 57-A . . . . Detroit
LU 124-A . . . . Detroit
LU 151-LDC . . . . . . Kalamazoo
LU 688 Catering, Hospitality
  Workers & Bartenders . . Bay City
LU 748-A . . . . Detroit
LU 2402 . . . . Detroit
LU 2411 . . . . Detroit
LU 2562 . . . . Detroit
LU 2563 . . . . Detroit

Utility Workers
LU 101 . . . . Jackson
LU 103 . . . . Moskegon
LU 104 . . . . Bay City
LU 105 . . . . Fenton
LU 106 . . . . Battle Creek
LU 107 . . . . Byron Center
LU 119 . . . . Burton
LU 123 . . . . Eagle
LU 124 . . . . Scottville
LU 129 . . . . Ithaca
LU 144 . . . . Bay City
LU 150 . . . . Kalamazoo
LU 154 . . . . Cadillac
LU 223 . . . . Dearborn
LU 223 Buildings & Properties
  Division . . . . Detroit
LU 223 Enrico Fermi
  Division . . . . . . Petersburg
LU 223 Maintenance
  Division . . . . Dearborn
LU 223 Meter Department
  Division . . . . Riverview
LU 223 Motor Transportation
  Division . . . . Gaines
LU 223 Office, Professional &
  Technical Division . . . Dearborn
LU 223 Stores & Transportation
  Division . . . . Detroit
LU 223 Substation
  Division . . . . Dearborn
LU 223 Underground Lines
  Division . . . . Dearborn
LU 223 Warren Service Shops
  Division . . . . Northville
LU 253 . . . . Owosso
LU 254 . . . . . . Clinton Township
LU 257 . . . . Hastings
LU 258 . . . . Newport
LU 261 . . . . Hubbardston
LU 286 . . . . Alpena
LU 295 . . . . Traverse City
LU 337 . . . . Fremont
LU 346 . . . . Cheboygan
LU 347 . . . . Traverse City
LU 358 . . . . Ypsilanti
LU 388 . . . . Grand Haven
LU 417 . . . . Newport
LU 445 . . . . East Leroy
LU 473 . . . . Port Huron
LU 517 . . . . Erie
LU 521 . . . . Traverse City
LU 532 . . . . Clyde
LU 542 . . . . Bay City
LU 543 . . . . Monroe
LU 564 . . . . Midland
STC Michigan . . . . Burton

Weather Service Employees
BR 03-19 . . . . . . Grand Rapids
BR 03-33 . . . . White Lake
BR 03-57 . . . . Gaylord
BR 03-69 . . . . Negaunee

Westinghouse Salaried Employees
ASSN Detroit . . . . . . Southfield

Unaffiliated Labor Organizations

Applewood Employee
  Association . . . . . . Brownstown
Barbers State Association
  Independent LU 90 . . . . Holland
Bay County Public Health Registered
  Nurses . . . . Bay City
Central Michigan Community
  Hospital Registered Nurses
  Association . . . . Mount Pleasant
Central Office Staff
  Association . . . . Lansing
Citation Tool Employees Bargaining
  Committee . . . . Southfield
Clerical Association LU 214 . Detroit
Clerical-Technical Union of
  Michigan State
  University . . . . . . East Lansing
Dean Transportation Employees
  Association . . . . Lansing
Executone of Northeastern Michigan
  Employee Association
  LU 101 . . . . Frankenmuth
Executone of Northeastern Michigan
  Employee Association
  International . . . . Frankenmuth
Gratiot Community Hospital
  Registered Nurse
  Association . . . . Riverdale
Great Lakes Licensed Officers
  Organization . . . . Detroit
Independent Union Local
  One . . . . Belleville
Independent Union of Plant
  Protection Employees
  LU 136 . . . . Fowlerville
International Association of Tool
  Craftsmen LU 6 . . . . . Charlotte
International Association of Tool
  Craftsmen LU 8 . . . . . . Morley
Lakehead Pipe Line Company
  Inc. Employees
  Representative . . . . . Marshall
Licensed Practical Nurse Association
  Oakwood Hospital . . . . . Canton
Licensed Practical Nurses
  Association of Hutzel
  Hospital . . . . Detroit
Magline Standish Employees
  Association . . . . Standish
Manchester Plastics Independent
  Union . . . . Manchester
Michigan Association of Police
  911 . . . . Southfield
Michigan Association of Police 911
  Mount Clemens General Security
  Office . . . . Detroit
Michigan Association of Police
  Henry Ford Health System
  Police . . . . Detroit
Michigan Association of Police
  Loomis Armored Guards
  Association . . . . Holly
Michigan Association of Police
  St. Joseph Mercy-Oakland
  Public . . . . Pontiac
Michigan Executive Directors
  Association . . . . . Auburn Hills
Michigan Nurses Association Lapeer
  Registered Nurse Staff
  Council . . . . Lapeer

North Ottawa Community Hospital
Employees Association
(NOCHEA) . . . . . Grand Haven
Nucraft Committee Nucraft
Furniture Company
Employees. . . . . Comstock Park
Paper Products Workers Association
LU 1 . . . . Livonia
Pico Employees
Association . . . . . Wyandotte
Pine Knoll Convalescent Center Inc.
Employees Association. . . Taylor

Plant Protection Independent
LU 255 . . Brownstown Township
Plant Protection Independent
Ford Sterling Plant
LU 598 . . . . . . Grosse Pointe
Precase Concrete Products Union LU
14 . . . . Flint
Professional Representatives
Organization . . . . Warren
Rapid Engineering Employees
Association . . . Comstock Park

Registered Nurses Staff Council
Spectrum Health-Kent Community
Camp . . . . Grand Rapids
Renaissance Police Officers
Association. . . . . . . Detroit
Representatives Organizers &
Clerical (ROCU) . . . Stockbridge
Rochester Crittenton Medical Lab
Employees Association . Rochester
Rochester Crittenton
Radiologic Employees
Association . . . . Rochester Hills

Starr Commonwealth Employees
Association. . . . . Albion
UAW Staff Council . . . . . Detroit
United Protective Workers of
America LU 1 . . . . . . Dearborn
University of Detroit Police Officers
Association Inc. . . . . . . Detroit
Westland Convalescent Center
Employees Association . Westland
Wisne Automation Employees . Novi
Wolverine Products Pipe Line
Union . . . . Manchester

Minnesota

AFL-CIO Trade and Industrial Departments

Building and Construction Trades Department
BCTC Brainerd . . . . . . Laporte
BCTC Duluth. . . . . Duluth
BCTC Iron Range. . . . . Virginia
BCTC Mankato-Minnesota
  Valley . . . . Mankato
BCTC Minneap Building &
  Construction Trades
  Council . . . . Minneapolis
BCTC Minnesota State . . . St. Paul
BCTC Northwest
  Minnesota . . . . St. Cloud
BCTC Southeast Minnesota Building
  and Trades Council . . . Rochester
BCTC St. Cloud . . . . . . St. Cloud
BCTC St. Paul . . . . St. Paul
BCTC Willmar . . . . Willmar

Affiliated Labor Organizations

Actors and Artistes
LU Minneapolis . . . . Minneapolis

Agricultural Employees
BR 38 . . . . St. Paul

Air Traffic Controllers
LU DLH . . . . Duluth
LU FCM . . . . Eden Prairie
LU M98. . . . . Minneapolis
LU MIC . . . . Crystal
LU MSP . . . . Minneapolis
LU RST . . . . Rochester
LU STP . . . . St. Paul
LU ZMP . . . . Farmington

Aircraft Mechanics
LU 33 MSP . . . . . Bloomington
LU 35. . . . . Duluth

Asbestos Workers
LU 34 . . . . St. Paul
LU 49 . . . . Duluth
LU 133 . . . . Crookston
LU 205 Asbestos & Hazardous Waste
  Abatement. . . . . St. Paul

Automobile, Aerospace Workers
C Minnesota State CAP
  Council . . . . St. Paul
LU 125. . . . . St. Paul
LU 241 . . . . Esko
LU 349 . . . . Hibbing
LU 683 . . . . Minneapolis
LU 763 . . . . South St. Paul
LU 867 Albert Lea-Austin
  Local . . . . Austin
LU 879. . . . . St. Paul
LU 958 . . . . Houston
LU 1016 . . . . Fairmont
LU 2125. . . . . Rochester
LU 2340 . . . . Dakota

Bakery, Confectionery, Tobacco Workers and Grain Millers
LU 1-G . . . . Minneapolis
LU 13-G . . . . Cannon Falls
LU 22 . . . . Minneapolis
LU 55-G . . . . Burnsville

LU 62-G . . . . Lake Crystal
LU 133-G . . . . Winona
LU 265-G . . . . Shakopee
LU 266-G . . . . Moorhead
LU 267-G . . . . Crookston
LU 360-G . . . . Worthington
LU 369-G . . . . Danube

Boilermakers
LG 3 . . . . Pequot Lakes
LG 647 . . . . Ramsey
LG 650 . . . . Lake City

Bricklayers
LU 1 Minnesota and North
  Dakota . . . . Minneapolis

Carpenters
DC Lakes and Plains Regional
  Council . . . . St. Paul
LU 87 . . . . St. Paul
LU 190-L . . . . Minneapolis
LU 361 . . . . Hermantown
LU 464 . . . . Mankato
LU 548 . . . . New Brighton
LU 596 . . . . Roseville
LU 606 . . . . Virginia
LU 766 . . . . Albert Lea
LU 851 . . . . Anoka
LU 930 . . . . St. Cloud
LU 1348. . . . . Virginia
LU 1382. . . . . Rochester
LU 1644 . . . . Minneapolis
LU 1847 . . . . Richfield
LU 1865 Twin City Cabinetmakers
  and Millmen. . . . . . St. Paul

Christian Labor Association
LU 78 Highway Construction
  Workers. . . . . Willmar
LU 84 United Construction
  Workers. . . . . Willmar

Civilian Technicians
CH 21 Tony Kempenich
  Memorial. . . . . . . Little Falls
CH 73 Duluth. . . . . Duluth

Communications Workers
LU 7200 . . . . Minneapolis
LU 7201 . . . . St. Paul
LU 7202. . . . . . . Meadowlands
LU 7203 . . . . Rochester
LU 7204 . . . . Windom
LU 7205 . . . . Spicer
LU 7212 . . . . St. Cloud
LU 7214 . . . . Duluth
LU 7219 . . . . Brainerd
LU 7250 . . . . Minneapolis
LU 7270 . . . . Farmington
LU 7272 . . . . Gully
LU 14725 Duluth Typographical
  Union. . . . . Duluth
LU 14726 . . . . Hibbing
LU 14727. . . . International Falls
LU 14728. . . . . Mankato
LU 14733. . . . . Duluth
LU 37002 Twin Cities . St. Anthony
LU 37008 Lake Superior . . . Duluth
LU 57411 . . . . . . St. Louis Park
LU 87042 . . . . St. Paul
LU 87140 . . . . Minneapolis
LU 87160 . . . . . . Mountain Iron
STC Minnesota . . . . Minneapolis

Electrical Workers
LU 23 . . . . St. Paul
LU 31 . . . . Duluth
LU 110. . . . . St. Paul
LU 160 . . . . Minneapolis
LU 242 . . . . Duluth
LU 292 . . . . Minneapolis
LU 294 . . . . Hibbing
LU 343 . . . . Rochester
LU 366 . . . . Esko
LU 506 . . . . Roseville
LU 731 . . . . . International Falls
LU 783. . . . . St. Paul
LU 886 . . . . New Hope
LU 949 . . . . Burnsville
LU 1999 . . . . North Mankato
STC 16 Minnesota . . . . . Hastings

Electrical, Radio and Machine Workers
LU 1139 . . . . Minneapolis

Elevator Constructors
LU 9 . . . . Little Canada

Federal Employees
LU 14 . . . . Fort Snelling
LU 1441. . . . . Red Wing
LU 2138 . . . . Silver Bay

Food and Commercial Workers
LU 6 . . . . Albert Lea
LU 9 . . . . Austin
LU 134. . . . . Plymouth
LU 199 . . . . Rochester
LU 228-C . . . . Dakota
LU 335 . . . . Red Wing
LU 442-P . . . . Owatonna
LU 527 . . . . Red Wing
LU 653 . . . . Plymouth
LU 789 . . . . South St. Paul
LU 1116 . . . . Duluth
LU 1161 . . . . Worthington

Glass, Molders, Pottery and Plastics Workers
CONBD Midwest . . . Minneapolis
CONBD Twin Cities . . Minneapolis
LU 21-B. . . . . Hibbing
LU 37-B. . . . . Virginia
LU 63-B . . . . Minneapolis
LU 129. . . . . Chaska
LU 142-B. . . . . Mankato

Government Employees
C 259 VA, Eighth
  District . . . . Minneapolis
LU 368 USDA . . . . . Albert Lea
LU 390 VA . . . . . . Sauk Rapids
LU 488 USDA . . . . Long Prairie
LU 683 DoJ. . . . . Duluth
LU 800 . . . . Minneapolis
LU 801 Council of Prisons . Waseca
LU 1969 VA . . . . St. Paul
LU 1997 DoD . . . . . Minneapolis
LU 2265 DoD . . Inver Grove Heights
LU 2999 DoD . . . . . . St. Paul
LU 3015 USDA . . . . Worthington
LU 3105 DoJ . . . . . Owatonna
LU 3129 SSA . . . . . . St. Paul
LU 3381 HHS . . . . . Minneapolis
LU 3419 HUD . . . . . Minneapolis
LU 3669 VA . . . . . . Minneapolis
LU 3935 DoJ . . . . Duluth

LU 3947 Council of
  Prisons . . . . Rochester

Government Security Officers
LU 24 . . . . Red Wing
LU 28. . . . . Monticello
LU 158. . . . . St. Paul

Graphic Communications
LU 1-B . . . . Minneapolis
LU 1-M Upper Midwest. . . St. Paul
LU 29-C . . . . St. Paul
LU 76-C . . . . Duluth
LU 379-C Mankato Pressman's
  Union . . . . North Mankato

Independent Unions
LU 220 American Musicians Union
  of Minnesota . . . . . . Rochester
LU 440 American Musicians Union
  of Minnesota . . . . . Zimmerman

Iron Workers
DC North Central
  Minnesota. . . . . Oakdale
LU 512. . . . . St. Paul
LU 535. . . . . St. Paul

Laborers
DC Minnesota-North
  Dakota . . . . Lino Lakes
LU 68 . . . . Wells
LU 132. . . . . St. Paul
LU 405 . . . . Rochester
LU 563 . . . . Minneapolis
LU 1091 . . . . Duluth
LU 1097. . . . . Virginia

Letter Carriers
BR 9 . . . . Minneapolis
BR 28 . . . . St. Paul
BR 90 . . . . Mankato
BR 114 . . . . Duluth
BR 350 . . . . Faribault
BR 388 . . . . St. Cloud
BR 401 . . . . Red Wing
BR 440 . . . . Rochester
BR 679 . . . . Crookston
BR 717 . . . . Austin
BR 718 . . . . Albert Lea
BR 776 . . . . Owatonna
BR 806 . . . . Fergus Falls
BR 864 . . . . Brainerd
BR 911 . . . . Northfield
BR 956 . . . . New Ulm
BR 1051. . . . . Moorhead
BR 1058. . . . . Chisholm
BR 1092. . . . . Bemidji
BR 1109 . . . . Lake City
BR 1113 . . . . Sleepy Eye
BR 1117. . . . . Willmar
BR 1243 . . . . Cloquet
BR 1246. . . . . Virginia
BR 1317. . . . . . . Detroit Lakes
BR 1418. . . . . . Thief River Falls
BR 1446. . . . . Montevideo
BR 1447 . . . . Waseca
BR 1451. . . . . Eveleth
BR 1532. . . . . Inver Grove Heights
BR 1581. . . . . Marshall
BR 1722. . . . . Pipestone
BR 1927 . . . . Morris
BR 1959 . . . . Warren
BR 2013. . . . . . . Redwood Falls
BR 2065 . . . . Worthington

BR 2121 . . . . Breckenridge
BR 2149 . . . . . International Falls
BR 2166 . . . . Tracy
BR 2377 . . . . St. James
BR 2415 . . . . Ada
BR 2548 . . . . Hutchinson
BR 2590 . . . . Springfield
BR 2637 . . . . Le Sueur
BR 2870 . . . . Staples
BR 2937 . . . . Blue Earth
BR 2938 . . . . Spring Valley
BR 2939 . . . . Luverne
BR 2942 . . . . Hopkins
BR 3140 . . . . . East Grand Forks
BR 3193 . . . . Waterville
BR 3196 . . . . New Prague
BR 3263 . . . . Montgomery
BR 3270 . . . . Park Rapids
BR 3283 . . . . Melrose
BR 3304 . . . . Madison
BR 3522 . . . . Caledonia
BR 3531 . . . . Litchfield
BR 3610 . . . . Grand Rapids
BR 3697 . . . . Le Center
BR 4095 . . . . Glencoe
BR 4096 . . . . Ortonville
BR 4185 . . . . Granite Falls
BR 4545 . . . . Aitkin
BR 4833 . . . . Olivia
BR 4967 . . . . Kenyon
BR 5204 . . . . Babbitt
BR 5213 . . . . Hoyt Lakes
BR 5237 . . . . Silver Bay
BR 5249 . . . . Waconia
BR 5370 . . . . Aurora
BR 5519 . . . . Appleton
BR 5545 . . . . Perham
BR 5556 . . . . La Crescent
BR 5626 . . . . Canby
BR 5692 . . . . Plainview
BR 5776 . . . . Cannon Falls
BR 5945 . . . . Bayport
BR 5946 . . . . Pine City
BR 6090 . . . . Stewartville
BR 6141 . . . . Warroad
BR 6172 . . . . St. Charles
BR 6182 . . . . Kasson
BR 6183 . . . . Chatfield
BR 6228 . . . . Fosston
BR 6229 . . . . Wheaton
SA Minnesota . . . . . . Northrop

Locomotive Engineers
DIV 9 . . . . St. James
DIV 27 . . . . St. Cloud
DIV 117 BLET . . . . . Albert Lea
DIV 163 . . . . Duluth
DIV 164 . . . . Duluth
DIV 290 . . . . Duluth
DIV 333 . . . . Minneapolis
DIV 357 . . . . Eagan
DIV 369 . . . . St. Paul
DIV 403 . . . . Waseca
DIV 494 . . . . . West St. Paul
DIV 517 . . . . Oakdale
DIV 549 . . . . Spicer
DIV 768 . . . . . . Middle River
GCA Chicago & Northwestern
    Railroad . . . . Blaine
GCA Division of Rail Confer of
    Teamster . . . . Albert Lea
SLB Minnesota . . . . . Maplewood

Longshoremen
LU 1279 . . . . Duluth
LU 2061 . . . . Duluth

Machinists
DLG 77 . . . . . . Vadnais Heights
DLG 143 . . . . . Mendota Heights
DLG 165 . . . . St. Cloud
LG 112 . . . . Burnsville
LG 197 . . . . Brainerd
LG 459 Capitol City & Minneapolis
    Metal Workers . . Vadnais Heights
LG 623 . . . . St. Cloud
LG 737 . . . . . . Vadnais Heights
LG 760 . . . . . . International Falls
LG 924 . . . . Madison Lake
LG 1030 . . . . Winona
LG 1037 . . . . . . Vadnais Heights
LG 1416 . . . . Owatonna
LG 1502 . . . . Esko
LG 1575 . . . . Duluth
LG 1833 . . . . Bloomington
LG 1956 . . . . . . Bingham Lake
LG 2036 Hastings . . . . Hastings
LLG W-33
    Woodworkers . International Falls
LLG W-62
    Woodworkers . . . Detroit Lakes
LLG W-150
    Woodworkers . . . . . Shoreview
STC Minnesota . . . Vadnais Heights

Maintenance of Way Employes
LG 91 . . . . Aitkin
LG 364 . . . . Crookston
LG 397 . . . . Motley
LG 519 . . . . Heron Lake
LG 1296 . . . . St. Cloud
LG 1488 . . . . Eden Valley
LG 1965 . . . . Hokah
SD Duluth Missabe Iron
    Range . . . . Duluth
SD Soo Line . . . . Richfield
SF Burlington
    Northern . . . . . . Minneapolis
SF Chicago-Milwaukee-St. Paul-
    Pacific . . . . Elk River
SLG 144 . . . . Maplewood
SLG 182 . . . . Fertile
SLG 278 . . . . Waseca
SLG 322 . . . . Baudette
SLG 331 . . . . Wabasha
SLG 343 . . . . Belle Plaine
SLG 420 . . . . Glencoe
SLG 472 . . . . Proctor
SLG 706 . . . . Hibbing
SLG 928 . . . . Minneapolis
SLG 1055 . . . . Willmar
SLG 1132 . . . . Bemidji
SLG 1490 . . . . Fosstan
SLG 1662 . . . . Barnum
SLG 1710 . . . . Duluth
SLG 1879 . . . . Burnsville

Musicians
LU 18 Duluth Musicians
    Association . . . . Duluth
LU 30-73 Twin Cities . Minneapolis
LU 382 . . . . Moorhead
LU 536 . . . . Swanville
LU 567 . . . . Faribault

National Staff Organization
ASSN Minnesota Professional
    Staff . . . . Duluth

NLRB Professional Association
LU 18 . . . . Minneapolis

Nurses
SA Minnesota . . . . St. Paul

Office and Professional Employees
LU 12 . . . . St. Anthony

Operating Engineers
LU 49 . . . . Minneapolis
LU 50 . . . . Ranier
LU 70 . . . . St. Paul
LU 756 . . . . Rochester

Painters
DC 82 . . . . Little Canada
LU 61 . . . . Little Canada
LU 106 . . . . Duluth
LU 259 . . . . Rochester
LU 386 . . . . Little Canada
LU 681 . . . . Rochester
LU 880 . . . . Little Canada
LU 884 . . . . Milaca
LU 1324 . . . . Little Canada
LU 2002 . . . . Stewartville

Plasterers and Cement Masons
LU 265 . . . . Minneapolis
LU 633 . . . . Minneapolis
STCON Midwest Multi-State
    Conference . . . . . Minneapolis

Plumbing and Pipe Fitting
DC 3 Twin City Pipe
    Trades . . . . St. Paul
LU 6 . . . . Rochester
LU 11 . . . . Duluth
LU 15 . . . . Minneapolis
LU 34 . . . . St. Paul
LU 340 . . . . Champlin
LU 417 . . . . Minneapolis
LU 455 . . . . St. Paul
LU 539 . . . . Minneapolis
LU 589 . . . . Virginia
SA Minnesota Pipe Trades . . Duluth

Postal Mail Handlers
LU 323 . . . . St. Paul

Postal Workers
LU Twin Cities Postal Data
    Center . . . . Eagan
LU 65 St. Paul . . . . . . St. Paul
LU 125 Minneapolis . . Minneapolis
LU 142 Duluth Area . . . . . Duluth
LU 207 International
    Falls . . . . International Falls
LU 597 Morris . . . . Morris
LU 606 Moorhead . . . . Moorhead
LU 631 Willmar . . . . . . Willmar
LU 647 St. Cloud Area . . Rockville
LU 798 Brainerd . . . . . Brainerd
LU 897 Rochester . . . . Rochester
LU 933 Worthington . . Worthington
LU 1006 Mankato . . . . Mankato
LU 1036 Winona . . . . . . Winona
LU 1080 Austin . . . . Austin
LU 1130 Thief River
    Falls . . . . . . Thief River Falls
LU 1333 Detroit
    Lakes . . . . Detroit Lakes
LU 1544 Litchfield . . . Litchfield
LU 2885 Windom . . . . Windom
LU 3142 Fergus Falls . . Fergus Falls
LU 3890 Hutchinson . . Hutchinson
LU 5425 Wayzata . . . . Wayzata
SA Minnesota . . . . . . Rochester

Railroad Signalmen
LLG 154 . . . . Hawley
LLG 168 . . . . Jackson
LLG 226 . . . . Paynesville

**Roofers, Waterproofers and Allied
Workers**
LU 96 . . . . Minneapolis

Rural Letter Carriers
AREA 1 South and Southeast
    Minnesota . . . . . New Richland
AREA 2 South and Southwest
    Minnesota . . . . Lakefield
AREA 3 East and Central
    Minnesota . . . . . Bloomington
AREA 4 Minnesota . . . . Appleton
AREA 5 North and Northwest
    Minnesota . . . . Callaway
AREA 6 North and Central
    Minnesota . . . . Carlton
LU Aitkin County . . . . . . Esko
LU Anoka-Sherburn-Isanti
    Counties . . . . Elk River
LU Beltrami County . . . Bemidji
LU Benton County . . . . . Foley
LU Big Stone-Traverse
    Counties . . . . Dumont
LU Blue Earth-Nicollet
    Counties . . . . Nicollet
LU Carver County . . . . . Chaska
LU Clay County . . . . Moorhead
LU Clearwater County . . . Gonvick
LU Dakota-Scott
    Counties . . . . . . Northfield
LU Dodge-Olmsted
    Counties . . . . Rochester
LU Douglas & Pope
    County . . . . . . Glenwood
LU Fillmore County . . . Peterson
LU Freeborn County . New Richland
LU Houston County . . . Caledonia
LU Hubbard County . . Park Rapids
LU Jackson-Nobles-Rock
    Counties . . . . . . Rushmore
LU Kandiyohi County . New London
LU Le Sueur County . . . Lonsdale
LU Lyon-Lincoln Counties . . Tyler
LU McLeod County . . Hutchinson
LU Meeker County . . . . . Dassel
LU Morrison-Crow Wing
    Counties . . . . Bertha
LU Norman-Mahnomen
    Counties . . . . . Twin Valley
LU Northeastern Minnesota . Aurora
LU Northern Minnesota
    Counties . . . . Badger
LU Ottertail County . . Underwood
LU Polk County . . . . . . Fertile
LU Redwood County . Walnut Grove
LU Rice County . . . . . Faribault
LU Sibley County . . . . Henderson
LU Stearns County . . . . . Avon
LU Swift County . . . . . Benson
LU Todd County . . . . Eagle Bend
LU Wadena County . . . . Wadena
LU Western Minnesota . Montevideo
LU Winona County . . . Winona
LU 5-B Becker
    County . . . . . . Detroit Lakes
LU 17 Fairbault-Martin
    Counties . . . . . . Sherburn
LU 22 Hennepin County . Plymouth
LU 26 Kanabec-Pine-Mille Lacs
    Counties . . . . Milaca
LU 53 Washington-Ramsey
    Counties . . . . . . Stillwater
LU 58 Wright County . . . Buffalo
LU 60 Murray-Pipestone
    Counties . . . . Fulda
LU 61 Cass County . . . Pine River
SA Minnesota . . . . . . Freeport

Security, Police and Fire Professionals
LU 201 . . . . Cottage Grove
LU 553 . . . . St. Paul

Service Employees
JC 7 . . . . St. Paul
LU 26 . . . . Minneapolis
LU 113 . . . . Minneapolis
LU 259 Firemen & Oilers . . Duluth
LU 284 School
  Service . . . . . . South St. Paul
LU 292 Firemen &
  Oilers . . . . St. Francis
LU 532 Firemen & Oilers . Andover
LU 937 . . . . . International Falls
LU 939 Firemen & Oilers . . Cloquet
LU 970 Firemen & Oilers . . Canyon

Sheet Metal Workers
C North Central States . Maplewood
C Sign Industry
  Council . . . . Maplewood
LU 10 . . . . St. Paul
LU 209 . . . . Inver Grove Heights
LU 480 . . . . Kenyon

State, County and Municipal Employees
C 5 Minnesota . . . South St. Paul
C 65 Minnesota . . . . . . Eveleth
LU 8 St. Paul City & Ramsey County
  Employees . . . . Elko
LU 9 . . . . Minneapolis
LU 105 MLPNA . . . . Paynesville
LU 395 Ely-Bloomenson Community
  Hospital Employees . . Embarrass
LU 722 St. Paul Ramsey Hospital
  Employees . . . . St. Paul
LU 753 St. Cloud State University
  Employees . . . . Rice
LU 791 City of Hibbing . . Hibbing
LU 1119 Hibbing-Big Fork Hospital
  Employees . . . . . . Hibbing
LU 1149 Lake Region Hospital
  Employees . . . . . Fergus Falls
LU 1949 Bemidji State University
  Employees . . . . . . Bemidji
LU 2219 Eveleth Hospital
  Employees . . . . Eveleth
LU 2385 Southwest Minnesota State
  College Employees . . . Marshall
LU 3481 . . . . South St. Paul
LU 3532 Walker Methodist
  Employees . . . . St. Louis Park
LU 3558 Arrowhead Region
  Non-Profit Employees . . . Duluth
LU 3931 North Central Blood
  Services . . . Inver Grove Heights

Steelworkers
LU 7-75 . . . . St. Paul
LU 07-49 . . . . International Falls
LU 07-63 . . . . Cloquet
LU 07-79 Brainerd . . . . Brainerd
LU 07-118 . . . . New Ulm
LU 07-159 . . . . International Falls
LU 07-264 . . . . St. Paul
LU 07-274 . . . . St. Cloud
LU 07-409 . . . . Stillwater
LU 07-418 . . . . . . Cottage Grove
LU 07-505 . . . . Fairmont
LU 07-528 . . . . Hastings
LU 07-578 . . . . Austin
LU 07-662 Pine Bend . . . Hastings
LU 07-717 . . . . Hastings
LU 07-776 . . . . Duluth
LU 07-970 . . . . Duluth
LU 07-1095 . . . . . Grand Rapids
LU 07-1259 Minneapolis
  Local . . . . Blaine
LU 07-1417 . . . . . . Belle Plaine
LU 07-1976 . . . . Avon
LU 11-31-L . . . . Red Wing
LU 11-133-T . . . . Shakopee
LU 11-460-G . . . . Kasota
LU 11-1028-S . . . . Duluth
LU 11-1938-S . . . . Virginia
LU 11-2002 . . . . . . Minneapolis
LU 11-2127-S . . . Vadnais Heights
LU 11-2175-S . . . . . Farmington
LU 11-2660-S . . . . . . Keewatin
LU 11-2705-S . . . . . . Chisholm
LU 11-6115-S . . . . Virginia
LU 11-6803-S . . . . . . Albert Lea
LU 11-6860-S . . . . Eveleth
LU 11-7090-S . . . . Eveleth
LU 11-7263-S . . . . Cottage Grove
LU 11-7505-S . . . . Crosby
LU 11-7796-S . . . White Bear Lake
LU 11-8392-S . . . . Melrose
LU 11-9115-S . . . . . Mount Iron
LU 11-9225-S . . . . . . Royalton
LU 11-9230-S . . . . Pierz
LU 11-9273-S . . . . Hewitt
LU 11-9333-S . . . . . . Onamia
LU 11-9349-S . . . . . . Chisholm
LU 11-9359-S . . . . Pierz
LU 11-9454 . . . . . . New Prague
LU 11-9460 . . . . Duluth
LU 11-12106-S . . . . . . Eveleth
LU 11-12571-S . . . . . Little Falls
LU 11-13241-S . . . North Mankato
LU 33-5859-S . . . . Aitkin

Teachers
LU 3468 Breck Federation of
  Teachers . . . . . . Minneapolis

Teamsters
CONF Bakery &
  Laundry . . . . . . Minneapolis
JC 32 . . . . Minneapolis
LU 4 Minneapolis-St. Paul Mailers
  Union . . . . Minneapolis
LU 120 . . . . St. Paul
LU 160 . . . . Rochester
LU 289 . . . . Minneapolis
LU 346 . . . . Duluth
LU 471 . . . . Minneapolis
LU 638 . . . . Minneapolis
LU 792 . . . . Minneapolis
LU 970 . . . . Minneapolis
LU 974 . . . . Minneapolis
LU 1145 . . . . St. Paul
LU 2000 Airline
  Division . . . . . . Minneapolis

Theatrical Stage Employees
LU 13 . . . . Minneapolis
LU 219 . . . . Minneapolis
LU 416 . . . . Rochester
LU 490 Studio
  Mechanics . . . . . Minneapolis

Train Dispatchers
SCOM Soo Line . . . . Eagan

Transport Workers
LU 543 . . . . Bloomington

Transportation Communications Union
LG 319 . . . . Duluth
LG 325 . . . . Ramsey
LG 593 . . . . Stillwater
LG 838 . . . . Minneapolis
LG 1085 . . . . Dilworth
LG 6004 Carvers Cave . Coon Rapids
LG 6615 Hiawatha . . . Woodbury
LG 6811 Lakehead . . . . . . Duluth
SBA 46 Consolidated Burlington
  Northern . . . . Fridley

Transportation Union
GCA GO-261 . . . . . . Woodbury
GCA GO-270 . . . . Mankato
GCA GO-315 Duluth Missabe & Iron
  Range . . . . . . Two Harbors
GCA GO-321 Duluth Missabe
  & Iron Range-Missabe
  D . . . . Hermantown
GCA GO-325 Duluth Winnipeg &
  Pacific Railway . . . . . Duluth
GCA GO-387 Burlington Northern
  Railroad . . . . Forest Lake
LU 650 . . . . Shakopee
LU 911 . . . . Maplewood
LU 1000 . . . . Woodbury
LU 1067 . . . . Duluth

LU 1177 . . . . Willmar
LU 1292 . . . . Hermantown
LU 1614 . . . . Bloomington
LU 1976 . . . . Circle Pines
SLB LO-26 Minnesota . . . St. Paul

Treasury Employees
CH 29 . . . . St. Paul
CH 157 . . . . Baudette
CH 167 . . . . Duluth
CH 170 . . . . Eagan

UNITE HERE
LU 17 . . . . Minneapolis
LU 21 . . . . Rochester
LU 99 . . . . Duluth
STC Minnesota . . . . Minneapolis

Weather Service Employees
BR 3-99 . . . . Chanhassen
BR 03-29 . . . . Chanhassen
BR 03-52 . . . . Duluth
BR 03-83 . . . . Chanhassen

Unaffiliated Labor Organizations
A M P I Employees
  Union . . . . New Ulm
Diagnostic Imaging
  Technologists . . . . . Andover
Education Minnesota . . . . St. Paul
Faribault Woolen Mill Workers
  Guild . . . . Faribault
Garlook Employees Union
  Independent . Inver Grove Heights
Honeywell Plant Protection
  Association Independent
  Honeywell Plant . . . . Burnsville
International Guards Union of
  America LU 32 . . . . . Eagan
International Guards Union of
  America LU 51 . . . . Minneapolis
International Guards Union of
  America RC Fifth . . Minneapolis
Milk Producers Inc. Association
  Employees . . . . . . Paynesville
Minnesota Arrowhead District
  Council 96 Staff Employee's
  Union . . . . Duluth
Minnesota Nurses Association Staff
  Organization LU 1 . . . . St. Paul
Northwest Airlines Meteorologists
  Association . . . . St. Paul
Prior Lake Secretary Association LU
  4887 . . . . Prior Lake
Professional Flight Attendants
  Association (PFAA) . Bloomington
Soo Line Locomotive & Car
  Foremen's . . . . . Mounds View
Technical Employees Association of
  Minnesota . . . . . Minneapolis
Union de Trabajadores del
  Norte . . . . Awatonna

Mississippi

AFL-CIO Trade and Industrial Departments

Building and Construction Trades Department
BCTC Central Mississippi . Jackson
BCTC Mississippi Gulf
   Coast . . . . Gulfport

Metal Trades Department
MTC Pascagoula. . . . . Pascagoula
MTC South Central
   Mississippi . . . . Gulfport

Affiliated Labor Organizations

Air Traffic Controllers
LU HCF. . . . . Gulfport
LU JAN . . . . Jackson
LU NMM . . . . Meridian

Asbestos Workers
LU 114 . . . . Columbus

Automobile, Aerospace Workers
LU 1724 . . . . Clarksdale
LU 1956 . . . . Pearl
LU 2190. . . . . Laurel
LU 2402 . . . . Brandon

Boilermakers
LG 110 . . . . Hattiesburg
LG 693 . . . . Pascagoula
LG 903 . . . . West Point

Carpenters
C Southern Industrial Workers
   4065. . . . . Jackson
LU 234 . . . . Pascagoula
LU 303 Mississippi . . . . Vicksburg
LU 1409 . . . . Greenwood
LU 1464 . . . . Columbia
LU 2086. . . . . Taylorsville
LU 2116. . . . . Grenada
LU 2153 . . . . Raleigh
LU 2272 . . . . Shuqualak
LU 2285 . . . . Vicksburg
LU 2305 . . . . Columbus
LU 2335 . . . . Columbus
LU 2445 . . . . Columbus
LU 2568. . . . . Grenada
LU 3031 . . . . Bentonia
LU 3181 . . . . Louisville
LU 3213 . . . . Jackson

Communications Workers
LU 3490 . . . . Florence
LU 3504 . . . . Columbus
LU 3505 . . . . Corinth
LU 3509 . . . . Hattiesburg
LU 3510 . . . . Indianola
LU 3511 . . . . Jackson
LU 3514 . . . . Meridian
LU 3516. . . . . Thaxton
LU 3517 . . . . Guntown
LU 3518 . . . . Vicksburg
LU 3519 . . . . D'Iberville
LU 3550 . . . . Jackson
LU 14330. . . . . Gulfport
LU 83655 . . . . Jackson
LU 83698 . . . . Clinton
LU 83718 . . . . Brookhaven
LU 83770 . . . . Columbus

LU 83792 . . . . Jackson
LU 83799 . . . . . Crystal Springs

Electrical Workers
LU 480 . . . . Jackson
LU 605 . . . . Jackson
LU 733 . . . . Pascagoula
LU 852. . . . . Corinth
LU 903 . . . . Gulfport
LU 917 . . . . Meridian
LU 985. . . . . Boyle
LU 1028 . . . . Tupelo
LU 1204 . . . . Hattiesburg
LU 1209 . . . . Collinsville
LU 1210. . . . . Laurel
LU 1211 . . . . Gulfport
LU 1317. . . . . Laurel
LU 1873 . . . . Vicksburg
LU 2164 . . . . Brandon
LU 2198 . . . . Mendenhall
LU 2265 . . . . Vicksburg
SC U-21 Mississippi Power
   Company . . . . Gulfport

Federal Employees
LU 589 . . . . Bolton
LU 943 . . . . Biloxi

Fire Fighters
LU 92-F . . . . Biloxi

Food and Commercial Workers
C Gas Employees Independent
   Union. . . . . Brandon
LU 361-G. . . . . Hazlehurst
LU 790-C Chemical
   Council . . . . Brandon
LU 982-C. . . . . Canton
LU 1000-C . . . . Laurel
LU 1191-T . . . . Shuqualak
LU 1991 . . . . West Point

Government Employees
LU 589 AFGE, Local 0589 . Jackson
LU 1009 HUD. . . . . . . Jackson
LU 1027 Armed Forces Retirement
   Home-Gulfport . . . . . Biloxi
LU 1028 DoD. . . . . . . Gulfport
LU 1031 . . . . Louin
LU 1045 . . . . Gulfport
LU 1296. . . . . Columbus
LU 2053 DoD. . . . . . . Gulfport
LU 2244 DoD . . . . . . Meridian
LU 2504 USDA . . . . . . Jackson
LU 2519 DoL. . . . . . . Brandon
LU 2543 USDA . . . . . . Raleigh
LU 2670 DoD . . . . Biloxi
LU 3190 USDA . . . . . Nettleton
LU 3200 Hattiesburg Circuit Food
   Inspectors . . . . . . Hattiesburg
LU 3310 DoD. . . . . . . Vicksburg

Government Employees Association
LU 5-125-R . . . . Gautier

Government Security Officers
LU 106 . . . . Biloxi

Graphic Communications
LU 223-M . . . . Horn Lake
LU 231-M . . . . . . Olive Branch
LU 734-S. . . . . Clinton

Iron Workers
LU 469 . . . . Jackson

Laborers
LU 145 . . . . Jackson
LU 693 . . . . Collins

Letter Carriers
BR 94 . . . . Vicksburg
BR 217 Magnolia Capital
   City . . . . Jackson
BR 260 . . . . Lucedale
BR 476 . . . . Natchez
BR 487 . . . . Collinsville
BR 516 . . . . Greenville
BR 938 . . . . Petal
BR 1080 . . . . Greenwood
BR 1195 . . . . Clarksdale
BR 1374 . . . . Gulfport
BR 1437. . . . . Laurel
BR 1593 . . . . Tupelo
BR 1682 . . . . McComb
BR 1692 . . . . Columbus
BR 1963 . . . . Okolona
BR 2202 . . . . Corinth
BR 2241 . . . . Pascagoula
BR 2291 . . . . Starkville
BR 2396. . . . . Brookhaven
BR 2403 . . . . Lumberton
BR 2543 . . . . Charleston
BR 2832 . . . . Leland
BR 2842 . . . . New Albany
BR 2896. . . . . Cleveland
BR 2995 . . . . Winona
BR 3090. . . . . Louisville
BR 3150 . . . . Indianola
BR 3152 . . . . Aberdeen
BR 3184 . . . . Philadelphia
BR 3548 . . . . Macon
BR 3773 . . . . Hazlehurst
BR 3827 . . . . Ocean Springs
BR 4107 . . . . Hernando
BR 4475 . . . . Forest
BR 4597 . . . . Drew
BR 4610 . . . . Ruleville
BR 4927 . . . . Olive Branch
BR 5257 . . . . Mendenhall
BR 5511 . . . . Magee
BR 5842 . . . . Marks
BR 6299. . . . . Fulton
BR 6362 . . . . Tylertown
BR 6441 . . . . Hernando
SA Mississippi . . . . . . Natchez

Locomotive Engineers
DIV 23 . . . . Southaven
DIV 99 . . . . Water Valley
DIV 196 . . . . Smithdale
DIV 203 . . . . Terry
DIV 230 . . . . Meridian
DIV 450 . . . . Louisville
DIV 593 . . . . Meridian
DIV 672 . . . . Byhalia
DIV 762 . . . . Senatobia
DIV 827 . . . . Lucedale
DIV 919 . . . . Amory
SLB Mississippi State Legislative
   Board. . . . . Southaven

Longshoremen
LU 1303 . . . . Gulfport
LU 1752 . . . . Pascagoula
LU 1967 . . . . Pascagoula

Machinists
DLG 73 . . . . Pascagoula
LG 14 . . . . Olive Branch
LG 18 . . . . Meridian
LG 1133 . . . . Pascagoula
LG 1343 . . . . Richton
LG 2249 . . . . Sandy Hook
LG 2386 . . . . Daleville
LLG 50 . . . . Columbus
LLG W-50 Woodworkers . Meridian
LLG W-349 Woodworkers . Gloster
LLG W-376 Woodworkers . Oxford
LLG W-443 Woodworkers . . Laurel
STC Mississippi State
   Council . . . . Marion

Maintenance of Way Employes
LG 616 . . . . Meridian
LG 657 . . . . Batesville
LG 660 . . . . Ovett
LG 1171 . . . . West Point
LG 1539 . . . . Brookhaven
SLG 615 . . . . Lucedale
SLG 637 . . . . Kilmichael
SLG 652 . . . . Union
SLG 916 . . . . Waveland
SLG 1600 . . . . Smithville
SLG 2838 . . . . Iuka

Musicians
LU 579 . . . . Jackson
LU 777 Association of the Gulf
   Coast . . . . Ocean Springs

National Staff Organization
LU Staff Organization, Mississippi
   Educators . . . . . Water Valley

Office and Professional Employees
LU 204 . . . . Pascagoula

Operating Engineers
LU 624 . . . . Jackson

Painters
LU 1225 . . . . Pascagoula
LU 1967. . . . . Grenada

Plasterers and Cement Masons
LU 311 . . . . Jackson

Plumbing and Pipe Fitting
LU 436 . . . . Pascagoula
LU 568 . . . . Gulfport
LU 619 . . . . Vicksburg
LU 714 . . . . Brandon
SA Mississippi . . . . . . Gulfport

Postal and Federal Employees
D 4. . . . . Jackson
LU 401 . . . . Jackson
LU 405 . . . . Jackson
LU 414 Tupelo . . . . . . Saltillo
LU 415 Mississippi Gulf Coast
   Local . . . . Long Beach

Postal Mail Handlers
LU 325 . . . . Jackson

Postal Workers
LU 54 Greenville . . . . . Greenville
LU 204 Gulfport . . . . . . Saucier
LU 440 East Central Mississippi Area
   Local. . . . . Meridian
LU 968 McComb . . . . . McComb

LU 1200 Mississippi Gulf Coast Area Local . . . . Pass Christian
LU 1207 Jackson . . . . . Jackson
LU 1280 Tupelo . . . . . . Tupelo
LU 1311 Hattiesburg . . Hattiesburg
LU 1371 Laurel . . . . Laurel
LU 2070 Northeast Mississippi Area . . . . Columbus
LU 2075 Philadelphia . Philadelphia
LU 2092 Brockhaven . . Brookhaven
LU 2415 Grenada . . . . . Grenada
LU 2424 Greenwood . . Greenwood
LU 2685 Cleveland . . . . Cleveland
LU 2772 Carthage . . . . Carthage
LU 2862 Batesville . . . . Batesville
LU 2864 Ripley . . . . Ripley
LU 2865 Pontotoc . . . . . Pontotoc
LU 2867 Houston . . . . . Houston
LU 2992 Senatobia . . . Senatobia
LU 4807 University . . . University
LU 4924 Louisville . . . . Louisville
LU 4961 Calhoun City . . . . Calhoun City
LU 5844 Oxford . . . . . . Oxford
SA Mississippi . . . . Clinton

Railroad Signalmen
LLG 107 . . . . Sontag

Rural Letter Carriers
D 1 . . . . Gattman
D 2 . . . . New Albany
D 3 . . . . Cleveland
D 4 . . . . French Camp
D 5 . . . . Decatur
D 6 . . . . Perkinston
D 7 . . . . Bogue Chitto
D 8 . . . . Florence
SA Mississippi . . . . . New Albany

Security, Police and Fire Professionals
LU 711 . . . . Carriere
LU 712 . . . . Clinton

Service Employees
LU 572 . . . . Jackson

Sheet Metal Workers
LU 406 . . . . Jackson

Steelworkers
LU 4-313 . . . . Mendenhall
LU 02-206-A . . . . Iuka
LU 04-371 . . . . Sontag
LU 04-632 . . . . Caledonia
LU 04-927 . . . . Woodville
LU 04-1076 . . . . McCool
LU 04-1080 . . . . Vicksburg
LU 04-1113 . . . . Natchez
LU 04-1369 . . . . . . Monticello
LU 04-1384 . . . . McComb
LU 04-1418 . . . . Houston
LU 04-1452 . . . . Ackerman
LU 04-1578 . . . . Marion
LU 04-1699 . . . . Natchez
LU 09-202-A . . . . Grenada
LU 09-204-A . . . . . . Hernando
LU 09-245 . . . . D'Iberville
LU 09-303-L . . . . Amory
LU 09-363-L . . . . Jackson
LU 09-523-G . . . . . Plantersville
LU 09-556-L . . . . . Clarksdale
LU 09-748-L . . . . . Columbus
LU 09-759-L . . . . Corinth
LU 09-975-L . . . . Ripley
LU 09-1011-L . . . . Ripley
LU 09-1061-L . . . . . Port Gibson
LU 09-7477-S . . . . Amory
LU 09-7772-S . . . . Philadelphia
LU 09-7891-S . . . . . Winona
LU 09-8420-S . . . . Fulton
LU 09-8421-S . . . . . Inverness
LU 09-8630-S . . . . . . Amory
LU 09-15198-S . . . . Aberdeen
LU 36-8958 . . . . Jackson

Teamsters
JC 87 . . . . Jackson
LU 119 Memphis Mailers Union . . . . Southaven
LU 258 . . . . Hattiesburg
LU 891 . . . . Jackson

Theatrical Stage Employees
LU 589 . . . . Madison
LU 616 . . . . Meridian
LU 674 . . . . Kiln

Transit Union
LDIV 1208 . . . . Jackson

Transportation Communications Union
D 5513 . . . . Carriere

LG 6164 Bulletin . . . . Hernando
LG 6178 New Year . . . . Jackson
LG 6724 Chickasaw . . Olive Branch

Transportation Union
GCA GO-436 Illinois Central Railroad . . . . Jackson
LU 427 . . . . Smithdale
LU 584 . . . . Pontotoc
LU 853 . . . . Prairie
LU 1334 . . . . Hattiesburg
LU 1557 . . . . Southaven
SLB LO-27 Mississippi . . . Jackson

Treasury Employees
CH 13 . . . . Clinton

UNITE HERE
LU 708-A . . . . Jackson
LU 944-C . . . . Jackson
LU 1148-C . . . . Jackson
LU 2550 . . . . Jackson
LU 2576 . . . . Jackson

Weather Service Employees
BR 02-52 . . . . Jackson

Unaffiliated Labor Organizations
Guards & Watchmen-Mississippi Gulf Coast LU 1 . . . . Pascagoula
International Guards Union of America LU 123 . . . Port Gibson
Meridian Association of Flight Training Instructions . . Naval Air Station Meridian

Missouri

AFL-CIO Trade and Industrial Departments

Building and Construction Trades Department
BCTC Columbia . . . . . Westphalia
BCTC Greater Kansas
   City . . . . Independence
BCTC Joplin Area. . . . . . . Joplin
BCTC Missouri State . Jefferson City
BCTC Northeastern
   Missouri . . . . Hannibal
BCTC Sedalia . . . . Sedalia
BCTC Springfield . . . . Springfield
BCTC St. Joseph . . . . St. Joseph
BCTC St. Louis . . . . . . St. Louis

Food and Allied Service Trades Department
FASTC Eastern Missouri . St. Louis

Maritime Trades Department
PC Greater Saint Louis
   Area . . . . St. Louis

AFL-CIO Directly Affiliated Locals

AFL-CIO
DALU 20711 Advertising Publicity
   & News Representatives . St. Louis

Affiliated Labor Organizations

Air Traffic Controllers
LU ECE . . . . Kansas City
LU MCI . . . . Kansas City
LU MKC . . . . Kansas City
LU SGF . . . . Springfield
LU STP . . . . Bridgeton
LU SUS . . . . Chesterfield
LU TKI . . . . St. Charles

Asbestos Workers
CONF Midwestern
   States . . . . Independence
LU 1 . . . . St. Louis
LU 27 . . . . Independence
LU 63 . . . . Springfield

Automobile, Aerospace Workers
C Greater Kansas City . Kansas City
C Greater Saint Louis . . Hazelwood
C Missouri . . . . Hazelwood
LU 25 . . . . Hazelwood
LU 110 . . . . Fenton
LU 136 . . . . Fenton
LU 249 . . . . . Pleasant Valley
LU 282 . . . . Florissant
LU 325 . . . . Hazelwood
LU 597 Saint Louis-Fenton
   Local . . . . Catawissa
LU 691 . . . . St. Charles
LU 710 . . . . Kansas City
LU 1070 . . . . Neosho
LU 1760 . . . . Pacific
LU 1887 . . . . St. Louis
LU 1930 . . . . Dexter
LU 2250 . . . . Wentzville
LU 2379 . . . . Jefferson City

Bakery, Confectionery, Tobacco Workers and Grain Millers
LU 4 . . . . St. Louis
LU 8-G . . . . St. Joseph
LU 16-G . . . . Kansas City
LU 51-G . . . . Carthage
LU 194-G . . . . Trenton
LU 235 . . . . Springfield
LU 348-G . . . . Palmyra

Boilermakers
LG 13-M . . . . St. Louis
LG 27 . . . . St. Louis
LG 27-D Cement
   Workers . . . . Kansas City
LG 83 . . . . Kansas City
LG 146-M . . . . Independence
LG 229-D Cement Workers . Willard
LG 455-D Cement
   Workers . . . . Bloomsdale
LG 469-D Cement
   Workers . . . . Louisiana

Bricklayers
LU 1 . . . . St. Louis
LU 15 . . . . Kansas City
LU 18 . . . . St. Louis
LU 23 . . . . . Cape Girardeau

Carpenters
DC Kansas City . . . . Kansas City
DC St. Louis . . . . . . St. Louis
LU 5 . . . . St. Louis
LU 27-L . . . . Oak Grove
LU 47 . . . . St. Louis
LU 61 . . . . Grain Valley
LU 73 . . . . St. Louis
LU 73-L . . . . St. Louis
LU 110 . . . . St. Joseph
LU 185 . . . . St. Louis
LU 311 . . . . Joplin
LU 412 . . . . St. Charles
LU 417 . . . . St. Louis
LU 602 . . . . St. Louis
LU 607 . . . . Palmyra
LU 777 . . . . Harrisonville
LU 795 . . . . St. Louis
LU 945 . . . . Jefferson City
LU 978 . . . . Springfield
LU 1008 . . . . . . Bowling Green
LU 1181 . . . . Independence
LU 1310 . . . . St. Louis
LU 1312 ACE Educators . Florissant
LU 1329 . . . . Independence
LU 1529 . . . . Kansas City
LU 1596 . . . . St. Louis
LU 1635 . . . . Kansas City
LU 1739 . . . . St. Louis
LU 1770 . . . . . Cape Girardeau
LU 1795 . . . . Farmington
LU 1839 . . . . Washington
LU 1875 . . . . Elsberry
LU 1899 . . . . Parkville
LU 1925 . . . . Columbia
LU 1987 . . . . St. Charles
LU 2016 . . . . Naylor
LU 2030 . . . . St. Mary
LU 2119 . . . . St. Louis
LU 2214 . . . . Festus
LU 2298 . . . . Rolla
LU 2301 . . . . Jefferson City
LU 3202 . . . . Warrenton

Catholic School Teachers
ASSN St. Louis
   Archdiocesan . . . . . Hazelwood

Civilian Technicians
CH 92 Missouri Show Me
   Army . . . . Jefferson City
CH 93 St. Louis Show Me
   Air . . . . St. Louis
CH 94 Pony Express . . . St. Joseph

Communications Workers
C Greater St. Louis City . . St. Louis
CONF Heartland Typographical &
   Mailer . . . . St. Louis
LU 6301 . . . . Ladue
LU 6310 . . . . St. Louis
LU 6311 . . . . Fulton
LU 6312 . . . . Springfield
LU 6314 . . . . Sedalia
LU 6316 . . . . . Cape Girardeau
LU 6320 . . . . St. Louis
LU 6327 . . . . Kansas City
LU 6350 . . . . St. Louis
LU 6360 . . . . Kansas City
LU 6372 . . . . Warrensburg
LU 6373 . . . . Cameron
LU 6374 . . . . Princeton
LU 6377 . . . . Bridgeton
LU 6390 . . . . St. Louis
LU 6391 . . . . Kansas City
LU 6450 . . . . Kansas City
LU 6477 . . . . Camdenton
LU 14612 . . . . Webb City
LU 14615 . . . . St. Louis
LU 14616 . . . . St. Louis
LU 14618 . . . . Strafford
LU 14620 St. Louis Mailers
   Union . . . . Florissant
LU 36047 St. Louis Newspaper
   Guild . . . . St. Louis
LU 84818 . . . . High Ridge
LU 86104 . . . . St. Louis
LU 86114 . . . . Washington
LU 86116 . . . . St. Joseph
LU 86820 . . . . Moberly
LU 86821 . . . . Centralia
LU 86823 . . . . St. Louis

Electrical Workers
LU 1 . . . . St. Louis
LU 2 . . . . St. Louis
LU 4 . . . . St. Louis
LU 53 . . . . Kansas City
LU 95 . . . . Joplin
LU 124 . . . . Kansas City
LU 257 . . . . Jefferson City
LU 350 . . . . Hannibal
LU 412 . . . . Kansas City
LU 453 . . . . Springfield
LU 545 . . . . St. Joseph
LU 695 . . . . St. Joseph
LU 753 . . . . Springfield
LU 778 . . . . Ash Grove
LU 814 . . . . Sedalia
LU 866 . . . . Kansas City
LU 1439 . . . . St. Louis
LU 1455 . . . . St. Louis
LU 1464 . . . . Kansas City
LU 1474 . . . . Joplin
LU 1553 . . . . Springfield
LU 1613 . . . . Kansas City
LU 1832 . . . . Liberty

Elevator Constructors
LU 3 . . . . St. Louis
LU 12 . . . . Kansas City

Federal Employees
LU 29 . . . . Kansas City
LU 405 Independent . . . . St. Louis
LU 858 . . . . Kansas City
LU 1763 . . . . St. Louis

Fire Fighters
LU 34-I . . . . Kansas City
LU 108-F . . . . Lebanon

Food and Commercial Workers
C View Insurance Workers Area
   XI . . . . St. Charles
LU 2 . . . . Kansas City
LU 74-A . . . . Weston
LU 81-C . . . . St. Louis
LU 88 . . . . St. Louis
LU 432-C . . . . Imperial
LU 655 . . . . Manchester
LU 796-C . . . . . Cape Girardeau
LU 871-C . . . . St. Louis
LU 887-C . . . . Hannibal

Glass, Molders, Pottery and Plastics Workers
LU 20 . . . . Pleasant Valley
LU 30 . . . . Festus
LU 43 . . . . Parma
LU 372 . . . . Nevada

Government Employees
C 245 St. Louis Area . . . . St. Louis
LU 96 VA . . . . St. Louis
LU 104 NARS . . . . . . Overland
LU 226 9th District VA
   Council . . . . Kansas City
LU 638 USDA . . . . St. Joseph
LU 900 Army Human Resource
   Command . . . . . . St. Louis
LU 903 . . . . Columbia
LU 905 . . . . St. Louis
LU 908 . . . . Fort Leonard Wood
LU 910 . . . . Kansas City
LU 1336 HHS . . . . . Kansas City
LU 1612 DoJ . . . . Willard
LU 1711 DLA . . . . . Kansas City
LU 1748 . . . . Kansas City
LU 1910 . . . . Independence
LU 2192 VA . . . . St. Louis
LU 2338 VA . . . . . Poplar Bluff
LU 2361 DoD . . . . Whiteman Air
                    Force Base
LU 2663 VA . . . . . Kansas City
LU 2754 . . . . Kansas City
LU 2761 DoD . . . . . . St. Louis
LU 2904 DoD . . . . . Kansas City
LU 3353 USDA . . . . . Neosho
LU 3354 USDA . . . . . St. Louis
LU 3399 VA . . . . Columbia
LU 3479 . . . . Springfield
LU 3502 USDA . . . . . Marshall
LU 3521 HHS . . . . . Sikeston
LU 3529 DoD . . . . . Hazelwood
LU 3838 ACE . . . . Monroe City
LU 3892 DoE . . . . . Kansas City
LU 3934 HUD . . . . . St. Louis
LU 3949 USDA . . . . . Liberal
LU 3983 Immigration &
   Naturalization . . . . Kansas City
LU 4059 . . . . Kansas City

Government Employees Association
LU 14-32 . . . . Fort Leonard Wood
LU 14-96 . . . . St. Louis
LU 14-139 . . . Fort Leonard Wood
LU 14-149 . . . Fort Leonard Wood
LU 14-150 . . . Fort Leonard Wood

Government Security Officers
LU 11 . . . . Fulton
LU 20 . . . . St. Louis
LU 220 . . . . Kansas City

Graphic Communications
DJC Missouri Kansas Iowa
   Nebraska . . . . Kansas City
LU 16-C . . . . Kansas City
LU 16-H . . . . St. Louis
LU 38-N St. Louis . . . . . St. Louis
LU 235-M . . . . Independence
LU 6505-M . . . . Maryland Heights

Iron Workers
DC St. Louis and Vicinity . St. Louis
LU 10 . . . . Kansas City
LU 396 . . . . St. Louis
LU 518 . . . . St. Louis
LU 520 . . . . Kansas City

Laborers
DC Eastern Missouri Laborers
   District Council . . . . . Bridgeton
DC Western Missouri-Kansas. Joplin
LU 42 . . . . St. Louis
LU 53 . . . . Bridgeton
LU 110 . . . . St. Louis
LU 264 . . . . Kansas City
LU 319 . . . . Joplin
LU 424 . . . . Hannibal
LU 509 . . . . St. Louis
LU 579 . . . . St. Joseph
LU 660 . . . . St. Charles
LU 662 . . . . Jefferson City
LU 663 . . . . Kansas City
LU 676 . . . . Springfield
LU 718 . . . . De Soto
LU 829 . . . . Ste. Genevieve
LU 830 . . . . Ste. Genevieve
LU 840 . . . . Rolla
LU 916 . . . . Farmington
LU 955 . . . . Rocheport
LU 1104 . . . . Cape Girardeau
LU 1290 . . . . Kansas City

Letter Carriers
BR 30 . . . . Kansas City
BR 127 . . . . Jefferson City
BR 139 . . . . Sedalia
BR 195 . . . . St. Joseph
BR 203 . . . . Springfield
BR 244 . . . . Frankford
BR 291 Tom Sawyer . . . . Hannibal
BR 335 . . . . Moberly
BR 343 . . . . St. Louis
BR 366 . . . . Joplin
BR 511 . . . . Chillicothe
BR 639 . . . . Kirksville
BR 763 . . . . Columbia
BR 827 . . . . Independence
BR 984 . . . . St. Charles
BR 1005 . . . . Macon
BR 1015 . . . . Cape Girardeau
BR 1016 . . . . Poplar Bluff
BR 1215 . . . . Brookfield
BR 1217 . . . . . Excelsior Springs
BR 1264 . . . . Liberty
BR 1287 . . . . Lexington
BR 1369 . . . . Monett

BR 1675 . . . . Caruthersville
BR 1678 . . . . Charleston
BR 1715 . . . . . . Mountain Grove
BR 1878 . . . . Monroe City
BR 1938 . . . . Lebanon
BR 2027 . . . . Marceline
BR 2140 . . . . . . Bowling Green
BR 2170 . . . . Kennett
BR 2257 . . . . Kahoka
BR 2292 . . . . Harrisonville
BR 2302 . . . . Savannah
BR 2311 . . . . Albany
BR 2327 . . . . Canton
BR 2354 . . . . Shelbina
BR 2362 . . . . Memphis
BR 2477 . . . . Slater
BR 2601 . . . . Rich Hill
BR 2604 . . . . Eldon
BR 2667 . . . . Dexter
BR 2706 . . . . Paris
BR 2741 . . . . Windsor
BR 2915 . . . . Marshfield
BR 2934 . . . . Centralia
BR 2985 . . . . Perryville
BR 3014 . . . . Appleton City
BR 3198 . . . . . . Sweet Spring
BR 3236 . . . . Stanberry
BR 3242 . . . . Milan
BR 3351 . . . . Norborne
BR 3441 . . . . Glasgow
BR 3442 . . . . Montgomery City
BR 3563 . . . . Mound City
BR 3566 . . . . Edina
BR 3567 . . . . Salisbury
BR 3576 . . . . Hermann
BR 3606 . . . . Vandalia
BR 3629 . . . . La Plata
BR 3711 . . . . Malden
BR 3767 . . . . Brunswick
BR 3778 . . . . Tarkio
BR 4050 . . . . Imperial
BR 4159 . . . . Greenfield
BR 4216 . . . . Palmyra
BR 4472 . . . . Huntsville
BR 4474 . . . . Elsberry
BR 4659 . . . . Hayti
BR 4839 . . . . Florissant
BR 4940 . . . . Belton
BR 5050 . . . . Ballwin
BR 5053 . . . . . Mountain View
BR 5056 . . . . Versailles
BR 5267 . . . . Grandview
BR 5510 . . . . Fort Leonard Wood
BR 5657 . . . . Owensville
BR 5671 . . . . Doniphan
BR 5743 . . . . Keytesville
BR 5847 . . . . Florissant
BR 5903 . . . . . . Portageville
BR 6054 . . . . Bevier
BR 6062 . . . . Houston
BR 6325 . . . . Ironton
BR 6396 . . . . Thayer
BR 8010 . . . . Shrewsbury
D East Central Missouri . . St. Ann
D Missouri State
   Association . . . . . . Springfield
D Northeast Missouri . . . Shelbina
D Northwest Missouri . . St. Joseph
D Southeast Missouri . . . Kennett
D West Central Missouri . . Sedalia
SA Missouri . . . . O'Fallon

Locomotive Engineers
DIV 8 . . . . Marshall
DIV 17 . . . . Smithville
DIV 42 . . . . Arnold
DIV 48 . . . . St. Louis
DIV 61 . . . . Kansas City

DIV 75 . . . . Smithville
DIV 80 . . . . St. Catherine
DIV 81 . . . . Liberty
DIV 83 . . . . Springfield
DIV 86 . . . . Moberly
DIV 107 . . . . Smithville
DIV 120 . . . . Kansas City
DIV 147 . . . . Parkville
DIV 152 . . . . Plattsburg
DIV 178 . . . . Golden City
DIV 285 BLET . . . . Thayer
DIV 336 . . . . Lawson
DIV 428 . . . . Manchester
DIV 442 . . . . Scott City
DIV 491 . . . . Kansas City
DIV 502 . . . . Gladstone
DIV 507 . . . . Joplin
DIV 567 . . . . Springfield
DIV 595 . . . . Scott City
DIV 609 . . . . Fulton
DIV 629 . . . . Hannibal
DIV 674 . . . . De Soto
DIV 708 . . . . Kansas City
DIV 777 . . . . Gladstone
DIV 930 . . . . Lees Summit
GCA St. Louis-San Francisco
   Railway . . . . Granby
SLB Missouri . . . . Moberly

Longshoremen
DC St. Louis . . . . St. Louis
LU 1765 . . . . St. Louis

Machinists
CONF Midwest States . . Bridgeton
DLG 9 . . . . Bridgeton
DLG 142 . . . . Kansas City
DLG 837 . . . . Hazelwood
LG 17 Deer Lake . . . . Brookline
LG 27 . . . . Grain Valley
LG 41 . . . . Bridgeton
LG 176 Harley
   Davidson . . . . . . Kansas City
LG 561 . . . . Kansas City
LG 688 . . . . Union
LG 777 . . . . Bridgeton
LG 778 . . . . Kansas City
LG 837-A . . . . Hazelwood
LG 837-B . . . . Hazelwood
LG 949 . . . . Bridgeton
LG 1345 . . . . Bridgeton
LG 1745 . . . . Warrenton
LG 2782 . . . . West Plains
STC Missouri . . . . . . Bridgeton

Maintenance of Way Employes
LG 493 . . . . Springfield
LG 745 . . . . Bloomfield
LG 996 . . . . Bland
LG 1137 . . . . Lilbourn
LG 1217 . . . . Brunswick
LG 1365 . . . . Lees Summit
LG 1523 . . . . Belle
LG 1601 . . . . Belton
LG 2402 . . . . Marceline
LG 2403 . . . . Pleasant Hill
LG 2621 . . . . Hannibal
SLG 224 . . . . St. Louis
SLG 230 . . . . St. Joseph
SLG 301 . . . . Jacksonville
SLG 344 . . . . Kansas City
SLG 353 . . . . Lawson
SLG 450 . . . . De Soto
SLG 662 . . . . Orrick
SLG 800 . . . . Kansas City
SLG 1041 . . . . California
SLG 1067 . . . . Martinsburg
SLG 1097 . . . . Dearborn

SLG 1306 . . . . Chillicothe
SLG 1353 . . . . Lexington
SLG 1700 . . . . St. Louis
SLG 1701 . . . . St. Ann

Mine Workers
LU 1122 . . . . Montrose
LU 2452 . . . . St. Charles
LU 7688 . . . . Clifton Hill

Musicians
LU 34-627 . . . . Kansas City
LU 197-2 Musicians Association of
   St. Louis . . . . St. Louis

National Staff Organization
LU Staff Organization,
   Missouri . . . . . Holts Summit

NLRB Professional Association
LU 14 . . . . St. Louis

Nurses
SA Missouri . . . . . . Jefferson City

Office and Professional Employees
LU 13 . . . . Bridgeton
LU 320 . . . . Blue Springs

Operating Engineers
BR Missouri State Branch
   IUOE . . . . Bridgeton
LU 2 . . . . St. Louis
LU 101 . . . . Kansas City
LU 513 . . . . Bridgeton

Painters
DC 2 . . . . St. Louis
DC 3 . . . . Raytown
LU 9 . . . . Raytown
LU 46 . . . . St. Charles
LU 98 . . . . St. Joseph
LU 115 . . . . Dittmer
LU 137 . . . . Hillsboro
LU 203 . . . . Springfield
LU 513 . . . . St. Louis
LU 558 Glaziers &
   Glassworkers . . . . . . Raytown
LU 604 . . . . St. Louis
LU 774 . . . . St. Louis
LU 820 . . . . Raytown
LU 861 . . . . Kansas City
LU 980 . . . . St. Louis
LU 1156 . . . . St. Charles
LU 1179 . . . . Raytown
LU 1185 . . . . Holts Summit
LU 1199 . . . . St. Louis
LU 1265 . . . . Waynesville
LU 1292 . . . . . . Cape Girardeau
LU 1786 . . . . Springfield
LU 2341 . . . . St. Louis

Plant Protection
LU 251 . . . . Independence

Plasterers and Cement Masons
LU 3 . . . . St. Louis
LU 518 . . . . Independence
LU 527 . . . . Bridgeton
LU 908 . . . . Cape Girardeau
STCON Missouri . . . . . Bridgeton

Plumbing and Pipe Fitting
LU 8 . . . . Kansas City
LU 45 . . . . St. Joseph
LU 178 . . . . Springfield
LU 268 Sprinkler Fitters &
   Apprentices . . . . . . St. Louis

LU 314 . . . . Kansas City
LU 533 . . . . Kansas City
LU 562 . . . . St. Louis
LU 781 . . . . Kansas City

Postal and Federal Employees
LU 912 . . . . St. Louis

Postal Mail Handlers
LU 297 . . . . Kansas City
LU 314 . . . . Hazelwood

Postal Workers
LU St. Louis Gateway District
   Area . . . . St. Louis
LU 2 Hannibal Area Local . Hannibal
LU 67 Greater Kansas City Metro
   Area . . . . Kansas City
LU 248 Joplin . . . . Joplin
LU 253 Nevada . . . . Nevada
LU 254 St. Joseph . . . . St. Joseph
LU 333 Sedalia . . . . Sedalia
LU 336 Jefferson
   City . . . . Jefferson City
LU 697 Moberly . . . . . Moberly
LU 700 Chillicothe . . . . Chillicothe
LU 786 Warrensburg . Warrensburg
LU 888 Springfield . . . Springfield
LU 1475 Harrisonville . Harrisonville
LU 1487 California . . . . California
LU 1841 Poplar . . . . . Poplar Bluff
LU 1888 Kirksville . . . Kirksville
LU 2082 Rolla . . . . Rolla
LU 2140 Dexter . . . . . . Dexter
LU 2188 Flat River . . . . Park Hills
LU 2271 Palmyra . . . . . Palmyra
LU 2272 Maryville . . . . Maryville
LU 3454 Savannah . . . . Savannah
LU 3698 West Plains . . West Plains
LU 4088 Cape
   Girardeau . . . . . Cape Girardeau
LU 4110 Boonville . . . . Boonville
LU 4783 Belton . . . . Belton
LU 4853 St. Charles . . . St. Charles
LU 5402 Sikeston . . . . . Sikeston
LU 7043 Saint Louis Bulk Mail
   Center . . . . Hazelwood
LU 7065 Mid Missouri General Mail
   Facility . . . . Ashland
SA Missouri . . . . . Jefferson City

Railroad Signalmen
LLG 55 . . . . Paris
LLG 129 . . . . Chaffee

Retail, Wholesale and Department
Store
LU 125 . . . . St. Joseph

Roofers, Waterproofers and Allied
Workers
DC North Central States . . Raytown
LU 2 . . . . St. Louis
LU 20 . . . . Raytown

Rural Letter Carriers
D 1 . . . . Excelsior Springs
D 2 . . . . Chillicothe
D 3 . . . . Holliday
D 4 . . . . Amsterdam
D 5 . . . . Berger
D 6 . . . . Mount Vernon
D 7 . . . . Elkland
D 8 . . . . Burfordville
D 9 . . . . Foristell
LU 45 Knox County . . . Knox City
SA Missouri . . . . Fairfax

Security, Police and Fire
Professionals
LU 249 . . . . Kansas City
LU 250 . . . . St. Louis
LU 251 . . . . Harrisonville
LU 257 . . . . Jackson
LU 259 . . . . St. Louis

Service Employees
JC 29 . . . . St. Louis
LU 359 . . . . St. Louis
LU 642 Firemen &
   Oilers . . . . Stewartsville
LU 716-A Firemen &
   Oilers . . . . Kansas City
LU 896 Firemen &
   Oilers . . . . Bonne Terre
LU 1106 Firemen &
   Oilers . . . . Springfield
LU 1122 Firemen &
   Oilers . . . . Springfield
LU 1142 Firemen &
   Oilers . . . . Kansas City
LU 2000 . . . . St. Louis
SC 19 Firemen & Oilers . Springfield

Sheet Metal Workers
LU 2 . . . . Kansas City
LU 36 . . . . St. Louis
LU 202 . . . . St. Louis
LU 208 . . . . Springfield
LU 419 . . . . Springfield

State, County and Municipal
Employees
C 72 . . . . Jefferson City
LU 410 Institutional & Public
   Employees . . . . St. Louis

Steelworkers
LU 01-437 . . . . Bridgeton
LU 05-6 Gas Workers . . . St. Louis
LU 05-107 . . . . Potosi
LU 05-152 . . . . Imperial
LU 05-164 . . . . Jackson
LU 05-194 . . . . St. Louis
LU 05-205 . . . . Hannibal
LU 05-266 . . . . St. Joseph
LU 05-500 . . . . Carthage
LU 05-531 . . . . St. Louis
LU 05-617 . . . . Excelsior Springs
LU 05-713 . . . . Louisiana
LU 05-726 . . . . Kansas City
LU 05-760 . . . . Kansas City
LU 05-770 . . . . Marshfield
LU 05-856 . . . . Grandview
LU 05-884 . . . . Farmington
LU 05-937 . . . . Oran
LU 07-300-B . . . . Bridgeton
LU 11-13-S . . . . Kansas City
LU 11-25-U . . . . St. Louis
LU 11-39-U . . . . St. Louis
LU 11-77 . . . . Festus
LU 11-169-G . . . . Ste. Genevieve
LU 11-400-G . . . . Ste. Genevieve
LU 11-433-B . . . . High Hill
LU 11-434 . . . . Bridgeton
LU 11-469-G . . . . Bridgeton
LU 11-662-L . . . . Springfield
LU 11-790-S . . . . Mexico
LU 11-812-L . . . . Joplin
LU 11-853-S . . . . Curryville
LU 11-990 . . . . Independence
LU 11-1004-T . . . . Sedalia
LU 11-5783-S . . . . St. Joseph
LU 11-7033-S . . . . Annapolis
LU 11-7044-S . . . . Bridgeton
LU 11-7450-S . . . . . . Annapolis

LU 11-7686-S . . . . Marston
LU 11-8139 . . . . St. Clair
LU 11-8612-S . . . . . . Bridgeton
LU 11-8734-S . . . . Park Hills
LU 11-9014-S . . . . . . Bridgeton
LU 11-13558-S . . . Independence
LU 11-14228-S . . . . Carterville
LU 11-15485-S . . . . . Springfield

Teachers
LU 3576 Park College Faculty,
   Federation of . . . . . . Parkville
LU 5126 Nurses United/Improved
   Patient Care . . . . . Raytown
LU 6006 Lindbergh Federation of
   Food Service . . . . . . St. Louis
LU 6095 St. Vincents Federation of
   Day Care Providers . . Kansas City
SFED 8023 Missouri . Jefferson City

Teamsters
CONF MO-KAK Conference of
   Teamsters . . . . . . Springfield
JC 13 . . . . St. Louis
JC 56 . . . . Kansas City
LU 6 . . . . St. Louis
LU 41 . . . . Kansas City
LU 245 . . . . Springfield
LU 303 Soft Drink and Mineral
   Water Workers . . . . . St. Louis
LU 541 . . . . Kansas City
LU 600 . . . . . . Maryland Heights
LU 604 . . . . St. Louis
LU 610 . . . . . . Maryland Heights
LU 618 . . . . St. Louis
LU 682 . . . . St. Louis
LU 688 . . . . St. Louis
LU 823 . . . . Joplin
LU 833 . . . . Jefferson City
LU 838 . . . . Kansas City
LU 955 . . . . Kansas City

Television and Radio Artists
LU St. Louis . . . . St. Louis
LU 213 Kansas City . . Kansas City

Theatrical Stage Employees
LU . . . . St. Louis
LU 2-B . . . . St. Louis
LU 6 . . . . St. Louis
LU 31 . . . . Kansas City
LU 143 . . . . St. Louis
LU 774 . . . . St. Louis
LU 805 . . . . St. Louis
LU 810 . . . . Kansas City

Transit Union
LDIV 788 . . . . St. Louis
LDIV 1498 . . . . . Independence
LU 847 . . . . St. Joseph
LU 1287 . . . . Kansas City

Transport Workers
LU 529 . . . . Bridgeton
LU 530 . . . . Kansas City
LU 1647 . . . . St. Louis

Transportation Communications
Union
D 126 Allied Services
   Division . . . . Kansas City
D 326 . . . . Granview
LG 121 . . . . Gladstone
LG 149 . . . . Springfield
LG 284 . . . . Independence
LG 6034 Violet . . . . . St. Peters
LG 6078 De Soto . . . . . De Soto

LG 6343
   Shippers . . . . North Kansas City

Transportation Union
GCA GO-1 . . . . Springfield
GCA GO-9 Atchison Topeka Santa
   Fe-P-E & W . . . . . Kansas City
GCA GO-341 . . . . . St. Joseph
LU 5 . . . . Blue Springs
LU 185 . . . . Rothville
LU 219 . . . . Hannibal
LU 226 . . . . Moberly
LU 259 . . . . Kansas City
LU 303 . . . . Springfield
LU 330 . . . . Poplar Bluff
LU 349 . . . . Blue Springs
LU 412 . . . . Kansas City
LU 607 . . . . Thayer
LU 933 . . . . California
LU 947 . . . . Jackson
LU 1216 . . . . Lees Summit
LU 1388 . . . . Arnold
LU 1403 . . . . Lees Summit
LU 1823 . . . . St. Louis
LU 1975 . . . . Lees Summit
SLB LO-28 Missouri . Jefferson City

Treasury Employees
CH 14 . . . . St. Louis
CH 36 . . . . Kansas City
CH 66 . . . . Kansas City
CH 121 . . . . St. Louis
CH 182 . . . . Kansas City
CH 217 . . . . Kansas City
CH 264 . . . . Kansas City
CH 274 . . . . Kansas City

UNITE HERE
LU 64 . . . . Kansas City
LU 74 . . . . St. Louis

Utility Workers
LU 335 . . . . Florissant
LU 398 . . . . Fredericktown
LU 455 . . . . St. Charles

Weather Service Employees
BR 03-28 . . . . Kansas City
BR 03-35 . . . . Pleasant Hill
BR 03-62 . . . . Pleasant Hill
BR 03-70 . . . . Kansas City
BR 03-71 . . . . Kansas City
BR 03-89 . . . . St. Charles
BR 03-97 . . . . Kansas City

Unaffiliated Labor
Organizations

Bowling Lane Resurfacer Installers
   Associated St. Louis . . St. Louis
Congress of Independent Unions LU
   18 Musicians . . . . Jefferson City
Craftsman Independent Union
   LU 1 . . . . Cape Girardeau
Craftsman International
   Union . . . . . . Cape Girardeau
Electric Protective Association
   Independent . . . . Calverton Park
FMCS Association of Federal
   Mediators . . . . Ballwin
Fuse Workers Inc.
   Independent . . . . Ellisville
Independent Store Employees
   Association . . . . O'Fallon
Independent Union of Plant
   Protection Employees LU
   267 . . . . Hazelwood

International Guards Union of
   America LU 36 . . . . . St. Louis
Jewish Community Center
   Employees Union . . Creve Coeur

Mink Pipe Trades
   Association . . . . . Springfield
Missouri Professional Staff
   Organization . . . . Independence

Railway Exchange Building
   Employees Association
   Independent . . . . . . St. Louis
Surgical Instrument Workers
   Inc. . . . . Fenton

Theatre Musicians
   Association. . . . . . . St. Louis
United Health Care Workers of
   Greater St. Louis LU 1 . . De Soto
Wehrenberg Alliance of Motion
   Picture Machine
   Operation . . . . St. Louis

Montana

AFL-CIO Trade and Industrial Departments

Building and Construction Trades Department
BCTC Montana State . . . . . Butte
BCTC North Central
  Montana . . . . Great Falls
BCTC Southeastern
  Montana. . . . . Billings
BCTC Southwestern Montana . Butte
BCTC Western Montana. . Missoula

Affiliated Labor Organizations

Air Traffic Controllers
LU BIL . . . . Billings
LU GTF . . . . Great Falls
LU HLN . . . . Helena

Bakery, Confectionery, Tobacco Workers and Grain Millers
LU 109-G . . . . Belt
LU 285-G. . . . . Sidney
LU 466 . . . . Billings

Boilermakers
LG 11 . . . . East Helena
LG 239-D Cement
  Workers. . . . . . . Three Forks
LG 435-D Cement
  Workers. . . . . . . East Helena
LG 599. . . . . Edgar

Bricklayers
LU 5. . . . . Three Forks

Carpenters
LU 28 . . . . Missoula
LU 112 . . . . Butte
LU 153 . . . . Helena
LU 286 . . . . Great Falls
LU 557. . . . . Bozeman
LU 1172 . . . . Billings
LU 2446. . . . . Laurel
LU 3038 . . . . Missoula

Civilian Technicians
CH 29 Montana Air . . . Great Falls
CH 57 Treasure State
  Chapter. . . . . Clancy

Communications Workers
LU 14734 . . . . Billings
LU 14737 . . . . Havre
LU 14740 Missoula Typographical
  Union . . . . Missoula

Electrical Workers
LU 44 . . . . Butte
LU 152 . . . . Glendive
LU 206 . . . . Helena
LU 233 . . . . Helena
LU 532 . . . . Billings
LU 653 . . . . Miles City
LU 758 . . . . Wolf Point
LU 768 . . . . Kalispell
LU 958. . . . . Baker
LU 988 . . . . Sidney
LU 1050 . . . . Glendive
LU 1155 . . . . Roundup
LU 1638 . . . . Colstrip
LU 1856 . . . . Havre

Federal Employees
LU 58 Fort Belknap Service
  Unit . . . . Harlem
LU 224 . . . . Crow Agency
LU 478 . . . . Hardin
LU 1150 . . . . Park City
LU 1241 . . . . Whitefish
LU 1398 . . . . Libby
LU 1492 . . . . Conner
LU 1585 . . . . Belgrade
LU 2107. . . . . Browning

Fire Fighters
LU 25-A State Association-State-
  Affiliate . . . . Great Falls

Food and Commercial Workers
LU 4 . . . . Butte
LU 8 . . . . Great Falls
LU 301 . . . . Butte

Government Employees
C 201 Food Inspection Locals,
  Northern . . . . Butte
LU 1124 . . . . Billings
LU 2609 DoD . . . . . . Great Falls
LU 3355 USDA . . . . . . Billings
LU 3570 VA. . . . . Fort Harrison

Government Employees Association
LU 14-84 . . . . Helena

Government Security Officers
LU 128 . . . . Missoula
LU 227 . . . . Lakeside
LU 239 United Government Security
  Officers . . . . Billings

Graphic Communications
LU 227-C . . . . Billings
LU 242-C . . . . Missoula

Iron Workers
LU 841 . . . . Helena

Laborers
DC 43 Montana . . . . . . Helena
LU 98 . . . . Billings
LU 254 . . . . Helena
LU 1334 . . . . Great Falls

Letter Carriers
BR 220 . . . . Helena
BR 621 . . . . Butte
BR 623 . . . . Anaconda
BR 650 . . . . Great Falls
BR 701 . . . . Missoula
BR 815 . . . . Billings
BR 948 . . . . Kalispell
BR 968 . . . . Livingston
BR 1028 . . . . Bozeman
BR 1160 . . . . Lewistown
BR 1281 . . . . Miles City
BR 1425 . . . . Havre
BR 1643 . . . . Glendive
BR 1680 . . . . Hamilton
BR 1698 . . . . Glasgow
BR 1778 . . . . Dillon
BR 2328 . . . . Roundup
BR 2382 . . . . Kalispell
BR 3204 . . . . Conrad
BR 3839 . . . . Deer Lodge
BR 4305 . . . . Sidney
BR 4537. . . . . Stevensville

Locomotive Engineers
DIV Montana Rail Link . . Missoula
DIV 180 . . . . Glendive
DIV 195 . . . . Forsyth
DIV 232 . . . . Billings
DIV 262 . . . . Missoula
DIV 298 . . . . Glasgow
DIV 392 Milk River. . . . . Havre
DIV 499 . . . . Whitefish
DIV 504 . . . . Great Falls
SLB Montana . . . . Forsyth

Machinists
DLG 86. . . . . Butte
LG 88 . . . . Butte
LG 169 . . . . Livingston
LG 231 . . . . Helena
LG 430 . . . . Havre
LG 509 . . . . Glendive
LG 622. . . . . Shepherd
LG 701-FL . . . . Dillon
LG 1760 . . . . . Columbia Falls
LG 1801. . . . . Busby
LG 2171 . . . . Poplar
LLG FL-60. . . . . Missoula
LLG FL-1697 . . . . . . Anaconda

Maintenance of Way Employes
LG 16 . . . . Harlem
LG 272 . . . . Missoula
LG 295 . . . . Hardin
LG 297 . . . . Miles City
SLG 158 . . . . Helena
SLG 735 . . . . Great Falls
SLG 1092 . . . . Whitefish
SLG 1189. . . . . Glasgow

Mine Workers
LU 1575 . . . . Forsyth

Musicians
LU 498 . . . . Missoula
LU 642 . . . . Helena
LU 709. . . . . Bozeman

National Staff Organization
LU Staff Organization, Professional,
  Montana Education
  Association . . . . . . Glendive

Nurses
SA Montana Nurses
  Association. . . . . Helena

Operating Engineers
LU 400 . . . . Helena

Painters
LU 260 . . . . Great Falls
LU 720 Butte-Anaconda . . . Butte
LU 1922 . . . . Billings

Plasterers and Cement Masons
LU 119 . . . . Anaconda

BR 4890 . . . . Cut Bank
BR 4891 . . . . Shelby
BR 4892 . . . . Wolf Point
BR 5157. . . . . Laurel
BR 5193 . . . . Plentywood
BR 5265 . . . . Hardin
BR 5387 . . . . Libby
BR 5533 . . . . Corvallis
BR 6560 . . . . Troy
SA Montana . . . . Billings

Plumbing and Pipe Fitting
LU 30 . . . . Billings
LU 41 . . . . Butte
LU 459 . . . . Missoula
SA Montana . . . . Billings

Postal Mail Handlers
LU 327 . . . . Billings

Postal Workers
LU 82 Butte . . . . Butte
LU 113 Missoula. . . . . . Missoula
LU 119 Miles City . . . . Miles City
LU 132 Billings . . . . Billings
LU 208 Great Falls. . . . Great Falls
LU 649 Helena . . . . Helena
LU 651 Sidney . . . . Sidney
LU 680 Bozeman . . . . . Bozeman
LU 683 Kalispell. . . . . . Kalispell
LU 728 Glendive. . . . . . Glendive
LU 843 Lewistown. . . . Lewistown
LU 922 Wolf Point. . . . Wolf Point
LU 4679 Dillon . . . . Dillon
LU 6505 Polson . . . . Polson
SA Montana . . . . Lewistown

Railroad Signalmen
LLG 87 . . . . Billings

Roofers, Waterproofers and Allied Workers
LU 229 . . . . Billings
LU 250 . . . . Butte

Rural Letter Carriers
D 1 . . . . Corvallis
D 2 . . . . Great Falls
D 3 . . . . Bozeman
D 4 . . . . Billings
SA Montana . . . . Sidney

Security, Police and Fire Professionals
LU 15 . . . . Butte

Service Employees
LU 468 Firemen & Oilers . Glendive
LU 840 Firemen & Oilers . . Billings
LU 911 Firemen & Oilers . . . Havre

Sheet Metal Workers
LU 103 . . . . Helena
LU 140 . . . . Glendive

State, County and Municipal Employees
LU 398 Montana Health
  Care Employees
  Association . . . . . . Stevensville
LU 4016 Eastern Montana Industries,
  Inc. Employees. . . . . . Helena
STC 9 . . . . Helena

Steelworkers
LU 8-443 Pace Pioneer
  Local . . . . Laurel
LU 08-1 . . . . Columbus
LU 08-470. . . . . Billings
LU 08-491 . . . . Great Falls
LU 08-493 . . . . Cut Bank
LU 08-885 Hellgate . . . . Missoula
LU 08-1509 . . . . Missoula
LU 11-320-A . . . . Columbia Falls

LU 11-3169-S . . . . Billings

Teachers
LU 5005 Butte Silverbow Federation
    of LPN . . . . Butte
SFED Montana . . . . Helena

Teamsters
LU 2 . . . . Butte
LU 190 . . . . Billings

Theatrical Stage Employees
LU 240 . . . . Billings

LU 339 . . . . Great Falls

**Transportation Communications
   Union**
LG 43 . . . . Missoula
LG 656 . . . . Havre
LG 6476 Laurel . . . . Laurel
LG 6670 Bear Paw . . . . . . Havre

Transportation Union
LU 486 . . . . Glendive
LU 544 . . . . Chinook
LU 730 . . . . Great Falls

LU 891 . . . . Whitefish
LU 1840 . . . . Glasgow
SLB LO-29 Montana . . . . Kalispell

Treasury Employees
CH 42 . . . . Helena
CH 231 . . . . Eureka

UNITE HERE
LU 427 . . . . Missoula

Weather Service Employees
BR 04-5 . . . . Missoula

BR 04-6 . . . . Great Falls
BR 04-7 . . . . Billings
BR 04-73 . . . . Glasgow

**Unaffiliated Labor
Organizations**
Aluminum Workers Trades
    Council . . . . . Columbia Falls
Big Sky Pilots
    Association . . . . Billings
John Muir LU 100 . . . . . Bozeman
Oil Basin Pipeliners Union . Billings
Rocky Mountain Union-Exxon
    Pipeline Company . . . . . Bridger

Nebraska

AFL-CIO Trade and Industrial Departments

Building and Construction Trades Department
BCTC Lincoln . . . . Lincoln
BCTC Omaha . . . . Omaha

Affiliated Labor Organizations

Air Traffic Controllers
LU LOU . . . . Lincoln
LU OMA . . . . Omaha
LU R90 . . . . Bellevue

Asbestos Workers
LU 39 . . . . Blair

Bakery, Confectionery, Tobacco Workers and Grain Millers
LU 31-G . . . . Lincoln
LU 50-G . . . . Omaha
LU 80-G . . . . Pleasant Dale
LU 178-G . . . . Fremont
LU 433 . . . . . . South Sioux City

Boilermakers
LG 174-D Cement
   Workers . . . . Louisville
LG 561-D Cement
   Workers . . . . . Weeping Water

Bricklayers
LU 1 . . . . Omaha

Carpenters
LU 444 . . . . Omaha
LU 1055 . . . . Lincoln
LU 1463 . . . . Wahoo

Civilian Technicians
CH 88 Cornhusker . . . . . Lincoln

Communications Workers
LU 7150 . . . . Omaha
LU 7290 . . . . Omaha
LU 7400 . . . . Omaha
LU 7401 . . . . Grand Island
LU 7470 . . . . Lincoln
LU 7471 . . . . Kearney
LU 7476 . . . . Hastings
LU 14744 . . . . Omaha
LU 57045 . . . . Omaha

Electrical Workers
C Nebraska . . . . Omaha
LU 22 . . . . Omaha
LU 244 . . . . Lincoln
LU 265 . . . . Lincoln
LU 843 . . . . Scottsbluff
LU 1022 . . . . Elmwood
LU 1517 . . . . Alliance
LU 1525 . . . . Omaha
LU 1614 . . . . Omaha
LU 1920 . . . . North Platte
LU 1974 . . . . Omaha
LU 2001 . . . . Fremont
LU 2366 . . . . Lincoln

Elevator Constructors
LU 28 . . . . Omaha

Federal Employees
C Bureau of Indian Affairs
   Locals . . . . Rushville

Food and Commercial Workers
LU 22 . . . . Fremont
LU 271 . . . . Omaha
LU 815-C . . . . Beatrice

Government Employees
LU 771 USDA . . . . . Plattsmouth
LU 840 Council of DFAS . Offutt Air
                           Force Base
LU 1486 DoD . . . . Omaha
LU 2200 VA . . . . Lincoln
LU 2219 VA . . . . Lincoln
LU 2223 USDA . . . . . . La Vista
LU 2270 VA . . . . Omaha
LU 2601 VA . . . . . Grand Island
LU 2706 HHS . . . . Omaha
LU 3286 HUD . . . . Omaha
LU 3363 USDA . . . . . . Chadron
LU 3684 HHS . . . . Grand Island
LU 3717 USDA . . . . . Columbus
LU 3749 USDA . . . . . . Kenesaw
LU 3928 INS . . . . Lincoln

Graphic Communications
LU 543-M . . . . Omaha

Iron Workers
LU 21 . . . . Omaha
LU 553 . . . . Omaha

Laborers
LU 1140 . . . . Omaha

Letter Carriers
BR 5 . . . . Omaha
BR 8 . . . . Lincoln
BR 89 . . . . Ames
BR 93 . . . . Hastings
BR 312 . . . . Kearney
BR 390 . . . . Wood River
BR 593 . . . . Nebraska City
BR 896 . . . . York
BR 1014 . . . . Fairbury
BR 1020 . . . . Norfolk
BR 1043 . . . . Columbus
BR 1258 . . . . North Platte
BR 1278 . . . . McCook
BR 1300 . . . . Alliance
BR 1483 . . . . Broken Bow
BR 1525 . . . . Blair
BR 1582 . . . . Falls City
BR 1591 . . . . Aurora
BR 1774 . . . . Minden
BR 1883 . . . . Seward
BR 1885 . . . . Lexington
BR 1924 . . . . Wahoo
BR 1952 . . . . Schuyler
BR 2061 . . . . Superior
BR 2209 . . . . Chadron
BR 2261 . . . . Wymore
BR 2314 . . . . Crete
BR 2499 . . . . Wayne
BR 2692 . . . . St. Paul
BR 2726 . . . . . . South Sioux City
BR 2798 . . . . Gothenburg
BR 2907 . . . . Sidney
BR 2926 . . . . Oakland
BR 2956 . . . . Franklin
BR 2963 . . . . Auburn
BR 2964 . . . . West Point
BR 2966 . . . . Clay Center

BR 2967 . . . . Geneva
BR 3101 . . . . Ainsworth
BR 3141 . . . . Ord
BR 3171 . . . . Gordon
BR 3425 . . . . Tekamah
BR 4017 . . . . Ogallala
BR 4072 . . . . Mitchell
BR 4128 . . . . Plattsmouth
BR 4142 . . . . Red Cloud
BR 4152 . . . . Cozad
BR 4646 . . . . Valentine
BR 4904 . . . . O'Neill
SA Nebraska . . . . Lincoln

Locomotive Engineers
DIV 88 . . . . North Platte
DIV 98 . . . . Lincoln
DIV 183 . . . . Lincoln
DIV 303 . . . . Gering
DIV 621 . . . . Lincoln
DIV 622 . . . . Alliance
DIV 623 . . . . McCook
DIV 699 . . . . Elkhorn
SLB Nebraska . . . . Lincoln

Machinists
LG 19 PVC . . . . Morrill
LG 31 . . . . Matell
LG 180 . . . . Maywood
LG 543 . . . . Beatrice
LG 602 . . . . Alliance
LG 612 . . . . Lincoln
LG 1569 . . . . Geneva
LG 1826 . . . . Omaha
STC Nebraska State Council of
   Machinist . . . . Beatrice

Maintenance of Way Employes
LG 1214 . . . . Hastings
LG 1316 . . . . Odell
LG 1320 . . . . Lincoln
SD Burlington Railroad . . Hastings
SLG 216 . . . . Omaha
SLG 473 . . . . Central City
SLG 700 . . . . Fremont
SLG 899 . . . . Sidney
SLG 961 . . . . Gering
SLG 1105 . . . . La Vista
SLG 1108 . . . . Alliance
SLG 1133 . . . . Fairbury

Musicians
LU 70-558 . . . . Omaha
LU 463 . . . . Lincoln

National Staff Organization
LU Staff Association,
   Nebraska . . . . Lincoln

Office and Professional Employees
LU 53 . . . . Omaha

Operating Engineers
LU 571 . . . . Omaha

Painters
LU 109 . . . . Omaha

Plasterers and Cement Masons
LU 538 . . . . Omaha

Plumbing and Pipe Fitting
LU 16 . . . . Omaha
LU 464 Steamfitters . . . . Omaha

Postal Mail Handlers
LU 298 . . . . Omaha

Postal Workers
LU 9 Central Nebraska
   Area . . . . Grand Island
LU 11 Omaha Area . . . . Omaha
LU 112 Lincoln . . . . . . Lincoln
LU 310 Beatrice . . . . . Beatrice
LU 311 Hastings . . . . . Hastings
LU 313 Columbus . . . . Columbus
LU 314 Nebraska
   City . . . . Nebraska City
LU 319 York . . . . York
LU 430 Seward . . . . . . Seward
LU 480 Fremont . . . . . Fremont
LU 619 North Platte . . North Platte
LU 845 Scottsbluff . . . . Scottsbluff
LU 948 Alliance . . . . . Alliance
LU 1148 Valentine . . . . Valentine
LU 1187 Norfolk . . . . . Norfolk
LU 2813 O'Neil . . . . . . O'Neill
LU 4040 Ogallala . . . . . Ogallala
LU 4048 Blair . . . . Blair
LU 4072 Sidney . . . . . . Sidney
SA Nebraska City . . . . La Vista

Railroad Signalmen
LLG 8 . . . . Kimball
LLG 119 . . . . Omaha

Retail, Wholesale and Department Store
LU 1808 . . . . Lincoln

Roofers, Waterproofers and Allied Workers
LU 19 . . . . Omaha

Rural Letter Carriers
D 1 . . . . Crete
D 2 . . . . Prague
D 3 . . . . St. Edward
D 4 . . . . Holdrege
D 5 . . . . Gering
SA Nebraska . . . . Firth

Security, Police and Fire Professionals
LU 778 . . . . Lincoln

Service Employees
LU 226 . . . . Omaha
LU 403 Firemen &
   Oilers . . . . North Platte
LU 736 Firemen & Oilers . . Lincoln
LU 861 Firemen & Oilers . Alliance
LU 1204 Firemen & Oilers . Lincoln

Sheet Metal Workers
LU 3 . . . . Omaha
LU 259 . . . . Alliance
LU 334 . . . . North Platte
LU 402 . . . . Lincoln

Steelworkers
LU 05-309 . . . . Omaha
LU 05-699 . . . . Omaha
LU 05-974 . . . . Ralston
LU 05-1473 . . . . Omaha
LU 11-286-L . . . . Lincoln
LU 11-6257-S . . . . Ames

Teamsters
LU 554 . . . . Omaha

Television and Radio Artists
LU Omaha . . . . Omaha

Theatrical Stage Employees
LU 42. . . . . Omaha
LU 151. . . . . Lincoln
LU 343 . . . . Omaha
LU 831 . . . . Omaha
SA Nebraska. . . . . Lincoln

Transportation Communications Union
JPB 50 Burlington Northern
  Railway . . . . Lincoln
LG 112 . . . . North Platte
LG 471. . . . . Lincoln
LG 1288 Alliance District . Alliance
LG 5101 Union Pacific Consolidated
  Lodge. . . . . North Platte
LG 6577 Kenneth . . . . Bellevue
LG 6743 Box Butte. . . . . Alliance
LG 6799 Cornhusker . . . . Lincoln
LG 6832 Platte Valley . North Platte

SBA 106 Union Pacific Lines-
  East . . . . Omaha

Transportation Union
LU 7. . . . . North Platte
LU 200 . . . . North Platte
LU 257 . . . . Gering
LU 286 . . . . North Platte
LU 305. . . . . Lincoln
LU 367 . . . . Papillion
LU 418. . . . . . South Sioux City
LU 626 . . . . McCook
LU 627. . . . . Walton

LU 934 . . . . Alliance
LU 962 . . . . Alliance
LU 1503. . . . . Beatrice
SLB LO-30 Nebraska . . . . Lincoln

Treasury Employees
CH 3 . . . . Omaha

Weather Service Employees
BR 03-27 . . . . North Platte
BR 03-73 . . . . Valley
BR 03-92 . . . . Hastings

Unaffiliated Labor Organizations
International Guards Union of
  America LU 133 . . . . . . Omaha

Nevada

AFL-CIO Trade and Industrial Departments

Building and Construction Trades Department
BCTC Northern Nevada . . . Sparks
BCTC Southern Nevada . Henderson

AFL-CIO Directly Affiliated Locals

AFL-CIO
C Southern Nevada Central
   Labor. . . . . Henderson

Affiliated Labor Organizations

Air Traffic Controllers
LU L30 . . . . Las Vegas
LU LAS. . . . . Las Vegas
LU RNO . . . . Reno
LU VGT . . . . . North Las Vegas

Asbestos Workers
LU 135 . . . . Las Vegas

Automobile, Aerospace Workers
LU 2162 . . . . Reno

Boilermakers
LG 263-D Cement Workers . . Reno
LG 381-D Cement
   Workers . . . . North Las Vegas

Bricklayers
LU 13 . . . . Las Vegas
LU 13 . . . . Las Vegas

Carpenters
LU 971 . . . . Reno
LU 1780 . . . . Las Vegas
LU 1827 . . . . Las Vegas
LU 1977 . . . . Las Vegas

Civilian Technicians
CH 77 Silver Barons . . . . Reno
CH 78 Silver Sage . . . . . Reno

Communications Workers
LU 1119. . . . . Fallon
LU 9413 . . . . Sparks
LU 14922 . . . . Las Vegas
LU 87177 . . . . Fallon
LU 89118 . . . . Fallon

Electrical Workers
C TCC-3 Telephone
   Coordinating . . . . . Las Vegas
LU 357 . . . . Las Vegas

LU 396 . . . . Las Vegas
LU 401 . . . . Reno

Fire Fighters
LU 268-F . . . . Fernley

Food and Commercial Workers
LU 711 . . . . Las Vegas

Government Employees
C 147 Regional SS Field Operations
   Locals . . . . Henderson
LU 1199 DoD. Nellis Air Force Base
LU 1201. . . . . Fallon
LU 1978 DoI. . . . . Boulder City
LU 2152 VA . . . . Reno
LU 3062 DoI Lake Mead National
   Recreation Center . . Boulder City
LU 4000 AFGE Local 4000
   CPL33 . . . . Las Vegas

Government Security Officers
LU 76 . . . . Dayton

Laborers
DC Nevada . . . . Reno
LU 169 . . . . Reno
LU 872 . . . . Las Vegas

Letter Carriers
BR 709 . . . . Reno
BR 2502 . . . . Las Vegas
BR 2778 . . . . Sparks
BR 2862. . . . . Elko
BR 4515 . . . . . . Battle Mountain
BR 6390 . . . . Winnemucca
BR 6496 . . . . Ely
SA Nevada . . . . Reno

Locomotive Engineers
DIV 158 . . . . Reno
DIV 229 . . . . Winnemucca
DIV 766. . . . . Las Vegas
SLB California . . . . Reno
SLB Nevada State Legislative
   Board . . . . Sparks

Machinists
LG 845 . . . . Las Vegas
LLG 744 . . . . Las Vegas

Maintenance of Way Employes
LG 85 . . . . Sparks
LG 107 . . . . Wells
LG 1020 . . . . Henderson

Musicians
LU 368 . . . . Reno
LU 369 . . . . Las Vegas

National Staff Organization
ASSN Nevada Education . . . Reno

LU Staff Organization Clark
   County . . . . Las Vegas

Nurses
SA Nevada Nurses
   Association. . . . . Reno

Painters
DC 15. . . . . Henderson
LU 159 . . . . Henderson
LU 567 International Brotherhood of
   Painters . . . . Sparks
LU 2001 . . . . Henderson

Plasterers and Cement Masons
LU 241 . . . . Sparks
LU 797 . . . . Las Vegas

Plumbing and Pipe Fitting
LU 350 . . . . Sparks
LU 525 . . . . Las Vegas
SA Nevada State Pipe
   Trades . . . . Las Vegas

Postal Workers
LU 746 Winnemucca . Winnemucca
LU 761 Las Vegas Area . Las Vegas
LU 936 Reno . . . . Reno
LU 1992 Elko. . . . . Elko
LU 4636 Tonopah . . . . . Tonopah
LU 5085 Carson City . . Carson City
LU 5718 Sparks . . . . . . Sparks
LU 6668 Ely . . . . Ely
LU 6689 Zephyr Cove . Zephyr Cove
LU 6806 Hawthorne . . Hawthorne
LU 7125 Crystal Bay-Incline Village
   Area . . . . Incline Village
LU 7156 Pahrump Nevada . Pahrump
SA Nevada . . . . Las Vegas

Railroad Signalmen
LLG 179 . . . . Spring Creek

Roofers, Waterproofers and Allied Workers
LU 162 . . . . Las Vegas

Rural Letter Carriers
SA 48 Nevada . . . . Reno

Security, Police and Fire Professionals
LU 824 . . . . Laughlin
LU 888 . . . . Las Vegas
LU 1010 . . . . Reno

Service Employees
LU 1107 Nevada Service Employees
   Union. . . . . Las Vegas
LU 12-135 NAGE . . . . Las Vegas

Sheet Metal Workers
C Western States . . . . . . Sparks
LU 26 . . . . Sparks
LU 88 . . . . Las Vegas

Steelworkers
LU 12-233-S . . . . Ely
LU 12-711-A . . . . . . Las Vegas
LU 12-4856-S . . . . . Henderson
LU 12-5282-S . . . . . Henderson

Teamsters
LU 14 . . . . Las Vegas
LU 533 . . . . Reno
LU 631 . . . . Las Vegas
LU 995 . . . . Las Vegas

Theatrical Stage EmployeesLas Vegas
D 2 California-Nevada-Arizona-
   Hawaii . . . . Las Vegas
LU 363 . . . . Reno

Transit Union
LU 1637 . . . . Las Vegas
LU 1758 . . . . Las Vegas

Transportation Union
LU 1043 . . . . Reno
LU 1117 . . . . Las Vegas
LU 1775. . . . . Elko
SLB LO-31 Nevada . . . Las Vegas

Treasury Employees
CH 38 . . . . Reno
CH 85 . . . . Las Vegas

UNITE HERE
LJEB Las Vegas . . . . . Las Vegas
LU 165 . . . . Las Vegas
LU 226 Culinary . . . . Las Vegas
LU 227 Culinary & Casino Workers
   Union . . . . Las Vegas

Weather Service Employees
BR 04-54 . . . . Las Vegas
BR 04-59. . . . . Reno
BR 04-77 . . . . Elko

Unaffiliated Labor Organizations
Clark County Associate Staff
   Organization-Teachers
   Staff . . . . Las Vegas
Guard Association of Nevada
   Independent LU 1 . . . . Mercury
Nevada Security Inspectors
   Association LU 1 . . . . Tonopah
Professional Office Personnel
   Professional Nurses
   Alliance. . . . . Las Vegas
Security Police Association of
   Nevada . . . . Las Vegas
Transit Drivers Association of
   Nevada . . . . Las Vegas

New Hampshire

AFL-CIO Trade and Industrial Departments

Building and Construction Trades Department
BCTC New Hampshire . . Deerfield

Metal Trades Department
MTC Metal Trades Council Portsmouth New Hampshire. . . . . . Portsmouth

Affiliated Labor Organizations

Air Traffic Controllers
LU A90 . . . . Merrimack
LU LEB. . . . . Lebanon
LU NCT . . . . Manchester
LU ZBW . . . . Nashua

Aircraft Mechanics
NHQ. . . . . Laconia

Boilermakers
LG 920. . . . . Portsmouth

Carpenters
LU 3073 . . . . Portsmouth

Civilian Technicians
CH 19 Granite State . . . Manchester
CH 99 White Mountain . Manchester

Communications Workers
LU 1366 . . . . Plaistow
LU 1400 . . . . Portsmouth
LU 14131 . . . . Manchester
LU 14132 . . . . Auburn
LU 14133. . . . . Goffstown
LU 31167 . . . . Manchester
LU 81243 . . . . Dover

Electrical Workers
LU 490 . . . . Concord
LU 2320 . . . . Manchester

Electrical, Radio and Machine Workers
LU 278. . . . . Woodsville
LU 293 . . . . Gonic

Engineers
C Northeast . . . . . . Portsmouth
LU 4 . . . . Portsmouth
LU 4 Chapter 1 . . . . . . Hanover

LU 202 . . . . Concord

Food and Commercial Workers
LU 17-T . . . . Nashua
LU 952-C . . . . Nashua
LU 1046-C . . . . Boscawen

Glass, Molders, Pottery and Plastics Workers
LU 257-B . . . . Amherst

Government Employees
LU 2024 DoD . . . . . Portsmouth
LU 2551 DoD . . . . Keene
LU 3257 USDA . . . . . . Epping
LU 3698 VA . . . . . . Manchester

Government Employees Association
LU 01-17 . . . . Manchester

Graphic Communications
LU 271-M M.P.P. & A.U. . . . . Manchester

Iron Workers
LU 474 . . . . Manchester
LU 745 . . . . Rochester

Laborers
DC Maine-New Hampshire & Vermont . . . . . . Portsmouth
LU 668 . . . . Hooksett
LU 976. . . . . Portsmouth

Letter Carriers
BR 44 . . . . Manchester
BR 72. . . . . Concord
BR 161. . . . . Portsmouth
BR 230 . . . . Nashua
BR 570 . . . . Laconia
BR 590 . . . . Keene
BR 833 . . . . Claremont
BR 990 . . . . Rochester
BR 1027. . . . . Franklin
BR 1536. . . . . Berlin
BR 1597 . . . . Littleton
BR 1633 . . . . Lebanon
BR 1738 . . . . Lancaster
BR 2002 . . . . Plymouth
BR 2007 . . . . Newport
BR 2053 . . . . Tilton
BR 2247 . . . . Peterborough
BR 4516 . . . . Pittsfield
BR 4519 . . . . Suncook
BR 4713 . . . . Gorham
BR 4906 . . . . Jaffrey

BR 4917 . . . . Hudson
BR 5057 . . . . Rindge
BR 5174 . . . . Groveton
BR 5631 . . . . Colebrook
BR 5879 . . . . Whitefield
SA New Hampshire . . . . Hooksett

Longshoremen
LU 1947 . . . . Portsmouth

Machinists
LG 2450 . . . . Newmarket
LG 2503 . . . . Bedford

Maintenance of Way Employes
LG 2820 . . . . Dover

Musicians
LU 349 . . . . Manchester
LU 374 . . . . Concord

National Staff Organization
LU Staff Organization, New Hampshire Educational . Concord

Office and Professional Employees
LU 104 . . . . Merrimack

Plumbing and Pipe Fitting
LU 131 . . . . Hooksett
LU 788. . . . . Portsmouth

Postal Workers
LU . . . . Newmarket
LU 230 Manchester . . . Manchester
LU 242 Rochester . . . . Rochester
LU 355 Portsmouth Area Local . . . . . . Portsmouth
LU 494 Laconia . . . . . . Laconia
LU 1074 Keene . . . . . . Keene
LU 1214 Meredith . . . . Meredith
LU 2619 Littleton. . . . . Littleton
LU 2778 Bellows Falls . Charlestown
LU 2964. . . . . Durham
LU 3157 Woodsville . . Woodsville
LU 3403 Lancaster . . . . Lancaster
LU 3408 Conway . . . . . Conway
LU 3435 Hanover. . . . . Hanover
LU 5080 Lebanon . . . . Lebanon
SA New Hampshire . . . Manchester

Rural Letter Carriers
SA New Hampshire . . . . . Milford

Security, Police and Fire Professionals
LU 501 . . . . Portsmouth

LU 545 . . . . New Boston

Service Employees
LU 560. . . . . Grafton
LU 941 Firemen & Oilers . . Pelham
LU 1984 . . . . Concord

Sheet Metal Workers
LU 546. . . . . Portsmouth

Steelworkers
LU 01-61. . . . . Groveton
LU 01-75 . . . . Berlin
LU 01-270 . . . . . . Merrimack
LU 01-472 . . . . . . Bennington
LU 01-574 . . . . Tilton
LU 04-8566-S . . . . . Sanbornton
LU 04-8938-S . . . . . Manchester

Teachers
LU 2433 Rindge Faculty Federation . . . . Rindge
LU 8027 AFT New Hampshire . Bow

Teamsters
LU 633 . . . . Manchester

Theatrical Stage Employees
LU 195. . . . . Milford

Transportation Union
LU 254. . . . . New Ipswich
LU 898 . . . . . . East Hampstead

Treasury Employees
CH 11 . . . . Manchester

Utility Workers
LU 555. . . . . Seabrook

Weather Service Employees
BR 01-63. . . . . Nashua

Unaffiliated Labor Organizations
American Independent Cockpit Alliance Inc. . . . . . . Laconia
Guild Representatives Federation . . . . . . Goffstown
Independent Flight Attendants . . . . . . Laconia
Seabrook Dog Track Employees Association . . . . . . Seabrook
Security Officers Independent Union . . . . Manchester
United Flight Attendant Union (UFAU) . . . . Laconia

New Jersey

AFL-CIO Trade and Industrial Departments

Building and Construction Trades Department
BCTC Atlantic City . . Bordentown
BCTC Bergen County . Hackensack
BCTC Camden County . . Winslow
BCTC Elizabeth &
   Vicinity . . . . Westfield
BCTC Essex County. . . Bloomfield
BCTC Hudson County . . . . . Lodi
BCTC Mercer County . . Hamilton
BCTC Middlesex County . . Newark
BCTC Monmouth & Ocean
   Counties . . . . Howell
BCTC Morris County . . Parsippany
BCTC New Jersey State . . . . Clark
BCTC Passaic County . . . . . Lodi
BCTC Somerville . . . . Somerville
BCTC Warren County . Phillipsburg

Other Councils and Committees
C Essex West Hudson Labor
   Council . . . . Newark

AFL-CIO Directly Affiliated Locals

AFL-CIO
DALU 24356 Engineering
   Employees . . . . Edison

Affiliated Labor Organizations

Agricultural Employees
BR 39 . . . . Elizabeth

Air Traffic Controllers
LU . . . . Teterboro
LU ACY . . . . Atlantic City
LU CDW . . . . Fairfield
LU CXY. . . . . Pomona
LU MMU. . . . . . Lake Stockholm
LU NKT . . . . Newark
LU TTN . . . . . . West Trenton

Asbestos Workers
LU 32 . . . . Newark
LU 89 . . . . Trenton

Atlantic Independent Union
NHQ . . . . Palmyra

Automobile, Aerospace Workers
C 9 New Jersey CAP . . . . . Edison
LU 153 . . . . Wood Ridge
LU 260 . . . . Edison
LU 267. . . . . Bloomfield
LU 595 . . . . Linden
LU 980 . . . . Edison
LU 1038 . . . . Avenel
LU 1668 . . . . Spotswood
LU 2210. . . . . Lodi
LU 2315 . . . . Newfield
LU 2326 . . . . Edison
LU 2327 . . . . Bridgeton

Bakery, Confectionery, Tobacco Workers and Grain Millers
LU 50. . . . . Edison
LU 719 . . . . Glen Rock

Boilermakers
LG 28 . . . . Bayonne
LG 432-D Cement Workers. . Berlin
LG 661 . . . . Florence

Bricklayers
LU 2 . . . . Pennsville
LU 4 . . . . Fairfield
LU 5 . . . . Bordentown

Carpenters
C New Jersey Regional
   Council . . . . Edison
LU 6 . . . . North Bergen
LU 15 . . . . Hackensack
LU 31 . . . . Trenton
LU 39 . . . . Edison
LU 119 . . . . Edison
LU 121 . . . . Vineland
LU 124 . . . . Wayne
LU 155 . . . . Plainfield
LU 393 . . . . Gloucester City
LU 455 . . . . Somerville
LU 542 . . . . Pennsville
LU 620 . . . . Madison
LU 623 . . . . Atlantic City
LU 715 . . . . Cranford
LU 781 . . . . Princeton
LU 821 . . . . Edison
LU 1006 . . . . Milltown
LU 1050 . . . . Audubon
LU 1342 . . . . Montclair
LU 1489 . . . . Burlington
LU 1578. . . . . . Gloucester City
LU 1743 . . Cape May Court House
LU 2018 . . . . Toms River
LU 2098. . . . . . Gloucester City
LU 2212. . . . . Union
LU 2250 . . . . Red Bank

Catholic School Teachers
LU South Jersey . . . . . Audubon

Civilian Technicians
CH 70 Garden State . . Browns Mills
CH 124 New Jersey
   Air . . . . Egg Harbor Township

Communications Workers
C New Jersey Presidents
   Coordinating . . . . West Trenton
LU 1002 . . . . Rockaway
LU 1006 . . . . Union
LU 1009 . . . . Elizabeth
LU 1010 . . . . Paramus
LU 1012 . . . . Absecon
LU 1013 . . . . Cinnaminson
LU 1020 . . . . Bloomfield
LU 1022 . . . . Englishtown
LU 1023 . . . . Cranford
LU 1032. . . . . Ewing
LU 1034 . . . . Trenton
LU 1037 . . . . Newark
LU 1039 . . . . Trenton
LU 1040 . . . . Trenton
LU 1058 . . . . Bridgewater
LU 1060 . . . . . . North Plainfield
LU 1061 . . . . Bayonne
LU 1062 . . . . Holmdel
LU 1067. . . . . Camden
LU 1090 . . . Egg Harbor Township
LU 1091 New Jersey Nurses
   Union . . . . Livingston
LU 3263 Manufacturing President's
   Council . . . . Holmdel

LU 13590 . . . Woodbury Heights
LU 14142 . . . . Phillipsburg
LU 14143 . . . . Vineland
LU 14176 . . . . Newark
LU 14826 Philadelphia
   Typographical
   Union . . . . Mount Laurel
LU 34042 Hudson
   County . . . . Jersey City
LU 81103 . . . . Camden
LU 81110 . . . . Camden
LU 81134 . . . . Bellmawr
LU 81310 . . . . Springfield
LU 81416 . . . . North Brunswick
LU 81427 . . . . Montville
LU 81440 . . . . Blackwood
LU 81441 . . . . Woodbridge
LU 81447 . . . . Clifton
LU 81455 . . . . Trenton
LU 81467 . . . . Mahwah
LU 81496 . . . . Edison
LU 88106 . . . . Moorestown
LU LO-1025 . . . . . Washington

DuPont Workers
LU Chemical Workers Association
   Inc. . . . . Pennsville

Electrical Workers
LU 94 . . . . Hightstown
LU 102 . . . . Parsippany
LU 164 . . . . Paramus
LU 210 . . . . Absecon
LU 269 . . . . Trenton
LU 327 . . . . Phillipsburg
LU 351 . . . . Hammonton
LU 400 General Fund . . . . . Wall
LU 454 . . . . Glassboro
LU 456 . . . . . North Brunswick
LU 827 . . . . East Windsor
LU 864 . . . . Beachwood
LU 1153 . . . . Manalapan
LU 1158 . . . . Clifton
LU 1289 . . . . Trenton
LU 1293 . . . . Oceanview
LU 1303 . . . . Matawan
LU 1309. . . . . Wanamassa
LU 1684 . . . . West Orange
LU 1820. . . . . Toms River
LU 2066 . . . . Iselin
SA New Jersey . . . . . . Absecon
SA New Jersey State Construction
   Division . . . . Wall
SC U-3 Jersey Central Power & Light
   Company . . . . Phillipsburg

Engineers
C New Jersey/Pennsylvania Area
   Council . . . . Iselin
LU 18 . . . . Lawnside
LU 66 . . . . Clinton
LU 241 . . . . Maple Shade

Federal Employees
LU 476 . . . . . . Fort Monmouth
LU 1340 . . . . Atlantic City
LU 1431 . . . . . North Plainfield
LU 1437. . . . . Picatinny Arsenal
SFED New Jersey . . . . . Orange

Fire Fighters
LU 26-I Uniformed Fire Patrolmen's
   Association . . . . West Milford
LU 103-F . . . . . . Fort Monmouth
LU 106-F . . . . Wrightstown

LU 114-F . . . . Lakehurst
LU 115-F . . . . Fort Dix
LU 147-F . . . . Eatontown

Food and Commercial Workers
C Insurance Area
   2A. . . . . . Whitehouse Station
C Insurance Workers Area V . Berlin
DC New York and Northern New
   Jersey . . . . Little Falls
LU 9-C . . . . Totowa
LU 56 . . . . Cherry Hill
LU 100-R . . . . . . Green Brook
LU 153-C . . . . Bayonne
LU 209-D . . . . Linden
LU 220-T . . . . Clifton
LU 271-C . . . . Parlin
LU 276-T . . . . Clifton
LU 464-A . . . . Little Falls
LU 527-C . . . . Monroe Township
LU 825-C . . . . Totowa
LU 1245 . . . . Little Falls
LU 1262 . . . . Clifton
LU 1358 . . . . Atlantic City
LU 1360. . . . . West Berlin

Glass, Molders, Pottery and Plastics Workers
LU 6 . . . . Salem
LU 7 . . . . Millville
LU 21 . . . . Penns Grove
LU 40 . . . . Kearny
LU 103 . . . . Mays Landing
LU 111 . . . . Carteret
LU 126 . . . . Minotola
LU 145 . . . . Buena
LU 157 . . . . Carney's Point
LU 219 . . . . Millville
LU 227 . . . . Somerset
LU 236-A . . . . Egg Harbor City

Government Employees
C 157 National Mint . . . . . Erial
C 238 . . . . Trenton
LU 23 . . . . Lakehurst
LU 42 ID, Second District
   At-Large . . . . . New Brunswick
LU 84 R2-84 . . . . . . Lakehurst
LU 200 . . . . Atlantic City
LU 225 DoD . . . Picatinny Arsenal
LU 371 National Army-Air
   Technicians
   Association . . . . . Maplewood
LU 632 USDA. . . . . . . Milford
LU 644 DoL . . . . Sewell
LU 674 USDA . . . . . . Marlton
LU 1012 VA . . . . Lyons
LU 1659 DoD . . . . Colt's Neck
LU 1778 DoD . . . . Wrightstown
LU 1904 DoD . . . . . Eatontown
LU 1999 . . . . Fort Dix
LU 2001 . . . . Fort Dix
LU 2041 GSA . . . . . Burlington
LU 2149 DoJ . . . . . . Aberdeen
LU 2175 DoD . . . . . . Bayonne
LU 2335 DoT . . . . . . Pomona
LU 2369 HHS . . . . Brick
LU 2425 Non-
   Professional. . . . South Orange
LU 2442 VA. . . . . Newark
LU 2513 DoL. . . . . . . Edison
LU 2567 DoD . . . Union Beach
LU 2658 GSA . . . . . . Newark
LU 2735 USDA . . . . . Allentown
LU 3183 USDA . . . . . . Norma

LU 3451 Non-Professional &
  Professionals . . . . . . Newark
LU 3486
  DoD . . . Egg Harbor Township
LU 3564 USDA . . . . Bordentown
LU 3588 SBA . . . . Newark
LU 3975 . . . . Fairton

Government Employees
** Association**
LU 560 Police Officers. . . Bayonne
LU R2-84 . . . . Lakehurst

Government Security Officers
LU 14 . . . . Glassboro

Graphic Communications
LU 8-N . . . . Red Bank
LU 447-S . . . . Jersey City
LU 612-M . . . . . West Caldwell

Independent Unions
LU 152 American Musicians
  Union . . . . Dumont
LU 229 Sheridan Printing
  Company Employees'
  Association . . . . . . Phillipsburg

Iron Workers
DC Northern New
  Jersey . . . . Kenilworth
LU 11 . . . . Bloomfield
LU 45 . . . . Jersey City
LU 68 . . . . Trenton
LU 350 . . . . Atlantic City
LU 373 . . . . Perth Amboy
LU 399 . . . . Westville
LU 480 . . . . Union
LU 483 . . . . Paterson

Laborers
DC Building Laborers District
  Council . . . . Fort Lee
DC Building Laborers District
  Council . . . . Hamilton
DC Central New Jersey,
  Building . . . . . . East Brunswick
DC New Jersey . . . . . Cherry Hill
DC NJH & GCL . . . . . . Newark
LU Laborers' Eastern Region
  Organizing . . . Monroe Township
LU 137 . . . . Cherry Hill
LU 172 . . . . Trenton
LU 222 . . . . Camden
LU 305 . . . . . Scotch Plains
LU 325 . . . . Jersey City
LU 394 . . . . Elizabeth
LU 415 . . . . Pleasantville
LU 472 . . . . Newark
LU 592 Building & General
  Construction Craft . . . Fort Lee
LU 593 . . . . Hillsborough
LU 594 . . . . . East Brunswick
LU 595 Building & General
  Construction Craft . . Robbinsville
LU 734 . . . . Rochelle Park
LU 889 . . . . Newark
LU 1030 . . . . North Bergen
LU 1153 . . . . Newark
LU 1412 . . . . Belleville

Letter Carriers
BR 38 . . . . Springfield
BR 42 . . . . Brick
BR 65 . . . . Passaic
BR 67 . . . . Elizabeth
BR 120 . . . . Paterson
BR 268 . . . . Princeton

BR 272 . . . . Hopatcong
BR 342 . . . . Montclair
BR 370 . . . . Atlantic City
BR 380 . . . . Trenton
BR 396 . . . . Plainfield
BR 425 . . . . . South Hackensack
BR 444 . . . . . North Brunswick
BR 457 . . . . Perth Amboy
BR 534 . . . . Vineland
BR 540 . . . . Oaklyn
BR 673 . . . . South Orange
BR 754 . . . . Cranford
BR 768 . . . . Somerville
BR 769 . . . . Haddonfield
BR 903 . . . . Northfield
BR 908 . . . . Woodbury
BR 924 . . . . Freehold
BR 1089 . . . . Lakewood
BR 1492 . . . . Westfield
BR 1776 . . . . Atlantic Highlands
BR 1904 . . . . . Bradley Beach
BR 1908 . . . . Riverside
BR 1913 . . . . Bordentown
BR 2128 . . . . Toms River
BR 2138 . . . . Fort Lee
BR 2458 . . . . Garwood
BR 2653 . . . . Avon by the Sea
BR 2682 . . . . . . Mount Laurel
BR 2876 . . . . Linden
BR 3540 . . . . Bergenfield
BR 4089 . . . . Vauxhall
BR 4091 . . . . . . New Milford
BR 4102 . . . . . Scotch Plains
BR 4307 . . . . Frenchtown
BR 4378 . . . . Haskell
BR 4433 . . . . Wanaque
BR 4556 . . . . Berlin
BR 4623 . . . . Clementon
BR 4697 . . . . Demarest
BR 5363 . . . . Belford
BR 5420 . . . . Brick
BR 5554 . . . . Northvale
BR 5571 . . . . Hopewell
BR 5648 . . . . Lumberton
BR 5801 . . . . Willingboro
BR 5818 . . . . Norwood
BR 6311 . . . . Cherry Hill
BR 6339 . . . . Oakhurst
BR 6487 . . . . Gibbsboro
SA New Jersey . . . . . Northfield

Locomotive Engineers
DIV 11 . . . . Edison
DIV 53 . . . . South Belmar
DIV 54 . . . . Sussex
DIV 157 . . . . Forked River
DIV 171 . . . . Hackettstown
DIV 226 . . . . Belleville
DIV 231 . . . . Maple Shade
DIV 235 . . . . Dumont
DIV 272 . . . . Mount Tabor
DIV 353 . . . . Mickleton
DIV 373 . . . . . North Wildwood
DIV 387 . . . . Atco
DIV 497 . . . . Clark
DIV 601 . . . . Livingston
DIV 886 . . . . Beverly
GCA Amtrak . . . . . . Cherry Hill
GCA NJTRO . . . . South Belmar
SLB New Jersey . . . . Toms River

Longshoremen
DC New York . . . . North Bergen
LU 1 . . . . Newark
LU 1233-123 International
  Longshoremen . . . . Newark
LU 1235 . . . . Newark
LU 1478-2 . . . . Newark

LU 1588 . . . . Bayonne
LU 1804-1 . . . . . North Bergen
LU 1964 . . . . . Ridgefield Park
LU 2049 . . . . Newark

Machinists
LG 15-S . . . . Hoboken
LG 76-S . . . . Pitman
LG 95-S . . . . Pleasantville
LG 315 Phoenix . . . . . . Clark
LG 321 Aircrew Training
  Professionals . . . . . Burlington
LG 329 . . . . Morganville
LG 914 . . . . Colonia
LG 1041 . . . . West Long Branch
LG 1445 . . . . Newark
LG 1812 . . . . Vineland
LG 2339 . . . . Newark
LLG PT-1 PT-1 . . . . . Cherry Hill
STC New
  Jersey . . . . . Upper Saddle River

Maintenance of Way Employes
DIV Commuter Railroad
  System . . . . South Amboy
LG 705 . . . . Clark
SLG 305 . . . . North Middletown
SLG 2800 . . . . Moorestown
SLG 2905 . . . . Hillside
SLG 2906 . . . . . . Long Branch
SLG 2907 . . . . Newton
SLG 3012 . . . . . . Mount Laurel
SLG 3089 . . . . . . Collingswood

Musicians
LU 16 . . . . West Orange
LU 62 . . . . Trenton
LU 151 . . . . Union
LU 204-373 . . . . Edison
LU 248 . . . . Paterson
LU 336 . . . . Burlington
LU 399 Asbury Park Local . . Ocean
LU 595 . . . . Vineland
LU 661-708 . . . . Ventnor
LU 746 . . . . Plainfield
STCON New Jersey . . . . . Edison

National Staff Organization
ASSN New Jersey . . . Moorestown

NLRB Professional Association
LU 22 . . . . Newark

Novelty and Production Workers
LU 148 Production
  Workers . . . . Jersey City

Nurses
SA New Jersey . . . . . . Trenton
SA New Jersey State Nurses
  Association . . . . Trenton

Office and Professional Employees
LU 32 . . . . Union

Operating Engineers
C JNESO DC 1 . . . New Brunswick
CONF Northeastern
  State . . . . Springfield
LU JNEJO-Pri-Tech . . . Bloomfield
LU JNESO Arbor Glen Care &
  Rehabilitation Center . . Caldwell
LU JNESO Irvington Organization of
  Nurses . . . . Irvington
LU JNESO Kessler Unit . . Dorothy
LU JNESO Long Branch Public
  Health Nursing . . . Long Branch

LU JNESO MCOSS Nursing
  Services . . . . Red Bank
LU JNESO St. Marys
  Hospital . . . . Bayonne
LU JNESO St. Michaels . . . Kearny
LU JNESO United Hospitals . Edison
LU JNESO Zurbrugg Memorial
  Hospital . . . . . . Bordentown
LU JNESO-WJHS . . Mount Laurel
LU 25 . . . . Millstone
LU 68 . . . . West Caldwell
LU 825 . . . . Springfield
LU 910 JNESO BIR-RN . . Linwood

Painters
DC 711 . . . . Egg Harbor Township
LU 277 . . . . Egg Harbor Township
LU 345 . . . . Sicklerville
LU 694 . . . . Neptune
LU 1004 . . . . Bloomfield
LU 1005 . . . . Bloomfield
LU 1007 . . . . Bloomfield
LU 1009 State of New Jersey
  Glaziers . . . . Toms River
LU 1310 . . . . Bloomfield
LU 1331 . . . . Glassboro
LU 1976 . . . . Neptune

Plasterers and Cement Masons
LU 29 . . . . Jersey City

Plumbing and Pipe Fitting
LU 9 . . . . Englishtown
LU 14 . . . . Lodi
LU 24 . . . . Springfield
LU 274 . . . . Ridgefield
LU 322 . . . . Winslow
LU 475 Steamfitters, Pipefitters &
  Apprentices . . . . Warren
LU 696 . . . . Millburn
LU 855 . . . . Edison
SA New Jersey State Pipe
  Trades . . . . Winslow

Police
LU 173 U.S. Department of
  Defense . . . . . . Fort Monmouth

Postal and Federal Employees
LU 501 . . . . Atlantic City
LU 513 Kearny, New
  Jersey . . . . Newark

Postal Workers
LU 149 Central Jersey
  Area . . . . New Brunswick
LU 190 North Jersey Area . . Clifton
LU 361 Elizabeth . . . . . Elizabeth
LU 381 New Jersey Mid-State
  Area . . . . Plainfield
LU 483 Jersey City . . Jersey City
LU 526 South New Jersey
  Area . . . . Blackwood
LU 750 . . . . Ridgewood
LU 986 Red Bank . . . . . Red Bank
LU 1020 Trenton Metropolitan
  Area . . . . Trenton
LU 1153 Bloomfield . . . Bloomfield
LU 1270 Passaic . . . . . Passaic
LU 1593 Egg Harbor
  City . . . . . . Egg Harbor City
LU 1629 Clifton . . . . . . Clifton
LU 2434 Linden . . . . . . Linden
LU 2912
  Bernardsville . . . . Bernardsville
LU 3568 Keansburg . . Keansburg
LU 3617 Cape Atlantic
  Area . . . . Pleasantville

LU 3760 Millville . . . . . Millville
LU 4884 Rutherford . . . Woodridge
LU 5276 Paramus. . . . . Paramus
LU 6419 New Jersey Shore
   Area. . . . . Lakehurst
SA New Jersey . . . . . Red Bank

Railroad Signalmen
LLG 18 . . . . Turnersville
LLG 58 . . . . . . Egg Harbor City
LLG 60. . . . . Jersey City
LLG 84. . . . . Howell
LLG 102. . . . . Metuchen

**Retail, Wholesale and Department
  Store**
LU 108 . . . . Maplewood
LU 262 . . . . East Orange

**Roofers, Waterproofers and Allied
  Workers**
LU 4 . . . . Parsippany
LU 10 . . . . Haledon

Rural Letter Carriers
D 1 New Jersey . . . . . Blairstown
D 2 New Jersey. . . . . . . Edison
D 3 New Jersey . . . . . Bridgeton
SA New Jersey . . . . . Sicklerville

**Security, Police and Fire
  Professionals**
LU 125 . . . . Columbia

Service Employees
C New Jersey . . . . . . Newark
LU 164 . . . . Lambertville
LU 175 . . . . Trenton
LU 302 Firemen &
  Oilers . . . . Mount Laurel
LU 338 Firemen &
  Oilers . . . . Port Reading
LU 518 New Jersey State Motor
  Vehicles Employees
  Union . . . . Garfield
LU 617 . . . . Newark
LU 1050 Firemen &
  Oilers . . . . Mount Laurel
LU 1115 New Jersey
  Division . . . . Edison
LU 1199-NJ New Jersey Health Care
  Union . . . . Iselin
SC 2 Firemen & Oilers. Mount Laurel

Sheet Metal Workers
LU 25. . . . . Carlstadt
LU 27 . . . . Farmingdale
LU 396 . . . . . Jefferson Township
STC New Jersey . . . . . Carlstadt

**State, County and Municipal
  Employees**
C Hospital & Health Care
  Employees . . . . Newark
C 1. . . . . Trenton
C 52 . . . . Jersey City
C 71. . . . . Williamstown
C 73 Central New Jersey
  District. . . . . Hamilton
D 1199 United Nurses of
  Pennsylvania . . . . . . Newark
D 1199-J New Jersey Health Care
  Employees . . . . Newark
LU 956 Princeton University Library
  Assistants . . . Princeton Junction
LU 2252 Eastern Pines
  Convalescent. . . . . Atlantic City
LU 2254 . . . . Jersey City

LU 2303-B . . . . . . Atlantic City
LU 3043 Rider College Clerical
  Union. . . . . . . Lawrenceville
LU 3499 Bergen Regional Medical
  Center . . . . Paterson
LU 3666 National Prescription
  Administrators . . . East Hanover
LU 3965 Central Fill
  Inc.. . . . . West Orange

Steelworkers
C Merck Sharpe & Dohme . Rahway
LU 9473. . . . . . South Amboy
LU 2-138. . . . . Cranbury
LU 4-200 . . . . North Brunswick
LU 01-284 . . . . Newark
LU 01-300 . . . . . Martinsville
LU 01-417 . . . . . . Bloomfield
LU 01-870 . . . . Paterson
LU 01-1275 . . . . . . Paterson
LU 01-1564 . . . . South River
LU 02-149. . . . . . . Rahway
LU 02-380 . . . . . . Deptford
LU 02-397 . . . . Avenel
LU 02-406 . . . . Bayonne
LU 02-438. . . . North Brunswick
LU 02-562 . . . . Bayville
LU 02-575. . . . . . . Rahway
LU 02-657 . . . . Trenton
LU 02-716 . . . . Beverly
LU 02-948. . . . North Brunswick
LU 02-991. . . . . . . Thorofare
LU 02-1308 . . . . . Frenchtown
LU 02-1426. . . . . Woodbridge
LU 02-1482. . . . . Jamesburg
LU 02-1712. . . . . Bloomsbury
LU 02-1928 . . . . Kendall Park
LU 02-5570 . . . . . . Cranbury
LU 04-7. . . . . Millville
LU 04-107-L. . . . . . Hamilton
LU 04-129 . . . . . . Pennsville
LU 04-153-T . . . . . Greenwich
LU 04-154. . . . . . . Sayreville
LU 04-396. . . . . . Bloomfield
LU 04-420-U. . . . . Piscataway
LU 04-493-SB . . . . . . Trenton
LU 04-547-L . . . . . . Trenton
LU 04-591-T . . . . Franklinville
LU 04-637-L. . . . . . Stanhope
LU 04-701 . . . . Vineland
LU 04-770. . . . . . . Monroe
LU 04-2026-S . . . . Burlington
LU 04-2040-S . . . . Lumberton
LU 04-3297-S . . . . . Irvington
LU 04-3355-S . . . . . Trenton
LU 04-5210-S . . . . Perth Amboy
LU 04-6129-S . . . . . Monroe
LU 04-8228-S . . . . . Edison
LU 04-8972-S . . . . . . Erial
LU 04-9404-S. . . . . Phillipsburg
LU 04-12238-S. . . . Birmingham
LU 04-12886-S . . . . . Salem
LU 04-13742-S . . . . . Elizabeth
LU 04-15024-S . . . . . Edison
LU 04-15540-S . . . . . Somerset

Teachers
LU 5057 Hospital Professional &
  Allied Employees of New
  Jersey. . . . . Emerson
SFED New Jersey Hospital
  Professional & Allied
  Employees . . . . Emerson
SFED 8028 New Jersey
  State . . . . Edison

Teamsters
JC 73 . . . . Union

LU 11 . . . . . . North Haledon
LU 35 . . . . Trenton
LU 97 . . . . Union
LU 102 . . . . Fairlawn
LU 111 . . . . Rahway
LU 125 . . . . Totowa
LU 177 . . . . Hillside
LU 331 . . . . Pleasantville
LU 408 . . . . Union
LU 418 . . . . Nutley
LU 469 . . . . Hazlet
LU 478 . . . . Union
LU 522 . . . . Rahway
LU 531 . . . . Rahway
LU 560 . . . . Union City
LU 641 . . . . Union
LU 676 . . . . Collingswood
LU 701 . . . . . North Brunswick
LU 723 . . . . Montville
LU 863 . . . . Mountainside
LU 877 . . . . Linden
LU 945 . . . . Wayne
LU 966 . . . . Cresskill
LU 1100 New Jersey Mailers
  Union . . . . Piscataway

Theatrical Stage Employees
LU 21 . . . . Vauxhall
LU 59 . . . . Secaucus
LU 77. . . . . Linwood
LU 534 . . . . . . New Brunswick
LU 536 . . . . Keyport
LU 632 . . . . Hackensack
LU 645 . . . . Closter
LU 804 . . . . Stratford
LU 917 . . . . Atlantic City

Train Dispatchers
SCOM New Jersey Rail
  Transit. . . . . Hamilton
SCOM New Jersey Transit Power
  Supervisors . . . . . Rockaway
SCOM Trans-Hudson Port
  Authority . . . . . . Red Bank

Transit Union
LDIV 540 . . . . Mullica Hill
LDIV 820 . . . . Jersey City
LDIV 821 . . . . Jersey City
LDIV 822 . . . . Bloomfield
LDIV 824 . . . . Howell
LDIV 880 . . . . . Mount Ephraim
LDIV 1317 . . . . . . Montclair
LU 819 . . . . Irvington
LU 1614 . . . . Dover
LU 1626 . . . . Brick

Transport Workers
LU 225 . . . . Hackensack
LU 225 Branch 4. . . . . Brick

**Transportation Communications
  Union**
D 435 Conrail . . . . . . Bayonne
D 1351 Conrail . . . Haddon Heights
D 1475 . . . . Orange
LG 6053 Hoboken . . . . Keyport

Transportation Union
GCA GO-770 Conrail South . Delran
GCA GO-795 Path . . . . Howell
LU 60 . . . . . . Edgewater Park
LU 300 . . . . Turnersville
LU 419 . . . . Willingboro
LU 759 . . . . Clifton
LU 838 . . . . Woolwich Township
LU 1370 . . . . Belford
LU 1390 . . . . Jacobstown

LU 1413 . . . . Montclair
LU 1440. . . . . Hazlet
LU 1445 . . . . Toms River
LU 1558. . . . . Dumont
LU 1589 . . . . Somerset
LU 1949 . . . . . Union Beach
SLB LO-33 New Jersey. . . Trenton

Treasury Employees
CH 60 . . . . Springfield
CH 161. . . . . Elizabeth

UNITE HERE
JB Central & South Jersey . Somerset
LU Metropolitan Distribution and
  Trucking . . . . . . Union City
LU 3 . . . . Newark
LU 54 . . . . . . Atlantic City
LU 76. . . . . . West New York
LU 99-I. . . . . . . Union City
LU 102-E . . . . . . Union City
LU 162 . . . . Union City
LU 190 . . . . Union City
LU 630-A . . . . . . Somerset
LU 1298 . . . . Somerset
LU 1439 . . . . Somerset
LU 1528 . . . . Somerset

University Professors
CH Bloomfield College . Bloomfield
CH Monmouth College, Faculty
  Association of . West Long Branch
CH Rider College. . . Lawrenceville
CH Union College . . . . Cranford

Utility Workers
LU 375 . . . . . . Elmwood Park
LU 391 . . . . Vauxhall
LU 395 . . . . Belmar
LU 409 . . . . . Point Pleasant
LU 423 . . . . Middlesex
LU 424 . . . . Elizabeth
LU 503 . . . . . . Toms River
LU 601 . . . . Bloomfield

Weather Service Employees
BR 01-14. . . . . . Mount Holly

Westinghouse Salaried Employees
ASSN New York Engineering &
  Service. . . . . Matawan

Unaffiliated Labor
Organizations

195 Broadway Corporation
  Employees Council . . . Bayonne
Ball & Pebble Mill Workers
  Inc.. . . . . Little Falls
Bayonne Chemical
  Workers . . . . Bayonne
Bayway Employees Salary
  Union. . . . . Linden
Bell Telephone Lab Protective
  Union . . . . . . Scotch Plains
Best Foods Employees Association
  Independent . . . . . . Bayonne
Buckeye Tri-State Pipe Line
  Union. . . . . Sewell
Building Service Employees
  Association Westmill Management
  Company . . . . . West Orange
Building Trades International Union
  LU 777. . . . . Emerson
Catalyst Employees
  Association . . . . . . Gibbstown
Chemical & Industrial
  Union . . . . Gibbstown

Chemical Workers Independent
Union Delaware
Valley . . . . Monroeville
Colgate Chemical Workers
Independent Union
Inc. . . . . Mount Laurel
Comite Organizador de Trabajadores
Agricolas . . . . Bridgeton
Dairy Workers Association Inc.
Cream-O-Land Dairy . Burlington
Electromagnetic Steel Manufacturing
Employees Union LU
16. . . . . Moorestown
Exxon Employees Association of
New Jersey. . . . . Linden
Federation International Cooperative
Union . . . . Vineland
Fort Lee Taxi Drivers Union, Inc.
Independent . . . . . . Union City
Freedmans Bakery Association
Independent . . . . Belmar
Hayward Industrial Employees Union
Inc. Independent. . . . Elizabeth
Independent Dock Workers Union
LU 1 . . . . . . Gloucester City
Independent United Workers Union
of Leone Industries . . . Bridgeton
International Union of Aides Nurses
& Professional Employees LU
1199 . . . . Middletown
International Union of District 55,
Allied & Industrial Workers of the
U.S. & Canada . . . . Bergenfield
Joint Association of Boxers. Rahway
Laboratory Employees Union
Independent . . . . . . Annandale
Lay Faculty Organization of Our
Lady of Mercy School. Jersey City
Lay Teachers Association of St.
Josephs High School . . Metuchen
Licorice & Paper Employees
Association . . . . . Pennsauken
Mobilab Union Inc. . . . Clarksboro

Mona Employees
Association. . . . . . . Paterson
Mosstype Employees Association
New Jersey . . . . . . Waldwick
National Association Catholic School
Teachers (St. John Vianney High
School). . . . . Matawan
National Association of
Catholic School Teachers
Local . . . . . . New Providence
New Jersey Civil Service Association
Camden C 10 . . . . . . Camden
New Jersey Paralegal Association
Inc. Union LU 1 . . . Farmingdale
New Jersey Regional Council of
Carpenters . . . . Edison
Northeastern Hospital Nurses
Association . . . . . Cinnaminson
Oil & Chemical Workers
Independent Procter &
Gamble-Staten Island . . . Avenel
Oil Workers of
Paulsboro . . . . . . Gibbstown
Parlin Employees Association
Inc. . . . . Parlin
Paulette Fashions Inc. Union
Independent . . . . . Weehawken
Pfister Chemical Works Employees
Association. . . . . . . Ridgefield
Physicians & Dentists Union,
Independent Florida
SFED . . . . Newark
Presbyterian Hospital Professional
Dieticians Association . . Dumont
Production Clerical & Public
Employees International Union LU
911. . . . . Brick
Professional Employees
Guild . . . . Hackensack
Professional Health Care Union DC
JNESO Council Technical
Unit . . . . Matawan

Publishers Employees
Independent Association
Inc.. . . . . . Princeton Junction
Quaker Independent Union . Newark
Railway Independent Transit Union
Grand Lodge . . . . . . Colonia
Registered Professional Nurse UNIT
1 . . . . Sewell
Resilent Floor Layers LU
29 . . . . Atlantic City
Scientists & Professional
Engineers Personnel
Association . . . . . Mount Laurel
Security Police & Guards Union
Independent LU 1456 . . Bayonne
Security Police & Guards Union
Independent LU 1536 . . Camden
Security Police & Guards Union
Independent NHQ . . . . Bayonne
Service, Healthcare, and Public
Employees Union LU
925. . . . . Union City
Sheet Metal Workers of New Jersey
LU 22 . . . . Cranford
Sovac Petroleum Union of South
Jersey . . . . Clarksboro
Standard Refinery Union Inc.
Exxon . . . . Bayonne
Stationary Engineers LU
4. . . . . Midland Park
Sun Oil Company Employees
Association South Amboy
District. . . . . Piscataway
Tank Truck Workers
Union . . . . . . Carney's Point
The Grand Lodge Railway
Independent Transit
Union . . . . Colonia
Tool Die & Mold Makers
International Union LU
69984 . . . . Rahway
Trades Independent United LU
732 . . . . Union

Union de Trabajadores Agricolas y
del Hongo. . . . . . . Glassboro
Union Employees Union (UEU) LU
1. . . . . West Trenton
Union of Heat Stretch Ceiling
and Wall
Installers . . . Upper Saddle River
United Armed Guards of
America. . . . . Lyndhurst
United International Brotherhood All
Trades Technical, Services,
Administrative, and Medical
Workers. . . . . Northvale
United States Oil and Chemical
Workers . . . . Linden
United Workers of America LU
621. . . . . Clifton
Utility Co-Workers Association C
Bridgewater . . . . . Green Brook
Utility Co-Workers Association C
Claim . . . . Summit
Utility Co-Workers Association C
Cranford. . . . . . . Bloomfield
Utility Co-Workers Association C
Customer Payment
Processing. . . . . . Bloomfield
Utility Co-Workers Association C
East Gate . . . . . . Bloomfield
Utility Co-Workers Association C
Garrett Mountain. . . . Paterson
Utility Co-Workers Association C
Harmon Cove . . . . Bloomfield
Utility Co-Workers Association C
Newark . . . . Bloomfield
Utility Co-Workers Association C
Northern Center . . . . Cranford
Utility Co-Workers Association C
Paramus . . . . Bloomfield
Utility Co-Workers Association C
Princeton . . . . Trenton
Utility Co-Workers Association C
Roseland . . . . Middlesex
Utility Co-Workers Association C
Southern Center . . . . Bloomfield
Workers Committee of Campbell's
Fresh . . . . Glassboro

New Mexico

AFL-CIO Trade and Industrial Departments

Building and Construction Trades Department
BCTC Albuquerque . . Albuquerque

Metal Trades Department
MTC Atomic Projects & Production Workers . . . . Albuquerque

Affiliated Labor Organizations

Air Traffic Controllers
LU ABQ . . . . Albuquerque
LU KWA . . . . Farmington
LU ROW . . . . Roswell
LU SAF . . . . Santa Fe
LU ZAB . . . . Albuquerque

Asbestos Workers
CONF Western States . Albuquerque
LU 76 . . . . Albuquerque

Bakery, Confectionery, Tobacco Workers and Grain Millers
LU 351 . . . . Albuquerque

Carpenters
C Mountain West Region Council
   UBC 04031 . . . . . Albuquerque
LU 1245 . . . . Las Cruces
LU 1319 . . . . Albuquerque
LU 1353 . . . . Santa Fe
LU 2088 Nurses . . . Albuquerque
LU 2166 Health Care
   Workers . . . . . . Albuquerque
LU 2218 . . . . Albuquerque

Communications Workers
LU 1314 Associated Press
   System . . . . Albuquerque
LU 7001 . . . . Las Cruces
LU 7009 . . . . Roswell
LU 7011 . . . . Albuquerque
LU 7037 . . . . Santa Fe
LU 14745 . . . . . . Albuquerque

Electrical Workers
LU 611 . . . . Albuquerque
LU 1199 . . . . Belen
LU 1988 . . . . Albuquerque

Elevator Constructors
LU 131 . . . . Albuquerque

Federal Employees
C Darcom . . . . Chaparral
LU 1031 . . . . Alamogordo
LU 2049 . . . . White Sands
   Missile Range
LU 2148 . . . . Albuquerque

Fire Fighters
LU 164-F Holloman AFB
   Local . . Holloman Air Force Base

LU 294-F White Sands
   Missile Range Fire
   Department . . . . . White Sands
   Missile Range

Food and Commercial Workers
LU 1564 . . . . Albuquerque

Government Employees
C 219 VA, Thirteenth
   District . . . . Albuquerque
LU 83 DoJ . . . . Anthony
LU 1032 . . . . Albuquerque
LU 1257 DoL . . . . . Albuquerque
LU 2063 VA . . . . . Albuquerque
LU 2263 AFGE . . . . Albuquerque
LU 2308 DoD . . . . Clovis
LU 3137 USDA . . . . . . Coyote
LU 3309 IBWC . . . . Hatch
LU 4041 Mega-Teleservice
   Center . . . . Albuquerque

Government Employees Association
LU 14-40 . . . . Carlsbad

Government Security Officers
LU 244 . . . . Las Cruces

Iron Workers
LU 495 . . . . Albuquerque

Laborers
LU 16 . . . . Albuquerque
LU 1636 . . . . Santa Fe

Letter Carriers
BR 504 . . . . Albuquerque
BR 823 . . . . Las Vegas
BR 989 . . . . Santa Fe
BR 1069 . . . . Roswell
BR 1142 . . . . Raton
BR 1509 . . . . . . Silver City
BR 2290 . . . . Clayton
BR 2691 . . . . Clovis
BR 2905 . . . . Las Cruces
BR 2990 . . . . Gallup
BR 3144 . . . . Deming
BR 3244 . . . . Carlsbad
BR 3556 . . . . Tucumcari
BR 3703 . . . . Artesia
BR 3727 . . . . Hobbs
BR 3849 . . . . San Antonio
BR 3994 Rocket City . . Alamogordo
BR 4112 . . . . Los Alamos
BR 4278 . . Truth or Consequences
BR 4347 . . . . Santa Rosa
BR 4377 . . . . Farmington
BR 5331 . . . . Grants
BR 6230 . Holloman Air Force Base
BR 6504 . . . . Lordsburg
SA 1284 New Mexico . Albuquerque

Locomotive Engineers
DIV 15 . . . . Albuquerque
DIV 400 . . . . Edgewood
DIV 446 . . . . Belen
DIV 791 . . . . Belen
DIV 811 . . . . Clovis

Machinists
LG 331 . . . . Veguita
LG 392 . . . . Las Cruces
LG 485 . . . . Taos
LG 794 . . . . Albuquerque
LG 1635 Albuquerque . Albuquerque
LG 1689 . . . . Albuquerque
LG 2515 . . . . Alamogordo
STC New Mexico State Council of
   Machinists . . . . . Alamogordo

Maintenance of Way Employes
LG 2414 . . . . Las Vegas
LG 2415 . . . . Albuquerque
SLG 2416 . . . . Clovis

Mine Workers
LU 7949 . . . . Raton

Musicians
LU 618 . . . . Albuquerque

National Staff Organization
LU Staff Organization of New
   Mexico, National . . . . Santa Fe

Nurses
D 1199 New Mexico Hospital and
   Health . . . . Santa Fe

Office and Professional Employees
LU 251 . . . . Albuquerque

Operating Engineers
LU 953 . . . . Albuquerque

Painters
LU 823 . . . . Albuquerque

Plasterers and Cement Masons
LU 254 . . . . Albuquerque

Plumbing and Pipe Fitting
LU 412 . . . . Albuquerque

Postal Mail Handlers
LU 331 . . . . Albuquerque

Postal Workers
LU . . . . Socorro
LU 356 Raton . . . . . . Raton
LU 380 Albuquerque . Albuquerque
LU 402 Las Cruces . . . Las Cruces
LU 422 Santa Fe . . . . . Santa Fe
LU 434 Roswell . . . . . Roswell
LU 655 Silver City . . . Silver City
LU 689 Gallup . . . . . . Gallup
LU 1044 Alamogordo . Alamogordo
LU 1633 Portales . . . . Portales
LU 2263 Carlsbad . . . . Carlsbad
LU 2270 Las Vegas . . . Las Vegas
LU 2287 Clovis . . . . . . Clovis
LU 2342 Hobbs . . . . . . Hobbs
LU 2501 Taos . . . . Taos
LU 2882 Belen . . . . . . Belen
LU 2884 Farmington . . Farmington
LU 5538 Lovington . . . Lovington
LU 7148 . . . . Ruidoso
SA New Mexico Postal Workers
   Union . . . . Farmington

Rural Letter Carriers
SA New Mexico . . . . Las Cruces

Service Employees
LU 1173 Firemen &
   Oilers . . . . Albuquerque

Sheet Metal Workers
DC Rocky Mountain . . Albuquerque
LU 49 . . . . Albuquerque

State, County and Municipal Employees
D 1199-NM Hospital and Health
   Care . . . . Santa Fe

Steelworkers
LU 04-659 . . . . Questa
LU 04-9477 Wipp Site . . . Carlsbad
LU 12-187-S . . . . . . Carlsbad
LU 12-188-A . . . . . . Carlsbad
LU 12-8507-S . . . . . Carlsbad
LU 12-9424 . . . . . . Las Cruces

Teachers
LU 4524 Indian Educators
   Federation . . . . . . Albuquerque
SFED New Mexico . . Albuquerque

Teamsters
LU 492 . . . . Albuquerque

Theatrical Stage Employees
D 5 Wyoming-Colorado-Utah-New
   Mexico . . . . Albuquerque
LU 423 . . . . Albuquerque
LU 480 . . . . Santa Fe
LU 869 . . . . Albuquerque

Transportation Communications Union
LG 6846 Belen . . . . Belen

Transportation Union
LU 1168 . . . . Portales
LU 1687 . . . . Belen
LU 1745 . . . . Albuquerque
SLB LO-34 New Mexico . . . Belen

Treasury Employees
CH 41 . . . . Albuquerque

UNITE HERE
LU 436 . . . . Albuquerque

Weather Service Employees
BR 02-24 . . . . Santa Teresa
BR 02-31-A . . . . . . Albuquerque
BR 02-66 . . . . Albuquerque

Unaffiliated Labor Organizations
Independent Security Police
   Association LU 1 . . Albuquerque
International Guards Union of
   America LU 69 . . . . Los Alamos
International Guards Union of
   America LU 106 . . . . . Socorro
International Guards Union of
   America LU 122 . . . Albuquerque
International Guards Union of
   America LU 131 . . . Albuquerque

New York

AFL-CIO Trade and Industrial Departments

Building and Construction Trades Department
BCTC Binghamton-Oneonta
  Area . . . . Binghamton
BCTC Buffalo and
  Vicinity . . . . West Seneca
BCTC Building & Construction
  Trades . . . . New York
BCTC Dutchess County . Newburgh
BCTC Elmira . . . . Elmira
BCTC Hudson Valley Orange
  County, Dutchess. . . . Newburgh
BCTC Ithaca . . . . Ithaca
BCTC Mohawk Valley . . . . Utica
BCTC Nassau & Suffolk
  Counties . . . . Hauppauge
BCTC New York State . . . Albany
BCTC Niagara County . West Seneca
BCTC Orange County . . Newburgh
BCTC Plattsburgh . . . . Plattsburgh
BCTC Rochester . . . . . Rochester
BCTC Rockland County. . Harriman
BCTC Southwestern New
  York . . . . Jamestown
BCTC Syracuse . . . . . . Syracuse
BCTC Tri-Cities . . . . Albany
BCTC Ulster Sullivan Delaware
  Green Counties . . . Mountainville
BCTC Watertown . . . . Watertown

Maritime Trades Department
PC Buffalo . . . . Buffalo
PC Greater New York &
  Vicinity . . . . Brooklyn

Metal Trades Department
MTC New York . . Long Island City

Other Councils and Committees
C New York Hotel
  Trades . . . . New York
C Niagara Orleans . . . . . Buffalo
LU 1 Hotel Maintenance
  Carpenters . . . . . . New York

Affiliated Labor Organizations

Actors and Artistes
BR Actors Equity
  Association . . . . . . New York
BR Employees (LIFE) Local
  890. . . . . Brooklyn
NHQ . . . . New York

Agricultural Employees
BR 14 . . . . Jamaica
BR 35 . . . . Jackson Heights

Air Traffic Controllers
LU ALN . . . . Latham
LU BGM . . . . Johnson City
LU BUF . . . . Cheektowaga
LU EEA . . . . Eastchester
LU ELM . . . . Horseheads
LU FRG . . . . Farmingdale
LU ISP . . . . Ronkonkoma
LU JFK . . . . Jamaica
LU LGA . . . . Flushing
LU N90 . . . . Westbury
LU NATCA Local ACK . . . Ithaca

LU Newark Tower NATCA
  (EWR) . . . . Bohemia
LU POU . . . . . . Wappingers Falls
LU RME . . . . Rome
LU ROC . . . . Rochester
LU SYR . . . . Newburgh
LU SYR . . . . . North Syracuse
LU Y90 . . . . White Plains

Aircraft Mechanics
LU 1 . . . . Mineola

Asbestos Workers
CONF New York-New England
  States . . . . Rochester
LU 4 . . . . South Wales
LU 12 . . . . . Long Island City
LU 12-A . . . . Astoria
LU 26 Rochester, New
  York. . . . . Rochester
LU 30. . . . . Camillus
LU 40 . . . . Schenectady
LU 91 . . . . Tarrytown
LU 201 . . . . . Wappingers Falls

Automobile, Aerospace Workers
C Central New York CAP . Amherst
C New York State CAP . . Amherst
C Western New York CAP . Amherst
D 65 Distributive
  Workers . . . . New York
D 65 Legal Aid Attorneys, New York
  City . . . . New York
LU 55 . . . . Williamsville
LU 259 Schenectady-New York
  Local . . . . New York
LU 338 . . . . Jamestown
LU 365 Denville-Brooklyn
  Local. . . . . . Long Island City
LU 424 . . . . Buffalo
LU 465 . . . . Massena
LU 481 . . . . Batavia
LU 508 . . . . Buffalo
LU 604 . . . . Elmira
LU 624 . . . . East Syracuse
LU 629 . . . . Clymer
LU 686 . . . . Lockport
LU 774 . . . . Buffalo
LU 846 . . . . Buffalo
LU 854 . . . . East Syracuse
LU 897 . . . . Buffalo
LU 936 . . . . Buffalo
LU 1060 . . . . Munnsville
LU 1097 . . . . Rochester
LU 1128 . . . . Syracuse
LU 1326 . . . . Cortland
LU 1337 . . . . Elmira
LU 1416 . . . . Cheektowaga
LU 1508 . . . . Green Island
LU 1752 . . . . . . Elmira Heights
LU 1774 . . . . Truxton
LU 1826 . . . . Minoa
LU 2094 . . . . North Tonawanda
LU 2110 . . . . New York
LU 2110 Association of Ecumenical
  Employees . . . . . . New York
LU 2149 . . . . Syracuse
LU 2179 . . . . New York
LU 2231 . . . . Jamestown
LU 2243 . . . . Rome
LU 2300 . . . . Ithaca
LU 2320 Legal Services
  Workers . . . . New York
LU 2367 Mesa . . . . Rome
LU 2571 . . . . . . Niagara Falls

LU 3034 . . . . Canandaigua
LU 3039 . . . . Tappan
LU 7902 . . . . New York

Bakery, Confectionery, Tobacco Workers and Grain Millers
C East Central . . . . Cheektowaga
LU 3 . . . . Long Island City
LU 36-G . . . . Buffalo
LU 69 . . . . Port Chester
LU 102 . . . . Ozone Park
LU 110 . . . . Buffalo
LU 110-G . . . . Buffalo
LU 116 . . . . Rochester
LU 429 . . . . Cheektowaga

Baseball Players
NHQ . . . . New York

Basketball Players
NHQ . . . . New York

Boilermakers
LG 5 . . . . Floral Park
LG 7 . . . . Orchard Park
LG 18-M . . . . Buffalo
LG 50-D Cement Workers. . . Cairo
LG 82-S . . . . Corfu
LG 175 . . . . Oswego
LG 197 . . . . Albany
LG 308-D Cement
  Workers . . . . Cowlesville
LG 328-D . . . . Alden
LG 342-D Cement
  Workers. . . . . . . West Chazy
LG 1916. . . . . Ilion

Bricklayers
LU 1 . . . . Long Island City
LU 2 . . . . Albany
LU 3 . . . . Getzville
LU 5 New York. . . . Poughkeepsie
LU 7 . . . . Long Island City
LU 52 . . . . . . Long Island City
STCON 99 New
  York . . . . . . Long Island City

Carpenters
C Suburban New York
  Region . . . . Hauppauge
DC New York City & Vicinity
  4112 . . . . New York
DC New York City
  Industrial . . . . New York
LU 7 . . . . Hauppauge
LU 11 . . . . Hawthorne
LU 19 . . . . Rock Tavern
LU 20 . . . . Staten Island
LU 42 . . . . Hawthorne
LU 45 . . . . Queens Village
LU 52 . . . . Hauppauge
LU 66 . . . . Olean
LU 85 . . . . Rochester
LU 157 . . . . New York
LU 281 . . . . Binghamton
LU 289 Empire State Regional
  Council . . . . Lockport
LU 370 . . . . Albany
LU 608 . . . . New York
LU 740 . . . . Woodhaven
LU 747 . . . . Syracuse
LU 926 . . . . Brooklyn
LU 1042 . . . . Plattsburgh
LU 1163 . . . . Syracuse
LU 1456 . . . . New York

LU 1536 . . . . New York
LU 2090 . . . . Woodhaven
LU 2287 . . . . New York
LU 2682 . . . . Bronx
LU 2947 . . . . Jamaica
LU 3127 . . . . New York

Catholic School Teachers
ASSN Deta Diocesan
  Elementary . . . . Amherst
ASSN Secondary Lay Teachers of
  Diocese . . . . . . West Seneca

Civilian Technicians
CH 1 Vincent J. Paterno
  Memorial . . . . . Bernhards Bay
CH 2 New York City . . . Brooklyn
CH 4 Genesee Valley . . . . Ontario
CH 6 Capital District . Stoney Creek
CH 7 Harold E. Brooks
  Memorial . . . . . Westhampton
CH 8 Mid Hudson
  Valley . . . . . Cortlandt Manor
CH 9 Long Island . . . . . Islandia
CH 10 Western New York . . Depew
CH 11 Niagara . . North Tonawanda
CH 12 Northern New
  York . . . . Redwood
CH 17 Schenectady . . . . Alplaus
CH 37 Hancock Field . . Syracuse
CH 51 Stewart . . . Middletown
STC New York . . . Bernhards Bay

Communications Workers
C New York State Plant
  Coordinating . . . . . Farmingdale
C Western New York . Cheektowaga
COM Downstate Grievance
  Coordinating . . . . . Farmingdale
LU 3 . . . . New York
LU 301 IUE-CWA . . . Schenectady
LU 1100 . . . . . . Queens Village
LU 1101 . . . . New York
LU 1102 . . . . Staten Island
LU 1103 . . . . Port Chester
LU 1104 . . . . Farmingdale
LU 1105 . . . . Bronx
LU 1106 . . . . . . Queens Village
LU 1107 . . . . New City
LU 1108 . . . . Patchogue
LU 1109 . . . . Brooklyn
LU 1111 . . . . Elmira
LU 1113 . . . . Albany
LU 1114 . . . . Auburn
LU 1115 . . . . Olean
LU 1117 . . . . Lockport
LU 1118 . . . . Albany
LU 1120 . . . . . . Poughkeepsie
LU 1122 . . . . Buffalo
LU 1123 . . . . Syracuse
LU 1124 . . . . Watertown
LU 1126 . . . . New York Mills
LU 1128 . . . . Potsdam
LU 1133 . . . . Buffalo
LU 1139 . . . . . . Glens Falls
LU 1141 . . . . Cohoes
LU 1150 . . . . New York
LU 1152 . . . . Syracuse
LU 1153 . . . . Valhalla
LU 1168 . . . . Buffalo
LU 1170 . . . . Rochester
LU 1177 . . . . Brooklyn
LU 1180 . . . . New York
LU 1190 . . . . New York
LU 1191 . . . . Frankfort

LU 1701 Alliance at IBM. . Endicott
LU 14146 . . . . Batavia
LU 14147 . . . . Binghamton
LU 14148 . . . . Lancaster
LU 14156 . . . . New York
LU 14158 . . . . Olean
LU 14162 . . . . . Saratoga Springs
LU 14164 . . . . Sidney
LU 14165 . . . . Oneida
LU 14169 Buffalo
　　Mailers . . . . West Seneca
LU 14170 New York Mailers
　　Union . . . . New York
LU 14177 . . . . Derby
LU 31017 . . . . Rochester
LU 31026 . . . . Buffalo
LU 31034 . . . . Albany
LU 31129 . . . . . New Hartford
LU 31180 . . . . Kingston
LU 31222 Wire Service . New York
LU 51011 . . . . New York
LU 51016 NABET Local
　　16 . . . . New York
LU 51021 NABET Local 21 . Scotia
LU 51022 . . . . Rochester
LU 51024 . . . . Watertown
LU 51025 . . . . Buffalo
LU 51026 . . . . . Johnson City
LU 51211 NABET Local
　　211 . . . . Liverpool
LU 81045 . . . . Falconer
LU 81076 . . . . Jamaica
LU 81101 . . . . Schenectady
LU 81102 . . . Long Island City
LU 81300 . . . . Syracuse
LU 81302 . . . . Wayland
LU 81303 . . . . Albany
LU 81304 . . . . North Tonawanda
LU 81313 . . . . . Painted Post
LU 81319 . . . . . East Syracuse
LU 81320 . . . . Liverpool
LU 81321 . . . . Hastings
LU 81323 . . . . Rochester
LU 81326 . . . . Lancaster
LU 81327 . . . . Hudson
LU 81331 . . . . North Chili
LU 81336 . . . . Springville
LU 81340 . . . . Cuba
LU 81347 . . . . Depew
LU 81349 . . . . Mayville
LU 81353 . . . . Springville
LU 81359 . . . . Waterford
LU 81361 . . . . Buffalo
LU 81380 . . . . Waterford
LU 81384 . . . . . Cheektowaga
LU 81386 . . . . Irving
LU 81388 . . . . . Cheektowaga
LU 81396 . . . . . . West Valley
LU 81403 . . . . Buffalo
LU 81408 . . . . Schenectady
LU 81444 . . . . . New Hyde Park
LU 81463 . . . . Jamaica
LU 81475 . . . . Pelham
LU 81485 . . . . Brooklyn
LU 81495 . . . . Leroy
LU 81509 . . . . Rochester
LU 81981 . . . . Buskirk
STC Connecticut . . . . Port Chester

Commuter Rail Employees
LDIV 1 . . . . New York
LDIV 9 . . . . Brewster
LDIV 37 . . . . New York
LDIV 113 . . . . Brewster
NHQ . . . . New York

Education
ASSN East Ramapo School Lunch
　　Association . . . . . Spring Valley
ASSN New York Educators
　　Association . . . . Albany
LU Rehab Programs Employee
　　Association . . . . . Poughkeepsie

Electrical Workers
LU 3 . . . . Flushing
LU 25 Long Island
　　Local . . . . Hauppauge
LU 36 . . . . . East Rochester
LU 41 . . . . Orchard Park
LU 43 . . . . Clay
LU 83 . . . . Johnson City
LU 86 . . . . Rochester
LU 97 Oswego . . . . . Syracuse
LU 106 . . . . Jamestown
LU 139 . . . . Elmira
LU 236 . . . . Schenectady
LU 237 . . . . Niagara Falls
LU 241 . . . . Ithaca
LU 249 . . . . Newark
LU 320 . . . . Kingston
LU 325 . . . . Binghamton
LU 363 . . . . Harriman
LU 503 . . . . Nanuet
LU 544 . . . . Bath
LU 589 Electrical Workers
　　IBEW . . . . Hicksville
LU 604 . . . . Bellvale
LU 770 . . . . Slingerlands
LU 817 . . . . Tuckahoe
LU 840 . . . . Geneva
LU 910 . . . . Watertown
LU 966 . . . . Lockport
LU 1049 . . . . Hauppauge
LU 1143 . . . . Old Chatham
LU 1189 . . . . Fulton
LU 1212 . . . . New York
LU 1249 . . . . . East Syracuse
LU 1381 . . . . Hicksville
LU 1430 . . . . North White Plains
LU 1573 . . . . Yonkers
LU 1631 . . . . . Putnam Valley
LU 1632 . . . . Elmira
LU 1799 . . . . . Saratoga Springs
LU 1813 . . . . Buffalo
LU 1833 . . . . Elmira
LU 1922 . . . . Westbury
LU 1968 . . . . Amsterdam
LU 2084 . . . . Syracuse
LU 2154 . . . . Orchard Park
LU 2176 . . . . Champlain
LU 2180 . . . . Randolph
LU 2199 . . . . Orchard Park
LU 2213 . . . . Syracuse
LU 2230 . . . . Coram
LU 2374 . . . . Jamestown
SC TCC-2 Telephone
　　Coordinating . . . . . . Syracuse
SC U-7 New York State Electric &
　　Gas . . . . Newfane

**Electrical, Radio and Machine
　Workers**
LU 227 . . . . Elizabethtown
LU 319 . . . . . North Tonawanda
LU 329 . . . . Elmira
LU 332 . . . . Hudson Falls
LU 334 . . . . Rochester
LU 335 . . . . . North Tonawanda

Elevator Constructors
LU 1 . . . . Long Island City
LU 14 . . . . Buffalo
LU 27 . . . . Penfield

LU 35 . . . . Albany
LU 62 . . . . Syracuse
LU 138 . . . . Verbank

Engineers
LU 147 . . . . Glenville

Federal Employees
LU 346 . . . . Castle Point
LU 387 . . . . Northport
LU 1505 . . . . Hyde Park
LU 2109 . . . . Watervliet

Fire Fighters
LU 7-F . . . . . Cornwall-on-Hudson
LU 105-F . . . . . . Adams Center
LU 214-F 914 T A G . East Amherst
SA Professional Fire Fighters
　　Association, New York . . Albany

Food and Commercial Workers
DC Production, Services & Sales
　　District Council . . . . . Brooklyn
LU 1 . . . . Utica
LU 1-D . . . . Brooklyn
LU 2-D . . . . Brooklyn
LU 18-D . . . . Brooklyn
LU 61-C . . . . Catskill
LU 76-C . . . . North Tonawanda
LU 95-C . . . . Plattsburgh
LU 143-C . . . . Bardonia
LU 192-C . . . . Auburn
LU 251-C . . . . Norwich
LU 293-C . . . . . . Harpursville
LU 300-S Production, Services &
　　Sales District Council . . Brooklyn
LU 342-050 . . . . Mineola
LU 348-S . . . . Brooklyn
LU 350-I . . . . Verona
LU 359 Seafood-Smoked
　　Fish-Cannery Workers . New York
LU 422-S Production, Services &
　　Sales District Council . Brooklyn
LU 517-S Production, Services &
　　Sales District Council . Brooklyn
LU 621 . . . . Brooklyn
LU 815-S Production, Services &
　　Sales District Council . Brooklyn
LU 888 . . . . Mount Vernon
LU 1138-T . . . . Watervliet
LU 1139-T . . . . Albany
LU 1500 . . . . . . Queens Village

**Glass, Molders, Pottery and
　Plastics Workers**
LU 27 . . . . Martville
LU 77 . . . . Clifton Park
LU 80-B . . . . Canastota
LU 104 . . . . Elmira
LU 180 . . . . . Elmira Heights
LU 368 . . . . Whitesboro
LU 381-A . . . . Meridian

Government Employees
C Second District New York/New
　　Jersey Veteran Affairs . St. Albans
LU 201 . . . . Rome
LU 202 . . . . Syracuse
LU 400 . . . . Fort Drum
LU 491 VA . . . . Bath
LU 521 USDA . . . . . . Cicero
LU 538 USDA . . . . Whitestone
LU 862 . . . . Brooklyn
LU 913 HUD . . . . . . New York
LU 1119 VA . . . . . . Montrose
LU 1151 VA . . . . . . New York
LU 1168 VA . . . . Bronx
LU 1667 VA . . . . . . Brooklyn

LU 1760 HHS . . . . . . Jamaica
LU 1843 VA . . . . . . Northport
LU 1917 DoJ . . . . . New York
LU 1919 VA . . . . . Farmingdale
LU 1968 DoT . . . . . . Massena
LU 1988 VA . . . . . St. Albans
LU 2005 . . . . Brooklyn
LU 2094 VA . . . . . . New York
LU 2116 DoT . . . . . Kings Point
LU 2203 . . . . New York
LU 2204 DoD . . . . . Brooklyn
LU 2205 USDA . . . . . Kingston
LU 2245 Castle Point VA
　　Hospital . . . . . Castle Point
LU 2367 DoD . . . . . West Point
LU 2431 GSA . . . . . New York
LU 2440 VA . . . . . . Montrose
LU 2580 DoJ . . . North Tonawanda
LU 2612 DoD . . . . . . Rome
LU 2657 VA . . . . . . Batavia
LU 2693 DoD . . . . . Bethpage
LU 2724 DoJ . . . North Bangor
LU 2739 USAR . . . . Fort Totten
LU 2747 DoT . . . . Staten Island
LU 2828 DoE . . . . . New York
LU 2831 USDA, FHA . . . . Batavia
LU 2930 ACE . . . . . . Buffalo
LU 3134 SBA . . . . . New York
LU 3148 DoJ . . . . . New York
LU 3252 FTC . . . . . New York
LU 3306 VA . . . . . Canandaigua
LU 3314 VA . . . . . . Buffalo
LU 3342 HHS . . . . . Syracuse
LU 3343 HHS . . . . Troy
LU 3367 HUD . . . . . . Buffalo
LU 3369 HHS . . . . . Flushing
LU 3432 NPS . . . . . New York
LU 3477 CPSC . . . . . New York
LU 3555 EEOC . . . . . New York
LU 3613 SBA . . . . . . Syracuse
LU 3692 CNC, VA . . . . Calverton
LU 3732 DoC . . . . . Kings Point
LU 3740 DT, U.S. Mint . West Point
LU 3797 DoE . . . . . New York
LU 3827 CFTC . . . . . New York
LU 3882 DoJ . . . . . Ray Brook
LU 3883 DCAA . . . . . Bethpage
LU 3911 . . . . New York

**Government Employees
　Association**
LU 02-33 . . . . . . Niagara Falls
LU 02-56 . . . . . . Binghamton
LU 02-62 . . . . . . Evans Mills
LU R2-61 . . . . Fort Drum

Government Security Officers
LU 119 . . . . Brooklyn
LU 507 . . . . Ithaca

Graphic Artists
NHQ . . . . New York

Graphic Communications
LU 1-H Paper Handlers-Sheet
　　Straighteners . . . Long Island City
LU 1-SE 100SE . . . . . Merrick
LU 2-N . . . . New York
LU 17-B . . . . Buffalo
LU 26-H . . . . Depew
LU 27-C . . . . Buffalo
LU 51-23M . . . . . . New York
LU 76-SE . . . . . Orchard Park
LU 119-43B 43B Parent
　　Division . . . . . . New York
LU 259-M Albany-Schenectady
　　Local . . . . Clifton Park
LU 261-M . . . . Buffalo

LU 284-M. . . . . Cicero	LU 157 . . . . Schenectady	BR 3285 . . . . Homer	LG 522 . . . . Wynantskill
LU 406-C . . . . Melville	LU 186 . . . . Plattsburgh	BR 3289 . . . . Delhi	LG 585 . . . . Buffalo
LU 503-M . . . . Rochester	LU 190 . . . . Glenmont	BR 3366 . . . . . . Cazenovia	LG 588 . . . . Palmyra
LU 898-M . . . . . . Binghamton	LU 210 . . . . Buffalo	BR 3573 . . . . Wolcott	LG 753 . . Hopewell Junction
	LU 235 . . . . Elmsford	BR 4067 . . . . Avon	LG 754 . . . . . . Bay Shore
Hebrew Actors	LU 279 Association of Professional	BR 4747 . . . . Honeoye Falls	LG 761 . . . . Dexter
NHQ . . . . New York	& Specialty Workers . . New York	BR 4918. . . . . . Brookhaven	LG 838 . . . . Albany
	LU 322 . . . . Massena	BR 5151 . . . . Vestal	LG 948 . . . . . . Newburgh
Independent Unions	LU 435 . . . . Rochester	BR 5229 . . . . . . New City	LG 1018 . . . . . . Lynbrook
LU 2 Building Service Employees &	LU 589 . . . . Ithaca	BR 5463 . . . . Dundee	LG 1071 . . . . Elma
Factory Workers . . . Ozone Park	LU 601 Professional Service &	BR 5746 . . . . Belmont	LG 1145 . . . . . . Delanson
	Related Employees . New Rochelle	BR 5750 . . . . . . Scottsville	LG 1180 . . . . . . Gasport
Industrial Trade Unions	LU 621 . . . . Olean	BR 6000 Long Island. . Amityville	LG 1322 . . . . Valley Stream
LU 1 . . . . Jamaica	LU 633 . . . . . East Syracuse	BR 6077. . . . . Minoa	LG 1379 . . . . Nichols
LU 1-A . . . . Jamaica	LU 731 . . . . Astoria	BR 6559 . . . . . . Lakewood	LG 1509 . . . . Utica
LU 16 . . . . Jamaica	LU 754 . . . . . Spring Valley	D Joseph T. Tinnelly . . Schenectady	LG 1529 . . . . Sidney
LU 486 . . . . Jamaica	LU 1000 . . . . . Poughkeepsie	SA New York . . . . Poughkeepsie	LG 1555 . . . . Brocton
LU 528 . . . . Jamaica	LU 1010 . . . . Flushing		LG 1562 . . . . . . Kingston
NHQ. . . . . Jamaica	LU 1018 . . . . Flushing	**Locomotive Engineers**	LG 1580 . . . . . . Wellsville
	LU 1298 . . . . . . Hempstead	DIV 46 . . . . . . Feura Bush	LG 1607 . . . . Ithaca
Iron Workers	LU 1358 . . . . . . Elmira Heights	DIV 87 . . . . . . Stillwater	LG 1691 . . . . Depew
DC Greater New York and	LU 2133 Upstate New York	DIV 127 . . . . . . Fishkill	LG 1793 . . . . New Berlin
Vicinity . . . . . . Tarrytown	Organizing Coalition. . . Syracuse	DIV 169 . . . . . . Kirkville	LG 1838 . . . . . . Geneva
LU 6 . . . . West Seneca		DIV 227 . . . . . . Massena	LG 1882 . . . . . Lindenhurst
LU 9 . . . . . . Niagara Falls	**Letter Carriers**	DIV 269 . . North Massapequa	LG 1894 . . . . Wading River
LU 12 . . . . Albany	BR 3 . . . . Buffalo	DIV 311 . . . . . Binghamton	LG 2105 . . . . . Jamestown
LU 33 . . . . Rochester	BR 21 George B. Calveric . . Elmira	DIV 382 . . . North Tonawanda	LG 2189 . . . . . Unionville
LU 40 . . . . New York	BR 29 . . . . Troy	DIV 421 . . . . . . Depew	LG 2310 . . . . . . Clinton
LU 46 Metallic Lathers'	BR 36 . . . . New York	DIV 641 . . . . . . Ithaca	LG 2312 . . . . . Rochester
Union . . . . New York	BR 41 . . . . Brooklyn	DIV 659 . . . . . Amherst	LG 2401 . . . . Cattaraugus
LU 60 . . . . Syracuse	BR 97 . . . . Oneonta	DIV 752 . . . . . . Scotia	LG 2420 . . . . . Celoron
LU 197 . . . . Long Island City	BR 99 . . . . . Staten Island	DIV 867 . . . . Watervliet	LG 2495 . . . . . Falconer
LU 361 . . . . . Ozone Park	BR 134 . . . . . . Syracuse	DIV 895 . . . . . Delevan	LG 2656 . . . . Woodhaven
LU 417 . . . . Wallkill	BR 137 . . . . Poughkeepsie	GCA Consolidated Rail	LG 2671 . . . . . . Auburn
LU 440 . . . . Utica	BR 150 . . . . Dunkirk	Corporation . . . . . Buffalo	LG 2741 . . . . . Hornell
LU 455 . . . . Long Island City	BR 165 . . . . . Frewsburg	GCA Delaware & Hudson &	LLG 2001 . . . . . . Ithaca
LU 470 . . . . . Jamestown	BR 178 . . . . . Watervliet	Springfield Term. . . Greenwich	STC New York . . . . . Sidney
LU 576 . . . . Buffalo	BR 190 . . . . . . Oswego	GCA 269 Long Island	
LU 580 . . . . . New York	BR 210 . . . . . Rochester	Railroad. . . . . . Hicksville	**Maintenance of Way Employes**
LU 612 . . . . Pulaski	BR 294 . . . Fresh Meadows	SLB New York Legislative	LG 707 . . . . Albion
LU 824 . . . . . Gouverneur	BR 300 . . . . . . Corning	Board . . . . . . Tonawanda	LG 895 . . . . . Wellsville
	BR 301 . . . . Geneva		LG 1356 . . . . . Glenmont
Italian Actors	BR 302 1000 Islands	**Longshoremen**	LG 1368 . . . . Howes Cave
NHQ . . . . New York	Region . . . . . Watertown	D Atlantic Coast . . . . New York	LG 1466 . . . . . Kingston
	BR 303 . . . . Owego	DIV United Marine . . Staten Island	LG 1632 . . . . . Guilford
Journeymen and Allied Trades	BR 333 . . . . . Binghamton	JC Buffalo . . . . . . Buffalo	LG 1743 . . . . Poestenkill
LU 400 . . . . New York	BR 356 . . . . Mount Vernon	LU 3 . . . . . . Floral Park	LG 1934 . . Saratoga Springs
NHQ . . . . Briarwood	BR 357 . . . Long Island City	LU 217-A . . . . . Ogdensburg	LG 2957 . . . . . Goshen
	BR 358 . . . . . Schenectady	LU 333 . . . . . Staten Island	SF Northeastern. . . . Oneonta
Laborers	BR 375 . . . . Utica	LU 824 . . . . . New York	SLG 482 . . . . . Fredonia
DC Concrete Workers District	BR 376 . . . . . Port Jervis	LU 901 . . . . . New York	SLG 704 . . . . . . Sodus
Council . . . . Long Island City	BR 387 . . . . . . Yonkers	LU 901-1 . . . . . New York	SLG 866 . . . . . . Alden
DC Eastern New York . . Glenmont	BR 562 . . . . . . Jamaica	LU 920 . . . . . Staten Island	SLG 881 . . . . Fort Plain
DC Eastern New York Organizing	BR 661 . . . North Tonawanda	LU 928. . . . . . . Buffalo	SLG 882 . . . . Fultonville
Fund. . . . . . . Glenmont	BR 681 . . . . . . Penn Yan	LU 976 . . . . . New York	SLG 887 . . . . . Hornell
DC Mason Tenders of Greater New	BR 693 . . . . . . Peekskill	LU 1218 . . . . . . Buffalo	SLG 891 . . . East Syracuse
York . . . . New York	BR 740 . . . . . Fort Plain	LU 1294 . . . . . Albany	SLG 910 . . . . . Dexter
DC Pavers & Road	BR 922 . . . . Malone	LU 1518 . . . . . Albany	SLG 1042 . . . Red Creek
Builders . . . . . . Flushing	BR 1009 . . . . Lyons	LU 1570-A . . . . . Oswego	SLG 1079 . . . Port Jervis
DC Upstate New York	BR 1163. . . . . Gouverneur	LU 1730 . . . . . Ridgewood	SLG 1323 . . . . Willsboro
Laborers . . . . Syracuse	BR 1299 . . . . . . Deposit	LU 1809 . . . . . New York	SLG 1716 . . West Edmeston
LU 6-A. . . . . Long Island City	BR 1341 . . . . . . Walton	LU 1814 . . . . . Brooklyn	SLG 3068 . . . . Deer Park
LU 7 . . . . Binghamton	BR 1825 . . . . . . Warsaw	LU 1909 . . . . . New York	
LU 17 . . . . Newburgh	BR 1847 . . . . . Massena	LU 2000-A . . . . West Seneca	**Mine Workers**
LU 18-A . . . . Bronx	BR 1893 . . . . . Granville	LU 2007 . . . . Ransomville	LU 717 . . . . Ilion
LU 20 Cement & Concrete Local	BR 1905 . . . . Clyde	LU 2028 . . . . . . Buffalo	
Union . . . . Long Island City	BR 1940 . . . . Mount Morris	NHQ . . . . . . New York	**Musical Artists**
LU 29 . . . . Astoria	BR 2022 . . . . . . Groton		NHQ . . . . New York
LU 35 . . . . Utica	BR 2062 . . . . . . Elmont	**Machinists**	
LU 60 . . . . . . Hawthorne	BR 2189 . . . . Valley Stream	DLG 15 . . . . . . Brooklyn	**Musicians**
LU 66 . . . . Melville	BR 2281 . . . . . Hamilton	DLG 65 . . . . . Jamestown	LU 14 . . . . Albany
LU 78 . . . . New York	BR 2481 . . . . . Little Valle	LG 75 . . . . West Henrietta	LU 38-398 . . . . Larchmont
LU 79 . . . . New York	BR 2556 . . . . . Dolgeville	LG 226 . . . . . Staten Island	LU 51 . . . . Utica
LU 91 . . . . . Niagara Falls	BR 2654 . . . . . Coxsackie	LG 330 . . . . Cheektowaga	LU 66 . . . . . . Rochester
LU 103 . . . . Geneva	BR 3050 . . . . Sidney	LG 340 . . . . . Brooklyn	LU 78 . . . . . . Syracuse
LU 108 Waste Material Recycling &	BR 3105 . . . . Phelps	LG 434 . . . . Valley Stream	LU 85-133 . . . . Schenectady
General Industrial . . . New York	BR 3219 . . . . . . Ravena	LG 447 . . . . . Brooklyn	LU 92 . . . . Buffalo
LU 147 . . . . Bronx	BR 3246 . . . Castleton-on-Hudson	LG 490-DS . . . . . Eden	LU 97 . . . . Lockport

Local Unions   *New York*

LU 106-209 Greater
   Niagara . . . . . North Tonawanda
LU 132 . . . . Pine City
LU 134 . . . . Jamestown
LU 215 . . . . Kingston
LU 238 . . . . Poughkeepsie
LU 267-441 . . . . Mexico
LU 380 . . . . Vestal
LU 398 . . . . . Yorktown Heights
LU 443 . . . . Oneonta
LU 506 . . . . . . Saratoga Springs
LU 802 . . . . New York
LU 809 . . . . Middletown
LU 1000 North American Traveling
   Musicians . . . . New York
NHQ . . . . New York
STCON New York . . . . . Buffalo

National Staff Organization
LU Staff Organization of New York
   Educators . . . . Elmira

NLRB Professional Association
LU 2 . . . . New York
LU 3 . . . . Buffalo
LU 29 . . . . Brooklyn

Novelty and Production Workers
JB 18 . . . . Mineola
LU 3 Production & Maintenance &
   Service . . . . Mineola
LU 223 Toy & Novelty
   Workers . . . . New York
LU 231 Industrial Trades . . Mineola
LU 298 Amalgamated
   Workers . . . . . Valley Stream

Nurses
SA New York State Nurses
   Association . . . . Latham

Nurses, Professional
NHQ . . . . Lockport

Office and Professional Employees
LU 51 . . . . New York
LU 153 . . . . New York
LU 180 . . . . Massena
LU 210 . . . . Massapequa
LU 212 . . . . Buffalo

Operating Engineers
C Upstate New York . . . . Syracuse
CONF New York State . . . Albany
LU 14 . . . . Flushing
LU 15 . . . . New York
LU 17 . . . . Lake View
LU 30 . . . . Richmond Hill
LU 94 . . . . New York
LU 106 . . . . Glenmont
LU 137 . . . . . . Briarcliff Manor
LU 138 . . . . Farmingdale
LU 295 B, C, D . . . . . . Maspeth
LU 409 . . . . Buffalo
LU 463 . . . . Ransomville
LU 545 . . . . Syracuse
LU 832-ABC . . . . . . Rochester

Painters
CONF Eastern Region . . New York
DC 4 . . . . Cheektowaga
DC 9 . . . . New York
LU 8-28A . . . . New York
LU 17 Allied Printing Press
   Workers . . . . . . Cheektowaga
LU 18 . . . . New York
LU 19 . . . . New York
LU 20 . . . . East Rockaway

LU 24 . . . . Brooklyn
LU 25 . . . . Commack
LU 28 . . . . New York
LU 31 . . . . Syracuse
LU 38 . . . . Oswego
LU 43 . . . . Blasdell
LU 65 . . . . Cheektowaga
LU 112 . . . . Amherst
LU 113 District Council 9 . Peekskill
LU 150 . . . . Rochester
LU 155 . . . . Poughkeepsie
LU 178 . . . . Landor
LU 201 . . . . Albany
LU 466 . . . . Glens Falls
LU 490 . . . . New York
LU 515 . . . . Cheektowaga
LU 660 . . . . Lake View
LU 677 Glaziers and
   Glassworkers . . . . . Rochester
LU 806 . . . . New York
LU 829 . . . . New York
LU 1203 Allied Healthcare
   Workers . . . . . . Cheektowaga
LU 1281 . . . . New York
LU 1422 . . . . New York
LU 1456 . . . . Bronx
LU 1486 Long Island
   Local . . . . East Islip
LU 1969 . . . . New York
LU 1974 . . . . New York
LU 1990 . . . . Johnson City

Plant Protection
LU 175 . . . . New York

Plasterers and Cement Masons
LU 9 . . . . North Tonawanda
LU 111 . . . . . . North Tonawanda
LU 530 . . . . Bronx
LU 780 . . . . Whitestone
STCON New
   York . . . . North Tonawanda
STCON Northeast
   Conference . . . North Tonawanda

Plumbing and Pipe Fitting
LU 1 . . . . Howard Beach
LU 7 . . . . Latham
LU 13 . . . . Rochester
LU 21 . . . . Peekskill
LU 22 . . . . Orchard Park
LU 73 . . . . Oswego
LU 112 . . . . Binghamton
LU 128 . . . . Niskayuna
LU 200 . . . . Ronkonkoma
LU 267 . . . . Syracuse
LU 373 . . . . Mountainville
LU 638 . . . . Long Island City
LU 773 . . . . . . South Glens Falls
SA New York State Pipe
   Trades . . . . Latham

Police
LG 1 Federal Protective Service
   Committee . . . . New York

Postal and Federal Employees
D 8 . . . . New York
LU 802 . . . . Brooklyn
LU 803 . . . . Buffalo
LU 807 . . . . Jamaica
LU 809 . . . . New Rochelle
LU 810 Nassau/Suffolk . . Roosevelt
LU 813 . . . . New York
LU 814 . . . . New York

Postal Mail Handlers
LU 300 . . . . New York

LU 309 . . . . Buffalo

Postal Workers
LU Capital District Area . . . . Troy
LU Long Island New York
   Area . . . . Farmingdale
LU 10 New York Metro
   Area . . . . New York
LU 51 Mount
   Vernon . . . . Mount Vernon
LU 183 Niagara Frontier
   Area . . . . Niagara Falls
LU 212 Glens Falls
   Area . . . . Glens Falls
LU 215 Rochester Center
   Area . . . . Rochester
LU 231 Staten Island
   Area . . . . Staten Island
LU 234 Schenectady Area . Glenville
LU 251 Brooklyn . . . . . Brooklyn
LU 257 Central New York Area
   Local . . . . Syracuse
LU 374 Buffalo . . . . . . Buffalo
LU 390 Albany . . . . . . Albany
LU 522 Southern New York
   Area . . . . Ossining
LU 1022 Queens Area . . Ozone Park
LU 1091 White Plains . White Plains
LU 1151 Ithaca . . . . . . Ithaca
LU 1241 Long Island
   City . . . . Long Island City
LU 1249 Rockville
   Centre . . . . . Rockville Centre
LU 1820 Utica Area . . . . Utica
LU 1893 Malone . . . . . . Malone
LU 1894 Plattsburgh
   Area . . . . Plattsburgh
LU 2255 Elmira . . . . . . Elmira
LU 2286 Flushing Local . . Bayside
LU 2530 Canton . . . . . . Canton
LU 2577 The Greater Hicksville
   Mid-Island . . . . Farmingdale
LU 3095 Boonville . . . . Boonville
LU 3150 Rockland & Orange
   Area . . . . Monsey
LU 3197 Geneva . . . . . . Geneva
LU 3526 Jamestown . . Jamestown
LU 3722 Mid Hudson
   Area . . . . Newburgh
LU 4770 Kingston . . . Kingston
LU 5242 Port Jervis . . Port Jervis
LU 5668 Warwick . . . . Warwick
LU 6510 Hornell . . . . . Hornell
LU 7015 Woodbury . . . Woodbury
LU 7115 Western Nassau New York
   Area . . . . Uniondale
SA New York . . . . . . Rochester

Railroad Signalmen
LLG 56 Long Island
   Railroad . . . . Bay Shore
LLG 59 . . . . Callicoon
LLG 75 . . . . Oneonta
LLG 80 . . . . Rexford
LLG 86 . . . . New Hartford
LLG 93 . . . . Central Square
LLG 147 . . . . Gansevoort
LLG 225 . . . . Buffalo
LLG 230 . . . . Valatie

**Retail, Wholesale and Department
Store**
LU 1-S . . . . New York
LU 3 United Storeworkers
   Union . . . . New York
LU 88 . . . . Brooklyn

LU 116 Independent Production
   & Maintenance
   Employees . . . . Great Neck
LU 139 . . . . Lockport
LU 220 . . . . . . East Williamson
LU 305 . . . . . Hastings-on-Hudson
LU 338 . . . . Rego Park
LU 377 . . . . . Long Island City
LU 670 . . . . New York
LU 1102 . . . . Westbury
LU 1974 . . . . Fulton
LU 1975 Nestle United Laboratory
   Workers Union . . . . . . Fulton
NHQ . . . . New York

**Roofers, Waterproofers and Allied
Workers**
DC Northeast Roofers . Binghamton
LU 8 . . . . Brooklyn
LU 22 . . . . Rochester
LU 74 . . . . West Seneca
LU 154 . . . . Hauppauge
LU 195 . . . . Cicero
LU 241 . . . . Albany
LU 293 . . . . Binghamton

Rural Letter Carriers
LU Allegany County . Alfred Station
LU Cayuga County . . King Ferry
LU Chautauqua County . . Fredonia
LU Chemung County . . . Lowman
LU Chenango County . . . Greene
LU Clinton-Essex
   Counties . . . . . . Keeseville
LU Columbia County . . Kinderhook
LU Cortland County . . . . Cortland
LU Delaware County . . . . Walton
LU Dutchess County . Standfordville
LU Onondaga County . . . Truxton
LU Otsego
   County . . . . . Richfield Springs
LU Rensselaer County Unit
   04 . . . . Averill Park
LU Schenectady County . . . Berne
LU St. Lawrence County . . Potsdam
LU Sullivan County . . . . . Liberty
LU Washington-Saratoga-Warren
   Counties . . . . . Saratoga Springs
LU Wayne County . . . . Palmyra
LU 1 Tompkins County . . Freeville
LU 2 Oswego County . . . Pulaski
LU 3 Steuben County . . . Campbell
LU 5 Oneida County . . . . Clinton
LU 6 Broome County . Harpursville
LU 7 Monroe County . . . . Pittsford
LU 8 Niagara County . . . Newfane
LU 9 Fulton-Montgomery
   Counties . . . . Broadalbin
LU 10 Wyoming
   County . . . . Gainesville
LU 11 Ontario-Yates
   Counties . . . . . . Manchester
LU 12 Erie
   County . . . . . North Tonawanda
LU 15 Jefferson
   County . . . . Evans Mills
LU 18 Tioga County . . . Apalachin
LU 19 Genesee
   County . . . . . . East Bethany
LU 23 Cattaraugus
   County . . . . Great Valley
LU 25 Livingston County . . Pavilion
LU 26 Herkimer County . . Frankfort
LU 30 Ulster County . . Ulster Park
LU 32 Madison County . Bridgeport
LU 37 Schoharie
   County . . . . Cherry Valley

Directory of U.S. Labor Organizations   **119**

LU 38 Franklin
County . . . . St. Regis Falls
LU 39 Suffolk-Nassau
Counties . . . . Sag Harbor
LU 40 Orleans County . . . . Albion
LU 42 Greene County . . Saugerties
LU 46 Putnam/Westchester
County . . . . Mahopac
LU 49 Lewis County . . . . Lowville
LU 53 Orange County . Tuxedo Park
SA New York . . . . Byron

**Security, Police and Fire
Professionals**
LU 513 . . . . Staten Island
LU 514. . . . Annandale-on-Hudson
LU 516 . . . . Albany
LU 520 . . . . Oyster Bay
LU 528 . . . . Yonkers
LU 529 . . . . Cattaraugus
LU 530 . . . . Middletown
LU 531 . . . . . North Lawrence

Service Employees
C New York State . . . . New York
LU 4 . . . . New York
LU 27 Firemen & Oilers . . Falconer
LU 29 . . . . New York
LU 32-B . . . . New York
LU 51 . . . . Troy
LU 56 Firemen & Oilers . New York
LU 74 . . . . . . Long Island City
LU 105 Firemen &
Oilers . . . . Queensbury
LU 176 . . . . Forest Hills
LU 177. . . . . Brooklyn
LU 200 United . . . . . . Syracuse
LU 234 . . . . New Hartford
LU 266 Firemen & Oilers . Fredonia
LU 276 . . . . Levittown
LU 299-U . . . . Bethpage
LU 311 Firemen &
Oilers . . . . Staten Island
LU 348 . . . . Fonda
LU 363 . . . . Briarwood
LU 520 Firemen &
Oilers . . . . Poughkeepsie
LU 693 University College of
Physicians-Surgeons . . New York
LU 723 Bethpage UFSD Cafeteria
Employees . . . . . . Plainview
LU 731 . . . . Mount Vernon
LU 758 Hotel and Allied
Services. . . . . New York
LU 933 Firemen & Oilers . . Delmar
LU 1199 Drug Hospital & Health
Care Employees Union. New York

Sheet Metal Workers
C Air Conditioning Production
Workers . . . . Syracuse
DC 1 U.S. Railroads. . . . Merrick
LU 28 . . . . New York
LU 31 . . . . Buchanan
LU 38. . . . . Brewster
LU 46 . . . . Rochester
LU 58. . . . . Syracuse
LU 71 . . . . Buffalo
LU 83 . . . . Albany
LU 112 . . . . Elmira
LU 137. . . . . . . Long Island City
LU 149. . . . . Westbury
LU 398 . . . . Nassau
LU 530 . . . . Deer Park

**State, County and Municipal
Employees**
C 66 . . . . Rochester

DC 37 New York City . . New York
DC 82 New York State Law
Enforcement Officers
Union . . . . Albany
DC 1707 Commun & Social Agency
Employees Union . . . New York
LU 95 Head Start
Employees . . . . New York
LU 107 Federation of Shorthand
Reporters . . . . New York
LU 205 Dare Care Centers
Employees Union . . . New York
LU 215 Social Service
Employees . . . . New York
LU 253 Teaching & Related
Organizations. . . . . . New York
LU 374 . . . . New York
LU 389 Home Care
Employees . . . . New York
LU 702 . . . . Albany
LU 703 . . . . Middletown
LU 704 . . . . Newburgh
LU 706 . . . . Albany
LU 708 . . . . Schenectady
LU 709 . . . . Watkins Glen
LU 710. . . . . Buffalo
LU 712 . . . . West Falls
LU 715 . . . . Tonawanda
LU 716 . . . . Burt
LU 728 Schenectady Family Health
Services . . . . . . Schenectady
LU 745 CSEA Employees Local
Union 1000 . . . . . . Harrison
LU 751 CSEA Employees Local
Union 1000 . . . . . Highland
LU 891 CSEA . . . . Buffalo
LU 1000 Civil Service Employees
Association (CSEA) . . . . Albany
LU 1000 CSEA Association at
SUNY Cortland Local
631 . . . . Cortland
LU 1000 CSEA Local 734 Pioneer
Central Tran . . . . . . Delavan
LU 1000 CSEA Local 738. Hamburg
LU 1000 CSEA Local Union
737 . . . . Ronkonkoma
LU 1000 CSEA Region IV,
Capital. . . . . Latham
LU 1000 CSEA Region V,
Central . . . . . . East Syracuse
LU 1000 CSEA Region VI,
Western . . . . West Seneca
LU 1000 CSEA SLU 315 Health
Research. . . . . Buffalo
LU 1000 CSEA SLU 316 Health
Research . . . . West Coxsackie
LU 1000 CSEA SLU 620
Alfred Faculty-Student
Association . . . . Arkport
LU 1000 CSEA SLU 621 SUNY
Buffalo Faculty . . . . . Buffalo
LU 1000 CSEA SLU 622
Oswego Faculty-Student
Association . . . . Mexico
LU 1000 CSEA SLU 624 Brockport
State University . . . . . Albion
LU 1000 CSEA SLU 625
Potsdam College Food
Service . . . . . North Lawrence
LU 1000 CSEA SLU 627 Fredonia
State University. . . . . Dunkirk
LU 1000 CSEA SLU 628 Delhi
Technical College . . . Bloomville
LU 1000 CSEA SLU 629 Geneseo
Faculty-Student . . . . . Albany
LU 1000 CSEA SLU 630
St. Lawrence
University . . . . Hannawa Falls

LU 1000 CSEA SLU
701 . . . . East Patchogue
LU 1000 CSEA SLU 717 Nioga
Library System . . . . . . Olcott
LU 1000 CSEA SLU 733 Amsterdam
Head Start. . . . . . Amsterdam
LU 1000 CSEA SLU 735 Nassau
Library System . . . . Bellmore
LU 1000 CSEA SLU 888
Columbia-Greene
Medcenter. . . . . Catskill
LU 1000 Family & Children's
Services Inc. . . . . Buffalo
LU 1000 SLU 727 . . . Ogdensburg
LU 1306 . . . . New York
LU 1501 New York Zoological
Society . . . . Monroe
LU 1502 Brooklyn Museum
Employees. . . . . . . Brooklyn
LU 1503. . . . . Melville
LU 1559 American Museum of
Natural History. . . . New York
LU 1930 New York Public Library
Guild . . . . New York
LU 2786 Erie County Human Service
Agencies Employees. Lackawanna
LU 3124 . . . . Auburn
LU 3414 Saratoga County
EOC . . . . Saratoga Springs
LU 3755 Professional Services
Group . . . . Scotia
LU 3933 Albany Public Library
Employees. . . . . . . Albany
R 1 CSEA. . . . . Commack
R 2 CSEA Metropolitan Region
Local Union 1000 . . . New York

Steelworkers
LU 1034-T . . . . Corning
LU 4-420-A. . . . . . . Massena
LU 4-450-A. . . . . . . Massena
LU I-6992 . . . . Buffalo
LU 01-2 . . . . . . Hudson Falls
LU 01-5 . . . . Mineville
LU 01-6 . . . . Corinth
LU 01-17. . . . . . . Johnsonville
LU 01-18 . . . . . . Queensbury
LU 01-28 . . . Castleton-on-Hudson
LU 01-32. . . . . Auburn
LU 01-53. . . . . Oneida
LU 01-54 . . . . Fulton
LU 01-58 . . . . Lockport
LU 01-107 . . . . Brooklyn
LU 01-129 . . . . . . Ransomville
LU 01-140. . . . . Redford
LU 01-155 . . . . . Queensbury
LU 01-209 . . . . . Niagara Falls
LU 01-250 . . . . . Niagara Falls
LU 01-276 . . . . . . Carthage
LU 01-277 . . North Tonawanda
LU 01-318 . . . . . . Flushing
LU 01-381 . . . . Mineola
LU 01-387 . . . . . . Plattsburgh
LU 01-389 . . . . . . West Chazy
LU 01-390 . . . . Cohoes
LU 01-429 . . . . Alcove
LU 01-431 . . . . Calverton
LU 01-442 . . . . Utica
LU 01-497 . . . . . Ticonderoga
LU 01-503 . . . . . . Ogdensburg
LU 01-607 . . . . . . Tonawanda
LU 01-620 . . . . . . Leicester
LU 01-625 . . . . Silver Springs
LU 01-649 . . . . . . Granville
LU 01-687 . . . . . . Harrisville
LU 01-748. . . . . Akron
LU 01-828 . . . . Geneva
LU 01-955 . . . . Liverpool

LU 01-956 . . . . . . Port Leyden
LU 01-1066 . . . . Pulaski
LU 01-1186 . . . . Glen Aubrey
LU 01-1280 . . . . . . Verona
LU 01-1300 Rock City . . Herkimer
LU 01-1370 . . . . . Amsterdam
LU 01-1392 . . . Hoosick Falls
LU 01-1430 . . . . . . Syracuse
LU 01-1438 . . . . Cold Brook
LU 01-1450 . . . . . Watertown
LU 01-1478 . . South Glens Falls
LU 01-1479 . . . . . . Ancram
LU 01-1584 . . . . Spencertown
LU 01-1734 . . . . . Tonawanda
LU 01-1736 . . . . Cheektowaga
LU 01-1799 . . . . . Croghan
LU 01-1888 . . . . Glenfield
LU 01-1988 . . . . . Lowville
LU 01-2058 . . . . Niagara Falls
LU 01-6220 . . . . Lake View
LU 04-20-T . . . . . Port Jervis
LU 04-135-L . . . . Cheektowaga
LU 04-135-T . . . . Pine Valley
LU 04-151-G . . . . . . Olean
LU 04-222 . . . . . West Seneca
LU 04-500 . . . . Elmira
LU 04-522 . . . . . Port Jervis
LU 04-593-S. . . . . . . Buffalo
LU 04-897-S . . . . Orchard Park
LU 04-1000 . . . . Corning
LU 04-1013-T . . . . . . Bath
LU 04-1026 . . . . . . Canton
LU 04-1029. . . . . . Unadilla
LU 04-1160-L . . . . . . Utica
LU 04-1277-S . . . . Syracuse
LU 04-1498-S . . . Rochester
LU 04-1750-S . . . . . Utica
LU 04-2603-S . . . Woodlawn
LU 04-2604-S. . . . . Blasdell
LU 04-2693-S . . . Forestville
LU 04-2924-S . . . . Syracuse
LU 04-3298-S . . . . Geneva
LU 04-3482-S . . . . Auburn
LU 04-3609-S . . . Hamburg
LU 04-4146-S . . . Cheektowaga
LU 04-4447-S . . . Tonawanda
LU 04-4601-S . . . . . Olean
LU 04-4783-S . . . . Syracuse
LU 04-4831-S . . Richfield Springs
LU 04-4867-S . . . Amsterdam
LU 04-4979-S . . . . Hermon
LU 04-5376-S . . . . . Fulton
LU 04-5429-S . . . . . Olean
LU 04-6989 . . . . . Auburn
LU 04-7110-S . . . . Waterloo
LU 04-7338-S . . . Ellenville
LU 04-7474-S . . . . Fulton
LU 04-8090-S . . . . Hudson
LU 04-8823-S . . . . Buffalo
LU 04-9265-S . . . . Latham
LU 04-9367-S . . . Jamestown
LU 04-9374-S . . . Smithtown
LU 04-9436 . . . . Niagara Falls
LU 04-12230-S . . . Sanbory
LU 04-12460-S . . . Burdett
LU 04-12623-S . . . Jamesville
LU 04-12770-S . . . . Troy
LU 04-13226-S . . . Saugerties
LU 04-13833-S . . . . Buffalo
LU 04-14316-S . . . Kenmore
LU 04-14532-S . . . Syracuse
LU 04-14753-S . . . Huntington
LU 04-15135-S . . . Argyle
LU 04-15310-S . . . Syracuse
LU 08-763 . . . . . Geneseo
LU 11-43-U. . . . . New York
LU 14-15071 . . . . Niagara Falls

Teachers

ASSN Academy Teacher's Association . . . . Syracuse
LU St. Dominic's School Staff Association . . . . Blauvelt
LU 2 New York City Teachers . . . . New York
LU 105 Henry Viscardi School Faculty Association . . . Albertson
LU 120 Rochester School for the Deaf United Faculty Association . . . . . . Rochester
LU 1460 College Teachers . . . . Brooklyn
LU 2092 Federation of Catholic Teachers . . . . . . Staten Island
LU 2334 Professional Staff Congress/CUNY . . . New York
LU 2413 Suffolk Center Teachers Association . . . Smithtown
LU 3163 Cooper Union Federation College Teachers . . . New York
LU 3517 C.W. Post Collegial Federation . . . . . Brookville
LU 3552 Teachers, Lexington School for Deaf . . . . Jackson Heights
LU 3634 Kadimah Teachers Association . . . . Williamsville
LU 3721 Cerebral Palsy Employees . . . . . Cheektowaga
LU 3739 New York State United Teachers . . . . . . Hicksville
LU 3882 UCATS . . . . New York
LU 3888 Baker Hall United Teachers . . . . . . Lackawanna
LU 3890 Dowling College Chapter . . . . Oakdale
LU 3892 Mill Neck Manor Educational Association Mill Neck
LU 3918 Teachers, St. Marys School for Deaf . . . . Buffalo
LU 4064 Hallen Teachers Association . . . New Rochelle
LU 4228 Cornell University Adjunct Faculty Federation . . . New York
LU 4265 Association for Retarded Citizens Employees . Niagara Falls
LU 4503 New York Staff Public Employees Federation PEF . . . . Albany
LU 5077 Brookhaven Memorial Federation of Nurses . . Patchogue
LU 5123 United Center Employees Assn. . . . . Commack
LU 6079 Grove Street Academy Faculty Association . . Ulster Park
LU 6147 Campus Education Association . . . . . . Lockport
LU 8053 Overseas Federation . . . . . Staten Island
SFED New York State United Teachers . . . . Latham
SFED NYSUT Margaretville LPNs-Technicians . . . Prattsville
SFED NYSUT Margaretville Professional Nurses . . . . Arkville

Teamsters

JC 16 . . . . New York
JC 18 . . . . Albany
JC 46 . . . . Cheektowaga
LU 118 . . . . Rochester
LU 126 . . . . Troy
LU 182 . . . . Utica
LU 202 . . . . Bronx
LU 210 . . . . New York
LU 264 . . . . Cheektowaga
LU 272 . . . . New York

LU 282 . . . . Lake Success
LU 294 . . . . Albany
LU 295 . . . . Valley Stream
LU 317 . . . . Syracuse
LU 338 . . . . Bronxville
LU 375 . . . . Buffalo
LU 445 . . . . Newburgh
LU 449 . . . . Buffalo
LU 456 . . . . Elmsford
LU 529 . . . . Elmira
LU 550 . . . . . . New Hyde Park
LU 553 . . . . New York
LU 584 . . . . New York
LU 669 . . . . Albany
LU 687 . . . . Potsdam
LU 693 . . . . Binghamton
LU 707 Highway & Local Motor Freight . . . . Hempstead
LU 802 . . . . . . Long Island City
LU 803 . . . . Woodhaven
LU 804 . . . . . . Long Island City
LU 805 . . . . . . Long Island City
LU 807 . . . . . . Long Island City
LU 808 . . . . . . Long Island City
LU 810 . . . . New York
LU 812 . . . . Scarsdale
LU 813 . . . . . . Long Island City
LU 814 . . . . . . Long Island City
LU 817 . . . . Lake Success
LU 851 . . . . Valley Stream
LU 854 . . . . Baldwin
LU 917 . . . . Floral Park
LU 1149 . . . . Baldwinsville
LU 1205 . . . . Farmingdale

Television and Radio Artists

LU Buffalo . . . . Buffalo
LU Dallas-Fort Worth . . New York
LU New York . . . . . . New York
LU 223 Rochester . . . . Rochester
NHQ . . . . New York

Theatrical Stage Employees

D 10 New York . . . . Ballston Lake
LU East Coast Council . . New York
LU 1 Theatrical Protective Union . . . . New York
LU 4 . . . . Brooklyn
LU 9 . . . . Syracuse
LU 10 . . . . Cheektowaga
LU 14 . . . . Albany
LU 25 . . . . Rochester
LU 29 . . . . Schenectady
LU 52 . . . . New York
LU 54 . . . . Johnson City
LU 72-F . . . . East Meadow
LU 90-B . . . . Rochester
LU 100 TV Broadcasting Studio & Remote Employees . . . New York
LU 121 . . . . Amherst
LU 161 . . . . New York
LU 253 . . . . . . West Henrietta
LU 266 . . . . Jamestown
LU 272 . . . . Dryden
LU 289 . . . . Elmira
LU 306 . . . . New York
LU 311 . . . . . . Washingtonville
LU 324 . . . . Knox
LU 340 . . . . Rocky Point
LU 353 . . . . Narrowsburg
LU 499 . . . . Narrowsburg
LU 524 . . . . Queensbury
LU 592 . . . . Stillwater
LU 640 Motion Picture Projectionists . . . . . . Babylon
LU 665 . . . . New York
LU 702 . . . . New York
LU 749 . . . . Ogdensburg

LU 751 . . . . New York
LU 751-B . . . . New York
LU 764 . . . . New York
LU 783 . . . . . South Cheektowaga
LU 788 . . . . Rochester
LU 794 Television Broadcasting Studio . . . . New York
LU 798 . . . . New York
LU 829 Exhibition Employees Union . . . . New York
LU 838 . . . . Syracuse
LU 842-M . . . . West Fulton
LU 858 . . . . Lancaster
LU 936-AE . . . . Albany
LU 18032 Theatrical Press Agents & Managers . . . . . . New York
NHQ . . . . New York

Train Dispatchers

SCOM GCA CSXT-East System Committee . . . . Ravena
SCOM Staten Island Rapid Transit Railroad . . . . . . Brooklyn

Transit Union

LDIV 282 . . . . Rochester
LDIV 580 . . . . Syracuse
LDIV 1179 . . . . Jamaica
LDIV 1181 . . . . . . Ozone Park
LDIV 1342 . . . . . . West Seneca
LDIV 1493 . . . . Syracuse
LDIV 1592 . . . . . . Glen Aubrey
LDIV 1625 . . . . . Cheektowaga
LU 1636 . . . . Troy

Transport Workers

LU 100 . . . . New York
LU 101 Utility Division . . Brooklyn
LU 226 . . . . New York
LU 227 . . . . New York
LU 229 . . . . New York
LU 241 . . . . New York
LU 252 . . . . Westbury
LU 264 . . . . New York
LU 501 . . . . Whitestone
LU 504 . . . . Jamaica
LU 562 . . . . Jamaica
LU 721 . . . . New York
LU 1460 . . . . New York
LU 2001 . . . . Elmsford
LU 2020 . . . . Wyoming
NHQ . . . . New York

Transportation Communications Union

D 491 . . . . East Aurora
D 861 Conrail . . . . . . Ravena
LG United Service Workers of America . . . . Briarwood
LG 177 . . . . Holtsville
LG 255 United Service Workers . . . . Briarwood
LG 339 United Service Workers . . . . Briarwood
LG 355 United Service Workers . . . . Briarwood
LG 455 United Service Workers . . . . Briarwood
LG 955 United Service Workers . . . . Briarwood
LG 1212 United Service Workers . . . . Briarwood
LG 1444 . . . . Sayville
LG 5085 Arasa . . . . Troy
LG 5086 Amtrak . . New Windsor
LG 6983 Binghamton . . . . Vestal
SBA 167 Long Island . . . Hicksville

Transportation Union

GCA GO-299 Delaware & Hudson Railway . . . . . . Mechanicville
GCA GO-300 . . . . . . Oneonta
GCA GO-340 . . . . . . Warwick
GCA GO-342 . . . . . Woodhaven
GCA GO-505 Long Island Railroad . . . . Babylon
GCA GO-619 Conrail-PC-ED-NYC-E . Syracuse
GCA GO-621 . . . . Cheektowaga
GCA GO-867 . . . . . Salamanca
LU 1 . . . . East Aurora
LU 29 . . . . Levittown
LU 95 . . . . Rensselaer
LU 167 . . . . Watervliet
LU 211 . . . . Binghamton
LU 212 . . . . Valatie
LU 256 . . . . Mechanicville
LU 292 . . . . East Syracuse
LU 318 . . . . Vestal
LU 377 . . . . Buffalo
LU 385 . . . . Schenectady
LU 394 . . . . Kinderhook
LU 645 . . . . Babylon
LU 722 . . . . Farmingdale
LU 982 . . . . Auburn
LU 1007 . . . . Brewerton
LU 1393 . . . . West Seneca
LU 1491 . . . . Port Jervis
LU 1556 . . . . . . East Amherst
LU 1582 . . . . . . Hoosick Falls
LU 1831 . . . . Massapequa Park
LU 1908 . . . . Buffalo
LU 1951 . . . . Hamburg
LU 1978 . . . . Deer Park
SLB LO-35 New York . . . . Albany

Treasury Employees

CH 47 . . . . New York
CH 53 . . . . Garden City
CH 57 . . . . Syracuse
CH 58 . . . . East Amherst
CH 61 . . . . Poughkeepsie
CH 79 . . . . Rochester
CH 99 . . . . Holtsville
CH 138 . . . . Champlain
CH 148 . . . . Champlain
CH 153 . . . . Jamaica
CH 154 . . . . Buffalo
CH 181 Toronto Preclearance . . . . . Niagara Falls
CH 183 . . . . New York
CH 252 . . . . Hempstead
CH 255 . . . . New York
CH 271 Queens/Brooklyn . Brooklyn

UNITE HERE

JB Disability Service and Allied Work . . . . New York
JB Gloves Cities/Hudson District . . . . Gloversville
JB Greater Northern District . . . . Oswego
JB Laundry, Dry Cleaning & Allied Workers . . . . New York
JB New York . . . . . . New York
JB New York Metropolitan Area . . . . New York
JB Northeast Regional . . New York
JB Rochester . . . . . . Rochester
JB Western . . . . . . Cheektowaga
JC Dress Makers . . . . New York
LU 3-T . . . . Rochester
LU 4 . . . . Buffalo
LU 4 . . . . New York
LU 6 . . . . New York
LU 8 . . . . New York

LU 10 . . . . New York	LU 1095 . . . . Buffalo
LU 14 . . . . Rochester	LU 1126 . . . . Buffalo
LU 14-A . . . . Rochester	LU 1338 . . . . New York
LU 14-B . . . . Rochester	LU 1648 . . . . New York
LU 14-W . . . . Suffern	LU 1651 Local Branch . . New York
LU 19 . . . . Gloversville	LU 1712-C . . . . . . Gloversville
LU 23-25 . . . . New York	LU 1714-T . . . . . . Gloversville
LU 25 . . . . New York	LU 1733 . . . . New York
LU 37 . . . . New York	LU 1802 . . . . Buffalo
LU 41 . . . . New York	LU 1822 . . . . Oswego
LU 49 . . . . Buffalo	LU 1827 . . . . Oswego
LU 59 . . . . New York	LU 1904 . . . . New York
LU 62-32 . . . . New York	LU 1932 . . . . New York
LU 63 . . . . New York	LU 1939 . . . . New York
LU 69 . . . . New York	LU 1947 . . . . Oswego
LU 73 . . . . New York	LU 2342 . . . . Ancramdale
LU 75-87 . . . . New York	LU 2486 . . . . . . Gloversville
LU 76 . . . . New York	LU 2538 . . . . Rochester
LU 89-22 . . . . New York	LU 2541 . . . . Rochester
LU 92-T . . . . New York	LU 2585 . . . . New York
LU 100 . . . . New York	LU 2607 . . . . Rochester
LU 117 . . . . New York	LU 13298-102 . . . . New York
LU 124 Southwest . . . New York	NHQ . . . . New York
LU 150 . . . . Syracuse	STC New York . . . . . . Syracuse
LU 155-I . . . . New York	
LU 158-A . . . . New York	**University Professors**
LU 158-I . . . . New York	CH Adelphi University . Garden City
LU 163 . . . . Gloversville	CH Arnold & Marie Schwartz
LU 168-LDC . . . . Buffalo	College . . . . Brooklyn
LU 169-C . . . . New York	CH Bard
LU 178-C . . . . New York	College . . Annandale-on-Hudson
LU 189 . . . . Buffalo	CH College of Insurance . New York
LU 201 . . . . Buffalo	CH D'Youville College . . . Buffalo
LU 204 . . . . Rochester	CH Hofstra University . . Hempstead
LU 205 . . . . Rochester	CH Marymount College . Tarrytown
LU 207 . . . . Buffalo	CH St. John's University . . Jamaica
LU 215 . . . . Rochester	CH Utica College of Syracuse . Utica
LU 220 . . . . Rochester	JC New York Institute of
LU 221 . . . . Buffalo	Technology . . . . Greenvale
LU 227-A . . . . Rochester	
LU 230 . . . . Rochester	**Utility Workers**
LU 231 . . . . Rochester	C Long Island Water
LU 239-A . . . . New York	Workers . . . . Brookhaven
LU 245 . . . . Rochester	LU 1-2 . . . . New York
LU 246 . . . . New York	LU 355 . . . . Merrick
LU 246-S . . . . New York	LU 365 . . . . Lynbrook
LU 250-C . . . . New York	LU 447 . . . . Port Washington
LU 253-C . . . . New York	
LU 279 . . . . New York	**Variety Artists**
LU 284-LDC . . . . . . New York	NHQ . . . . New York
LU 300-C . . . . New York	
LU 324-J . . . . New York	**Weather Service Employees**
LU 325 . . . . New York	BR 01-17 . . . . Albany
LU 330-A . . . . New York	BR 01-18 . . . . Upton
LU 331 . . . . New York	BR 01-19 . . . . Rochester
LU 332 . . . . New York	BR 01-32 . . . . . . Johnson City
LU 340 . . . . New York	BR 01-35 . . . . Buffalo
LU 340-A . . . . New York	BR 01-58 . . . . Bohemia
LU 355 . . . . New York	BR 01-65 . . . . . . Ronkonkoma
LU 368 . . . . Gloversville	
LU 381 . . . . Rochester	**Westinghouse Salaried Employees**
LU 388 . . . . Rochester	ASSN Buffalo Salaried
LU 400 . . . . New York	Employees . . . . . Lackawanna
LU 446 . . . . New York	
LU 471 . . . . Broadway	**Writers, East**
LU 482 . . . . Buffalo	NHQ . . . . New York
LU 506-A . . . . New York	
LU 548-A . . . . New York	## Unaffiliated Labor Organizations
LU 563-SW . . . . . . New York	
LU 569 . . . . New York	318 Restaurant Workers
LU 574-A . . . . New York	Union . . . . Brooklyn
LU 646-T . . . . Gloversville	92nd Street Y Nursery School
LU 701-T . . . . Oswego	Association . . . . New York
LU 800-A . . . . New York	Adelphi Physical Plant Workers
LU 800-A . . . . New York	Labor Union . . . . East Meadow
LU 919 . . . . New York	Allied International Union . Mineola
LU 976-T . . . . Gloversville	
LU 1067 . . . . Buffalo	

Alternative Workers Alliance
Inc . . . . Long Beach
Amalgamated Lithographers of
America LU 1 . . . . . New York
Amalgamated Union LU
450-A . . . . Elmsford
Amalgamated Workers of North
America . . . . . New Rochelle
Amalgamated Workers of North
America LU 724 . . New Rochelle
American Federation of Railroad
Police Inc . . . . Woodbury
American Federation of School
Administrators LU 1 . . Brooklyn
American Guild of
Employees . . . . New City
Amex Employees
Association . . . . New York
Anti-Defamation League Professional
Staff Association . . . . New York
Asian Employee
Association . . . . New York
Association of Court Security
Officers of New York . Centereach
Attending Physicians
Association City Hospital at
Elmhurst . . . . Elmhurst
Benefit Fund Staff
Association . . . . New York
Braun Union Independent . . Depew
Brotherhood of Essential Workers
Union LU 1 . . . . . Hauppauge
Builders Woodworkers &
Millwrights LU
1 . . . . South Glens Falls
Campaign & Professional Workers
LU 1 . . . . Albany
Chemical Workers Independent
Union . . . . Schenectady
City Wholesale Distributors Union
Association . . . . Lancaster
Clerical Employees
Association . . . . Syracuse
Collective Negotiations Committee,
New York Chapter, American
Physical Therapy
Association . . . . Albany
Confort Employees
Association . . . Long Island City
Cornell Police Union . . . . Ithaca
Crafts & Industrial Workers Union,
United LU 91 . . . Williston Park
Culinary Craft
Association . . . . . . Hyde Park
Detectives Association Suffolk
County . . . . . . West Sayville
Diversified Employees Union LU
4 . . . . Selden
Doctors Council . . . . New York
Draftsmen's Association of
Syracuse . . . . Phoenix
Ellison Bronze Employees
Union . . . . Falconer
Elrae Employees Association
Independent Union . . . . . Alden
Entertainment & Amusement
Employees Association LU
99 . . . . Long Island City
Fabric Labor Committee . New York
Factory & Building Employees
Union LU 187 . . . . . Brooklyn
Faculty Association at St. Johns
University . . . . Jamaica
Field Staff
Association . . . . . Williamsville
Fordham Law School Bargaining
Committee . . . . New York
Frank Siviglia Employees . . . Bronx

General Union for International
Labor Development . . New York
Grove Street Academy Faculty
New York State United
Teachers . . . . Ulster Park
Guards & Plant Protection
Employees LU 1 . . . Schenectady
H.W. Wilson Employees
Association . . . . Bronx
Half Hollow Hills Library
Employees Association
Independent . . . . . . Dix Hills
Hassall Employees
Association . . . . Westbury
Headquarters Staff Union . . Albany
Health Care Professional Guild
Guild . . . . New Hartford
Hearst International Employees
Association . . . . New York
Huntington Hospital Nurses
Association . . . . . Huntington
Hunts Point Police Benevolent
Association . . . . Bronx
Independent Artists of
America . . . . New York
Independent Guard Union . Brooklyn
Independent Railway Supervisors
Association Grand Lodge
NHQ . . . . Plainview
Independent Railway Supervisors
Long Island Railroad LG
1 . . . . Bethpage
Independent School
Transportation Workers
Association . . . . . Staten Island
Independent Theatrical Employees of
America LU 1 . . . . Whitesboro
Independent Union of Court Security
Officers Northern District of New
York . . . . Syracuse
Independent Union of Plant
Protection Employees LU
18 . . . . Syracuse
Independent Union of Plant
Protection Employees
NHQ . . . . Syracuse
Independent Union Staff
Employees . . . . . Cheektowaga
Industrial Employees
Association . . . Long Island City
International Brotherhood of Trade
Unions LU 122 . . . East Meadow
International Brotherhood of Trade
Unions LU 713 . . . . Garden City
International Guards Union of
America LU 37 . . . . . Upton
International Guards Union of
America LU 107 . . . Schenectady
International Shield of Labor
Alliances (ISLA) . . . . . Glendale
International Workers Guild . Elmont
Interns and Residents Staff Union,
The Committee of . . . New York
Interns and Residents, Committee,
Einstein College of Medicine &
Logan Hospital . . . . . New York
IUISTHE D 6 . . . . . . New York
Jewish Committee Staff Organization
America . . . . New York
Kingsbrook Jewish Medical
Center Medical Staff
Association . . . . Brooklyn
Lay Faculty Association . . Flushing
League of Employees
Guild . . . . New York
League of International Federated
Employees . . . . Brooklyn
Legal Staff Association . . New York

Local One Security
  Officers . . . . Brooklyn
Machinists & Mechanics Independent
  Association . . . . Watervliet
Magtrol Employees
  Association . . . . . West Seneca
Marine Technicians Guild Marine
  Technicians . . North Massapequa
Models and Showroom Employees
  LU 1 . . . . Long Beach
Mount Sinai Hospital Pharmacy
  Association . . . . . . New York
Municipal Highway Inspectors LU
  1042 . . . . Jackson Heights
National Basketball Coaches
  Association . . . . . . New York
National Music Instructors Guild BR
  120 . . . . . Cold Springs Harbor
National Organization of
  Industrial Trade Unions LU
  36 . . . . Far Rockaway
National Security Officers &
  Protection Employees LU
  308 . . . . New York
National Trans Supervisors
  Association LG 78 . . . . Mineola
National Union of Security Officers
  and Guards . . . . Jamaica
National United Brotherhood of
  Section 3 Workers LU
  1888 . . . . Bronx
Neergaard Employees
  Association . . . . Brooklyn
New School Security Guards
  Independent Union . . . New York
New York Archdiocesan High School
  Lay Faculty Association . . Bronx
New York Physicians & Dentists
  SFED . . . . New York
New York Professional Nurses
  Union . . . . New York

New York Professional Nurses Union
  National . . . . New York
Newspaper & Mail Deliverers
  Union New York &
  Vicinity . . . . Long Island City
Niagara Frontier Sheet Metal
  Workers Union . . . Niagara Falls
Niagara Hooker Employees
  Union . . . . . . Niagara Falls
Niagara Plant Employees
  Union . . . . . . Niagara Falls
Niagara University Lay Teachers
  Association . . . . . Lake View
Olin Nigara Employees
  Union . . . . . . Niagara Falls
Onondaga Sheriff's Captain's
  Association. . . . . . . Syracuse
Organization of Union
  Representatives . . . . New York
Petroleum Workers Independent of
  Albany . . . . Delmar
Physicians for Responsible
  Negotiation . . . . . . New York
Pius XII Chester Campus Institution
  Unit A LU 725 . . . . . . Albany
Police and Security Guards
  International Union . . . Glendale
Police Benevolent Association
  Federal Protective
  Service . . . . New York
Presbyterian Hospital Occupational
  Therapy Association . . New York
Prismatic Employees
  Union . . . . . . Washingtonville
Private, Public & Professional
  Employees of America LU
  654 . . . . Elmsford
Production & Service Employees
  International Union Independent
  LU 143 . . . . Bronx

Production Industrial Technical
  Textile & Professional
  Employees . . . . Bronx
Production Maintenance & Technical
  Service Employees Union . Selden
Professional Association Holy Cross
  High School . . . . . . Flushing
Professional Service & Healthcare
  Employees International
  Union . . . . Jamaica
Professional Staff
  Association . . . . Latham
Real Benefits Association
  14-1900-957 . . . . . Staten Island
Retail Wholesale Warehouse and
  Production Employees
  International Union . . . Brooklyn
Rochester Telephone Workers
  Association . . . . Rochester
Security Officers Association
  University of Rochester . Webster
Security Personnel Brotherhood L.J.
  Overton & Associates . New York
Security Police & Guards Union
  Independent LU 2 . . . New York
Security Police & Guards Union
  Independent LU
  18 . . . . West Hempstead
Security Police & Guards Union
  Independent LU 55 . . . Brooklyn
Security Workers of America LU
  819 . . . . Bronx
Service Professionals Independent
  Union LU 726 . . . . Briarwood
Solidarity of Labor Organization LU
  947 . . . . . Huntington Station
Special & Superior Officers
  Benevolent Association . Babylon
Special Patrolmen Benevolent
  Association LU 1 . . . . . Bronx

St. John's Preparatory Teacher
  Association . . . . Astoria
Staff Union . . . . Buffalo
Stage Directors & Choreographers
  Society . . . . New York
Stage Performers Guild . Huntington
Sun Oil Company Employees
  Association Oceanside
  District . . . . Lawrence
Teachers Association of the Weekend
  School of Japanese Educational
  Institute of New York . Shoreham
Teachers Representatives
  Union . . . . New York
United Business Workers of
  America . . . . Nanuet
United Construction Trade LU
  1130 . . . . New York
United Construction Trades &
  Industrial Employees International
  Union . . . . Valley Stream
United Construction Trades Industrial
  LU 621 . . . . Glendale
United Federation of Security
  Officers, Inc. . . . Briarcliff Manor
United Production Workers LU
  17-18 . . . . Brooklyn
United Safety Inspectors Union LU
  1021 . . . . Hicksville
United Service Employees Union LU
  1222 . . . . Ronkonkoma
United Teachers Association of
  Solomon Schechter Day
  School . . . . East Meadow
Visiting Nurses Professional
  Guild . . . . Woodgate
Women's National Basketball Players
  Association . . . . . . New York
Workers of America Canada
  International Union LU
  11 . . . . Brooklyn

North Carolina

AFL-CIO Trade and Industrial Departments

Food and Allied Service Trades Department
FASTC Carolinas . . . . . Concord

Affiliated Labor Organizations

Agricultural Employees
BR 34 . . . . Willow Spring

Air Traffic Controllers
LU AVL . . . . Fletcher
LU CLT . . . . Charlotte
LU GSO . . . . Greensboro
LU ILM . . . . Wilmington
LU INT . . . . Winston-Salem
LU NATCA ITH Local . Fayetteville
LU NKT . . . . Havelock
LU RDU . . . . Morrisville

Asbestos Workers
LU 72 . . . . Hillsborough

Automobile, Aerospace Workers
LU 1597 . . . . Belews Creek
LU 2404 . . . . Charlotte
LU 2828 . . . . Charlotte
LU 3520 . . . . Cleveland
LU 5285 . . . . Mount Holly
LU 5286 . . . . Dallas
LU 5287 . . . . High Point

Bakery, Confectionery, Tobacco Workers and Grain Millers
LU 176-T . . . . Durham
LU 192-T . . . . Reidsville
LU 229-T . . . . Concord
LU 270-T . . . . Wilson
LU 274-T . . . . Farmville
LU 317-T . . . . Burlington
LU 503 . . . . Concord

Boilermakers
LG 30 . . . . Greensboro
LG 31 . . . . New London
LG 613 . . . . Rocky Point
LG 905 . . . . Wilmington

Carpenters
LU 312 . . . . Lexington

Civilian Technicians
CH 96 Old Hickory . . . . . St. Pauls

Communications Workers
C North Carolina
  Political . . . . Vanceboro
LU 3061 . . . . Greensboro
LU 3601 . . . . Asheville
LU 3602 . . . . Graham
LU 3603 . . . . Charlotte
LU 3605 . . . . Gastonia
LU 3606 . . . . Goldsboro
LU 3607 . . . . Greensboro
LU 3608 . . . . Morganton
LU 3609 . . . . Lumberton
LU 3610 . . . . Newton
LU 3611 . . . . Raleigh
LU 3613 . . . . Salisbury
LU 3615 . . . . Castle Hayne
LU 3616 . . . . . . Winston-Salem

LU 3617 . . . . Ellerbe
LU 3640 . . . . . . Winston-Salem
LU 3641 . . . . Charlotte
LU 3650 . . . . Greensboro
LU 3672 . . . . Hickory
LU 3673 . . . . Whittier
LU 3676 . . . . Mount Olive
LU 3680 . . . . Hope Mills
LU 3681 . . . . New Bern
LU 3682 . . . . Henderson
LU 3683 . . . . Marshville
LU 3684 . . . . Tobaccoville
LU 3685 . . . . . . Elizabeth City
LU 3695 . . . . Charlotte
LU 3790 . . . . . Pleasant Garden
LU 83181 . . . . Charlotte
LU 83188 . . . . Durham
LU 83265 . . . . Henderson

Education
ASSN Maxwell Education
  Association . . . . . Fayetteville
C OEA Germany South East
  Area . . . . Fayetteville
C OEA Pacific Area . . . Fayetteville
LU Benning Education
  Association . . . . . Fayetteville
LU Fort Bragg Association of
  Educators . . . . . . Fayetteville
LU Fort Knox Classified Personnel
  Association . . . . . Fayetteville
LU Fort Knox Education
  Association . . . . . Fayetteville
LU Fort Stewart Association of
  Educators . . . . . Fayetteville
LU Hampton, South
  Carolina . . . . . . Fayetteville
LU OEA Lejeune Education
  Association . . . . . Fayetteville
LU Stateside Region
  FEA . . . . Fayetteville

Electrical Workers
LU 238 . . . . Asheville
LU 289 . . . . Franklinton
LU 312 . . . . Mooresville
LU 342 . . . . . . Winston-Salem
LU 379 . . . . Concord
LU 495 . . . . Wilmington
LU 553 . . . Research Triangle Park
LU 962 . . . . Greensboro
LU 1183 . . . . Plymouth
LU 1537 . . . . Asheboro
LU 1863 . . . . Rockwell
LU 1902 . . . . Charlotte
LU 1912 . . . . Siler City
LU 1923 . . . . Hamlet

Electrical, Radio and Machine Workers
LU 150 North Carolina Public
  Service Workers Union . . Durham

Elevator Constructors
LU 80 . . . . Hillsborough
LU 135 . . . . Concord

Federal Employees
LU 1563 . . . . Nebo

Food and Commercial Workers
LU 204 . . . . Clemmons
LU 297-C . . . . Angier
LU 298-C . . . . . . Hillsborough
LU 426-T . . . . Tyner

LU 427-C . . . . Morganton
LU 528-C . . . . . . Weaverville
LU 954-C . . . . Concord
LU 955-C . . . . Statesville
LU 2598-T . . . . Enka

Glass, Molders, Pottery and Plastics Workers
LU 168 . . . . Germanton
LU 179 . . . . Henderson
LU 193 . . . . Wilson
LU 222 . . . . Oxford
LU 256 . . . . Rockingham
LU 291 . . . . Shelby
LU 420 . . . . Oxford

Government Employees
LU 405 . . . . Butner
LU 406 Azalea Station . Wilmington
LU 408 BoP . . . . Butner
LU 446 AFGE Local 446 . Asheville
LU 1708 DoD . . . . . Southport
LU 1770 DoD . . . . . Fort Bragg
LU 2065 DoD . . . . . Jacksonville
LU 2325 USDA . . . . . . Sanford
LU 2364 DoD . . . . Spring Lake
LU 2652 DT, Customs Inspectors
  Association . . . . Raleigh
LU 2923 HHS . . . . . . Durham
LU 3347
  EPA . . . . Research Triangle Park
LU 3409 HUD . . . . . Greensboro
LU 3696 DoJ . . . . . . Butner
LU 3977 FPG1, SJAFB . Goldsboro
LU VA-1738 . . . . . . Salisbury

Government Employees Association
LU 5-187 . . . . Pikeville
LU 04-75 . . . . Asheville
LU 05-160 . . . . . . Fayetteville
LU 05-188 . . . . Goldsboro

Government Security Officers
LU 90 . . . . Polkton
LU 94 . . . . Wilmington
LU 96 . . . . Asheville

Iron Workers
LU 812 . . . . Leichester
LU 843 . . . . Greensboro

Laborers
LU 104 . . . . Kenly
LU 1699 Cherokee Indian Health
  Services . . . . Cherokee

Letter Carriers
BR 248 . . . . Asheville
BR 382 . . . . Durham
BR 459 . . . . Raleigh
BR 461 . . . . . . Winston-Salem
BR 464 . . . . Wilmington
BR 545 . . . . Charlotte
BR 630 . . . . Greensboro
BR 780 . . . . New Bern
BR 876 . . . . Goldsboro
BR 934 . . . . Salisbury
BR 935 . . . . Statesville
BR 936 . . . . High Point
BR 1044 . . . . Dover
BR 1127 . . . . South Mills
BR 1128 . . . . Fayetteville
BR 1250 . . . . Hickory
BR 1286 . . . . Henderson

BR 1321 . . . . Rocky Mount
BR 1510 . . . . Oxford
BR 1512 . . . . Gastonia
BR 1670 . . . . Lumberton
BR 1719 . . . . Tarboro
BR 1729 . . . . Greenville
BR 1843 . . . . Morganton
BR 1852 . . . . Lenoir
BR 1898 . . . . Hamlet
BR 1957 . . . . Lincolnton
BR 2216 . . . . Taylorsville
BR 2262 . . . . Burlington
BR 2300 . . . . Laurinburg
BR 2307 . . . . Shelby
BR 2381 . . . . Rockingham
BR 2486 . . . . Newton
BR 2560 . . . . Asheboro
BR 2571 . . . . North Wilkesboro
BR 2613 . . . . Chapel Hill
BR 2659 . . . . Wadesboro
BR 2669 . . . . Reidsville
BR 2679 . . . . Mount Olive
BR 2731 . . . . Sanford
BR 2794 . . . . Kannapolis
BR 2893 . . . . . . Rutherfordton
BR 3114 . . . . . . Morehead City
BR 3119 . . . . Belhaven
BR 3145 . . . . Grover
BR 3155 . . . . Williamston
BR 3257 . . . . Whiteville
BR 3281 . . . . Albemarle
BR 3331 . . . . . . Roanoke Rapids
BR 3561 . . . . . Carolina Beach
BR 3712 . . . . Eden
BR 3813 . . . . Forest City
BR 3840 . . . . Plymouth
BR 3859 . . . . Elkin
BR 3970 . . . . Clinton
BR 3984 . . . . Richlands
BR 4122 . . . . Roxboro
BR 4141 . . . . Siler City
BR 4206 . . . . Windsor
BR 4243 . . . . Benson
BR 4244 . . . . Franklinton
BR 4264 . . . . Cherryville
BR 4392 . . . . Fairmont
BR 4460 . . . . St. Pauls
BR 4563 . . . . Ayden
BR 4637 . . . . Randleman
BR 4765 . . . . Enfield
BR 4883 . . . . Mayodan
BR 4970 . . . . Havelock
BR 5067 . . . . Tabor City
BR 5134 . . . . . . Scotland Neck
BR 5253 . . . . Carrboro
BR 5322 . . . . Maiden
BR 5367 . . . . . Black Mountain
BR 5425 . . . . Franklin
BR 5493 . . . . La Grange
BR 5529 . . . . Madison
BR 5544 . . . . Landis
BR 5629 . . . . Spindale
BR 5646 . . . . Red Springs
BR 5647 . . . . . . Murfreesboro
BR 5658 . . . . Sylva
BR 5673 . . . . China Grove
BR 5690 . . . . Dallas
BR 5771 . . . . Wallace
BR 6081 . . . . Snow Hill
BR 6345 . . . . Jonesville
BR 6369 . . . . Stanley
BR 6482 . . . . Maxton
BR 6528 . . . . . . Hillsborough
BR 6622 . . . . Aberdeen
BR 8009 . . . . Asheville

SA North Carolina . . . . . Durham

Locomotive Engineers
DIV 166 . . . . Charlotte
DIV 208 . . . . Winston-Salem
DIV 267 . . . . Arden
DIV 314 . . . . Rocky Mount
DIV 375 . . . . Faith
DIV 435 . . . . Hamlet
DIV 849 . . . . Raleigh
DIV 932 . . . . Wilmington
SLB North Carolina . . . . Asheville

Longshoremen
LU 1426 . . . . Wilmington
LU 1766 . . . . Wilmington
LU 1807 . . . . . . Morehead City
LU 1838 . . . . Southport
LU 1847 . . . . . . Morehead City
LU 1968 . . . . Southport

Machinists
DLG 110 . . . . Havelock
LG 108 . . . . Concord
LG 263 . . . . Vale
LG 641 . . . . Cleveland
LG 757 . . . . Durham
LG 1725 . . . . Charlotte
LG 1859 . . . . Havelock
LG 2203 . . . . . . Elizabeth City
LG 2296 . . . . Havelock
LG 2297 . . . . Havelock
LG 2444 . . . . . . Winston-Salem
LG 2541 . . . . Wilson
LG 2555 . . . . Havelock
LLG W-354
    Woodworkers . . . . Powellville
LLG W-369 Woodworkers . Sanford
STC North Carolina . Winston-Salem

Maintenance of Way Employes
LG 523 . . . . Reidsville
LG 525 . . . . Asheville
LG 537 . . . . Siloam
LG 563 . . . . Rocky Mount
LG 1993 . . . . Denton
LG 2003 . . . . Dobson
LG 2161 . . . . Wilmington
LG 2369 . . . . Littleton
SLG 524 . . . . Charlotte
SLG 600 . . . . Newport
SLG 2102 . . . . Lincolnton

Mine Workers
LU 140 . . . . Spruce Pine

Musicians
LU 342 Charlotte . . . . . Charlotte
LU 500 . . . . Cary

National Staff Organization
LU Staff Organization, North
    Carolina Association of
    Educators . . . . Raleigh

NLRB Professional Association
LU 11 . . . . Winston-Salem

Nurses
SA North Carolina Nurses
    Association . . . . Raleigh

Office and Professional Employees
LU 354 . . . . Plymouth

Operating Engineers
LU 415 . . . . Windsor
LU 465 . . . . Durham

Painters
LU 1865 . . . . High Point

Plasterers and Cement Masons
LU 477 . . . . Charlotte

Police Associations
LU 105 . . . . Chapel Hill

Postal and Federal Employees
LU 311 . . . . Charlotte
LU 316 . . . . Fayetteville
LU 317 . . . . Goldsboro
LU 318 Greensboro, North
    Carolina . . . . Greensboro
LU 324 . . . . Clayton

Postal Workers
LU 17 Elizabeth City . Elizabeth City
LU 24 Durham Area . . . . Durham
LU 145 Wilmington . . Wilmington
LU 220 Washington . . Washington
LU 277 Asheville . . . . . Asheville
LU 375 Charlotte Area . . . Charlotte
LU 523 Winston-
    Salem . . . . . . Winston-Salem
LU 591 Rocky Mount . Rocky Mount
LU 711 Greater Greensboro
    Area . . . . Greensboro
LU 984 Fayetteville . . . Fayetteville
LU 1046 Goldsboro . . . Goldsboro
LU 1078 Raleigh Cosmopolitan Area
    Local . . . . Raleigh
LU 1125 Statesville . . Statesville
LU 1129 Greenville . . . Greenville
LU 1217 Chapel Hill . . Chapel Hill
LU 1236 Salisbury . . . . Salisbury
LU 1305 Rockingham . Rockingham
LU 1537 Burlington . . Burlington
LU 1561 Mebane . . . . . Mebane
LU 1562 Lexington . . . Lexington
LU 1563 Eden . . . . Eden
LU 1564 Thomasville . . . Denton
LU 1615 Oxford . . . . . . Oxford
LU 1616 Roanoke
    Rapids . . . . . Roanoke Rapids
LU 1618 Wilson Area . . . . Wilson
LU 1631 Morehead
    City . . . . . . Morehead City
LU 1632 Franklin . . . . . Franklin
LU 1637 Smithfield . . . Smithfield
LU 1638 Shelby . . . . . . Shelby
LU 1641 Hamlet . . . . . Hamlet
LU 1661 Concord . . . . . Concord
LU 1665 North
    Wilkesboro . . . North Wilkesboro
LU 1768 Whiteville . . . Whiteville
LU 1772 Edenton . . . . Edenton
LU 1807 Hickory . . . . . Hickory
LU 1809 Murphy . . . . . Murphy
LU 1810 Newton . . . . . Newton
LU 1901 Reidsville . . . Reidsville
LU 1950 Boone . . . . . . Boone
LU 2095 Mount Airy . . Mount Airy
LU 2154 Waynesville . Waynesville
LU 2158 Beaufort . . . . Beaufort
LU 2187 Siler City . . . Siler City
LU 2196 Kinston . . . . . Kinston
LU 2197 Plymouth . . . Plymouth
LU 2375 Elkin . . . . Elkin
LU 2376 Lenoir . . . . . . Lenoir
LU 2508 Lincolnton . . Lincolnton
LU 2788 Asheboro . . . Asheboro
LU 2933 Laurinburg . . Laurinburg
LU 2934 Southern
    Pines . . . . . . Southern Pines
LU 2950 Sylva . . . . Sylva
LU 3268 Hillsborough . Hillsborough

LU 3284 Jacksonville . . Jacksonville
LU 3424 Lillington . . . . Lillington
LU 3483 Nashville . . . . Nashville
LU 3553 Mount Olive . Mount Olive
LU 3644 Havelock . . . . Havelock
LU 3648 Highlands . . . . Highlands
LU 3744 Maiden . . . . . . Maiden
LU 4560 High Point . . . High Point
LU 6184 Kernersville . . Kernersville
LU 6578 Weaverville . . Weaverville
LU 6645 Arden . . . . Arden
LU 6671 Carrboro . . . . . Carrboro
LU 7035 Greensboro Bulk Mail
    Center . . . . Greensboro
SA North Carolina
    Council . . . . . . Elizabeth City

Retail, Wholesale and Department Store
LU 1050 . . . . Rocky Mount

Rural Letter Carriers
D Rockingham County . . Reidsville
D 1 Alamance County . . . Mebane
D 2 Albemarle . . . . Elizabeth City
D 5 Peach Belt . . . . Hamlet
D 7 Roanoke Chowan . . . Ahoskie
D 10 Foothills . . . . . . Statesville
D 11 Smokey Mountain . . . . Otto
D 15 Catawba-Lincoln
    Counties . . . . Maiden
D 16 Central North Carolina Sanford
D 20 Cumerland-Hoke
    Counties . . . . . Southern Pines
D 23 Sea Level . . . . . . Garland
D 25 Tri-County
    Association . . . . . . Battleboro
D 28 Five County . . . . Henderson
D 42 Randolph County . Randleman
D 44 Roanoke . . . . . . Plymouth
D 50 Piedmont . . . . . China Grove
D 52 Tidewater . . . . . Handstead
LU Alleghany County . . . . Sparta
LU Ashe County . . . West Jefferson
LU Bushy Mountain . Hamptonville
LU Caswell County . . . Providence
LU Cleveland
    County . . . . . . Kings Mountain
LU Durham County . . . . Durham
LU French-Broad Counties . Canton
LU Guilford County . . . Gibsonville
LU Mecklenburg County . Charlotte
LU Orange County . . . . Durham
LU Polk-Rutherford
    Counties . . . . . Hendersonville
LU Tar River . . . . . . Greenville
LU Union County . . . . Waxhaw
LU Wake County . . . . . Erwin
LU Watauga-Avery Counties . Boone
LU Wayne County . . . Mount Olive
LU 8 Southeastern . . . Winnabow
LU 9 Burke
    County . . . . Connelly Springs
LU 26 Yadkin River . Winston-Salem
LU 29 Gaston County . . . . Dallas
LU 32 Harnett County . . Lillington
LU 34 Johnston County . . Clayton
LU 36 McDowell County . . Marion
LU 37 Mitchell County . . Burnsville
LU 41 Person County . . Timberlake
SA North Carolina . . . Stoneville

Service Employees
LU 576 Firemen & Oilers . Salisbury

Sheet Metal Workers
LU 393 . . . . Moyock
LU 449 . . . . Midland

State, County and Municipal Employees
LU 77 Duke University
    Employees . . . . Durham

Steelworkers
LU 1159-L . . . . Statesville
LU 02-425 . . . . . Roanoke Rapids
LU 02-428 . . . . Harrells
LU 02-429 . . . . Scotts
LU 02-507 Smoky
    Mountain . . . . Canton
LU 02-738 . . . . Riegelwood
LU 02-853 . . . . High Point
LU 02-1139 . . . . Wilson
LU 02-1167 . . . . . . New Bern
LU 02-1268 . . . . . . Rockingham
LU 02-1283 . . . . Seaboard
LU 02-1325 . . . . New Bern
LU 02-1356 . . . . . . Williamston
LU 02-1423 . . . . Plymouth
LU 02-1475 . . . . Whiteville
LU 02-1481 . . . . Whiteville
LU 02-1730 . . . . Linwood
LU 02-1821 . . . . Charlotte
LU 02-1870 . . . . Winston-Salem
LU 02-1947 . . . . Newton
LU 02-1971 . . . . Brevard
LU 08-831-L . . . . . . Providence
LU 09-45-T . . . . Clemmons
LU 09-47 . . . . Wilson
LU 09-55 . . . . Henderson
LU 09-303-S . . . . Badin
LU 09-345-L . . . . Hazelwood
LU 09-959-L . . . . . . Fayetteville
LU 09-1025 . . . . . . Wilmington
LU 09-1028-T . . . . Raleigh
LU 09-1133-L . . . Kings Mountain
LU 09-1811-S . . . . . . Charlotte
LU 09-7202-S . . . . . . Dillsboro
LU 09-8205 . . . . Burlington
LU 09-8498-S . . . Winston-Salem
LU 09-8573-S . . . Granite Quarry
LU 94- . . . . Laurinburg

Teachers
SFED 8031 North
    Carolina . . . . Kure Beach

Teamsters
JC 9 . . . . Charlotte
LU 61 . . . . Asheville
LU 71 . . . . Charlotte
LU 391 . . . . Greensboro

Theatrical Stage Employees
LU 278 . . . . Candler
LU 322 . . . . Charlotte
LU 417 . . . . Raleigh
LU 491 North Carolina Studio
    Mechanics . . . . . Wilmington
LU 574 . . . . Greensboro
LU 635 . . . . Winston-Salem
LU 870 . . . . Fayetteville

Transit Union
LDIV 1328 . . . . Angier

Transport Workers
LU 248 . . . . Winston-Salem
LU 569 . . . . Raleigh

Transportation Communications Union
LG 6142 Pee Dee . . . Rockingham
LG 6205 Spencer . . . . . Salisbury

Transportation Union
LU 782 . . . . Candler
LU 783 . . . . Salisbury
LU 1011 . . . . Hamlet
LU 1105 . . . . Wilmington
LU 1106 . . . . Nashville
LU 1129 . . . . Raleigh
LU 1166 . . . . Charlotte
LU 1715 . . . . Charlotte
SLB LO-36 . . . . Garner

Treasury Employees
CH 50 . . . . Greensboro
CH 203 . . . . Charlotte

UNITE HERE
LU 294-T . . . . Eden
LU 1391 . . . . Eden
LU 1867 . . . . Eden
LU 1994 . . . . Eden

LU 2398 . . . . Eden
LU 2604 . . . . Eden
LU 2605 . . . . Eden
LU 2639 . . . . Eden

Weather Service Employees
BR 01-33 . . . . Raleigh
BR 01-46 . . . . Wilmington
BR 01-52 . . . . Newport

Unaffiliated Labor Organizations

Exxon Employees Association
  Southeast . . . . Selma
Federal Education Association
  West Point School Support
  Staff . . . . Fayetteville
Federal Education Association, Inc.
  Dahlgren School Education
  Association . . . . . Fayetteville

Federal Education Association, Inc.
  Fort Campbell Education
  Association . . . . . Fayetteville
Federal Education Association, Inc.
  Fort Campbell Non-Certified
  Education Support . . Fayetteville
Federal Education Association, Inc.
  Fort Jackson Association of
  Educators . . . . . . Fayetteville
Federal Education Association, Inc.
  Fort Rucker Education
  Association . . . . . Fayetteville
Federal Education Association, Inc.
  Fort Stewart Educational Support
  Association . . . . . Fayetteville
Federal Education Association, Inc.
  Guam Education
  Association . . . . . Fayetteville

Federal Education Association, Inc.
  Lejeune Education Support
  Association . . . . . Fayetteville
Federal Education Association, Inc.
  Quantico Education
  Association . . . . . Fayetteville
Federal Education Association, Inc.
  Robbins Education
  Association . . . . . Fayetteville
Federal Education Association, Inc.
  Robins AFB Support Educational
  Association . . . . . Fayetteville
Federal Education Association, Inc.
  West Point Elementary School
  Teachers . . . . Fayetteville
Federation of Union
  Representatives . . . . . Charlotte
National Association of Aeronautical
  Examiners LU 2 . . . . . Newport
National Association of Government
  Inspectors UNIT 6 . . . . Havelock
National Federation of Licensed
  Practical Nurses NHQ . . . Garner

North Dakota

AFL-CIO Trade and Industrial Departments

Building and Construction Trades Department
BCTC Bismarck-Mandan . . Mandan
BCTC Grand Forks . . . Grand Forks
BCTC Minot . . . . Minot
BCTC North Dakota State . Mandan
BCTC Southeastern North
Dakota . . . . Fargo

AFL-CIO Directly Affiliated Locals

AFL-CIO
C Fargo-Moorhead Central
Labor . . . . Fargo

Affiliated Labor Organizations

Air Traffic Controllers
LU BIS . . . . Bismarck
LU FAR . . . . Fargo
LU GFK . . . . Grand Forks

Automobile, Aerospace Workers
LU 9429 . . . . Bismarck

Bakery, Confectionery, Tobacco Workers and Grain Millers
C -G District 2-Sugar
Council . . . . Hillsboro
LU 135-G . . . . Grand Forks
LU 264-G . . . . Manvel
LU 326-G . . . . Pembina
LU 372-G . . . . Cummings
LU 405-G . . . . Wahpeton

Carpenters
LU 1091 . . . . Bismarck
LU 1176 . . . . Fargo

Civilian Technicians
CH 112 Roughrider
Chapter . . . . Devils Lake

Communications Workers
LU 7301 . . . . Bismarck
LU 7303 . . . . Fargo
LU 7304 . . . . Grand Forks

Electrical Workers
LU 203 . . . . Devils Lake
LU 239 . . . . Spiritwood
LU 395 . . . . Dickinson
LU 524 . . . . Wahpeton
LU 714 . . . . Minot
LU 971 . . . . Williston

LU 975 . . . . Bismarck
LU 1426 . . . . Grand Forks
LU 1532 . . . . Minot
LU 1570 . . . . Beulah
LU 1593 . . . . Hazen
SC U-13 Montana-Dakota
Utilities . . . . Bismarck
SC U-27 Williston Basin Interst
Pipe . . . . Medina

Federal Employees
LU 225 . . . . Fargo

Government Employees
LU 888 . . . . Mandan
LU 1347 DoD . . . Grand Forks Air
Force Base
LU 1888 AFGE-ND-USDA-
RD . . . . Minot
LU 2789 DoJ . . . . Reynolds
LU 2989 DoD . . . . . West Fargo
LU 3413 USDA . . . . . . Mandan
LU 3748 USDA . . . . . . Mandan
LU 3884 VA . . . . Fargo
LU 4046 MAFB . . . . . . Surrey

Graphic Communications
LU 192-C . . . . Hatton
LU 240-C . . . . Bismarck

Letter Carriers
BR 205 . . . . Fargo
BR 517 . . . . Grand Forks
BR 957 . . . . Bismarck
BR 965 . . . . Jamestown
BR 1090 . . . . Valley City
BR 1152 . . . . Minot
BR 1253 . . . . Mandan
BR 1388 . . . . Wahpeton
BR 1463 . . . . Dickinson
BR 1494 . . . . Williston
BR 1657 . . . . Devils Lake
BR 2287 . . . . Grafton
BR 3057 . . . . Carrington
BR 3078 . . . . Harvey
BR 3594 . . . . Enderlin
BR 3922 . . . . Oakes
BR 3989 . . . . Rugby
BR 4806 . . . . Langdon
BR 5675 . . . . Bottineau
BR 6279 . . . . . . New Rockford
SA North Dakota . . . . Bismarck

Locomotive Engineers
DIV 69 . . . . Grand Forks
DIV 160 . . . . Harvey
DIV 202 . . . . Fargo
DIV 671 Ogema . . . . . Enderlin
DIV 695 . . . . Minot
DIV 746 . . . . Mandan
GCA Soo Line Railroad . . . Minot
SLB North Dakota . . . . Bismarck

Machinists
LG 810 . . . . Horace
LG 2525 . . . . Fargo
LLG W-384 Woodworkers . Pembina

Maintenance of Way Employes
LG 19 . . . . Minot
LG 750 . . . . Williston
LG 1326 . . . . Minot
LG 1334 . . . . Fargo
LG 1498 . . . . Max
LG 1654 . . . . Hannaford
SLG 249 . . . . Fargo
SLG 303 . . . . Jamestown
SLG 306 . . . . Mandan
SLG 1280 . . . . . . Grand Forks
SLG 1481 . . . . Minot
SLG 1524 . . . . Bismarck
SLG 1552 . . . . . . West Fargo

Mine Workers
LU 1101 . . . . Beulah
LU 8957 . . . . Velva

National Staff Organization
LU Staff Organization, Professional,
North Dakota Education
Association . . . . . . Dickinson

Painters
LU 1962 . . . . Beulah

Plumbing and Pipe Fitting
LU 300 . . . . Mandan
SA North Dakota Pipe Trades . Fargo

Postal Workers
LU 55 Devils Lake . . . Devils Lake
LU 88 Fargo . . . . Fargo
LU 137 Williston . . . . . Williston
LU 139 Grand Forks . . Grand Forks
LU 154 Jamestown . . . Jamestown
LU 157 Minot . . . . Minot
LU 349 Bismarck-Mandan Area
Local . . . . Bismarck
LU 590 Dickinson . . . . Dickinson
SA North Dakota . . . . Devils Lake

Rural Letter Carriers
LU Barnes County . . . . . Dazey
LU Big Four Unit . . . . . . Minot
LU Capital Tri-Counties . . Bismarck
LU Cass-Traill Counties . . Amenia
LU Dunn-Mercer Counties . . Hazen
LU Eddy-Foster Counties Carrington
LU Frontier Five
Association . . . . . . Dickinson
LU Griggs-Stelle Counties . Binford
LU Lake Region Four Unit . Brocket
LU McLean County . . . . Wilton
LU Missouri Slope
Counties . . . . Bismarck

LU Red River Tri-County
Association . . . . . . Fordville
LU Richland County . . Lidgerwood
LU Stutsman County . . . . Ypsilanti
LU 2 Southeast Four
Counties . . . . Lisbon
LU 12 Peace Garden Unit . Westhope
LU 15 Central Four Unit . . . Harvey
LU 21 Logan-McIntosh
Counties . . . . Wishek
LU 29 Northwest Tri Unit . Williston
SA North Dakota . . . . . Bismarck

Security, Police and Fire Professionals
LU 560 . . . . Park River

Service Employees
LU 52 . . . . Minot
LU 618 Firemen & Oilers . . Mandan

Steelworkers
LU 07-10 . . . . Mandan
LU 07-560 . . . . Gwinner
LU 07-566 . . . . Bismarck
LU 07-663 . . . . Bismarck
LU 07-953 . . . . Jamestown
LU 11-901 . . . . Hebron

Teamsters
LU 116 . . . . Fargo

Theatrical Stage Employees
LU 510 . . . . Fargo

Transportation Communications Union
LG 6440 Mandan . . . . . Bismarck

Transportation Union
LU 525 . . . . West Fargo
LU 887 . . . . Harvey
LU 980 . . . . Enderlin
LU 1059 . . . . Minot
LU 1137 . . . . West Fargo
LU 1344 . . . . Mandan
SLB LO-37 . . . . Bismarck

Treasury Employees
CH 2 . . . . Fargo

Weather Service Employees
BR 03-31 . . . . Bismarck
BR 03-53 . . . . Grand Forks
BR 03-90 . . . . Williston

Unaffiliated Labor Organizations
North Dakota Joint Legislative
Board of Railway Labor FED
73 . . . . Bismarck

Northern Mariana Islands

Affiliated Labor Organizations

Postal Workers
LU 7146 Saipan . . . . Saipan

Ohio

AFL-CIO Trade and Industrial Departments

Building and Construction Trades Department
BCTC Akron Tri-County . . . Akron
BCTC Butler County . . . Hamilton
BCTC Cincinnati . . . . . Cincinnati
BCTC Cleveland . . . . . Cleveland
BCTC Columbus . . . . . Columbus
BCTC Dayton . . . . Dayton
BCTC East Central Ohio. . . Canton
BCTC Lima . . . . Lima
BCTC Muskingum County . . . . Zanesville
BCTC North Central Ohio . . . . Sandusky
BCTC Northwestern Ohio . . Toledo
BCTC Ohio . . . . Columbus
BCTC Upper Ohio Valley . . . . Steubenville
BCTC Western Reserve. . . . . . . Youngstown

Maritime Trades Department
PC Cleveland . . . . Cleveland
PC Toledo . . . . Toledo

Metal Trades Department
MTC Atomic Trades & Labor . Ross

Affiliated Labor Organizations

Air Traffic Controllers
LU CAK. . . . . North Canton
LU CLE. . . . . Cleveland
LU CMH . . . . Columbus
LU DAY . . . . Dayton
LU MFD . . . . Mansfield
LU TOL . . . . Swanton
LU YNG . . . . Vienna
LU ZOB . . . . Oberlin

Asbestos Workers
LU 3. . . . . Cleveland
LU 8 . . . . Cincinnati
LU 44 . . . . Columbus
LU 45. . . . . Toledo
LU 79 . . . . Dayton
LU 84 Akron/Youngstown . . Akron

Automobile, Aerospace Workers
C Ashtabula Geauga Lake County CAP . . . . Willowick
C Butler Warren Highland County CAP . . . . Fairfield
C Central Ohio Area CAP . Delaware
C Columbia Mahoning & Trumbull CAP . . . . Warren
C Columbus Franklin County CAP. . . . . Columbus
C Cuyahoga Medina CAP . . . . Cleveland
C Dayton Metropolitan CAP. Dayton
C Defiance Area CAP . . . . Ottawa
C Fostoria Area CAP . . . Fostoria
C Greater Cincinnati CAP . Dayton
C Greater Springfield Area CAP . . . . Springfield
C Lima Troy Area CAP . . . Lima
C Lorain County CAP . . . . . . Sheffield Village
C Ohio State CAP . . . . Maumee

C Portage-Summit CAP . . . . Stow
C Stark Wayne CAP . . . . Canton
C Toledo Area CAP Council. Toledo
C Tri County Area CAP. . Sandusky
C UAW Southeastern Ohio CAP Council . . . . Byesville
LU . . . . Medina
LU 12. . . . . Toledo
LU 14. . . . . Toledo
LU 70 . . . . Bedford
LU 86 . . . . Napoleon
LU 91 . . . . Cleveland
LU 101 . . . . Elyria
LU 105 . . . . Wapakoneta
LU 118 . . . . Norton
LU 122 . . . . Twinsburg
LU 128 . . . . Troy
LU 169 . . . . Kent
LU 211 . . . . Defiance
LU 294 . . . . . Cuyahoga Falls
LU 336 . . . . Fostoria
LU 393 . . . . Sandusky
LU 402 . . . . Springfield
LU 420 . . . . Bedford
LU 425 . . . . Lorain
LU 493 . . . . Bellevue
LU 497 . . . . Port Clinton
LU 533 . . . . Fostoria
LU 549 . . . . Mansfield
LU 573 . . . . Streetsboro
LU 638 . . . . Defiance
LU 647 . . . . Cincinnati
LU 658 . . . . Springfield
LU 674 . . . . Fairfield
LU 696 . . . . Dayton
LU 775 . . . . Fostoria
LU 856 . . . . Akron
LU 863 . . . . Cincinnati
LU 877 . . . . Neapolis
LU 886 . . . . Byesville
LU 888 . . . . Dayton
LU 902 . . . . Springfield
LU 913 . . . . Sandusky
LU 959 . . . . Fremont
LU 962 . . . . Spencerville
LU 969 . . . . Columbus
LU 975 . . . . Lima
LU 996 . . . . Elyria
LU 1005 . . . . Parma
LU 1033 . . . . Mount Blanchard
LU 1037 . . . . Heath
LU 1040 . . . . Beavercreek
LU 1050 . . . . Cleveland
LU 1055 . . . . McArthur
LU 1094 . . . . Clinton
LU 1112 . . . . Warren
LU 1120 . . . . Marblehead
LU 1181 . . . . Fayette
LU 1196 . . . . Cleveland
LU 1216 . . . . Sandusky
LU 1219 . . . . Lima
LU 1224 . . . . . . West Liberty
LU 1239 . . . . Wooster
LU 1250 . . . . Brook Park
LU 1327 . . . . Bluffton
LU 1379 . . . . Norwalk
LU 1435 . . . . Perrysburg
LU 1437 . . . . Kenton
LU 1484 . . . . Fostoria
LU 1549 . . . . Logan
LU 1588 . . . . Delaware
LU 1619 . . . . Lodi
LU 1623 . . . . Bellevue
LU 1685 . . . . Gallipolis
LU 1686 . . . . Crooksville

LU 1714 . . . . Lordstown
LU 1765 . . . . Lima
LU 1802 . . . . . . Mount Gilead
LU 1803 . . . . Carey
LU 1825 . . . . Senecaville
LU 1834 . . . . Ashtabula
LU 1842 . . . . Greenfield
LU 1889 . . . . North Baltimore
LU 1892 . . . . Toledo
LU 1935 . . . . Hicksville
LU 1939 . . . . . . Mount Vernon
LU 1957 . . . . Sandusky
LU 1978 Obetz-Columbus Local . . . . Tarlton
LU 2000 . . . . Sheffield Village
LU 2005 . . . . Westerville
LU 2015 . . . . Cleveland
LU 2021 . . . . Tiffin
LU 2024 . . . . Byesville
LU 2029 . . . . Cincinnati
LU 2063 . . . . Bellevue
LU 2075 . . . . Lima
LU 2089 . . . . Archbold
LU 2147 . . . . Lima
LU 2192 . . . . Elyria
LU 2262 . . . . Euclid
LU 2269 . . . . Richwood
LU 2279 . . . . Delphos
LU 2308 . . . . Trenton
LU 2332 . . . . Franklin
LU 2333 . . . . Cleveland
LU 2352 . . . . Milan
LU 2359 Mesa . . . . . Eastlake
LU 2375 . . . . Deshler
LU 2387 . . . . Lebanon
LU 2391 . . . . Minster
LU 2413 . . . . Greenville
LU 2562 . . . . Cleveland
LU 2901 . . . . Girard
LU 3462 . . . . Coshocton
LU 4199 . . . . Salem
LU 4444 Mesa . . . . . Toledo

Bakery, Confectionery, Tobacco Workers and Grain Millers
LU 19 . . . . Cleveland
LU 33-A. . . . . Akron
LU 57 . . . . Columbus
LU 58-G . . . . Toledo
LU 138-G . . . . Wapakoneta
LU 208-G . . . . Cincinnati
LU 253 . . . . Cincinnati
LU 256-G . . . . Lebanon
LU 294-G . . . . Fremont
LU 336-G . . . . Delphos
LU 382-G . . . . Minster

Boilermakers
C State of Ohio 'Buckeye' Industrial. . . . . Canton
LG National Transient Lodge. . . . . Maumee
LU 2-M. . . . . Maumee
LG 3-M . . . . East Cleveland
LG 4-P . . . . Youngstown
LG 68-M . . . . Cincinnati
LG 85. . . . . Rossford
LG 105 . . . . Piketon
LG 106 . . . . Okeana
LG 301-M . . . . Bryan
LG 337-D Cement Workers . . . . Sandusky
LG 357-D Cement Workers . . . . Fairborn

LG 375-D Cement Workers . . . . Paulding
LG 416-D Cement Workers . Lorain
LG 597-D . . . . . . Clay Center
LG 744 . . . . Cleveland
LG 900 . . . . Barberton
LG 908 . . . . Wooster
LG 1073 . . . . . North Olmsted
LG 1086. . . . . Parma
LG 1603. . . . . Alliance
LG 1610 . . . . Beallsville
LG 1622 . . . . Minerva
LG 1664. . . . Warrensville Heights
LG 1666 . . . . . Huber Heights
LG 1667 . . . . Marion
LG 1702. . . . . Alliance
LG 1704 . . . . Cleveland

Bricklayers
DC Northern Ohio . . . . . Middleburg Heights
DC 96 Southern Ohio . . . Columbus
LU 1 . . . . Defiance
LU 2 . . . . Cincinnati
LU 3 . . . . Toledo
LU 5. . . . . Cleveland
LU 6 . . . . Canton
LU 6 Apprenticeship Fund . . Canton
LU 7 . . . . Akron
LU 7 . . . . Ironton
LU 8 . . . . Youngstown
LU 9 . . . . Bellaire
LU 10 . . . . East Liverpool
LU 16 . . . . Mentor
LU 18 . . . . Cincinnati
LU 22 . . . . Dayton
LU 32. . . . . Pomeroy
LU 35. . . . . Lima
LU 36 Tile Layers. . . . . Cleveland
LU 39 . . . . . . West Portsmouth
LU 40 . . . . Mansfield
LU 43 . . . . Warren
LU 44 . . . . Zanesville
LU 45 . . . Washington Court House
LU 46 . . . . Fremont
LU 52. . . . . Athens
LU 55 . . . . Columbus

Carpenters
C Ohio & Vicinity Regional Council . . . . Cleveland
LU 2 . . . . New Vienna
LU 21 . . . . Cleveland
LU 69 . . . . Akron
LU 95 . . . . Mentor
LU 104 . . . . Dayton
LU 113 . . . . Middletown
LU 126 . . . . Cincinnati
LU 171 . . . . Youngstown
LU 186 . . . . Steubenville
LU 200 . . . . Columbus
LU 212 . . . . Cleveland
LU 248 . . . . Rossford
LU 305 . . . . Norwalk
LU 356 . . . . Marietta
LU 372 . . . . Lima
LU 415 . . . . Cleves
LU 437 . . . . Portsmouth
LU 509 . . . . Cleveland
LU 639 . . . . Hartville
LU 650 . . . . Pomeroy
LU 684 . . . . Tipp City
LU 698 . . . . Lebanon
LU 712 . . . . Springfield
LU 735 . . . . Mansfield

LU 940. . . . . Sandusky
LU 1066. . . . . Monroe
LU 1138 . . . . Rossford
LU 1241 Millwright . . . Columbus
LU 1359 . . . . Perrysburg
LU 1365 . . . . Rossford
LU 1393 . . . . Rossford
LU 1519 Millwright & Machinery
   Erectors . . . . South Point
LU 1542 . . . . Fairview Park
LU 1581 . . . . Napoleon
LU 1871 . . . . Cleveland
LU 2077 . . . . Columbus
LU 2239 . . . . Fremont
LU 2380 . . . . Forest Park
LU 2420 . . . . Newark
LU 2506 . . . . Marion
LU 2540 . . . . Wilmington

Catholic School Teachers
LU 3504 . . . . Youngstown

Communications Workers
CONF General Motors . . Kettering
LU 724 District 14 . . . Youngstown
LU 4300 . . . . Canfield
LU 4302 . . . . Akron
LU 4309 . . . . Cleveland
LU 4310 . . . . Columbus
LU 4318 . . . . St. Clairsville
LU 4319 . . . . Rossford
LU 4320 . . . . Columbus
LU 4321 . . . . Zanesville
LU 4322 . . . . Dayton
LU 4323 . . . . Rawson
LU 4325 . . . . Lancaster
LU 4326 . . . . Springfield
LU 4340 . . . . Cleveland
LU 4352 . . . . Toledo
LU 4370 . . . . Lorain
LU 4371 . . . . Marion
LU 4372 . . . . Portsmouth
LU 4373 . . . . . . Mingo Junction
LU 4375 . . . . Athens
LU 4377 . . . . Celina
LU 4378 . . . . Bryan
LU 4379 . . . . Sylvania
LU 4385 . . . . . New Philadelphia
LU 4386 . . . . Urbana
LU 4390 . . . . Cleveland
LU 4400 . . . . Cincinnati
LU 4401 . . . . Cincinnati
LU 4404 . . . . Vandalia
LU 4470 . . . . Maumee
LU 4471 . . . . Pataskala
LU 4473 . . . . Bellefontaine
LU 4474 . . . . Smithville
LU 4475 . . . . Warren
LU 4484 . . . . Middleburg Heights
LU 4485 . . . . Elyria
LU 4487 . . . . Newark
LU 4488 . . . . Quaker City
LU 4501 . . . . Columbus
LU 4510 . . . . Portsmouth
LU 4527 . . . . Wintersville
LU 14323 . . . . Ironton
LU 14514 . . . . Akron
LU 14516 . . . . Cambridge
LU 14517 . . . . Canton
LU 14519 . . . . Cincinnati
LU 14522 Coshocton Typographical
   364 . . . . Coshocton
LU 14526 . . . . Shadyside
LU 14529 . . . . Niles
LU 14532 . . . . Sandusky
LU 14535 . . . . Toledo
LU 14537 . . . . Lisbon
LU 34001 . . . . . Brooklyn Heights

LU 34009 . . . . Cincinnati
LU 34011 . . . . Youngstown
LU 34043 Toledo Newspaper
   Guild/CWA . . . . Toledo
LU 34157 . . . . Dayton
LU 54042 NABET Local
   42 . . . . Massillon
LU 54047 . . . . Youngstown
LU 84689 . . . . Dayton
LU 84692 . . . . . Newcomerstown
LU 84704 . . . . Bucyrus
LU 84705 . . . . Dover
LU 84707 . . . . Cleveland
LU 84708 . . . . Mansfield
LU 84710 . . . . Jacksontown
LU 84715 . . . . Cleveland
LU 84716 . . . . Warren
LU 84717 . . . . Warren
LU 84719 . . . . Mansfield
LU 84722 . . . . Warren
LU 84725 . . . . Sidney
LU 84726 . . . . Lima
LU 84727 . . . . Cortland
LU 84729 . . . . Cincinnati
LU 84734 . . . . Youngstown
LU 84737 . . . . Euclid
LU 84742 . . . . Lima
LU 84745 . . . . Columbus
LU 84749 . . . . Tiffin
LU 84750 . . . . Alliance
LU 84755 . . . . Dayton
LU 84757 . . . . Cincinnati
LU 84758 . . . . Moraine
LU 84765 . . . . Cincinnati
LU 84768 . . . . Riverside
LU 84771 . . . . . Yellow Springs
LU 84773 IUE-CWA . . . Cincinnati
LU 84774 . . . . Norwood
LU 84775 . . . . Dayton
LU 84778 . . . . Cleveland
LU 84797 . . . . Dayton
LU 84798 . . . . Dayton
LU 84801 . . . . Kettering
LU 82-670 . . . . Chesapeake
STC Ohio . . . . Rossford

Education
SA Ohio Education
   Association . . . . . . Columbus

Electrical Workers
BD Ohio State Electrical
   Utility . . . . Rossford
LU 8 . . . . Rossford
LU 32 . . . . Lima
LU 38 . . . . Cleveland
LU 39 . . . . Cleveland
LU 64 . . . . Youngstown
LU 71 . . . . Galloway
LU 82 Electrical Workers IBEW
   AFL-CIO . . . . Dayton
LU 129 . . . . Lorain
LU 212 . . . . Cincinnati
LU 245 . . . . Rossford
LU 246 . . . . Steubenville
LU 306 . . . . Akron
LU 392 . . . . Greenville
LU 540 . . . . Massillon
LU 573 . . . . Warren
LU 575 . . . . Portsmouth
LU 578 . . . . Chillicothe
LU 648 . . . . Hamilton
LU 673 . . . . Mentor
LU 683 . . . . Columbus
LU 688 . . . . Mansfield
LU 696 . . . . Steubenville
LU 774 . . . . North Bend
LU 912 . . . . Mentor

LU 972 . . . . Reno
LU 986 . . . . Norwalk
LU 998 . . . . Vermilion
LU 1047 . . . . Perrysburg
LU 1105 . . . . Nashport
LU 1108 . . . . Greenwich
LU 1194 . . . . Milan
LU 1206 . . . . Nashport
LU 1224 . . . . Cincinnati
LU 1266 . . . . New Lebanon
LU 1347 . . . . Cincinnati
LU 1377 . . . . Cleveland
LU 1413 . . . . Oak Harbor
LU 1466 . . . . Columbus
LU 1507 . . . . Hudson
LU 1587 . . . . Pomeroy
LU 1643 . . . . Upper Sandusky
LU 1691 . . . . Bellefontaine
LU 1740 . . . . Urbana
LU 1825 . . . . Ross
LU 1842 . . . . Goshen
LU 1853 . . . . Newark
LU 1977 . . . . Tipp City
LU 1985 . . . . North Canton
LU 1996 . . . . Warren
LU 2020 . . . . Reynoldsburg
LU 2172 . . . . Bellevue
LU 2287 . . . . Oxford
LU 2303 . . . . Akron
LU 2359 . . . . Ashville

**Electrical, Radio and Machine
Workers**
DC 7 . . . . Yellow Springs
LU 704 . . . . Loveland
LU 705 . . . . Warren
LU 707 . . . . North Royalton
LU 712 Kenyon Maintenance Skilled
   Trades . . . . Bellville
LU 714 . . . . Sandusky
LU 715 . . . . Edon
LU 731 . . . . Ashtabula
LU 751 . . . . Niles
LU 766 . . . . Wapakoneta
LU 767 . . . . Yellow Springs
LU 792 . . . . Fairborn

Elevator Constructors
LU 11 . . . . Cincinnati
LU 17 . . . . Cleveland
LU 37 . . . . Grove City
LU 44 . . . . Toledo

Engineers
C NASA . . . . Cleveland
LU 7 . . . . Columbus

Farm Labor Committee
NHQ . . . . Toledo

Federal Employees
LU 75 . . . . Cincinnati
LU 2062 National Park
   Services . . . . Akron

Fire Fighters
LU 88-F . . . . Fairborn
LU 154-F . . . . Vienna

Food and Commercial Workers
C Chemical Workers Council . Akron
LU 7-A . . . . Cincinnati
LU 17-A . . . . Canton
LU 20-C . . . . . New Philadelphia
LU 32-D . . . . Cincinnati
LU 73-C . . . . Elyria
LU 83-I . . . . Portage
LU 207-C . . . . . Cuyahoga Falls

LU 343-C . . . . Caldwell
LU 418-C . . . . . Maple Heights
LU 419-C . . . . Mogadore
LU 501-C . . . . Blanchester
LU 554-C . . . . Cleveland
LU 560-C . . . . Akron
LU 561-C . . . . Fairfield
LU 776-C . . . . Circleville
LU 838-C . . . . Broadview Heights
LU 852-C . . . . Elyria
LU 880 . . . . Cleveland
LU 911 . . . . Holland
LU 1020-C . . . . Akron
LU 1033-C . . . . Akron
LU 1034-C . . . . Akron
LU 1059 . . . . Columbus
LU 1099 . . . . Monroe

**Glass, Molders, Pottery and
Plastics Workers**
CONBD Ohio . . . . East Liverpool
LU 7-A . . . . Tiffin
LU 45-B . . . . Columbus
LU 51 . . . . Defiance
LU 59 . . . . Toledo
LU 68-B . . . . Fairfield
LU 73 . . . . Euclid
LU 105 . . . . Nashport
LU 123 . . . . Union City
LU 127 . . . . Fairfield
LU 152 . . . . Yorkville
LU 159 . . . . Philo
LU 164 . . . . Howard
LU 170 . . . . Cincinnati
LU 172 . . . . Zanesville
LU 178 . . . . Zanesville
LU 191 . . . . Somerset
LU 207-A . . . . Roseville
LU 235 . . . . Laurelville
LU 241 . . . . East Palestine
LU 244 . . . . Newark
LU 249 . . . . . . New Lexington
LU 288 . . . . Pickerington
LU 292 . . . . Zanesville
LU 304 . . . . Carey
LU 314 . . . . Nashport
LU 333-A . . . . Wellsville
LU 343 . . . . New Bremen
LU 380-A . . . . Minerva
LU 384 . . . . Columbiana
LU 389 . . . . Newark
LU 417 . . . . East Liverpool
LU 419 . . . . East Liverpool

Government Employees
C 164 Guard-Reserve
   Technician . . . . . . Walbridge
C 172 Defense Commissary
   Agency . . . . . . Huber Heights
C 214 National AFLC
   Locals . . . . Wright-Patterson Air
                  Force Base
C 262 . . . . Dayton
LU 31 VAMC . . . . . Brecksville
LU 43 IAEP . . . . Akron
LU 519 USDA . . . . Huron
LU 600 . . . . Mason
LU 601 . . . . Dayton
LU 602 . . . . Lima
LU 604 . . . . Cleveland
LU 605 . . . . Cleveland
LU 607 . . . . Elkton
LU 1138 DoD . . . . Dayton
LU 1148 DoD . . . . . . Columbus
LU 1631 VA . . . . . . Chillicothe
LU 1952 DoD . . . . Vienna
LU 2031 VA . . . . Cincinnati
LU 2083 USDA . . . . . Cincinnati

Government Security Officers

LU 2089 DoL . . . . . . Columbus
LU 2182 NASA . . . . . Cleveland
LU 2187 DoD . . . . Bellaire
LU 2209 VA . . . . Dayton
LU 2221 DoD . . . . Heath
LU 2660 DoJ . . . . . . Cleveland
LU 2823 VA . . . . Cleveland
LU 2835 USDA . . . . . . Sardinia
LU 3283 DoD . . . . . . Cleveland
LU 3435 HUD . . . . . . Columbus
LU 3448 HHS . . . . . Painesville
LU 3701 HUD . . . . . Cleveland
LU 3840 HHS . . . . . Cincinnati
LU 3924 . . . . Chillicothe
LU 3970 Ohio Air and Army
   National Guard . . . . . Gahanna

Government Security Officers

LU 56 . . . . Cleveland
LU 114 . . . . Miamisburg
LU 127 . . . . Circleville
LU 137 Cincinnati . . . . Cincinnati
LU 231 . . . . Rawson

Graphic Communications

DC 3 Cincinnati . . . . . Cincinnati
LU 42-C . . . . Rootstown
LU 62-C . . . . Brice
LU 205-C . . . . Youngstown
LU 508-M . . . . Cincinnati
LU 544-C Offset Workers of Canton
   and Vicinity . . . . Canton
LU 546-M . . . . Cleveland
LU 566-M . . . . Fostoria
LU 638-S . . . . Poland
LU 731-S . . . . Norwalk
LU 789-S . . . . Shelby

Independent Unions

LU 5 Zanesville Armco Independent
   Organization . . . . . . Zanesville
LU 239 United Electro-Medical
   Workers . . . . Cincinnati

Iron Workers

DC Southern Ohio &
   Vicinity . . . . Franklin
LU 17 . . . . Cleveland
LU 44 . . . . Cincinnati
LU 55 . . . . Toledo
LU 172 . . . . Columbus
LU 207 . . . . Youngstown
LU 290 . . . . Dayton
LU 372 . . . . Cincinnati
LU 468 . . . . Cleveland
LU 522 . . . . Cincinnati
LU 550 . . . . Canton
LU 778 . . . . Lima
LU 820 . . . . Fredericktown

Laborers

DC Ohio . . . . Westerville
LU 83 . . . . Portsmouth
LU 125 . . . . Youngstown
LU 134 . . . . Newcomerstown
LU 141 Industrial & Service
   Employees . . . . Dayton
LU 245 . . . . North Kingsville
LU 265 . . . . Cincinnati
LU 310 . . . . Cleveland
LU 329 . . . . Lima
LU 423 . . . . Columbus
LU 480 . . . . Sandusky
LU 500 . . . . Toledo
LU 513 . . . . Winchester
LU 530 . . . . Zanesville
LU 534 . . . . Middletown
LU 574 . . . . Marion

LU 639 . . . . Marietta
LU 758 . . . . Lorain
LU 809 . . . . Steubenville
LU 860 . . . . Cleveland
LU 894 . . . . Akron
LU 935 . . . . Warren
LU 1015 . . . . Canton
LU 1216 . . . . Mansfield
LU 1410 . . . . Dayton

Letter Carriers

BR 40 . . . . Cleveland
BR 43 . . . . Cincinnati
BR 45 . . . . Springfield
BR 63 . . . . Zanesville
BR 66 . . . . St. Clairsville
BR 78 . . . . Columbus
BR 100 . . . . Toledo
BR 105 . . . . Lima
BR 118 . . . . Mansfield
BR 123 . . . . Piqua
BR 140 . . . . Ironton
BR 143 . . . . Findlay
BR 148 . . . . Akron
BR 154 . . . . Marietta
BR 164 . . . . Steubenville
BR 174 . . . . Norwalk
BR 182 . . . . Dayton
BR 184 . . . . Portsmouth
BR 196 . . . . Elyria
BR 238 . . . . Canton
BR 279 . . . . Fostoria
BR 280 . . . . Marion
BR 281 . . . . Newark
BR 288 . . Washington Court House
BR 297 . . . . Alliance
BR 298 . . . . Mount Vernon
BR 307 . . . . Urbana
BR 340 . . . . Bremen
BR 385 . . . . Youngstown
BR 413 . . . . Tiffin
BR 426 . . . . Hamilton
BR 452 . . . . Chillicothe
BR 465 . . . . Bellefontaine
BR 470 . . . . Defiance
BR 480 . . . . Wooster
BR 482 . . . . Ashtabula
BR 549 . . . . Painesville
BR 583 . . . . Lorain
BR 634 . . . . Cambridge
BR 647 . . . . Coshocton
BR 648 . . . . Van Wert
BR 711 . . . . . . New Philadelphia
BR 714 . . . . Bellaire
BR 721 . . . . Ashland
BR 800 . . . . Niles
BR 829 . . . . Greenfield
BR 897 . . . . Barberton
BR 898 . . . . Dover
BR 997 . . . . Athens
BR 1002 . . . . St. Marys
BR 1061 . . . . Martins Ferry
BR 1137 . . . . Bellevue
BR 1149 . . . . Xenia
BR 1224 . . . . Wellston
BR 1240 . . . . Uhrichsville
BR 1252 . . . . Jackson
BR 1354 . . . . Barnesville
BR 1380 . . . . Cadiz
BR 1387 . . . . West Chester
BR 1424 . . . . Gallipolis
BR 1460 . . . . Upper Sandusky
BR 1571 . . . . Logan
BR 1629 . . . . Cuyahoga Falls
BR 1634 . . . . Wadsworth
BR 1687 . . . . New London
BR 1716 . . . . Mount Gilead
BR 2017 . . . . Newcomerstown

BR 2055 . . . . Bradford
BR 2056 . . . . Covington
BR 2199 . . . . Carey
BR 2201 . . . . Leipsic
BR 2221 . . . . Toronto
BR 2238 . . . . Hicksville
BR 2250 . . . . Richwood
BR 2308 . . . . Paulding
BR 2537 . . . . Caldwell
BR 2575 . . . . . . New Lexington
BR 2618 . . . . Minerva
BR 2644 . . . . New Bremen
BR 2678 . . . . Pomeroy
BR 2754 . . . . Middleport
BR 2760 . . . . Shadyside
BR 2763 . . . . Byesville
BR 2969 . . . . Mingo Junction
BR 3095 . . . . Cardington
BR 3188 . . . . Manchester
BR 3422 . . . . Spencerville
BR 3433 . . . . Camden
BR 3437 . . . . Vermilion
BR 3440 . . . . Sabina
BR 3443 . . . . Dunkirk
BR 3497 . . . . Bluffton
BR 3595 . . . . Carrollton
BR 3688 . . . . Willowick
BR 3823 . . . . St. Clairsville
BR 3948 . . . . Cleves
BR 3999 . . . . Fredericktown
BR 4195 . . . . Mentor
BR 4343 . . . . Belpre
BR 4408 . . . . Lucas
BR 4592 . . . . Mechanicsburg
BR 4804 . . . . Ravenna
BR 5081 . . . . Jeffersonville
BR 5234 . . . . Peebles
BR 5401 . . . . Ashville
BR 5426 . . . . Chesapeake
BR 5698 . . . . Garrettsville
BR 5699 . . . . Baltimore
BR 5726 . . . . Bremen
BR 5727 . . . . Tiltonsville
BR 5728 . . . . Yorkville
BR 5729 . . . . Brilliant
BR 5730 . . . . Oak Hill
BR 5732 . . . . . West Alexandria
BR 6018 . . . . Brewster
BR 6071 . . . . West Lafayette
BR 6117 . . . . Johnstown
BR 6280 . . . . Roseville
BR 6501 . . . . West Union
BR 6520 . . . . Uniontown
BR 6597 . . . . Lakeside Marblehead
SA Ohio . . . . Akron

Locomotive Engineers

DIV 3 . . . . Medina
DIV 4 . . . . Perrysburg
DIV 34 . . . . Bremen
DIV 36 . . . . St. Louisville
DIV 79 . . . . Columbus
DIV 95 . . . . Cincinnati
DIV 234 . . . . Hilliard
DIV 257 . . . . Columbus
DIV 260 . . . . Geneva
DIV 273 . . . . Conneaut
DIV 281 . . . . Lima
DIV 282 . . . . Springdale
DIV 292 . . . . Brewster
DIV 306 . . . . Loudonville
DIV 447 . . . . Bellevue
DIV 457 . . . . Sylvania
DIV 480 . . . . Cincinnati
DIV 481 . . . . Marietta
DIV 511 . . . . Portsmouth
DIV 526 . . . . Brewster
DIV 565 . . . . Youngstown

DIV 607 . . . . . . North Royalton
DIV 678 . . . . Harrod
DIV 735 . . . . Minerva
DIV 894 . . . . Westerville
DIV 937 . . . . Millbury
GCA . . . . Lima
NHQ . . . . Cleveland
SLB Ohio . . . . Canton

Longshoremen

C Lake Erie Coal & Ore
   Dock . . . . Oregon
DC Great Lakes . . . . . . Cleveland
LU 153 . . . . Maumee
LU 1317 . . . . Cleveland
LU 1768 . . . . Oregon
LU 1913 . . . . Ashtabula
LU 1982 . . . . Toledo
LU 2000 . . . . Cleveland
LU 2052 . . . . Conneaut

Machinists

CONF Northeastern
   States . . . . New Lebanon
DLG 34 . . . . Columbus
DLG 54 . . . . Cleveland
LG 10-DS . . . . Rocky River
LG 22 . . . . Akron
LG 30-DS . . . . Alliance
LG 55 . . . . Columbus
LG 90 . . . . Mount Vernon
LG 105 . . . . Wauseon
LG 225 . . . . Dayton
LG 233 . . . . Cleveland
LG 244 . . . . Cleveland
LG 427 . . . . Marysville
LG 439 . . . . Cleveland
LG 523 . . . . Spencer
LG 584 . . . . Williamsfield
LG 813 . . . . New London
LG 912 . . . . Monroe
LG 956 . . . . Stryker
LG 986 . . . . McConnelsville
LG 1019 . . . . Alliance
LG 1042 . . . . Wauseon
LG 1130 . . . . Cleveland
LG 1151 . . . . Galion
LG 1203 . . . . Kent
LG 1210 . . . . Pemberville
LG 1234 . . . . Zanesville
LG 1280 . . . . Newark
LG 1285 . . . . Dover
LG 1297 . . . . Ashland
LG 1320 . . . . Columbus
LG 1329 . . . . Wauseon
LG 1346 . . . . Wauseon
LG 1347 . . . . Bellevue
LG 1349 . . . . Bryan
LG 1356 . . . . Wauseon
LG 1363 . . . . Cleveland
LG 1471 . . . . Columbus
LG 1539 . . . . South Amherst
LG 1581 . . . . Wooster
LG 1628 . . . . Zanesville
LG 1711 . . . . Sandusky
LG 1731 . . . . Cleveland
LG 1802 . . . . Vermilion
LG 1825 . . . . Medina
LG 1849 . . . . Elyria
LG 2050 . . . . West Lafayette
LG 2159 . . . . Wauseon
LG 2276 . . . . Urbana
LG 2334 Wright Lodge . . . Dayton
LG 2339-C Cleveland Inflight
   Aircraft Lodge . . . . . Cleveland
LG 2475 . . . . Newcomerstown
LG 2535 . . . . Middletown
LG 2787 . . . . Springfield

LG 2794 . . . . Gambier
LG 2910 . . . . Dalton
STC Ohio . . . . Cleveland

Maintenance of Way Employes
FED Nickel Plate-Wheeling & Lake
  Erie . . . . Oregon
LG 424 . . . . Hamilton
LG 499 . . . . Reedsville
LG 532 . . . . Delaware
LG 535 . . . . Peebles
LG 885 . . . . Cincinnati
LG 1047 . . . . Sardis
LG 1234 . . . . Salem
LG 1595 . . . . Ashland
LG 1650 . . . . Geneva
LG 1900 . . . . Loudonville
LG 1978 . . . . Dayton
LG 2307 . . . . Scion
LG 2705 . . . . Defiance
LG 2742 . . . . Portsmouth
LG 3016 . . . . Ashtabula
LG 3073 . . . . Wintersville
LG 3080 . . . . Uhrichsville
SF Consolidated Rail . . Port Clinton
SLG 267 . . . . Carey
SLG 566 . . . . Lucasville
SLG 580 . . . . Ironton
SLG 698 . . . . Reynoldsburg
SLG 741 . . . . Marietta
SLG 838 . . . . Zanesville
SLG 888 . . . . Pioneer
SLG 1037 . . . . Toledo
SLG 1264 . . . . Mansfield
SLG 1315 . . . . Hillsboro
SLG 1376 . . . . Willard
SLG 1377 . . . . Columbus Grove
SLG 1396 . . . . Port Clinton
SLG 1432 . . . . Akron
SLG 1562 . . . . Westerville
SLG 1657 . . . . South Euclid
SLG 1664 . . . . Oregon
SLG 1679 . . . . Navarre
SLG 1975 . . . . Greenville
SLG 2624 . . . . Millbury
SLG 3007 . . . . Canfield
SLG 3017 . . . . Greenville
SLG 3018 . . . . Cambridge
SLG 3027 . . . . Wellsville
SLG 3061 . . . . Gahanna

Mine Workers
LU 283 . . . . Cadiz
LU 310 . . . . Cambridge
LU 892 . . . . Langsville
LU 911 . . . . Gallipolis
LU 1188 . . . . Coshocton
LU 1304 . . . . Hopedale
LU 1340 . . . . Trimble
LU 1360 . . . . Adena
LU 1366 . . . . Trinway
LU 1506 . . . . Dillonvale
LU 1604 . . . . Duncan Falls
LU 1785 . . . . Bellaire
LU 1810 . . . . Barnesville
LU 1818 . . . . Dresden
LU 1857 . . . . Chester
LU 2262 . . . . Shadyside
LU 4994 . . . . Sherrodsville
LU 5400 District 17 . . . . Cheshire
LU 5400 District 17 . . . . Gallipolis
LU 5497 . . . . Bellaire
LU 6989 . . . . New Lexington
LU 7690 . . . . Cadiz
LU 9695 . . . . St. Clairsville

Musicians
LU 1 . . . . Cincinnati

LU 4 Cleveland Area
  Local . . . . Cleveland
LU 15-286 . . . . Toledo
LU 24 . . . . Stow
LU 31 . . . . Fairfield
LU 86-242 . . . . . . Youngstown
LU 101-473 . . . . Dayton
LU 103 . . . . Columbus
LU 111 Canton . . . . . . Canton
LU 118 . . . . Warren
LU 159 . . . . Mansfield
LU 160 . . . . Springfield
LU 179 . . . . Marietta
LU 320 . . . . Lima
LU 482 . . . . Wheelersburg
LU 657 . . . . Willowick

National Staff Organization
LU Staff Union, Professional,
  Ohio Education
  Association . . . . . Westerville
LU Staff Union/NSO, Association,
  Ohio . . . . Columbus

NLRB Professional Association
LU 8 . . . . Cleveland
LU 9 . . . . Cincinnati

Nurses
LU Ohio Nurses
  Association . . . . . . Cincinnati
LU Ohio Nurses Association Alliance
  Local Union Unit . East Rochester
SA Ohio Nurses
  Association . . . . . Columbus
UNIT Hillside Nurses
  Association . . . . . . Warren
UNIT Little Forest Medical Center
  Nursing Home . . . . Boardman
UNIT Logan County Hi-Point
  23 . . . . Bellefontaine
UNIT Ohio Geneva Nurses
  Association . . . . . Geneva
UNIT Ohio Nurses Association Allen
  Memorial Hospital . . . Lagrange
UNIT Ohio Nurses Association
  Ashtabula General . . . Ashtabula
UNIT Ohio Nurses Association PHN
  of CCBH . . . . . Strongsville
UNIT Ohio Nurses Association
  PPU St. Vincent
  Hospital . . . . . North Royalton
UNIT Ohio Professional Staff Nurses
  Association . . . . Akron
UNIT Ohio-CCMH Local RNA
  Unit . . . . Coshocton
UNIT Registered Nurse Coshocton
  County Memorial
  Hospital . . . . . . Coshocton
UNIT Salem Community Hospital
  Registered Nurses . . . . Salem
UNIT Visiting Nurse Service of
  Toledo . . . . Toledo
UNIT Youngstown General Duty
  (Ohio) . . . . . . Youngstown

Office and Professional Employees
LU 17 . . . . Parma
LU 19 . . . . Toledo
LU 98 . . . . Cincinnati
LU 339 . . . . Kent
LU 375 . . . . Cincinnati
LU 422 . . . . Chillicothe
LU 502 . . . . Oberlin
LU 514 . . . . Custar
LU 1313 . . . . Cincinnati
LU 1313 . . . . Oberlin
LU 1794 . . . . Cleveland

Operating Engineers
LU 18 . . . . Cleveland
LU 20 . . . . Cincinnati

Painters
DC 6 . . . . Strongsville
DC 12 . . . . Cincinnati
LU 7 . . . . Toledo
LU 50 . . . . Cincinnati
LU 128 . . . . Westlake
LU 181 . . . . Cleveland
LU 240 . . . . Elyria
LU 249 . . . . Dayton
LU 308 . . . . Hamersville
LU 356 . . . . Zanesville
LU 372 . . . . Pataskala
LU 387 . . . . Cincinnati
LU 406 . . . . Mansfield
LU 438 . . . . Steubenville
LU 476 . . . . Youngstown
LU 505 . . . . Washington
LU 555 . . . . Portsmouth
LU 603 . . . . Canton
LU 639 . . . . Strongsville
LU 765 . . . . Chesterland
LU 788 . . . . Sandusky
LU 841 . . . . Akron
LU 847 . . . . Youngstown
LU 867 . . . . Strongsville
LU 948 . . . . Toledo
LU 1020 . . . . Lima
LU 1103 . . . . Madison
LU 1162 . . . . Akron
LU 1275 . . . . Columbus

Plant Protection
LU 107 Cleveland Plants
  Unit . . . . Maple Heights
LU 108 Lima Plants Unit . . . Lima
LU 110 Lorain Plants Unit . Amherst
LU 111 Batavia Unit . . . . . Goshen
LU 112 Cleveland Casting Plants
  Unit . . . . Maple Heights

Plasterers and Cement Masons
LU 80 . . . . Cleveland
LU 109 . . . . Akron
LU 132 . . . . Washington
LU 179 . . . . Youngstown
LU 404 . . . . Cleveland
LU 886 . . . . Toledo
STCON
  Ohio . . Washington Court House

Plumbing and Pipe Fitting
LU 42 . . . . Norwalk
LU 50 . . . . Northwood
LU 55 . . . . Cleveland
LU 94 . . . . Canton
LU 120 . . . . Cleveland
LU 162 . . . . Dayton
LU 168 . . . . Marietta
LU 189 Plumbers and Pipe
  Fitters . . . . Columbus
LU 219 . . . . Akron
LU 392 . . . . Cincinnati
LU 396 . . . . Boardman
LU 495 . . . . Cambridge
LU 577 . . . . Portsmouth
LU 711 . . . . Westerville
LU 776 . . . . Lima
SA Ohio . . . . Westerville

Postal and Federal Employees
LU 601 . . . . Dayton
LU 603 . . . . Cincinnati
LU 604 . . . . Cleveland
LU 605 . . . . Columbus

LU 611 . . . . Toledo

Postal Mail Handlers
LU 304 . . . . Cincinnati

Postal Workers
LU Dayton Area . . . . . . Dayton
LU 72 Cleveland Area . . Cleveland
LU 120 Akron Area . . . . . Akron
LU 135 Defiance . . . . . Defiance
LU 164 Greater Cincinnati Ohio
  Area . . . . Cincinnati
LU 170 Toledo . . . . Toledo
LU 193 Steubenville . . Steubenville
LU 232 Columbus . . . Columbus
LU 315 Lorain County Area . Elyria
LU 318 Portsmouth . . . Portsmouth
LU 438 Lima . . . . Lima
LU 443 Youngstown . . Youngstown
LU 524 Canton . . . . . . Canton
LU 535 Zanesville . . . . Zanesville
LU 556 Cambridge . . . Cambridge
LU 603 Newark . . . . . . Newark
LU 872 Willoughby . . Willoughby
LU 903 Mansfield . . . . Mansfield
LU 1180 Ironton . . . . . Ironton
LU 1204 Lake Geauga Area . Mentor
LU 1268 Marietta . . . . . Marietta
LU 1399 Bryan . . . . . . Bryan
LU 1471 Geneva . . . . . Geneva
LU 1821 Wapakoneta . Wapakoneta
LU 1963 Cuyahoga
  Falls . . . . . . Cuyahoga Falls
LU 2360 Mogadore . . . Mogadore
LU 2548 Ravenna . . . . Ravenna
LU 2558 South Central Ohio
  Area . . . . Chillicothe
LU 2824 Ashtabula . . Ashtabula
LU 2836 Gallipolis . . . Gallipolis
LU 3120 St. Clairsville . St. Clairsville
LU 3291 Fostoria . . . . . Fostoria
LU 3352 Wickliffe . . . . Wickliffe
LU 3812 Martins Ferry . Bridgeport
LU 3913 Kenton . . . . . . Kenton
LU 3957 Findlay . . . . . . Findlay
LU 3972 Springfield, Ohio
  Local . . . . Springfield
LU 4743 Athens . . . . . . Athens
LU 4764 Hillsboro . . . . Hillsboro
LU 5705 Urbana . . . . . Urbana
LU 6528 Kent . . . . Kent
LU 6530 Marion . . . . . Marion
LU 6531 Tiffin . . . . . . Tiffin
LU 6691 Tallmadge . . . . Akron
LU 6891 Belpre . . . . Coolville
LU 7038 Tri County Ohio
  Area . . . . Cincinnati
LU 7105 Northfield . . . Northfield
SA Ohio . . . . Dayton

Railroad Signalmen
GC 58 Norfolk & Southern
  Railroad . . . . Bellevue
GC 60 United . . . . . Beavercreek
LLG 10 . . . . Swanton
LLG 35 . . . . Eastlake
LLG 52 . . . . Cincinnati
LLG 64 . . . . Tiro
LLG 94 . . . . Bellville
LLG 109 . . . . Creston
LLG 136 . . . . Chesapeake
LLG 216 . . . . Fostoria
LLG 231 . . . . Strasburg
LLG 237 Wheeling & Lake Erie
  Railroad Locomotive . . . Orrville

Retail, Wholesale and Department Store
LU 379 . . . . Columbus
LU 390 . . . . Cincinnati

Roofers, Waterproofers and Allied Workers
DC Mid-States
Roofers. . . . . Youngstown
LU 42 . . . . Cincinnati
LU 44 . . . . Cleveland
LU 71 . . . . Youngstown
LU 75 . . . . Dayton
LU 86 . . . . Columbus
LU 88 . . . . North Canton
LU 134 . . . . Toledo

Rural Letter Carriers
D 1 . . . . Chesterland
D 2 . . . . Toronto
D 3 . . . . Millersburg
D 4 . . . . Graysville
D 5 . . . . South Point
D 6 . . . . Baltimore
D 7 . . . . Galion
D 8 . . . . Valley City
D 9 . . . . Fostoria
D 10 . . . . Sedalia
D 11 . . . . Winchester
D 12 . . . . Somerville
D 13 . . . . New Bremen
D 14 . . . . Liberty Center
LU Delaware County . . . Delaware
LU Lorain County . . . . Wellington
LU Noble County . . . . Caldwell
LU 3 Ashland County. . . . Ashland
LU 9 Butler County . . . . . Attica
LU 20 Defiance County . . Defiance
SA Ohio . . . . Attica

Security, Police and Fire Professionals
LU 64 . . . . Warren
LU 67 . . . . Canton
LU 122 . . . . Springfield
LU 131 . . . . Sandusky
LU 137 . . . . Toledo
LU 141 . . . . Mansfield
LU 145 . . . . Cleveland
LU 166 . . . . Union

Service Employees
C Central States Building Service
Council . . . . Canfield
DALU 3042 Billposters &
Billers. . . . . . . Olmsted Falls
JC 25 . . . . Columbus
LU 3 . . . . Canfield
LU 85 . . . . Brecksville
LU 101 . . . . East Liverpool
LU 700 Firemen &
Oilers . . . . North Olmsted
LU 1199 NUHHCE, West Virginia/
Kentucky/Ohio . . . . Columbus

Sheet Metal Workers
C Ohio Valley . . . . Toledo
LU 24 . . . . Dayton
LU 33 . . . . Cleveland
LU 183 . . . . Cincinnati
LU 287 . . . . Columbus
LU 368 . . . . Avon Lake

State, County and Municipal Employees
C 8 Ohio . . . . Worthington
LU 4 . . . . Amherst

LU 4 OAPSE Chapter
782 . . . . Chillicothe
LU 4 Ohio Association of Public
School Employees . . . Columbus
LU 11 OCSEA 7820 Trumbull
Corrections Institute
Chapter . . . . Westerville
LU 11 Ohio Civil Service Employees
Association . . . . . Westerville
LU 33 Goshen (OAPSE) . Loveland
LU 101 Dayton Public Service
Union . . . . Dayton
LU 169 OAPSE Local Union 4
Defiance . . . . Defiance
LU 217 Ohio Council 8. . Cincinnati
LU 282 Cincinnati Zoological
Employees . . . . . . Cincinnati
LU 610 Rogus . . . . Canton
LU 684 Akron City Hospital
Employees . . . . Akron
LU 797 . . . . Columbus
LU 1039 Portsmouth City
Employees. . . . . . Portsmouth
LU 1252 O'Bleness Memorial
Hospital Employees . . . . Athens
LU 1881 Professional Personnel,
Association of. . . . Beachwood
LU 2028 Boardman Community Care
Center . . . . Youngstown
LU 2288 Hillside Hospital. . Warren
LU 2317 Barberton Citizens Hospital
Employees . . . . . . Barberton
LU 2804 Trumbull Memorial
Hospital Employees . . . Warren
LU 2934 Ohio Valley
Hospital Association
Employees . . . . . . Steubenville
LU 3098 Lucas County Non-Profit
Agency Employees. . . Walbridge
LU 3357 New York Council
66 . . . . Copley

Steelworkers
C . . . . Elisa
C Ashland Company
Wide . . . . Louisville
LU 530 . . . . Norwood
LU 979 . . . . Cleveland
LU 1493 . . . . Dayton
LU 9478. . . . . Minerva
LU 50634 . . . . Gibsonburg
LU 5-757 . . . . Cincinnati
LU 01-2-L. . . . . Akron
LU 01-4-T . . . . Newark
LU 01-7-L. . . . . Akron
LU 01-8-L . . . . Atwater
LU 01-9 . . . . Perrysburg
LU 01-24-A . . . . Bowling Green
LU 01-25 . . . . Rockbridge
LU 01-45 . . . . Carrollton
LU 01-48-U . . . . . Rocky River
LU 01-50-L . . . . . . Coshocton
LU 01-60 . . . . Lancaster
LU 01-65-T . . . . Toledo
LU 01-73 . . . . Lancaster
LU 01-76-L . . . . Akron
LU 01-87-G . . . . Toledo
LU 01-87-L . . . . Dayton
LU 01-98-L . . . . Warren
LU 01-105-T . . . . St. Louisville
LU 01-121-T . . . . . Zanesville
LU 01-134-S. . . . . . McDermott
LU 01-144. . . . . . . Lancaster
LU 01-156-U . . . . West Chester
LU 01-169-S . . . . . . Mansfield
LU 01-192 . . . . Springfield
LU 01-196-L . . . . Ashland
LU 01-200-L . . . . . . St. Marys

LU 01-207-L. . . . . Findlay
LU 01-241-L . . . . . Green Camp
LU 01-298-L . . . . . . Ravenna
LU 01-302-L . . . . . . Wooster
LU 01-341-S. . . . . Heath
LU 01-418-L. . . . . . Uniontown
LU 01-496-L . . . Newcomerstown
LU 01-502-T . . . . St. Clairsville
LU 01-505. . . . . New Lexington
LU 01-506. . . . . Logan
LU 01-516-T . . . . . Blanchester
LU 01-520 . . . . . . Zanesville
LU 01-521. . . . . . Tuscarawas
LU 01-524-L . . . . . . Mansfield
LU 01-525 . . . . Newark
LU 01-538-B . . . . Stone Creek
LU 01-540 . . . . . . Lancaster
LU 01-550-L . . . . . . Navarre
LU 01-557-L . . . . . . Chardon
LU 01-561 . . . . . . Lancaster
LU 01-563-L . . . . . . Crestline
LU 01-575 . . . . . . Lancaster
LU 01-576 . . . . . . Lancaster
LU 01-577 . . . . . . Lancaster
LU 01-578. . . . . Logan
LU 01-582-L . . . . . Johnstown
LU 01-598 . . . . . . Lancaster
LU 01-600-T . . . . . . Maumee
LU 01-667-L . . . . . Bowerston
LU 01-673-L . . . . . . Bucyrus
LU 01-700-T . . . . . . Toledo
LU 01-725-L . . . . . Union City
LU 01-731-L . . . . . . Akron
LU 01-735-S . . . . . Cleveland
LU 01-820-L . . . . . . Jackson
LU 01-843-L . . . . . Marysville
LU 01-890-L. . . . . West Unity
LU 01-898-L . . . . . Rushsylvania
LU 01-905-L. . . . . . . Geneva
LU 01-931-L. . . . . New London
LU 01-982-L . . . . . Wapakoneta
LU 01-1014-L. . . . . . . Akron
LU 01-1017 . . . . Logan
LU 01-1020-L . . . . . Conneaut
LU 01-1033-T. . . . . . . Hiram
LU 01-1042-L. . . . Bowling Green
LU 01-1045-L . . . . . . Akron
LU 01-1046-S. . . . . . Louisville
LU 01-1104-S. . . . . . . Lorain
LU 01-1117-L. . . . . Marblehead
LU 01-1123-L . . . . Piqua
LU 01-1123-S . . . . . . Canton
LU 01-1124-S . . . . . Massillon
LU 01-1152-L. . . . Bowling Green
LU 01-1170-S . . . . . Wadsworth
LU 01-1179-S . . . . . . Elyria
LU 01-1190-S . . . . . Steubenville
LU 01-1200-S . . . . . . Canton
LU 01-1223-S . . . . . . Yorkville
LU 01-1238-S. . . . . Martins Ferry
LU 01-1331-S . . . . . . Niles
LU 01-1375-S . . . . . . Warren
LU 01-1538-S . . . . . . Salem
LU 01-1618-S . . . . . . Niles
LU 01-1761-S. . . . . . Niles
LU 01-1858-S . . . . . Cincinnati
LU 01-1915-S . . . . . . Clyde
LU 01-1949 . . . . Marion
LU 01-2116-S . . . . New Boston
LU 01-2155-S . . . . . . Niles
LU 01-2163-S . . . . . Lowellville
LU 01-2173-S. . . . . Columbus
LU 01-2211-S . . . . . . Alliance
LU 01-2243-S . . . . . . Fowler
LU 01-2310-S . . . . . Youngstown
LU 01-2324-S . . . . . . Jackson
LU 01-2332-S . . . . . Austintown
LU 01-2342-S . . . . Columbus

LU 01-2345-S . . . . . . Canton
LU 01-2354-S. . . . . . . Lorain
LU 01-2377-S . . New Middletown
LU 01-2463-S . . . . . . Canfield
LU 01-2737-S . . . . . . Dover
LU 01-2887-S . . . . . . Navarre
LU 01-3047-S . . . . . . Niles
LU 01-3057-S. . . . . . Ashland
LU 01-3059-S . . . . . . Alliance
LU 01-3081-S . . . . . Ashtabula
LU 01-3210-S . . . . . . Minster
LU 01-3241-S . . . St. Clairsville
LU 01-3320-S . . . . . . Dayton
LU 01-3372-S. . . . . Columbiana
LU 01-3404-S . . . . . Hamilton
LU 01-3446-S . . . . . Carrollton
LU 01-3523-S . . . . . . Girard
LU 01-3610-S . . . . . . Canton
LU 01-3816-S . . . . . . Salem
LU 01-4195-S . . . . Wintersville
LU 01-4372-S . . . . . Lebanon
LU 01-4427-S . . . . . Hubbard
LU 01-4545-S . . . . . Trotwood
LU 01-4564-S . . . . . . Girard
LU 01-4708-S . . . Junction City
LU 01-4836-S . . . . Sarahsville
LU 01-4839-S. . . . . Coldwater
LU 01-4960-S . . . . Youngstown
LU 01-5000-S . Middleburg Heights
LU 01-5025-S. . . . . . Boardman
LU 01-5154-S . . . . . Campbell
LU 01-5439-S . . . . . Magnolia
LU 01-5541-S . . . . Middletown
LU 01-5644-S . . . . . . Toronto
LU 01-5724-S . . . . . Clarington
LU 01-5760-S . . . . . . Sardis
LU 01-5962-S . . . . . Cortland
LU 01-6037-S . . . . . . Stow
LU 01-6197. . . . . . . Racine
LU 01-6413-S . . . . . . Goshen
LU 01-6463-S . . . . . . Sabina
LU 01-6621-S. . . . . . . Lorain
LU 01-6821-S . . . . . . Salem
LU 01-6931-S . . . . . . Xenia
LU 01-7008-S . . . . . Ashland
LU 01-7014-S . . . . . . Fresno
LU 01-7187-S . . . New Straitsville
LU 01-7248-S . . . . . Montpelier
LU 01-7318-S . . . . . Addyston
LU 01-7334-S . . . . . Austinburg
LU 01-7540-S . . . . . Lexington
LU 01-7620-S . . . . . Greenville
LU 01-7679-S . . . . . Mansfield
LU 01-7697-S. . . . . Cincinnati
LU 01-7993-S. . . . . . Ashville
LU 01-8130-S . . . . . . Negley
LU 01-8316-S . . . . Whitehouse
LU 01-8530-S . . . . . Mansfield
LU 01-8565-S . . . . . Mantua
LU 01-8645-S . . . East Liverpool
LU 01-8772-S . . . . . Litchfield
LU 01-8845-S . . . . . . Elyria
LU 01-8869-S . . . . West Salem
LU 01-9110-S . . . . . Columbus
LU 01-9126-S . . . . . Cleveland
LU 01-9130-S . . . . . Crestline
LU 01-9187-S . . . . . . Canton
LU 01-9306-S . . . . . . Warren
LU 01-9309-S . . . . . . Carroll
LU 01-9354. . . . . Garrettsville
LU 01-9401-S . . . . . Struthers
LU 01-9419 . . . . Powhatan Point
LU 01-9433 . . . . . . Bocryus
LU 01-9456 . . . . . . Trotwood
LU 01-12049-S . . . . . Cincinnati
LU 01-12081 . . . . . . Creston
LU 01-12319-S . . . . Steubenville
LU 01-12833-S. . . . . Painesville

LU 01-12965-S . . . . . Gibsonburg
LU 01-13029-S . . . . . Van Wert
LU 01-13656-S . . . . . . Toronto
LU 01-13983-S . . . . . . Yorkville
LU 01-14362-S. . . Maple Heights
LU 01-14734-S . . . . . . Milford
LU 01-14742-S . . . . . Van Wert
LU 01-14765-S . . . East Palestine
LU 01-14919-S . . . . . . Bedford
LU 01-14964-S. . . . . Painesville
LU 01-14976-S . . . . Belpre
LU 01-15050-S . . . . Carey
LU 01-15519-S . . . . West Union
LU 05-48 . . . . Trenton
LU 05-55 . . . . Franklin
LU 05-60 . . . . Millbury
LU 05-78 . . . . Tallmadge
LU 05-98 . . . . Maineville
LU 05-99. . . . . Goshen
LU 05-108 . . . . Montpelier
LU 05-109 . . . . Kenton
LU 05-112 . . . . Middletown
LU 05-139 Region VIII . . Jefferson
LU 05-141 . . . . Bryan
LU 05-142 . . . . Willowick
LU 05-150 . . . . Creston
LU 05-211 . . . . Sandusky
LU 05-220 . . . . Massillon
LU 05-243 . . . . Valley City
LU 05-266 . . . . . . Miamisburg
LU 05-293 . . . . Troy
LU 05-332 . . . . . Upper Sandusky
LU 05-346 . . . . Toledo
LU 05-363 . . . . Bayview
LU 05-377 . . . . Collins
LU 05-435 . . . . Lorain
LU 05-438 . . . . Brunswick
LU 05-443 . . . . Elyria
LU 05-450 . . . . Canton
LU 05-460 . . . . Malvern
LU 05-498 . . . . Bethel
LU 05-513 . . . . Cleveland
LU 05-524 . . . . Van Wert
LU 05-525. . . . . Huron
LU 05-526 . . . . . Upper Sandusky
LU 05-587 . . . . Cable
LU 05-592 . . . . Kinsman
LU 05-598 . . . . Youngstown
LU 05-607 . . . . Tallmadge
LU 05-609 . . . . Cincinnati
LU 05-621 . . . . Girard
LU 05-622. . . . . Mayfield Heights
LU 05-624 . . . . Lima
LU 05-626. . . . . . . Cridersville
LU 05-639 . . . . Coolville
LU 05-662 . . . . Orrville
LU 05-672 . . . . Aurora
LU 05-673 . . . . . Olmsted Falls
LU 05-689 . . . . Piketon
LU 05-701 . . . . Bryan
LU 05-711 . . . . Madison
LU 05-712 . . . . Hicksville
LU 05-716 . . . . Thurston
LU 05-718 . . . . . New London
LU 05-728 . . . . Eaton
LU 05-730 . . . . Columbus
LU 05-731 . . . . Chillicothe
LU 05-756 . . . . Dalton
LU 05-781 . . . . Middletown
LU 05-801 . . . . Orrville
LU 05-811 . . . . Andover
LU 05-823 . . . . Franklin
LU 05-826 . . . . Mentor
LU 05-829. . . . . Milford
LU 05-854 . . . . Van Wert
LU 05-864 . . . . Cincinnati
LU 05-912 . . . . Toledo
LU 05-962 . . . . Lorain

LU 05-966 . . . . Madison
LU 05-967. . . . . Parma
LU 05-988 . . . . Chillicothe
LU 05-989 . . . . Cincinnati
LU 05-995 . . . . Steubenville
LU 05-1070. Washington Court House
LU 05-1114 . . . . . . Middletown
LU 05-1152 . . . . Lancaster
LU 05-1193 . . . . Trotwood
LU 05-1195 . . . . Pique
LU 05-1206 . . . . Franklin
LU 05-1228 . . . . Van Wert
LU 05-1237 . . . . Conneaut
LU 05-1240 . . . . Zanesville
LU 05-1250 . . . . Mantua
LU 05-1258 . . . . Ravenna
LU 05-1263 . . . . Toledo
LU 05-1270 . . . . Ashtabula
LU 05-1313 . . . . Marion
LU 05-1377 . . . . Salem
LU 05-1462 . . . . Cincinnati
LU 05-1467 . . . . Conover
LU 05-1494 . . . . Dayton
LU 05-1525 . . . . Mount Vernon
LU 05-1528 . . . . . North Benton
LU 05-1544 . . . . . Valley View
LU 05-1560 . . . . Ashland
LU 05-1567 . . . . Batavia
LU 05-1676 . . . . . Middletown
LU 05-1738 . . . . Batavia
LU 05-1824 . . . . Elyria
LU 05-1838 . . . . Reading
LU 05-1967 . . . . Hamilton
LU 05-1968 . . . . Hamilton
LU 05-1973 . . . . . Germantown
LU 05-1974 . . . New Philadelphia
LU 05-2001 . . . Bedford Heights
LU 05-4200 . . . . Franklin
LU 06-1108 . . . . Edgerton
LU 07-490 . . . . Andover
LU 08-508-T . . . . Belpre
LU 08-859-L . . . . . Rio Grande
LU 08-1651-S. . . . . . . Belpre
LU 08-8851-S . . . . . Yorkville
LU 23-1307 . . . . Hubbard

Teachers
LU 1960 Professional Guild of
Ohio . . . . Columbus
LU 3499 Dyke College Federation of
Teachers . . . . Cleveland
SFED 8033 Ohio . . . . . Columbus

Teamsters
CONF Ohio Conference of
Teamsters . . . . Canton
JC 26 . . . . Cincinnati
JC 41. . . . . Brook Park
JC 44 . . . . Toledo
LU 20. . . . . Toledo
LU 24 . . . . Akron
LU 40 . . . . Mansfield
LU 52 . . . . Brook Park
LU 92. . . . . Canton
LU 100 . . . . Cincinnati
LU 113 . . . . Canton
LU 114 . . . . Cincinnati
LU 244 . . . . Cleveland
LU 284 . . . . Columbus
LU 293 . . . . Cleveland
LU 336 . . . . Independence
LU 348 . . . . Akron
LU 377 . . . . Youngstown
LU 400 . . . . Cleveland
LU 407 . . . . Cleveland
LU 413 . . . . Columbus
LU 416 . . . . Cleveland
LU 422 . . . . Cleveland

LU 436 . . . . Valley View
LU 473 . . . . Cleveland
LU 507 . . . . Cleveland
LU 510 . . . . Orrville
LU 637 . . . . Zanesville
LU 654 . . . . Springfield
LU 661 . . . . Cincinnati
LU 908 . . . . Lima
LU 957 . . . . Dayton
LU 964 Auto Transportation
Union . . . . Brook Park
LU 1108 Netjet Pilots and
Affiliares . . . . Columbus
LU 1135 . . . . Perrysburg
LU 1164 . . . . Cleveland
LU 1199 . . . . Cincinnati
LU 1224 Flight Deck Crew Members
ABX Air . . . . . . Wilmington
LU 1717 Cincinnati Mailers
Union . . . . Cincinnati

Television and Radio Artists
LU Cleveland . . . . Cleveland
LU Tri State. . . . . . . Cincinnati

Theatrical Stage Employees
LU 5 . . . . Cincinnati
LU 12 . . . . Columbus
LU 24 . . . . Toledo
LU 27 . . . . Cleveland
LU 27-B . . . . Cleveland
LU 48 . . . . Akron
LU 66 . . . . Dayton
LU 101 . . . . Struthers
LU 148-B . . . . Bedford
LU 160 . . . . Cleveland
LU 209 . . . . Cleveland
LU 364 . . . . Akron
LU 747 . . . . Gahanna
LU 754-B . . . . Cincinnati
LU 756 . . . . . . North Royalton
LU 864 . . . . Cincinnati
LU 883 . . . . . . North Olmsted
LU 886 Theatrical
Wardrobe . . . . . Spring Valley
SA Ohio . . . . Columbus

Train Dispatchers
NHQ . . . . Cleveland

Transit Union
LU 627 . . . . Cincinnati
LU 697 . . . . Toledo

Transport Workers
LU 212 . . . . Columbus
LU 2005 . . . . Columbus
LU 2008 . . . . Steubenville
LU 2019 . . . . . . South Euclid
LU 2022 . . . . Malvern

**Transportation Communications
Union**
D 105 Chesapeake & Ohio System
Board 146 . . . . . . Perrysburg
D 234 Southeastern . . . . Oregon
D 562 Southeastern System Board
96 . . . . North Bend
D 610 . . . . Worthington
D 725 . . . . Kirtland
D 823 . . . . Circleville
D 866 . . . . Austintown
LG 6132 Tankers . . . . . Marion
LG 6546 Bellevue . . . . Sandusky
LG 6731 Willard . . . . . . Shelby

Transportation Union
GCA GO-348 . . . . Sunbury

GCA GO-687 Norfolk
Southern Corporation-Nickel
Plate . . . . Bellevue
LLG GO-247 Yardmasters
Department. . . . . Poland
LU 2 . . . . Bowling Green
LU 27 . . . . Medina
LU 138 . . . . Elida
LU 145 . . . . Bellville
LU 225 . . . . Bellevue
LU 284 . . . . Valley City
LU 378 . . . . Beachwood
LU 421. . . . . Conneaut
LU 440 . . . . Hamilton
LU 586 . . . . Crestline
LU 601 . . . . Mansfield
LU 792 . . . . Brunswick
LU 991 . . . . . . Mingo Junction
LU 1365 . . . . Canfield
LU 1376 . . . . Galloway
LU 1386 . . . . Marietta
LU 1397 . . . . Columbus
LU 1529 . . . . Curtice
LU 1638 . . . . Timberlake
LU 1816 . . . . Oregon
LU 1928 . . . . Oregon
LU 1962 . . . . Sandusky
NHQ . . . . Cleveland
SLB LO-38 Ohio . . . . Columbus

Treasury Employees
CH 9 . . . . Cincinnati
CH 27 . . . . Columbus
CH 37 . . . . Cleveland
CH 44 . . . . Toledo
CH 74 . . . . Akron
CH 75 . . . . Dayton
CH 88 . . . . Cincinnati
CH 100 . . . . Youngstown
CH 155 . . . . Middleburg Heights
CH 224 Staff Attorneys Office of
Hearings/Appeals. . . . Cleveland
CH 279 . . . . Cincinnati
CH 285 . . . . Cincinnati

UNITE HERE
LU 10 . . . . Macedonia
LU 12 . . . . Cincinnati
LU 84 . . . . Summit Station

University Professors
CH Wilberforce University Faculty
Association . . . . . . Wilberforce

Utility Workers
JC American Electric Power
Affiliates. . . . . Canton
JC Ohio Edison . . . . . Shadyside
LU 111 . . . . Tiffin
LU 116 . . . . Dover
LU 118 . . . . Youngstown
LU 126 . . . . Akron
LU 175 . . . . Dayton
LU 270 . . . . Cleveland
LU 308 . . . . Lima
LU 349 . . . . Toledo
LU 350 . . . . . . St. Clairsville
LU 351 . . . . Lorain
LU 397 . . . . Ashtabula
LU 425 . . . . Austintown
LU 427 . . . . Massillon
LU 428 . . . . Mentor
LU 430 . . . . Rutland
LU 434 . . . . Marion
LU 436 . . . . Bellaire
LU 438 . . . . Geneva
LU 457 . . . . East Liverpool
LU 463 . . . . Celina

LU 469 . . . . Sidney
LU 477. . . . . Hillsboro
LU 477-W . . . . Hillsboro
LU 478. . . . . Cadiz
LU 496 . . . . Steubenville
LU 544 . . . . Martins Ferry
LU 555-G. . . . . . . Valley View
LU 560 . . . . Salem

Weather Service Employees
BR 01-34 . . . . Cleveland
BR 01-39. . . . . Oberlin
BR 01-61 . . . . Wilmington
BR 01-66 . . . . Wilmington

Unaffiliated Labor Organizations

Accurate Printing Union . Cleveland
AFSCME Council 8 Staff Employees
    Ohio. . . . . Austintown
Allied Chemical & Alkali
    Workers. . . . . Barberton
Allied Chemical & Alkali Workers
    LU 1. . . . . Barberton
Armco Employees Independent
    Federation Inc. . . . . Middletown
Association of Managed Care
    Pharmacists . . . . Galloway
Association of WEWS News
    Reporters . . . . Cleveland
Bardol Employees Association
    Inc. . . . . Solon
Bettchers Union
    Independent . . . . . . Brook Park
Building & Construction Workers
    American Association LU 1. Tiffin
Business and Organizing
    Representatives Union
    LU 1 . . . . Akron
Carmen Steering
    Committee . . . . Brewster
Cincinnati Shaper
    Independent . . . . Harrison
Cleveland High School & Academy
    Lay Teachers Association . Mentor
Columbus Diocesan Education
    Association . . . . . . Westerville

Concrete Vault and Sewage System
    Installers Union of Valley
    City . . . . Valley City
Conveyor Workers Association
    United . . . . Geneva
Dupont Systems Unions
    Independent Fort Hill Bargaining
    Agency . . . . North Bend
Electrical Construction Workers
    Union . . . . . . New Middletown
Employees Organization
    Independent . . . . Amelia
Exxon Radio Officers
    Association . . . . Campbell
Federated Union of Correctional
    Officers LU 1 . . . . Youngstown
Fram Employees Independent
    Union. . . . . Greenville
General Organizers
    Association . . . . Monroe
Girard Machine Company Union
    Independent . . . . . . McDonald
Globe Industries Employees
    Independent . . . . Dayton
Grafton Ready Mix Drivers . Grafton
Hancock-Wood Electric Employees
    Group . . . . . North Baltimore
Hull Coal Builders Supply
    Employees Association . Sandusky
Independent Supervisor's
    Union . . . . Oregon
Independent Union of Metal Carbides
    Employees . . . . Poland
Industrial Workers Union LU
    52 . . . . Defiance
Industrial Workers Union
    NHQ . . . . Defiance
International Chemical Workers Staff
    Union. . . . . Cincinnati
International Guards Union of
    America LU 14 . . . . . Cincinnati
International Union of
    Labor Organization
    Employees . . . . . . Columbus
International Union of Residential
    Construction & Affiliated Trades
    LU 100. . . . . Jamestown

Ivorydale & St. Bernard
    Employees Representation
    Association. . . . . . . Cincinnati
Latex Employees Union Chemionics
    Corporation . . . . Munroe Falls
Lewis Engineers & Scientists
    Association . . . . . . Cleveland
Lima Memorial Professional Nurses
    Association . . . . Delphos
Malco Employees Independent
    Union . . . . Akron
Marietta Truckers Independent
    LU 1 . . . . Beverly
Masonry Institute of Dayton . Dayton
Metal Workers Alliance
    Inc. . . . . Minerva
Monarch Electric Blue Collar
    Union . . . . Brook Park
National Allied Union Allied
    Professional Associates
    LU 33 . . . . Columbus
Norwood Police Wage & Benefit
    Committee. . . . . Norwood
Ohio Association of Public School
    Employees LU 180 . . . Columbus
Ohio Association of Public School
    Employees LU 358 . . . . . Zoar
Ohio Nurses Employee
    Association . . . . Columbus
Ohio Physicians and Dentists
    Guild . . . . Youngstown
Oil Workers Association Independent
    LU 1 . . . . Dayton
Oil Workers of Cincinnati
    Independent . . . . . Cincinnati
Physical Plant Employees
    Union . . . . Springfield
Piqua Quarries Division, Armco Steel
    Corporation Employees
    Association . . . . Piqua
Protection Workers of America,
    United LU 50059. . . . Smithville
Public Employees Representative
    Union. . . . . Columbus
Representatives & Organizers
    Union . . . . St. Louisville

Rubber Molders of
    America. . . . . Highland Heights
School Employees Service Union
    Independent. . . . . . Columbus
Security, Police, Fire
    Professional . . . . Piketon
Soft Drink Workers Independent
    Coca Cola Bottling
    Works. . . . . Cincinnati
Southern California Engineering
    Association . . . . Akron
Springfield Newspapers Editorial
    Association . . . . . . Springfield
St. Mary Education
    Association . . . . Lancaster
Sun Council . . . . Toledo
Sun Oil Company Employees
    Association. . . . . Toledo
Sun Oil Company Employees
    Association Akron Terminal
    Operating Employees. . . . Akron
Sun Oil Company Employees
    Association Operating Employees
    of Cleveland . . . . . . Amherst
Sun Oil Company Employees
    Association Warehouse-
    Maintenance-Drivers . . Columbus
Textile Processors LU 1 . Cleveland
Transit Employees Union
    Independent. . . . . . . Bedford
Tremco Employees Association
    Inc. . . . . Cleveland
Truck Drivers Operating
    Maintenance Workers
    United . . . . Cadiz
Union Hospital Nurses
    Association . . . . Navarre
United Archaeological Field
    Technicians. . . . . Middletown
United Building Trades
    Group . . . . Toledo
United Diversified Labor. . Defiance
Warehouse Maintenance & Drivers
    Independent Association . Dayton
Wayne Professional Nurses
    Association. . . . . . Greenville
Wittenberg University Physical Plant
    Employees. . . . . . Springfield

Oklahoma

AFL-CIO Trade and Industrial Departments

Building and Construction Trades Department
BCTC Eastern Oklahoma . . . Tulsa
BCTC Western
  Oklahoma . . . . . Oklahoma City

Affiliated Labor Organizations

Air Traffic Controllers
LU ADM . . . . Moore
LU EAC . . . . Wheatland
LU OKC . . . . . . Oklahoma City
LU RVS . . . . Tulsa
LU TUL . . . . Tulsa

Asbestos Workers
LU 64 . . . . Tulsa
LU 94 . . . . . . Oklahoma City

Automobile, Aerospace Workers
C Oklahoma CAP . . Broken Arrow
LU 286 . . . . Oklahoma City
LU 952 . . . . Tulsa
LU 1558 . . . . McAlester
LU 1895 . . . . . . Broken Arrow
LU 1999 . . . . . . Oklahoma City

Bakery, Confectionery, Tobacco Workers and Grain Millers
LU 65 . . . . Tulsa
LU 117-G . . . . Shawnee
LU 142-G . . . . El Reno
LU 346 . . . . Poteau
LU 356-G . . . . Enid
LU 366-G . . . . Edmond

Boilermakers
LG 114-D Cement Workers . . . Ada
LG 414-D Cement Workers . . Rose
LG 421-D Cement Workers . . Tulsa
LG 465-D Cement
  Workers . . . . . . Midwest City
LG 546-D Cement Workers . . Pryor
LG 592 . . . . Tulsa

Bricklayers
LU 5 . . . . Oklahoma City

Carpenters
LU 329 . . . . . . Oklahoma City
LU 943 . . . . Tulsa
LU 1686 . . . . Stillwater

Civilian Technicians
CH 1 Oklahoma Army 127 . Wewoka
CH 126 Oklahoma Air . . . . Tulsa

Communications Workers
C CWA City Council of Oklahoma
  City . . . . . . Oklahoma City
LU 6007 . . . . Drummond
LU 6009 . . . . Lawton
LU 6012 . . . . Tulsa
LU 6015 . . . . Shawnee
LU 6016 . . . . . . Oklahoma City
LU 6313 . . . . Vinita
LU 6500 . . . . Sallisaw
LU 14622 . . . . Enid
LU 14625 . . . . Tulsa
LU 86017 . . . . . Midwest City

LU 86027 . . . . . Oklahoma City

Electrical Workers
LU 444 . . . . Ponca City
LU 584 . . . . Tulsa
LU 976 . . . . Pryor
LU 1002 . . . . Tulsa
LU 1141 . . . . . . Oklahoma City
SA Oklahoma . . . . . Ponca City

Elevator Constructors
LU 63 . . . . Oklahoma City
LU 83 . . . . Tulsa

Federal Employees
LU 273 . . . . Fort Sill
LU 386 . . . . Tulsa
LU 2097 . . . . . . Oklahoma City

Fire Fighters
LU 211-F . . . Tinker Air Force Base

Flint Glass Workers
LU 120 . . . . Muskogee
LU 145 . . . . Sapulpa

Glass, Molders, Pottery and Plastics Workers
LU 48 . . . . Okmulgee
LU 195 . . . . Muskogee
LU 239 . . . . Sapulpa
LU 286 . . . . Mill Creek
LU 325 . . . . Tulsa

Government Employees
LU 171 DoJ . . . . El Reno
LU 689 USDA . . . . Enid
LU 904 . . . . Fort Sill
LU 916 DoD . . . Oklahoma City
LU 2250 VA . . . . . Muskogee
LU 2282 DoT . . . Oklahoma City
LU 2505 HHS . . . . . Crescent
LU 2562 VA . . . . Oklahoma City
LU 2586 DoD . . . . Altus
LU 2815 DoD . . . . . McAlester
LU 2900 . . . . Ada
LU 3053 DoD . . . Oklahoma City
LU 3138 HUD . . . Oklahoma City
LU 3141 USDA . . . Broken Bow
LU 3266 DoD . . . . . . Sallisaw
LU 3506 HHS . . . . . McAlester
LU 3601 PHS, Indian
  Hospital . . . . Claremore
LU 3950 HUD . . . . Tulsa

Government Employees Association
LU 20 Emergency Medical
  Technicians & Paramedics . Yukon
LU 8-1-R AAFES (Army Air Force
  Exchange Service) . . . . Lawton

Government Security Officers
LU 66 . . . . Tulsa
LU 130 . . . . Oklahoma City
LU 201 . . . . Oklahoma City
LU 243 . . . . Oklahoma City

Graphic Communications
LU 226-M . . . . Tulsa
LU 286-C . . . . Enid
LU 562-C . . . . Lawton

Iron Workers
LU 48 . . . . Oklahoma City

Laborers
LU 107 . . . . Tulsa
LU 888 . . . . Tahlequan

Letter Carriers
BR 458 . . . . . . Oklahoma City
BR 858 . . . . Enid
BR 883 . . . . Shawnee
BR 973 . . . . Calumet
BR 985 . . . . Ardmore
BR 1042 . . . . Cookson
BR 1053 . . . . Chickasha
BR 1123 . . . . Lawton
BR 1166 . . . . McAlester
BR 1336 . . . . Blackwell
BR 1355 . . . . Okmulgee
BR 1358 . . . . Tulsa
BR 1491 . . . . Norman
BR 1551 . . . . Mangum
BR 1595 . . . . Stillwater
BR 1631 . . . . . . Pauls Valley
BR 1646 . . . . Hugo
BR 1713 . . . . Nowata
BR 1725 . . . . Clinton
BR 1730 . . . . Ponca City
BR 1958 . . . . Miami
BR 2040 . . . . Holdenville
BR 2087 . . . . Tonkawa
BR 2173 . . . . Woodward
BR 2337 . . . . Sulphur
BR 2422 . . . . Okemah
BR 2460 . . . . Newkirk
BR 2607 . . . . Thomas
BR 2789 . . . . Drumright
BR 2840 . . . . Atoka
BR 2918 . . . . Coalgate
BR 2988 . . . . Kingfisher
BR 3237 . . . . Heavener
BR 3264 . . . . Guymon
BR 3324 . . . . Sayre
BR 3605 . . . . Morris
BR 3990 . . . . Idabel
BR 4155 . . . . Marietta
BR 4242 . . . . Lindsay
BR 4353 . . . . Madill
BR 4667 . . . . Skiatook
BR 4702 . . . . Dewey
BR 5277 . . . . Wetumka
BR 5313 . . . . Konawa
BR 5315 . . . . Hartshorne
BR 5320 . . . . Tishomingo
BR 5403 . . . . Nardin
BR 5422 . . . . Watonga
BR 5481 . . . . Waynoka
BR 5873 . . . . Antlers
BR 6231 . . . . Hennessey
BR 6251 . . . . Wilson
BR 6262 . . . . Davis
SA Oklahoma . . . . . Weatherford

Locomotive Engineers
DIV 141 . . . . . . Oklahoma City
DIV 201 . . . . Wilson
DIV 523 . . . . Chickasha
DIV 569 . . . . Hodgen
DIV 578 . . . . Tulsa
DIV 604 . . . . Lone Grove
DIV 721 . . . . Enid
GCA Kansas City Southern
  Railroad . . . . Poteau
SLB Oklahoma . . . . . . Wagoner

Machinists
DLG 171 . . . . Enid
LG 457 . . . . Mannford
LG 850 . . . . Oklahoma City
LG 898 . . . . Enid
LG 1461 . . . . Porter
LG 2909 . . . . . . Oklahoma City
STC Oklahoma . . . . . . Porter

Maintenance of Way Employes
LG 1251 . . . . Tulsa
LG 2408 . . . . Noble
SF Frisco . . . . Tulsa
SLG 355 . . . . Checotah
SLG 361 . . . . Enid
SLG 522 . . . . Enid
SLG 1025 . . . . . South Coffeyville
SLG 1254 . . . . Indiahoma
SLG 1540 . . . . Poteau
SLG 1547 . . . . Kenefic

Mine Workers
LU 1329 . . . . Stigler
LU 1593 . . . . Adair

Musicians
LU 94 . . . . Tulsa
LU 375-703
  Oklahoma . . . . . Oklahoma City

National Staff Organization
LU Associate Staff
  Organization . . . Oklahoma City
LU Staff Organization, Professional,
  Oklahoma . . . . . Oklahoma City

Office and Professional Employees
LU 330 . . . . Tulsa
LU 381 . . . . Oklahoma City

Operating Engineers
LU 627-ABC . . . . Tulsa
LU 670 . . . . Ardmore

Painters
LU 807 . . . . Oklahoma City

Plumbing and Pipe Fitting
LU 344 . . . . Oklahoma City
LU 430 . . . . Tulsa
LU 798 . . . . Tulsa

Postal Mail Handlers
LU 324 . . . . Oklahoma City

Postal Workers
LU 7 Muskogee Area . . . Muskogee
LU 14 McAlester . . . . McAlester
LU 30 Durant . . . . Durant
LU 37 Norman . . . . . . Norman
LU 84 Enid . . . . Enid
LU 86 Oklahoma City
  Area . . . . . . Oklahoma City
LU 344 . . . . Ada
LU 726 Ponca City
  Local . . . . Ponca City
LU 727 Chickasha . . . . Chickasha
LU 990 Ardmore Area . . . Ardmore
LU 1348 Tulsa . . . . Tulsa
LU 1402 El Reno . . . . . El Reno
LU 1499 Clinton . . . . . . Clinton
LU 1565 Shawnee Area . . Shawnee
LU 1931 Lawton Area . . . Lawton
LU 2281 Mangum . . . . . Mangum
LU 2900 Woodward . . . Woodward

LU 3973 Stillwater . . . . Stillwater
LU 4791 Elk City . . . . . . Elk City
SA Oklahoma . . . . Lawton

Roofers, Waterproofers and Allied Workers
LU 143 . . . . Oklahoma City

Rural Letter Carriers
D Northeast Oklahoma . . Glenpool
D Southeast Oklahoma . . . Tupelo
D Southwest Oklahoma . . Cheyenne
D 6 Northwest Oklahoma . Guymon
SA Oklahoma . . . . Alva

Security, Police and Fire Professionals
LU 796 . . . . McAlester

Sheet Metal Workers
LU 124 . . . . Oklahoma City
LU 270 . . . . Tulsa
LU 464 . . . . Ponca City

State, County and Municipal Employees
LU 2406 Greater Oklahoma City Public Employees . Oklahoma City

Steelworkers
LU 63-T . . . . Sapulpa
LU 05-162 . . . . Valliant

LU 05-174 . . . . Pryor
LU 05-391 . . . . Barnsdall
LU 05-401 . . . . Bartlesville
LU 05-428 . . . . Jay
LU 05-432 . . . . Bartlesville
LU 05-467 . . . . Arkoma
LU 05-606 . . . . Spiro
LU 05-627 . . . . . . North Miami
LU 05-669 . . . . Pryor
LU 05-746 . . . . Muskogee
LU 05-857 . . . . Ponca City
LU 05-930 . . . . Pryor
LU 05-959 . . . . Sapulpa
LU 05-1141 . . . . . Locust Grove
LU 05-1480 . . . . Wagoner
LU 12-57 . . . . Sapulpa
LU 12-157-S . . . . Ardmore
LU 12-716 . . . . Sapulpa
LU 12-985-L . . . . Ada
LU 12-998-L . . . . Oklahoma City
LU 12-2741-S . . . . . Sand Springs
LU 12-4430-S . . . . Inola
LU 12-4785-S . . . Broken Arrow
LU 12-4800-S . . . . Enid
LU 12-4992-3 . . . . . . Claremore
LU 12-6157-S . . . . . . Claremore
LU 12-7570-S . . . . . . Henryetta
LU 12-8509-S . . . . Guthrie
LU 12-8511-S . . . . Pryor
LU 12-9227-S . . . . Tulsa
LU 12-9368 . . . . Saline
LU 12-9402 . . . . Morris

LU 12-9467 . . . . Mustang

Teachers
SFED 8034 Oklahoma Federation of Teachers . . . . . Oklahoma City

Teamsters
LU 516 . . . . Muskogee
LU 523 . . . . Tulsa
LU 886 Oklahoma City, Oklahoma . . . . . Oklahoma City

Theatrical Stage Employees
LU 60-B . . . . . . Oklahoma City
LU 112 . . . . Oklahoma City
LU 354 . . . . Tulsa
LU 387 . . . . Lawton
LU 904 . . . . Tulsa

Transit Union
LDIV 993 . . . . . . Oklahoma City

Transport Workers
LU 514 . . . . Tulsa

Transportation Communications Union
D 218 . . . . Oklahoma City
LG 6747 Will Rogers . . . Mannford

Transportation Union
LU 770 . . . . Shady Point

LU 794 . . . . Blackwell
LU 894 . . . . Sand Springs
LU 1016 . . . . Enid
LU 1042 . . . . Norman
LU 1188 . . . . Purcell
LU 1289 . . . . Sand Springs
SLB LO-39 Oklahoma . . . Mustang

Treasury Employees
CH 45 . . . . Oklahoma City

Weather Service Employees
BR 02-13 . . . . Tulsa
BR 02-34 . . . . Norman
BR 02-37 . . . . . Oklahoma City
BR 02-78 . . . . Norman
BR 02-83 . . . . Norman

Unaffiliated Labor Organizations

Exxon Employees Federation Central Division Tyler Area . . . . Stigler
Professional Association Aeronautical Center Employees Independent . . . . Oklahoma City
Radiographers of America . . . . Henryetta
Standish Pipe Line Guild Oklahoma LU 999 . . . . Cushing
Transport Drivers Employees Union . . . . Tulsa
Vance Instructor Association . Vance Air Force Base

Oregon

AFL-CIO Trade and Industrial Departments

Building and Construction Trades Department
BCTC Central Oregon . . . . . Bend
BCTC Columbia Pacific . . Portland
BCTC Eugene . . . . Eugene
BCTC Oregon State. . . . . Tualatin
BCTC Salem . . . . Tangent
BCTC Southern
 Oregon. . . . . . . Central Point

Metal Trades Department
MTC Portland & Vicinity . Portland

Affiliated Labor Organizations

Air Traffic Controllers
LU EUG . . . . Eugene
LU HIO . . . . Hillsboro
LU P80 . . . . Portland
LU PDX. . . . . Portland

Aircraft Mechanics
LU 17 . . . . Portland

Asbestos Workers
LU 36 . . . . Portland

Automobile, Aerospace Workers
LU 492 Beaverton-Portland
 Local . . . . Beaverton

Bakery, Confectionery, Tobacco Workers and Grain Millers
C Western. . . . . Portland
LU 63-G. . . . . Pendleton
LU 114 . . . . Portland
LU 364 . . . . Portland

Boilermakers
LG 500 . . . . Portland

Bricklayers
LU 1. . . . . Portland
STCON 99 Washington-
 Oregon . . . . Portland

Carpenters
C Industrial Coalition. . . . Portland
DC Western Council/Lumber-
 Production-Industrial
 Workers. . . . . Portland
LU 190 . . . . Klamath Falls
LU 247 . . . . Portland
LU 306 . . . . Bend
LU 711 Millwrights & Machine
 Erectors . . . . Portland
LU 1001 . . . . North Bend
LU 1017. . . . . Portland
LU 1065 . . . . Salem
LU 1273 . . . . Eugene
LU 1388 . . . . Oregon City
LU 1411. . . . . Salem
LU 2058 . . . . Prineville
LU 2067 . . . . Central Point
LU 2130 . . . . Hillsboro
LU 2154. . . . . Portland
LU 2197 Western
 Council . . . . Sublimity
LU 2416. . . . . Portland
LU 2522. . . . . St. Helens

LU 2714. . . . . Dallas
LU 2750 . . . . Springfield
LU 2780 . . . . Elgin
LU 2784 . . . . Coquille
LU 2791 . . . . Coburg
LU 2835 . . . . Salem
LU 2851 . . . . La Grande
LU 2910 . . . . Elgin
LU 2949 . . . . Roseburg
LU 2961. . . . . St. Helens
LU 3091 . . . . Saginaw

Classified School Employees
CH 201 South Umpqua Contract
 Employees. . . . . . Myrtle Creek
CH 302 Coos Bay Area Contracted
 School Employees . . . . Salem
NHQ . . . . Springfield
SA Oregon (OSEA). . . . . Salem

Communications Workers
C Oregon . . . . Portland
LU 7901. . . . . Portland
LU 7904. . . . . Salem
LU 7906 . . . . Eugene
LU 7908 . . . . Medford
LU 7955. . . . . Portland
LU 7970 . . . . Hood River
LU 7990. . . . . Beaverton
LU 14752 . . . . Eugene
LU 14754 . . . . Coos Bay
LU 37194 . . . . Eugene

Electrical Workers
LU 48 . . . . Portland
LU 125 . . . . Gresham
LU 280 . . . . Tangent
LU 659. . . . . Central Point
LU 799 . . . . Hermiston
LU 932 . . . . North Bend

Elevator Constructors
LU 23 . . . . Portland

Federal Employees
LU 447. . . . . Hines
LU 454 . . . . Yachats
LU 457. . . . . Oakridge
LU 642 . . . . Klamath Falls
LU 1379. . . . . Winston
LU 1888. . . . . Portland
LU 2079 Umpqua National
 Forest . . . . Roseburg
LU 2085 . . . . Grants Pass
SFED Oregon . . . . . . Corvallis

Food and Commercial Workers
LU 555 . . . . Tigard

Glass, Molders, Pottery and Plastics Workers
LU 112 . . . . Portland
LU 139-B . . . . Portland

Government Employees
LU 928 DoE . . . . Portland
LU 1042 VA. . . . . . . Roseburg
LU 1089 VA . . . . . White City
LU 1104 . . . . Albany
LU 1126 . . . . Keizer
LU 1188 USDA. . . . . . Dallas
LU 1417 DoD . . . . . Hermiston
LU 1911 . . . . Eugene
LU 2023 . . . . Medford
LU 2157 VA . . . . . . Portland

LU 2336 DoL . . . . Portland
LU 2583 VA . . . . . . Portland
LU 2986 DoD. . . . . . Portland
LU 3116 DoD. . . . . . Portland
LU 3781 USDA. . . . . . Portland
LU 3917 HUD . . . . . Portland
LU 3979 BoP, FCI,
 Sheridan . . . . Sheridan

Government Security Officers
LU 38 . . . . Portland
LU 228 . . . . Springfield

Graphic Communications
LU 116-C . . . . Eugene

Iron Workers
LU 29 . . . . Portland
LU 516 . . . . Portland

Laborers
LU 121 . . . . Bend
LU 296 . . . . Portland
LU 320 . . . . Portland
LU 483 . . . . Portland
LU 1400 . . . . Central Point

Letter Carriers
BR 82 . . . . Portland
BR 295 . . . . Astoria
BR 347 . . . . Salem
BR 743 . . . . Baker City
BR 909 . . . . Pendleton
BR 916 . . . . Eugene
BR 954 . . . . The Dalles
BR 959 . . . . Albany
BR 1248 . . . . La Grande
BR 1274 . . . . Corvallis
BR 1349 . . . . Grants Pass
BR 1433 . . . . Medford
BR 1450 . . . . Coos Bay
BR 1518 . . . . Roseburg
BR 1784 Crater Lake
 Branch . . . . . . Klamath Falls
BR 1937 . . . . Bend
BR 2296. . . . . Dallas
BR 2342 . . . . North Bend
BR 2558 . . . . Tillamook
BR 2855 . . . . Monmouth
BR 2912 . . . . Lebanon
BR 3518 . . . . Vernonia
BR 3601 . . . . . . Independence
BR 3607 . . . . Enterprise
BR 3750 . . . . Ontario
BR 4163 . . . . Newport
BR 4229 . . . . Sheridan
BR 4416 . . . . Reedsport
BR 4425 . . . . Nyssa
BR 4483 . . . . Toledo
BR 4500 . . . . John Day
BR 4797 . . . . . . Myrtle Point
BR 5093 . . . . Burns
BR 5464 . . . . Florence
BR 6225. . . . . Vale
BR 6418 . . . . . . Lincoln City
SA Oregon . . . . Astoria

Locomotive Engineers
DIV 236 . . . . Portland
DIV 362 . . . . La Grande
DIV 476. . . . . St. Helens
DIV 842 . . . . . . Klamath Falls
SLB Oregon . . . . . . Eagle Point

Longshore and Warehouse
DC Columbia River. . . . . Portland
LU 8. . . . . Portland
LU 12 . . . . North Bend
LU 28 . . . . Portland
LU 40 . . . . Portland
LU 50 . . . . Astoria
LU 53 . . . . Newport
LU 92 . . . . Portland
LU 200 Unit 84 . . . . . . Medford

Machinists
DLG 1 . . . . Gladstone
DLG 24 . . . . Portland
LG 12-W . . . . . . Klamath Falls
LG 63 . . . . Portland
LG 246-W . . . . Springfield
LG 261-W Woodworkers . Reedsport
LG 1005. . . . . Portland
LG 1110 . . . . Prineville
LG 1179 . . . . Astoria
LG 1311 . . . . Eugene
LG 1333 . . . . Hermiston
LG 1432. . . . . Portland
LG 1885 . . . . Portland
LG 2911. . . . . Portland
LLG 450 NFFE. . . . . . Joseph
LLG 2187 . . . . Roseburg
LLG FL-7 NFFE . . . . . Portland
LLG FL-1966 . . . . . North Bend
STC Oregon. . . . . . . Portland

Maintenance of Way Employes
LG 236 . . . . Klamath Falls
LG 1054 . . . . Roseburg
LG 1066 . . . . Molalla
SLG 227 . . . . Eugene
SLG 369 . . . . Hood River
SLG 799 . . . . Milwaukie
SLG 874 . . . . Hermiston
SLG 1381 . . . . Nyssa

Musicians
LU 99 . . . . Portland
LU 560 . . . . Pendleton
LU 689. . . . . Eugene

National Staff Organization
LU Oregon Education
 Association . . . . Tigard

NLRB Professional Association
LU 36 . . . . Portland

Nurses
SA Oregon Nurses
 Association . . . . Tualatin

Office and Professional Employees
LU 11 . . . . Portland

Operating Engineers
LU 701 . . . . Gladstone

Painters
LU 10 . . . . Portland
LU 724 . . . . Salem
LU 740 . . . . Portland
LU 1236. . . . . Portland
LU 1277 . . . . Eugene

Plasterers and Cement Masons
LU 82 . . . . Portland
LU 555 . . . . Portland

STCON Northwest
Conference . . . . Portland

Plumbing and Pipe Fitting
LU 290 . . . . Tualatin

Postal Mail Handlers
LU 315 . . . . Portland

Postal Workers
LU 128 Portland . . . . . Portland
LU 342 Medford . . . . . Medford
LU 410 Coos Bay Local. . Coos Bay
LU 431 Roseburg . . . . Roseburg
LU 457 Klamath
Falls. . . . . Klamath Falls
LU 475 La Grande . . . La Grande
LU 499 Grants Pass . . Grants Pass
LU 540 Oregon Postal Workers
Union . . . . Salem
LU 555 Bend . . . . Bend
LU 557 Corvallis. . . . . Corvallis
LU 604 Salem . . . . Salem
LU 679 Eugene . . . . . . Eugene
LU 720 Hood River . . . Hood River
LU 921 Cottage
Grove . . . . Cottage Grove
LU 3806 Seaside. . . . . Seaside
LU 4973 Forest Grove . Forest Grove
LU 6264 Boring . . . . . . Boring

Pulp and Paper Workers
LU. . . . . Portland
LU 1. . . . . St. Helens
LU 3 . . . . Albany
LU 13 . . . . Toledo
LU 60 . . . . Newberg
LU 68 . . . . Oregon City
LU 89 . . . . Eagle Point
LU 396 . . . . Salem
LU 467 . . . . Dallas
LU 677 . . . . Springfield
LU 680 . . . . Portland
LU 1000. . . . . Portland
NHQ . . . . Portland

Railroad Signalmen
LLG 152 . . . . Eugene
LLG 155 . . . . Hermiston

Roofers, Waterproofers and Allied Workers
LU 49 . . . . Portland
LU 156 . . . . Springfield

Rural Letter Carriers
D 1 Oregon . . . . Hillsboro

D 2 . . . . Eagle Creek
D 3 . . . . Hood River
D 4 . . . . Woodburn
D 5 . . . . Bend
D 6 . . . . Pendleton
D 7 . . . . Pleasant Hill
D 8 . . . . Chiloquin
SA Oregon. . . . . . . Dundee

Security, Police and Fire Professionals
LU 2 . . . . Cascade Locks

Service Employees
C Oregon Service . . . . . Portland
LU 49 . . . . Portland
LU 503 . . . . Salem
LU 999 Firemen & Oilers . Stanfield

Sheet Metal Workers
LU 16 . . . . Portland

State, County and Municipal Employees
LU 88 Multnomah County
Employees Union. . . . Portland
LU 835 Good Shepherd Hospital
Local . . . . Hermiston
LU 2479 Morrow County
Employees . . . . Heppner
LU 2746 . . . . Astoria
LU 3115 Oregon Environmental
Research Employees. . . Corvallis
LU 3213 Oregon Committee Support
Inc. Employees Salem . . . Salem
LU 3214 Albertina Kerr-Plane
County. . . . . Eugene
LU 3505 . . . . Coos Bay
LU 3668 Metro Public Defenders Inc.
Employee. . . . . Portland
LU 3670 Trabajadores Unidos y
Organization. . . . Forest Grove
LU 4002 Oregon LPN
Association . . . . . . Portland
LU 4003 . . . . Hillsboro
LU 4004 St. Charles Medical Center
LPN's . . . . La Pine
LU 4005 Council 75 . . . . Ontario
STC 75 Oregon . . . . . . Salem

Steelworkers
LU 04-1199 . . . . Corvallis
LU 08-1097 . . . . Westport
LU 08-1146. . . . . . Brownsville
LU 08-1171. . . . . Halsey
LU 08-1189 Halsey. . . . . Halsey

LU 08-1234 Maintenance
Local . . . . Halsey
LU 11-330. . . . . . . Troutdale
LU 11-504-L . . . . Mulino
LU 11-5074-S. . . . . Canyonville
LU 11-6163-S . . . . . . Albany
LU 11-7150-S . . . . . . Albany
LU 11-8378-S . . . . McMinnville
LU 11-9170-S . . . . . The Dalles

Teachers
LU 3432 Willamette Valley Child
Care Federation. . . . . Portland
LU 3809 Western States Chiropractic
Faculty . . . . Portland
LU 4912 Lewis & Clark College
Support Staff . . . . . . Portland
LU 5017 Oregon Federation of
Nurses-Kaiser . . . . Clackamas
SFED 8035 Oregon. . . . . Tigard

Teamsters
JC 37 . . . . Portland
LU 81 . . . . Portland
LU 162 . . . . Portland
LU 206 . . . . Portland
LU 223 . . . . Portland
LU 305 . . . . Portland
LU 324 . . . . Salem
LU 670 . . . . Salem
LU 962 . . . . Central Point

Television and Radio Artists
LU Portland. . . . . . . Portland

Theatrical Stage Employees
LU 20-B. . . . . Portland
LU 28 . . . . Portland
LU 488 . . . . Portland
LU 675 . . . . Eugene

Transit Union
LDIV 757 . . . . Portland

Transportation Communications Union
D 5501 Oregon . . . . . . Portland
LG 1380 . . . . Gresham
LG 6486 McNary. . . . Hermiston

Transportation Union
LU 283 . . . . Portland
LU 471 . . . . Eugene
LU 473 . . . . La Grande
LU 1573. . . . . . . Klamath Falls
LU 1841. . . . . . . Klamath Falls
SLB LO-40 Oregon . . . Island City

Treasury Employees
CH 40 . . . . Portland
CH 156 . . . . Portland
CH 273 San Francisco
Chapter . . . . . . Lake Oswego

UNITE HERE
LU 9. . . . . Portland

Utility Workers
LU 197 . . . . Coos Bay

Weather Service Employees
BR 04-9 . . . . Portland
BR 04-11 . . . . Medford
BR 04-31 . . . . Pendleton

Unaffiliated Labor Organizations
Associated Field
Representatives. . . . . Portland
Foundry & Warehouse Employees of
Esco . . . . Aloha
IBT Titan United Staff LU
223 . . . . Cove
Industrial Chrome Union
Independent. . . . . . . Portland
Industrial Workers of the World
Portland Public Service
Workers. . . . . Portland
National Staff
Organization . . . . . . Portland
Northwest Boot & Shoe Workers
LU 1 . . . . Scappoose
Northwest Paramedic
Alliance. . . . . Portland
Oregon Court Security
Officers . . . . Gresham
Oregon Federation of Teachers Staff
Union United Employees
Guild . . . . Tigard
Pacific Northwest Employee
Association Salem
LU 1 . . . . Independence
Pacific Northwest Employees
Association LU 1. . . . . Dexter
Pacific Northwest Employees
Association Portland
LU 2 . . . . Portland
Pacific Stainless Products Employee
Association Inc. LU
304 . . . . Beaverton
Pineros y Campesinos Unidos del
Noroeste Inc. . . . . Woodburn
Staff Union, Oregon School
Employees Association . . . Elgin
The Aviators Group . . McMinnville
United Shop & Service Employees
Union. . . . . Portland
Valley Imaging Professionals
UNIT 1. . . . . Albany

Pennsylvania

AFL-CIO Trade and Industrial Departments

Building and Construction Trades Department
BCTC Altoona Area . . . . Altoona
BCTC Beaver County . . . . Beaver
BCTC Berks County . . . . Reading
BCTC Butler Venango
  Counties. . . . . Butler
BCTC Central
  Pennsylvania. . . . . Harrisburg
BCTC Erie. . . . . Erie
BCTC Johnstown . . . . Pittsburgh
BCTC Lawrence County New Castle
BCTC Lehigh-Northampton-Pike-
  Monroe Counties. . . . Allentown
BCTC Mechanical
  Trades . . . . Newportville
BCTC Mercer County . . . . Sharon
BCTC North Central
  Pennsylvania . . . . . . Clearfield
BCTC Northeastern
  Pennsylvania . . . . Wilkes-Barre
BCTC Pennsylvania
  State . . . . Harrisburg
BCTC Philadelphia. . . Philadelphia
BCTC Pittsburgh . . . . Pittsburgh
BCTC Scranton. . . . . . Scranton

Maritime Trades Department
PC Delaware Valley &
  Vicinity. . . . . Philadelphia

Metal Trades Department
MTC Philadelphia . . . . . Limerick

AFL-CIO Directly Affiliated Locals

AFL-CIO
DALU 221 Cereal
  Workers. . . . . Mechanicsburg
DALU 1242 Slag Workers . Munhall
LJEB Brewery
  Workers . . . . . . Allison Park

Affiliated Labor Organizations

Agricultural Employees
BR 7 . . . . Philadelphia

Air Traffic Controllers
LU ABE . . . . Allentown
LU AGC . . . . Pittsburgh
LU AVP . . . . Scranton
LU CCR. . . . . . New Cumberland
LU ERI . . . . Erie
LU MDT . . . . Middletown
LU PHL . . . . Philadelphia
LU PIT . . . . Pittsburgh
LU PNE. . . . . Philadelphia
LU RDG . . . . Reading

Aircraft Mechanics
LU 39 AMFA Local . . . . Hanover

Asbestos Workers
CONF Middle Atlantic
  States . . . . Philadelphia
LU 2 . . . . Clinton
LU 14 . . . . Philadelphia

LU 15 . . . . Pittsburgh
LU 23 . . . . Middletown
LU 38 . . . . Wilkes-Barre

Automobile, Aerospace Workers
C Central Pennsylvania
  CAP . . . . Williamsport
C Erie County CAP . . . . . . Erie
C Lehigh Valley Pennsylvania
  CAP . . . . Allentown
C Southeastern Pennsylvania
  CAP . . . . . . Fort Washington
C Southwestern Pennsylvania
  CAP. . . . . Pittsburgh
C 121-UAW Pennsylvania State
  CAP . . . . . . Fort Washington
LU 56 . . . . Bradenville
LU 204 . . . . Greensburg
LU 502 . . . . Levittown
LU 544 . . . . Dravosburg
LU 644 . . . . Pottstown
LU 677 . . . . Allentown
LU 714 . . . . Erie
LU 739 . . . . Erie
LU 786 . . . . York
LU 787. . . . . Williamsport
LU 832 . . . . Erie
LU 929 . . . . Philadelphia
LU 1039. . . . . Collegeville
LU 1059 . . . . Jeannette
LU 1069 . . . . Eddystone
LU 1098. . . . . Lehighton
LU 1186 . . . . McKean
LU 1191 . . . . . . Perkiomenville
LU 1193 . . . . Eynon
LU 1206 . . . . Northampton
LU 1242 . . . . Moosil
LU 1282 . . . . Bellefonte
LU 1296 . . . . Waynesboro
LU 1311 . . . . Imperial
LU 1443 . . . . Cumberland
LU 1561 . . . . Drums
LU 1612 . . . . . . Fort Washington
LU 1695 . . . . Lansdale
LU 1799 . . . . Greensburg
LU 1872 . . . . York
LU 1968 . . . . Abbottstown
LU 2177. . . . . Bensalem
LU 2255 . . . . Warminster
LU 2412. . . . . Larksville
LU 3303 Butler Armco
  Independent. . . . . . . Butler
LU 8275. . . . . Levittown

Bakery, Confectionery, Tobacco Workers and Grain Millers
C Candy Confectionery and
  Pasta . . . . Philadelphia
LU 6 . . . . Philadelphia
LU 357-G . . . . . . Shiremanstown
LU 374-G . . . . Lancaster
LU 386-G . . . . Mount Joy
LU 387-G . . . . Lancaster
LU 401-G. . . . . Muncy
LU 464 . . . . Hershey
LU 492 . . . . Philadelphia
LU 10-175-G . . . . . . Greensburg

Boilermakers
C Pennsylvania Industrial. Pittsburgh
LG 13 . . . . Newportville
LG 19 . . . . Philadelphia
LG 87 . . . . Aston
LG 88 . . . . Boothwyn

LG 92-D Cement
  Workers. . . . . Milesburg
LG 151 . . . . Erie
LG 154 . . . . Pittsburgh
LG 159 . . . . . West Wyoming
LG 173-D Cement
  Workers. . . . . . . Ellwood City
LG 196 . . . . Athens
LG 282-D Cement
  Workers. . . . . Wind Gap
LG 295 . . . . York
LG 397 . . . . Stroudsburg
LG 398 . . . . Stroudsburg
LG 508-D Cement
  Workers. . . . . Darlington
LG 596-D . . . . Chester
LG 608 . . . . Hanover
LG 659 . . . . Warren
LG 677 . . . . Shavertown
LG 802 . . . . Crum Lynne
LG 906 . . . . Donora
LG 1032 . . . . Sharon Hill
LG 1393 . . . . Gallitzin
LG 1506. . . . . Lehighton
LG 2000 . . . . Philadelphia

Bricklayers
LU 1 Pennsylvania/
  Delaware . . . . . . Philadelphia
LU 5 . . . . Harrisburg
LU 9. . . . . Pittsburgh

Carpenters
DC Greater Pennsylvania Regional
  Council . . . . Pittsburgh
DC Metropolitan
  Philadelphia . . . . Philadelphia
LU 8 . . . . Philadelphia
LU 37 . . . . Philadelphia
LU 76. . . . . Hazleton
LU 81 . . . . Erie
LU 84 . . . . Pittsburgh
LU 86 . . . . Pittsburgh
LU 99. . . . . Scranton
LU 122 . . . . Collegeville
LU 142 . . . . Pittsburgh
LU 165 . . . . Pittsburgh
LU 211 . . . . Pittsburgh
LU 214 . . . . Harrisburg
LU 230 . . . . West Mifflin
LU 240 . . . . Pittsburgh
LU 268 . . . . Sharon
LU 333 . . . . New Kensington
LU 359 . . . . Philadelphia
LU 454 . . . . Philadelphia
LU 462 . . . . Greensburg
LU 465 . . . . Audubon
LU 600 . . . . Bethlehem
LU 645 . . . . Scranton
LU 845 . . . . Springfield
LU 922 . . . . Baden
LU 947 . . . . Reynoldsville
LU 950 Tyrone . . . . . Ashville
LU 1059 . . . . Port Carbon
LU 1073 . . . . Philadelphia
LU 1160 . . . . Pittsburgh
LU 1233 . . . . Pittsburgh
LU 1419 . . . . Johnstown
LU 1462 . . . . Bensalem
LU 1595 . . . . . . Conshohocken
LU 1759 . . . . Pittsburgh
LU 1806 . . . . Red Lion
LU 1823 . . . . Philadelphia
LU 1856 . . . . Philadelphia
LU 1906 . . . . Philadelphia

LU 1936 . . . . Lewistown
LU 2187 . . . . Montandon
LU 2216 . . . . Red Lion
LU 2235 . . . . Pittsburgh
LU 2240 . . . . Home
LU 2274 . . . . Pittsburgh
LU 2515 . . . . Bristol
LU 2539 . . . . Coalport
LU 2786 . . . . Auburn
LU 2799 . . . . . Middlebury Center
LU 2837 . . . . Mifflinburg
LU 2900. . . . . Sunbury
STC Pennsylvania . . . . Pittsburgh

Catholic School Teachers
ASSN Scranton
  Diocese . . . . . . Wilkes-Barre
LU 1776 . . . . Philadelphia
LU 2400. . . . . Pittsburgh
NHQ . . . . Philadelphia

Civilian Technicians
CH 27 Pittsburgh . . . Monongahela
CH 28 Greater
  Pittsburgh . . . . . . Saxonburg
CH 35 Central
  Pennsylvania. . . . Hummelstown
CH 43 Philadelphia
  Chapter. . . . . . . Lebanon
CH 46 Blue Mountain Chapter
  A.C.T. . . . . Jonestown
CH 52 Willow Grove. Willow Grove
CH 53 Flood City . . . . . Tyrone
STC Pennsylvania . . . . Jonestown

Communications Workers
LU 23 . . . . Wilkes-Barre
LU 452 . . . . . . Natrona Heights
LU 683 . . . . Erie
LU 13000 . . . . Philadelphia
LU 13302. . . . . Coraopolis
LU 13500 AT&T
  Division. . . . . . . Pittsburgh
LU 13500 Central
  Division. . . . . . . Pittsburgh
LU 13500 Eastern
  Division. . . . . . . Pittsburgh
LU 13500 Philadelphia
  Division. . . . . . . Pittsburgh
LU 13500 Pittsburgh/Western
  Division. . . . . . . Pittsburgh
LU 13500 Statewide
  Local . . . . Pittsburgh
LU 13550 . . . . Pittsburgh
LU 13552. . . . . Boothwyn
LU 13570 . . . . Bangor
LU 13571 . . . . Duryea
LU 13572 . . . . Orwigsburg
LU 13573 . . . . Middlebury Center
LU 13591 . . . . Cheswick
LU 14167 . . . . Sayre
LU 14802 . . . . Altoona
LU 14803 . . . . Beaver Falls
LU 14804 Bradford Typographical
  Union . . . . Bradford
LU 14806 . . . . Upper Darby
LU 14807 . . . . Curwensville
LU 14812 . . . . Hunker
LU 14813 . . . . Harrisburg
LU 14814 . . . . Mountain Top
LU 14815 . . . . Johnstown
LU 14816 . . . . Kittanning
LU 14817 . . . . Mountville
LU 14819 . . . . Elizabeth

LU 14821 Monongahela Valley
  Typographical . . . . Fayette City
LU 14822 New Castle Typographical
  Union . . . . New Castle
LU 14827 . . . . Pittsburgh
LU 14829 . . . . Ringtown
LU 14830 . . . . West Lawn
LU 14831 . . . . Scranton
LU 14836 . . . . Washington
LU 14837 . . . . . . Swoyersville
LU 14838 . . . . . . Jersey Shore
LU 14840 . . . . Erie
LU 14842 . . . . . . Allison Park
LU 14845 Printers & Bindery
  Workers Union . . . . . . Easton
LU 38010 Newspapers Guild
  Philadelphia . . . . Philadelphia
LU 38016 . . . . . . Middletown
LU 38061 Newspaper Guild of
  Pittsburgh . . . . Pittsburgh
LU 38120 . . . . . . Wilkes-Barre
LU 38177 Scranton . . . . Scranton
LU 38187 . . . . Erie
LU 38216 . . . . Hazleton
LU 38218 . . . . York
LU 58012 . . . King of Prussia
LU 58028 . . . . Erie
LU 58213 . . . . Harrisburg
LU 81311 . . . . Sayre
LU 84155 . . . Conshohocken
LU 88022 Brewery
  Workers . . . . Latrobe
LU 88064 . . . . . . Bechtelsville
LU 88101 . . . . St. Marys
LU 88120 . . . . . . Philadelphia
LU 88123 . . . . Jenkintown
LU 88135 . . . . Lykens
LU 88144 . . . . . . Allison Park
LU 88177 . . . . . Mountain Top
LU 88329 . . . . . . Coudersport
LU 88389 . . . . Wellsboro
LU 88400 . . . . Harrisburg
LU 88502 . . . . St. Marys
LU 88601 . . . . Trafford
LU 88607 . . . . Emporium
LU 88609 . . . . Kane
LU 88611 . . . . Indiana
LU 88612 . . . . . . Coudersport
LU 88623 . . . . Munhall
LU 88628 . . . . . Williamsport
LU 88630 . . . . Creighton
LU 88640 . . . . . . Bridgeville
LU 88643 . . . . Sarver
LU 88648 . . . . Sharon
LU 88651 . . . . . Manns Choice
LU 88666 . . . . Latrobe
LU 88667 . . . . Latrobe
LU 88681 . . . . Corry
LU L-13301 . . . . . Prospect Park

DuPont Workers
NHQ . . . . Philadelphia

Education
LU Katharine Dean
  Tillotson . . . . Bethel Park
LU Milton Hershey Education
  Association . . . . Hershey
LU 720 PSEA Polyclinic Medical
  Center . . . . . New Cumberland
SA Pennsylvania . . . . . Harrisburg

Electrical Workers
C TCC-6 Telephone
  Coordinating . . . . . Meadville
LU 5 . . . . Pittsburgh
LU 29 . . . . Pittsburgh
LU 56 . . . . Erie

LU 81 General Fund . . . . Scranton
LU 98 . . . . Philadelphia
LU 126 . . . . Collegeville
LU 143 . . . . Harrisburg
LU 163 . . . . Wilkes-Barre
LU 201 . . . . Beaver
LU 229 . . . . York
LU 272 . . . . Midland
LU 375 . . . . Allentown
LU 380 . . . . Collegeville
LU 385 . . . . Butler
LU 459 . . . . Johnstown
LU 607 . . . . Shamokin
LU 654 . . . . Boothwyn
LU 712 . . . . Beaver
LU 743 . . . . Reading
LU 744 . . . . Philadelphia
LU 777 . . . . Middletown
LU 812 . . . . Montoursville
LU 1024 . . . . Pittsburgh
LU 1096 . . . . Blairsville
LU 1298 . . . . Easton
LU 1319 . . . . . . Wilkes-Barre
LU 1451 . . . . York
LU 1456 . . . . Allentown
LU 1522 . . . . Allentown
LU 1585 . . . . Meadville
LU 1600 . . . . Trexlertown
LU 1602 . . . . Mount Joy
LU 1633 . . . . Howard
LU 1635 . . . . Johnstown
LU 1637 . . . . Erie
LU 1666 . . . . Lancaster
LU 1671 . . . . Birdsboro
LU 1690 . . . . . . Duke Center
LU 1898 . . . . Reading
LU 1914 . . . . Harwick
LU 1919 . . . . Pittsburgh
LU 1927 . . . . Feasterville
LU 1929 . . . . Clarksville
LU 1941 . . . . Harrisburg
LU 1944 . . . . Harrisburg
LU 1956 . . . . Pittsburgh
LU 1957 . . . . Chicora
LU 1963 . . . . Youngwood
LU 2005 . . . . . . Philadelphia
LU 2007 . . . . Altoona
LU 2009 . . . . Huntingdon
LU 2089 . . . . Meadville
LU 2118 . . . . Boyertown
LU 2179 . . . . . . Sandy Lake
LU 2241 . . . . . . New Castle
LU 2244 . . . . . . Mehoopany
LU 2269 . . . . Dornsife
LU 2271 . . . . . . Philadelphia
LU 2273 . . . . Altoona
SC T-1 General Telephone Company
  of Pennsylvania . . . . . . York
SC U-22 U.G.I.
  Corporation . . . . . Bethlehem
SC 7 Railroad . . . . Philadelphia

**Electrical, Radio and Machine
Workers**
DC 1 . . . . Conshohocken
DC 6 . . . . East Pittsburgh
LU 404 . . . . . . Conshohocken
LU 506 . . . . Erie
LU 610 . . . . Wilmerding
LU 613 WPSBC . . East Pittsburgh
LU 615 . . . . . . East Pittsburgh
LU 618 . . . . Erie
LU 622 . . . . . . East Pittsburgh
LU 623 . . . . . . East Pittsburgh
LU 625 . . . . . . East Pittsburgh
LU 626 . . . . . . East Pittsburgh
LU 645 . . . . . . East Pittsburgh
LU 684 . . . . . . East Pittsburgh

LU 689 . . . . East Pittsburgh
LU 690 . . . . East Pittsburgh
LU 697 . . . . Erie
NHQ . . . . Pittsburgh

Elevator Constructors
LU 5 . . . . Philadelphia
LU 6 . . . . Pittsburgh
LU 59 . . . . Harrisburg
LU 84 . . . . Kempton

Engineers
LU 3 . . . . Philadelphia
LU 96 . . . . Pittsburgh
LU 117 . . . . Quakertown
LU 138 . . . . Erie

Federal Employees
LU 1429 . . . . . . Chambersburg
LU 1430 . . . . Lester
LU 1442 . . . . . . Chambersburg

Fire Fighters
LU 17-I . . . . Trainer
LU 61-F . . . . Philadelphia
LU 109-F . . . . Carlisle
LU 170-F . . . . . Chambersburg
LU 221-F . . . . New Cumberland
LU 246-F . . . . Moscow

Food and Commercial Workers
DC Northeastern . . . . Wilkes-Barre
LU 23 . . . . Canonsburg
LU 31-T . . . . Kulpsville
LU 38 . . . . Milton
LU 144-C . . . . Easton
LU 195-T . . . . . . Wilkes-Barre
LU 211-C . . . . Glassport
LU 283-G . . . Schuylkill Haven
LU 325 . . . . Pittsburgh
LU 406-T . . . . . . Wilkes-Barre
LU 416-C . . . . Oaks
LU 477-C . . . . Catasauqua
LU 570-C . . . . Pottsville
LU 619-C . . . . Gilbertsville
LU 724-T . . . . . . Swoyersville
LU 727-T . . . . . . Wilkes-Barre
LU 737-T . . . . Sheppton
LU 740-T . . . . Stowe
LU 741-T . . . . . . Wilkes-Barre
LU 959-C . . . . Gilbertsville
LU 1776 . . . . Plymouth Meeting
LU 2635-T . . . . . Wilkes-Barre

**Glass, Molders, Pottery and
Plastics Workers**
LU 1 . . . . Philadelphia
LU 2-B . . . . Ellwood City
LU 28 . . . . Brockway
LU 36 . . . . Wrightville
LU 38-B . . . . Erie
LU 46 . . . . Pittsburgh
LU 54 . . . . Port Allegany
LU 61 . . . . Albion
LU 75 . . . . Port Allegany
LU 90 . . . . Hazleton
LU 99 . . . . Beaver Falls
LU 107 . . . . . South Connellsville
LU 110 . . . . Brockway
LU 120 . . . . Clarion
LU 124 . . . . . . Mount Pleasant
LU 130 . . . . . . New Enterprise
LU 132 . . . . Pottstown
LU 134 . . . . Lower Burrell
LU 136 . . . . Grindstone
LU 149 . . . . Connellsville
LU 185-A . . . . Bensalem
LU 188 . . . . Connellsville

LU 201-B . . . . Mont Alto
LU 237 . . . . Nuremberg
LU 238-B . . . . Boyertown
LU 240 . . . . Cumbola
LU 243 . . . . Plains
LU 246 . . . . Sligo
LU 247 . . . . Brookville
LU 272 . . . . Washington
LU 273 . . . . Greenville
LU 275 . . . . Grove City
LU 287 . . . . Lancaster
LU 295 . . . . Macungie
LU 297 . . . . Knox
LU 304-B . . . . Wellsboro
LU 313 . . . . Friedens
LU 326 . . . . Media
LU 337 . . . . Washington
LU 361 . . . . . . Lenhartsville
LU 365-A . . . . . . New Castle
LU 366-B . . . . Drums
LU 375 . . . . Willow Street
LU 376 . . . . Mount Joy
LU 422 . . . . Drums
LU 454 . . . . Pottsville
NHQ . . . . Media

Government Employees
C 169 Defense Supply
  Agency . . . . Philadelphia
C 264 3rd District of Veterans
  Affairs . . . . Pittsburgh
LU 62 . . . . Philadelphia
LU 63 . . . . Mechanicsburg
LU 148 DoJ . . . . . . Lewisburg
LU 304 . . . . Philadelphia
LU 305 . . . . Philadelphia
LU 306 . . . . White Deer
LU 307 USP
  Allenwood . . . . . . White Deer
LU 940 VA . . . . . . Philadelphia
LU 1018 USDA . . . . Monroeville
LU 1023 DoI . . . . . Philadelphia
LU 1156 DoD . . . . Mechanicsburg
LU 1331 USDA . . . . Wyndmoor
LU 1627 VA . . . . . . Pittsburgh
LU 1647 DoD . . . . . Tobyhanna
LU 1698 DoD . . . . Philadelphia
LU 1699 VA . . . . . Wilkes-Barre
LU 1793 VA . . . . . Philadelphia
LU 1862 VA . . . . Altoona
LU 1902 DoD . . . . Philadelphia
LU 1916 DoI . . . . . South Park
LU 1927 USDA . . . Tunkhannock
LU 1966 VA . . . . Lebanon
LU 2004 DoD . . . New Cumberland
LU 2006 HHS . . . . Philadelphia
LU 2012 DoJ . . . . . Essington
LU 2028 VA . . . . . . Pittsburgh
LU 2032 HUD . . . . Philadelphia
LU 2058 DoI . . . . . Philadelphia
LU 2304 DoD . . . . . Pittsburgh
LU 2316 DoD . . . . . Coraopolis
LU 2450 OPM . . . . . Boyers
LU 2495 DoD . . . . . Oakdale
LU 2502 DoL . . . . . Ebensburg
LU 2531 USDA . . Mechanicsburg
LU 2541 GSA . . . . Pittsburgh
LU 2764 HUD . Cranberry Township
LU 2809 HHS . . . . Wilkes-Barre
LU 2935 USDA . . . . . Ulster
LU 3020 . . . . Hazleton
LU 3034 . . . . Chalk Hill
LU 3145 DoI . . . . Gettysburg
LU 3434 VA . . . . . Pittsburgh
LU 3493 USDA . . . . Fairview
LU 3617 USDA . . . . Claysburg
LU 3631 EPA Region
  III . . . . Philadelphia

LU 3848 DoL . . . . . . Pittsburgh
LU 3860 DoJ . . . . . Beach Lake
LU 3895 DoE . . . . Philadelphia
LU 3951 DoJ . . . . Altoona
LU 3974 BoP, FCI,
   McKean . . . . Bradford
LU 4047 Council of
   Prison . . . . White Deer

Government Employees
Association
LU 358 Police
   Officers . . . . . . Chambersburg
LU 03-15 . . . . . . Willow Grove
LU 03-32 . . . . Wears
LU 03-35 . . . . Coatesville
LU 03-74 . . . . Butler
LU 03-76 . . . . Elkins Park
LU 03-120 . . . . . King of Prussia
LU 03-354 Association of Physicians
   & Surgeons . . . . . Coatesville

Government Security Officers
LU 12 . . . . Stowe
LU 58 . . . . Philadelphia
LU 73 . . . . Hanover Township
LU 129 . . . . Scranton
LU 139 . . . . Pittsburgh
LU 168 . . . . . East Springfield
LU 204 Local . . . . . Middletown

Graphic Communications
LU 4-C . . . . . . Clifton Heights
LU 9-N . . . . Pittsburgh
LU 14-M . . . . . . Philadelphia
LU 16-N . . . . . . Philadelphia
LU 24-M . . . . Pittsburgh
LU 64-C . . . . Pittsburgh
LU 73-C . . . . Erie
LU 137-C . . . . . . Shavertown
LU 138-B . . . . Millersville
LU 188-C . . . . Windber
LU 241-M . . . . Clarks Summit
LU 329-C . . . . Dover
LU 330-C . . . . Lewis Run
LU 338-C . . . . Meadville
LU 350-C . . . East Stroudsburg
LU 493-M . . . . . . Clearfield
LU 594-S . . . . Mount Wolf
LU 726-S . . . . Shamokin
LU 732-C . . . . . . Bloomsburg
LU 735-S . . . . Hazleton

Independent Unions
ASSN United Independent
   Union . . . . Philadelphia
LU Merck Sharpe &
   Dohme Employees
   Organization . . . . . West Point
LU 1 United Independent
   Union . . . . Philadelphia
LU 2 United Independent
   Union . . . . Philadelphia
LU 5 United Independent
   Union . . . . Philadelphia
LU 22 . . . . Philadelphia
NHQ . . . . Philadelphia

Iron Workers
DC East Ohio-West Pennsylvania-
   Northern West
   Virginia . . . . Canonsburg
DC Philadelphia &
   Vicinity . . . . Allentown
LU 3 . . . . Pittsburgh
LU 36 . . . . Whitehall
LU 401 . . . . Philadelphia
LU 404 . . . . Harrisburg

LU 405 . . . . Philadelphia
LU 420 . . . . Reading
LU 489 . . . . Avoca
LU 502 . . . . . . Conshohocken
LU 521 . . . . Dickson City
LU 527 . . . . Pittsburgh
LU 594 . . . . Hellertown
LU 621 . . . . Montrose
LU 642 . . . . Erie
LU 772 . . . . Clearfield
LU 822 . . . . Milton

Laborers
DC Eastern
   Pennsylvania . . . . . Harrisburg
DC Federal Public Service
   Employees . . . . . Philadelphia
DC Metropolitan
   Philadelphia . . . . . Philadelphia
DC Western
   Pennsylvania . . . . . Pittsburgh
LU 57 . . . . Philadelphia
LU 130 . . . . Scranton
LU 135 . . . . Norristown
LU 158 . . . . Harrisburg
LU 286 . . . . Brownsville
LU 323 . . . . Butler
LU 332 . . . . Philadelphia
LU 373 . . . . Pittsburgh
LU 413 . . . . Chester
LU 419 . . . . Somerset
LU 603 . . . . Erie
LU 824 . . . . Bellefonte
LU 833 . . . . New Brighton
LU 910 . . . . Johnstown
LU 952 . . . . Kittanning
LU 964 . . . . New Castle
LU 1012 . . . . Philadelphia
LU 1058 . . . . Pittsburgh
LU 1170 . . . . . . Mechanicsburg
LU 1174 . . . . Allentown
LU 1180 . . . . Harrisburg
LU 1300 Public Service
   Employees . . . . . Wilkes-Barre
LU 1305 . . . . Ebensburg
LU 1319 . . . . Chester
LU 1451 . . . . Latrobe

Letter Carriers
BR 17 . . . . Scranton
BR 22 . . . . New Castle
BR 50 . . . . Williamsport
BR 84 . . . . Pittsburgh
BR 115 . . . . Wilkes-Barre
BR 146 . . . . Corry
BR 157 Keystone . . . . Philadelphia
BR 162 . . . . Pittston
BR 163 . . . . Carbondale
BR 177 . . . . Mahanoy City
BR 253 . . . . Hazleton
BR 254 . . . . Bethlehem
BR 258 . . . . Reading
BR 267 . . . . Meadville
BR 273 . . . . Lancaster
BR 274 . . . . Allentown
BR 277 . . . . Chester
BR 284 . . . . Erie
BR 293 . . . . Bradford
BR 332 . . . . McKeesport
BR 389 . . . . Easton
BR 451 . . . . Johnstown
BR 500 . . . . Harrisburg
BR 509 . . . . York
BR 520 . . . . Uniontown
BR 542 . . . . Norristown
BR 575 . . . . Towanda
BR 725 . . . . Holmes
BR 771 . . . . Ridgway

BR 812 . . . . Kane
BR 920 . . . . Souderton
BR 961 . . . . Huntingdon
BR 1029 . . . . Tarentum
BR 1045 . . . . Honesdale
BR 1048 . . . . Athens
BR 1124 . . . . . Mount Pleasant
BR 1133 . . . . Wellsboro
BR 1139 . . . . . New Kensington
BR 1218 . . . . Hollidaysburg
BR 1330 . . . . Montrose
BR 1384 . . . . Meyersdale
BR 1403 . . . . . Cambridge Springs
BR 1430 . . . . Donora
BR 1473 . . . . East Pittsburgh
BR 1495 . . . . State College
BR 1500 . . . . St. Marys
BR 1645 . . . . Smethport
BR 1796 . . . . Mount Union
BR 1929 . . . . Morton
BR 1964 . . . . Everett
BR 1993 . . . . Johnsonburg
BR 2248 . . . . Weatherly
BR 2249 . . . . Hawley
BR 2258 . . . . Houtzdale
BR 2531 . . . . Mifflinburg
BR 2572 Morrisville . . . Morrisville
BR 2641 . . . . McAdoo
BR 2657 . . . . Clarion
BR 2771 . . . . . . Willow Grove
BR 2873 . . . . Mansfield
BR 3013 . . . . Turtle Creek
BR 3024 . . . . Montgomery
BR 3034 . . . . . . Port Allegany
BR 3068 . . . . Gallitzin
BR 3073 . . . . Coaldale
BR 3225 . . . . Tremont
BR 3337 . . . . White Haven
BR 3392 . . . . West Newton
BR 3449 . . . . Tidioute
BR 3487 . . . . Pittsburgh
BR 4094 . . . . Glen Lyon
BR 4104 . . . . North Wales
BR 4105 . . . . Clymer
BR 4109 . . . . Burnham
BR 4207 . . . . Forest City
BR 4317 . . . . Paoli
BR 4452 . . . . Coplay
BR 4663 . . . . Trevorton
BR 4680 . . . . . New Bethlehem
BR 4931 . . . . Langhorne
BR 4973 . . . . Levittown
BR 5101 . . . . Sykesville
BR 5482 . . . . Point Marion
BR 5791 . . . . Horsham
BR 5848 . . . . . . Crooked Creek
BR 5931 . . . . Matamoras
BR 6027 . . . . . McConnellsburg
BR 6144 . . . . . . Merion Station
BR 6252 . . . . Christiana
BR 6286 . . . . Saltsburg
BR 6338 . . . . Mifflintown
BR 6353 . . . . Creighton
BR 6371 . . . . Lyndora
BR 6574 . . . . Shrewsbury
SA Pennsylvania . . . . Philadelphia

Locomotive Engineers
DIV 50 . . . . Acme
DIV 52 . . . . York
DIV 71 . . . . Fairless Hills
DIV 74 . . . . Enola
DIV 108 . . . . Saxonburg
DIV 146 . . . . Mohnton
DIV 250 . . . . . . Montoursville
DIV 259 . . . . Easton
DIV 263 . . . . Shavertown
DIV 276 . . . . Allentown

DIV 287 . . . . . . Hollidaysburg
DIV 325 . . . . Elrama
DIV 335 . . . . Pittsburgh
DIV 370 . . . . Bellevue
DIV 459 . . . . . . Mechanicsburg
DIV 521 . . . . Forest City
DIV 590 . . . . Aliquippa
DIV 700 . . . . Pittsburgh
DIV 730 . . . . . . Duncansville
DIV 757 . . . . New Castle
DIV 851 . . . . Philadelphia
GCA Septa . . . . . Fairless Hills
SLB Pennsylvania . . . . Pittsburgh

Longshoremen
DC Philadelphia . . . Philadelphia
LU 1242 . . . . Philadelphia
LU 1242-1 . . . . . . Philadelphia
LU 1291 . . . . Philadelphia
LU 1566 . . . . Philadelphia
LU 2064
   Warehousemen . . . Philadelphia

Machinists
DLG 1 . . . . Philadelphia
DLG 98 . . . . York
LG 52 . . . . Pittsburgh
LG 101 . . . . North East
LG 159 . . . . Philadelphia
LG 175 . . . . York
LG 212 . . . . Bedford
LG 243 . . . . . . East Prospect
LG 380 . . . . Carbondale
LG 648 . . . . Philadelphia
LG 847 . . . . Scranton
LG 917 . . . . Allentown
LG 928 Garden Spot . . . Mount Joy
LG 993 . . . . Warren
LG 998 . . . . Marble
LG 1044 . . . . Ambridge
LG 1060 . . . . Pittsburgh
LG 1070 . . . . Harrisburg
LG 1092 . . . . Lansdale
LG 1174 . . . . Greenville
LG 1190 . . . . Canton
LG 1211 . . . . Girard
LG 1352 . . . . Wycombe
LG 1400 . . . . Spring Grove
LG 1403 . . . . Spring Grove
LG 1582 . . . . Kent
LG 1602 . . . . Pittston
LG 1639 . . . . Altoona
LG 1644 . . . . Eldred
LG 1653 . . . . Carbondale
LG 1671 . . . . New Castle
LG 1676 Conway
   Lodge . . . . . . Allison Park
LG 1776 . . . . Essington
LG 1778 . . . . Lebanon
LG 1780 Moravian Lodge . . Easton
LG 1799 . . . . Christiana
LG 1830 . . . . Fogelsville
LG 1842 . . . . Franklin
LG 1869 . . . . Ducannon
LG 1968 . . . . Erie
LG 1971 . . . . Dunmore
LG 1976 Potomac Air
   Lodge . . . . Moon Township
LG 1985 . . . . Red Lion
LG 2058 . . . . . . Mechanicsburg
LG 2067 . . . . Athens
LG 2171 . . . . Boynton
LG 2200 . . . . Shavertown
LG 2304 . . . . Warren
LG 2305 . . . . Scranton
LG 2348 . . . . . . Duncansville
LG 2367 . . . . . . Hummelstown
LG 2394 . . . . Danville

LG 2430 . . . . Karns City
LG 2439 . . . . Leeper
LG 2448 . . . . Ridgway
LG 2462 . . . . Scranton
LG 2530 . . . . Waynesboro
LG 2779 . . . . Portage
LG 2780 . . . . . . Union City
LG 2905 . . . . . . Mountain Top
LG 2906 . . . . Lititz
STC Pennsylvania . . . Philadelphia

Maintenance of Way Employes
FED Pennsylvania . . . Philadelphia
LG 400 . . . . Bethlehem
LG 935. . . . . Jim Thorpe
LG 1115. . . . . Sarver
LG 1923. . . . . Frackville
LG 1957 . . . . Harrisburg
LG 1997 . . . . Cranesville
LG 2779. . . . . Brownsville
LG 3006. . . . . Brownsville
LG 3008. . . . . Greensburg
LG 3014 . . . . Langhorne
LG 3024 . . . . York
LG 3039 . . . . Coatesville
LG 3047 . . . . Gallitzin
LG 3062 . . . . Irwin
LG 3072. . . . . . . Sinnamahoning
LG 3082. . . . . Saylorsburg
LG 3084 . . . . Jersey Shore
LG 3099 . . . . Oil City
SD Bessemer & Lake
Erie . . . . Grove City
SLG 275 . . . . Pittston
SLG 362 . . . . Athens
SLG 737 . . . . South Park
SLG 1045 . . . . Clifford
SLG 1049 . . . . North Huntingdon
SLG 1350 . . . . Peckville
SLG 1551 . . . . Carbondale
SLG 1556 . . . . . . Buffalo Mills
SLG 1904 . . . . Meadville
SLG 2775 . . . . New Castle
SLG 2780 . . . . Temple
SLG 2908 . . . . Morrisville
SLG 3002 . . . . Mifflintown
SLG 3004 . . . . Carnegie
SLG 3009 . . . . . . Duncansville
SLG 3011 . . . . Lititz
SLG 3015 . . . . Pittsburgh
SLG 3020 . . . . Anita
SLG 3023 . . . . Leechburg
SLG 3030 . . . . Woodland
SLG 3063 . . . . Broomall
SLG 3091 . . . . Millmont
SLG 3094. . . . . . . Beaver Falls
SLG 3098 . . . . . . Mechanicsburg

Mine Workers
LU . . . . Nanty Glo
LU 316. . . . . Uniontown
LU 488 . . . . Homer City
LU 600 . . . . Penn Run
LU 616 . . . . Ebensburg
LU 713 . . . . Pittsburgh
LU 762 . . . . Waynesburg
LU 803 . . . . . . Beaver Brook
LU 819 . . . . Kittanning
LU 850 . . . . Revloc
LU 998 . . . . Johnstown
LU 1117 . . . . Mahaffey
LU 1197 . . . . Cokeburg
LU 1248 . . . . . McClellandtown
LU 1257 . . . . Bolivar
LU 1269 . . . . Northern Cambria
LU 1318 . . . . Lilly
LU 1319 . . . . Uniontown
LU 1368. . . . . St. Benedict

LU 1378 . . . . Avonmore
LU 1386 . . . . Nanty Glo
LU 1488. . . . . Pittsburgh
LU 1520. . . . . Houtzdale
LU 1686 . . . . Pottsville
LU 1742 . . . . Friedens
LU 1875 . . . . Garrett
LU 1901 . . . . . . Waltersburg
LU 1914 . . . . South Park
LU 1957 . . . . Windber
LU 1980 . . . . Crucible
LU 1994 . . . . Sligo
LU 1998 . . . . . . Monongahela
LU 2003 Pittsburgh District
Office . . . . Masontown
LU 2004 . . . . Brookville
LU 2022 . . . . Ohiopyle
LU 2193 . . . . Clymer
LU 2200 . . . . Broad Top
LU 2244. . . . . . . Bentleyville
LU 2258 . . . . Carmichaels
LU 2283 . . . . Rural Valley
LU 2291 . . . . Martin
LU 2300 . . . . Uniontown
LU 2350. . . . . Pittsburgh
LU 2485 . . . . Cokeburg
LU 2494 . . . . Nicktown
LU 2587 . . . . Minersville
LU 2874 . . . . Marianna
LU 3123 . . . . Knox
LU 3246. . . . . . . Carrollton
LU 3333 . . . . . . Merritts Town
LU 3548. . . . . . . Homer City
LU 4004 . . . . Tamaqua
LU 4426 . . . . Cheswick
LU 4963 . . . . Butler
LU 6132 . . . . Greensburg
LU 6159 . . . . Bobtown
LU 6290 . . . . Nemacolin
LU 6310. . . . . Spraggs
LU 6321 . . . . Masontown
LU 6330 . . . . Clarksville
LU 6359 . . . . St. Michael
LU 6410 . . . . Central City
LU 6461 . . . . Shelocta
LU 6754 . . . . Washington
LU 6986 . . . . Apollo
LU 7226 . . . . Hazleton
LU 7891 . . . . Pottsville
LU 7925 . . . . Salix
LU 8923 . . . . Ridgway
LU 9113 . . . . New Salem
LU 9636. . . . . Oakdale
LU 9873. . . . . Pittsburgh

Musicians
LU 17 . . . . Erie
LU 27 . . . . New Castle
LU 41. . . . . Johnstown
LU 60-471 . . . . Pittsburgh
LU 77. . . . . Philadelphia
LU 82-545 Beaver Valley Musicians
Union. . . . . Beaver
LU 120 . . . . Scranton
LU 130 . . . . Archbald
LU 135 . . . . Wernersville
LU 140 . . . . Ashley
LU 269 . . . . Harrisburg
LU 294 . . . . Mountville
LU 339 . . . . Export
LU 341 . . . . Norristown
LU 401-750. . . . . . . Lebanon
LU 472 . . . . York
LU 515 . . . . Pottsville
LU 561 . . . . Allentown
LU 577 Pocono
Musicians. . . . . . Stroudsburg
LU 592 . . . . New Salem

LU 596. . . . . Uniontown
LU 630. . . . . . New Kensington
LU 660. . . . . State College

National Staff Organization
LU Pennsylvania State Education
Association Staff
Organization . . Montgomeryville

NLRB Professional Association
LU 4 . . . . Philadelphia
LU 6. . . . . Pittsburgh

Nurses
LU 701 PNA Berks Visiting
Nurse . . . . Wyomissing
LU 702 PNA Braddock
Hospital . . . . . . West Mifflin
LU 703 PNA Braddock
Hospital . . . . Allentown
LU 706 PNA Centre County Home
Health Service . . . . Bellefonte
LU 707 PNA-Charles Cole Memorial
Hospital . . . . Galeton
LU 708 PNA Clearfield
Hospital. . . . . Houtzdale
LU 710 PNA Highlands Hospital &
Health Center . . . . . Scottdale
LU 711 J.C. Blair Unit of
Pennsylvania. . . . . Alexandria
LU 712 PNA . . . . . . Philadelphia
LU 715 PNA-Hazelton General
Hospital . . . . Freeland
LU 717 PNA Pocono
Hospital. . . . . . . Stroudsburg
LU 718 PNA Pottsville Hospital &
Warne Clinic . . . . Pine Grove
LU 719 PNA Pottsville School of
Nursing . . . . Pottsville
LU 722 PNA Suburban General
Hospital . . . . Bridgeport
LU 725 PNA Wayne County
Memorial Hospital . . . Tyler Hill
LU 728 PNA Fulton County Medical
Center . . . . . McConnellsburg
LU 729 PNA John F. Kennedy
Memorial Hospital . . Philadelphia
LU 730 PNA Sun Health Services
Inc. . . . . Sunbury

Office and Professional Employees
LU 112 . . . . Allentown
LU 112 Healthcare
Profession. . . . . . . Frackville
LU 426 . . . . Levittown
LU 457. . . . . Fredricktown
LU 471 . . . . Hiller

Operating Engineers
LU 66 . . . . Monroeville
LU 95-95A . . . . Pittsburgh
LU 367 Brewery Workers . Scranton
LU 542 . . . . . . Fort Washington
LU 835. . . . . Drexel Hill

Painters
DC 21. . . . . Philadelphia
DC 57 . . . . Carnegie
LU 6. . . . . Pittsburgh
LU 41 . . . . Drums
LU 218 . . . . Scranton
LU 252 . . . . Philadelphia
LU 409 . . . . Carnegie
LU 411 . . . . Harrisburg
LU 426 . . . . Philadelphia
LU 479 Sign, Pictorial & Display
Artists. . . . . Pittsburgh
LU 530 . . . . Carnegie

LU 549 . . . . Erie
LU 587 . . . . Philadelphia
LU 641 . . . . Conshohocken
LU 703 . . . . Philadelphia
LU 751 . . . . Carnegie
LU 921 . . . . Philadelphia
LU 997 . . . . Ridley Park
LU 1107 . . . . Horsham
LU 1159 . . . . Warminster
LU 1269 . . . . Nazareth
LU 1309 . . . . Leesport
LU 1955 . . . . Philadelphia
LU 1970 . . . . Philadelphia
LU 2006 . . . . Carnegie

Plasterers and Cement Masons
LU 8 . . . . Philadelphia
LU 31 . . . . Munhall
LU 526 . . . . Pittsburgh
LU 592 . . . . Philadelphia
STCON Plasterers & Cement Masons
Tri-State Conference . . . Munhall

Plumbing and Pipe Fitting
LU 27. . . . . Coraopolis
LU 47 . . . . Monaca
LU 354 . . . . Youngwood
LU 420 . . . . Philadelphia
LU 449 Steamfitters
Local . . . . Pittsburgh
LU 520 . . . . Harrisburg
LU 524 . . . . Scranton
LU 542 Pittsburgh Sprinkle
Fitters. . . . . Pittsburgh
LU 600 . . . . Wernersville
LU 690 . . . . Philadelphia
LU 692 . . . . Philadelphia
SA Pennsylvania . . . . Philadelphia

Police
LG 1-F First Federal,
Pennsylvania. . . . . Philadelphia
LG 113 University of Pennsylvania
Police. . . . . Philadelphia

Postal and Federal Employees
D 5 . . . . Pittsburgh
LU 208 . . . . Archbald
LU 507 . . . . Warrendale
LU 509 . . . . Philadelphia
LU 510 Pittsburgh
Pennsylvania . . . . . Pittsburgh

Postal Mail Handlers
LU 308 . . . . Philadelphia
LU 322 . . . . Pittsburgh

Postal Workers
LU 81 Pittsburgh Area . . Pittsburgh
LU 89 Philadelphia. . . Philadelphia
LU 95 Lancaster. . . . . Lancaster
LU 101 Scranton . . . . Scranton
LU 104 McKeesport . . McKeesport
LU 175 Wilkes-Barre . Wilkes-Barre
LU 227 New Castle . . . New Castle
LU 268 Lehigh Valley
Area . . . . Lehigh Valley
LU 269 Erie Area . . . . . . Erie
LU 500 Grove City . . . Grove City
LU 776 Altoona . . . . . Altoona
LU 853 Oil City. . . . . Oil City
LU 869 Sharon . . West Middlesex
LU 956 Kittanning . . . . Kittanning
LU 1027 Reading . . . Reading
LU 1244 York . . . . . . York
LU 1566 Keystone Area . Harrisburg
LU 1759 Pottsville. . . . Pottsville
LU 1948 Greensburg . . Greensburg

LU 2007 Williamsport. Williamsport
LU 2013 State
  College . . . . . . State College
LU 2057 Titusville . . . . Titusville
LU 2059 Brookville . . Brookville
LU 2061 Du Bois . . . . . DuBois
LU 2063 Bradford . . . . Bradford
LU 2065 St. Marys . . . St. Marys
LU 2146 Greenville . . Greenville
LU 2153 Washington . . Washington
LU 2171 Donora. . . . . Donora
LU 2179 Warren. . . . . . Warren
LU 2185 Jim Thorpe . . Jim Thorpe
LU 2233 Eastern Montgomery
  County. . . . Plymouth Meeting
LU 2776 West
  Chester . . . . . . West Chester
LU 2781 Upper Darby . Upper Darby
LU 3193 Perkasie. . . . . Perkasie
LU 3285 Hanover. . . . . Hanover
LU 3712 Archbald . . . . Archbald
LU 3800 Tri County . . . . Media
LU 4285 Langhorne . . Langhorne
LU 4469 Johnstown . . . Johnstown
LU 5225 Indiana. . . . . Indiana
LU 6728 Bensalem . . . . Bensalem
LU 7048 Philadelphia Bulk Mail
  Center . . . . Philadelphia
LU 7067 Wilkes-Barre
  PDC . . . . Wilkes-Barre
SA Pennsylvania . . . Wilkes-Barre

Railroad Signalmen
GC 4 Baltimore & Ohio
  Railroad . . . . Connellsville
GC 62 Amtrak Eastern . . . Lansdale
LLG 1. . . . . Mifflintown
LLG 2 . . . . Pittsburgh
LLG 26 . . . . . Schuylkill Haven
LLG 40. . . . . Jeannette
LLG 53. . . . . Drexel Hill
LLG 57 . . . . Northampton
LLG 63. . . . . Williamsport
LLG 105. . . . . . Mechanicsburg
LLG 106 . . . . . . Elizabethtown
LLG 134 . . . . Castanea
LLG 150 . . . . Carnegie
LLG 193. . . . . Aliquippa

Retail, Wholesale and Department Store
JB Allegheny Regional . . Pittsburgh
LU 101 . . . . Pittsburgh
LU 1034 . . . . Philadelphia
LU 1718. . . . . Berlin

Roofers, Waterproofers and Allied Workers
LU 30. . . . . Philadelphia
LU 37. . . . . Bellevue
LU 210 . . . . Erie

Rural Letter Carriers
LU Allegheny County . . . . . Mars
LU Armstrong County . . East Brady
LU Beaver County . . New Brighton
LU Bedford County. . . . . Bedford
LU Berks County . . . Boyertown
LU Blair County . . . Hollidaysburg
LU Bradford-Sullivan
  Counties . . . . Gillett
LU Bucks County . . Doylestown
LU Butler County . . . . Evans City
LU Cambria County . . . . . Patton
LU Centre County . . . . Bellefonte
LU Clearfield County . . . Gramplan
LU Columbia-Montour
  Counties . . . . Danville

LU Cumberland-Dauphin
  Counties . . . . Harrisburg
LU Delaware-Chester
  Counties . . . . Narvon
LU Elk-Cameron
  Counties . . . . Weedville
LU Fayette County. . . . Uniontown
LU Franklin-Fulton
  Counties . . . . . Chambersburg
LU Huntingdon
  County . . . . . Mapleton Depot
LU Indiana County . . . . Armagh
LU Jefferson-Clarion. Punxsutawney
LU Lancaster County . . . Lancaster
LU Lebanon County . . Myerstown
LU Lehigh-Pocono . . Northampton
LU Luzerne County . Mountain Top
LU Lycoming-Clinton
  Counties . . . . Hughesville
LU Mercer-Lawrence
  Counties . . . . Fredonia
LU Montgomery
  County . . . . . Schwenksville
LU Perry-Juanita-Mifflin
  Counties . . . . . . Port Royal
LU Potter-McKean Counties . Eldred
LU Schuylkill County. . Orwigsburg
LU Somerset County . . . . Friedens
LU Susquehanna
  County . . . . . Little Meadows
LU Tioga County . . . . . Ulysses
LU Union-Snyder-Northumberland
  Counties . . . . Lewisburg
LU Venango-Crawford
  Counties . . . . Linesville
LU Warren-Forest
  Counties . . . . . . Sugar Grove
LU Washington County . McDonald
LU Wayne-Pike
  Counties . . . . Lake Ariel
LU Westmoreland County. . Latrobe
LU Wyoming County . Tunkhannock
LU York County . . . . . Glenville
LU 1 Adams County . . . . Fairfield
LU 21 Erie County. . . . . Edinboro
LU 24 Greene County . Carmichaels
SA Pennsylvania . . . Hollidaysburg

Security, Police and Fire Professionals
LU 502 . . . . Baden
LU 506 . . . . Philadelphia

Service Employees
JC 45 . . . . Harrisburg
LU 16 . . . . Pittsburgh
LU 22 Firemen & Oilers . . . . Erie
LU 40 Firemen &
  Oilers. . . . . Philadelphia
LU 61 . . . . Philadelphia
LU 69 . . . . Greensburg
LU 75 Firemen & Oilers . Pittsburgh
LU 188 . . . . Pittsburgh
LU 252 . . . . Wynnewood
LU 344 Firemen &
  Oilers. . . . . Lansdowne
LU 473 Firemen &
  Oilers. . . . . Philadelphia
LU 504 MH/MR/DD Home Care
  Workers-Pennsylvania . Pittsburgh
LU 508 . . . . North Versailles
LU 612 . . . . Philadelphia
LU 668 . . . . Harrisburg
LU 1199 NUHHCE,
  Pennsylvania Health Care
  Employees . . . . Harrisburg
LU 1206 Firemen & Oilers. Scranton

LU 1215 Firemen &
  Oilers. . . . . Harrisburg
LU 1216 Firemen & Oilers . Altoona
LU 1218 Firemen & Oilers . . Baden
LU 1250 Firemen & Oilers . Tyrone

Sheet Metal Workers
LU 12 . . . . Pittsburgh
LU 19 . . . . Philadelphia
LU 44 . . . . Wilkes-Barre
LU 194 . . . . Cheltenham
LU 520 . . . . Harrisburg
LU 525 . . . . Tyrone

State, County and Municipal Employees
C 13 Pennsylvania Public
  Employees . . . . Harrisburg
D 1199-C Philadelphia Health Care
  Employees . . . . . . Philadelphia
DC 33. . . . . Philadelphia
DC 47 Philadelphia Administrative,
  Professional & Technical
  Association. . . . . . Philadelphia
DC 83 Pennsylvania Public
  Employees,
  Southwestern. . . . . Harrisburg
DC 84 Pennsylvania Public
  Employees, Western . . Harrisburg
DC 85 Pennsylvania Public
  Employees,
  Northwestern. . . . . . Harrisburg
DC 86 Pennsylvania Public
  Employees, North
  Central . . . . Harrisburg
DC 87 Pennsylvania Public
  Employees,
  Northeastern. . . . . Harrisburg
DC 88 Pennsylvania Public
  Employees,
  Southeastern . . . . . Harrisburg
DC 89 Pennsylvania Public
  Employees, Southern . Harrisburg
DC 90 Pennsylvania Public
  Employees, Dauphin
  County . . . . Harrisburg
LU United Child Care
  Union. . . . . Philadelphia
LU 45 Mercy Hospital
  Employees . . . . Altoona
LU 54 University of Pennsylvania
  Cafeteria Workers . . Philadelphia
LU 285 . . . . Brookville
LU 471 . . . . Berlin
LU 488 . . . . Philadelphia
LU 590 University of Pennsylvania
  Employees . . . . . . Philadelphia
LU 752 Philadelphia Zoo
  Employees . . . . . . Philadelphia
LU 816 Hillview Care Center
  Employees. . . . . . . Bellwood
LU 1278 Johnstown Water Works
  Employees . . . . . . Johnstown
LU 1723 Temple University
  Employees . . . . . . Philadelphia
LU 1739 Community & Social
  Agency Employees. . Philadelphia
LU 1807 . . . . Carnegie
LU 2309 . . . . Indiana
LU 2482 Ashland Regional Medical
  Center . . . . Pottsville
LU 2562 Child Development Center
  of Northeast Pennsylvania
  Employees . . . . Berwick
LU 2631 Shippensburg Area
  Pennsylvania Employees. Carlisle
LU 2665 . . . . Clearfield

LU 3070 Sieman Lakeview Manor
  Estates . . . . Somerset
LU 3156 Hospital & Mobile
  Emergency Medicine
  Employees . . . . . . Altoona
LU 3397 Faculty Federation of Art
  Institute. . . . . . . Philadelphia
LU 3853 . . . . Philipsburg
LU 3950 Central Fill Inc.
  Pennsylvania
  Employees . . . . . Hummelstown

Steelworkers
C Delaware Valley Oil. . . Linwood
C Industry . . . . Alburtis
C Pennsylvania Grade Crude
  Regional . . . . Karns City
C Region 111
  Council. . . . . . Northumberland
DC 1 . . . . Northampton
LU 782-008 . . . . . White Haven
LU 2-1 . . . . Linwood
LU 02-18 . . . . Wind Gap
LU 02-29. . . . . . . Walnutport
LU 02-54 . . . . Fleetwood
LU 02-68 . . . . Philadelphia
LU 02-73 Horse Nail
  Makers . . . . . New Brighton
LU 02-74 . . . . Beaver
LU 02-100 . . . . . Wernersville
LU 02-179 . . . . . Spring Grove
LU 02-234 . . . . Linwood
LU 02-240. . . . . . . Glenshaw
LU 02-286 . . . . . Philadelphia
LU 02-296 . . . . . . Pittsburgh
LU 02-304 . . . . Center Valley
LU 02-308 . . . . . Williamsburg
LU 02-326 . . . . Columbia
LU 02-333 . . . . . Honeybrook
LU 02-348 . . . . Erie
LU 02-373 . . . . Aliquippa
LU 02-375 . . . . . Philadelphia
LU 02-376 . . . . . . Allentown
LU 02-412 . . . . . East Bangor
LU 02-422. . . . . East Freedom
LU 02-441 . . . . . . Emlenton
LU 02-448 . . . . Chester
LU 02-455 . . . . . . Rouseville
LU 02-456 . . . . . . Gettysburg
LU 02-488 . . . . . . Martinsburg
LU 02-504 . . . . Roaring Spring
LU 02-529. . . . . . Eighty Four
LU 02-547 . . . . . . Lehighton
LU 02-554 . . . . . . Fogelsville
LU 02-578 . . . . Easton
LU 02-580 . . . . Northumberland
LU 02-583 . . . . . . Bradford
LU 02-604 . . . . . . Darlington
LU 02-607 . . . . . Smethport
LU 02-614 Yorktowne . . . . York
LU 02-615 . . . . . . Nescopeck
LU 02-623 . . . . Beaver
LU 02-629 . . . . . . Gardners
LU 02-635 . . . . Mount Carmel
LU 02-667 . . . . . Philadelphia
LU 02-670 . . . . . Mount Joy
LU 02-690. . . . . . Rochester
LU 02-701 . . . . . Johnsonburg
LU 02-714 . . . . Aston
LU 02-719 . . . . . Minersville
LU 02-729 . . . . Easton
LU 02-788 . . . . . White Haven
LU 02-789 . . . . North Versailles
LU 02-807 . . . . . Phoenixville
LU 02-839 . . . . . Biglerville
LU 02-859 . . . . . . Charleroi
LU 02-875 . . . . . Williamsport
LU 02-886 . . . . Jeannette

LU 02-889. . . . . Cranberry
LU 02-890 . . . . Bristol
LU 02-892. . . . . Monaca
LU 02-901 . . . . Linwood
LU 02-902 . . . . Hanover
LU 02-940 . . . . . Downingtown
LU 02-993 . . . . . Monroeville
LU 02-1098 . . . . Mechanicsburg
LU 02-1130 . . Delaware Water Gap
LU 02-1160 . . . . Latrobe
LU 02-1281 . . . . Erie
LU 02-1303. . . . . York
LU 02-1338 . . . . Shamokin
LU 02-1419 . . . . Sinking Spring
LU 02-1442 . . . . . Alexandria
LU 02-1443. . . . . . Laureldale
LU 02-1448 . . . . . . Pittston
LU 02-1531 . . . . . Sugarloaf
LU 02-1754 . . . . . . Brogue
LU 02-1811. . . . . York
LU 02-1815 . . . . . Claysville
LU 04-90-T . . . . . . Pittsburgh
LU 04-8936-S . . . . . . Holmes
LU 04-12781-S . . Marcus Hook
LU 05-843 . . . . Waynesburg
LU 07-198-G. . . . . . Dunbar
LU 08-26-L . . . . . . Springs
LU 08-86 . . . . Lansdale
LU 08-240 . . . New Kensington
LU 08-9016-S . . . . . Hanover
LU 10-12-G . . . . . Creighton
LU 10-21 . . . . Butler
LU 10-22-L . . . . . Jeannette
LU 10-52-T . . . . . Pittsburgh
LU 10-53-G . . . . . Charleroi
LU 10-67-T . . . . . Freedom
LU 10-71 . . . . . Falls Creek
LU 10-88-S . . . . Bristol
LU 10-100 . . . . . Shippenville
LU 10-102-T . . Mount Pleasant
LU 10-103-T . . . . Jeannette
LU 10-112-G . . . . . . Arnold
LU 10-117-T. . . . Connellsville
LU 10-142 . . . . . Washington
LU 10-146-T . . . . Washington
LU 10-148. . . . . Erie
LU 10-150-T . . . Port Allegany
LU 10-158 . . . . . Kittanning
LU 10-256-L . . . Beaver Falls
LU 10-285-L . . . . Lancaster
LU 10-404-U . . Philadelphia
LU 10-409-G . . . . . Butler
LU 10-480-A . . . Shenandoah
LU 10-482-A. . . . . Tamaqua
LU 10-485-A . . . . Lehighton
LU 10-500-L. . . Ellwood City
LU 10-505-T . . . . . Latrobe
LU 10-512-T . . . Beaver Falls
LU 10-532-T. . . . West Mifflin
LU 10-535-T . . . . . . Irwin
LU 10-537 . . . Mount Pleasant
LU 10-544 . . . . . Washington
LU 10-545. . . . . . Greensburg
LU 10-547-T . . . Mount Morris
LU 10-555-T . . . Enon Valley
LU 10-580 . . . Ellwood City
LU 10-590-T . . . . . Jeannette
LU 10-930-B. . . . Shoemakersville
LU 10-1001. . . . . . Wellsboro
LU 10-1016-S . . . . New Castle
LU 10-1019 . . . . . Smethport
LU 10-1024 . . . . Greencastle
LU 10-1035-S . . . . Lancaster
LU 10-1138-S . . . . Leechburg
LU 10-1145-S . . . . Jeannette
LU 10-1165-S . . . . Coatesville
LU 10-1187-S . . . . . Allenport
LU 10-1196-S . . . Brackenridge

LU 10-1211-S . . . . Beaver Falls
LU 10-1212-S. . . . . . Midland
LU 10-1219-S . . . . . Braddock
LU 10-1324-S . . New Kensington
LU 10-1355-S . . . . Sharpsville
LU 10-1408-S . . North Versailles
LU 10-1537-S . . . . . Latrobe
LU 10-1557-S . . . . . Clairton
LU 10-1660-S . . . . Hermitage
LU 10-1688-S . . . . . Steelton
LU 10-1852-S . . . . York
LU 10-1913-S . . North Braddock
LU 10-1917-S . . . . Meadville
LU 10-1928-S . . . . . . Milton
LU 10-1940-S . . . . Lewistown
LU 10-2227-S . . . West Mifflin
LU 10-2229-S . . . . . Oil City
LU 10-2599-S . . . . Bethlehem
LU 10-2632-S . . . . Johnstown
LU 10-2635-S . . . . Johnstown
LU 10-3199-S . . . . Erie
LU 10-3403-S. . . . Fayette City
LU 10-3657-S. . . . . Pittsburgh
LU 10-3713-S . . . . Greenville
LU 10-4889-S . . . Fairless Hills
LU 10-4907-S . . . Williamsport
LU 10-5032 . . . Moon Township
LU 10-5306-S . . . . Harrisville
LU 10-5652-S . . . Wilkes-Barre
LU 10-5852-S. . . . . Pittsburgh
LU 10-6346-S . . . . Eau Claire
LU 10-6521-S. . . . . . Altoona
LU 10-6816-S . . . . Norristown
LU 10-6996-S . . . Wyomissing
LU 10-7139-S . . . . Washington
LU 10-7274-S . . . . . Lebanon
LU 10-7312-S . . . . . . Corry
LU 10-7343-S . . . . Gettysburg
LU 10-7687-S . . . Spring Grove
LU 10-8041-S . . North Charleroi
LU 10-8042-S . . . . . Butler
LU 10-8166-S. . . . . Brockway
LU 10-8183-S . . West Bridgewater
LU 10-8567-S . . . West Hazleton
LU 10-9305-S . . . . Beaver Falls
LU 10-9445 . . . New Kensington
LU 10-9455. . . . . Collegeville
LU 10-9462 . . . Conshohocken
LU 10-12050-S . . . . Pittsburgh
LU 10-12698-S . . . . Boothwyn
LU 10-13836-S . . . . Uniontown
LU 10-14034-S . . . . Pittsburgh
LU 10-14040-S . . . . . Eldred
LU 10-14372-S . . . . Ashland
LU 10-14693-S . . . Canonsburg
LU 10-15253-S . . Wilkes-Barre
NHQ . . . . Pittsburgh

Teachers
LU 2208 Moore College of Art &
   Design . . . . . . Philadelphia
LU 3412 Robert Morris College
   Faculty Federation . . . . Freedom
LU 3505 Akiba Hebrew Academy
   Faculty Association . . . Merion
LU 3578 Perelman Jewish Day
   School . . . . Jenkintown
LU 3845 Lincoln Technical
   Institute. . . . . . Philadelphia
LU 3942 Western Penn School for
   Blind Child . . . . Pittsburgh
LU 4531 Temple
   University . . . . Philadelphia
LU 4802 . . . . . . Philadelphia
LU 4973 Woodhaven Federation
   of Human Service
   Professionals . . . . Philadelphia
LU 6290 Tugsa . . . . Philadelphia

LU 8036 Pennsylvania . Philadelphia

Teamsters
CONF Pennsylvania Conference of
   Teamsters . . . . . . Harrisburg
JC 40 . . . . Mars
JC 53 . . . . Philadelphia
LU 30 . . . . Jeannette
LU 107 . . . . Philadelphia
LU 110 . . . . Ebensburg
LU 115 . . . . Philadelphia
LU 169. . . . . . . Elkins Park
LU 205 . . . . White Oak
LU 211 . . . . Pittsburgh
LU 229. . . . . Scranton
LU 249 . . . . Pittsburgh
LU 250 . . . . Pittsburgh
LU 261 . . . . New Castle
LU 312 . . . . Chester
LU 341 . . . . Ambridge
LU 384 . . . . Norristown
LU 397 . . . . Erie
LU 401 . . . . . . Wilkes-Barre
LU 429 . . . . . . Wyomissing
LU 463 . . . . Fort Washington
LU 470 . . . . Philadelphia
LU 491 . . . . Uniontown
LU 500 . . . . Philadelphia
LU 538 . . . . Worthington
LU 585 . . . . Washington
LU 623 . . . . Philadelphia
LU 628 . . . . Philadelphia
LU 636 . . . . . . McKees Rocks
LU 764 . . . . Milton
LU 771 . . . . Lancaster
LU 773 . . . . Allentown
LU 776 . . . . Harrisburg
LU 830 . . . . Philadelphia
LU 837 Industrial Workers
   Union . . . . . . Philadelphia
LU 926 . . . . Pittsburgh
LU 929 . . . . Philadelphia
LU 1414 . . . . . . Philadelphia

Television and Radio Artists
LU Philadelphia . . . . Philadelphia
LU Pittsburgh . . . . . . Pittsburgh

Theatrical Stage Employees
D 4 Pennsylvania-Delaware-
   Maryland-Virginia-West
   Virginia-DC . . . . Philadelphia
LU 3. . . . . Pittsburgh
LU 8 . . . . Philadelphia
LU 29-B . . . . Philadelphia
LU 82 . . . . Wilkes-Barre
LU 97 . . . . Reading
LU 98 . . . . Harrisburg
LU 113 . . . . Erie
LU 152 . . . . Beaver Meadows
LU 200 Allentown-
   Easton . . . . Allentown
LU 218 . . . . . . Shenandoah
LU 283 . . . . York
LU 329 . . . . Dalton
LU 451 . . . . New Castle
LU 489 . . . . Pittsburgh
LU 627 IATSE . . . . . Strabane
LU 636 . . . . . . State College
LU 752 . . . . Philadelphia
LU 787 . . . . Pittsburgh
LU 799 . . . . Philadelphia
LU 820 . . . . Pittsburgh
LU 862 . . . . Pittsburgh
LU 902 . . . . Johnstown

Train Dispatchers
SCOM Conrail System . . . Hatfield

SCOM GCA N & W
   North. . . . . Carnegie

Transit Union
CONBD Pennsylvania
   Legislative . . . . Salix
LDIV 85 . . . . . . Pittsburgh
LDIV 89 . . . . . . New Castle
LDIV 801 . . . . . . Altoona
LDIV 956 . . . . . . Whitehall
LDIV 1119 . . . . Wilkes-Barre
LDIV 1195 . . . . Harrisburg
LDIV 1241 . . . . . Lancaster
LDIV 1345 . . . . . Reading
LDIV 1496 . . . . Williamsport
LDIV 1552 . . . . . Pittsburgh
LU 1603 . . . . Lehigh Valley
LU 1729. . . . . . Pittsburgh
LU 1738 . . . . . . Latrobe
LU 1743 . . . . . . Pittsburgh
LU 1753 . . . . . South Park

Transport Workers
LU 234 . . . . Philadelphia
LU 289 . . . . East Lansdowne
LU 290 . . . . . Philadelphia
LU 545 . . . . Moon Township
LU 700 . . . . . Philadelphia
LU 2009 Railroad
   Division . . . . North Huntingdon
LU 2013 . . . . . . Broomall
LU 2016 . . . . Enola
LU 2017. . . . . . . Altoona
LU 2035. . . . . . . Conway

**Transportation Communications
Union**
D 133 . . . . Monroeville
D 518 . . . . Lansdowne
D 718 Conrail . . . . Langhorne
D 747 . . . . . . Coraopolis
D 821 . . . . Altoona
D 878 . . . . . . Philadelphia
D 1218 Conrail . . . . Langhorne
LG 5075 Port Authority Trans
   Hudson . . . . Bushkill
LG 6965 Oak Island . . . Bethlehem

Transportation Union
GCA GO-769 Conrail-PC-Lines
   East-PLE . . . Philadelphia
GCA GO-969 Union
   Railroad-Pittsburgh . . . . Verona
LU 61 . . . . . King of Prussia
LU 309 . . . . Ashville
LU 340 . . . . . Connellsville
LU 386 . . . . . . Pottsville
LU 498 . . . . . . Nazareth
LU 596 . . . . . . Jamestown
LU 602 . . . . . Montoursville
LU 632 . . . . Windber
LU 800 . . . . Bangor
LU 816 . . . . . Elizabethtown
LU 830 . . . . . . Harrisburg
LU 997 . . . . . . Camp Hill
LU 1006 . . . . . Finleyville
LU 1074 . . . . Lower Burrell
LU 1373 . . . . . Philadelphia
LU 1374 . . . . . New Castle
LU 1375 . . . . . Havertown
LU 1379 . . . . . Uniontown
LU 1418 . . . . . . Conway
LU 1447 . . . . . Allentown
LU 1590 . . . . . . Vanport
LU 1594 . . . . Upper Darby
LU 1628 . . . . . Monroeville
LU 1722 . . . . . Lancaster
LU 1948 . . . . . New Castle

SLB LO-41
Pennsylvania . . . . . . Harrisburg

Treasury Employees
CH 22 . . . . Philadelphia
CH 34 . . . . Pittsburgh
CH 71 . . . . Philadelphia
CH 89 . . . . Levittown
CH 90 . . . . Philadelphia
CH 110 . . . . Philadelphia
CH 135 . . . . Pittsburgh
CH 232 . . . . Philadelphia
CH 299 Northeast
   District . . . . Pittsburgh

UNITE HERE
JB Pennsylvania Ohio & South
   Jersey . . . . Philadelphia
JB Philadelphia . . . . . Philadelphia
LU 15-88 . . . . Philadelphia
LU 26-I . . . . Philadelphia
LU 33-T . . . . Philadelphia
LU 45 . . . . Philadelphia
LU 57 . . . . Pittsburgh
LU 75-A . . . . Philadelphia
LU 93 . . . . Philadelphia
LU 108-I . . . . Philadelphia
LU 109-I . . . . Dunmore
LU 111 . . . . Allentown
LU 125 . . . . Philadelphia
LU 126-333 . . . . Philadelphia
LU 148-C . . . . Philadelphia
LU 170-A . . . . Philadelphia
LU 170-I . . . . Philadelphia
LU 185 . . . . Dunmore
LU 196 . . . . Philadelphia
LU 197 . . . . Philadelphia
LU 225 . . . . Meadville
LU 225-I . . . . Dunmore
LU 227-I . . . . Philadelphia
LU 234 . . . . Allentown
LU 237 . . . . Philadelphia
LU 241-LDC . . . . . . Mount Wolf
LU 243-I . . . . Allentown
LU 249 . . . . Dunmore
LU 274 . . . . Philadelphia
LU 295 . . . . Dunmore
LU 352 . . . . Philadelphia
LU 391 . . . . Allentown
LU 424 . . . . Philadelphia
LU 634 School Cafeteria Employees
   Union . . . . Philadelphia
LU 1034-T . . . . Huntingdon
LU 1700 . . . . Bloomsburg
LU 2520 . . . . Philadelphia
STC Pennsylvania . . . Philadelphia

University Professors
CH Delaware Valley College
   Chapter . . . . Doylestown
DIV Pennsylvania . . . . . Leesport

Utility Workers
JC Columbia Gas System . Pittsburgh
LU 102 . . . . Rector
LU 102-B . . . . . . Lower Burrell
LU 102-C . . . . St. Marys
LU 102-D . . . . Greensburg
LU 102-F . . . . Scottdale
LU 102-G . . . . Clarksville
LU 102-H . . . . . . Washington
LU 102-I . . . . Kittanning
LU 102-J . . . . Fenelton
LU 102-K . . . . Ruffsdale
LU 102-L . . . . Howard
LU 102-M . . . . . . Uniontown
LU 102-N . . . . . . Mercersburg

LU 102-R Cumberland,
   Oakland . . . . Meyersdale
LU 140 . . . . Butler
LU 180 . . . . Altoona
LU 242 . . . . . . Sprankle Mills
LU 262 . . . . Shickshinny
LU 285 . . . . Hermitage
LU 287 . . . . Uniontown
LU 332 . . . . Forty Fort
LU 334 . . . . Shamokin
LU 406 . . . . Wilkes-Barre
LU 407 . . . . South Williamsport
LU 408 . . . . . Northumberland
LU 435 . . . . Lewistown
LU 437 . . . . Midland
LU 456 . . . . Clairton
LU 475 . . . . Wampum
LU 479 . . . . Pittsburgh
LU 489 . . . . Harrisburg
LU 506 . . . . . . Rochester Mills
LU 516 . . . . Berwick
LU 529 . . . . Millville
LU 537 . . . . Washington
LU 540 . . . . Baden
LU 554 . . . . Stroudsburg
LU 563 . . . . Sayre

Weather Service Employees
BR 01-8 . . . . . Moon Township
BR 01-51 . . . . Allentown
BR 01-56 . . . . . State College
BR 01-86 . . . . . State College

Westinghouse Salaried Employees
ASSN East Pittsburgh Plaza
   Employees . . . . East Pittsburgh
NHQ . . . . Pittsburgh

Unaffiliated Labor Organizations

African American Workers
   Union . . . . Pittsburgh
Armco Butler Independent Salary
   Union . . . . Butler
Associated Services for the Blind
   Employees Group . . Philadelphia
Bakers Independent
   Union . . . . . . King of Prussia
Beaver Salaried Employees
   Association . . . . Beaver
Berry Metal Employees
   Association . Cranberry Township
Bethlehem Corporation Employees
   Association . . . . Bethlehem
Broadcast Employees Staff
   Team . . . . Indiana
Brownsville Nurses
   Association . . . . . Belle Vernon
Butler Armco Plant Protection
   Employees, Armco Steel
   Corporation . . . . . Saxonburg
C.A. Spalding Company Employees'
   Association . . . . Croydon
Carnegie Mellon Campus Police
   Association . . . . . . Pittsburgh
Choice Hospitality Independent
   People . . . . Southampton
Commercial Kitchen Equipment
   Workers United
   LU 1 . . . . Philadelphia
Concrete Product Workers
   Union . . . . Fredonia
D.G. Nicholas Employees
   Association . . . . . Carbondale
Delaware County Prison Employees
   Independent Union . . . Thornton

Fellow Employees Labor
   Organization . . . . . New Castle
Fitzgerald Mercy Hospital Nurses
   Association PSEA . . . . Chester
Fraternal Association of Professional
   Paramedics LU 4 . . . Turtle Creek
Fraternal Association of Professional
   Paramedics LU 8 . . . . Cheswick
General Partitions Manufacturing
   Corporation Shop Union . . . Erie
Guards & Plant Protection
   Employees LU 3 . . . . Erie
Hamilton Watch Workers
   Independent . . . . . . Lancaster
Homer Center Riverside Employees
   Independent . . . . . Homer City
Immco Employees
   Association . . . . . . Allentown
Independent Cryogenics
   Workers . . . . Bethlehem
Independent Mixed Drivers
   Union . . . . Quakertown
Independent Wire Workers
   Union . . . . Mount Joy
Indiana Registered Nurses PSEA or
   IHPEA . . . . Bolivar
Industrial Workers of the World
   NHQ . . . . Philadelphia
Jeannette Professional Nurses
   Association . . . . . . Ruffsdale
Keystone Rustproofing Independent
   Union . . . . Arnold
Lady Ester-Undergarment Workers
   Association . . . . Berwick
Legal Services Plan Professional
   Employees Union DC 33 . . Media
Lower Bucks Hospital Nurses
   Association . . . . . . Croydon
Major League Umpires
   Association . . . . . Bala Cynwyd
McCauley Truck Drivers Dock &
   Mechanics Union
   Independent . . . New Bethlehem
Mechanics Union Independent
   LU 1 . . . . . . West Alexander
Melrath Employees Union
   Independent . . . . . Philadelphia
Montour Cafeteria Educational
   Support Personnel Association
   (PSEA/NEA) . . . McKees Rocks
National Association of Catholic
   School Teachers Greensburg
   Catholic Teachers
   Association . . . . . . Greensburg
National Education Association
   Abington Cafeteria/
   ESPA . . . . Philadelphia
National Education Association
   Bethel Park/ESPA-PSEA-
   NEA . . . . Bethel Park
National Education Association
   Elizabeth-For-Food-Service/PSEA/
   NEA . . . . Elizabeth
National Education Association
   Elwyn EA/PSEA 65-23-
   200 . . . . Aston
National Education Association
   Lackawanna Junior College/PSEA/
   NEA . . . . . Madison Township
National Education Association
   Shaler Area/SSPA/PSEA/
   ESPA . . . . Allison Park
National Education Association
   South Allegheny ESPA, PSEA,
   NEA . . . . Elizabeth
National Forge Employees Union
   Independent . . . . Warren

Norwin School Bus Drivers
   Association . . . . Larimer
Nurses, Pennsylvania State
   LP, Independent DIV
   701 . . . . Wyomissing
Penn Iron Employees Union
   Association . . . . . Wyomissing
Pennsylvania Association of Staff
   Nurses and Allied
   Professionals . . . . Conshohocken
Pennsylvania Independent
   Nurses . . . . Butler
Pennsylvania State Education
   Association Armstrong Nurses
   Association-PSEA or
   ANA . . . . Kittanning
Pennsylvania State Education
   Association Dallas
   Cafeteria/ESPA/PSEA/
   NEA . . . . Dallas
Pennsylvania State Education
   Association Somerset Professional
   Nurses Association . . . . Boswell
Pitt Police Association
   Inc. . . . . Pittsburgh
PNI Security Union . Conshohocken
Professional Association of Golf
   Agronomy . . . . . Bala Cynwyd
Salesmen's Committee
   Inc. . . . . Warminster
Shaw Industries Union
   Independent . . . . . . Franklin
Staff Representatives
   Union . . . . Pittsburgh
Steel Workers Union of Beaver
   Valley Independent . New Brighton
Sun Oil Company Employees
   Association Blawnox District
   Operating Employees . . Pittsburgh
Sun Oil Company Employees
   Association Research &
   Development
   Employees . . . . . Marcus Hook
Sun Oil Employees Association Twin
   Oaks . . . . Aston
Temple University Hospital Nurses
   Association . . . . . . Philadelphia
Textile Garment Workers
   Association . . . . Millville
Union de Trabajadores de
   Kaolin Kaolin Workers
   Union . . . . . . Kennett Square
Union Employees Union
   LU 1 . . . . Pittsburgh
United Independent Aerosol
   Workers . . . . Somerset
United Independent Union
   LU 8 . . . . Philadelphia
United Independent Union
   LU 9 . . . . Philadelphia
United States Womens National
   Soccer Team Players
   Association . . . . . . Philadelphia
Utility Coordinating Council 2 IBEW
   Utility Locals Unions . Middletown
Valley Nurses
   Association . . . . Wyoming
Warren General Hospital Professional
   Employees Association . . Warren
Westfield Tanning Company
   Employees Association . Westfield
WUSA Players
   Association . . . . . . Philadelphia
Yorkco Salaried Employees
   Association . . . . York

Puerto Rico

Affiliated Labor Organizations

Agricultural Employees
BR 13 . . . . Toa Baja

Air Traffic Controllers
LU SJU . . . . San Juan
LU ZSU . . . . Carolina

Automobile, Aerospace Workers
LU 103 . . . . Canovanas
LU 1850 . . . . Carolina
LU 2286 . . . . Manati
LU 2311 . . . . Corozal
LU 2312 Hato Rey Community
    Hospital . . . . Caguas
LU 2429 Union Empleados Suiza
    Dairy . . . . Toa Baja

Civilian Technicians
CH 119 Puerto Rico National
    Guard . . . . Juana Diaz

Communications Workers
LU 3010 Union Trabajadores de Los
    Com de Puerto Rico. . . Aquadilla
LU 3150 . . . . Caguas
LU 33225 Puerto Rico . . . San Juan

Commuter Rail Employees
LDIV . . . . San Juan

Education
LU Antilles Consolidated Education
    Association. . . . . . . San Juan

Federal Employees
LU 523 International Institute of
    Tropical Forestry. . . . San Juan
LU 2158 . . . . Vega Baja

Fire Fighters
LU 97-F . . . . Fajardo

Food and Commercial Workers
LU 481 Asociacion de Peloteros
    Profesionales . . . . . Bayamon
LU 481 Federacion Americana de
    Empleados Publicos . . . San Juan

Government Employees
LU 55 . . . . Mayaguez
LU 1503 GSA Center . . . San Juan
LU 2408 VA . . . . San Juan
LU 2598 DoL . . . . . . Trujillo Alto
LU 2608 HHS . . . . Caguas
LU 2614 DoD . . . . San Juan
LU 2698 DoJ . . . . San Juan
LU 2837 HUD . . . . . . San Juan
LU 2951 SBA . . . . San Juan
LU 3408 USDA . . . . Caguas
LU 3936 AFB. . . . . Carolina
LU L-4052 Council of Prisons Locals
    C-33 . . . . San Juan

Government Security Officers
LU 33 . . . . San Juan
LU 72 . . . . Vega Alta

Letter Carriers
BR 826 . . . . Ponce
BR 869 . . . . San Juan

Longshoremen
DC Puerto Rico . . . . . . San Juan
LU 1575 . . . . San Juan
LU 1740 . . . . San Juan
LU 1856 . . . . Fajardo
LU 1901 Empleados de
    Muelles. . . . . San Juan
LU 1902 . . . . San Juan
LU 1903 . . . . Ponce
LU 1904 Union Trabajadores
    Muelles y Ramas
    Anexas . . . . Mayaguez
LU 1965 . . . . Vieques
LU 2012 . . . . Lajas

Machinists
LG 2725 . . . . Rio Grande

Musicians
LU 555 . . . . San Juan

NLRB Professional Association
LU 24 . . . . San Juan

Office and Professional Employees
LU 402 . . . . Santurce
LU 506 . . . . Rio Grande

Postal Mail Handlers
LU 313 . . . . San Juan

Postal Workers
LU 1070 Puerto Rico Area
    Local . . . . San Juan
LU 5898 Gurabo . . . . . . Gurabo

Seafarers
LU Puerto Rico Caribbean & Latin
    America . . . . San Juan

Steelworkers
LU 04-5954-S . . . . . . Toa Baja
LU 04-6873 . . . . Bayamon
LU 04-7797-S . . . . . . Bayamon
LU 04-8201-S . . . . Trujillo Alto
LU 04-9058 . . . . San Juan
LU 04-9242 . . . . Bayamon
LU 04-9314-S . . . . . Hato Rey
LU 09-6135-S . . . . Trujillo Alto
LU 09-6588-S . . . . Vega Baja
LU 09-6871 . . . . Dorado
LU 09-8198-S . . . . . . Ponce

Teamsters
LU 901 . . . . Santurce

Treasury Employees
CH 188 . . . . San Juan
CH 193 . . . . San Juan

UNITE HERE
LU 610 . . . . San Juan

Weather Service Employees
BR 02-30 . . . . Carolina

Unaffiliated Labor Organizations

Abono Super A
    Independent . . . . Aguada
Asociacion de Empleados del Fondo
    de Bienestar y Pension
    I L A . . . . Bayamon
Asociacion Empleados Casinos
    Puerto Rico . . . . . Puerto Nuevo
Cemento Mezclado Union Obreros
    Independent . . . . San Juan
Cemento Union de Operadores y
    Canteros de la Industria . . . Ponce
Confederacion General de
    Trabajadores de Puerto Rico LU
    Empleados de Drogeria y
    Farmacia . . . . . . Puerto Nuevo
Confederacion General de
    Trabajadores de Puerto Rico LU
    Union Trabajadores Ready
    Mix . . . . Puerto Nuevo
Confederacion General de
    Trabajadores de Puerto Rico LU
    1964 Trabajadores de la Industria
    del Abono . . . . Ensenada
Confederacion General de
    Trabajadores de Puerto Rico
    NHQ . . . . Puerto Nuevo
Congreso de Uniones Industriales de
    Puerto Rico LU 965 Trabajadores
    de Molinos . . . . Santurce
Congreso de Uniones Industriales de
    Puerto Rico NHQ . . . . Catano
Empleados Supermercados Pueblo
    Inc. . . . . San Juan
Equipo Pesado Construccion y
    Ramas . . . . Rio Piedras
Federacion del Trabajo de Puerto
    Rico Inc. (Federation of Union
    Local Unions) . . . . . San Juan
Federacion Puertorriquena de
    Trabajadores LU 412 Union de
    Empleadosmepsi Center . Toa Alta
Federacion Puertorriquena de
    Trabajadores LU 957 Union
    Empleados Auxilio
    Mutuo . . . . Trujillo Alto
Federacion Puertorriquena de
    Trabajadores NHQ. . . San Juan
Federacion Trabajadores de Empresa
    Privada (FETEMP) . Puerto Nuevo
Guardias de Seguridad del Hotel
    Caribe Hilton . . . . . . Vieques
Hermandad Independiente de
    Empleados Telefonicos
    HIETEL . . . . San Juan
Laborista de Puerto Rico,
    Confederacion, Independent
    NHQ . . . . Mayaguez
Los Gladiadores Inc. . . . . San Juan
Sindicato de Guardias de Seguridad
    de Puerto Rico. . . . Rio Piedras
Sindicato de Obreros Unidos del Sur
    de Puerto Rico LU 5 . . . . Ponce
Sindicato de Obreros Unidos del Sur
    de Puerto Rico LU 14 Trabajadores
    de la Industria Azucarera . Salinas
Sindicato de Obreros Unidos del Sur
    de Puerto Rico NHQ. . . . Salinas

Sindicato de Trabajadores de la
    Industria Electronica de Puerto
    Rico . . . . Aquadilla
Sindicato de Uniones
    Autonomas . . . . Ponce
Sindicato Puertorriqueno de
    Trabajadores LU Tecnicos y
    Profesionales Hospital . . . Ponce
Sindicato Puertorriqueno de
    Trabajadores LU Trabajadores de
    la Puerto Rico Cement
    Company . . . . Ponce
Sindicato Puertorriqueno de
    Trabajadores LU 929 Trabajadores
    de Borinquen Biscuits . . . Yauco
Sindicato Puertorriqueno de
    Trabajadores LU 999 Empleados
    Clemente Santisteban . . San Juan
Sindicato Puertorriqueno de
    Trabajadores NHQ. . . San Juan
Solaridad General de Trabajadores
    de Puerto Rico y Sus
    Afiliadas . . . . Trujillo Alto
Trabajadores de Estacionamiento
    Independent . . . . . Trujillo Alto
Trabajadores de la Cerveceria India
    Inc. Independent . . . . Mayaguez
Trabajadores de Servicios Legales
    Union Independiente. . . San Juan
Trabajadores Industriales y
    Construcciones
    Electricas . . . . Guaynabo
Trabajadores Petroquimicos Union
    Carbide . . . . Ponce
Unidad Laboral de Enfermeras (OS)
    Empleados de la Salud de Puerto
    Rico . . . . San Juan
Union de Abogados de Servicios
    Legales de Puerto Rico
    UASLPR . . . . San Juan
Union de Carpinteros de Puerto Rico
    CH 27 . . . . San Juan
Union de Carpinteros de Puerto Rico
    CH 0025 . . . . San Juan
Union de Carpinteros de Puerto Rico
    Inc. . . . . San Juan
Union de Construccion de Concreto
    Mixto y Equipo Pesado de Puerto
    Rico. . . . . Mayaguez
Union de Detectives y Guardias de
    Seguridad . . . . Dorado
Union de Empleados de la
    Bombonera . . . . San Juan
Union de Empleados de la Industria
    Petrolera y Sus Derivados. Bayamon
Union de Empleados del Hipodromo
    el Comandante . . . . . . Carolina
Union de Trabajadores Borinquen
    Macaroni . . . . Guanica
Union General de Trabajadores UGT
    4444 . . . . Rio Piedras
Union Independiente de Abogados
    de la Sociedad Para Asistencia
    Legal . . . . San Juan
Union Independiente de Empleados
    de la Cruz Azul. . . . . Guaynabo
Union Independiente de Trabajadores
    de la Industria de la Sal . Boqueron
Union Independiente Empleados
    Telefonicos de Puerto Rico
    Inc. . . . . Rio Piedras
Union Nacional de Trabajadores de
    Puerto Rico . . . . . . Rio Piedras
Union Trabajadores Industria
    Licorera . . . . Mercedita

Rhode Island

AFL-CIO Trade and Industrial Departments

Building and Construction Trades Department
BCTC Providence . . . . . Cranston

Affiliated Labor Organizations

Air Traffic Controllers
LU PVD . . . . Warwick

Automobile, Aerospace Workers
LU 7770 . . . . Newport

Bricklayers
LU 1 . . . . Cranston

Carpenters
LU 94 . . . . Warwick

Civilian Technicians
CH 22 Rhode
    Island . . . . . North Kingstown

Communications Workers
LU 14174 . . . . Woonsocket
LU 31041 . . . . Providence
LU 31182 . . . . Woonsocket
LU 32185 . . . . Pawtucket

Education
ASSN Rhode Island School of
    Design Faculty . . . . Providence
LU 845 Roger Williams University
    Faculty . . . . Bristol
LU 850 Roger Williams University
    Physical Plant . . . . . Bristol
LU 892 Roger Williams College
    Association Clericals/
    Technicals . . . . Bristol
LU 895 Part Time Faculty
    Association . . . . . . Providence
SA Rhode Island National Education
    Association . . . . Cranston

Electrical Workers
LU 99 . . . . Cranston
LU 1203 . . . . Pawtucket
LU 1274 . . . . Warwick
LU 2323 . . . . Cranston

Elevator Constructors
LU 39 . . . . Chepachet

Fire Fighters
LU 100-F . . . . Newport

Food and Commercial Workers
C New England . . . . Providence
LU 328 . . . . Providence

Government Employees
LU 190 DoD . . . . . Middletown
LU 2910 USDA . . East Providence

Government Employees Association
LU 01-134 . . . . . . Middletown
LU 01-144 . . . . Portsmouth
LU 01-240 . . . . . . Narragansett

Graphic Communications
LU 12-N . . . . Providence

Iron Workers
LU 37 . . . . East Providence
LU 523 . . . . Pawtucket

Laborers
DC Rhode Island . . . . Providence
LU New England
    Region . . . . Providence
LU 15 . . . . Westerly
LU 226 Lunch Program & Service
    Employees . . . . Providence
LU 271 . . . . Providence
LU 673 . . . . Middletown
LU 1322 . . . . Providence

Letter Carriers
BR 15 . . . . Cranston
BR 54 . . . . Woonsocket
BR 55 . . . . Pawtucket
BR 57 . . . . Portsmouth
BR 2158 . . . . . . West Warwick
BR 3166 . . . . Warwick
BR 3501 . . . . Manville
BR 6529 . . . . Harrisville
SA Rhode Island . . . . . Warwick

Locomotive Engineers
DIV 439 . . . . Woonsocket

Longshoremen
LU 1329 . . . . Providence
LU 1996-1 . . . . North Kingstown
LU 2001 . . . . Johnston

Machine Printers and Engravers
NHQ . . . . Providence

Machinists
LG 129 . . . . Riverside
LG 147 . . . . . . East Providence
LG 1017 . . . . Cranston
LG 2363 Human Service
    Providers . . . . Cranston
LG 2705 . . . . Ashaway

Maintenance of Way Employes
SLG 228 . . . . Pawtucket

Musicians
LU 198-457 Providence Federation
    of Musicians . . . . . . Cranston
LU 262 . . . . Woonsocket
LU 529 . . . . Middletown

National Staff Organization
LU Staff Organization of Rhode
    Island, National . . . . Cranston

Nurses, Professional
LU 5067 . . . . . North Smithfield

LU 5098 Rhode Island Hospital
    UNAP . . . . Providence

Office and Professional Employees
LU 25 . . . . Providence

Operating Engineers
LU 57 . . . . Providence

Plasterers and Cement Masons
LU 40 . . . . Cranston

Plumbing and Pipe Fitting
LU 51 . . . . East Providence
SA New England States Pipe
    Trades . . . . . East Providence

Postal Workers
LU 387 Providence
    Area . . . . Providence
LU 391 Newport . . . Middletown
LU 395 Woonsocket . . Woonsocket
LU 621 Westerly . . . . . Westerly
LU 2039 Wakefield . . . . Wakefield
LU 2318 East
    Greenwich . . . . East Greenwich
LU 3739 Warwick . . . . Warwick
LU 5615 Barrington . . . Barrington
LU 6363 North
    Scituate . . . . . North Scituate
SA Rhode Island . . . . Wakeland

Rural Letter Carriers
SA Rhode Island . . . . Cumberland

Service Employees
C 10 Rhode Island . . . . Providence
LU 69 . . . . Coventry
LU 334 . . . . Woonsocket

State, County and Municipal Employees
C 94 Rhode
    Island . . . . . . North Providence
LU 911 Newport Public Employees
    Union . . . . Newport

Steelworkers
LU 01-1407 . . . . Tiverton
LU 01-1410 . . . . . . Cumberland
LU 04-1007 . . . . . . Cumberland
LU 04-4543-S . . . . . . Lincoln
LU 04-12431-S . . . . Providence
LU 04-14845-S . . . . . . Warren
LU 04-15509-S . . . . . Riverside
LU 04-16031-S . . . West Warwick

Teachers
LU 195 Rhode Island
    Painters . . . . Warwick
LU 1769 Bryant Faculty
    Federation . . . . . . Smithfield
LU 4940 Northern Rhode
    Island Collaborative
    Employees . . . North Providence
LU 5018 Nurses & Health
    Professionals, St.
    Josephs . . . . Cranston

LU 5022 Nurses & Health
    Professionals, Visiting . . Warwick
LU 5075 Federation of Nurses &
    Health Professionals . . . Westerly
LU 5082 Nurses & Health
    Professionals, Memorial Hospital
    Federation . . . . . . Pawtucket
LU 5090 Visiting Nurses . Providence
SFED Rhode Island . . . Providence

Teamsters
LU 251 . . . . East Providence

Theatrical Stage Employees
LU 23 . . . . . . North Providence
LU 424 . . . . Bristol
LU 830 . . . . Coventry

Transit Union
LDIV 174 . . . . . Little Compton
LDIV 1116 . . . . . . West Warwick

Transportation Union
LU 679 . . . . Johnston
LU 1672 . . . . Westerly

Treasury Employees
CH 54 . . . . Providence

Utility Workers
LU 359 . . . . East Providence

Unaffiliated Labor Organizations

Ashton Cable Workers Union LU
    533 . . . . Cumberland
My Bread Salesmens Union
    Independent . . . . Lincoln
New England Social Security
    Management
    Association . . . . . . Providence
Newport Firefighting School
    Maintenance Workers
    Association . . . . . . Middletown
Rhode Island Private Correctional
    Officers Union Independent
    Local . . . . Providence
Roger William University
    Department of Public Safety
    Employees Association . . Bristol
Sealol Shop Union . . . . Warwick
Sun Oil Company Operating,
    Maintenance & Delivery
    Employees Association of New
    England . . . . . . East Providence
United Nurses & Allied Professional
    (Westerly) 5104 . . . . . Westerly
United Nurses & Allied Professional
    Greater Woonsocket Visiting
    Nurses LU 5201 . . North Scituate
United Nurses and Allied
    Professionals . . . . . Providence
United Nurses and Allied
    Professionals 5110 . . . . Johnston
United Service and Allied Workers of
    Rhode Island . . . . . . Rumford
Utility Workers Council LU
    310 . . . . Providence
Utility Workers Council
    NHQ . . . . Warwick

South Carolina

AFL-CIO Trade and Industrial Departments

Building and Construction Trades Department
BCTC Charleston . . . . Charleston
BCTC South
Carolina . . . . . North Charleston

Affiliated Labor Organizations

Agricultural Employees
BR 19 . . . . . . North Charleston

Air Traffic Controllers
LU CAE . . . . . . West Columbia
LU Chicago Tracon
(C90) . . . . . North Charleston
LU CRE . . . . Myrtle Beach
LU FLO . . . . Florence
LU GTF . . . . Greenville
LU MYR . . . . . . Myrtle Beach

Asbestos Workers
LU 92 . . . . McCormick

Automobile, Aerospace Workers
LU 4616 . . . . Carlisle
LU 5841 . . . . Winnsboro

Boilermakers
LG 687 . . . . Charleston

Carpenters
LU 1468 . . . . Alcolu
LU 1778 . . . . Columbia
LU 2221 Hampton
Council . . . . North Charleston
LU 2224 . . . . Ridgeville
LU 3130 . . . . Hampton

Communications Workers
LU 3702 . . . . Anderson
LU 3704 . . . . Hanahan
LU 3706 . . . . . . West Columbia
LU 3708 . . . . Florence
LU 3710 . . . . Greenville
LU 3716 . . . . Spartanburg
LU 3719 . . . . Orangeburg
LU 83175 . . . . Sumter
LU 83709 . . . . Landrum

Electrical Workers
LU 248 . . . . Georgetown
LU 382 . . . . Florence
LU 398 . . . . Charleston
LU 772 . . . . Lexington
LU 776 . . . . Charleston
LU 1431 . . . . Johnsonville
LU 1588 . . . . Trenton
LU 1591 . . . . Conway
LU 1649 . . . . Hampton
LU 1753 . . . . . North Charleston
LU 2277 . . . . Lancaster

Federal Employees
LU 117 . . . . Eastover
LU 1214 . . . . Gilbert
LU 1639 . . . . Columbia

Fire Fighters
LU 4158-L Fire Officers of North
Charleston . . . . North Charleston

Food and Commercial Workers
LU 1800-T . . . . Winnsboro
LU 2014-T . . . . Newberry

Glass, Molders, Pottery and Plastics Workers
LU 15 . . . . Anderson
LU 387 . . . . Spartanburg

Government Employees
C 29 South Carolina State . Beaufort
C 179 Fifth D Veteran
Affairs . . . . Columbia
C 235 AFGE/AAFES . . . Columbia
LU 56 . . . . Columbia
LU 429 DoD . . . . . Parris Island
LU 510 . . . . Edgefield
LU 520 . . . . Columbia
LU 1869 DoD . . . . Charleston Air
Force Base
LU 1872 DoD . Shaw Air Force Base
LU 1909 DoD . . . . Fort Jackson
LU 1915 VA . . . . Columbia
LU 1951 DoD . . . . . Charleston
LU 2176 DoD Clarkshill-
Hartwell . . . . Starr
LU 2298 DoD . . . . . Goose Creek
LU 2510 DoD . . . . . Charleston
LU 2796 DoD . . . . . . Beaufort
LU 3509 HHS . . . . . . Anderson
LU 3654 . . . . Columbia
LU 3976 Council of Prisons Federal
Corrections Institute-EST . . Estill

Government Employees Association
LU 5-150-R . . . . . . Charleston
LU R-145-5 . . . . North Charleston
LU 05-136 . . . . . . Charleston

Government Security Officers
LU 97 . . . . Charleston

Iron Workers
LU 601 . . . . Charleston

Letter Carriers
BR 233 . . . . Columbia
BR 439 . . . . Greenville
BR 628 . . . . Spartanburg
BR 904 . . . . Sumter
BR 1003 . . . . Chester
BR 1145 . . . . Greenwood
BR 1212 . . . . Chester
BR 1416 . . . . Florence
BR 1569 . . . . Aiken
BR 1590 . . . . Bennettsville
BR 1666 . . . . Darlington
BR 1746 . . . . Clinton
BR 1782 . . . . Orangeburg
BR 1871 . . . . Anderson
BR 1914 . . . . Laurens
BR 2190 . . . . Gaffney
BR 2533 . . . . Lancaster
BR 2553 . . . . Greer
BR 2745 . . . . Winnsboro
BR 2804 . . . . York
BR 3082 . . . . Inman
BR 3161 . . . . Lyman
BR 3262 . . . . Beaufort
BR 3393 . . . . Woodruff
BR 3648 . . . . Clover
BR 3649 . . . . Conway
BR 3822 . . . . Kershaw
BR 3902 . . . . . North Charleston

BR 3927 . . . . Loris
BR 3996 . . . . Liberty
BR 4119 . . . . Whitmire
BR 4223 . . . . Kingstree
BR 4401 . . . . . . Honea Path
BR 4616 . . . . . . West Columbia
BR 4645 . . . . Myrtle Beach
BR 4974 . . . . Saluda
BR 4975 . . . . Pelzer
BR 5104 . . . . Ruby
BR 5292 . . . . Ware Shoals
BR 5321 . . . . Calhoun Falls
BR 5411 . . . . Allendale
BR 5413 . . . . St. Matthews
BR 5423 . . . . . . Travelers Rest
BR 5486 . . . . Branchville
BR 5527 . . . . Fountain Inn
BR 5823 . . . . . . North Augusta
BR 5826 . . . . Andrews
BR 5857 . . . . McColl
BR 6113 . . . . Islandton
BR 6123 . . . . Walterboro
BR 6423 . . . . Chesterfield
BR 6490 . . . . Joanna
BR 6549 . . . . Great Falls
SA South Carolina . . Timmonsville

Locomotive Engineers
DIV 84 . . . . Greer
DIV 85 . . . . Columbia
DIV 265 . . . . Lamar
DIV 321 . . . . . . Summerville
DIV 498 . . . . Abbeville
DIV 598 . . . . Pickens
DIV 717 . . . . Belvedere

Longshoremen
LU 1422 . . . . Charleston
LU 1422-A . . . . . . Charleston
LU 1751 . . . . Georgetown
LU 1771 . . . . Charleston

Machinists
LG 183 . . . . . North Charleston
LG 659 . . . . Quinby
LG 1002 . . . . Hemingway
LG 1879 . . . . Cayce
LLG 2775 . . . . Yemassee
LLG W-52 Woodworkers . Kingstree
LLG W-77 Woodworkers . Florence
LLG fl-379 . . . . Columbia
STC South Carolina . . . . Florence

Maintenance of Way Employes
LG 1618 . . . . . . West Columbia
SLG 544 . . . . Whitmire
SLG 562 . . . . Nichols
SLG 624 . . . . Clark Hill
SLG 1187 . . . . Donalds
SLG 2042 . . . . Huger

Musicians
LU 502 . . . . Charleston

National Staff Organization
LU Staff Organization, South
Carolina . . . . Columbia

Nurses
SA South Carolina Nurses
Association . . . . . . Columbia

Office and Professional Employees
LU 233 . . . . Georgetown

Operating Engineers
LU 470 . . . . Aiken

Painters
LU 1756 . . . . New Ellenton
LU 1946 . . . . New Ellenton

Plumbing and Pipe Fitting
LU 421 . . . . . North Charleston

Postal and Federal Employees
LU 304 . . . . Quinby
LU 313 . . . . Columbia
LU 319 . . . . Greenville
LU 326 . . . . Sumter

Postal Mail Handlers
LU 334 . . . . . . West Columbia

Postal Workers
LU Spartanburg Area . . Spartanburg
LU 18 Anderson . . . . . Anderson
LU 168 Upper Piedmont
Area . . . . Greenville
LU 566
Charleston . . . . North Charleston
LU 795 Sumter . . . . . . Sumter
LU 807 Columbia . . . . Columbia
LU 1429 Marion . . . . . Marion
LU 1581 Aiken . . . . . . Aiken
LU 1628 . . . . Gaffney
LU 1649 . . . . Laurens
LU 1796 Georgetown . . Georgetown
LU 1798 Bennettsville . Bennettsville
LU 2003 Conway . . . . . Conway
LU 2214 Lancaster . . . Lancaster
LU 2225 Greer . . . . . . Greer
LU 2408 Florence . . . . Florence
LU 2444 Clemson . . . . Clemson
LU 2755 Myrtle
Beach . . . . . . Myrtle Beach
LU 2841 Beaufort . . . . Beaufort
LU 5591 . . . . . . Mount Pleasant
LU 7064 North Myrtle
Beach . . . . North Myrtle Beach
LU 7076 Hilton Head
Island . . . . Hilton Head
SA South Carolina . . . . Greenville

Rural Letter Carriers
D 1 . . . . Huger
D 2 . . . . Columbia
D 3 . . . . Wagener
D 4 . . . . Simpsonville
D 5 . . . . Rock Hill
D 6 6th District South
Carolina . . . . . Galivants Ferry
LU Abbeville County . . . Abbeville
LU Allendale-Hampton
Counties . . . . Gifford
LU Anderson County . . . . Belton
LU Beaufort-Jasper
Counties . . . . Seabrook
LU Chester-Fairfield
Counties . . . . . Blackstock
LU Darlington-Lee
Counties . . . . Hartsville
LU Florence County . . . Florence
LU Greenville County . Fountain Inn
LU Kershaw-Lancaster
Counties . . . . . . Lancaster
LU Laurens County . . . . Laurens
LU Lexington-Richland
Counties . . . . Columbia
LU Newberry County . . . Prosperity

LU Pickens County. . . . Greenville
LU Spartanburg County. . . . Inman
LU Sumter County. . . . . Sumter
SA South Carolina . . . . . Inman

Security, Police and Fire Professionals
LU 330 . . . . Jackson

Sheet Metal Workers
C Nuclear & Hazardous
  Material . . . . . North Charleston
LU 399 . . . . Charleston

Steelworkers
LU 02-1089. . . . . York
LU 03-216 . . . . St. George
LU 03-357 . . . . . . Georgetown
LU 03-377 . . . . . . Georgetown
LU 03-378 . . . . . . Georgetown
LU 03-477 . . . . . . Georgetown
LU 03-478. . . . . . New Ellenton
LU 03-508 . . . . Eutawville
LU 03-663 . . . . . . Johns Island

LU 03-674 . . . . Florence
LU 03-713. . . . . Pelion
LU 03-925 . . . . Lancaster
LU 03-997 . . . . Wellford
LU 03-1425 . . . . . . Silverstreet
LU 03-1435 . . . . . Goose Creek
LU 03-1569. . . . . Catawba
LU 03-1877 . . . . . . Darlington
LU 03-1879. . . . . Florence
LU 03-1924 . . . . Rock Hill
LU 09-850-L . . . . Fort Mill
LU 09-863-S. . . . North Charleston
LU 09-7898-S . . . . . Georgetown
LU 09-8634-S . . . . . . Bishopville

Teamsters
LU 28 . . . . Taylors
LU 509 . . . . Cayce

Theatrical Stage Employees
D 7 Tennessee-Alabama-Georgia-
  Florida-North Carolina-South
  Carolina-Mississippi-
  Louisiana . . . . . . Walterboro

LU 333 . . . . Charleston
LU 347 . . . . Columbia

Transit Union
LDIV 610. . . . . Charleston

Transportation Communications Union
D 115 . . . . Florence
JPB 200 Norfolk Southern Joint
  Protect Board . . . Boiling Springs
LG 6474 Florence . . . . . Florence

Transportation Union
LLG 1971 Yardmasters
  Department . . . . . Cottageville
LU 407. . . . . St. Stephen
LU 793 . . . . Irmo
LU 931 . . . . Pelzer
LU 942 . . . . Darlington
LU 970 . . . . Greenwood
LU 1814 . . . . Iva
SLB LO-45 South
  Carolina. . . . . Mount Pleasant

Treasury Employees
CH 55 . . . . Lexington
CH 166 . . . . Charleston
CH 276 . . . . Columbia

UNITE HERE
LU 710-T . . . . . West Columbia
LU 860-A . . . . . West Columbia
LU 1093-T. . . . . Rock Hill
LU 1120. . . . . . West Columbia

Weather Service Employees
BR 01-3 . . . . West Columbia
BR 01-40. . . . . Greer
BR 01-50. . . . . Charleston

Unaffiliated Labor Organizations

HarperCollins Sales
  Association . . . . Inman
Motion Picture Actors Guild of
  America . . . . Cross

South Dakota

AFL-CIO Trade and Industrial Departments

Building and Construction Trades Department
BCTC West River . . . . Rapid City

Affiliated Labor Organizations

Air Traffic Controllers
LU FSD . . . . Sioux Falls

Bricklayers
LU 1 . . . . Sioux Falls
LU 2 . . . . Yankton
LU 3 . . . . Aberdeen
LU 4 . . . . Rapid City
LU 5 . . . . Watertown
STCON South Dakota . . . Brandon

Carpenters
LU 587 . . . . Sioux Falls

Communications Workers
LU 7500 . . . . Sioux Falls
LU 7505 . . . . Rapid City

Electrical Workers
LU 423 . . . . Mobridge
LU 426 . . . . Sioux Falls
LU 690 . . . . Mitchell
LU 706 . . . . Aberdeen
LU 754 . . . . Yankton
LU 766 . . . . Huron
LU 1250 . . . . Rapid City
LU 1616 . . . . Rapid City
LU 1688 . . . . Pierre
LU 1959 . . . . Watertown
SC U-26 Northwestern Public
    Service Company . . . . Mitchell

Electrical, Radio and Machine Workers
LU 1128 . . . . Sioux Falls
LU 1187 . . . . Elk Point

Food and Commercial Workers
LU 304-A . . . . Sioux Falls
LU 353-C . . . . . . Belle Fourche
LU 394 . . . . Rapid City

Government Employees
LU 901 USDA . . . . . Sioux Falls
LU 1509 VA . . . . . Sioux Falls
LU 1539 VA . . . . . Hot Springs
LU 2228 DoD . . . . . Rapid City
LU 2342 VA . . . . . . Fort Meade
LU 3035 DoD . . . . . Sioux Falls
LU 3185 DoD . . . . . . Yankton
LU 3365 USDA . . . . Rapid City
LU 3807 DoE . . . . . Watertown
LU 4040 BoP, FPC,
    Yankton . . . . Yankton

Laborers
LU 1050 . . . . Mitchell

Letter Carriers
BR 491 . . . . Sioux Falls
BR 498 . . . . Mitchell
BR 502 . . . . Aberdeen
BR 659 . . . . Yankton
BR 724 . . . . Deadwood
BR 751 . . . . Wolsey
BR 1064 . . . . Pierre
BR 1088 . . . . Brookings
BR 1114 . . . . Watertown
BR 1225 . . . . Rapid City
BR 1308 . . . . Madison
BR 1480 . . . . Hot Springs
BR 1485 . . . . Vermillion
BR 1673 . . . . Redfield
BR 2011 . . . . Flandreau
BR 2205 . . . . Canton
BR 2762 . . . . Milbank
BR 3015 . . . . Mobridge
BR 3124 . . . . Belle Fourche
BR 3526 . . . . Sisseton
BR 3597 . . . . Sturgis
BR 3622 . . . . Clark
BR 3630 . . . . Chamberlain
BR 3737 . . . . Gregory
BR 4298 . . . . Custer
BR 4488 . . . . Webster

BR 4711 . . . . Spearfish
BR 4976 . . . . Dell Rapids
BR 4995 . . . . Miller
BR 4996 . . . . Lemmon
BR 5160 . . . . Winner
BR 5209 . . . . Beresford
BR 6174 . . . . Gettysburg
BR 8001 . . . . Rosholt
SA South Dakota . . . . Aberdeen

Locomotive Engineers
DIV 213 . . . . Edgemont
DIV 726 . . . . Aberdeen

Machinists
DLG 5 . . . . Aberdeen
LG 862 . . . . Aberdeen
LG 2357 . . . . Watertown
STC Joint Dakota . . . . Aberdeen

Maintenance of Way Employes
LG 2825 . . . . Aberdeen
SLG 908 . . . . Sioux Falls
SLG 1071 . . . . Black Hawk
SLG 2852 . . . . Custer

National Staff Organization
LU Staff Association Professional,
    South Dakota . . . . Sioux Falls
LU Staff Organization, South
    Dakota . . . . Rapid City

Postal Mail Handlers
LU 328 . . . . Sioux Falls

Postal Workers
LU . . . . Winner
LU Mitchell . . . . Mitchell
LU Sioux Falls Area . . . Sioux Falls
LU 68 Aberdeen . . . . Aberdeen
LU 144 Watertown . . . Watertown
LU 160 Huron . . . . Huron
LU 760 Rapid City . . . . Rapid City
LU 1235 Mobridge . . . . Mobridge
LU 2787 Pierre . . . . . . Pierre
LU 2874 Spearfish . . . . Spearfish
LU 4113 Vermillion . . . Vermillion
LU 7141 . . . . Huron

SA South Dakota . . . . Sioux Falls

Rural Letter Carriers
SA South Dakota . . . . . Garretson

Service Employees
LU 217 Firemen &
    Oilers . . . . Sioux Falls

Steelworkers
LU 7-1060 . . . . Gregory
LU 07-738 . . . . Lennox
LU 07-1078 . . . . . . Chamberlain
LU 07-1457 . . . . Hartford
LU 11-7833-S . . . . . . Rapid City
LU 11-8188-S . . . . . . Spearfish

Teamsters
LU 749 . . . . Sioux Falls

Theatrical Stage Employees
LU 220 . . . . Sioux Falls
LU 731 . . . . Rapid City

Transit Union
LDIV 1356 . . . . Tea

Transportation Union
LU 64 . . . . Huron
LU 233 . . . . Aberdeen
LU 375 . . . . Hot Springs
SLB LO-46 South
    Dakota . . . . Edgemont

Treasury Employees
CH 8 . . . . Aberdeen

Weather Service Employees
BR 03-30 . . . . Sioux Falls
BR 03-74 . . . . Rapid City
BR 03-93 . . . . Aberdeen

Unaffiliated Labor Organizations
Eros Laborers Number
    One . . . . Sioux Falls
Eros Laborers Number
    Two . . . . Dell Rapids

Tennessee

AFL-CIO Trade and Industrial Departments

Building and Construction Trades Department
BCTC Chattanooga. . . Chattanooga
BCTC East Tennessee . . Blountville
BCTC Knoxville . . . . . Knoxville
BCTC Memphis . . . . . . Memphis
BCTC Nashville . . . . . . Nashville

Metal Trades Department
MTC Air Engineering . . Tullahoma
MTC Atomic Trades &
  Labor. . . . . Oak Ridge

Affiliated Labor Organizations

Air Traffic Controllers
LU BNA . . . . Nashville
LU CHA . . . . Chattanooga
LU MEM . . . . Memphis
LU MQY . . . . Smyrna
LU TRI. . . . . Blountville
LU TYS . . . . Louisville
LU ZME . . . . Memphis

Aircraft Mechanics
LU 38 . . . . Memphis

Asbestos Workers
LU 46 . . . . Harriman
LU 52 . . . . Knoxville
LU 86 . . . . Hermitage
LU 90 . . . . Memphis

Automobile, Aerospace Workers
C Region 8 CAP . . . . . . Lebanon
LU 342 . . . . . Castalian Springs
LU 737 . . . . Nashville
LU 1086 . . . . Memphis
LU 1407 . . . . Cookeville
LU 1577 . . . . . Spring Hill
LU 1617 . . . . Morristown
LU 1621 . . . . Lawrenceburg
LU 1676. . . . . Cleveland
LU 1832 . . . . Madison
LU 1853 . . . . Spring Hill
LU 1989 . . . . Memphis
LU 2155 . . . . Johnson City
LU 2303 . . . . Smyrna
LU 2314 . . . . . . Madisonville
LU 2406 . . . . Memphis
LU 2409 . . . . Cookeville
LU 3031 . . . . Spring Hill
LU 3033 . . . . Sparta
LU 3036 Ford Motor Co. Parts &
  Distributor. . . . . . . Memphis
LU 6519 Auto Workers . . Memphis

Bakery, Confectionery, Tobacco Workers and Grain Millers
C Fourth Regional . . . Chattanooga
LU 25 . . . . Chattanooga
LU 149. . . . . Memphis
LU 252-G . . . . Memphis
LU 352-G . . . . Arlington
LU 390-G . . . . Memphis
LU 407-G . . . . Memphis

Boilermakers
C TVIC. . . . . Lewisburg
DLG 57. . . . . Chattanooga

LG 2-S . . . . Ashland City
LG 14. . . . . Hixson
LG 140-D Cement
  Workers. . . . . Knoxville
LG 234-S . . . . Dickson
LG 251-S. . . . . Bolivar
LG 263. . . . . Memphis
LG 272-S . . . . La Vergne
LG 453 . . . . Knoxville
LG 454 . . . . Chattanooga
LG 586 . . . . Copperhill
LG 656 . . . . Chattanooga
LG 679 . . . . Chattanooga

Bricklayers
LU 5 Joint Apprenticeship Training
  Committee. . . . . . . Nashville

Carpenters
DC Tennessee . . . . . . Nashville
LU 50. . . . . Oak Ridge
LU 74. . . . . Hixson
LU 223. . . . . Nashville
LU 345. . . . . Memphis
LU 654 . . . . Hixson
LU 1544 . . . . Nashville
LU 2394 . . . . Paris
LU 2509 . . . . Jackson
LU 2825 . . . . Ashland City
LU 2919 . . . . Memphis
LU 3100 . . . . Lafayette

Civilian Technicians
CH 103 Volunteer . . . . . Smyrna
CH 110 Army Aviation . . Humboldt
CH 114 Smokey
  Mountain . . . . Louisville
CH 115 Memphis . . . . . Memphis
CH 116 Music City Air . . Nashville

Communications Workers
LU 3802 . . . . Chattanooga
LU 3803 . . . . Columbia
LU 3804 . . . . Jackson
LU 3805 . . . . Knoxville
LU 3806 . . . . Memphis
LU 3808 . . . . Nashville
LU 3871 . . . . Bluff City
LU 3879 . . . . Nashville
LU 3890 . . . . Brentwood
LU 14347 . . . . Kingsport
LU 14348 . . . . Memphis
LU 14351 . . . . Powell
LU 33076 . . . . Knoxville
LU 33091 . . . . Memphis
LU 83282 . . . . Memphis
LU 83703 . . . . . . Murfreesboro
LU 83706. . . . . Oneida
LU 83791 . . . . Greeneville
LU 83796 . . . . Greeneville
LU 8-369 . . . . Allons

Electrical Workers
LU 175 . . . . Chattanooga
LU 270 . . . . Oak Ridge
LU 311. . . . . Birchwood
LU 318 . . . . Knoxville
LU 365 . . . . Morristown
LU 429. . . . . Nashville
LU 474. . . . . Memphis
LU 760 . . . . Knoxville
LU 881. . . . . Memphis
LU 934. . . . . Blountville
LU 1087 . . . . Cookeville
LU 1288 . . . . Memphis

LU 1323 . . . . Knoxville
LU 1749 . . . . Springville
LU 1925 . . . . Martin
LU 2080 . . . . White House
LU 2113 . . . . Manchester
LU 2143. . . . . Sparta

Elevator Constructors
LU 30 . . . . Bartlett
LU 93 . . . . Nashville

Engineers
LU 2 Judicial Council 2 . . Memphis
LU 259. . . . . Memphis

Federal Employees
LU 1930 . . . . Bristol

Fire Fighters
LU 2-I X-10 Industrial
  Firefighters. . . . . . Oak Ridge
LU 14-F . . . . Fayetteville
LU 1346. . . . . Knoxville

Food and Commercial Workers
C Textile and Garment . . Hermitage
LU 194-C . . . . Memphis
LU 252-C . . . . Oak Ridge
LU 272-T . . . . Russellville
LU 297-T . . . . Lenoir City
LU 387-C . . . . Alcoa
LU 397-C . . . . Bartlett
LU 515. . . . . Memphis
LU 522-G . . . . White House
LU 663-T . . . . Bean Station
LU 700-C . . . . . . New Market
LU 701-C . . . . . . New Market
LU 715-C . . . . Kingston
LU 815-T . . . . Morristown
LU 1036-C . . . . Washburn
LU 1529 . . . . Cordova
LU 1995 . . . . Hermitage
LU 2207-T . . . . Hermitage

Glass, Molders, Pottery and Plastics Workers
LU 53. . . . . Chattanooga

Government Employees
C 61 Tennessee . . . . . Knoxville
C 222 AFGE Council of HUD
  Locals . . . . Dandridge
LU 530 HUD . . . . . . Knoxville
LU 850 USDA. . . . . . Memphis
LU 1687 VA . . . . Mountain Home
LU 1788 USDA . . . . . . Smyrna
LU 1844 VA . . . . Murfreesboro
LU 2172 DoD . . . . . . Millington
LU 2400 VA. . . . . . . Nashville
LU 2470 VA. . . . . . . Nashville
LU 3136 USDA . . . . . . Talbott
LU 3496 DoL . . . . . . Jacksboro
LU 3599 EEOC . . . . . Memphis
LU 3731 DoJ. . . . . . . Memphis
LU 3930 VA, Medical Center Staff
  Nurse Association. . . Collierville
LU 3980 CoP . . . . . Nashville

Government Employees Association
LU 05-66. . . . . Memphis
LU 05-147. . . . . Maryville

Government Security Officers
LU 25 . . . . Oakdale

LU 26. . . . . Soddy Daisy
LU 68 . . . . Memphis
LU 88 . . . . Rogersville

Graphic Communications
LU 118-C . . . . Knoxville
LU 197-M . . . . . . Chattanooga
LU 290-M . . . . . . Clarksville
LU 400-C . . . . Rogersville
LU 513-S . . . . . . Murfreesboro
LU 521-M. . . . . Dickson

Iron Workers
DC Tennessee Valley &
  Vicinity. . . . . . . Chattanooga
LU 167. . . . . Memphis
LU 384 . . . . Knoxville
LU 492. . . . . Nashville
LU 526 . . . . Chattanooga
LU 704 . . . . Chattanooga
LU 733. . . . . Nashville

Laborers
DC. . . . . Nashville
DC 8 Regional Organizing
  Committee. . . . . . . Nashville
LU 386 . . . . Madison
LU 818 . . . . Knoxville
LU 846 . . . . Chattanooga

Letter Carriers
BR 4 . . . . Nashville
BR 27 . . . . Memphis
BR 62. . . . . Hixson
BR 364 . . . . Clarksville
BR 419 . . . . Knoxville
BR 807 Bristol . . . . . . Bristol
BR 1110. . . . . . . Jonesborough
BR 1256. . . . . Morristown
BR 1402. . . . . . . Murfreesboro
BR 1710. . . . . Humboldt
BR 1819. . . . . Franklin
BR 1838. . . . . Rockwood
BR 1853. . . . . Shelbyville
BR 1879. . . . . Etowah
BR 1897. . . . . Athens
BR 1994. . . . . Dyersburg
BR 1995. . . . . Cleveland
BR 1999. . . . . Kingsport
BR 2332. . . . . La Follette
BR 2585. . . . . McKenzie
BR 2684. . . . . Sweetwater
BR 2831. . . . . . . Elizabethton
BR 2910. . . . . Clinton
BR 2917. . . . . Erwin
BR 3157. . . . . Rogersville
BR 3174. . . . . Dresden
BR 3214. . . . . Livingston
BR 3229. . . . . Huntingdon
BR 3255. . . . . Carthage
BR 3259. . . . . Watertown
BR 3339. . . . . Greenfield
BR 3408. . . . . Kenton
BR 3431. . . . . Newbern
BR 3503. . . . . Loudon
BR 3509. . . . . Sevierville
BR 3549. . . . . Sparta
BR 3552. . . . . . . Jonesborough
BR 3644. . . . . Halls
BR 3707. . . . . Oneida
BR 3718. . . . . Bolivar
BR 3800. . . . . Portland
BR 4070. . . . . Bruceton
BR 4164. . . . . Centerville
BR 4209. . . . . Smithville

BR 4210 . . . . Selmer
BR 4215 . . . . Parsons
BR 4884 . . . . Monterey
BR 5106 . . . . Lancaster
BR 5173 . . . . Lookout Mountain
BR 5404 . . . . Clarksville
BR 6164 . . . . Madisonville
BR 6271 . . . . Rockford
BR 6435 . . . . Woodlawn
SA Tennessee . . . . . . Knoxville

Locomotive Engineers
DIV 41 . . . . Cross Plains
DIV 129 . . . . Smyrna
DIV 170 . . . . Memphis
DIV 198 . . . . Ooltewah
DIV 205 . . . . Chattanooga
DIV 239 . . . . Seymour
DIV 473 . . . . Columbia
DIV 508 . . . . South Fulton
DIV 547 . . . . Englewood
DIV 610 . . . . Huntingdon
DIV 781 . . . . Gray
DIV 782 . . . . Riceville
GCA 4-175 Norfolk Southern
    Railway . . . . Powell
SLB Kentucky . . . . . South Fulton
SLB Tennessee . . . . . Ooltewah

Longshoremen
LU 1671 . . . . Memphis

Machinists
DLG 2 . . . . Memphis
DLG 711 . . . . Nashville
LG 3 Desoto Lodge . . . . Memphis
LG 56 Success . . . . . Chattanooga
LG 58 . . . . Luttrell
LG 61 . . . . Memphis
LG 154 . . . . Murfreesboro
LG 480 . . . . Oak Ridge
LG 735 . . . . Nashville
LG 792 . . . . Lebanon
LG 798 . . . . Nashville
LG 879 . . . . Nashville
LG 1296 . . . . Clarksville
LG 1387 . . . . Paris
LG 1443 . . . . Erwin
LG 1450 . . . . Harrison
LG 1458 Chickamauga . Chattanooga
LG 1479 Old Hickory . . . . Burns
LG 1501 . . . . Tullahoma
LG 1538 . . . . Erin
LG 1640 . . . . Dover
LG 1647 . . . . Beech Bluff
LG 2212 . . . . Nashville
LG 2325 . . . . Waynesboro
LG 2356 . . . . . Tennessee Ridge
LG 2385 . . . . Fayetteville
LG 2419 . . . . Humboldt
LG 2544 . . . . Chattanooga
LG 2709 . . . . . . Oliver Springs
LG 2763 . . . . Memphis
LLG 259 . . . . Memphis
LLG 1-2545 Machinists . . . Loudon
STC Tennessee . . . . . Nashville

Maintenance of Way Employes
LG 546 . . . . Evensville
LG 546 . . . . Knoxville
LG 654 . . . . Halls
LG 667 . . . . Winchester
LG 670 . . . . Smyrna
LG 676 . . . . Camden
SF Allied Eastern
    Federation . . . . . Hendersonville
SLG 558 . . . . Unicoi
SLG 567 . . . . Sevierville

SLG 725 . . . . Lewisburg
SLG 986 . . . . White Bluff
SLG 1854 . . . . Jacksboro
SLG 2600 . . . . Millington
SLG 2606 . . . . Clarfield

Mine Workers
LU 1070 . . . . Cosby

Musicians
LU 71 . . . . Memphis
LU 80 . . . . Chattanooga
LU 257 . . . . Nashville
LU 546 . . . . Knoxville

National Staff Organization
ASSN Memphis
    Education . . . . Memphis
LU Staff Organization of the
    Tennessee Educators
    Association . . . . . . Kingsport

NLRB Professional Association
LU 26 . . . . Memphis

Office and Professional Employees
LU 144 . . . . Knoxville
LU 182 . . . . Nashville
LU 367 . . . . Memphis
LU 2001 . . . . Knoxville

Operating Engineers
LU 369 . . . . Memphis
LU 900 . . . . Oak Ridge
LU 912 . . . . Columbia
LU 917 . . . . Chattanooga

Painters
LU 49 . . . . Memphis
LU 226 . . . . Chattanooga
LU 437 . . . . Knoxville
LU 456 . . . . Nashville
LU 1805 . . . . Harriman

Plasterers and Cement Masons
LU 78 . . . . Knoxville
LU 647 . . . . Church Hill
LU 909 . . . . Nashville

Plumbing and Pipe Fitting
LU 17 . . . . Memphis
LU 43 . . . . Chattanooga
LU 102 . . . . Knoxville
LU 538 . . . . Johnson City
LU 572 . . . . Nashville
LU 614 . . . . Memphis
LU 702 . . . . Nashville
LU 718 . . . . Lake City
LU 854 . . . . Henderson
SA Tennessee Pipe
    Trades . . . . Nashville

Postal and Federal Employees
LU 403 . . . . Chattanooga
LU 406 . . . . Knoxville
LU 407 . . . . Memphis
LU 410 . . . . Nashville

Postal Mail Handlers
LU 329 . . . . Memphis

Postal Workers
LU The Hermitage . . . . Hermitage
LU 5 Nashville . . . . . Nashville
LU 96 Memphis Area
    Local . . . . Memphis
LU 192 Chattanooga
    Area . . . . Chattanooga

LU 245 Jackson . . . . . . Jackson
LU 263 Knoxville . . . . Knoxville
LU 308 Clarksville . . . . Clarksville
LU 353 Columbia . . . . . Columbia
LU 365 Johnson City . Johnson City
LU 736 Elizabethton . Elizabethton
LU 757 Paris . . . . Paris
LU 974 Murfreesboro . Murfreesboro
LU 977 Cookeville . . . . Cookeville
LU 1113 Fayetteville . . Fayetteville
LU 1335 Jefferson
    City . . . . Jefferson City
LU 1384 Maryville . . . . Maryville
LU 1540 Gallatin . . . . . Gallatin
LU 1596 Sparta . . . . . . Sparta
LU 1663 Lewisburg . . . Lewisburg
LU 1728 McMinnville . McMinnville
LU 2335 Lexington . . . . Lexington
LU 2394 Dresden . . . . . Dresden
LU 2395 Humboldt . . . . Humboldt
LU 2464 Crossville . . . . Crossville
LU 2509 Dickson . . . . . Dickson
LU 2692 McKenzie . . . . McKenzie
LU 2932 Savannah . . . . Savannah
LU 3097 Milan . . . . Milan
LU 3955 Smithville . . . Smithville
LU 4059 Dyersburg . . . Dyersburg
LU 4426 Mountain
    City . . . . Mountain City
LU 4728 Tiptonville . . . Tiptonville
LU 5060 Gatlinburg . . . Gatlinburg
LU 6783
    Hendersonville . . Hendersonville
SA Tennessee . . . . Jackson

Railroad Signalmen
LLG 49 . . . . Ooltewah
LLG 67 . . . . Portland
LLG 110 . . . . Sweetwater
LLG 158 . . . . Clinton
LLG 162 . . . . Martin
LLG 198 . . . . Erwin

**Retail, Wholesale and Department
  Store**
C Central States . . . . . Knoxville
DC Tennessee . . . . . Knoxville
LU 150 . . . . Nashville
LU 323 . . . . Knoxville
LU 910 . . . . Memphis
LU 23444 Guards and Watchmen's
    Union . . . . Chattanooga

**Roofers, Waterproofers and Allied
  Workers**
LU 176 . . . . Nashville

Rural Letter Carriers
LU Bedford County . . . Shelbyville
LU Blount County . . . . Lenoir City
LU Campbell County . . La Follette
LU Carter County . . . Elizabethton
LU Cheatham
    County . . . . . . Chapmansboro
LU Chester County . . . . . Finger
LU Claiborne
    County . . . . . Cumberland Gap
LU Clay County . . . . . . Celina
LU Cumberland County . Crossville
LU Davidson County . Goodlettsville
LU Decatur County . . . . Parsons
LU Dyer County . . . . Dyersburg
LU Fayette County . . . . Oakland
LU Gibson County . . . Humboldt
LU Greene County . . Parrottsville
LU Hamblen County . . . Bulls Gap
LU Hamilton-Bradley-Polk
    Counties . . . . . . Cleveland

LU Hancock County . . . Sneedville
LU Hardin County . . . . . Enville
LU Hawkins County . . . Rogersville
LU Henderson County . . Lexington
LU Henry County . . . . Buchanan
LU Hickman County . . . Centerville
LU Jefferson County . . . . Talbott
LU Lauderdale County . . . Ripley
LU Loudon County . . . . . Powell
LU Marion County . . . . . Whitwell
LU Marshall County . . . . Belfast
LU Maury County . . . . Lynnville
LU Montgomery County . Clarksville
LU Morgan County . . . Wartburg
LU Putnam County . . . Cookeville
LU Rhea County . . . . . Dayton
LU Roane County . . Oliver Springs
LU Robertson County . Cross Plains
LU Scott County . . . . . Oneida
LU Stewart-Houston Counties . Erin
LU Sumner County . . . . Gallatin
LU Union County . . . . . Luttrell
LU Washington
    County . . . . . . Johnson City
LU Wilson County . . Mount Juliet
LU 1 Anderson
    County . . . . . . Maynardville
LU 9 Carroll County . . . McKenzie
LU 15 Cocke County . . Parrottsville
LU 16 Coffee-Grundy
    Counties . . . . . . Manchester
LU 22 Dickson County . White Bluff
LU 26 Franklin-Moore
    Counties . . . . . Estill Springs
LU 29 Grainger
    County . . . . . . Bean Station
LU 47 Knox County . . . . Seymour
LU 52 Lincoln County . Fayetteville
LU 54 Macon
    County . . . . Red Boiling Springs
LU 55 Madison County . . . Jackson
LU 60 McNairy
    County . . . . . . Morris Chapel
LU 61 Meigs County . . . Ten Mile
LU 69 Pickett . . . . . . Byrdstown
LU 75 Rutherford County . . Smyrna
LU 78 Sevier County . . . Seymour
LU 79 Shelby County . . Brighton
LU 82 Sullivan
    County . . . . . Mount Carmel
LU 84 Tipton County . . . Millington
LU 88-89 Warren & Van Buren
    Counties . . . . . Woodbury
LU 91 Wayne County . . Collinwood
LU 92 Weakley County . . . Dresden
SA Tennessee . . . . . . Bethpage

**Security, Police and Fire
  Professionals**
LU 108 . . . . Kingsport
LU 109 . . . . Oak Ridge
LU 403 . . . . Spring Hill

Service Employees
C 4 Tennessee State . . . Nashville
LU 166 . . . . Oak Ridge
LU 177 Firemen & Oilers . Knoxville
LU 205 . . . . Nashville
LU 784 Firemen & Oilers . Memphis
LU 1160 Firemen &
    Oilers . . . . Nashville

Sheet Metal Workers
LU 4 . . . . Memphis
LU 5 . . . . Knoxville
LU 177 . . . . Nashville
LU 211 . . . . Antioch
LU 227 . . . . Arlington

LU 267 . . . . Chattanooga
LU 424 . . . . Bradyville
LU 483 . . . . Morrison
LU 555 . . . . Knoxville

State, County and Municipal
Employees
LU 1733 Memphis Public Employees
   Union . . . . Memphis

Steelworkers
LU 288 . . . . Oak Ridge
LU 3006 . . . . Dyer
LU 5001 . . . . Chattanooga
LU 9457 . . . . Milan
LU 5-7 . . . . Waverly
LU 5-714 . . . . Memphis
LU 5-772 . . . . Memphis
LU 5-777 . . . . Millington
LU 5-899 . . . . Charleston
LU 5-951 . . . . Johnson City
LU 05-80 . . . . Mount Juliet
LU 05-122 . . . . Soddy Daisy
LU 05-212 . . . . Jackson
LU 05-357 . . . . Arlington
LU 05-362 . . . . Harrison
LU 05-466 Humboldt Boxmakers
   Union . . . . Bells
LU 05-566 . . . . Brighton
LU 05-590 . . . . Jackson
LU 05-631 . . . . Memphis
LU 05-677 . . . . Erwin
LU 05-722 . . . . Collierville
LU 05-724 . . . . Del Rio
LU 05-733 . . . . Talbott
LU 05-771 . . . . Memphis
LU 05-790 . . . . Athens
LU 05-978 . . . . Counce
LU 05-983 . . . . Oak Ridge
LU 05-984 . . . . Memphis
LU 05-987 . . . . Columbia
LU 05-990 . . . . Rockwood
LU 05-992 . . . . Counce
LU 05-993 . . . . Savannah
LU 05-1197 . . . . Bruceton
LU 05-1274 . . . . Memphis
LU 05-1276 . . . . Corryton
LU 05-1289 . . . . Memphis
LU 05-1337 . . . . Cleveland
LU 05-1411 . . . . Newport
LU 05-1766 . . . . Memphis
LU 05-1816 . . . . Memphis
LU 09-90-G . . . . Knoxville
LU 09-109-S . . . . Kingsport
LU 09-117-S . . . . Corryton
LU 09-122-S . . . Elizabethton
LU 09-194-L . . . . Palmyra
LU 09-234-A . . . . . . Greeneville
LU 09-244 . . . . Waverly
LU 09-299 . . . . Kingsport
LU 09-309-S . . . . Alcoa

LU 09-440-G . . . . Jackson
LU 09-456-G . . . . . Church Hill
LU 09-496 . . . . Kingsport
LU 09-507-G . . . . . Greeneville
LU 09-634 . . . . . . Soddy Daisy
LU 09-641-L . . . . Pulaski
LU 09-672-L . . . . Grand Junction
LU 09-878-L . . . . . . Union City
LU 09-1002-L . . . . Newport
LU 09-1008-L . . . . Obion
LU 09-1055-L . . . . . La Vergne
LU 09-1155-L . . . . . . Morrison
LU 09-2360-S . . . . . Moscow
LU 09-3115-S . . . . . Harrison
LU 09-3508-S . . . . . Chattanooga
LU 09-4586-S . . . . . Bluff City
LU 09-4802-S . . . . . . Gallatin
LU 09-5887-S . . . . . Nashville
LU 09-5945-S . . . . . . Erwin
LU 09-6638-S . . . . Tellico Plains
LU 09-6817-S . . . . . . Decherd
LU 09-6884-S . . . . . Greeneville
LU 09-7198-S . . . . . . Newport
LU 09-7573-S . . . . . Savannah
LU 09-7655-S . . . . . . Memphis
LU 09-7739-S . . . . . Johnson City
LU 09-7894-S . . . . Bristol
LU 09-8681-S . . . . . . Knoxville
LU 09-8915-S . . . . . . McKenzie
LU 09-9137-S . . . . . Manchester
LU 09-9147-S . . . . . Harriman
LU 09-9410 . . . . . . Harriman
LU 09-9426-S . . . . . Nashville
LU 09-9496 . . . . Athens
LU 09-12943-S . . . . . Kingsport
LU 09-14597-S. . . . . . Oneida
LU 09-15120-S . . . Chattanooga
LU 50-784 . . . . . . Dowelltown

Teachers
SFED Tennessee . . . . . . Jellico

Teamsters
LU 217 . . . . Jackson
LU 327 . . . . Nashville
LU 480 . . . . Nashville
LU 515 . . . . Chattanooga
LU 519 . . . . Knoxville
LU 549 . . . . Blountville
LU 667 . . . . Memphis
LU 984 . . . . Memphis
LU 1196 Brewery and Soft Drink
   Workers . . . . Memphis

Television and Radio Artists
LU Nashville . . . . . . Nashville

Theatrical Stage Employees
LU 46 . . . . Nashville
LU 69 . . . . Memphis
LU 140 . . . . Chattanooga

LU 197 . . . . Knoxville
LU 492 . . . . Nashville
LU 825 Theater Wardrobe
   Union . . . . Germantown
LU 894 . . . . Seymour
LU 915 . . . . Hermitage

Transit Union
LDIV 713 . . . . Memphis
LDIV 1164 . . . . Knoxville
LDIV 1212 . . . . . . Chattanooga
LDIV 1235 . . . . Nashville
LU 1285 . . . . Jackson

Transport Workers
LU 590 . . . . Nashville

Transportation Communications
Union
D 22 . . . . Knoxville
D 24 Southeastern . . . Chattanooga
D 228 . . . . Nolensville
D 1293 . . . . Moscow
LG 6047 Marble City . . . Cleveland
LG 6477 Clinchfield . . . . Erwin
LG 6673 Nashville . . . . Smyrna

Transportation Union
GCA G6-346 . . . . Whitwell
GCA GO-433 Illinois Central Gulf
   Railroad . . . . Memphis
GCA GO-898 Southern
   Railway . . . . . . Maryville
LU 338 . . . . Hixson
LU 339 . . . . Jackson
LU 750 . . . . Norris
LU 753 . . . . Munford
LU 950 . . . . Cordova
LU 974 . . . . Antioch
LU 1162 . . . . Erwin
LU 1301 . . . . Knoxville
LU 1308 . . . . Huntingdon
LU 1314 . . . . Athens
LU 1345 . . . . Etowah
LU 1346 . . . . Chapel Hill
LU 1420 . . . . Collierville
LU 1525 . . . . South Fulton
SLB LO-47 Tennessee . . . Gallatin

Treasury Employees
CH 39 . . . . Nashville
CH 98 . . . . Memphis
CH 270 . . . . Nashville
CH 277 . . . . Cordova

UNITE HERE
LU 338 . . . . Knoxville
LU 609-A . . . . Knoxville
LU 623 . . . . Knoxville
LU 775 . . . . Nashville
LU 847 . . . . Memphis

LU 906 . . . . Knoxville
LU 1418 . . . . Knoxville
LU 1742 . . . . Knoxville
LU 1933-A . . . . Knoxville
LU 2102 . . . . Knoxville
LU 2408 . . . . Knoxville
LU 2537 . . . . Knoxville
LU 2548 . . . . Knoxville
LU 2614 . . . . Knoxville
LU 2633 . . . . Knoxville

Utility Workers
LU 461 . . . . Harrison

Weather Service Employees
BR 02-2 . . . . Memphis
BR 02-43 . . . . Old Hickory
BR 02-55 . . . . Memphis
BR 02-82 . . . . Morristown

Unaffiliated Labor
Organizations

C12 Aviation Inc. MKL-Air Traffic
   Control Tower . . . . . . Jackson
Drivers Warehousemen Maintenance
   Workers LU 1 . . . . . . Nashville
Employees Independent Association
   Joint Council . . . . . . Newbern
Independent Union of Graphic
   Industry International
   Personnel . . . . Nashville
Independent Union of Plant
   Protection Employees LU
   402 . . . . Nashville
International Association of Tool
   Craftsmen LU 20 . . . . Sevierville
International Guards Union of
   America LU 3 . . . . . Oak Ridge
International Guards Union of
   America LU 46 . . . . Winchester
International Guards Union of
   America LU 100 . . . . . Athens
International Guards Union of
   America LU 137 . . . . Nashville
International Guards Union of
   America LU 138 . . . . Nashville
International Guards Union of
   America LU 147 . . . . . Milan
International Guards Union of
   America LU 148 . . . Spring City
International Guards Union of
   America RC Tenth . . . Oak Ridge
Old Hickory Clerk & Technical
   Workers Union . . . . Old Hickory
Old Hickory Rayon Employees
   Council . . . . Old Hickory
Petroleum Marketing Employees
   Union . . . . Millington
Trades and Labor Council for Annual
   of TVA . . . . Chattanooga
USWA . . . . Nashville

Texas

AFL-CIO Trade and Industrial Departments

Building and Construction Trades Department
BCTC Arkansas-Louisiana-
Texas . . . . Longview
BCTC Central Texas . . . . . Austin
BCTC Dallas . . . . Dallas
BCTC El Paso . . . . El Paso
BCTC Fort Worth . . . . . Burleson
BCTC Houston . . . . Houston
BCTC Sabine Area . . . . Nederland
BCTC San Antonio . . . San Antonio
BCTC South Texas . . . . Harlingen
BCTC Texas State . . . . . Austin
BCTC West Texas Building &
Construction Trades . . . Amarillo

Maritime Trades Department
PC West Gulf . . . . Houston

Metal Trades Department
MTC Freeport . . . . . Lake Jackson
MTC Galveston . . . . . La Marque
MTC Houston . . . . Houston
MTC Metal Trades Council of
Amarillo . . . . Amarillo
MTC Texas City . . . . . Texas City

Other Councils and Committees
C Ellis County Labor . . . . . Ennis
C San Antonio . . . . . San Antonio

Affiliated Labor Organizations

Agricultural Employees
BR 4 . . . . Harlingen
BR 5 . . . . Laredo
BR 10 . . . . Edinburg
BR 15 . . . . El Paso
BR 21 . . . . Pearland
BR 27 . . . . Eagle Pass
BR 42 . . Dallas-Fort Worth Airport

Air Traffic Controllers
LU ABI . . . . Abilene
LU ACT . . . . Waco
LU ADS . . . . Addison
LU AFW . . . . Fort Worth
LU AMA . . . . Amarillo
LU AUS . . . . Austin
LU BPT . . . . Beaumont
LU BRO . . . . Brownsville
LU CRP . . . . . . Corpus Christi
LU D21 . Dallas-Fort Worth Airport
LU DFW . Dallas-Fort Worth Airport
LU DWH . . . . Tomball
LU ELP . . . . El Paso
LU ESW . . . . Fort Worth
LU FTW . . . . Fort Worth
LU GGG . . . . Longview
LU HOU . . . . Houston
LU IAD . . . . Houston
LU IAH . . . . Houston
LU LBB . . . . Lubbock
LU MAF . . . . Midland
LU MFE . . . . McAllen
LU NATCA Engineers . . . . Dallas
LU SAT . . . . San Antonio
LU SJU . . . . San Angelo
LU TKI . . . . McKinney
LU ZFW . . . . Fort Worth

LU ZHU . . . . Houston

Aircraft Mechanics
LU 11 . . . . Dallas
LU 18 . . . . Houston

Asbestos Workers
LU 21 . . . . Dallas
LU 22 . . . . Pasadena
LU 66 . . . . Lubbock
LU 87 . . . . New Braunfels

Automobile, Aerospace Workers
C Texas UAW State CAP
Council . . . . Dallas
LU 119 . . . . Fort Worth
LU 129 . . . . Fort Worth
LU 218 . . . . Hurst
LU 276 . . . . Grand Prairie
LU 317 . . . . Hurst
LU 514 . . . . Fort Worth
LU 816 . . . . Fort Worth
LU 848 . . . . Grand Prairie
LU 864 . . . . Houston
LU 870 . . . . Cedar Hill
LU 967 . . . . Greenville
LU 2157 . . . . Wichita Falls
LU 2346 . . . . Cedar Hill
LU 2360 . . . . Fort Worth

Bakery, Confectionery, Tobacco Workers and Grain Millers
LU 111 . . . . Dallas
LU 163 . . . . Houston
LU 257-G . . . . Kenedy
LU 356 . . . . El Paso

Boilermakers
DLG . . . . Spring
LG 69-D Cement Workers . . Waco
LG 74 . . . . Houston
LG 78-D Cement Workers . Quanah
LG 132 . . . . La Marque
LG 437-D Cement Workers . Palmer
LG 476-D Cement Workers . Odessa
LG 531 . . . . Amarillo
LG 587 . . . . Orange
LG 682 . . . . Lake Jackson
LG 5200 . . . . Electra

Bricklayers
LU 1 Texas Louisiana New
Mexico . . . . Kemp

Carpenters
DC Texas . . . . Arlington
LU 14 . . . . San Antonio
LU 429 . . . . Arlington
LU 502 . . . . Port Arthur
LU 551 . . . . Houston
LU 665 . . . . Amarillo
LU 724 . . . . Houston
LU 1266 . . . . Austin
LU 1421 . . . . Arlington
LU 1751 . . . . Austin
LU 2104 . . . . Mesquite
LU 2232 . . . . Houston
LU 2440 . . . . Wimberly
LU 2713 . . . . . . San Augustine
LU 2743 . . . . . . San Antonio
LU 2848 . . . . Mesquite

Civilian Technicians
CH 100 Texas Lone Star . . . Austin

Communications Workers
LU 1000 . . . . San Antonio
LU 6001 Association Passenger
Service Agents . . . . . . Euless
LU 6110 . . . . Laredo
LU 6113 . . . . Greenville
LU 6118 . . . . Longview
LU 6127 . . . . Midland
LU 6128 . . . . Amarillo
LU 6132 . . . . Austin
LU 6137 . . . . . . Corpus Christi
LU 6139 . . . . Beaumont
LU 6143 . . . . San Antonio
LU 6150 . . . . Dallas
LU 6151 . . . . Dallas
LU 6171 . . . . Krum
LU 6174 . . . . Killeen
LU 6178 . . . . Dallas
LU 6182 . . . . Austin
LU 6186 . . . . Austin
LU 6200 . . . . Henrietta
LU 6201 . . . . Fort Worth
LU 6202 . . . . Abilene
LU 6203 . . . . Lubbock
LU 6206 . . . . Temple
LU 6210 . . . . Gainesville
LU 6214 . . . . Tyler
LU 6215 . . . . Dallas
LU 6218 . . . . Lufkin
LU 6222 . . . . Houston
LU 6225 . . . . Waco
LU 6228 . . . . Texas City
LU 6229 . . . . Harlingen
LU 6290 . . . . Dallas
LU 6733 . . . . El Paso
LU 14628 . . . . Austin
LU 14630 . . . . El Paso
LU 14631 Fort Worth . . Fort Worth
LU 14635 . . . . Waco
LU 14642 . . . . Waco
LU 86029 . . . . . Corpus Christi
LU 86129 . . . . Marion
LU 86780 . . . . . . San Antonio
LU 86782 . . . . Tyler
LU 86787 . . . . Richardson
LU 86788 . . . . Dallas

Electrical Workers
LU 20 . . . . Dallas
LU 60 . . . . San Antonio
LU 66 . . . . Pasadena
LU 69 . . . . Dallas
LU 72 . . . . Waco
LU 278 . . . . Corpus Christi
LU 301 . . . . Nash
LU 386 . . . . Texarkana
LU 418 . . . . Academy
LU 479 . . . . Beaumont
LU 520 . . . . Austin
LU 527 . . . . Galveston
LU 547 . . . . Amarillo
LU 583 . . . . El Paso
LU 602 . . . . Wichita Falls
LU 681 . . . . Wichita Falls
LU 716 . . . . Houston
LU 726 . . . . El Paso
LU 738 . . . . Linden
LU 898 . . . . San Angelo
LU 942 . . . . Arlington
LU 960 . . . . El Paso
LU 1015 . . . . Weslaco
LU 1146 . . . . Amarillo
LU 1151 . . . . Tyler
LU 1548 . . . . San Marcos
LU 1645 . . . . Lufkin

LU 1794 . . . . Paris
LU 1814 . . . . Houston
LU 1911 . . . . San Antonio
LU 2078 . . . . Rockdale
LU 2286 . . . . Beaumont
LU 2337 . . . . Tatum

Elevator Constructors
LU 21 . . . . Grand Prairie
LU 31 . . . . Houston
LU 81 . . . . San Antonio
LU 133 . . . . Austin

Federal Employees
LU 513 . . . . Carrollton
LU 516 . . . . Austin
LU 797 . . . . . . Corpus Christi
LU 1138 . . . . Amarillo

Fire Fighters
LU 89-F . . . . San Antonio
LU 341 . . . . Houston
LU 1117-I . . . . Amarillo

Food and Commercial Workers
C Region 5 . . . . Grapevine
LU 3-C . . . . . . Grand Saline
LU 130-C . . . . Marshall
LU 408 . . . . Houston
LU 455 . . . . Houston
LU 514-T . . . . San Angelo
LU 526-C . . . . Texarkana
LU 540 . . . . Dallas
LU 780-C . . . . Bryan
LU 900-C . . . . Baytown
LU 1000 . . . . Dallas

Glass, Molders, Pottery and Plastics Workers
LU 57 . . . . Hearne
LU 58 . . . . Tyler
LU 125 . . . . Waxahachie
LU 201 . . . . Waxahachie
LU 209 . . . . Hondo
LU 216 . . . . Cleburne
LU 220 . . . . Waco
LU 259 . . . . Waco
LU 283 . . . . Houston
LU 284 . . . . Longview
LU 429 . . . . Lufkin

Government Employees
C 17 Food Inspection Locals,
Southwest . . . . . San Antonio
C 83 National Border Patrol . Laredo
C 141 Texas Air National Guard
Locals . . . . San Antonio
C 200 National Meat
Graders . . . . Weslaco
C 216 National EEOC Locals . Dallas
C 227 VA, Tenth District . . Houston
LU 1 TSA . . . . Harlingen
LU 10 ID . . . . Boerne
LU 33 . . . . Galveston
LU 571 . . . . College Station
LU 681 USDA . . . . Joshua
LU 756 USDA . . . . . . Houston
LU 779 . . Sheppard Air Force Base
LU 1003 EPA Employees
Region 6 . . . . Dallas
LU 1004 . . . . . Fort Sam Houston
LU 1006 . . . . Fort Worth
LU 1010 . . . . Nederland
LU 1029 Red River Army Depot
Firefighters . . . . . . Texarkana

LU 1030. . . . . Houston	LU 3941 USDA, Food	BR 1367 . . . . Denton	BR 5210 . . . . Bellville
LU 1038 . . . . Amarillo	Inspectors . . . . Mount Pleasant	BR 1389 . . . . Brownwood	BR 5351 . . . . Post
LU 1210 DoJ. . . . . . . El Paso	LU 3961 . . . . San Antonio	BR 1456. . . . . . . Brownsville	BR 5397. . . . . Azle
LU 1298 DoJ. . . . . . Fort Worth	LU 3978 FPC . . . . Bryan	BR 1487 . . . . Alpine	BR 5414 . . . . Seymour
LU 1361 USAF . . . . Fort Worth	LU 4032 VA, Hospital Professional	BR 1550 . . . . Brenham	BR 5435. . . . . . . Jacksboro
LU 1364 DoD . . . . . Fort Worth	Unit. . . . . . . San Antonio	BR 1558 . . . . Taylor	BR 5445 . . . . Atlanta
LU 1367 DoD . . . . Lackland Air	LU 4042 . . . . Waco	BR 1568 . . . . Belton	BR 5487 . . . . Granbury
Force Base	LU 4044 FPC, FCI. . . Three Rivers	BR 1757 . . . . Bryan	BR 5593 . . . . Rockdale
LU 1617 DoD . . . . Helotes	LU LU-1055 . . . . Boerne	BR 1872 . . . . Vernon	BR 5695. . . . . College Station
LU 1633 VA . . . . Houston		BR 1891 . . . . Big Spring	BR 5734 . . . . Copperas Cove
LU 1637 DoJ. . . . . . Seagoville	**Government Employees**	BR 1903 . . . . Ranger	BR 5827 . . . . Weimar
LU 1656 DoJ. . . . . . Converse	**Association**	BR 1966 . . . . Cisco	BR 5938. . . . . . . Bedford
LU 1731 DoD . . . . Sheppard Air	LU 14-52 . . . . Hooks	BR 2036 . . . . Clarksville	BR 6083 . . . . Morton
Force Base	LU 14-89 . . . . Fort Bliss	BR 2130 . . . . McAllen	BR 6272 . . . . . Denver City
LU 1735 DoD. . . . . . Kingsville	LU 14-151 . . . . . Texarkana	BR 2271 . . . . Mexia	BR 6421 . . . . Llano
LU 1745 AFGE Local 1745 . Austin		BR 2279 . . . . Lufkin	BR 6479 . . . . Ferris
LU 1749 DoD . . . . . . Del Rio	**Government Security Officers**	BR 2309 . . . . Arlington	BR 6570 . . . . . . Abernathy
LU 1757 DoD . . . . San Antonio	LU 78. . . . . Desoto	BR 2501 . . . . Crockett	SA Texas . . . . Humble
LU 1816 DoD . . . . . San Angelo	LU 85 . . . . Waco	BR 2511 . . . . Del Rio	
LU 1822 VA . . . . Waco	LU 86 . . . . Texarkana	BR 2562 . . . . Mercedes	**Locomotive Engineers**
LU 1840 DoD . . . . Randolph Air	LU 203 . . . . Fort Worth	BR 2589 . . . . Lubbock	DIV 22 . . . . El Paso
Force Base		BR 2623. . . . . Mineola	DIV 62 . . . . Deer Park
LU 1903 USDA . . . College Station	**Graphic Communications**	BR 2712 . . . . Gilmer	DIV 139. . . . . Spring
LU 1920 DoD . . . . . . Killeen	DJC South Western . . . . . Ennis	BR 2805 . . . . New Braunfels	DIV 172 . . . . . . Fort Worth
LU 1929 DoJ. . . . . . . El Paso	LU 4-B . . . . Fort Worth	BR 2977 . . . . Childress	DIV 177 . . . . Sherman
LU 1934 VA . . . . . Big Spring	LU 71-M . . . . Houston	BR 2983 . . . . Harlingen	DIV 187 . . . . . . Fort Worth
LU 1944 DoJ . . . . Elsa	LU 88-N . . . . Waco	BR 3028 . . . . Kerrville	DIV 192 . . . . El Paso
LU 2109 VA . . . . Temple	LU 167-C . . . . Gilmer	BR 3053 . . . . Lamesa	DIV 194 . . . . . . Magnolia
LU 2128 DoD . . . . Fort Worth	LU 367-M . . . . Dallas	BR 3094 . . . . Pampa	DIV 197 . . . . . San Antonio
LU 2142 DoD . . . Corpus Christi	LU 439-S . . . . Ennis	BR 3096 . . . . Dalhart	DIV 206 . . . . Temple
LU 2258 HEW . . . . San Antonio	LU 528-M. . . . . Austin	BR 3147 . . . . Uvalde	DIV 212 . . . . . Big Spring
LU 2281 VA . . . . . . Kerrville	LU 737-S . . . . . . San Antonio	BR 3177 . . . . Slaton	DIV 242 . . . . Ennis
LU 2284 NASA. . . . . . Houston		BR 3185 . . . . . . Whitesboro	DIV 249 . . . . . . La Porte
LU 2356 DoD . . . . . Dyess Air	**Iron Workers**	BR 3271 . . . . . . Commerce	DIV 249 . . . . . Montgomery
Force Base	DC Texas . . . . . . Georgetown	BR 3296 . . . . Luling	DIV 264 . . . . El Paso
LU 2366 DoJ . . . . . . Del Rio	LU 66 . . . . San Antonio	BR 3303 . . . . . . Perryton	DIV 299 D.H. Nichols . . Amarillo
LU 2413 DoC. . . . . Nederland	LU 84 . . . . Houston	BR 3305 . . . . Elgin	DIV 350. . . . . . Kingsville
LU 2427 DoD . . . . Fort Worth	LU 135 . . . . . . Texas City	BR 3307 . . . . . . Eastland	DIV 366 . . . . . Missouri City
LU 2437 VA . . . . Dallas	LU 263. . . . . . . Arlington	BR 3309 . . . . . . Ladonia	DIV 475. . . . . . Smithville
LU 2455 DoJ . . . . Laredo	LU 482 . . . . Austin	BR 3318 . . . . . . Navasota	DIV 500 . . . . . Springtown
LU 2459 DoJ . . . . . Texarkana	LU 536. . . . . . Wichita Falls	BR 3467 . . . . . . Caldwell	DIV 530 . . . . . Commerce
LU 2466 USDA . . . . . . Lufkin		BR 3709 . . . . Hearne	DIV 566 . . . . . Sanderson
LU 2488 GSA . . . . Fort Worth	**Laborers**	BR 3764 . . . . West	DIV 573 . . . . . Caddo Mills
LU 2509 MARFA. . . . . Marfa	LU 28. . . . . Fort Sam Houston	BR 3792 . . . . Midland	DIV 574 . . . . . . Amarillo
LU 2516 VA . . . . El Paso	LU 154. . . . . . . Arlington	BR 3843 . . . . Bay City	DIV 592 . . . . Dalhart
LU 2571 VA. . . . . Waco	LU 350 . . . . . . Mauriceville	BR 3844 . . . . Borger	DIV 612 . . . . Vidor
LU 2727 HHS. . . . . . . Dallas	LU 1095 . . . . . . San Antonio	BR 3867 . . . . . . Pasadena	DIV 620 . . . . . . Cleburne
LU 2732 DoD . . . . Sam Rayburn	LU 1168 . . . . Wichita	BR 3888 . . . . Brady	DIV 636 . . . . . Beaumont
LU 2759 USDA . . . . . El Paso		BR 3964 . . . . Odessa	DIV 703 . . . . . . Teague
LU 2771 USDA . . . . Plainview	**Letter Carriers**	BR 3993 . . . . Garland	DIV 711 . . . . . . Baytown
LU 2836 VA . . . . . . Bonham	BR 23 . . . . Galveston	BR 4065 . . . . Plano	DIV 736 . . . . . Wichita Falls
LU 2911 DoD . . . . San Antonio	BR 132 . . . . Dallas	BR 4100 . . . . . . Stephenville	DIV 775 City of Roses . . . Victoria
LU 2921 DoD . . . . . . Dallas	BR 181 . . . . Austin	BR 4101 . . . . Dublin	DIV 776 . . . . . . Santa Fe
LU 2959 SBA . . . . Fort Worth	BR 226 . . . . Fort Worth	BR 4168 . . . . . Raymondville	DIV 834. . . . . . Mineola
LU 3000 DoD . . . . Fort Worth	BR 251 . . . . Denison	BR 4217 . . . . Killeen	DIV 857 . . . . . . Whitehouse
LU 3027. . Lackland Air Force Base	BR 283 . . . . Houston	BR 4240 . . . . Irving	DIV 863 . . . . . . Abilene
LU 3060 IBWC . . . . . Harlingen	BR 354 . . . . Laredo	BR 4245 . . . . . . Monahans	DIV 871 . . . . . . Lubbock
LU 3097 DoD. . . . . . Houston	BR 404. . . . . Waco	BR 4263 . . . . . . La Grange	DIV 910 . . . . Nome
LU 3106 USDA . . . . . Hidalgo	BR 421 . . . . . . San Antonio	BR 4274 . . . . Lubbock	DIV 918. . . . . . Beeville
LU 3165 GSA . . . . . El Paso	BR 493 . . . . Tyler	BR 4326 . . . . Kermit	DIV 944 . . . . . Fort Worth
LU 3184 HHS. . . . . . . Dallas	BR 501 . . . . Paris	BR 4357 . . . . . . Smithville	GCA Union Pacific Railroad,
LU 3307 DoJ . . . . . Harlingen	BR 505 . . . . El Paso	BR 4504 . . . . . Wellington	Southern Region . . . San Antonio
LU 3320 HUD . . . . San Antonio	BR 569 . . . . . . Texarkana	BR 4511 . . . . . . Hondo	GCA 177 Southern Pacific
LU 3332 DoJ. . . . . . Baytown	BR 643. . . . . . . Temple	BR 4531. . . . . . Junction	Transportation Company . El Paso
LU 3377 National Immigration	BR 697 . . . . . . Weatherford	BR 4549 . . . . . . Hamilton	GCA 244 . . . . . . Laredo
Naturalization. . . . . . Dallas	BR 699 . . . . Palestine	BR 4561 . . . . . . Nocona	SLB Texas . . . . . . Mineola
LU 3388 SSA . . . . . . Vinton	BR 752. . . . . . . Cleburne	BR 4723 . . . . . Lake Jackson	
LU 3511 VA . . . . San Antonio	BR 842 . . . . . . Beaumont	BR 4728 . . . . . Schulenburg	**Longshoremen**
LU 3523 USDA . . . . . Amarillo	BR 890 . . . . Terrell	BR 4783 . . . . Edna	C Central Dock &
LU 3637 EEOC . . . . . Dallas	BR 950 . . . . Abilene	BR 4784 . . . . . Richardson	Marine . . . . . Galveston
LU 3769 USDA . . . . . Crosby	BR 1032. . . . . . . Bonham	BR 4809 . . . . . . Andrews	C Houston Dock &
LU 3809 DoJ . . . . Big Spring	BR 1037 Palo Duro	BR 4908 . . . . . . Deleon	Marine . . . . . . Pasadena
LU 3828 BoP, FCI, Bastrop . Bastrop	Branch . . . . . . Amarillo	BR 4909 . . . . . Columbus	C Sabine Dock & Marine . Beaumont
LU 3839 USDA . . . . Fort Worth	BR 1179 . . . . Groves	BR 4977 . . . . . Seminole	D South Atlantic & Gulf
LU 3885 USDA . . . . Weslaco	BR 1203 . . . . . San Angelo	BR 4979 . . . . . . Teague	Coast . . . . . . Galveston
LU 3897 DoE Regional Office	BR 1221 . . . . Victoria	BR 5109 . . . . . Memphis	LU 20 . . . . . . Galveston
VI. . . . . Dallas	BR 1227 T.T. Morris . Burkburnett	BR 5111 . . . . West Columbia	LU 21 . . . . . . Beaumont
LU 3921 FDA . . . . . . Tyler	BR 1259 . . . . . Corpus Christi	BR 5112 . . . . . . Wills Point	LU 24 . . . . Houston

LU 25 . . . . Port Arthur
LU 26. . . . . Corpus Christi
LU 28 . . . . Pasadena
LU 29 . . . . Brownsville
LU 30 . . . . Freeport
LU 31 . . . . Houston
LU 440. . . . . Port Arthur
LU 1316. . . . . Beaumont
LU 1351. . . . . Houston
LU 1395. . . . . Brownsville
LU 1438. . . . . Pasadena
LU 1453. . . . . Galveston
LU 1494. . . . . Galveston
LU 1504. . . . . Galveston
LU 1530. . . . . Houston
LU 1544 Clerk-
  Checkers . . . . . . Brownsville
LU 1665. . . . . Houston
LU 1692 . . . . Corpus Christi
LU 1817. . . . . Freeport
LU 1924. . . . . Port Neches
LU 2014 . . . . Corpus Christi
LU 2022. . . . . Houston

Machinists
DLG 37 . . . . Houston
DLG 776 . . . . Fort Worth
LG 12 . . . . La Porte
LG 36 Alamo City . . . . Fort Worth
LG 517 . . . . Richmond
LG 526 . . . . Fort Worth
LG 643 . . . . Lott
LG 776-A . . . . Fort Worth
LG 776-B . . . . Fort Worth
LG 776-C . . . . Fort Worth
LG 791 . . . . Fort Worth
LG 823 . . . . Beaumont
LG 975 . . . . Fort Worth
LG 1051 . . . . Baytown
LG 1243. . . . . Hooks
LG 1255 Panhandle . . . . Amarillo
LG 1727 . . . . West Columbia
LG 1786 . . . . Pasadena
LG 1792. . . . . Port Neches
LG 1808 . . . . Wells
LG 1999 . . . . Lufkin
LG 2049 . . . . Fort Worth
LG 2082 . . . . Fort Worth
LG 2121 . . . . Fort Worth
LG 2198. . . . . Houston
LG 2208. . . . . Bedford
LG 2210 . . . . San Antonio
LG 2251 . . . . Fort Worth
LG 2317 . . . . Fort Worth
LG 2340 . . . . Fort Worth
LG 2427 . . . . Eddy
LG 2483 . . . . Fort Worth
LG 2513 . . . . Fort Worth
LG 2576 . . . . Tyler
LG 2641 . . . . Henderson
LG 2768 . . . . Fort Worth
LG 2771 . . . . Wichita Falls
LLG 2341 . . . . Fort Worth
LLG H-2339
  Woodworkers. . . . . . Houston
LLG W-2916
  Woodworkers . . . . Aransas Pass
LLG FL-2189 NFFE . . . . Hooks
LLG LL-15 . . . . Houston
STC Texas . . . . Fort Worth

Maintenance of Way Employes
FED Southern Pacific
  Atlantic . . . . Houston
LG . . . . League City
LG 526 . . . . Childress
LG 644 . . . . Luling
LG 675 . . . . Ballinger

LG 1058 . . . . Waller
LG 1099 . . . . Grapeland
LG 1252 . . . . Lumberton
LG 1732 . . . . Keller
LG 2409 . . . . Aledo
LG 2410 . . . . Rockdale
LG 2413 . . . . Amarillo
LG 2710 . . . . Van Horn
LG 2754. . . . . . . Brownsville
SF Missouri Pacific . . . . Longview
SLG 44 . . . . Del Rio
SLG 115 . . . . El Paso
SLG 203 . . . . Ennis
SLG 366 . . . . San Antonio
SLG 732 . . . . Amarillo
SLG 927 . . . . . Sulphur Springs
SLG 1011 . . . . Highlands
SLG 1012 . . . . Channelview
SLG 1021 . . . . Pleasanton
SLG 1082 . . . . Byers
SLG 1338 . . . . Waller
SLG 1405 . . . . Houston
SLG 1507 . . . . Humble
SLG 1563 . . . . Laredo
SLG 1571 . . . . Eagle Lake
SLG 1634 . . . . Laredo
SLG 1715 . . . . Beaumont
SLG 1862 . . . . El Paso
SLG 2286 . . . . Benbrook
SLG 2411 . . . . Silsbee
SLG 2421 . . . . Sealy
SLG 2762 . . . . Flint

Musicians
LU 23 . . . . San Antonio
LU 65-699 . . . . Houston
LU 72 . . . . Arlington
LU 74 . . . . Galveston
LU 433 . . . . Austin
LU 466 . . . . El Paso
LU 644 . . . . Corpus Christi
STCON Texas . . . . . . Arlington

National Staff Organization
LU Staff Association, Professional,
  Texas Teachers
  Association . . . . Plano
LU Staff Organization, Association,
  Texas Teachers
  Association . . . . Austin

NLRB Professional Association
LU 16 . . . . Fort Worth

Nurses
SA Texas Nurses
  Association . . . . Austin

Office and Professional Employees
LU 27 . . . . Galveston
LU 66. . . . . Groves
LU 129. . . . . Pasadena
LU 277 . . . . Fort Worth
LU 298 . . . . Austin
LU 303 . . . . Hooks
LU 306 . . . . Amarillo

Operating Engineers
LU 178 . . . . Fort Worth
LU 340 . . . . Amarillo
LU 347 . . . . Texas City
LU 351 . . . . Borger
LU 450 . . . . Houston
LU 564 . . . . Lake Jackson

Painters
DC 88 . . . . Georgetown
LU 53 . . . . Dallas

LU 130 . . . . Houston
LU 400 Professional, Legal &
  Clerical Union . . . . . . Houston
LU 550 . . . . Houston
LU 756 . . . . Dallas
LU 1778. . . . . Houston
LU 2348 Professional & Clerical
  Workers . . . . . . Georgetown

Plant Protection
LU 299 Dallas. . . . . Dallas

Plasterers and Cement Masons
LU 79 . . . . Houston
LU 681 . . . . Kingwood
LU 783 . . . . Austin
STCON Texas . . . . Austin

Plumbing and Pipe Fitting
DC Gulf Coast Multi State Pipe
  Trade Council . . . . . . Houston
LU 68 . . . . Houston
LU 100 . . . . Garland
LU 142 . . . . San Antonio
LU 146 . . . . Fort Worth
LU 195 . . . . Nederland
LU 196 . . . . Amarillo
LU 211 . . . . Houston
LU 231 . . . . El Paso
LU 286 . . . . Austin
LU 390 . . . . Lake Jackson
LU 529. . . . . Waco
LU 629 . . . . Lubbock
LU 654 . . . . Abilene
LU 823 . . . . Harlingen
SA Texas . . . . Harlingen

Postal and Federal Employees
LU 103 . . . . Beaumont
LU 104 . . . . Dallas
LU 105 . . . . Fort Worth
LU 106 . . . . Galveston
LU 107 . . . . Houston
LU 109 . . . . Lubbock
LU 111 Orange. . . . . . . Orange
LU 113 . . . . San Antonio

Postal Mail Handlers
LU 311 . . . . Dallas

Postal Workers
LU 87 Paris. . . . . Paris
LU 98 Fort Worth . . . . Fort Worth
LU 114 Amarillo. . . . . . Amarillo
LU 180 El Paso . . . . . . El Paso
LU 185 Houston . . . . . Houston
LU 195 San Antonio . San Antonio
LU 246 Bowie . . . . Bowie
LU 299 Austin Area . . . . Austin
LU 469 Beaumont Sectional Center
  Area. . . . . Beaumont
LU 471 Eagle Pass . . . . Eagle Pass
LU 578 Texarkana . . . . Texarkana
LU 652 Vernon . . . . . . Vernon
LU 732 Dallas Area. . . . . Dallas
LU 739 Waco . . . . Waco
LU 741 Denison . . . . . Denison
LU 742 Sherman . . . . . Sherman
LU 754 Wichita Falls . Wichita Falls
LU 779 Corpus Christi
  Area . . . . Corpus Christi
LU 787 Galveston. . . . . Galveston
LU 800 Del Rio . . . . . . Del Rio
LU 802 Uvalde. . . . . . . Uvalde
LU 811 Arlington . . . . . Arlington
LU 812 Denton. . . . . . Denton
LU 826 Greater East Texas
  Area. . . . . Longview

LU 827 Abilene . . . . . . Abilene
LU 952 Lubbock Area . . . Lubbock
LU 1045 Temple. . . . . . Temple
LU 1093 Brownsville. . Brownsville
LU 1354 Borger . . . . . . Borger
LU 1437 Pampa . . . . . . Pampa
LU 1453 Plainview . . . . Plainview
LU 1477 Tyler . . . . Tyler
LU 1485 Pecos . . . . . . Pecos
LU 1573 Hereford . . . . Hereford
LU 1624 Dalhart. . . . . Dalhart
LU 1696 Midland. . . . . Midland
LU 1726 Comanche . . . Comanche
LU 1778 Huntsville. . . . Huntsville
LU 1784 Angleton . . . . Angleton
LU 1849 Liberty . . . . . Liberty
LU 1868 San Angelo . . San Angelo
LU 1870 Edinburg . . . . Edinburg
LU 1871 Mission . . . . . Mission
LU 1882 Athens . . . . . . Athens
LU 1933 Freeport . . . . Freeport
LU 1971 Jasper . . . . . . Jasper
LU 2030 Kilgore. . . . . . Kilgore
LU 2066 Canyon . . . . . Canyon
LU 2248 Laredo . . . . . . Laredo
LU 2260 Conroe . . . . . . Conroe
LU 2421 Harlingen . . . . Harlingen
LU 2476 College
  Station. . . . . . . College Station
LU 2518 McKinney . . McKinney
LU 2622 Lockhart . . . . Lockhart
LU 2633 Palestine . . . Palestine
LU 2640 Llano . . . . . . Llano
LU 2806 Bay City . . . . Bay City
LU 2808 El Campo . . . El Campo
LU 2869 Alpine . . . . . . Alpine
LU 2944 Center. . . . . . Center
LU 2945 Lufkin Area. . . . Lufkin
LU 2952 Gilmer . . . . . . Gilmer
LU 3219 Odessa . . . . . Odessa
LU 3231 Mineral
  Wells. . . . . . Mineral Wells
LU 3288 Gainesville. . . Gainesville
LU 3419 Sonora . . . . . Sonora
LU 3607 Greenville . . . Greenville
LU 3608 Daingerfield . Daingerfield
LU 4084 Pasadena . . . . Pasadena
LU 4126 Bonham. . . . . Bonham
LU 4138 Brenham . . . . Brenham
LU 4171 Victoria . . . . . Victoria
LU 4326 McAllen . . . . McAllen
LU 4478 Nacogdoches. Nacogdoches
LU 4962 Killeen . . . . . Killeen
LU 5173 Kerrville . . . . Kerrville
LU 5300 Weslaco. . . . . Weslaco
LU 5845 Belton. . . . . . Belton
LU 6192 Brazoria. . . . . Brazoria
LU 6197 Rosenberg. . . . . Wallis
LU 6551 Bryan . . . . . . Bryan
LU 6552 Cisco. . . . . . . Cisco
LU 6553 Cuero . . . . . . Cuero
LU 6557 Mount
  Pleasant. . . . . Mount Pleasant
LU 6558 San Benito . . . San Benito
LU 6707 Clarksville . . . Clarksville
LU 6768 Plano. . . . . . . Plano
LU 8004 Texoma . . . . . . Dallas
SA Texas . . . . McAllen

Railroad Signalmen
LLG 121 . . . . Temple
LLG 133 . . . . Fort Worth
LLG 141 . . . . Weatherford
LLG 161 . . . . Amarillo
LLG 182 . . . . El Paso
LLG 185 . . . . Elysian Fields
LLG 206 . . . . Houston

Roofers, Waterproofers and Allied Workers
LU 123 . . . . Fort Worth

Rural Letter Carriers
LU Alamo Association . San Antonio
LU Angelina County . . . . . Diboll
LU Bell-Milam-Falls
  Counties . . . . Salado
LU Concho Valley . . . San Angelo
LU Denton County . . . . . Krum
LU Eastland-Stephens
  Counties . . . . Rising Star
LU Fayette County . . . . Columbus
LU Grayson-Fannin Counties . Savoy
LU Gulf Coast . . . . . . Wharton
LU Hamilton-Coryell
  Counties . . . . Lampasas
LU Hill County . . . . . . Malone
LU Johnson County . . . Burleson
LU Kaufman County . . . Kaufman
LU Lavaca-Dewitt
  Counties . . . . Yoakum
LU Palo Duro Association . Amarillo
LU Sam Houston
  Association . . . . Dayton
LU South Plains
  Association . . . . . Hale Center
LU Southeast Texas
  Association . . . . Vidor
LU Tarrant-Dallas
  Counties . . . . . . Richardson
LU West Texas . . . . . Levelland
LU Wise County . . . . . . Chico
LU 4 Austin County . . Hempstead
LU 9 Bosque County . . . Kopperl
LU 10 Brazos Valley . . Hermleigh
LU 13 Bi-Stone
  Association . . . . . . Fairfield
LU 15 Coastal Bend . . . . . Cuero
LU 17 Collin-Rockwall
  Counties . . . . Anna
LU 21 Cooke County . . Gainesville
LU 28 El Paso Association . El Paso
LU 31 Foard-Hardeman-Wilbarger
  Counties . . . . Quanah
LU 36 Gregg-Rusk-Smith
  Association . . . . . . Henderson
LU 39 Harris-Fort Bend-Waller
  Counties . . . . Houston
LU 40 Harrison-Marion-Panola
  Counties . . . . Jefferson
LU 41 Henderson County . . Larue
LU 44 Houston County . . Lovelady
LU 45 Hunt-Rains Counties . Emory
LU 50 Lamar-Delta
  Association . . . . . Arthur City
LU 53 Llano-Burnet
  County . . . . . . Buchanan Dam
LU 54 Lower Rio Grande
  Valley . . . . Mission
LU 55 McLennan County . . . Waco
LU 61 Nacogdoches
  County . . . . . . Nacogdoches
LU 62 Navarro County . . . Kerens
LU 65 Panhandle
  Association . . . . . . Childress
LU 66 Northeast Texas
  Association . . . . . New Boston
LU 69 Robertson-Brazos
  Counties . . . . . College Station
LU 71 South Texas
  Association . . . . Tynan
LU 75 Southwest Texas
  Association . . . . . . Odessa
LU 77 Taylor-Callahan
  Counties . . . . Abilene
LU 78 Capitol Area . . . . . Austin

LU 79 Tyler-Jasper-Newton-Hardin
  Counties . . . . Jasper
LU 80 Upshur County . . . . Diana
LU 81 Van Zandt
  County . . . . Murchison
LU 82 Laredo . . . . Laredo
LU 83 Washington
  County . . . . Brenham
LU 86 Texas . . . . Austin
LU 86 Williamson County
  Local . . . . Austin
LU 14- Cherokee
  County . . . . . . Jacksonville
LU 67- Parker
  County . . . . Weatherford
SA Texas . . . . Georgetown

Security, Police and Fire Professionals
LU 48 . . . . Dallas
LU 126 . . . . Big Spring
LU 256 . . . . Fort Worth
LU 258 . . . . Daingerfield
LU 262 . . . . Wichita Falls
LU 263 . . . . . . Grand Prairie
LU 267 . . . . Austin
LU 268 . . . . Angleton
LU 269 . . . . Austin
LU 300 . . . . Texas City
LU 723 . . . . Fort Worth
LU 724 . . . . El Paso
LU 725 . . . . El Paso
LU 727 . . . . Los Fresnos
LU 728 . . . . Bay City

Service Employees
LU 5 Arizona . . . . . San Antonio
LU 713 Firemen & Oilers . . El Paso
LU 1016 Firemen & Oilers . Houston
LU 1045 Firemen &
  Oilers . . . . Carrollton

Sheet Metal Workers
DC Southwest . . . . . . Houston
LU 54 . . . . Houston
LU 67 . . . . San Antonio
LU 68 . . . . Euless
LU 121 . . . . Joshua
LU 337 . . . . Tyler
LU 440 . . . . Humble

State, County and Municipal Employees
LU 2399 San Antonio Area Public
  Employees . . . . . San Antonio

Steelworkers
C Mobile Oil Company
  Wide . . . . Baytown
C Standard Oil of
  Indiana-Nationwide . . Texas City
C TML . . . . Orange
LU 9479 . . . . Dallas
LU 4-424 . . . . Cleburne
LU 04-1 . . . . Pasadena
LU 04-23 . . . . Port Arthur
LU 04-74 . . . . Rotan
LU 04-100 . . . . Longview
LU 04-153 . . . . . Corpus Christi
LU 04-202 . . . . Tyler
LU 04-208 . . . . Irving
LU 04-211 . . . . Denton
LU 04-227 . . . . Pasadena
LU 04-228 . . . . . . Port Neches
LU 04-243 . . . . . . Beaumont
LU 04-314 . . . . Edinburg
LU 04-316 . . . . . . Aransas Pass
LU 04-391 . . . . Orange

LU 04-487 . . . . Dumas
LU 04-759 . . . . Desoto
LU 04-771 . . . . Burleson
LU 04-780 . . . . . . Glen Rose
LU 04-801 . . . . Evadale
LU 04-825 . . . . Evadale
LU 04-895 . . . . Dallas
LU 04-1147 . . . . Tyler
LU 04-1148 . . . . . . Queen City
LU 04-1149 . . . . . . Atlanta
LU 04-1398 . . . . . . Mauriceville
LU 04-1401 . . . . Lufkin
LU 04-1856 . . . . Wylie
LU 04-6000 . . . . . . Pasadena
LU 08-1199 . . . . . . McGregor
LU 12-37-T . . . . Waco
LU 12-75 . . . . Baytown
LU 12-166-S . . . . . . Houston
LU 12-173-S . . . . . Sweetwater
LU 12-235-A . . . . Corpus Christi
LU 12-312-L . . . . . . Waco
LU 12-422-S . . . . . . Dallas
LU 12-430-S . . . . . Fort Worth
LU 12-626-B . . . . Mineral Wells
LU 12-746-L . . . . . . Tyler
LU 12-1027-L . . . . . Corsicana
LU 12-1157-L . . . . . . Tyler
LU 12-1822-S . . . . . Rosebud
LU 12-2083-S . . . . . Houston
LU 12-4134-S . . . . . Lone Star
LU 12-4370-S . . . . Point Comfort
LU 12-4654-S . . . . Daingerfield
LU 12-4895-S . . . . . Rockdale
LU 12-5022-S . . . . Corpus Christi
LU 12-5613-S . . . . . Amarillo
LU 12-6635-S . . . . . Houston
LU 12-7982-S . . . . . . Waco
LU 12-8586-S . . . . . Beaumont
LU 12-8618-S . . . . . Denison
LU 12-8923-S . . . . . Shepherd
LU 12-9448 . . . . . Queen City

Teachers
LU 2415 Houston Federation of
  Teachers . . . . Houston
SFED Texas . . . . Austin

Teamsters
JC 58 . . . . Houston
JC 80 . . . . Dallas
LU 19 . . . . Houston
LU 577 . . . . Amarillo
LU 657 . . . . San Antonio
LU 745 . . . . Dallas
LU 747 Professional Flight Deck
  Crewmember . . . . . . Houston
LU 767 . . . . Forest Hill
LU 919 . . . . Houston
LU 968 . . . . Houston
LU 988 . . . . Houston
LU 997 . . . . Fort Worth

Television and Radio Artists
LU Houston . . . . Houston

Theatrical Stage Employees
D 6 Texas . . . . Dallas
LU 51 . . . . Houston
LU 76 . . . . San Antonio
LU 126 . . . . Fort Worth
LU 127 . . . . Dallas
LU 153 . . . . El Paso
LU 183 . . . . Port Neches
LU 184-B Front House/
  Ushers . . . . Houston
LU 205 . . . . Austin
LU 249 . . . . Dallas
LU 330 . . . . Weatherford

LU 331 . . . . Killeen
LU 378 . . . . Wichita Falls
LU 484 . . . . Austin
LU 604 . . . . Corpus Christi
LU 803 . . . . Dallas
LU 865 . . . . Odessa
LU 896 . . . . Houston

Train Dispatchers
SCOM Burlington Northern
  Railroad . . . . Paradise

Transit Union
LDIV 1031 . . . . Beaumont
LDIV 1091 . . . . Austin
LDIV 1338 . . . . Dallas
LDIV 1549 . . . . Austin

Transport Workers
LU 276 . . . . Waco
LU 513 Air Transport
  Division . . . . Southlake
LU 541 . . . . Euless
LU 542 . . . . Euless
LU 555 Southwest Airlines Ramp
  Operations . . . . Dallas
LU 556 Texas . . . . Dallas
LU 565 . . . . Bedford
LU 567 . . . . Fort Worth
LU 575 DFW/LAX . . . . . Dallas
LU 576 . . . . Grapevine

Transportation Communications Union
D 317 . . . . Laredo
D 5509 . . . . El Paso
D 5515 . . . . San Antonio
JPB 320 Missouri
  Pacific . . . . San Antonio
LG 67 . . . . Palestine
LG 84 . . . . Laredo
LG 805 . . . . Saginaw
LG 886 . . . . Somerville
LG 5511 Houston . . . . . Houston
LG 6005 Pecos Valley . . . Amarillo
LG 6023 Fort Worth . . . . Burleson
LG 6077 . . . . San Antonio
LG 6452 San Jacinto . . Friendswood
LG 6495 Sycamore . . . . Elkhart
LG 6793 Bird Creek . . . . Temple
SBA 500 American Rail &
  Airway Supervisors . . Rockport
SBA 555 Western Railway
  Supervisors . . . . . Pinehurst

Transportation Union
GCA GO-343 . . . . . . Texarkana
GCA GO-393 Atchison Topeka Santa
  Fe-W-N & S . . . . . . Temple
GCA GO-457 Kansas City Southern
  Railway . . . . Rockwall
GCA GO-577 . . . . Spring
GCA GO-803 Port Terminal Railroad
  Association . . . . . . Houston
GCA GO-927 Union Pacific Railroad
  (T&P) . . . . Tyler
LU 9 . . . . Lubbock
LU 18 . . . . El Paso
LU 20 . . . . Beaumont
LU 243 . . . . Keller
LU 293 . . . . Houston
LU 331 . . . . Temple
LU 439 . . . . Longview
LU 489 . . . . La Vernia
LU 508 . . . . Smithville
LU 513 . . . . Gainesville
LU 524 . . . . Conroe
LU 564 . . . . Fort Worth

LU 569 . . . . Ennis
LU 594 . . . . Mineola
LU 733 . . . . Hooks
LU 756 . . . . Helotes
LU 773 . . . . Friendswood
LU 818 . . . . Keller
LU 821 . . . . Del Rio
LU 823 . . . . Big Spring
LU 857 . . . . San Antonio
LU 878 . . . . Richardson
LU 923 . . . . Dalhart
LU 937 . . . . Fort Worth
LU 940 . . . . Wichita Falls
LU 949 . . . . Whitesboro
LU 953 . . . . Victoria
LU 965 . . . . Terrell
LU 1092 . . . . Teague
LU 1205 . . . . Nursery
LU 1313 . . . . Amarillo
LU 1458 . . . . Klein
LU 1524 . . . . New Caney
LU 1571 . . . . El Paso
LU 1593 . . . . Brownwood
LU 1697 . . . . Amarillo
LU 1886 . . . . Tomball
LU 1892 . . . . Houston
LU 1904 . . . . Katy
LU 1918 . . . . El Paso
LU 1957 . . . . Silsbee
LU 1974 . . . . Hurst
SLB LO-48 . . . . Austin

Treasury Employees

CH 46 . . . . Dallas
CH 52 . . . . Austin
CH 72 . . . . Austin
CH 140 . . . . Dallas
CH 143 . . . . El Paso
CH 145 . . . . Laredo
CH 149 . . . . Pharr
CH 160 . . . . Brownsville
CH 163 . . . . Houston
CH 178 . . . . Eagle Pass
CH 179 . . . . Roma
CH 180 . . . . Del Rio
CH 219 . . . . Dallas
CH 222 . . . . Houston
CH 247 . . . . Austin
CH 260 . . . . Dallas
CH 265 . . . . Dallas
CH 275 FDIC . . . . Houston
CH 298 . . . . Dallas

UNITE HERE
JB Southwest Regional . . . . Dallas

LU 14-K . . . . Dallas
LU 50-002 . . . . Dallas
LU 50-003 . . . . Dallas
LU 50-004 . . . . Dallas
LU 50-005 . . . . Dallas
LU 50-006 . . . . Dallas
LU 128-H . . . . Dallas
LU 129-H . . . . Dallas
LU 174 . . . . Dallas
LU 211-A . . . . Dallas
LU 251 . . . . Dallas
LU 353 . . . . Dallas
LU 371 . . . . Dallas
LU 441 . . . . Amarillo
LU 848-T . . . . Dallas
LU 931-A . . . . Dallas
LU 1022-C . . . . Dallas
LU 1117 . . . . Dallas
LU 1129-C . . . . Dallas
LU 1131 . . . . Dallas
LU 1162 . . . . Dallas
LU 1414-D . . . . Dallas
LU 1798 . . . . Dallas
LU 2368 . . . . Dallas
LU 2623 . . . . Dallas
LU 2629 . . . . Dallas
LU 2630 . . . . Dallas
LU 2631 . . . . Dallas
LU 2632 . . . . Dallas
LU 2638 . . . . Dallas
LU 2645 . . . . Dallas
LU 2647 . . . . Dallas
LU 2672 . . . . Dallas
LU 2700 . . . . Dallas
LU 2705 . . . . Dallas
LU 2711 . . . . Dallas
LU 2712 . . . . Dallas
LU 2726 . . . . Dallas

Weather Service Employees
BR 02-3 . . . . Brownsville
BR 02-4 . . . . Lubbock
BR 02-8 . . . . Amarillo
BR 02-14 . . . . . . New Braunfels
BR 02-16 . . . . Fort Worth
BR 02-20 . . . . Abilene
BR 02-22 . . . . Midland
BR 02-27 . . . . San Angelo
BR 02-33 . . . . Dickinson
BR 02-63 . . . . . . Corpus Christi
BR 02-67 . . . . Fort Worth
BR 02-70 . . . . Houston
BR 02-74 . . . . Houston
BR 02-80 . . . . Fort Worth

Unaffiliated Labor Organizations

Allied Pilots Association
  NHQ . . . . Fort Worth
Allied Pilots Association (Domicile)
  Chicago (ORD) . . . . Fort Worth
Allied Pilots Association (Domicile)
  Dallas (DFW) . . . . Fort Worth
Allied Pilots Association (Domicile)
  Los Angeles (LAX) . . Fort Worth
Allied Pilots Association (Domicile)
  Miami (MIA) . . . . . Fort Worth
Allied Pilots Association (Domicile)
  New York (LGA) . . . Fort Worth
Allied Pilots Association (Domicile)
  San Francisco (SFO) . Fort Worth
Allied Pilots Association (Domicile)
  St. Louis (STL) . . . . Fort Worth
Allied Pilots Association Domicile
  (Boston) (BOS) . . . . Fort Worth
Allied Pilots Association Washington
  DC (DCA) Domicile . . Fort Worth
Allied Pilots Staff Employees
  Association APSEA . . Fort Worth
Association of Union
  Representative . . . . . . Houston
Bell Production Engineering
  Association . . . . Hurst
Champlin Corpus Christi
  Refinery Employees
  Federation . . . . . Corpus Christi
Currency & Security Handlers
  Association . . . . Houston
Exxon Employees Association
  Western Division. . . . . Seguin
Exxon Employees Federation General
  Services Department . . . Houston
Exxon Employees Federation South
  Texas Division . . . . . Kingsville
Exxon Seamens
  Association . . . . Seabrook
Exxon Southwestern Employees
  Federation Southwestern
  Division. . . . . Midland
Federated Texas Unions LU 900
  Aircraft Workers. . . . Fort Worth
Federated Texas Unions
  NHQ . . . . Fort Worth
Flight Attendants Professional
  Association . . . . Euless
Fort Hood Barbers
  Association . . . . Killeen
Fraternal Order of Police National
  Labor Texas LG 50 . Weatherford

Guards of the United States
  Associated . . . . . . Texas City
Gulf Coast Industrial Workers
  Union . . . . Baytown
Ingleside Association of Maintenance
  Personnel . . . . Robstown
International Guards Union of
  America LU 38 . . . . . Amarillo
International Guards Union of
  America LU 50 . . . . Texarkana
International Guards Union of
  America LU 80 . . . . . Karnack
International Guards Union of
  America LU 124 . . . . . Hooks
International Guards Union of
  America NHQ . . . . . Amarillo
International Guards Union of
  America RC Eighth . . . . Avery
Manufacturing and Industrial Worker
  Union . . . . Bryan
National Air Traffic
  Controllers Local Council
  Harlinger . . . . Harlingen
Petroleum Employees
  Associated . . . . Hull
Phillips Pipe Line Company
  Employees Chocolate Bayou
  District . . . . La Porte
Phillips Pipe Line Company
  Employees Federation West
  Texas-Borger District . . . Borger
Phillips Pipeline Employees Union
  LU 66. . . . . Goldsmith
Radio & Television Broadcast
  Group. . . . . Houston
Randolph Courseware Developers
  Association RCDA . . . . Schertz
Schulenberg Plant Shop
  Committee . . . . . . La Grange
Shell Pipe Line Employees
  Federation Independent, West
  Texas Division. . . . . . Odessa
Southwest Airlines Employee
  Association . . . . Dallas
Southwest Airlines Pilots
  Association . . . . Dallas
Sun Pipe Line Employees
  Association Texas
  Area. . . . . Longview
Sunoco Terminals Independent
  Association . . . . . . Nederland
Technical Control Union . Nederland
Texas Employees Federation of
  Exxon Pipe Line UNIT 2. La Porte
United Workers Union . Brownsville

Utah

AFL-CIO Trade and Industrial Departments

Building and Construction Trades Department
BCTC Utah. . . . . . Salt Lake City

Affiliated Labor Organizations

Air Traffic Controllers
LU SAF. . . . . Salt Lake City
LU SLC. . . . . Salt Lake City
LU ZLC . . . . Salt Lake City

Asbestos Workers
LU 510 . . . . Salt Lake City

Bakery, Confectionery, Tobacco Workers and Grain Millers
LU 19-G . . . . Roy
LU 401 . . . . Salt Lake City

Boilermakers
LG 182 . . . . Murray
LG 374-D Cement
  Workers . . . . West Jordan

Bricklayers
LU 1 . . . . Salt Lake City

Carpenters
LU 184 . . . . West Jordan
LU 1498 . . . . Provo
LU 1507 . . . . . West Jordan

Communications Workers
LU 7704 . . . . Salt Lake City
LU 7705 . . . . Ogden
LU 14759. . . . . . . Salt Lake City

Electrical Workers
LU 57. . . . . Salt Lake City
LU 354 . . . . . West Valley City
LU 650 . . . . Layton
LU 1619 . . . . Delta

Elevator Constructors
LU 38 . . . . Salt Lake City

Federal Employees
LU 125 . . . . Pleasant View
LU 1724 . . . . Kearns
LU 1933 . . . . Cedar City

Glass, Molders, Pottery and Plastics Workers
LU 231-B . . . . . West Valley City

Government Employees
LU 1592 DoD . . Hill Air Force Base
LU 2118. . . . . Brigham City
LU 2118 DCMC
  Thiokol . . . . . . Brigham City
LU 2185 DoD . . . . Tooele

LU 2199 VA. . . . West Valley City
LU 3052 USDA . . . . . Providence
LU 3251 HHS . . . . Salt Lake City

Government Employees Association
LU 14-9 . . . . Dugway

Iron Workers
LU 27. . . . . Salt Lake City

Laborers
LU 295 . . . . Salt Lake City

Letter Carriers
BR 68 . . . . Morgan
BR 111 . . . . . . Salt Lake City
BR 887. . . . . Provo
BR 970 . . . . Logan
BR 1765. . . . . Kanab
BR 2112 . . . . Brigham City
BR 2171 . . . . . . East Carbon
BR 2339 . . . . . . Spanish Fork
BR 2376 . . . . Payson
BR 2609 . . . . . . American Fork
BR 2821 . . . . Springville
BR 2863 . . . . Richfield
BR 3143 . . . . Manti
BR 3252 . . . . Nephi
BR 3574 . . . . Cedar City
BR 3928 . . . . Clearfield
BR 3931 . . . . Tremonton
BR 3932 . . . . Vernal
BR 4012 . . . . . . Heber City
BR 4032 . . . . Helper
BR 4043 . . . . St. George
BR 4235 . . . . Orem
BR 4506 . . . . Layton
BR 4789 . . . . Roosevelt
BR 5360 . . . . . . Pleasant Grove
BR 5964 . . . . Moab
BR 6308 . . . . Smithfield
SA Utah. . . . . North Salt Lake

Locomotive Engineers
DIV 51. . . . . Morgan
DIV 55. . . . . Roy
DIV 136 . . . . . Salt Lake City
DIV 222 . . . . . West Bountiful
DIV 349 . . . . Sandy
DIV 374 . . . . Morgan
DIV 681 . . . . Milford
DIV 713 . . . . . Salt Lake City
DIV 794 . . . . Layton
DIV 846 . . . . . Salt Lake City
DIV 888 . . . . Helper
GCA 221 . . . . Springville
SLB Utah State . . . . Salt Lake City

Machinists
LG 568 . . . . Salt Lake City
LG 1287 Air
  Transport . . . . . Salt Lake City
LG 1497 . . . . . . Salt Lake City
LG 1976 . . . . Cedar City
STC Utah. . . . . . Salt Lake City

Maintenance of Way Employes
LG 968. . . . . Spanish Fork
LG 1227. . . . . Midvale
LG 1709 . . . . Price
SLG 779 . . . . Price
SLG 1348 . . . . South Weber

Mine Workers
LU 1206 . . . . Wellington
LU 1261 . . . . Ferron
LU 1681 . . . . Helper
LU 1769 . . . . Huntington
LU 2176 . . . . Orangeville
LU 6363 . . . . Ferron
LU 6788 . . . . Helper
LU 8622 . . . . Helper
LU 9958 . . . . Sunnyside

Musicians
LU 104 . . . . Salt Lake City

National Staff Organization
LU Staff Organization, Professional,
  Utah . . . . Murray

Office and Professional Employees
LU 286 . . . . Midvale

Painters
LU 77. . . . . Salt Lake City
LU 755 . . . . Erda

Plasterers and Cement Masons
LU 568 . . . . Salt Lake City

Postal Mail Handlers
LU 332 . . . . . West Valley City

Postal Workers
LU 6 Salt Lake City . Salt Lake City
LU 42 . . . . Provo
LU 75 Utah Area . . . . . . Ogden
LU 1568 Price . . . . Price
LU 1934 Vernal . . . . . . Vernal
LU 2350 St. George . . . St. George
LU 2513 Tooele . . . . . Tooele
LU 5192 Orem. . . . . Orem
SA Utah . . . . . Salt Lake City

Pulp and Paper Workers
LU 700 . . . . Salt Lake City

Railroad Signalmen
LLG 24 . . . . West Jordan

Roofers, Waterproofers and Allied Workers
LU 91 . . . . Salt Lake City

Rural Letter Carriers
SA Utah . . . . South Jordan

Service Employees
LU 651 Firemen & Oilers . . Murray

Sheet Metal Workers
LU 312 . . . . Salt Lake City

Steelworkers
C Chevron Coordinating
  Council . . . . . West Valley City
LU 8593 . . . . Magna
LU 08-286. . . . . Roy
LU 08-578 . . . . . . Woodscross
LU 08-931 . . . . . Salt Lake City
LU 12-392-S . . . . Magna
LU 12-876-S . . . . . . Wendover
LU 12-1654-S . . . . Orem
LU 12-3318-S . . . . American Fork
LU 12-4265-S . . . . . Payson
LU 12-6162-S. . . . . Ogden
LU 12-8319 . . . . . . Grantsville

Teamsters
LU 222 . . . . Salt Lake City

Theatrical Stage Employees
LU 99 . . . . Salt Lake City

Transit Union
LU 1700 . . . . . . American Fork

Transportation Communications Union
D 1223 Union Pacific-Eastern Lines
  SD 106 . . . . Riverton
D 5517. . . . . Sandy
LG 6542 Carman
  Division . . . . Harrisville

Transportation Union
LU 166 . . . . Salt Lake City
LU 238 . . . . Ogden
LU 1038 . . . . Kearns
LU 1294 . . . . Minersville
LU 1366 . . . . Santaquin
LU 1554 . . . . Ogden
SLB LO-49 Utah . . . Salt Lake City

Treasury Employees
CH 17. . . . . Salt Lake City
CH 67. . . . . Ogden

Weather Service Employees
BR 04-39 . . . . . . Salt Lake City
BR 04-71 . . . . . . Salt Lake City
BR 04-78 . . . . . . Salt Lake City

Unaffiliated Labor Organizations
Ballet West Dancers
  Association. . . . . Salt Lake City
Concrete Handlers Drivers &
  Operators Independent Union. Roy
International Association of United
  Workers Union . West Valley City
International Association of United
  Workers Union LU
  1-02 . . . . Huntington
Moon Lake Employees
  Association . . . . . . Roosevelt

Vermont

AFL-CIO Trade and Industrial Departments

Building and Construction Trades Department
BCTC Vermont
   State . . . . . . South Burlington

Affiliated Labor Organizations

Air Traffic Controllers
LU BTV . . . . . South Burlington

Boilermakers
LG 449-D Cement Workers . Chester

Civilian Technicians
CH 66 Green
   Mountain . . . . South Burlington

Communications Workers
LU 81170 . . . . Brandon
LU 81248 . . . . Colchester

Education
SA Vermont-National Education
   Association . . . . . Montpelier

Electrical Workers
LU 300 . . . . . South Burlington
LU 2326 . . . . Essex Junction

Electrical, Radio and Machine Workers
LU 203 City Market/Onion River
   Coop Workers . . . . Burlington
LU 218 . . . . Colchester
LU 221 . . . . Burlington
LU 225 . . . . Rutland

LU 234 . . . . St. Johnsbury
LU 255 . . . . Montpelier
LU 267 . . . . Burlington

Government Employees
LU 2076 DoJ . . . . . . St. Albans
LU 2604 VA . White River Junction

Government Employees Association
LU 01-175 . . . . Colchester

Government Security Officers
LU 16 . . . . Vernon

Graphic Communications
LU 745-C . . . . Montpelier

Laborers
LU 522 . . . . Williston

Letter Carriers
BR 37 . . . . Brattleboro
BR 252 . . . . Bennington
BR 495 . . . . Rutland
BR 521 . . . . Burlington
BR 617 . . . . Middlesex
BR 777 . . . . Bellows Falls
BR 837 . . . . St. Johnsbury
BR 1365 . . . . Newport
BR 1828 . . . . White River Junction
BR 2244 . . . . Northfield
BR 2245 . . . . Woodstock
BR 3133 . . . . Fair Haven
BR 3490 . . . . Brandon
SA Vermont . . . . . . Burlington

Machinists
LG 1829 . . . . Newport
LG 2704 . . . . Starksboro

Maintenance of Way Employees
LG 356 . . . . Newport

Musicians
LU 351 . . . . Burlington

National Staff Organization
LU 3 Vermont Staff
   Organization . . . . . Montpelier

Nurses
LU 5109 Copley
   Hospital . . . . Morrisville

Nurses, Professional
LU 5050 . . . . Brattleboro

Plumbing and Pipe Fitting
LU 693 . . . . . South Burlington

Postal Workers
LU 520 White River
   Junction . . . White River Junction
LU 570 Burlington . . . . Burlington
LU 759 Montpelier
   Vermont . . . . . . Montpelier
LU 765 Barre . . . . Barre
LU 3173 Rutland . . . . . Rutland
LU 3178 Bennington . . Bennington
LU 3184 Springfield . . Springfield
LU 3535 Brattleboro . . Brattleboro
LU 4000 Lyndonville . . Lyndonville
LU 6322 Manchester
   Center . . . . Manchester Center
SA Vermont . . White River Junction

Rural Letter Carriers
SA Vermont . . . . . . Grand Isle

State, County and Municipal Employees
LU 1674 Vermont Community
   Health Care Centers
   Employees . . . . . Essex Junction

Steelworkers
LU 4-4-S . . . . Barre
LU 01-340 . . . . St. Albans
LU 01-345 . . . . St. Albans
LU 01-944 . . . . . West Brattleboro
LU 01-1862 . . . . . Bellows Falls
LU 04-5518-S . . . . Lyndon Center
LU 08-296 Granite Cutters
   Association . . . . Barre

Teachers
LU 5064 Nurses, Brattleboro
   Federation of . . . . . Brattleboro
LU 5221 Vermont Nurses and Health
   Professon . . . . Burlington
LU 8043 State
   Federation . . . . . . Burlington

Teamsters
LU 597 . . . . South Barre

Theatrical Stage Employees
LU 919 . . . . Burlington

Treasury Employees
CH 19 . . . . Burlington
CH 142 . . . . Swanton

Weather Service Employees
BR 01-7 . . . . Burlington

Unaffiliated Labor Organizations

Brattleboro Retreat United Nurses &
   Allied Professionals LU
   5086 . . . . Putney
Independent Union of Plant
   Protection Employees LU
   20 . . . . Burlington

Virgin Islands

Affiliated Labor Organizations

Agricultural Employees
BR 44 . . . . Kingshill

Air Traffic Controllers
LU STT . . . . St. Thomas

Civilian Technicians
LU 87 Virgin Islands Chapter of
   Association. . . . . . . St. Croix

Government Employees
C 228 National SBA
   Locals . . . . Kingshill

Government Security Officers
LU 60 . . . . St. Thomas

Letter Carriers
BR 6412 . . . . St. Thomas
BR 6413 . . . . Christiansted

Postal Workers
LU 6176 Virgin Island
   Area . . . . St. Thomas

Steelworkers
LU . . . . Christiansted
LU 03-9488 . . . . . . St. Thomas
LU 09-8248-S . . . . . . St. Croix
LU 09-8249-S . . . . . St. Thomas
LU 09-8526-S . . . . . . St. Croix
LU 09-8545-S . . . . . Kingshill
LU 09-8677-S . . . . . St. Thomas
LU 09-8713-S . . . . . St. Thomas

Treasury Employees
CH 200 . . . . St. Croix

UNITE HERE
LU 611 . . . . Christiansted

Unaffiliated Labor Organizations

Our Virgin Island Labor
   Union . . . . Christiansted

Virginia

AFL-CIO Trade and Industrial Departments

Building and Construction Trades Department
BCTC Hampton
  Roads . . . . Newport News
BCTC North Carolina . . . Roanoke
BCTC Richmond . . . . . Richmond
BCTC Southwestern
  Virginia . . . . Roanoke
BCTC Virginia State . . . Richmond

Maritime Trades Department
PC Hampton Roads . . . . . Norfolk

Metal Trades Department
MTC Tidewater Virginia Federal
  Employees. . . . . . . Portsmouth

Affiliated Labor Organizations

Agricultural Employees
BR 32 . . . . Norfolk

Air Traffic Controllers
LU DCC . . . . Herndon
LU HEF . . . . Manassas
LU ORF . . . . . . Virginia Beach
LU PCT . . . . Warrenton
LU PHF . . . . . Newport News
LU RIC . . . . Richmond
LU ROC . . . . Roanoke
LU ZDC . . . . Leesburg

Asbestos Workers
LU 9 . . . . Chesapeake
LU 85 . . . . Chesterfield
LU 129 . . . . . . Colonial Heights

Automobile, Aerospace Workers
LU 26 . . . . Suffolk
LU 149 . . . . Winchester
LU 919 . . . . Norfolk
LU 2069 . . . . Dublin
LU 2123 . . . . . Fredericksburg
LU 2389 . . . . . . Clifton Forge
LU 2807 . . . . Lebanon
LU 2999 . . . . Strasburg
LU 3041 . . . . Pulaski
LU 3151 . . . . . . Christiansburg

Bakery, Confectionery, Tobacco Workers and Grain Millers
LU 203-T . . . . Richmond
LU 233-T . . . . Danville
LU 255-T . . . . . Lawrenceville
LU 321-T . . . . Blackstone
LU 348-T . . . . Danville
LU 358 . . . . Richmond
LU 359-T . . . . . Colonial Heights

Boilermakers
LG 45 . . . . Richmond
LG 57 . . . . Portsmouth
LG 191-D Cement
  Workers . . . . Chesapeake
LG 314-D Cement
  Workers . . . . Roanoke
LG 538 . . . . Roanoke
LG 684 . . . . Chesapeake
LG 1999 . . . . Portsmouth

Carpenters
C East Coast Industrial. . . . Marion
LU 319 . . . . Roanoke
LU 388 . . . . Richmond
LU 613 . . . . Norfolk
LU 1078 . . . . . . Fredericksburg
LU 1402 . . . . Richmond
LU 1665 . . . . Alexandria
LU 2033 . . . . Front Royal
LU 2316 . . . . Boykins
LU 2488 . . . . Berryville
LU 2514 . . . . Chesapeake
LU 8222 . . . . Cana

Civilian Technicians
CH 49 Old Dominion . . . Sandston
CH 59 Robert C. Atkinson
  Memorial . . . . . Mechanicsville
CH 95 Potomac . . . . . Fort Belvoir
CH 102 Southside Virginia . Victoria
NHQ . . . . Woodbridge

Communications Workers
C Virginia State . . . . . Roanoke
LU 2201 . . . . Richmond
LU 2202 . . . . . . Virginia Beach
LU 2203 . . . . Lynchburg
LU 2204 . . . . Roanoke
LU 2205 . . . . . Newport News
LU 2206 . . . . Melfa
LU 2222 . . . . Annandale
LU 2252 . . . . Chesterfield
LU 2272 . . . . Middletown
LU 2275 . . . . Woodbridge
LU 2277 . . . . Martinsville
LU 2390 . . . . Fairfax
LU 14208 . . . . Norfolk
LU 82160 . . . . . . Christiansburg
LU 82161 . . . . Salem
LU 82162 . . . . Roanoke
LU 82167 . . . . Vinton
LU 82173 . . . . Verona
LU 82174 . . . . . . Shenandoah

DuPont Workers
LU United Workers
  Inc. . . . . Waynesboro

Electrical Workers
LU 50 . . . . Richmond
LU 80 . . . . Chesapeake
LU 121 . . . . Stephens City
LU 464 . . . . Covington
LU 666 . . . . . Highland Springs
LU 734 . . . . Portsmouth
LU 813 . . . . Goodview
LU 1142 . . . . Norfolk
LU 1181 . . . . . . Charlottesville
LU 1340 . . . . . Newport News
LU 1434 . . . . Chesterfield
LU 1737 . . . . Manassas
LU 2173 Lynchburg . . . Concord
LU 2240 . . . . Windsor

Electrical, Radio and Machine Workers
LU 123 . . . . Verona

Elevator Constructors
LU 51 . . . . Richmond
LU 52 . . . . Norfolk

Engineers
LU 1 . . . . Portsmouth
LU 10 . . . . Portsmouth

Federal Employees
C GSA Locals . . . West Springfield
LU 1028 . . . . Norfolk
LU 1309 . . . . Reston
LU 1332 . . . . . . Fort Belvoir
LU 1627 . . . . Springfield
LU 1642 . . . . Arlington
LU 1800 . . . . West Springfield
LU 1861 . . . . Roanoke
LU 1887 . . . . Alexandria
LU 1957 . . . . Reston
LU 1993 . . . . Springfield

Fire Fighters
LU 25-F . . . . . . Virginia Beach
LU 45-I Newport News Professional
  Shipyard . . . . Seaford
LU 287-F Fort Lee Fire &
  Emergency Services . . . Fort Lee
LU 3217 Metro Washington
  Airports . . . . Arlington

Food and Commercial Workers
LU 94-C . . . . Shenandoah
LU 591-C . . . . . . Prince George
LU 845-C . . . . Brookneal
LU 851-C . . . . Stony Creek

Glass, Molders, Pottery and Plastics Workers
LU 33 . . . . Barhamsville
LU 89 . . . . Danville

Government Employees
C 4 VA, Fourth District . . . . Salem
C 53 National VA . . . . . . Salem
C 215 National SSA-BHA
  Locals . . . . Falls Church
C 240 National U.S. Marine Corps
  Locals . . . . Quantico
LU 2 Army Pentagon-
  DoD . . . . Arlington
LU 22 ID . . . . Norfolk
LU 53 DoD . . . . Norfolk
LU 65 ID Retirees . . . . . . Hayes
LU 407 National Park Service
  Virginia and West Virginia . Luray
LU 1052 . . . . Fort Belvoir
LU 1178 DoD . . . . Fort Lee
LU 1356 USDA . . . . . Richmond
LU 1402 . . . . Arlington
LU 1643 DoD . . . . . Fort Eustis
LU 1739 VA . . . . Salem
LU 1754 FEMA . . . . . Winchester
LU 1786 DoD . . . . . . Quantico
LU 1924 DoJ . . . . . . Arlington
LU 1992 . . . . Richmond
LU 2052 DoJ . . . . . . Petersburg
LU 2096 DoD . . . . . . Dahlgren
LU 2100 USDA . . . . . Timberville
LU 2145 VA . . . . . . Richmond
LU 2328 VAMC . . . . . Hampton
LU 2449 DLA . . . . Lorton
LU 2755 NASA . . . . . Hampton
LU 2785 DoJ . . . . . . Arlington
LU 2817 USDA . . . . . Windsor
LU 2902 DoD . . . Bowling Green
LU 3316 DoL . . . . Norton
LU 3380 HUD . . . . . Richmond
LU 3403 NSF . . . . . . Arlington
LU 3525 DoJ . . . . . Falls Church
LU 3615 SSA . . . . . Falls Church
LU 4015 DoD . . . . . Portsmouth

Government Employees Association
LU . . . . Hampton
LU 03-118 Service Employees
  Intern. . . . . Alexandria
LU 04-1 . . . . Lackey
LU 04-2 . . . . . Newport News
LU 04-6 . . . . Fort Eustis
LU 04-11 . . . . . . Fort Monroe
LU 04-12 . . . . . . Fort Monroe
LU 04-17 . . . . Hampton
LU 04-19 . . . . . Virginia Beach
LU 04-26 . Langley Air Force Base
LU 04-27 . . . . Petersburg
LU 04-45 . . . . Norfolk
LU 04-47 . . . . Fort Eustis
LU 04-68 . . . . . . Williamsburg
LU 04-69 . . . . Hampton
LU 04-86 . . . . Alexandria
LU 04-106 . Langley Air Force Base
LU 04-109 . . . . . . Portsmouth
LU 04-114 . . . . Hampton
LU 04-123 . . . . . Virginia Beach
LU 04-124 . . . . . . Chesapeake

Government Security Officers
LU 40 . . . . Roanoke
LU 84 . . . . Chesterfield

Graphic Communications
LU 40-N . . . . Richmond
LU 210-C . . . . Vinton
LU 538-C . . . . Woodbridge
LU 642-S . . . . Grottoes
LU 670-C . . . . Richmond

Iron Workers
DC Mid Atlantic States . . . Fairfax
LU 28 . . . . Richmond
LU 79 . . . . Norfolk
LU 228 . . . . Portsmouth
LU 486 . . . . McLean
LU 697 . . . . Roanoke
LU 753 . . . . Bristol
LU 781 . . . . Norfolk

Laborers
DC Virginia & North
  Carolina . . . . . . Williamsburg
LU Mid Atlantic Region Organizing
  Coalition . . . . Reston
LU 11 Construction & Master
  Laborers . . . . Alexandria
LU 307 . . . . Williamsburg
LU 388 . . . . Norfolk
LU 404 Industrial & Commercial
  Employees . . . . . Williamsburg
LU 572 . . . . Williamsburg
LU 980 . . . . Roanoke
LU 1046 . . . . Williamsburg
LU 1225 Aviation Maintenance
  Technicians . . . . Sterling

Letter Carriers
BR 247 Tidewater . . . . Hampton
BR 325 . . . . Lynchburg
BR 326 . . . . Petersburg
BR 456 Norfolk . . . . . Norfolk
BR 496 . . . . Richmond
BR 513 . . . . Staunton
BR 518 . . . . Charlottesville
BR 524 . . . . Hardy
BR 567 Cavalier . . . . Alexandria
BR 595 . . . . Danville
BR 609 . . . . Newport News

BR 685 . . . . Fredericksburg
BR 694 . . . . Winchester
BR 880 . . . . Bluefield
BR 1112 . . . . . . Virginia Beach
BR 1185 . . . . Bedford
BR 1605 . . . . Salem
BR 1793 . . . . Pulaski
BR 2091 . . . . Franklin
BR 2153 . . . . Hopewell
BR 2280 . . . . Martinsville
BR 2500 . . . . . . Cape Charles
BR 2727 . . . . Front Royal
BR 2819 . . . . . . Virginia Beach
BR 3005 . . . . Wytheville
BR 3138 . . . . Crewe
BR 3170 . . . . . South Boston
BR 3376 . . . . Woodstock
BR 3379 . . . . Strasburg
BR 3387 . . . . Norton
BR 3508 . . . . . Big Stone Gap
BR 3520 . . . . Annandale
BR 3621 . . . . Galax
BR 3686 . . . . Radford
BR 3864 . . . . Emporia
BR 3882 . . . . Onancock
BR 4053 . . . . Bluefield
BR 4276 . . . . Blacksburg
BR 4292 . . . . . Christiansburg
BR 4575 . . . . Tazewell
BR 4576 . . . . Pennington Gap
BR 4577 . . . . . . Rocky Mount
BR 4581 . . . . Altavista
BR 4582 . . . . Appalachia
BR 4654 . . . . South Hill
BR 4798 . . . . Springfield
BR 4989 . . . Chincoteague Island
BR 4990 . . . . Chase City
BR 4991 . . . . . Lawrenceville
BR 5282 . . . . Spencer
BR 5447 . . . . Smithfield
BR 5457 . . . . Richlands
BR 5661 . . . . Orange
BR 5825 . . . . . . Collinsville
BR 5917 . . . . Narrows
BR 5920 . . . . . Colonial Beach
BR 5921 . . . . . . Woodbridge
BR 6009 . . . . Pearisburg
BR 6066 . . . . Chesapeake
BR 6434 . . . . Ridgeway
SA Virginia . . . . Newport News

Locomotive Engineers
DIV 14 . . . . Spotsylvania
DIV 26 . . . . Richmond
DIV 37 . . . . Coeburn
DIV 38 . . . . Hot Springs
DIV 143 . . . . Culpeper
DIV 167 . . . . . Big Stone Gap
DIV 217 . . . . Elkton
DIV 291 . . . . Victoria
DIV 301 . . . . Vinton
DIV 456 . . . . . Virginia Beach
DIV 483 . . . . . . Locust Grove
DIV 532 . . . . . Mechanicsville
DIV 561 . . . . Montpelier
GCA Norfolk & Western
    Railway . . . . Salem

Longshoremen
DC Hampton Roads &
    Vicinity . . . . Norfolk
LU 846 . . . . . Newport News
LU 862 . . . . . Newport News
LU 970 . . . . Norfolk
LU 1248 . . . . Norfolk
LU 1458 . . . . Norfolk
LU 1624 . . . . Norfolk
LU 1736 . . . . . Newport News

LU 1784 . . . . Hampton
LU 1963 . . . . Chesapeake
LU 1970 . . . . Norfolk

Machinists
DLG 74 . . . . Norfolk
LG 10 . . . . Richmond
LG 97 . . . . . . Virginia Beach
LG 165 . . . . Roanoke
LG 680 . . . . . . Virginia Beach
LG 696 . . . . Powhatan
LG 1747 . . . . Herndon
LG 1759 . . . . Herndon
LG 2461 . . . . . Newport News
LG 2531 . . . . Hampton
LG 2552 . . . . . Wallops Island
LG 2708 . . . . Norfolk
LG 2914 . . . . Norfolk
LLG 67 . . . . Dublin
LLG W-216
    Woodworkers . . . Mechanicsville
LLG W-331 Woodworkers . Emporia
LLG W-391 Woodworkers . . . Ivor
LLG W-2533 Woodworkers . . Floyd
LLG FL-2143 . . . . . Alexandria
STC Virginia . . . . Hampton

Maintenance of Way Employes
LG 75 . . . . Eagle Rock
LG 568 . . . . Dublin
LG 571 . . . . Bluefield
LG 572 . . . . Farmville
LG 577 . . . . Stanley
LG 588 . . . . La Crosse
LG 598 . . . . Crewe
LG 2925 . . . . Midlothian
SLG 153 . . . . Scottsville
SLG 338 . . . . Richmond
SLG 586 . . . . Gate City
SLG 594 . . . . . Virginia Beach
SLG 599 . . . . Salem
SLG 995 . . . . Chesapeake

Mine Workers
LU 218 . . . . . . Martinsville
LU 325 . . . . Lebanon
LU 1055 . . . . Pennington Gap
LU 1259 . . . . Lebanon
LU 1374 . . . . Grundy
LU 1405 . . . . . Big Stone Gap
LU 1470 . . . . Castlewood
LU 1509 . . . . Lebanon
LU 1594 . . . . . . Jewell Ridge
LU 1607 . . . . Appalachia
LU 1640 . . . . Honaker
LU 1671 . . . . Oakwood
LU 1760 . . . . . . Swords Creek
LU 1976 . . . . . Big Stone Gap
LU 2158 . . . . Appalachia
LU 2232 . . . . Grundy
LU 2274 . . . . Coeburn
LU 2322 . . . . . . Cedar Bluff
LU 2354 . . . . Clintwood
LU 2490 . . . . Clintwood
LU 2888 . . . . Abingdon
LU 6025 . . . . Bandy
LU 6229 . . . . Wise
LU 6354 . . . . Norton
LU 6375 . . . . Keokee
LU 6633 . . . . Bandy
LU 6843 . . . . Mavisdale
LU 7170 . . . . Haysi
LU 7276 . . . . Wise
LU 7327 . . . . Rosedale
LU 7950 . . . . Coeburn
LU 8017 . . . . Wise
LU 8181 . . . . Appalachia
LU 8761 . . . . . Pennington Gap

LU 9127 . . . . . . East Stone Gap
LU 9967 . . . . Wise
NHQ . . . . Fairfax

Musicians
LU 123 . . . . Richmond
LU 125 . . . . Norfolk

National Staff Organization
LU Virginia Professional Staff
    Association . . . . . . Richmond

Office and Professional Employees
LU 334 . . . . Richmond

Operating Engineers
LU 147 . . . . Norfolk

Painters
LU 474 . . . . Portsmouth
LU 890 . . . . Springfield
LU 1100 . . . . Norfolk
LU 1846 . . . . . Virginia Beach

Pilots, Air Line
LEC 1 Northwest Airlines . Herndon
LEC 5 United Airlines . . . Herndon
LEC 7 Fedex . . . . Herndon
LEC 11 United Airlines . . Herndon
LEC 12 United Airlines . . Herndon
LEC 15 Sun Country Local Executive
    Council . . . . Herndon
LEC 16 Delta Airlines . . . Herndon
LEC 17 Astar Air Cargo . . Herndon
LEC 18 Spirit Local Executive
    Council . . . . Herndon
LEC 20 Northwest
    Airlines . . . . Herndon
LEC 22 Fedex . . . . Herndon
LEC 23 Polar Air Cargo Local Exec
    Council . . . . Herndon
LEC 25 Champion Air . . . Herndon
LEC 26 Fedex Local Executive
    Council . . . . Herndon
LEC 27 United Airlines . . Herndon
LEC 28 Piedmont Airlines . Herndon
LEC 29 Piedmont Airlines . Herndon
LEC 30 Midwest Airlines Local
    Executive Council . . . . Herndon
LEC 32 USAirways . . . Herndon
LEC 33 United Airlines . . Herndon
LEC 34 United Airlines . . Herndon
LEC 35 Piedmont Local Executive
    Council . . . . Herndon
LEC 37 Comair . . . . . . Herndon
LEC 38 Trans States Local Exec
    Council . . . . Herndon
LEC 39 Trans States . . . Herndon
LEC 41 USAirways . . . . Herndon
LEC 44 Delta Airlines . . . Herndon
LEC 46 Ryan Airlines . . . Herndon
LEC 48 Delta . . . . Herndon
LEC 50 Air Wisconsin . . . Herndon
LEC 51 Air Wisconsin
    Local . . . . Herndon
LEC 52 United Airlines . . Herndon
LEC 53 Air Wisconsin . . . Herndon
LEC 55 Northwest Airlines . Herndon
LEC 57 United Airlines . . Herndon
LEC 60 Skyway Local Executive
    Council . . . . Herndon
LEC 61 PSA Local Executive
    Council . . . . Herndon
LEC 62 America West . . . Herndon
LEC 63 Alaska Airlines . . Herndon
LEC 64 Alaska Airlines . . Herndon
LEC 65 Hawaiian Airlines . Herndon
LEC 66 Delta Airlines . . . Herndon

LEC 67 Alaska Airlines . . Herndon
LEC 69 PSA . . . . Herndon
LEC 70 PSA . . . . Herndon
LEC 72 Atlas Air Local Executive
    Council . . . . Herndon
LEC 74 Northwest
    Airlines . . . . Herndon
LEC 78 Allegheny . . . . Herndon
LEC 79 Fedex . . . . Herndon
LEC 80 Aloha Airlines . . Herndon
LEC 81 Delta Airlines . . . Herndon
LEC 82 America West . . . Herndon
LEC 83 American Eagle . . Herndon
LEC 84 Mesa . . . . Herndon
LEC 85 Mesa Air Group . . Herndon
LEC 86 Mesa . . . . Herndon
LEC 87 Florida Gulf . . . Herndon
LEC 88 Mesa . . . . Herndon
LEC 90 US Airways . . . Herndon
LEC 93 United Airlines . . Herndon
LEC 94 USAirways . . . . Herndon
LEC 95 Allegheny Local Executive
    Council . . . . Herndon
LEC 96 ATA Airlines Local Exec
    Council . . . . Herndon
LEC 97 ATA Airlines Local Exec
    Council . . . . Herndon
LEC 98 ATA Airlines Local Exec
    Council . . . . Herndon
LEC 99 Fedex . . . . Herndon
LEC 100 Fedex Local Executive
    Council . . . . Herndon
LEC 104 Mesaba . . . . . Herndon
LEC 105 American Eagle . Herndon
LEC 106 Mesaba Airlines . Herndon
LEC 107 Mesaba Airlines . Herndon
LEC 108 Delta Airlines . . Herndon
LEC 109 Spirit Local Executive
    Council . . . . Herndon
LEC 111 Kitty Hawk . . . . Herndon
LEC 112 Atlantic Southeast
    Airlines . . . . Herndon
LEC 113 Atlantic Southeast
    Airlines . . . . Herndon
LEC 117 Gemini Local . . . Herndon
LEC 121 American Eagle . Herndon
LEC 126 American Eagle . Herndon
LEC 128 Pinnacle Local Executive
    Council . . . . Herndon
LEC 129 Pinnacle Local Executive
    Council . . . . Herndon
LEC 130 Pinnacle Local Executive
    Council . . . . Herndon
LEC 131 American Eagle . Herndon
LEC 133 American Eagle . Herndon
LEC 135 US Airways . . . Herndon
LEC 138 US Airways . . . Herndon
LEC 141 Independence
    Air . . . . Herndon
LEC 146 Island Air Local Executive
    Council . . . . Herndon
LEC 155 American Eagle . Herndon
LEC 170 Continental . . . . Herndon
LEC 171 Continental
    Express . . . . Herndon
LEC 172 Continental
    Express . . . . Herndon
LEC 173 Continental . . . . Herndon
LEC 175 Continental
    Express . . . . Herndon
LEC 176 Continental
    Express . . . . Herndon
LEC 177 Continental
    Express . . . . Herndon
LEC 178 Continental
    Instructors . . . . Herndon
LEC 179 Continental Express
    Instructors . . . . Herndon

MEC Air Wisconsin . . . . Herndon
MEC Alaska Airlines. . . . Herndon
MEC Allegheny . . . . . . Herndon
MEC Aloha Airlines . . . . Herndon
MEC Aloha Island Air . . . Herndon
MEC America West . . . . Herndon
MEC American Eagle . . . Herndon
MEC American Trans Air . Herndon
MEC Astar Air Cargo . . . Herndon
MEC Atlantic Coast . . . . Herndon
MEC Atlantic Southeast . . Herndon
MEC Atlas Air . . . . . . Herndon
MEC Champion Air . . . . Herndon
MEC Comair . . . . Herndon
MEC Continental. . . . . . Herndon
MEC Delta Airlines . . . . Herndon
MEC Express Airlines . . . Herndon
MEC Expressjet . . . . . . Herndon
MEC Fedex Master Executive
    Council . . . . Herndon
MEC Flying Tiger Airlines. Herndon
MEC Gemini . . . . Herndon
MEC Hawaiian Airlines . . Herndon
MEC Kitty Hawk . . . . . . Herndon
MEC Mesa . . . . Herndon
MEC Mesaba Airlines . . . Herndon
MEC Midway Airlines . . . Herndon
MEC Midwest Express . . . Herndon
MEC Northwest Airlines . . Herndon
MEC Pan American . . . . Herndon
MEC Piedmont Airlines . . Herndon
MEC Polar Air Cargo . . . Herndon
MEC PSA . . . . Herndon
MEC Republic Airlines . . Herndon
MEC Ryan . . . . Herndon
MEC Skyway Master. . . . Herndon
MEC Spirit . . . . Herndon
MEC Sun Country . . . . . Herndon
MEC Trans States . . . . . Herndon
MEC Trans World Airlines. Herndon
MEC United Airlines. . . . Herndon
MEC USAirways . . . . . . Herndon
NHQ . . . . Herndon

Plant Protection
LU 757 National. . . . . . Norfolk

Plumbing and Pipe Fitting
LU 10 . . . . Richmond
LU 110 . . . . Norfolk
LU 272. . . . . . . Virginia Beach
LU 376 . . . . Norfolk
LU 477. . . . . Portsmouth
LU 491 . . . . Roanoke
LU 540. . . . . . Newport News
LU 851 . . . . Dinwiddie
SA Virginia State Pipe
    Trades . . . . Richmond

Police Associations
LU 122 Metropolitan Special
    Police . . . . Alexandria
NHQ . . . . Alexandria

Postal and Federal Employees
D 2 . . . . Chesapeake
LU 206 . . . . Norfolk
LU 210 Northern Virginia . Stafford

Postal Mail Handlers
LU 305 . . . . Richmond

Postal Workers
LU 171 Portsmouth . . . Portsmouth
LU 199 Richmond . . . . Richmond
LU 262 Norfolk . . . . . . Norfolk
LU 482 Roanoke . . . . . Roanoke

LU 559
    Fredericksburg . . Fredericksburg
LU 713 Petersburg . . . . Petersburg
LU 823 Wytheville. . . . Wytheville
LU 830 Cape Charles . Cape Charles
LU 834 Culpeper. . . . . Culpeper
LU 862 Hopewell . . . . Hopewell
LU 867 Clifton Forge . Clifton Forge
LU 875 Orange. . . . . . Orange
LU 883 Marion. . . . . . Marion
LU 1040 Danville. . . . . Danville
LU 1376 Suffolk. . . . . . Suffolk
LU 1383 Emporia. . . . . Emporia
LU 1490 Ashland . . . . Ashland
LU 1491 Chatham . . . . Chatham
LU 1492 Salem . . . . . . Salem
LU 1493 Blacksburg. . . Blacksburg
LU 1495
    Harrisonburg . . . Harrisonburg
LU 1518 Virginia
    Beach . . . . . . Virginia Beach
LU 1602 Lynchburg . . . Lynchburg
LU 1604 Galax . . . . . . Galax
LU 1606 Coeburn. . . . . Coeburn
LU 1608 Saltville. . . . . Saltville
LU 1609 Pulaski . . . . . Pulaski
LU 1610 Martinsville
    Area. . . . . . . Martinsville
LU 1611 Radford . . . . . Radford
LU 1657
    Charlottesville . . . Charlottesville
LU 2023 Winchester. . . Winchester
LU 2024 Front Royal . . Front Royal
LU 2193 Bristol . . . . . . Bristol
LU 2245 Covington . . . Covington
LU 2299
    Christiansburg . . Christiansburg
LU 3484 Gate City . . . . Gate City
LU 4759 Chester. . . . . Chester
LU 6324 Woodbridge . Woodbridge
LU 6600 Chesapeake . Chesapeake
LU 6638
    Mechanicsville . . Mechanicsville
LU 6726 Peninsula Facility
    Area. . . . . Williamsburg
LU 6803 The Northern Virginia
    Area . . . . Annandale
LU 7163 Southwest Virginia
    Area. . . . . . . Cedar Bluff
SA Virginia . . . . . . Chesapeake

Railroad Signalmen
GC 36 . . . . Front Royal
LLG 15 . . . . Front Royal
LLG 34 . . . . Front Royal
LLG 77 . . . . Front Royal
LLG 99 . . . . Front Royal
LLG 138 . . . . . Fredericksburg
LLG 148 . . . . . . Chesterfield
LLG 194 . . . . . . Front Royal

Rural Letter Carriers
LU Albemarle-Greene-Nelson
    Counties . . . . . . Ruckersville
LU Amelia-Powhatan
    Counties . . . Amelia Court House
LU Amherst-Appomattox-Campbell
    Counties . . . . . Appomattox
LU Augusta-Highland
    Counties . . . . . . Staunton
LU Bedford County. . . . Bedford
LU Clarke-Frederick-Warren
    Counties . . . . . Stephens City
LU Fairfax-Prince William-Loudoun
    Counties . . . . . . Vienna
LU Fairystone Park County
    Association . . . . Patrick Springs
LU Halifax County. . . . Virgilina

LU Mount Rogers . . . . Austinville
LU New River Valley-Tri-County
    Association . . . . Christiansburg
LU Piedmount . . . . . . Richmond
LU Pittsylvania County. . . Danville
LU Richmond-Henrico-Chesterfield
    Association . . . . . Midlothian
LU Rockbridge
    County . . . . Rockbridge Baths
LU Rockingham County . Broadway
LU Southampton County . Newsoms
LU Southside Virginia . . . . Rice
LU Tidewater
    Association . . . Virginia Beach
LU Washington-Scott
    Counties. . . . . . Abingdon
LU 8 Fredericksburg. Fredericksburg
LU 10 Charlotte County . . Keysville
LU 11 Clinch Valley . . . St. Paul
LU 12 Rappahannock County . Reva
LU 13 Dinwiddie-Prince George
    Counties . . . . . . Richmond
LU 21 Colonial Area
    Association . . . Providence Forge
LU 22 Mecklenburg
    County . . . . . . Lawrenceville
LU 29 Roanoke-Craig
    Counties . . . . . . Goodview
LU 32 Shenandoah
    County. . . . . . . Strasburg
LU 36 Sussex-Surry Counties . Surry
LU 37 Tazewell County. Cedar Bluff
LU 41 Accomack-Northampton
    Counties . . . Chincoteague Island
LU 42 Bristol . . . . . . Abingdon
NHQ . . . . Alexandria
SA Virginia . . . . Windsor

Security, Police and Fire
Professionals
LU 287 . . . . Annandale
LU 290 . . . . Front Royal
LU 451 . . . . Suffolk
LU 452. . . . . Portsmouth

Service Employees
LU 117. . . . . . . Newport News
LU 176 Firemen &
    Oilers. . . . . . . Smithfield
LU 513 Firemen & Oilers . . Vinton
LU 741 Firemen & Oilers . Roanoke
SC 6 Firemen & Oilers . . . . Vinton

Sheet Metal Workers
LU 52. . . . . Vinton

State, County and Municipal
Employees
LU 2027 Action Employees
    Union . . . . Alexandria

Steelworkers
C International Paper
    Union. . . . . Franklin
LU 2-36. . . . . Waynesboro
LU 2-486. . . . . Richmond
LU 8-1305 . . . . Rosedale
LU 02-2 . . . . Pulaski
LU 02-10 . . . . Yorktown
LU 02-294. . . . . . . Chesapeake
LU 02-410 . . . . Covington
LU 02-467 . . . . West Point
LU 02-490 . . . . Covington
LU 02-495. . . . . Radford
LU 02-496 . . . . . . Clifton Forge
LU 02-505 . . . . Franklin
LU 02-515 . . . . Salem
LU 02-543. . . . . Chesapeake

LU 02-573 . . . . Eagle Rock
LU 02-666 . . . . Richmond
LU 02-675 . . . . Covington
LU 02-694 . . . . Amelia Court House
LU 02-695. . . . . . . Collinsville
LU 02-699. . . . . Highland Springs
LU 02-747 . . . . Providence Forge
LU 02-843. . . . . Hardy
LU 02-884 . . . . Covington
LU 02-986 . . . . Wytheville
LU 02-1013 . Natural Bridge Station
LU 02-1014 . . . . Lynchburg
LU 02-1153 . . . . Hopewell
LU 02-1372 . . . . Jarratt
LU 02-1374 . . . . Buena Vista
LU 02-1389. . . . . . . Covington
LU 02-1408 . . . . Richmond
LU 02-1488 . . . . Franklin
LU 02-1550 . . . . Richmond
LU 02-1553 . . . . Richmond
LU 02-1666 . . . . . Newport News
LU 02-1692 . . . . Richmond
LU 02-1831 . . . . Richmond
LU 02-1853 . . . . Ridgeway
LU 02-1895 . . . . Lynchburg
LU 02-1898 . . . . Chester
LU 02-1941 . . . . Petersburg
LU 08-64 . . . . Williamsburg
LU 08-78 . . . . Danville
LU 08-240-L . . . . Bedford
LU 08-400-A . . . . Richmond
LU 08-440-A . . . . Sutherland
LU 08-1014-T . . . . Danville
LU 08-1022 . . . . Blacksburg
LU 08-1023 . . . . Salem
LU 08-2864-S . . . Madison Heights
LU 08-5886-S. . . . . . Damascus
LU 08-6891-S . . . . . Glade Spring
LU 08-8270-S . . . . . Lynchburg
LU 08-8544-S . . . . . . Honaker
LU 08-8888-S . . . . Newport News
LU 08-9336-S. . . . . . . Radford
LU 08-9428 . . . . Chatham
LU 08-12103-S . . . . . . Hopewell
LU 08-13061-S . . Colonial Heights
LU 08-14187-S . . . . . . Franklin
LU 08-14440-S . . . . . . Elliston
LU 08-14459-S. . . . . . . Norton
LU 08-14842-S. . . . Sugar Grove
LU 08-15094-S. . . . . . Chilowie

Teamsters
JC 83 . . . . Richmond
LU 22 . . . . Collinsville
LU 29 . . . . Waynesboro
LU 95 . . . . Williamsburg
LU 101 . . . . Hopewell
LU 171 . . . . Salem
LU 322 . . . . Richmond
LU 592 . . . . Richmond
LU 822 . . . . Norfolk

Theatrical Stage Employees
LU 55. . . . . Roanoke
LU 87 . . . . Sandston
LU 264 . . . . Hampton
LU 699 . . . . Bristol

Transit Union
CONBD Virginia . . Virginia Beach
JCONF ATU Joint
    Conference . . . . Virginia Beach
LDIV 1220 . . . . Richmond
LU 1177. . . . . Norfolk

Transport Workers
LU 510 . . . . Alexandria

Transportation Communications Union

D 304 Chesapeake & Ohio System Board 146 . . . . Richmond
D 500 Southeastern System Board 96 . . . . Virginia Beach
D 537 Southeastern System Board 96. . . . . Roanoke
D 619 Southeastern System Board 96 . . . . Bluefield
FED 622 Western Regional-General Chairmen . . . . Suffolk
LG 1090 . . . . Roanoke
LG 6061 Roanoke. . . . . . . Salem
LG 6185 Salt Water . Newport News
LG 6465 Pocahontas. Virginia Beach
SBA 96 Southeastern . . . . Suffolk

Transportation Union

GCA GO-679 Norfolk & Western Railway-P . . . . Roanoke
GCA GO-680 Norfolk & Western Railway-P . . . . Roanoke
LU 48 . . . . Norfolk
LU 363 . . . . Pembroke
LU 623 . . . . Millboro
LU 655 . . . . Falls Mills
LU 662 . . . . Richmond

LU 706 . . . . Roanoke
LU 769 . . . . Centreville
LU 854. . . . . Portsmouth
LU 924 . . . . Richmond
LU 971. . . . . Keysville
LU 1522 . . . . Lorton
LU 1601. . . . . Duffield
LU 1933. . . . . Ashland
SLB LO-10 District of Columbia . . . . . . Gainesville
SLB LO-51 Virginia . . . . . Vinton

Treasury Employees

CH 48 . . . . Richmond
CH 130. . . . . Fredericksburg
CH 136 . . . . Norfolk
CH 207 . . . . Arlington
CH 226. . . . . Alexandria
CH 243 . . . . Arlington
CH 245 Trademark Society. . . . . Alexandria
CH 302. . . . . Alexandria

UNITE HERE

LU 524 . . . . Petersburg
LU 1398 . . . . Elkton
LU 2024 . . . . Narrows

Utility Workers

LU 102-P Madison Luray Front Royal . . . . Madison

Weather Service Employees

BR 01-1 . . . . Sterling
BR 01-38. . . . . Blacksburg
BR 01-64. . . . . Leesburg
BR 01-87 . . . . Wakefield
BR 06-1 . . . . . . Wallops Island

Unaffiliated Labor Organizations

Amthill Rayon Workers, Inc. . . . . Hopewell
Exxon Industrial Employees Delaware-Maryland-DC. . . . . Fredericksburg
Exxon Oil Workers Union of Virginia. . . . . Richmond
Federal Employees Tobacco Organization . . . . South Boston
Government Workers National Association Independent . Norfolk
Independent Union of Pension Employees . . . . Stafford
Martinsville Dupont Employees Union . . . . Collinsville

Motor Carrier Workers Union Inc. . . . . Staunton
National Association of Independent Labor . . . . Virginia Beach
Patent Office Professional Association . . . . . . Arlington
Richmond Newspapers Professional Association. . . . . . Richmond
Socony Mobil Boatmens Union. . . . . . . Port Haywood
Telephone Workers Association Independent Waynesboro-Covington-Clifton Forge. . . . . Waynesboro
Transparent Film Workers Inc. . . . . Richmond
Tri City Local 1 Independent . . . . . . Petersburg
Union of Alpa Professional & Administrative Employees UNIT 1 . . . . Herndon
Union of Alpa Professional & Administrative Employees UNIT 2 . . . . Herndon
United Defense Workers of America LU 1 . . . . Marion
Virginia Loomis Fargo Employees Union. . . . . Roanoke

Washington

AFL-CIO Trade and Industrial Departments

Building and Construction Trades Department
BCTC Central Washington . . Pasco
BCTC Longview-Kelso . . Longview
BCTC Northeastern Washington & Northern Idaho . . . . . . Spokane
BCTC Northwest Washington . . . . Everett
BCTC Olympia . . . . . . Olympia
BCTC Olympic Peninsula . . . . Silverdale
BCTC Pendleton . . . . . Kennewick
BCTC Pierce County . . . . Tacoma
BCTC Seattle . . . . Seattle
BCTC Washington . . . . . Olympia

Maritime Trades Department
PC Puget Sound District . . . Seattle

Metal Trades Department
MTC Bremerton . . . . . Bremerton
MTC Hanford Atomic . . . Richland
MTC Puget Sound . . . . . Seattle

Other Councils and Committees
C Aluminum Trades . . . . . East Wenatchee
C Longview Federated Aluminum . . . . Longview

AFL-CIO Directly Affiliated Locals

AFL-CIO
C Columbia Basin Irrigation Council . . . . Seattle

Affiliated Labor Organizations

Agricultural Employees
BR 31 . . . . Seattle
BR 45 . . . . Blaine

Air Traffic Controllers
LU BFI . . . . Seattle
LU ENM . . . . Renton
LU GEG . . . . . Airway Heights
LU GRB . . . . Moses Lake
LU PAE . . . . Everett
LU PSC . . . . Pasco
LU S46 . . . . Burien
LU SEA . . . . Seattle
LU ZSE . . . . Auburn

Aircraft Mechanics
LU 14 . . . . Seatac

Asbestos Workers
LU 7 . . . . Renton
LU 62 . . . . Silverdale
LU 82 . . . . Spokane
LU 120 . . . . Benton City

Bakery, Confectionery, Tobacco Workers and Grain Millers
C-G Pacific . . . . Spokane
LU 9 . . . . Seattle
LU 98-G . . . . Spokane

Boilermakers
LG 37-D Cement Workers . . . . . Port Orchard
LG 104 . . . . Seattle
LG 242 . . . . Spokane
LG 290 . . . . Bremerton
LG 502 . . . . Puyallup

Bricklayers
LU 1 Washington . . . . . Tukwila
LU 3 . . . . Spokane

Carpenters
DC Pacific Northwest Regional . . . . Kent
LU 69 AWPPW Building . . . . Kennewick
LU 98 . . . . Spokane
LU 131 . . . . Seattle
LU 151 . . . . Shelton
LU 204 . . . . Renton
LU 317 . . . . Aberdeen
LU 360 . . . . Olympia
LU 456 . . . . Renton
LU 470 . . . . Tacoma
LU 562 . . . . Everett
LU 756 . . . . Bellingham
LU 770 . . . . Yakima
LU 816 . . . . Federal Way
LU 1136 . . . . Kettle Falls
LU 1144 . . . . Seattle
LU 1148 . . . . Olympia
LU 1184 . . . . Seattle
LU 1303 . . . . Port Angeles
LU 1532 . . . . . . Mount Vernon
LU 1597 . . . . Bremerton
LU 1699 . . . . Pasco
LU 1707 . . . . Longview
LU 1715 . . . . Vancouver
LU 1797 . . . . Renton
LU 1849 . . . . Pasco
LU 2084 United Brotherhood of Carpenters . . . . Aberdeen
LU 2127 . . . . Centralia
LU 2205 . . . . Wenatchee
LU 2317 . . . . Bremerton
LU 2382 . . . . Spokane
LU 2396 . . . . Yakima
LU 2403 . . . . Richland
LU 2594 . . . . Kettle Falls
LU 2633 . . . . Tacoma
LU 2659 Lumber & Sawmill Workers . . . . Roslyn
LU 2667 . . . . Bellingham
LU 2739 . . . . Yakima
LU 2761 . . . . McCleary
LU 2767 . . . . Morton
LU 3099 . . . . Aberdeen

Civilian Technicians
CH 107 Evergreen Chapter . . . . . . Fairchild Air Force Base
CH 108 Ranier . . . . . . Tillicum

Communications Workers
C Washington-North Idaho . Tacoma
LU 7800 . . . . Seattle
LU 7803 . . . . Renton
LU 7804 . . . . Tacoma
LU 7810 . . . . Olympia
LU 7812 . . . . Vancouver
LU 7816 . . . . Yakima
LU 7817 . . . . Medical Lake
LU 7818 . . . . Spokane

[Boilermakers continued]
LU 14760 . . . . Aberdeen
LU 14764 . . . . Yakima
LU 14766 . . . . . Nine Mile Falls
LU 37082 Pacific Northwest . Seattle
LU 37083 Washington Alliance of Technology Workers . . . . Seattle
LU 89002 . . . . Pacific

Electrical Workers
C Pacific Coast Marine . . . . Kent
LU 46 . . . . Kent
LU 73 . . . . Spokane
LU 76 . . . . Tacoma
LU 77 . . . . Seattle
LU 89 . . . . Everett
LU 112 . . . . Kennewick
LU 191 . . . . Everett
LU 483 . . . . Tacoma
LU 574 . . . . Bremerton
LU 970 . . . . Longview
LU 984 . . . . Richland
LU 1769 . . . . Auburn
LU 1782 . . . . Battle Ground

Elevator Constructors
LU 19 . . . . Seattle

Engineers
LU 6 . . . . Bremerton
LU 8 . . . . Seattle
LU 12 . . . . Bremerton
LU 89 . . . . Grand Coulee
LU 2001 SPEEA . . . . . Tukwila

Federal Employees
LU 34 . . . . Darrington
LU 181 . . . . Walla Walla
LU 1156 . . . . Colville
LU 1174 . . . . Twisp
LU 1641 . . . . Spokane
LU 2014 . . . . Forks

Fire Fighters
LU 24-I Hanford Industrial Fire Fighters . . . . Richland
LU 282-F . . . . Keyport
LU 283-F . . . . Fort Lewis

Food and Commercial Workers
DC Oregon & Washington . Bellevue
LU 21 . . . . Bellevue
LU 44 . . . . Mount Vernon
LU 49 . . . . Spokane
LU 81 . . . . Auburn
LU 110-C . . . . Tacoma
LU 121-C . . . . Bellingham
LU 141 . . . . Federal Way
LU 367 . . . . Tacoma
LU 747-C . . . . Kalama
LU 1439 . . . . Spokane

Glass, Molders, Pottery and Plastics Workers
LU 50 . . . . Seattle
LU 87 . . . . Seattle
LU 289 . . . . Deer Park

Government Employees
C 249 VA, Eleventh District . . . . Tacoma
LU 40 HHS . . . . Spanaway
LU 48 DoD . . . . Bremerton
LU 181 . . . . Walla Walla
LU 498 VA . . . . Tacoma

[Government Employees continued]
LU 1102 Federal Detention Center . . . . Seattle
LU 1108 . . . . Spokane
LU 1170 HHS . . . . Seattle
LU 1176 USDA . . . . . . Yakima
LU 1196 USDA . . . Mount Vernon
LU 1501 DoD . . . . McChord Air Force Base
LU 1502 DoD . . . . Tillicum
LU 1504 DoD . . . . Fort Lewis
LU 1589 . . . . Vancouver
LU 2600 GSA . . . . . . Auburn
LU 2913 DoJ . . . . Custer
LU 3196 SBA . . . . Seattle
LU 3197 VA . . . . Seattle
LU 3294 HUD . . . . . . Seattle
LU 3593 DoD . . . . Fort Lewis
LU 3900 . . . . Seattle
LU 3937 SSA . . . . Seattle

Government Security Officers
LU 71 . . . . Seattle
LU 124 . . . . Tacoma
LU 133 . . . . Richland
LU 134 . . . . Spokane

Graphic Communications
LU 262-C . . . . Aberdeen
LU 767-M . . . . Kent

Iron Workers
DC Pacific Northwest . . Lakewood
LU 14 . . . . Spokane
LU 86 . . . . Tukwila
LU 506 . . . . Lakewood

Laborers
DC Washington & Northern Idaho . . . . Mill Creek
LU 238 . . . . Spokane
LU 242 . . . . Seattle
LU 252 . . . . Tacoma
LU 276 . . . . Bellingham
LU 292 . . . . Everett
LU 335 . . . . Vancouver
LU 348 . . . . Pasco
LU 440 . . . . Seattle
LU 614 Laborers . . . . . Yakima
LU 791 . . . . Longview
LU 901 . . . . . . Mount Vernon
LU 1239 . . . . Seattle

Letter Carriers
BR 79 . . . . Seattle
BR 130 . . . . Tacoma
BR 351 Clark V. Savidge, Branch 351 . . . . Olympia
BR 442 . . . . Spokane
BR 450 . . . . Bellingham
BR 736 . . . . . . Walla Walla
BR 791 . . . . Everett
BR 852 . . . . Yakima
BR 853 . . . . Aberdeen
BR 1104 . . . . Vancouver
BR 1266 . . . . Centralia
BR 1302 . . . . Hoquiam
BR 1350 . . . . Wenatchee
BR 1414 . . . . Bremerton
BR 1484 . . . . Puyallup
BR 1515 . . . . . Port Townsend
BR 1527 . . . . Anacortes
BR 1528 . . . . Pasco
BR 1606 . . . . Raymond
BR 1906 . . . . . . Port Angeles
BR 1947 . . . . Clarkston

BR 2030 . . . . . . Sedro Woolley
BR 2038 . . . . Kent
BR 2103 . . . . Kelso
BR 2214. . . . . Longview
BR 2914 . . . . Dayton
BR 2935 . . . . Montesano
BR 2948 . . . . Cle Elum
BR 3008 . . . . Camas
BR 3127 . . . . Sumner
BR 3320 . . . . . . Leavenworth
BR 3877 . . . . . West Richland
BR 4118 . . . . Prosser
BR 4132 . . . . Lynden
BR 4213 . . . . Ephrata
BR 4232 . . . . Grandview
BR 4513 . . . . Cashmere
BR 4573. . . . . . Moses Lake
BR 5194 . . . . . . Oak Harbor
BR 5262 . . . . Othello
BR 5479 . . . . . . Castle Rock
BR 5705 . . . . . . Washougal
BR 6008 . . . . Quincy
SA Washington . . Bainbridge Island

Locomotive Engineers
DIV 58 . . . . Wishram
DIV 60 . . . . . Anderson Island
DIV 104. . . . . Spokane Valley
DIV 238 . . . . Tacoma
DIV 402 . . . . Pasco
DIV 518 . . . . Edmonds
DIV 758 . . . . Vancouver
DIV 892 . . . . Renton
SLB Washington State . . Newcastle

Longshore and Warehouse
DC Puget Sound . . . . . Longview
DIV Inlandboatmen's Union of the
   Pacific . . . . Seattle
LU 4 . . . . Vancouver
LU 7 . . . . Bellingham
LU 19 . . . . Seattle
LU 21 . . . . Longview
LU 21 Kalama Grainhandlers
   Division . . . . Kalama
LU 21 Peavey Grain
   Division . . . . Kalama
LU 23 . . . . Fife
LU 24 . . . . Hoquiam
LU 25 . . . . Anacortes
LU 27 . . . . Port Angeles
LU 32. . . . . Everett
LU 47. . . . . Olympia
LU 51 . . . . Allyn
LU 52. . . . . Seattle
LU 98 . . . . Seatac

Machinists
DLG 160 . . . . Seattle
DLG 751 . . . . Seattle
LG 2 Woodworkers . . . Aberdeen
LG 79 . . . . Seattle
LG 86 . . . . Spokane
LG 130 . . . . Seattle
LG 130-W Woodworkers . Centralia
LG 157-W . . . . Tacoma
LG 239 . . . . Seattle
LG 282 . . . . Bremerton
LG 289 . . . . Lynnwood
LG 297 . . . . Tacoma
LG 536-W . . . . Longview
LG 591 . . . . Puyallup
LG 637 . . . . Spokane Valley
LG 695 . . . . Seattle
LG 751-A . . . . Seattle
LG 751-C . . . . Seattle
LG 751-E . . . . Seattle
LG 751-F . . . . Seattle

LG 1040 . . . . Federal Way
LG 1123 . . . . Rock Island
LG 1350 . . . . Kelso
LG 1351 . . . . Seattle
LG 1374 . . . . Vancouver
LG 1951 . . . . Richland
LG 2202 . . . . Kent
LG 2379 . . . . Ferndale
LLG W-38 . . . . Shelton
LLG EL-762 NFFE . . . . Sequim
LLG FL-271 . . . Walla Walla
LLG FL-758 NFFE . . . Vancouver
LLG FL-1373 . . . . . Trout Lake
LLG FL-1968 NFFE . . Vancouver
LLG FL-1998 NFFE . . . . Seattle
STC Washington . . . . . . Seattle

Maintenance of Way Employes
LG 159 . . . . Kennewick
LG 325 . . . . Spokane
LG 389 . . . . Tacoma
LG 757 . . . . Vancouver
LG 1763 . . . . . . Battle Ground
SLG 104 . . . . Spokane
SLG 309 . . . . Centralia
SLG 683 . . . . Colville
SLG 1218 . . . . Tukwila
SLG 1426 . . . . Arlington

Musicians
LU 76 . . . . Seattle
LU 105 . . . . Spokane
LU 461 . . . . . . Mount Vernon

National Staff Organization
LU Staff Organization, Washington
   Education Association . . . . Kent

NLRB Professional Association
LU 19 . . . . Seattle

Nurses
SA Washington State Nurses
   Association . . . . Seattle

Office and Professional Employees
LU 8 . . . . Seattle
LU 10 . . . . Spokane
LU 23 . . . . Tacoma

Operating Engineers
LU 280 . . . . Richland
LU 286 . . . . Auburn
LU 302 . . . . Bothell
LU 370 . . . . Spokane
LU 612 . . . . Tacoma

Painters
CONF Fourth District
   Western . . . . Seattle
DC 5 . . . . Seattle
LU 64 . . . . Tacoma
LU 78 . . . . Longview
LU 188 . . . . Tukwila
LU 269 . . . . . Spokane Valley
LU 300 . . . . Seattle
LU 339 . . . . . Mount Vernon
LU 360 . . . . Vancouver
LU 427 . . . . Pasco
LU 995 . . . . Yakima
LU 1094 . . . . Seattle
LU 1208 . . . . Belfair
LU 1238 . . . . Tukwila
LU 1982 . . . . Renton

Plasterers and Cement Masons
LU 72 . . . . Spokane
LU 77 . . . . Seattle

LU 478 . . . . Pasco
LU 528 . . . . Tukwila

Plumbing and Pipe Fitting
DC Northwest . . . . . Spokane
LU 26 Western Washington . Everett
LU 32 . . . . Renton
LU 44 . . . . Spokane
LU 598 . . . . Pasco
LU 699 . . . . Seattle
SA Washington . . . . . Everett

Postal and Federal Employees
LU 1012 . . . . Tacoma

Postal Mail Handlers
LU 316 . . . . Seatac

Postal Workers
LU 28 Greater Seattle Area . . Burien
LU 36 Walla Walla . . . Walla Walla
LU 298 Puget Sound Area . Tacoma
LU 338 . . . . Spokane
LU 484 Everett . . . . . Everett
LU 709 Bellingham . . . Bellingham
LU 751 Wenatchee . . . . Wenatchee
LU 763 Yakima Area Local . Yakima
LU 905 Pullman . . . . . Pullman
LU 962 Centralia . . . . Centralia
LU 1686 Kent . . . . Kent
LU 2293 Tri Cities Area . . . Pasco
LU 2354 Olympia . . . . Olympia
LU 2568 Auburn . . . . . Auburn
LU 2779 Camas . . . . . Camas
LU 3302 Shelton . . . . . Shelton
LU 3463 Vancouver . . . Vancouver
LU 3734 Renton . . . . . . Renton
LU 4996 Washougal . . . Washougal
LU 5086 Enumclaw . . . . Enumclaw
LU 5213 Bellevue . . . Bellevue
LU 6110 Sequim . . . . . . Sequim
LU 6231 Stanwood . . . Stanwood
LU 7042 Seattle Bulk
   Mail . . . . Federal Way
LU 7160 Green River Valley . . Kent
SA Washington State . . . . Colville

Pulp and Paper Workers
LU 5 . . . . Camas
LU 28 . . . . Sumner
LU 69 . . . . Kennewick
LU 153 . . . . Longview
LU 155 . . . . Port Angeles
LU 183 . . . . . . Camano Island
LU 194 . . . . Bellingham
LU 211 . . . . Cosmopolis
LU 225 . . . . Woodland
LU 293 . . . . Ridgefield
LU 309 . . . . Bellingham
LU 580 . . . . Longview
LU 633 . . . . Longview
LU 644 . . . . Everett
LU 817 . . . . Bonney Lake
LU 913 . . . . Hoquiam

Railroad Signalmen
LLG 188 . . . . Ephrata

**Roofers, Waterproofers and Allied
   Workers**
DC Northwest Roofers . . . . Seattle
LU 54 . . . . Seattle
LU 153 . . . . Tacoma
LU 189 . . . . Spokane

Rural Letter Carriers
LU Chelan-Douglas Counties . Entiat

LU Clallam-Jefferson
   Counties . . . . Sequim
LU Garfield-Columbia-Walla Walla
   Counties . . . . Waitsburg
LU Kitsap County . . . Port Orchard
LU Lincoln-Grant-Adams
   Counties . . . . Moses Lake
LU Lower Columbia
   County . . . . Castle Rock
LU Mutual County . . . . Lakewood
LU Northeast
   Washington . . . . . . Chewelah
LU Okanogan County . . . Tonasket
LU Skagit-San Juan
   Counties . . . . Anacortes
LU Snohomish-King-Island
   Counties . . . . Vashon
LU Spokane County . . . . Spokane
LU Whatcom County . . Bellingham
LU Whitman-Asotin
   Counties . . . . Endicott
LU Yakima Valley . . West Richland
SA Washington . . . . . . Spokane

**Security, Police and Fire
   Professionals**
LU 5 . . . . Seattle
LU 9 . . . . Everett
LU 11 . . . . Spokane Valley
LU 12 . . . . Kennewick

Service Employees
C 14 Northwestern States . . . Seattle
LU 6 . . . . Seattle
LU 6 Staff Union . . . . . Seattle
LU 51 . . . . Seattle
LU 193 Firemen & Oilers . Seattle
LU 202 . . . . Spokane
LU 634 Firemen & Oilers . Spokane
LU 690 Firemen & Oilers . Spokane
LU 714 Firemen & Oilers . Spokane
LU 764 Firemen & Oilers . Seattle
LU 775 . . . . Seattle
LU 775 Staff Union . . . Seattle
LU 801 Firemen &
   Oilers . . . . Vancouver
LU 920 Firemen & Oilers . Spokane
LU 925 . . . . Seattle
LU 1184 Firemen & Oilers . Sumner
LU 1199-NW NUHHCE, District
   1199-NW . . . . Renton
SC 15 Firemen & Oilers . . Spokane

Sheet Metal Workers
DC Northwest . . . . . . Kirkland
LU 66 . . . . Kirkland

**State, County and Municipal
   Employees**
LU 2 Washington State
   Council . . . . Everett
LU 780 Spokane City School Bus
   Drivers . . . . Spokane
LU 2699 Columbia River Mental
   Health . . . . Vancouver

Steelworkers
LU 4959 . . . . Olympia
LU 08-167 . . . . Spangle
LU 08-171 . . . . Vancouver
LU 08-175 . . . . . Port Townsend
LU 08-237 . . . . Tacoma
LU 08-279 . . . . Tacoma
LU 08-369 . . . . Richland
LU 08-562 . . . . Elk
LU 08-586 . . . . Tacoma
LU 08-590 . . . . Ferndale
LU 08-591 . . . . . . Anacortes

LU 08-592 . . . . Fife
LU 08-600 . . . . Vancouver
LU 08-712 . . . . Clarkston
LU 08-784 . . . . . East Wenatchee
LU 08-990 . . . . Kennewick
LU 08-1103 . . . . Sumner
LU 08-1689 . . . . Ridgefield
LU 11-68-T . . . . Renton
LU 11-305-A . . . . Longview
LU 11-310-A . . . East Wenatchee
LU 11-315-A . . . East Wenatchee
LU 11-329-S . . . . Spokane
LU 11-338-S . . . Spokane Valley
LU 11-532-B . . . . Kent
LU 11-556 . . . . Spokane
LU 11-5089-S . . . . . . Spokane
LU 11-8147-S . . . . . Goldendale
LU 11-9041-S . . . . Auburn
LU 11-9241-S . . . . . . Silverdale

Teachers
SFED Washington . . . . . Tukwila

Teamsters
JC 28 . . . . Seattle
LU 38 . . . . Everett
LU 58 . . . . Vancouver
LU 117 . . . . Seattle
LU 174 . . . . Seattle
LU 231 . . . . Bellingham
LU 252 . . . . Centralia
LU 313 . . . . Tacoma
LU 589 . . . . Port Angeles
LU 690 . . . . Spokane
LU 760 . . . . Yakima
LU 763 . . . . Seattle
LU 839 . . . . Pasco

Television and Radio Artists
LU Seattle . . . . Seattle

Theatrical Stage Employees
D 1 Montana-Idaho-Oregon-
   Washington-Alaska . . . . Seattle
LU 15 . . . . Seattle
LU 93 . . . . Spokane
LU 887 . . . . Seattle

Transit Union
LDIV 1384 . . . . Olympia
LDIV 1576 . . . . Everett
LDIV 1599 . . . . Tri Cities
LU 587 . . . . Seattle
LU 758 . . . . Lakewood

**Transportation Communications
   Union**
D 2505 . . . . Seattle
D 2513 . . . . Seattle
LG 34 . . . . Colbert
LG 894 Seattle Emerald
   City . . . . Auburn
LG 6294 Sagebrush . . . . . Pasco
LG 6697 . . . . Granite Falls
LG 6748 Van-Port . . . . Vancouver

Transportation Union
GCA GO-386 . . . . . Vancouver
LU 117 . . . . Vancouver
LU 161 . . . . Covington
LU 324 . . . . Granite Falls
LU 426 . . . . Cheney
LU 556 . . . . Sumner
LU 845 . . . . Auburn
LU 855 . . . . Spokane Valley
LU 977 . . . . Pasco
LU 1238 . . . . Vancouver
LU 1348 . . . . Seattle
LU 1468 . . . . Walla Walla
LU 1505 . . . . . Nine Mile Falls
LU 1574 . . . . Heisson
LU 1637 . . . . Vancouver

LU 1713 . . . . Marysville
LU 1977 . . . . Kent
SLB LO-54 Washington . Longview

Treasury Employees
CH 30 . . . . Seattle
CH 139 . . . . Seattle
CH 164 . . . . Blaine
CH 215 . . . . Bothell

UNITE HERE
LU 8 . . . . Seattle
LU 14 . . . . Seattle
LU 360 . . . . Seattle
LU 791 . . . . Aberdeen

Weather Service Employees
BR 04-1 . . . . Seattle
BR 04-3 . . . . Spokane
BR 08-9 . . . . Seattle

Unaffiliated Labor
Organizations

1199 Northwest Staff Union . Renton
Air Cushion Workers Union . Seattle
Association of Western Pulp and
   Paper Workers Washington/
   Alaska . . . . Kelso
Boeing Pilots Association . . Seattle
Columbia Basin Trades
   Council . . . . Kennewick
Deep Sea Fishermens Union Pacific
   Coast District . . . . Seattle
Fairchild Federal Employees
   Union . . Fairchild Air Force Base
Fellow Associates Involved in
   Representation . . . . Yelm
Industrial Workers of the World
   Puget Sound GMB . . . . . Seattle

International Guards Union of
   America LU 21 . . . . . Richland
International Guards Union of
   America RC First . . . . Richland
International Guild of
   Symphony . . . . Seattle
Medical Engineers Association of
   Spokane . . . . Spokane
National Council of Security
   Inspectors . . . . Selah
Northwest Mechanical Services
   Union LU 77 . . . . Kent
Ownership Union . . . Brush Prairie
Pacific Northwest Employees
   Association Portland LU 1 . Yacolt
Portland Pattern Maker's
   Association . . . . . Battle Ground
Public School Employees . . Auburn
Public School Employees Staff
   Organization . . . . Auburn
Public School Employees,
   Washington CH 58 . . Vancouver
Spokane Editorial Society . Spokane
Symphony Opera & Ballet
   Musicians Seattle Players
   Organization . . . . Seattle
Symphony Opera and Ballet
   Musicians Pacific Northwest Ballet
   Players Organization . . . . Seattle
The Demil Trades
   Council . . . . Kennewick
Union of Union
   Representatives . . . Marysville
United Power Trades Organization
   Association, Pacific
   Northwest . . . . Connell
Washington Farm Workers
   Union . . . . Granger
Washington Federation of State
   Employees Staff Union . Olympia
Washington Legal
   Workers . . . . Kennewick

West Virginia

AFL-CIO Trade and Industrial Departments

Building and Construction Trades Department
BCTC Kanawha County . Charleston
BCTC North Central West
 Virginia . . . . Clarksburg
BCTC Parkersburg-
 Marietta. . . . . . . Parkersburg
BCTC West Virginia
 State . . . . Charleston

Affiliated Labor Organizations

Air Traffic Controllers
LU CKB . . . . Bridgeport
LU CRW . . . . Charleston
LU HTS . . . . Ceredo

Asbestos Workers
LU 80 . . . . Winfield

Automobile, Aerospace Workers
LU 3399 . . . . Nitro

Bakery, Confectionery, Tobacco Workers and Grain Millers
LU 2-T . . . . Wheeling

Boilermakers
LG 208-D Cement
 Workers . . . . Hedgesville
LG 249 . . . . Wayne
LG 271-D Cement
 Workers . . . . Hedgesville
LG 667 . . . . Winfield

Bricklayers
DC West Virginia . . . . Fairmont
LU 1 . . . . Valley Grove
LU 5 . . . . Fairmont
LU 6 . . . . Fairmont
LU 9 . . . . Fairmont
LU 11 . . . . Wellsburg
LU 15 . . . . Fairmont

Carpenters
LU 3 . . . . Wheeling
LU 302 . . . . Huntington
LU 476 . . . . Shinnston
LU 604 . . . . Morgantown
LU 899 . . . . Parkersburg
LU 1159 . . . . Point Pleasant
LU 1207 . . . . Charleston
LU 1755 . . . . Parkersburg
LU 1911 . . . . Beckley
LU 2101 . . . . Moorefield
LU 2528 . . . . Rainelle

Civilian Technicians
CH 89 Mountaineer . . . . . . Nitro
CH 90 Mountain
 State . . . . Point Pleasant
CH 91 Shenandoah . . . Martinsburg

Communications Workers
C West Virginia State . . Clarksburg
LU 620 . . . . Charleston
LU 2001 . . . . Charleston
LU 2002 . . . . Logan
LU 2003 . . . . Parkersburg
LU 2004 . . . . Fairview

LU 2006 . . . . Wheeling
LU 2007 . . . . Beckley
LU 2009 . . . . Huntington
LU 2010 . . . . Glenville
LU 2011 . . . . Clarksburg
LU 2276 . . . . Bluefield
LU 14210 . . . . Charleston
LU 14211 . . . . Clarksburg
LU 14215 . . . . Parkersburg
LU 14217 . . . . Wheeling
LU 52027 . . . . Ona
LU 52212 . . . . Triadelphia
LU 82627 . . . . Fairmont
LU 82647 . . . . Bluefield

Electrical Workers
LU 141 . . . . Wheeling
LU 317 . . . . Huntington
LU 466 . . . . Charleston
LU 549 . . . . Barboursville
LU 596 . . . . Clarksburg
LU 736 . . . . Princeton
LU 968 . . . . Parkersburg
LU 978 . . . . Charleston
LU 1935 . . . . Salem
LU 2035 . . . . Romney
LU 2357 . . . . Terra Alta

Electrical, Radio and Machine Workers
LU 611 . . . . Newell

Elevator Constructors
LU 48 . . . . Charleston

Food and Commercial Workers
LU 45-C . . . . Middlebourne
LU 566-C . . . . Moundsville
LU 698-C . . . . Littleton
LU 864-C . . . . Moundsville
LU 888-C . . . . Benwood
LU 967-C . . . . Moundsville

Glass, Molders, Pottery and Plastics Workers
LU 16-A . . . . Chester
LU 24 . . . . Newell
LU 302 . . . . Independence
LU 328 . . . . Chester

Government Employees
LU 43 . . . . Martinsburg
LU 404 Council of Prison . . Beaver
LU 420 Council of
 Prisons . . . . . . Bruceton Mills
LU 1494 DoJ . . . . Alderson
LU 1938 DoD . . . . . . Gassaway
LU 1995 DoE . . . . . Morgantown
LU 2198 VA . . . . Beckley
LU 2344 VA . . . . . . Huntington
LU 2384 VA . . . . . . Clarksburg
LU 2441 DoJ . . . . . Morgantown
LU 3181 DoL . . . . Madison
LU 3430 HHS . . . . . Morgantown
LU 3610 HHS . . . . Bruceton Mills
LU 3729 DoD . . . . . Huntington

Government Employees Association
LU 04-78 . . . . Martinsburg
LU 04-88 . . . . Elkins

Government Security Officers
LU 87 . . . . Clarksburg
LU 92 . . . . Charleston

LU 92 Amalgamated . . . . Kenova

Graphic Communications
LU 53-C . . . . Huntington
LU 95-C . . . . Salem
LU 360-C . . . . Flat Top
LU 392-C . . . . Fairmont
LU 443-C Fairmont Printing
 Pressmen . . . . Fairmont

Iron Workers
LU 301 . . . . Charleston
LU 549 . . . . Wheeling
LU 787 . . . . Parkersburg

Laborers
DC Charleston . . . . . Charleston
LU 379 . . . . Morgantown
LU 453 . . . . Beckley
LU 543 . . . . Huntington
LU 814 . . . . Westover
LU 984 . . . . Clarksburg
LU 1085 . . . . Parkersburg
LU 1149 . . . . Wheeling
LU 1182 . . . White Sulphur Springs
LU 1311 . . . . Ceredo
LU 1353 . . . . Charleston

Letter Carriers
BR 359 . . . . Lesage
BR 481 . . . . Parkersburg
BR 531 . . . . Charleston
BR 783 . . . . Morgantown
BR 817 . . . . Clarksburg
BR 893 . . . . Moundsville
BR 910 . . . . Fairmont
BR 1183 . . . . Elkins
BR 1475 . . . . Martinsburg
BR 1854 . . . . New Martinsville
BR 2042 . . . . Mannington
BR 2420 . . . . Oak Hill
BR 2936 . . . . Marlinton
BR 3087 . . . . . . Point Pleasant
BR 3535 . . . . Williamstown
BR 3677 . . . . Weirton
BR 4303 . . . . . Berkeley Springs
BR 4458 . . . . Clarksburg
BR 4980 . . . . Paden City
BR 5283 . . . . Man
BR 5599 . . . . Milton
BR 5677 . . . . . Webster Springs
BR 5792 . . . . Parsons
SA West Virginia . . . . . Glasgow

Locomotive Engineers
DIV 101 . . . . Pipestem
DIV 124 . . . . Bluefield
DIV 190 . . . . Huntington
DIV 255 Mingo Jet Ohio . Follansbee
DIV 284 . . . . Grafton
DIV 401 . . . . Ragland
DIV 448 . . . . Bluefield
DIV 477 . . . . Parkersburg
DIV 714 . . . . Dunbar
DIV 751 . . . . Exchange
SLB Virginia . . . . . Harpers Ferry
SLB West Virginia . . . . . . Nitro

Machinists
LG 87-S . . . . Halltown
LG 104 . . . . Huntington
LG 598 . . . . . South Charleston
LG 656 . . . . Nitro
LG 818 . . . . Benwood
LG 1027 . . . . Clarksburg

LG 1370 . . . . Milton
LG 1798-FL . . . . . . Martinsburg
LG 2798 . . . . Barboursville
STC West Virginia . . . . . . Nitro

Maintenance of Way Employes
LG 61 . . . . Clarksburg
LG 551 . . . . Bluefield
LG 1509 . . . . Parkersburg
LG 1550 . . . . Elkins
SLG 76 . . . . Leon
SLG 112 . . . . Salt Rock
SLG 130 . . . . Danese
SLG 710 . . . . Berkeley Springs
SLG 1029 . . . . Arthurdale
SLG 1064 . . . . Belington
SLG 1300 . . . . Sutton

Mine Workers
LU 93 . . . . Peach Creek
LU 340 . . . . Montgomery
LU 633 . . . . Hewett
LU 750 . . . . Eskdale
LU 781 . . . . Oceana
LU 1058 . . . . Westover
LU 1110 . . . . Moundsville
LU 1123 . . . . Beckley
LU 1160 . . . . Oceana
LU 1289 . . . . Newburg
LU 1302 . . . . Amherstdale
LU 1330 . . . . Daniels
LU 1335 . . . . Rainelle
LU 1352 . . . . Nettie
LU 1440 . . . . Matewan
LU 1444 . . . . Gormania
LU 1466 . . . . Craigsville
LU 1473 . . . . Wheeling
LU 1501 . . . . Fairmont
LU 1503 . . . . Madison
LU 1570 . . . . Rivesville
LU 1582 . . . . Alum Creek
LU 1597 . . . . Mannington
LU 1638 . . . . Moundsville
LU 1643 . . . . Fairmont
LU 1648 . . . . Worthington
LU 1687 . . . . Mannington
LU 1698 . . . . Rupert
LU 1702 . . . . Westover
LU 1713 . . . . Herndon
LU 1717 . . . . Star City
LU 1751 . . . . Accoville
LU 1766 . . . . St. Albans
LU 1852 . . . . Paynesville
LU 1886 . . . . Hartford
LU 1938 . . . . Buckhannon
LU 1949 . . . . Fairmont
LU 1971 . . . . Man
LU 2059 . . . . Summersville
LU 2236 . . . . Charleston
LU 2286 . . . . Danville
LU 2542 . . . . Seth
LU 2903 . . . . Ridgeview
LU 2935 . . . . Hamlin
LU 3029 . . . . Charleston
LU 3196 . . . . Shinnston
LU 4047 . . . . Grant Town
LU 4172 . . . . Buckhannon
LU 4921 District 17 . . . . . Scarbro
LU 5396 . . . . Letart
LU 5770 . . . . Scarbro
LU 5817 . . . . Delbarton
LU 5850 . . . . Accoville
LU 5921 . . . . Barnabus
LU 5958 . . . . Omar
LU 5997 . . . . Welch

LU 6029 . . . . Thorpe
LU 6046 . . . . Lochgelly
LU 6105 . . . . Midway
LU 6196 . . . . Princeton
LU 6243 . . . . Jodie
LU 6362 . . . . West Liberty
LU 6426 . . . . Seth
LU 6608 . . . . Dorothy
LU 6869 . . . . Amigo
LU 7086 . . . . Beckley
LU 7555 . . . . Verner
LU 7604 . . . . Matheny
LU 7635 . . . . Gary
LU 7692 . . . . Pineville
LU 8190 . . . . Craigsville
LU 8783 . . . . Bradshaw
LU 8843 . . . . Cannelton
LU 9108 . . . . Rainelle
LU 9177 . . . . Bolt
LU 9462 . . . . Lenore
LU 9735 . . . . Madison
LU 9781 . . . . Beckley
LU 9909 . . . . Shinnston

Musicians
LU 136 . . . . Charleston
LU 142 . . . . Benwood
LU 259 . . . . Vienna
LU 362-691 . . . . Huntington
LU 492 . . . . Moundsville
LU 580 . . . . Clarksburg

National Staff Organization
LU Staff Union, United, West
  Virginia . . . . Charleston

Nurses
LU 201 Registered Nurse Collective
  Bargaining Unit
  Association . . . . . Shady Spring
LU 202 Man ARH
  Unit . . . . Amherstdale
LU 203 West Virginia . Martinsburg
LU 205 West Virginia . . . . Hinton
SA West Virginia Nurses
  Association. . . . . . . Charleston
UNIT East Liverpool City
  Hospital. . . . . New Cumberland

Operating Engineers
LU 132 . . . . Charleston

Painters
DC 53. . . . . Charleston
LU 91 . . . . Wheeling
LU 93 . . . . Parkersburg
LU 804 . . . . Horner
LU 970 . . . . Charleston
LU 1072 . . . . Kenova
LU 1144 . . . . Parkersburg
LU 1195 . . . . Charleston

Plasterers and Cement Masons
LU 39 . . . . Middlebourne
LU 887 . . . . Charleston

Plumbing and Pipe Fitting
LU 83 . . . . Wheeling
LU 152 . . . . Morgantown
LU 521 . . . . Huntington
LU 565 . . . . Parkersburg
LU 625 . . . . Charleston
SA West Virginia . . . Morgantown

Postal and Federal Employees
LU 203 . . . . Charleston

Postal Workers
LU Clarksburg . . . . . Clarksburg
LU 99 Elkins . . . . Elkins
LU 133 Charleston . . . . Charleston
LU 1350 Fairmont . . . . Fairmont
LU 1488 Kyowva Area . Huntington
LU 1509 Beckley . . . . . Beckley
LU 1580 Cecil F. Romine
  Area. . . . . Parkersburg
LU 1734 Morgantown . Morgantown
LU 2669 Buckhannon . Buckhannon
LU 3339 Keyser . . . . . Keyser
LU 4134 Bluefield Area . . . Athens
LU 4343 Weirton . . . . . Weirton
LU 4571 Wheeling . . . . Wheeling
LU 4755 Martinsburg. . Martinsburg
LU 5448 Petersburg . . Moorefield
SA West Virginia . . . . Fairmont

Railroad Signalmen
GC 16 Northeast-Chesapeake & Ohio
  Railroad . . . . . Jumping Branch
LLG 89 . . . . Hilltop

**Retail, Wholesale and Department
Store**
LU 21 . . . . Huntington
LU 550 . . . . Fairmont

**Roofers, Waterproofers and Allied
Workers**
LU 34 . . . . Ridgeley
LU 185 . . . . Charleston
LU 188. . . . . Wheeling
LU 242 . . . . Parkersburg

Rural Letter Carriers
D 1 Buckwheat
  Association . . . . Morgantown
D 2 Central West
  Virginia . . . . . . Walkersville
D 3 West Virginia . Berkeley Springs
D 5 Southwestern West
  Virginia. . . . . Milton
D 6 West Virginia . New Martinsville
LU Allegany-Garrett
  Counties . . . . Ridgeley
LU Tri-County . . . . Martinsburg
LU 4 West Central . . Parkersburg
LU 7 Black Diamond . . . . . Rock
SA West Virginia . . . Walkersville

**Security, Police and Fire
Professionals**
LU 65 . . . . Middlebourne
LU 400 . . . . Keyser
LU 405 . . White Sulphur Springs
LU 406 . . . . Martinsburg

Service Employees
LU 553 . . . . Ranson

Sheet Metal Workers
LU 339 . . . . Ridgeley
LU 462 . . . . Huntington

Steelworkers
LU 01-3664-S . . . . . Huntington
LU 01-14200-S . . . Williamstown
LU 02-225 . . . . . Bruceton Mills

LU 02-1449 . . . . . . Peterstown
LU 05-89 . . . . Boomer
LU 05-180 . . . . Milton
LU 05-276 . . . . . . Mount Clare
LU 05-295 . . . . Shinnston
LU 05-499 . . . . St. Marys
LU 05-628 . . . . Charleston
LU 05-721 . . . . Branchland
LU 05-753 . . . . . . Moatsville
LU 05-887 Congo. New Cumberland
LU 05-957 . . . . . . Morgantown
LU 05-973 . . . . Ridgeley
LU 05-997 . . . . . . Ravenswood
LU 05-1673 . . . . . . Beech Bottom
LU 05-2971 . . . . . . Wellsburg
LU 08-1-S . . . . Fairmont
LU 08-22-T . . . . Vienna
LU 08-26 . . . . Westover
LU 08-37-S . . . . . . Huntington
LU 08-40-S . . . . . . Huntington
LU 08-53-T . . . . Wheeling
LU 08-477-S . . . . . Buckhannon
LU 08-516-S . . . . . Harrisville
LU 08-518 . . . . . . Clarksburg
LU 08-542 . . . . . . Morgantown
LU 08-567 . . . . . . Clarksburg
LU 08-570 . . . . . . Barboursville
LU 08-604 . . . . . . Buckhannon
LU 08-644-L . . . . . Henderson
LU 08-874-L . . . . . . Cowen
LU 08-1017-L . . . . . Petersburg
LU 08-1280-S . . . . . Follansbee
LU 08-1652-S . . . . . Huntington
LU 08-2383-S . . . . . Parkersburg
LU 08-4842-S . . . . . Follansbee
LU 08-5171-S . . . . . Huntington
LU 08-5668-S . . . . Ravenswood
LU 08-5712-S . . . . . Redhouse
LU 08-7047-S. . . . . . Prichard
LU 08-8360-S. . . . . . Augusta
LU 08-8621-S . . . . . . Nitro
LU 08-8984-S . . . . . Jane Lew
LU 08-12315-S . . . . . Wellsburg
LU 08-12424-S. . . . . Alderson
LU 08-12610-S . . . . Barboursville
LU 08-12625-S . . South Charleston
LU 08-13252-S . . . Middlebourne
LU 08-14310-S . . . . . Beckley
LU 08-14400-S . . . . . Williamson
LU 08-14505-S . . . . . Logan
LU 08-14614-S. . . . . . Nitro
LU 08-14811-S . . . Point Pleasant
LU 08-15229-S . . . . Wellsburg
LU 08-15293-S . . . . . Richwood
LU 10-36 . . . . Benwood

Teachers
LU 6053 Job Corps Employees
  Federation . . . . . . Charleston
SFED West Virginia . . . Charleston

Teamsters
LU 175 . . . . . South Charleston
LU 505. . . . . Huntington
LU 697. . . . . Wheeling

Theatrical Stage Employees
LU 64 . . . . Wheeling
LU 271 . . . . Charleston
LU 369 . . . . Huntington
LU 578 . . . . Morgantown

Transit Union
LDIV 103 . . . . Wheeling
LDIV 812 . . . . Clarksburg

**Transportation Communications
Union**
D 308 Chesapeake & Ohio System
  Board . . . . Ona
D 403 . . . . Shepherdstown
LG 5056 Arasa Division . . . . Ona
LG 6454 Williamson . . . Delbarton

Transportation Union
GCA GO-201 Chesapeake & Ohio
  Railway-P . . . . Kenova
LU 118 . . . . Hinton
LU 430 . . . . Keyser
LU 504 . . . . Moundsville
LU 605 . . . . Fairmont
LU 631 . . . . Ranson
LU 860 . . . . Nitro
LU 915 . . . . Poca
LU 1172 . . . . Princeton
LU 1327 . . . . Branchland
SLB LO-55 West Virginia . Grafton

Treasury Employees
CH 64 . . . . Bridgeport
CH 82 . . . . Kearneysville
CH 190 . . . . Parkersburg

UNITE HERE
LU 863 . . . White Sulphur Springs
LU 2392 . . . . Clay

Utility Workers
LU 102-O Martinsburg . Martinsburg
LU 176 . . . . Huntington
LU 264 . . . . Wheeling
LU 296 . . . . . . Point Pleasant
LU 420 . . . . Moundsville
LU 468 . . . . Moundsville
LU 492 . . . . Moundsville

Weather Service Employees
BR 01-16 . . . . Charleston

**Unaffiliated Labor
Organizations**
Appalred Staff Employees
  Union. . . . . Charleston
Chemical Employees
  Association. . . . . Belle
Craig Motor Service Company
  Automotive Parts & Service
  Workers. . . . . Beckley
Greenbrier Security Union SPFPA
  LU 405 . . White Sulphur Springs
Nurse Anesthetists Association of
  West Virginia Association of Nurse
  Anesthetists Inc. . . . . Charleston
Steelworkers Union
  Independent. . . . . Weirton
Swanson Plating Employees
  Association . . . . Bluefield
Swanson Plating Workers
  Independent Union . Morgantown
Weirton Steel Corporation Guard
  Union Inc.. . . . . Weirton
West Virginia Professional Staff
  Union . . . . Jane Lew

Wisconsin

AFL-CIO Trade and Industrial Departments

Building and Construction Trades Department

BCTC Eau Claire . . . . . Eau Claire
BCTC Kenosha . . . . Kenosha
BCTC La Crosse . . . . . La Crosse
BCTC Milwaukee . . . . Milwaukee
BCTC Northeast
  Wisconsin . . . . Appleton
BCTC Northern . . . . . . Superior
BCTC South Central
  Wisconsin . . . . Madison
BCTC Southern
  Wisconsin . . . . Janesville

Other Councils and Committees

JC Badger Ordnance
  Works . . . . Sauk City

AFL-CIO Directly Affiliated Locals

AFL-CIO

DALU 19806 Smith Steel
  Workers . . . . Milwaukee
DALU 24111 Newspaper
  Editors . . . . . . Random Lake

Affiliated Labor Organizations

Air Traffic Controllers

LU CWA . . . . Mosinee
LU ENW . . . . Kenosha
LU GRB . . . . Green Bay
LU MKE . . . . Milwaukee
LU MSN . . . . Madison

Asbestos Workers

LU 19 . . . . Milwaukee
LU 127 . . . . Merrill

Automobile, Aerospace Workers

C Fox River Valley Area
  CAP . . . . Fond du Lac
C Janesville Madison Area
  CAP . . . . Janesville
C Rockford Area . . . . . Beloit
C Sheboygan Area CAP . . Sheboygan
C UAW Southeastern Wisconsin
  Area CAP Council . . . Oak Creek
LU 9 . . . . West Allis
LU 46 . . . . Beloit
LU 72 . . . . Kenosha
LU 75 . . . . Milwaukee
LU 77 . . . . Clinton
LU 82 . . . . Racine
LU 95 . . . . Janesville
LU 108 . . . . Cleveland
LU 173 . . . . Kenosha
LU 180 . . . . Racine
LU 291 . . . . Oshkosh
LU 316 . . . . La Crosse
LU 407 . . . . Milwaukee
LU 413 . . . . Marinette
LU 438 . . . . Oak Creek
LU 443 . . . . Evansville
LU 469 . . . . Oak Creek
LU 557 . . . . Racine
LU 578 . . . . Oshkosh
LU 627 . . . . Racine

LU 646 . . . . Fond du Lac
LU 722 St. Paul-Minneapolis
  Local . . . . New Richmond
LU 833 . . . . Sheboygan
LU 1076 . . . . Sheboygan
LU 1092 West Allis-
  Milwaukee . . . . . . Oak Creek
LU 1102 . . . . Green Bay
LU 1108 . . . . Oshkosh
LU 1291 . . . . Plymouth
LU 1332 . . . . Sheboygan
LU 1472 . . . . Sheboygan
LU 1548 . . . . Saurville
LU 1866 . . . . Oak Creek
LU 2020 . . . . Stevens Point
LU 2132 . . . . Fond du Lac
LU 2183 . . . . Marinette
LU 2376 . . . . Sheboygan

Bakery, Confectionery, Tobacco Workers and Grain Millers

C Third Region . . . . . West Allis
LU 118-G . . . . Superior
LU 205 . . . . West Allis
LU 244 . . . . Milwaukee

Boilermakers

C Metal Polishers Northshore
  Conference . . . . Elkhorn
LG 10-M . . . . Milwaukee
LG 94-M . . . . Elkhorn
LG 107 . . . . Waukesha
LG 117 . . . . Superior
LG 177 . . . . Green Bay
LG 443 . . . . Manitowoc
LG 449 . . . . Sturgeon Bay
LG 487 . . . . Pulaski
LG 696 . . . . Marinette
LG 697 . . . . Auburndale
LG 1509 . . . . . South Milwaukee

Bricklayers

DC District Council of
  Wisconsin . . . . . . New Berlin
LU 1 . . . . West Salem
LU 2 . . . . Iron River
LU 3 . . . . Green Bay
LU 4 . . . . Racine
LU 5 . . . . Germantown
LU 6 . . . . Merrill
LU 7 . . . . Janesville
LU 8 . . . . New Berlin
LU 9 Fox River Valley . . Menasha
LU 11 Wisconsin . . . . Sheboygan
LU 13 . . . . Madison
LU 19 . . . . Eau Claire
LU 21 . . . . Watertown
LU 34 . . . . Reedsburg

Carpenters

3 Midwestern District Promotional
  Commit . . . . Kaukauna
C Midwestern Council of
  Independent Workers . . Oshkosh
C Northern Wisconsin
  Regional . . . . Kaukauna
LU 161 . . . . Kenosha
LU 264 . . . . Pewaukee
LU 310 . . . . Westboro
LU 314 . . . . Madison
LU 344 . . . . Pewaukee
LU 646 . . . . Rhinelander
LU 731 . . . . Sheboygan
LU 804 . . . . Stevens Point
LU 955 . . . . Appleton

LU 1025 . . . . Medford
LU 1053 . . . . Brookfield
LU 1056 Millwright . . . . De Pere
LU 1074 . . . . Eau Claire
LU 1143 . . . . La Crosse
LU 1146 . . . . Green Bay
LU 1349 . . . . Two Rivers
LU 1363 . . . . Oshkosh
LU 1435 . . . . Ladysmith
LU 1488 . . . . Medford
LU 1521 . . . . Kewaunee
LU 1533 . . . . Two Rivers
LU 1594 . . . . Wausau
LU 1733 . . . . Marshfield
LU 1801 . . . . Hawkins
LU 2190 . . . . Madison
LU 2283 . . . . Fredonia
LU 2337 . . . . Milwaukee
LU 2344 . . . . Wausau
LU 2794 . . . . Antigo
LU 2832 . . . . Oshkosh
LU 2958 . . . . Auburndale
LU 2979 . . . . Merrill
LU 3157 . . . . Wausau
STC Wisconsin . . . . . . Madison

Civilian Technicians

CH 26 Wisconsin Army . . . Viroqua
CH 80 Mad City . . . . . . Madison
CH 81 Badger State . . . Milwaukee

Communications Workers

C Wisconsin Political . . Milwaukee
LU 4603 . . . . Milwaukee
LU 4611 . . . . Racine
LU 4620 . . . . Green Bay
LU 4621 . . . . Appleton
LU 4622 . . . . Fond du Lac
LU 4630 . . . . Madison
LU 4640 . . . . Eau Claire
LU 4641 . . . . Beldenville
LU 4642 . . . . Vesper
LU 4670 . . . . Nekoosa
LU 4671 . . . . Sun Prairie
LU 4672 . . . . Mosinee
LU 4674 . . . . Rice Lake
LU 4675 . . . . Mishicot
LU 7206 . . . . Holmen
LU 14547 . . . . Kenosha
LU 14550 . . . . Sheboygan
LU 14551 Superior Printing
  Publishing Media . . . . Superior
LU 34051 Milwaukee . . Milwaukee
LU 34159 . . . . Kenosha
LU 34179 . . . . Sheboygan
LU 82846 . . . . Waukesha
LU 84038 . . . . Hales Corners
LU 84101 . . . . Milwaukee
LU 84161 . . . . Seymour
LU 84800 . . . . Sheboygan
LU 84811 Local 84811-
  801FW . . . . Janesville

Electrical Workers

LU 14 . . . . Fall Creek
LU 127 . . . . Kenosha
LU 158 . . . . Green Bay
LU 159 . . . . Madison
LU 388 . . . . Stevens Point
LU 430 . . . . Racine
LU 494 . . . . Milwaukee
LU 577 . . . . Appleton
LU 663 . . . . . . South Milwaukee
LU 715 . . . . Milwaukee
LU 890 . . . . Janesville

LU 953 . . . . Eau Claire
LU 965 . . . . Madison
LU 1060 . . . . Sheboygan
LU 1147 . . . . . Wisconsin Rapids
LU 1559 . . . . Superior
LU 1791 . . . . Wausau
LU 2150 . . . . Waukesha
LU 2221 . . . . Florence
LU 2304 . . . . Madison
SC EM-5 General Electric . Big Bend
STCON Wisconsin . . Stevens Point

Electrical, Radio and Machine Workers

LU 1107 . . . . Necedah
LU 1111 . . . . Milwaukee
LU 1112 . . . . Oak Creek
LU 1121 . . . . La Crosse
LU 1125 . . . . Milwaukee
LU 1135 . . . . Milwaukee
LU 1161 . . . . Sparta
LU 1172 . . . . Milwaukee

Elevator Constructors

LU 15 . . . . New Berlin
LU 132 . . . . Cottage Grove

Engineers

LU 1 Administrative Law Judges
  Judicial Council . . . . . Sussex
LU 92 . . . . Cudahy

Federal Employees

LU 3 . . . . Milwaukee
LU 276 . . . . Madison
LU 1920 . . . . Greendale
LU 2137 Blackwell Job
  Corporation . . . . Laona
LU 2165 . . . . Hayward

Fire Fighters

LU 415 . . . . Wausau

Food and Commercial Workers

C 4 Great Lakes District
  Council . . . . Bay City
DC Midwestern . . . . Appleton
LU 1-I . . . . Wauwatosa
LU 73-A . . . . Milwaukee
LU 78-T . . . . Kaukauna
LU 147-T . . . . Cleveland
LU 215-T . . . . Casco
LU 236-T . . . . Two Rivers
LU 245 . . . . Green Bay
LU 268 . . . . Chippewa Falls
LU 349-C . . . . Rio
LU 538 . . . . Madison
LU 625-T . . . . Sheboygan
LU 665-T . . . . Manitowoc
LU 688 . . . . Merrill
LU 717 . . . . Marshfield
LU 1444 . . . . Milwaukee

Glass, Molders, Pottery and Plastics Workers

CONF Wisconsin . . . . . Cudahy
LU 6-B . . . . Cudahy
LU 14-B . . . . Jackson
LU 113-B . . . . . Richland Center
LU 121-B . . . . Neenah
LU 125-B . . . . . South Milwaukee
LU 226 . . . . Burlington
LU 261 . . . . Cedar Grove
LU 271 . . . . De Pere
LU 301 . . . . Manitowoc

LU 437 . . . . Onalaska

Government Employees
C 33 Prison Locals . . . . . Danbury
LU 3 . . . . Milwaukee
LU 666 USDA . . . . . Wauwatosa
LU 675 USGA . . . . . Lake Mills
LU 1346 HHS . . . . . . Franksville
LU 1732 VA . . . . . . Madison
LU 1882 VA . . . . . Fort McCoy
LU 2144 DoD . . . . . Milwaukee
LU 2722 USDA . . . . . Green Bay
LU 2882 DoL . . . . . . Green Bay
LU 3289 USDA . . . . Dallas
LU 3495 DoJ . . . . . . Necedah

Government Security Officers
LU 157 . . . . Muskego

Graphic Communications
LU 7-C . . . . West Allis
LU 23-N . . . . Milwaukee
LU 77-P Fox Valley . . . . Neenah
LU 254-M . . . . Racine
LU 370-C . . . . Schofield
LU 577-M . . . . Milwaukee
LU 585-S . . . . Rhinelander

Iron Workers
LU 8 . . . . Milwaukee
LU 383 . . . . Madison
LU 665 . . . . Stoughton
LU 811 . . . . Wausau
LU 825 . . . . La Crosse

Laborers
DC Wisconsin . . . . . . De Forest
LU 113 . . . . Milwaukee
LU 140 . . . . La Crosse
LU 268 . . . . Eau Claire
LU 330 . . . . Menasha
LU 464 . . . . Madison

Letter Carriers
BR 2 . . . . Milwaukee
BR 59 . . . . La Crosse
BR 102 . . . . Sheboygan
BR 125 . . . . Fond du Lac
BR 173 . . . . Oshkosh
BR 215 . . . . Wausau
BR 242 Ashland Area
  Local . . . . Marengo
BR 337 . . . . Superior
BR 346 . . . . Marinette
BR 381 . . . . Stevens Point
BR 397 . . . . Waukesha
BR 436 . . . . Racine
BR 490 . . . . Manitowoc
BR 507 . . . . Madison
BR 572 . . . . Janesville
BR 574 . . . . Kenosha
BR 619 . . . . Green Bay
BR 649 . . . . Watertown
BR 700 . . . . Neenah
BR 715 Conrad Hansen . . . . Beloit
BR 728 . . . . Eau Claire
BR 729 . . . . Fort Atkinson
BR 778 . . . . Irma
BR 822 . . . . Menasha
BR 944 . . . . Beaver Dam
BR 978 . . . . Marshfield
BR 983 . . . . Antigo
BR 1033 . . . . Menomonie
BR 1083 . . . . . Wisconsin Rapids
BR 1144 . . . . Berlin
BR 1181 . . . . Monroe
BR 1208 . . . . Ripon
BR 1222 . . . . . Port Washington

BR 1233 . . . . Sparta
BR 1241 . . . . Oconto
BR 1267 . . . . Oconomowoc
BR 1272 . . . . Platteville
BR 1298 . . . . Waupaca
BR 1345 . . . . Two Rivers
BR 1370 . . . . Plymouth
BR 1613 . . . . Hudson
BR 1662 . . . . Rice Lake
BR 1890 . . . . Clintonville
BR 1949 . . . . Columbus
BR 2025 . . . . . Prairie du Chien
BR 2186 . . . . Mayville
BR 2284 . . . . Spooner
BR 2285 . . . . Hurley
BR 2316 . . . . Medford
BR 2454 . . . . Durand
BR 2478 . . . . Horicon
BR 2491 . . . . . . Mineral Point
BR 2504 . . . . Arcadia
BR 2516 . . . . Black River
BR 2544 . . . . Park Falls
BR 2565 . . . . Viroqua
BR 2576 . . . . River Falls
BR 2594 . . . . Chilton
BR 2674 . . . . Phillips
BR 2884 . . . . Darlington
BR 2965 . . . . . . New Holstein
BR 2972 . . . . Tomah
BR 3002 . . . . Stanley
BR 3035 . . . . . Sturgeon Bay
BR 3100 . . . . Niagara
BR 3231 . . . . Lodi
BR 3647 . . . . Boscobel
BR 3740 . . . . . . Oconto Falls
BR 3806 . . . . Algoma
BR 4123 . . . . Bloomer
BR 4124 . . . . Barron
BR 4225 . . . . Little Chute
BR 4329 . . . . Westby
BR 4630 . . . . Brillion
BR 4668 . . . . . . New Richmond
BR 4811 . . . . Brookfield
BR 4852 . . . . Nekoosa
BR 4880 . . . . Peshtigo
BR 5123 . . . . Arlington
BR 5125 . . . . Fennimore
BR 5129 . . . . Pewaukee
BR 5354 . . . . Prescott
BR 5371 . . . . Crandon
BR 5372 . . . . Brodhead
BR 5436 . . . . . Camp Douglas
BR 5787 . . . . . . Port Edwards
BR 5871 . . . . Mosinee
BR 5941 . . . . Waterford
BR 5942 . . . . Delafield
BR 6216 . . . . Amery
BR 6217 . . . . Randolph
BR 6292 . . . . Oregon
BR 6342 . . . . . Prairie du Sac
BR 6352 . . . . Cuba City
SA Wisconsin . . . . . . Madison

Locomotive Engineers
DIV 13 . . . . Trempealeau
DIV 173 . . . . Eden
DIV 174 . . . . . Stevens Point
DIV 175 . . . . Neenah
DIV 176 . . . . Friendship
DIV 188 . . . . Superior
DIV 209 . . . . De Pere
DIV 241 . . . . Eau Claire
DIV 253 . . . . Madison
DIV 405 . . . . Waukesha
DIV 861 . . . . . . South Range
DIV 882 A.C.
  Blainey . . . South Milwaukee
SLB Wisconsin . . . . . Oak Creek

Longshoremen
LU 815 . . . . Milwaukee
LU 1000 . . . . Superior
LU 1014 . . . . Green Bay
LU 1037 . . . . Superior
LU 1295 . . . . Cudahy

Machinists
DLG 3 Woodworkers . . . Schofield
DLG 10 . . . . Milwaukee
DLG 66 . . . . La Crosse
DLG 121 . . . . Sun Prairie
LG 21 . . . . La Crosse
LG 34 . . . . Kenosha
LG 66 . . . . Milwaukee
LG 78 . . . . Milwaukee
LG 140-DS . . . . Greenfield
LG 419 . . . . Milwaukee
LG 437 Belle City . . . . . Racine
LG 510 . . . . West Allis
LG 516 . . . . Manitowoc
LG 621 . . . . Ashland
LG 655 . . . . Junction City
LG 672 . . . . Superior
LG 747 . . . . Appleton
LG 873 . . . . Horicon
LG 908 . . . . St. Francis
LG 957 . . . . . . Fort Atkinson
LG 1061 Cream City . . . Milwaukee
LG 1115 . . . . La Crosse
LG 1217 . . . . . New Richmond
LG 1259 . . . . . . New Holstein
LG 1266 . . . . Janesville
LG 1326 . . . . West Bend
LG 1367 . . . . Watertown
LG 1377 Spring City
  Lodge . . . . Waukesha
LG 1406 . . . . . . New Glarus
LG 1430 . . . . Cedarburg
LG 1438 . . . . Merrill
LG 1493 . . . . Burlington
LG 1516 . . . . Cambria
LG 1543 . . . . . Wisconsin Rapids
LG 1564 . . . . . . Fort Atkinson
LG 1668 . . . . Milwaukee
LG 1713 . . . . Tomahawk
LG 1771 . . . . Bangor
LG 1798 . . . . Seymour
LG 1845 . . . . Brookfield
LG 1855 . . . . Sherwood
LG 1862 . . . . Cudahy
LG 1904 . . . . Milwaukee
LG 1916 . . . . Milwaukee
LG 1947 . . . . . . Fond du Lac
LG 2052 . . . . Mayville
LG 2053 . . . . Mayville
LG 2054 . . . . Watertown
LG 2073 . . . . Seymour
LG 2110 . . . . Cudahy
LG 2180 . . . . . Wisconsin Dells
LG 2185 . . . . Chilton
LG 2191 . . . . La Crosse
LG 2269 . . . . Loganville
LG 2362 . . . . Merrill
LG 2560 . . . . Sussex
LG 2575 . . . . . . New London
LLG 1260 . . . . . New Holstein
LLG W-67
  Woodworkers . . . . Abbotsford
LLG W-110 Woodworkers . Stratford
LLG W-223
  Woodworkers . . . . . White Lake
LLG W-335
  Woodworkers . . . . South Range
LLG W-401 Woodworkers . Phillips
STC Wisconsin . . . . . Milwaukee

Maintenance of Way Employes
LG 298 . . . . Rice Lake
LG 320 . . . . Superior
LG 509 . . . . Holmen
LG 1841 . . . . Jefferson
LG 2643 . . . . Madison
LG 2857 . . . . Genoa City
LG 2927 . . . . Fond du Lac
LG 2928 . . . . Green Bay
LG 2929 . . . . . . Chippewa Falls
LG 2930 . . . . Burlington
LG 2932 . . . . Argonne
SD Wisconsin Central System
  Division . . . . . . Stevens Point
SLG 99 . . . . Racine
SLG 239 . . . . Eau Claire
SLG 410 . . . . West Allis
SLG 425 . . . . Manitowoc
SLG 893 . . . . Merrill
SLG 1034 . . . . . . Cottage Grove
SLG 1125 . . . . Friendship
SLG 1906 . . . . River Falls

Musicians
LU 8 . . . . Milwaukee
LU 42 Racine . . . . Racine
LU 166 . . . . Madison
LU 193 . . . . Waukesha
LU 205 . . . . Green Bay
LU 469 . . . . Watertown
STCON Wisconsin . . . . . Monona

NLRB Professional Association
LU 30 . . . . Milwaukee

Nurses
LSC Bay Area Medical Center,
  Professional . . . . . . Marinette
SA Wisconsin Nurses
  Association . . . . Madison

Office and Professional Employees
LU 9 . . . . Milwaukee
LU 35 . . . . Butler
LU 39 . . . . Madison
LU 74 . . . . Fall Creek
LU 95 . . . . Wisconsin Rapids

Operating Engineers
LU 139 . . . . Pewaukee
LU 305 . . . . Superior
LU 310 . . . . Green Bay
LU 317 . . . . Milwaukee

Painters
DC 7 . . . . New Berlin
LU 108 . . . . Kenosha
LU 579 . . . . New Berlin
LU 770 . . . . New Berlin
LU 781 . . . . New Berlin
LU 802 . . . . Sun Prairie
LU 934 . . . . Kenosha
LU 941 Glaziers &
  Glassworkers . . . . Sun Prairie
LU 1204 . . . . Pewaukee
LU 1355 Glaziers Architectural
  Metal . . . . Janesville

Plasterers and Cement Masons
LU 599 . . . . Wauwatosa

Plumbing and Pipe Fitting
LU 75 . . . . Milwaukee
LU 118 . . . . Kenosha
LU 183 Milwaukee Area
  Local . . . . . Menomonee Falls
LU 400 Fox River Valley . Kaukauna
LU 434 . . . . Mosinee

LU 601 . . . . Milwaukee
SA Wisconsin Pipe
  Trades . . . . Milwaukee

Postal and Federal Employees
LU 708 . . . . Milwaukee

Postal Workers
LU 3 Milwaukee . . . . . Milwaukee
LU 90 Appleton . . . . . Appleton
LU 102 Eau Claire Area . Eau Claire
LU 178 Oshkosh . . . . . Oshkosh
LU 241 Madison Area . . . Madison
LU 360 La Crosse . . . . La Crosse
LU 577 Sheboygan . . . . Sheboygan
LU 778 Racine . . . . . . Racine
LU 840 Kenosha . . . . . Kenosha
LU 878 West Bend . . . West Bend
LU 1030 Manitowoc . . . Manitowoc
LU 1041 Ashland . . . . . Ashland
LU 2100 Plymouth . . . Plymouth
LU 2218 Sturgeon
  Bay . . . . Sturgeon Bay
LU 2247 Northeastern Wisconsin
  Area Local . . . . . . Green Bay
LU 3452 Port
  Washington . . . Port Washington
LU 4532 Wausau . . . . . Wausau
LU 4763 Spooner . . . . . Spooner
LU 5341 Whitewater . . Whitewater
LU 6196 Portage . . . . . Portage
SA Wisconsin . . . . . . Madison

Railroad Signalmen
LLG 9 . . . . West Bend
LLG 39 . . . . Randolph
LLG 236 . . . . Ripon

Roofers, Waterproofers and Allied Workers
LU 65 . . . . New Berlin

Rural Letter Carriers
LU Adams-Marquette
  Counties . . . . Adams
LU Barron-Washburn
  County . . . . Rice Lake
LU Calumet-Manitowoc-Sheboygan
  Counties . . . . Chilton
LU Chippewa-Eau Claire
  Counties . . . . . Chippewa Falls
LU Columbia
  County . . . . . Wisconsin Dells
LU Dodge County . . . . . Neosho
LU Door-Kewaunee
  Counties . . . . Luxemburg
LU Fond du Lac-Green Lake
  Counties . . . . . Campbellsport
LU Forest-Tri-County
  Association . . . . . Three Lakes
LU Grant County . . . . Lone Rock
LU Jefferson County . . . . Ivonia
LU Juneau County . . . . Mauston
LU La Crosse County . . . Onalaska
LU Lake Superior . . . . Iron River
LU Milwaukee-Waukesha
  Counties . . . . . Oconomowoc
LU Monroe County
  Association . . . . Tomah
LU Oconto County . . . . . Oconto
LU Outagamie County . . . Shiocton
LU Ozaukee County . . . Fredonia
LU Polk County . . . . . Centuria
LU Price-Taylor Counties . . Gilman
LU Racine-Kenosha
  Counties . . . . Bristol
LU Rock-Walworth
  Counties . . . . Elkhorn

LU Rusk County . . . . . Sheldon
LU Sawyer County . . . Stone Lake
LU St. Croix County . . . River Falls
LU Trempealeau-Buffalo County
  Association . . . . Eleva
LU Vernon County . . . . . Viola
LU Washington County . . . Lannon
LU Waupaca County . . . . Amherst
LU Waushara County . . Redgranite
LU 3 Chisago County . Grantsburg
LU 4 Brown County . . . Denmark
LU 11 Dane County . . . Middleton
LU 15 Dunn County . . . . Colfax
LU 22 Jackson County . . . Hixton
LU 27 Green-Lafayette
  Counties . . . . Monroe
LU 28 Lincoln-Langlade
  Counties . . . . . . Tomahawk
LU 30 Marathon County . . . Edgar
LU 38 Pierce-Pepin
  Counties . . . . Nelson
LU 47 Sauk-Richland . . . Baraboo
LU 49 McHenry
  County . . . . . . Lake Geneva
LU 49 Shawano County . . . Eland
LU 61 Winnebago County . . Omro
LU 62 Wood-Portage
  Counties . . . . . Stevens Point
SA 51 Wisconsin . . . Eau Claire
UNIT 10 Crawford
  County . . . . . . Soldiers Grove

Security, Police and Fire Professionals
LU 203 . . . . Milwaukee
LU 554 . . . . Beloit
LU 555 . . . . Mukwonago
LU 556 . . . . Kenosha
LU 557 . . . . Genoa
LU 558 . . . . Two Rivers
LU 563 . . . . Park Falls

Service Employees
JC 4 Wisconsin State
  Council . . . . Milwaukee
LU 47 . . . . Milwaukee
LU 150 . . . . Milwaukee
LU 152 . . . . Racine
LU 168 . . . . Kenosha
LU 1199-W District 1199-W,
  SEIU . . . . Madison

Sheet Metal Workers
LU 18 . . . . Milwaukee
LU 565 . . . . Madison

State, County and Municipal Employees
C 40 Wisconsin State
  Council . . . . Madison
DC 48 Milwaukee
  Wisconsin . . . . . . Milwaukee
LU 216 Ashland City and County
  Employees . . . . . . Marengo
LU 255 The Wisconsin Childcare
  Union . . . . Madison
LU 366 Milwaukee, Wisconsin,
  Sewerage Commission
  Employees . . . . . Oak Creek
LU 412 Madison Area Rehabilitation
  Center . . . . Madison
LU 524 . . . . Janesville
LU 524-B Beloit Jelco Bus
  Drivers . . . . Beloit
LU 526 Milwaukee Public Museum
  Employees . . . . . Milwaukee
LU 621 Family Heritage Nursing
  Home Employees . . . Merrillian

LU 727-D American Lutheran
  Homes, Inc. . . . . . Elk Mound
LU 913 Rivers Bend
  Employees . . . . . . Manitowoc
LU 1146 Middle River Health Care
  Center . . . . Poplar
LU 1155 Memorial Medical
  Center . . . . Marengo
LU 1205 Clara Barton
  Brigade . . . . Green Bay
LU 1440 . . . . Milwaukee
LU 1558 Badger Regional Blood
  Center Employees . . . Madison
LU 1760 St. Mary Hospital of
  Superior . . . . Superior
LU 1760-A . . . . Superior
LU 1954 Rehabilitation & Social
  Service Workers . . . Milwaukee
LU 2236 Lakeside Nursing and
  Rehabilitation . . . . . Cadott
LU 2276 Wyalusing Academy Child
  Care Worker . . . Prairie du Chien
LU 2418 Jefferson County
  Institutions Employees . Jefferson
LU 2425 Spooner Health System
  Employees . . . . . . Minong
LU 3152 Pepin Manor Care Center
  Employees . . . . . . Pepin
LU 3305 Bay Area Medical
  Center . . . . Marinette
LU 3382 Dental Associates, Ltd.
  Employees . . . . . . New Berlin
LU 3635 Chequamegon Bay Area
  Nursing Employees . . . Ashland
LU 3635-A . . . . Washburn
LU 3902 Homme Home Employees
  Union . . . . Wittenberg

Steelworkers
C Kimberly Clark . . . Stevens Point
DC 330 Region Ten . . Fond du Lac
LU 794 . . . . Wisconsin Rapids
LU 70009 Paper Mill
  Workers . . . . Kimberly
LU 7-69 . . . . . West Milwaukee
LU 7-666 . . . . Wausau
LU 7-850 . . . . Kewaskum
LU 01-1279 . . . . Neenah
LU 02-14-L . . . . . La Crosse
LU 02-29-U . . . . . . Cudahy
LU 02-29-U . . . . . . Cudahy
LU 02-125-A . . . . . Manitowoc
LU 02-133-U . . . . . Sheboygan
LU 02-146-S . . . . . . Niagara
LU 02-175-A . . . . . Kewaunee
LU 02-333-U . . . . Stevens Point
LU 02-460-L . . . . Chippewa Falls
LU 02-642-U . . . . New London
LU 02-741-L . . . . Chippewa Falls
LU 02-892-L . . . . . Burlington
LU 02-904-L . . . . . Sun Prairie
LU 02-1114-S . . . West Milwaukee
LU 02-1327-S . . . . . Ripon
LU 02-1343-S . . South Milwaukee
LU 02-1527-S . . . . West Allis
LU 02-1533-S . . . . . Beloit
LU 02-1569-S . . . . St. Francis
LU 02-1610-S . . . . Milwaukee
LU 02-2138-S . . . . Eau Claire
LU 02-3168-S . . . . . Niagara
LU 02-3205-S . . . . Oak Creek
LU 02-3245-S . . . . . Beloit
LU 02-3740-S . . . . Pewaukee
LU 02-4547-S . . . . Oak Creek
LU 02-4845-S . . . . Waukesha
LU 02-4846-S . . . . Marshall
LU 02-6050-S . . . . . Suring
LU 02-6499-S . . . . Manitowoc

LU 02-7076-S . . . . . East Troy
LU 02-7875-S . . . . Milwaukee
LU 02-8149-S . . . . . Fredonia
LU 02-9040-S . . Menomonee Falls
LU 02-9184-S . . . . . Crivitz
LU 02-9435 . . . . . . Beloit
LU 02-12005-S . . . . . Eagle
LU 07-15 . . . . Tomahawk
LU 07-16 . . . . Appleton
LU 07-18 . . . . Milwaukee
LU 07-20 . . . . Hilbert
LU 07-42 . . . . . Chippewa Falls
LU 07-47 . . . . Green Bay
LU 07-53 Brewers &
  Maltsters . . . . . Fort Atkinson
LU 07-59 . . . . Nekoosa
LU 07-86 . . . . Marinette
LU 07-111 Lake Geneva
  Local . . . . Twin Lakes
LU 07-116 . . . . . Stevens Point
LU 07-131 . . . . Adams
LU 07-144 Appleton
  Coated . . . . Combined Locks
LU 07-145 . . . . . Campbellsport
LU 07-148 . . . . Neenah
LU 07-150 . . . . . Camp Douglas
LU 07-169 . . . . Oshkosh
LU 07-187 . . . . Wisconsin Rapids
LU 07-200 . . . . . . Milwaukee
LU 07-201 . . . . Neenah
LU 07-204 . . . . . . Green Bay
LU 07-209 . . . . . . West Allis
LU 07-213 . . . . . . Green Bay
LU 07-221 . . . . . . Mosinee
LU 07-224 . . . . . . Mosinee
LU 07-227 . . . . . . Peshtigo
LU 07-231 . . . . . . Burlington
LU 07-232 . . . . . . Milwaukee
LU 07-248 . . . . . . Tomahawk
LU 07-273 . . . . . . Appleton
LU 07-295 . . . . . . Brookfield
LU 07-316 . . . . . . Mosinee
LU 07-319 . . . . . . Rothschild
LU 07-324 . . . . . . Appleton
LU 07-327 . . . . . . De Pere
LU 07-331 . . . . . . Holmen
LU 07-342 . . . . . . Watertown
LU 07-345 . . . . . . Two Rivers
LU 07-356 . . . . . . Milwaukee
LU 07-359 . . . . . Stevens Point
LU 07-364 . . . . . . Milwaukee
LU 07-366 . . . . . . Berlin
LU 07-368 . . . . . . Two Rivers
LU 07-369 . . . . . . Slinger
LU 07-370 . . . . . Stevens Point
LU 07-380 . . . . . . Sauk City
LU 07-432 . . . . . . Fremont
LU 07-445 . . . . . . Butternut
LU 07-460 . . . . . . Tomahawk
LU 07-465 . . . . . . Appleton
LU 07-469 . . . . . . Appleton
LU 07-475 . . . . . . Brillion
LU 07-482 . . . . . . Appleton
LU 07-484 . . . . . . Oshkosh
LU 07-535 . . . . . . Antigo
LU 07-550 . . . . . . Waupaca
LU 07-579 . . . . . . Allenton
LU 07-588 . . . . . . Manawa
LU 07-597 . . . . . . Pulaski
LU 07-598 . . . . . . Lomira
LU 07-614 . . . . . . Redgranite
LU 07-631 . . . . . . Marathon
LU 07-681 . . . . . . Mequon
LU 07-695 . . . . Menomonee Falls
LU 07-696 . . . . . . Marshfield
LU 07-727 . . . . . . Menasha
LU 07-748 . . . . . . Winneconne
LU 07-765 . . . . . . Milwaukee

LU 07-779 . . . . Richfield
LU 07-790 . . . . Marion
LU 07-803 . . . . Dorchester
LU 07-812 . . . . Neenah
LU 07-815 . . . . Marion
LU 07-851 . . . . Portage
LU 07-852 . . . . Waukesha
LU 07-857 . . . . Kimberly
LU 07-888 . . . . Neenah
LU 07-889 . . . . Clintonville
LU 07-902 . . . . West Bend
LU 07-932 . . . . Winneconne
LU 07-945 . . . . Malone
LU 07-995 . . . . Shiocton
LU 07-1004 . . . . Marinette
LU 07-1096 . . . . . . Green Bay
LU 07-1166 . . . . Niagara
LU 07-1170 . . . . . New London
LU 07-1203 . . . . De Pere
LU 07-1207 . . . . . . Stoughton
LU 07-1260 . . . . Merrill
LU 07-1306 . . . . . Stevens Point
LU 07-1316 . . . . Shawano
LU 07-1319 . . . . Green Bay
LU 07-1321 . . . . Green Bay
LU 07-1324 . . . . Menasha
LU 07-1381 . . . . Wausau
LU 07-1477 . . . . Appleton
LU 07-1517 . . . . Green Bay
LU 07-1670 . . . . Appleton
LU 07-1778 . . . . . Eagle River
LU 07-1822 . . . . Fremont
LU 07-1970 . . . . . New London
LU 07-1980 . . . . Appleton
LU 07-7152 . . . . . . Fond du Lac
LU 70-322 Regional 10 . Milwaukee

Teachers
LU 5012 Nurses & Health
  Professionals . . . . . Burlington
LU 5032 Veterans Administration
  Staff Nurses Council . Milwaukee
LU 5034 Eagle River Memorial
  Hospital Professional
  Nurses . . . . . Land O'Lakes
LU 5040 Federation of Nurses &
  Health Professionals . Cumberland

SFED Nurses & Health Professionals,
  Wisconsin Federation
  of . . . . West Allis

Teamsters
CONF Dairy Conference, USA and
  Canada . . . . Green Bay
JC 39 . . . . Milwaukee
LU 23 Milwaukee Mailers
  Union . . . . Milwaukee
LU 43 . . . . Racine
LU 75 . . . . Green Bay
LU 200 . . . . Milwaukee
LU 344 . . . . Milwaukee
LU 563 . . . . Appleton
LU 579 . . . . Janesville
LU 662 . . . . Eau Claire
LU 695 . . . . Madison

Theatrical Stage Employees
LU 18 . . . . Milwaukee
LU 32 . . . . Superior
LU 141 . . . . La Crosse
LU 164 . . . . Milwaukee
LU 251 . . . . Madison
LU 470 . . . . Oshkosh
LU 777 . . . . Milwaukee

Transit Union
LDIV 998 . . . . Milwaukee
LDIV 1635 . . . . Madison

**Transportation Communications
  Union**
LG 415 . . . . Solon Springs
LG 6013 . . . . Fond du Lac
LG 6595 Madison . . . . . . Ripon

Transportation Union
GCA GO-225 Chicago &
  Northwestern Trans
  Company-P . . . . . Milwaukee
GCA GO-987 Wisconsin
  Central . . . . . . New London
LLG GO-256 Yardmasters
  Department . . . . . . Prescott
LU 311 . . . . West Salem

LU 312 . . . . Friendship
LU 322 . . . . Hubertus
LU 581 . . . . Marinette
LU 582 . . . . Milladore
LU 583 . . . . Oshkosh
LU 590 . . . . Portage
LU 832 . . . . Poplar
LU 1175 . . . . . Lake Nebagamon
LU 1293 . . . . Eau Claire
LU 1382 . . . . Hartland
SLB LO-56 Wisconsin . . . Madison

Treasury Employees
CH 1 . . . . Milwaukee

UNITE HERE
LU 122 . . . . Milwaukee
LU 228-LDC . . . . . . Eau Claire
LU 315 . . . . Nekoosa
LU 361 . . . . River Falls
LU 414 . . . . Omro
LU 479 United H.E.R.E. . La Crosse
LU 517 . . . . Osseo

Weather Service Employees
BR 03-9 . . . . Dousman
BR 03-10 . . . . Green Bay
BR 03-64 . . . . La Crosse

World Umpires Association
NHQ . . . . Neenah

Unaffiliated Labor
Organizations

Atlas Workers
  Association . . . . . . Green Bay
Bank Employees Union Firststar
  Bank . . . . Milwaukee
Business Agent Association LU
  662 . . . . Altoona
Council Employees Union . Madison
Duo Safety Ladder Independent
  Bargaining Unit
  (DSLIBU) . . . . Oshkosh
Employee Committee . . Sheboygan

Employees Association of B & T
  Mail Services, Inc . . . Mukwonago
Frigo Cheese Corporation Lena
  Independent LU 101 . Oconto Falls
Independent Employees Union of
  Hillshire Farm Company
  Inc . . . . New London
Independent Loomis Security
  Employees Union . . . . Cudahy
Independent Pattern Makers Union of
  Neenah Wisconsin . . . . Menasha
International Association of Tool
  Craftsmen LU 2 . . . . . Racine
International Association of Tool
  Craftsmen NHQ . . . . . Racine
International Guards Union of
  America LU 10 . . . . . . Portage
Kenosha School Bus Drivers
  Union . . . . Kenosha
Lake Superior Professional Nurses
  Association . . . . Ashland
Northland College Faculty
  Senate . . . . Ashland
Office Employees Carpenters
  Independent . . . . Altoona
Packerland Packing Company
  Inc. Drivers Union
  Independent . . . . . . Pulaski
Postal Supervisors, National
  Association LU 549 . . Green Bay
Professional Football Referees
  Association . . . . . Shorewood
Progressive Organization of
  Workers Representatives
  (POWR) . . . . Milwaukee
Staff Representatives Union
  (AFSCME) DC 48 . . . Milwaukee
Technical Engineers
  Association . . . . . Wauwatosa
Telemarketers Union of
  Wisconsin . . . . . . Milwaukee
Tosca Limited Employees
  Union . . . . Green Bay
United Business Representatives
  Union . . . . Monona
United Staff Union . . . . . Oregon
Western States Envelope Company
  Employees Association . . Butler
Wisconsin Council 40 Field Staff
  Union . . . . Madison

Wyoming

AFL-CIO Trade and Industrial Departments

Building and Construction Trades Department
BCTC Wyoming . . . Rock Springs

Affiliated Labor Organizations

Air Traffic Controllers
LU CPR . . . . Casper

Bakery, Confectionery, Tobacco Workers and Grain Millers
LU 279-G. . . . . Worland
LU 280-G. . . . . Torrington

Boilermakers
LG 495-D Cement Workers . Lovell

Bricklayers
LU 1. . . . . Cheyenne
LU 2 . . . . Big Horn
LU 3 . . . . Casper
STCON 99 Wyoming . . . Cheyenne

Carpenters
LU 1564 . . . . Casper

Civilian Technicians
CH 113 Wyoming Air. . . Cheyenne

Communications Workers
LU 7601 . . . . Cheyenne

Electrical Workers
C Wyoming State. . . . . . Casper
LU 322 . . . . Casper
LU 415 . . . . Cheyenne
LU 612 . . . . Wheatland
LU 775 . . . . Rawlins
LU 1759 . . . . Mills

Federal Employees
LU 2159 . . . . Casper

Government Employees
C 171 DFAS . . . . . . Wheatland

LU 1014 VA . . . . . . Cheyenne
LU 1219 VA . . . . Sheridan
LU 2354 DoD . . . . . . Cheyenne

Government Employees Association
LU 14-82 . . . . Guernsey

Iron Workers
LU 454 . . . . Casper

Laborers
LU 1271 . . . . Cheyenne

Letter Carriers
BR 463 . . . . Laramie
BR 555 . . . . Carpenter
BR 1006 . . . . Sheridan
BR 1372 . . . . . . Rock Springs
BR 1548 . . . . Gillette
BR 1681 . . . . Casper
BR 2177 . . . . Evanston
BR 2580. . . . . Douglas
BR 2779. . . . . Rawlins
BR 2929 . . . . Kemmerer
BR 3139 . . . . Cody
BR 3670 . . . . Torrington
BR 4387 . . . . Wheatland
BR 4456 . . . . Thermopolis
BR 4482 . . . . Powell
BR 5384 . . . . Worland
BR 5923 . . . . Riverton
BR 6116. . . . . Lovell
BR 6175 . . . . . . Green River
BR 6587 . . . . Greybull
SA Wyoming . . . . Casper

Locomotive Engineers
DIV 31 . . . . Douglas
DIV 44 . . . . Cheyenne
DIV 94 . . . . Gillette
DIV 103 BLET . . . . . Cheyenne
DIV 115 . . . . Cheyenne
DIV 142 . . . . Rawlins
DIV 207 . . . . Casper
DIV 245. . . . . Green River
DIV 624 . . . . Sheridan
DIV 869 . . . . Basin
GCA Union Pacific Railroad, Central
   Region . . . . Cheyenne

SLB Wyoming. . . . . . . Gillette

Machinists
LG 2190-FL . . . . Jackson

Maintenance of Way Employes
LG 1074 . . . . Dayton
LG 2933. . . . . Cheyenne
SD Union Pacific Railroad. . Lyman
SLG 686. . . . . Cheyenne
SLG 918 . . . . Evanston
SLG 1142. . . . . Douglas
SLG 1292. . . . . Greybull

Mine Workers
LU 1307. . . . . . Diamondville
LU 1972 . . . . Sheridan
LU 2055 . . . . Sheridan
LU 3010 Office of Allied
   Workers . . . . . . Kemmerer
LU 4893 Office of Allied
   Workers . . . . . . Rock Springs
LU 7404 . . . . . . Rock Springs

National Staff Organization
LU Staff Organization, Wyoming
   Education Association . Cheyenne

Operating Engineers
LU 800 . . . . Bar Nunn

Plumbing and Pipe Fitting
LU 192 . . . . Cheyenne

Postal Mail Handlers
LU 319 . . . . Cheyenne

Postal Workers
LU 580 Casper . . . . . . Casper
LU 769 Cheyenne. . . . Cheyenne
LU 1317 Rock
   Springs . . . . . . Rock Springs
LU 1762 Rawlins . . . . . Rawlins
LU 2204 Laramie . . . . . Laramie
LU 2338 Worland Area . . Worland
LU 2340 Sheridan . . . . Sheridan
LU 2463 Gillette. . . . . . Gillette
LU 2564 Wheatland . . . Wheatland
LU 2621 Cody . . . . Cody
LU 3781 Jackson . . . . . Jackson

LU 7135 Evanston. . . . Evanston
SA Wyoming. . . . . Casper

Rural Letter Carriers
LU Laramie . . . . Laramie
SA Wyoming. . . . . Cody

Steelworkers
LU 02-656 . . . . Shell
LU 08-574. . . . . Cheyenne
LU 08-952 . . . . Powell
LU 11-72 . . . . . . Rock Springs
LU 11-5427-S . . . . Rock Springs
LU 11-8499-S. . . . . . Green River
LU 11-8810-S . . . . . . Worland
LU 11-13214-S . . . . Green River
LU 11-13531-S . . . Diamondville
LU 11-15184-S . . . Rock Springs
LU 11-15320-S . . . Rock Springs

Theatrical Stage Employees
LU 426 . . . . Casper

Transportation Union
LU 28 . . . . Cheyenne
LU 446 . . . . Cheyenne
LU 465. . . . . Gillette
LU 866 . . . . Rawlins
LU 951 . . . . Sheridan
LU 1279 . . . . Greybull
LU 1280 . . . . Casper
LU 1857 . . . . Green River
SLB LO-57 Wyoming . . . Sheridan

Treasury Employees
CH 31 . . . . Cheyenne

Utility Workers
LU 127 . . . . Casper

Weather Service Employees
BR 03-5 . . . . Cheyenne
BR 03-20 . . . . Riverton
BR 03-43 . . . . Casper

Unaffiliated Labor Organizations
Western Energy Workers
   Union . . . . Rock Springs

Foreign

Affiliated Labor Organizations

Air Traffic Controllers
LU KWA. . . . . . Marshall Islands

Education
ASSN Teacher Education
Association Korea . . South Korea

LU OEA American Education
Association Okinawa . . . . Japan
LU OEA North East Asia Teachers
Association . . . . Japan

Federal Employees
LU 1363 . . . . South Korea

Government Employees
LU 3712 ID . . . . Italy

Sheet Metal Workers
C Mid-Western States Production
Workers . . . . Canada

Teachers
LU 1495 Naples Federation of
Teachers . . . . Italy
LU 1619 Vincenza Federation . Italy
LU 1628 Izmir Federation of
Teachers . . . . Turkey

LU 1862 Rota Chapter
Overseas. . . . . Spain

Unaffiliated Labor Organizations
Major Indoor Lacrosse League
Players Association . . . . Canada
Professional Hockey Players
Association . . . . Canada

PART IV. American Federation of Labor-Congress of Industrial Organizations (AFL-CIO)

American Federation of Labor-Congress of Industrial Organizations

815 16th St., N.W.
Washington, DC 20006
Phone: (202) 637-5000
Fax: (202) 637-5058
Web: www.aflcio.org
Convention: Quadrennially (2005)
Publication: *America@work*

President: John J. Sweeney

Secretary-Treasurer: Richard L. Trumka

Executive Vice President: Linda Chavez-Thompson

Executive Council

Baxter M. Atkinson
    President, American Federation of School Administrators
John M. Bowers
    President, International Longshoremen's Association
Andrea E. Brooks
    National Vice President for Women and Fair Practices, American Federation of Government Employees
R. Thomas Buffenbarger
    President, International Association of Machinists and Aerospace Workers
Elizabeth Bunn
    Secretary-Treasurer, United Automobile, Aerospace and Agricultural Implement Workers of America
William Burrus
    President, American Postal Workers Union
Larry Cohen
    President, Communications Workers of America
John J. Flynn
    President, International Union of Bricklayers and Allied Craftworkers
Patricia A. Friend
    President, Association of Flight Attendants
John Gage
    President, American Federation of Government Employees
Warren S. George
    President, Amalgamated Transit Union

Leo W. Gerard
    President, United Steel, Paper and Forestry, Rubber, Manufacturing, Energy, Allied Industrial and Service Workers International Union
Ron Gettelfinger
    President, United Automobile, Aerospace and Agricultural Implement Workers of America
Vincent J. Giblin
    President, International Union of Operating Engineers
Melissa Gilbert
    Former President, Screen Actors Guild
Michael Goodwin
    President, Office and Professional Employees International Union
Edwin D. Hill
    President, International Brotherhood of Electrical Workers
William P. Hite
    General President, United Association of Journeymen and Apprentices of the Plumbing and Pipe Fitting Industry of the United States and Canada
Joseph J. Hunt
    President, International Association of Bridge, Structural, Ornamental and Reinforcing Iron Workers
Frank Hurt
    President, Bakery, Confectionery, Tobacco Workers and Grain Millers International Union
Cheryl L. Johnson, R.N.
    President, United American Nurses

Gregory J. Junemann
    President, International Federation of Professional and Technical Engineers
Nat LaCour
    Secretary-Treasurer, American Federation of Teachers
William Lucy
    Secretary-Treasurer, American Federation of State, County and Municipal Employees
Leon Lynch
    Former Vice President, United Steel, Paper and Forestry, Rubber, Manufacturing, Energy, Allied Industrial and Service Workers International Union
Michael J. Sullivan
    President, Sheet Metal Workers International Association
Paul C. Thompson
    President, United Transportation Union
Gene Upshaw
    President, Federation of Professional Athletes
James A. Williams
    President, International Union of Painters and Allied Trades
Capt. Duane Woerth
    President, Air Line Pilots Association International
Nancy Wohlforth
    Secretary-Treasurer, Office and Professional Employees International Union
William H. Young
    President, National Association of Letter Carriers

Trade and Industrial Departments

Building and Construction Trades Department
815 16th St., N.W., Suite 600,
Washington, DC 20006
Phone: (202) 347-1461
Fax: (202) 628-0724
Web: www.buildingtrades.org
President: Edward C. Sullivan
Secretary-Treasurer: Sean McGarvey

Food and Allied Service Trades Department
1925 K St., N.W., Suite 400,
Washington, DC 20006
Phone: (202) 737-7200
Fax: (202) 737-7208
Web: www.fastaflcio.org
President: Jeffrey L. Fiedler
Secretary-Treasurer: Gene Bruskin

Maritime Trades Department
815 16th St., N.W., Washington, DC
20006
Phone: (202) 628-6300
Fax: (202) 637-3989
Executive Secretary-Treasurer: Frank
Pecquex

Metal Trades Department
888 16th St., N.W., Suite 690,
Washington, DC 20006
Phone: (202) 974-8030
Fax: (202) 974-8035
Web: www.metaltrades.org
President: Ronald Ault

Professional Employees, Department for
1025 Vermont Ave., N.W., Suite 1030,
Washington, DC 20005
Phone: (202) 638-0320
Fax: (202) 628-4379
Web: www.dpeaflcio.org
President: Paul E. Almeida
First Vice President: William Lucy
Treasurer: Linda Foley

Transportation Trades Department
888 16th St., N.W., Suite 650,
Washington, DC 20006
Phone: (202) 628-9262
Fax: (202) 628-0391
Web: www.ttd.org
President: Edward Wytkind
Secretary-Treasurer: Michael A. Ingrao

Union Label and Service Trades Department
815 16th St., N.W., Washington, DC
20006
Phone: (202) 628-2131
Fax: (202) 638-1602
Web: www.unionlabel.org
President: Charles E. Mercer
Secretary-Treasurer: Matthew C. Bates

Field Mobilization and Community Services Regional Offices

Midwest Region

940 W. Adams St., Suite 404, Chicago, IL 60607
Phone: (312) 492-6569
Fax: (312) 492-6610
Area: Illinois, Indiana, Iowa, Kansas, Michigan, Minnesota, Missouri, Nebraska, North Dakota, Ohio, Oklahoma, South Dakota, Wisconsin
Director: Todd Anderson
Community Services Liaison: Nancy I. McCormick
6551 S. Base Rd., Lynn, IN 47355
Phone: (765) 874-1989
Fax: (765) 874-2710

Northeast Region

211 E. 43rd St., Room 300, New York, NY 10017
Phone: (212) 661-1555
Fax: (212) 661-5213
Area: Connecticut, Delaware, District of Columbia, Maine, Maryland, Massachusetts, New Hampshire, New Jersey, New York, Pennsylvania, Puerto Rico, Rhode Island, Vermont, West Virginia
Director: José Alvarez
Deputy Director: Merrilee Milstein
56 Town Line Rd., Rocky Hill, CT 06067
Phone: (860) 571-8467
Fax: (860) 529-2548
Community Services Liaison: William R. Hauenstein
2311 E. Tilden Rd., Harrisburg, PA 17112
Phone: (717) 657-9116
Fax: (717) 657-9747

Southern Region

2314 Sullivan Rd., Suite 100, College Park, GA 30337
Phone: (404) 766-5050
Fax: (404) 766-2049
Area: Alabama, Arkansas, Florida, Georgia, Kentucky, Louisiana, Mississippi, North Carolina, South Carolina, Tennessee, Texas, Virginia
Director: Ken Johnson
Deputy Director: Cathy Howell
Community Services Liaison: J. Robert Miller
2471 Beachview Dr., Grand Prairie, TX 75054
Phone: (682) 518-0673
Fax: (682) 518-0674

Western Region

2800 First Ave., Suite 220, Seattle, WA 98121
Phone: (206) 770-7666
Fax: (206) 448-9250
Area: Alaska, Arizona, California, Colorado, Hawaii, Idaho, Montana, Nevada, New Mexico, Oregon, Utah, Washington, Wyoming
Director: Ron Judd
Deputy Director: Jerry Acosta
5818 N. 7th St., Suite 200, Phoenix, AZ 85014
Phone: (602) 200-8325
Fax: (602) 789-9301
Community Services Liaison: Armando Olivas
3325 Wilshire Blvd., Suite 1208, Los Angeles, CA 90010
Phone: (213) 387-1974
Fax: (213) 387-3525

Allied Organizations

A. Philip Randolph Institute
815 16th St., N.W., Washington, DC 20006
Phone: (202) 508-3710
Fax: (202) 508-3711
Web: www.apri.org
President: Norman Hill

AFL-CIO Working for America Institute
815 16th St., N.W., Washington, DC 20006
Phone: (202) 508-3717
Fax: (202) 508-3719
Web: www.workingforamerica.org
President: John J. Sweeney
Secretary-Treasurer: Richard L. Trumka
Executive Director: Nancy Mills

Alliance for Retired Americans
815 16th St., N.W., 4th Floor, Washington, DC 20006
Phone: (202) 637-5399
Web: www.retiredamericans.org
President: George J. Kourpias
Secretary-Treasurer: Ruben Burks
Executive Director: Edward F. Coyle

American Center for International Labor Solidarity
1925 K St., N.W., Suite 300, Washington, DC 20006
Phone: (202) 778-4500
Fax: (202) 778-4525
Web: www.solidaritycenter.org
Chair: John J. Sweeney
Vice-Chair: William Lucy
Secretary-Treasurer: Richard L. Trumka
Executive Director: Barbara Shailor

Asian Pacific American Labor Alliance
815 16th St., N.W., Washington, DC 20006
Phone: (202) 974-8051
Fax: (202) 974-8056
Web: www.apalanet.org
President: Tony Saguibo, Jr.
Executive Director: Juliet Huang

Coalition of Black Trade Unionists
1625 L St., N.W., Washington, DC 20036
Phone: (202) 429-1203
Fax: (202) 429-1102
Web: www.cbtu.org
President: William Lucy
Executive Director: Michael Williams

Coalition of Labor Union Women
815 16th St., N.W., 2nd Floor, Washington, DC 20006
Phone: (202) 508-6969
Fax: (202) 508-6968
Web: www.cluw.org
President: Marsha Zakowski
Executive Director: Carol Rosenblatt

International Labor Communications Association
815 16th St., N.W., 4 North, Washington, DC 20006
Phone: (202) 637-5068
Fax: (202) 637-5069
Web: www.ilcaonline.org
President: Steve Stallone
Secretary-Treasurer: Michael Kuchta

Labor Council for Latin American Advancement
815 16th St., N.W., 4th Floor, Washington, DC 20006
Phone: (202) 508-6919
Fax: (202) 508-6922
Web: www.lclaa.org
President: Milton Rosado
Executive Director: Jesse Rios

National Labor College
10000 New Hampshire Ave., Silver Spring, MD 20903
Phone: (301) 431-6400;
(800) 462-4237
Fax: (301) 431-5411
Web: www.georgemeany.org
President: Susan J. Schurman, Ph.D.

Pride at Work
815 16th St., N.W., Washington, DC 20006
Phone: (202) 637-5014
Fax: (202) 508-6923
Web: www.prideatwork.org
Co-President: Josh Cazares
Co-President: Nancy Wohlforth

Union Privilege
1125 15th St., N.W., Suite 300, Washington, DC 20005
Phone: (202) 293-5330;
(800) 452-9425
Fax: (202) 293-5311
Web: www.unionprivilege.org
Chair: John J. Sweeney
Vice Chair: Linda Chavez-Thompson
Vice Chair: Richard L. Trumka
President: Leslie A. Tolf

State Federations

Alabama AFL-CIO
435 S. McDonough St., Montgomery, AL 36104
Phone: (334) 834-1061
Fax: (334) 834-1065
Web: www.alaflcio.com
President: D. Stewart Burkhalter
Secretary-Treasurer: Al Henley

Alaska State AFL-CIO
2501 Commercial Dr., Anchorage, AK 99501
Phone: (907) 258-6284
Fax: (907) 274-0570
Executive President: Jim Sampson
Secretary-Treasurer: Bruce Ludwig

Arizona AFL-CIO
5818 N. 7th St., Suite 200, Phoenix, AZ 85014
Phone: (602) 631-4488
Fax: (602) 631-4490
Web: www.azaflcio.org
Executive Director: Michael McGrath
President: Rebekah Friend

Arkansas AFL-CIO
1115 Bishop St., Little Rock, AR 72202
Phone: (501) 375-9101
Fax: (501) 375-8217
Web: www.arkansasafl-cio.org
President: Alan B. Hughes
Secretary-Treasurer: Jean Lee

California Labor Federation, AFL-CIO
600 Grand Ave., Suite 410, Oakland, CA 94610
Phone: (510) 663-4000
Fax: (510) 663-4099
Web: www.calaborfed.org
Executive Secretary-Treasurer: Art Pulaski
President: Connie Leyva

Colorado AFL-CIO
140 Sheridan Blvd., Suite 201, Denver, CO 80226
Phone: (303) 433-2100
Fax: (303) 433-1260
Web: www.coaflcio.org
President: Steve Adams
Secretary-Treasurer: Paul J. Mendrick

Connecticut AFL-CIO
56 Town Line Rd., Rocky Hill, CT 06067
Phone: (860) 571-6191
Fax: (860) 571-6190
Web: www.ctaflcio.org
President: John Olsen
Secretary-Treasurer: Lori Pelletier

Delaware State AFL-CIO
698 Old Baltimore Pike, Newark, DE 19702
Phone: (302) 283-1330
Fax: (302) 283-1335
Web: www.deaflcio.com
President: Samuel E. Lathem
Secretary-Treasurer: E. Jackie Canada-Reaves

Florida AFL-CIO
135 S. Monroe St., Tallahassee, FL 32301
Phone: (850) 224-6926
Fax: (850) 224-2266
Web: www.flaflcio.org
President: Cynthia Hall
Secretary-Treasurer: Dwayne Sealy

Georgia State AFL-CIO
501 Pulliam St., S.W., Suite 549, Atlanta, GA 30312
Phone: (404) 525-2793
Fax: (404) 525-5983
Web: www.gaaflcio.org
President: Richard A. Ray
Secretary-Treasurer: Charlie Key

Hawaii State AFL-CIO
320 Ward Ave., Suite 209, Honolulu, HI 96814
Phone: (808) 597-1441
Fax: (808) 593-2149
Web: www.hawaflcio.org
President: Randy P. Perreira

Idaho State AFL-CIO
412 E. 41st St., Suite 5, Boise, ID 83714
Phone: (208) 321-4814
Fax: (208) 321-4827
Web: www.idaflcio.org
President: David Whaley
Secretary-Treasurer: Cindy Hedge

Illinois AFL-CIO
55 W. Wacker Dr., Suite 716, Chicago, IL 60601
Phone: (312) 251-1414
Fax: (312) 251-1420
Web: www.ilafl-cio.org
President: Margaret Blackshere
Secretary-Treasurer: Michael T. Carrigan

Indiana State AFL-CIO
1701 W. 18th St., Indianapolis, IN 46202
Phone: (317) 632-9147
Fax: (317) 638-1217
Web: www.inaflcio.org
President: Ken Zeller
Secretary-Treasurer: Joe Breedlove

Iowa Federation of Labor, AFL-CIO
2000 Walker St., Suite A, Des Moines, IA 50317
Phone: (515) 262-9571
Fax: (515) 262-9573
Web: www.iowaaflcio.org
President: Mark Smith
Secretary-Treasurer: Ken Sagar

Kansas AFL-CIO
2131 S.W. 36th St., Topeka, KS 66611
Phone: (785) 267-0100
Fax: (785) 267-2775
Web: www.kansasaflcio.org
President: Ron Eldridge
Executive Secretary-Treasurer: Jim DeHoff

Kentucky State AFL-CIO
340 Democrat Dr., Frankfort, KY 40601
Phone: (502) 695-6172
Fax: (502) 695-6176
Web: www.kyaflcio.org
President: William Londrigan
Secretary-Treasurer: Larry Jaggers

Louisiana AFL-CIO
P.O. Box 3477, Baton Rouge, LA 70821
Phone: (225) 383-5741
Fax: (225) 383-8847
President: Louis Reine

Maine AFL-CIO
P.O. Box 2669, Bangor, ME 04402
Phone: (207) 947-0006
Fax: (207) 623-4137
Web: www.maineaflcio.org
President: Edward Gorham
Secretary-Treasurer: Ned McCann

Maryland State and D.C. AFL-CIO
7 School St., Annapolis, MD 21401
Phone: (410) 269-1940
Fax: (410) 280-2956
Web: www.mddcaflcio.org
President: Fred Mason
Secretary-Treasurer: Donna Edwards

Massachusetts AFL-CIO
389 Main St., Malden, MA 02148
Phone: (718) 324-8230
Fax: (718) 324-4010
Web: www.massaflcio.org
President: Robert J. Haynes
Treasurer: Kathleen A. Casavant

Michigan State AFL-CIO
419 Washington Sq. S., Suite 200,
Lansing, MI 48933
Phone: (517) 487-5966
Fax: (517) 487-5213
Web: www.miaflcio.org
President: Mark Gaffney
Secretary-Treasurer: Tina Abbott

Minnesota AFL-CIO
175 Aurora Ave., St. Paul, MN 55103
Phone: (651) 227-7647
Fax: (651) 227-3801
Web: www.mnaflcio.org
President: Ray Waldron
Secretary-Treasurer: Steve Hunter

Mississippi AFL-CIO
826 N. West St., Jackson, MS 39202
Phone: (601) 948-0517
Fax: (601) 948-8588
President: Robert Shaffer

Missouri AFL-CIO
227 Jefferson St., Jefferson City, MO
65101
Phone: (573) 634-2115
Fax: (573) 634-5618
Web: www.moaflcio.org
President: Hugh M. McVey
Secretary-Treasurer: Herb Johnson

Montana State AFL-CIO
P.O. Box 1176, Helena, MT 59624
Phone: (406) 442-1708
Fax: (406) 449-3324
Web: www.mtaflcio.org
Executive Secretary: Jim McGarvey
President: Jacquie Helt

Nebraska State AFL-CIO
5418 S. 27th St., Suite 1, Omaha, NE
68107
Phone: (402) 734-1300
Fax: (402) 734-1205
President: Ken Mass
Secretary-Treasurer: James Tylski

Nevada State AFL-CIO
602 E. John St., Carson City, NV
89706
Phone: (775) 882-7490
Fax: (775) 882-1701
Web: www.aflcionevada.org
Executive Secretary-Treasurer: Danny L.
Thompson
President: Roberta West

New Hampshire AFL-CIO
161 Londonderry Tpke., Hooksett, NH
03106
Phone: (603) 623-7302
Fax: (603) 623-7304
Web: www.nhaflcio.org
President: Mark MacKenzie
Secretary-Treasurer: William Stetson

New Jersey State AFL-CIO
106 W. State St., Trenton, NJ 08608
Phone: (609) 989-8730
Fax: (609) 989-8734
Web: www.njaflcio.org
President: Charles Wowkanech
Secretary-Treasurer: Laurel Brennan

**New Mexico Federation of Labor,
AFL-CIO**
130 Alvarado Dr., N.E., Suite 200,
Albuquerque, NM 87108
Phone: (505) 262-2629
Fax: (505) 266-7155
Web: www.nmfl.org
Executive Director: Daniel Rivera
President: Christine Trujillo
Secretary-Treasurer: Michelle Gutierrez

New York State AFL-CIO
50 Broadway, 35th Floor, New York,
NY 10004
Phone: (212) 777-6040
Fax: (212) 777-8422
Web: www.nysaflcio.org
President: Denis M. Hughes

North Carolina State AFL-CIO
P.O. Box 10805, Raleigh, NC 27605
Phone: (919) 833-6678
Fax: (919) 828-2102
Web: www.aflcionc.org
President: James Andrews
Secretary-Treasurer: MaryBe McMillan

North Dakota AFL-CIO
1323 E. Front Ave., Bismarck, ND
58504
Phone: (701) 223-0784
Fax: (701) 223-9387
Web: www.ndaflcio.org
President: David Kemnitz

Ohio AFL-CIO
395 E. Broad St., Suite 300, Columbus,
OH 43215
Phone: (614) 224-8271
Fax: (614) 224-2671
Web: www.ohaflcio.org
President: William A. Burga
Secretary-Treasurer: Pierrette Talley

Oklahoma State AFL-CIO
501 N.E. 27th St., Oklahoma City, OK
73105
Phone: (405) 528-2409
Fax: (405) 525-2810
Web: www.okaflcio.org
President: Jimmy C. Curry

Oregon AFL-CIO
2110 State St., Salem, OR 97301
Phone: (503) 585-6320
Fax: (503) 585-1668
Web: www.oraflcio.org
President: Tom Chamberlain
Secretary-Treasurer: Barbara Byrd

Pennsylvania AFL-CIO
231 State St., 7th Floor, Harrisburg, PA
17101
Phone: (717) 231-2840
Fax: (717) 238-8541
Web: www.paaflcio.org
President: Bill George
Secretary-Treasurer: Richard W.
Bloomingdale

**Puerto Rico Federation of Labor,
AFL-CIO**
P.O. Box 19689, Fernandez Juncos
Sta., San Juan, PR 00910
Phone: (787) 764-2545
Fax: (787) 753-9676
President: José M. Rodriguez Baez

Rhode Island AFL-CIO
194 Smith St., Providence, RI 02908
Phone: (401) 751-7100
Fax: (401) 331-8533
Web: www.riafl-cio.org
President: Frank J. Montanaro
Secretary-Treasurer: George H. Nee

South Carolina AFL-CIO
254 LaTonea Dr., Columbia, SC 29210
Phone: (803) 798-8300
Fax: (803) 798-2231
Web: www.unionvoice.org/sclabor
President: Donna DeWitt
Secretary-Treasurer: Mike Godfrey
80 Persimmon Rd., Great Falls, SC
29055

South Dakota State Federation of Labor, AFL-CIO
P.O. Box 1445, Sioux Falls, SD 57101
Phone: (605) 339-7284
Fax: (605) 339-7285
President and Financial Secretary: Paul
Aylward

Tennessee AFL-CIO Labor Council
1901 Lindell Ave., Nashville, TN
37203
Phone: (615) 269-7111
Fax: (615) 269-8534
Web: www.tnaflcio.org
President: Lindsay Jerry Lee
Secretary-Treasurer: Eddie Bryan

Texas AFL-CIO
1106 Lavaca St., Suite 200, Austin, TX
78701
Phone: (512) 477-6195
Fax: (512) 477-2962
Web: www.texasaflcio.org
President: Emmett Sheppard
Secretary-Treasurer: Becky Moeller

Utah State AFL-CIO
2261 S. Redwood Rd., Suite M, Salt
Lake City, UT 84119
Phone: (801) 972-2771
Fax: (801) 972-9344
President and Secretary-Treasurer: Ed
Mayne

Vermont State Labor Council, AFL-CIO
P.O. Box 858, Montpelier, VT 05601
Phone: (802) 223-5229
Fax: (802) 223-1123
Web: www.vtafl-cio.org
President: Dan Brush
Secretary-Treasurer: Marty Scanlon

Virginia AFL-CIO
5400 Glenside Dr., Suite E, Richmond,
VA 23228
Phone: (804) 755-8001
Fax: (804) 755-8005
Web: www.va-aflcio.org
President: James R. Leaman
Secretary-Treasurer: Doris Crouse-Mays

Washington State Labor Council, AFL-CIO
314 First Ave., W., Seattle, WA 98119
Phone: (206) 281-8901
Fax: (206) 352-9415
Web: www.wslc.org
President: Rick S. Bender
Secretary-Treasurer: Alan O. Link

West Virginia AFL-CIO
501 Leon Sullivan Way, Suite 304,
Charleston, WV 25301
Phone: (304) 344-3557
Fax: (304) 344-3550
Web: www.wvaflcio.org
President: Kenneth M. Perdue
Secretary-Treasurer: Larry K. Matheney

Wisconsin State AFL-CIO
6333 W. Bluemound Rd., Milwaukee,
WI 53213
Phone: (414) 771-0700
Fax: (414) 771-1715
Web: www.wisaflcio.org
President: David Newby
Secretary-Treasurer: Phil Neuenfeldt

Wyoming State AFL-CIO
1021 W. 23rd St., Suite A, Cheyenne,
WY 82001
Phone: (307) 635-2823
Fax: (307) 635-8516
Web: www.wyomingaflcio.org
Executive Secretary: Kim A. Floyd
President: Dale Hill

Central Labor Councils

Alabama

Jefferson County Labor Council
210 Summit Pkwy., Birmingham, AL 35209
Phone: (205) 942-5252
Fax: (205) 942-3431

Mid-State Labor Council
200 Fulton Gap Cir., Sylacauga, AL 35150
Phone: (256) 245-2551

Montgomery Central Labor Council
475 George Ryals Rd., Titus, AL 36080
Phone: (334) 240-7151
Fax: (334) 567-8413

North Alabama Area Labor Council
108 Fontana Ln., Huntsville, AL 35811
Phone: (256) 461-8476

Northeast Alabama Labor Council
536 Hollingsworth Dr., Gadsden, AL 35905
Phone: (256) 492-2685

Shoals Area Central Labor Council
P.O. Box 831, Sheffield, AL 35660
Phone: (256) 383-2758
Fax: (256) 383-2758

Southwest Alabama Labor Council
P.O. Box 7688, Mobile, AL 36670
Phone: (251) 478-9060
Fax: (251) 476-0606

West Alabama Labor Council
15351 Sylvan Loop Rd., Foster, AL 35463
Phone: (205) 752-7395

West Central Alabama Labor Council
681 Outers Rd., Hamilton, AL 35570
Phone: (205) 622-3206

Wiregrass Labor Council
415 Christopher Dr., Dothan, AL 36301
Phone: (334) 792-6233

Alaska

Anchorage Central Labor Council
P.O. Box 91136, Anchorage, AK 99509
Phone: (907) 777-7248
Fax: (907) 777-7255

Fairbanks Central Labor Council
60 Hall St., Fairbanks, AK 99701
Phone: (907) 452-2300
Fax: (907) 452-2307

Juneau Central Labor Council
1751 Anka St., Juneau, AK 99801
Phone: (907) 586-2874
Fax: (907) 463-5116

Kenai Peninsula Central Labor Council
P.O. Box 1162, Kenai, AK 99611
Phone: (907) 283-4238

Ketchikan Central Labor Council
317 Stedman St., Suite A, Ketchikan, AK 99901
Phone: (907) 225-4010
Fax: (907) 225-3924

Arizona

Maricopa Area Labor Federation
5818 N. Seventh St., Phoenix, AZ 85014
Phone: (602) 631-4488

Nal-Nishii Federation of Labor
25 County Rte. 5817, Farmington, AZ 87401
Phone: (505) 598-8710
Fax: (505) 598-8698

Pima Area Labor Federation
369 W. Ajo Way, Tucson, AZ 85713
Phone: (520) 294-7696
Fax: (520) 294-4797

Arkansas

Central Arkansas Labor Council
1315 W. Second St., Little Rock, AR 72201
Phone: (501) 371-0424
Fax: (501) 374-8046

East Central Arkansas Labor Council
622 Mann St., Forrest City, AR 72335
Phone: (870) 633-5714

Jefferson County Trades and Labor Council
1504 Dancing Rapid Dr., Pine Bluff, AR 71603
Phone: (870) 247-9987
Fax: (870) 247-9635

Northeast Arkansas Central Trades and Labor Council
2996 Hwy. 115, Pocahontas, AR 72455
Phone: (870) 248-0027

Northwest Arkansas Joint Labor Council
1780 N. Walnut Ave., Fayetteville, AR 72701
Phone: (479) 466-1131
Fax: (479) 442-0134

Sebastian-Crawford Counties AFL-CIO Labor Council
P.O. Box 6251, Fort Smith, AR 72906
Phone: (479) 646-6143
Fax: (479) 646-8739

Texarkana Central Trades and Labor Council
1103 Grim St., Texarkana, AR 71854
Phone: (903) 278-8132

Union County Labor Council
P.O. Box 30, El Dorado, AR 71731
Phone: (870) 863-6169
Fax: (870) 862-6408

California

Alameda County AFL-CIO, Central Labor Council
100 Hegenberger Rd., Suite 150, Oakland, CA 94621
Phone: (510) 632-4242
Fax: (510) 632-3993

Butte and Glenn Counties AFL-CIO Central Labor Council
1009 Sycamore St., Chico, CA 95928
Phone: (530) 873-3680
Fax: (530) 873-3680
Web: www.northvalley.net/bgclc

Contra Costa County AFL-CIO, Central Labor Council
1333 Pine St., Suite E, Martinez, CA 94553
Phone: (925) 228-0161
Fax: (925) 228-0224
Web: www.cclabor.net

Five Counties Labor Council
900 Locust St., Room 7, Redding, CA 96001
Phone: (530) 241-0319
Fax: (530) 241-0319

Fresno-Madera-Tulare-Kings Central Labor Council
3485 W. Shaw Ave., Suite 101, Fresno, CA 93711
Phone: (559) 275-1151
Fax: (559) 276-2150

Humboldt and Del Norte Counties AFL-CIO, Central Labor Council
840 E St., Suite 9, Eureka, CA 95501
Phone: (707) 443-7371
Fax: (707) 443-0819

Kern, Inyo and Mono Counties Central Labor Council
200 W. Jeffrey St., Bakersfield, CA 93305
Phone: (661) 324-6451
Fax: (661) 327-8379

Los Angeles County Federation of Labor
2130 W. James M. Wood Blvd., Los Angeles, CA 90006
Phone: (213) 381-5611
Fax: (213) 383-0772

Marysville Central Labor Council
468 Century Park Dr., Yuba City, CA 95991
Phone: (530) 671-6228
Fax: (530) 671-4655

Merced-Mariposa County Central Labor Council
625 W. Olive Ave., Suite 103, Merced, CA 95348
Phone: (209) 722-3636
Fax: (209) 722-9640

Monterey Bay Central Labor Council
10353 Merritt St., Castroville, CA 95012
Phone: (831) 633-1869
Fax: (831) 633-1859
Web: www.mbclc.org

Napa and Solano Counties AFL-CIO, Central Labor Council
945 Empire St., Fairfield, CA 94533
Phone: (707) 428-1055
Fax: (707) 428-1393

North Bay Labor Council, AFL-CIO
1700 Corby Ave., Suite C, Santa Rosa, CA 95407
Phone: (707) 545-6970
Fax: (707) 544-6336
Web: northbayclc.home.mindspring.com

Orange County AFL-CIO, Central Labor Council
2020 W. Chapman Ave., Orange, CA 92868
Phone: (714) 385-1534
Fax: (714) 385-1544

Sacramento Central Labor Council
2840 El Centro Rd., Suite 111, Sacramento, CA 95833
Phone: (916) 927-9772
Fax: (916) 927-1643

San Bernardino and Riverside Counties, Central Labor Council
1074 E. La Cadena Dr., Suite 1, Riverside, CA 92501
Phone: (909) 825-7871
Fax: (909) 825-0110

San Diego-Imperial Counties Labor Council
4305 University Ave., Suite 340, San Diego, CA 92105
Phone: (619) 283-5411
Fax: (619) 283-2782
Web: www.unionyes.org

San Francisco Labor Council
1188 Franklin St., Suite 203, San Francisco, CA 94109
Phone: (415) 440-4809
Fax: (415) 440-9297
Web: www.sflaborcouncil.org

San Joaquin and Calaveras Counties, Central Labor Council
1045 N. El Dorado St., Suite 8, Stockton, CA 95202
Phone: (209) 948-5526
Fax: (209) 948-2652

San Mateo County Central Labor Council
1153 Chess Dr., Suite 200, Foster City, CA 94404
Phone: (650) 572-8848
Fax: (650) 572-2481

South Bay AFL-CIO, Labor Council
2102 Almaden Rd., Suite 107, San Jose, CA 95125
Phone: (408) 266-3790
Fax: (408) 266-2653
Web: www.atwork.org

Stanislaus and Tuolumne Counties Central Labor Council
1125 Kansas Ave., Modesto, CA 95351
Phone: (209) 523-8079
Fax: (209) 523-2619

Tri-Counties Central Labor Council
21 S. Dos Caminos St., Ventura, CA 93003
Phone: (805) 641-3712
Fax: (805) 643-9426

Colorado

Boulder Area Labor Council
P.O. Box 1106, Boulder, CO 80306
Phone: (303) 440-1309
Fax: (303) 365-0096

Colorado Springs Area Labor Council
2150 Naegele Rd., Colorado Springs, CO 80904
Phone: (719) 633-3872
Fax: (719) 633-2553
Web: www.csalc.com

Denver Area Labor Federation
140 Sheridan Blvd., Suite 304, Denver, CO 80226
Phone: (303) 477-6111
Fax: (303) 477-6123

Northern Colorado Central Labor Council
P.O. Box 271007, Fort Collins, CO 80527
Phone: (970) 222-4176
Fax: (970) 225-7874

Southern Colorado Labor Council
108 Broadway Ave., Pueblo, CO 81004
Phone: (719) 543-6053
Fax: (719) 542-7064

Western Colorado Trades and Labor Assembly
3123 Perkins Dr., Grand Junction, CO 81504
Phone: (970) 314-3572

Connecticut

Bristol Labor Council (Greater)
30 Walnut St., Bristol, CT 06010
Phone: (860) 493-1570
Fax: (860) 953-1777

Central Connecticut Labor Council
66 Mattabasset Dr., Meriden, CT 06450
Phone: (203) 634-8830

Danbury Central Labor Council
1 Padanaram Rd., Suite 114, Danbury, CT 06811
Phone: (203) 317-4750
Fax: (203) 748-2988

Fairfield County Labor Council
290 Post Rd. W., Westport, CT 06880
Phone: (203) 226-4751

Hartford Labor Council (Greater)
77 Huyshope Ave., Suite 210,
Hartford, CT 06106
Phone: (860) 727-8785
Fax: (860) 965-8098

New Britain Central Labor Council
29 N. Wellington St., New Britain, CT
06053
Phone: (860) 305-5917

**New Haven Central Labor Council
(Greater)**
267 Chapel St., New Haven, CT 06513
Phone: (203) 865-3259
Fax: (203) 776-6438

**Northeastern Connecticut Central Labor
Council**
167 Hickory Ln., Marlborough, CT
06447
Phone: (860) 295-8483

**Southeastern Connecticut Central Labor
Council**
P.O. Box 7275, Groton, CT 06340
Phone: (860) 448-0552
Fax: (860) 448-3721

**Western Connecticut Central Labor
Council**
P.O. Box 1027, Waterbury, CT 06721
Phone: (203) 756-1600
Fax: (203) 755-2120

District of Columbia

Metropolitan Washington Council
1925 K St., N.W., Suite 410,
Washington, DC 20006
Phone: (202) 756-4150
Fax: (202) 756-4151
Web: www.dclabor.org

Florida

Broward County AFL-CIO
1700 N.W. 66th Ave., Suite 100,
Plantation, FL 33313
Phone: (954) 327-9007
Fax: (954) 327-9081

Central Florida AFL-CIO
231 E. Colonial Dr., Orlando, FL
32801
Phone: (407) 649-8557
Fax: (407) 647-8510

**North Central Florida AFL-CIO, Central
Labor Council**
1910 N.W. 53rd Ave., Gainesville, FL
32653
Phone: (352) 372-6888
Fax: (352) 376-7114

North Florida Central Labor Council
P.O. Box 60188, Jacksonville, FL
32236
Phone: (904) 390-3242
Fax: (904) 390-7360

Northwest Florida Federation of Labor
Plaza Bldg., Suite 311, 3300 N. Pace
Blvd., Pensacola, FL 32505
Phone: (850) 433-0596
Fax: (850) 433-1991

Palm Beach-Treasure Coast AFL-CIO
1001 W. 15th St., Riviera Beach, FL
33404
Phone: (561) 841-8626
Fax: (561) 842-7652
Web: www.palmbeachtcaflcio.org

South Florida AFL-CIO
7910 N.W. 25th St., Suite 201, Doral,
FL 33122
Phone: (305) 593-8886
Fax: (305) 593-7806

Space Coast AFL-CIO Labor Council
P.O. Box 3787, Cocoa, FL 32924
Phone: (321) 631-0110
Fax: (321) 631-0103

West Central Florida Federation of Labor
10108 U.S. Hwy. 92 E., Tampa, FL
33610
Phone: (813) 740-2233
Fax: (813) 740-2234

Georgia

Albany/Southwest Georgia Labor Council
P.O. Box 50081, Albany, GA 31703
Phone: (229) 432-0799
Fax: (229) 435-3273

Athens Area Central Labor Council
227 Huntington Dr., Temple, GA 30179
Phone: (404) 584-0005
Fax: (404) 584-0009

**Atlanta-North Georgia Labor Council,
AFL-CIO**
501 Pulliam St., S.W., Suite 517,
Atlanta, GA 30312
Phone: (404) 525-3559
Fax: (678) 623-0158

Augusta Federation of Trades
1250 Reynolds St., Augusta, GA 30901
Phone: (706) 722-8087
Fax: (706) 724-9792

**Central Georgia Federation of Trades and
Labor Council**
P.O. Box 13385, Macon, GA 31208
Phone: (404) 584-0005
Fax: (404) 584-0009

**Northwest Georgia Labor Council,
AFL-CIO**
2315 Church Rd., Smyrna, GA 30080
Phone: (404) 794-7985
Fax: (404) 792-8025

**Savannah and Vicinity, AFL-CIO Trades
and Labor Assembly**
P.O. Box 22654, Savannah, GA 31403
Phone: (912) 507-8037
Fax: (912) 921-7802
Web: www.savannahclc.org

South Georgia Labor Council
P.O. Box 1447, Valdosta, GA 31603
Phone: (229) 559-7108

Southeast Georgia Central Labor Council
P.O. Box 5772, St. Mary's, GA 31558
Phone: (912) 269-0207

Idaho

Boise Central Trades and Labor Council
225 N. 16th St., Suite 114B, Boise, ID
83702
Phone: (208) 343-1561
Fax: (208) 429-6877

East Idaho Central Labor Council
4484 N. Fifth St., Idaho Falls, ID
83401
Phone: (208) 521-0075

**Lewiston, Idaho-Clarkston, Washington
Central Labor Council**
1618 Idaho St., Suite 102, Lewiston, ID
83501
Phone: (208) 746-7357

Magic Valley Central Labor Council
41 E. 700 N., Rupert, ID 83350
Phone: (208) 532-4386

Northern Idaho Central Labor Council
1802 N. Fifth St., Coeur d'Alene, ID
83814
Phone: (208) 667-6947

Pocatello Central Labor Union
P.O. Box 1574, Pocatello, ID 83204
Phone: (208) 232-6806
Fax: (208) 232-6807

Western Idaho Central Labor Council
3430 N. Buckboard Way, Boise, ID
83713
Phone: (208) 378-9749

Illinois

**Bloomington-Normal Trades and Labor
Assembly**
P.O. Box 3396, Bloomington, IL 61702
Phone: (309) 828-8813
Fax: (309) 829-0377
Web: www.bntrades.org

Champaign County AFL-CIO
404 W. Church St., Champaign, IL
61820
Phone: (217) 351-4810
Fax: (217) 328-4339

**Chicago Federation of Labor and
Industrial Union Council**
130 E. Randolph Dr., Suite 2600,
Chicago, IL 60601
Phone: (312) 222-1000
Fax: (312) 565-6769
Web: www.cflonline.org

**Decatur Trades and Labor Assembly,
AFL-CIO of Macon County**
P.O. Box 2847, Decatur, IL 62524
Phone: (217) 422-8953
Fax: (217) 422-8955

Elgin Trades Council
2400 Big Timber Rd., Bldg. B, Suite
202, Elgin, IL 60123
Phone: (847) 741-7430
Fax: (847) 741-1622

Galesburg Trades and Labor Assembly
2243 Grand Ave., Galesburg, IL 61401
Phone: (309) 342-7015

**Illinois Valley Federation of Labor,
AFL-CIO**
P.O. Box 17, LaSalle, IL 61301
Phone: (312) 952-1140
Fax: (815) 434-1240
Web: www.illinoisvalleyaflcio.org

Kankakee Federation of Labor
1390 Stanford Dr., Kankakee, IL 60901
Phone: (815) 932-1726
Fax: (815) 932-1840

**Madison County Federation of Labor
(Greater)**
132 S. Thorngate Dr., Granite City, IL
62040
Phone: (618) 931-1068
Fax: (618) 931-7657

Mideastern Illinois Labor Council
813 C St., Charleston, IL 61920
Phone: (217) 348-8366

North Central Illinois Labor Council
28600 Bella Vista Pkwy., Suite 1601,
Warrenville, IL 60555
Phone: (630) 393-0952
Fax: (630) 393-3560

**Northeastern Illinois Federation of Labor,
AFL-CIO**
248 Ambrogio Dr., Gurnee, IL 60031
Phone: (224) 628-2223

**Northwest Illinois Central Labor
Council**
214 W. Main St., Freeport, IL 61032
Phone: (815) 235-4030

**Quad-City, Illinois and Iowa Federation of
Labor**
311½ 21st St., Rock Island, IL 61201
Phone: (309) 788-1303
Fax: (309) 788-6433

Rockford United Labor
212 S. First St., Rockford, IL 61104
Phone: (815) 968-1411

**South Central Illinois Trades and Labor
Council**
3150 Deadmond Rd., Odin, IL 62870
Phone: (618) 548-5425
Fax: (618) 775-6210

Southern Illinois Central Labor Council
106 N. Monroe St., West Frankfort, IL
62896
Phone: (618) 932-2102
Fax: (618) 932-2311

**Southwestern Illinois Central Labor
Council**
1605 Mascoutah Ave., Belleville, IL
62220
Phone: (618) 235-1905
Fax: (618) 235-6898

**Springfield and Central Illinois Trades
and Labor Council**
P.O. Box 6128, Springfield, IL 62708
Phone: (217) 522-2100

Vermilion County Federation of Labor
P.O. Box 1575, Danville, IL 61834
Phone: (217) 260-9343

West Central Illinois Labor Council
400 N.E. Jefferson Ave., Suite 408,
Peoria, IL 61603
Phone: (309) 673-3691
Fax: (309) 673-4747

Western Trades and Labor Assembly
2929 N. Fifth St., Quincy, IL 62305
Phone: (217) 222-0497
Fax: (217) 222-1094

**Will-Grundy Counties Central Trades and
Labor Council**
724 Railroad St., Joliet, IL 60436
Phone: (815) 723-3232
Fax: (815) 723-3239

Indiana

Central Indiana Labor Council
1701 W. 18th St., Indianapolis, IN
46202
Phone: (317) 638-3455
Fax: (317) 638-1053

East Central Indiana AFL-CIO Council
2412 Briar Rd., Anderson, IN 46011
Phone: (765) 707-2038
Fax: (765) 643-3731

Grant County, Central Labor Union of
P.O. Box 5141, Huntington, IN 46750
Phone: (219) 358-3473

Hoosier Heartland Central Labor Council
357 W. Main St., Peru, IN 46970
Phone: (765) 473-9214

**Howard and Tipton Counties, Indiana,
Central Labor Council of**
P.O. Box 755, Kokomo, IN 46901
Phone: (765) 452-4866
Fax: (765) 452-4691

North Central Indiana AFL-CIO Council
209 Marycrest Bldg., 2015 Western
Ave., South Bend, IN 46629
Phone: (574) 289-6414
Fax: (574) 233-5543

Northeast Indiana Central Labor Council
1520 Profit Dr., Fort Wayne, IN 46808
Phone: (260) 482-5588
Fax: (260) 471-3957

Northwest Central Labor Council
2535 S. 30th St., Suite 8A, Lafayette,
IN 47909
Phone: (765) 742-2762
Fax: (765) 742-5792

Northwest Indiana Federation of Labor
6415 Kennedy Ave., Hammond, IN
46323
Phone: (219) 989-7920
Fax: (219) 989-7925
Web: www.nifl.info

**South Central Indiana Central Labor
Council**
2209 Glen Abbey, Jeffersonville, IN
47130
Phone: (502) 931-3799
Fax: (812) 282-4493

**Southern Indiana, Central Labor Council
of**
210 N. Fulton Ave., Evansville, IN
47710
Phone: (812) 422-2552
Fax: (812) 425-9797

Wabash Valley Central Labor Council
31 S. 13th St., Terre Haute, IN 47807
Phone: (812) 235-9559
Fax: (812) 235-9559

White River Central Labor Council
840 W. 17th St., Suite 9, Bloomington,
IN 47404
Phone: (812) 333-8494
Fax: (812) 333-6229

**Whitewater Valley Indiana AFL-CIO
Council**
813 W. Sixth St., Connersville, IN
47331
Phone: (765) 825-0859

Iowa

Black Hawk Union Council
1695 Burton Ave., Waterloo, IA 50703
Phone: (319) 232-2484
Fax: (319) 232-6845

Clinton Labor Congress
752 Breezy Point Dr., Clinton, IA
52732
Phone: (563) 243-2790

**Des Moines-Henry County Labor Council,
AFL-CIO**
315 Broadway St., West Burlington, IA
52655
Phone: (319) 754-7034

Dubuque Federation of Labor
1610 Garfield Ave., Dubuque, IA
52001
Phone: (563) 557-9823
Fax: (563) 583-9399

Hawkeye Labor Council
1211 Wiley Blvd., S.W., Cedar Rapids,
IA 52404
Phone: (319) 396-8461
Fax: (319) 396-3380

Iowa City Federation of Labor
102 Second Ave., Coralville, IA 52241
Phone: (319) 351-3238

Lee County Labor Council
1380 Francis Sartory Rd., Warsaw, IA
62379
Phone: (217) 256-3446
Fax: (319) 524-8028

North Central Federation of Labor
P.O. Box 387, Fort Dodge, IA 50501
Phone: (515) 955-8301

**North Iowa Nine Labor Council,
AFL-CIO**
P.O. Box 1531, Mason City, IA 50402
Phone: (641) 423-0883

Northwest Iowa Central Labor Council
3038 S. Lakeport Rd., Suite 100, Sioux
City, IA 51106
Phone: (712) 276-0473
Fax: (712) 276-2173

South Central Iowa Federation of Labor
300 E. Locust St., Suite 120, Des
Moines, IA 50309
Phone: (515) 265-1862
Fax: (515) 263-2670
Web: www.scifl.org

Southern Iowa Labor Council
411 N. Court St., Ottumwa, IA 52501
Phone: (641) 683-4630
Fax: (641) 683-6390

Southwest Iowa Labor Council
P.O. Box 351, Council Bluffs, IA
51502
Phone: (712) 242-2138

Kansas

Lawrence Central Labor Council
14805 27th St., Perry, KS 66073
Phone: (785) 843-7743
Fax: (785) 843-3421

Salina Central Labor Union
201 Hawkes St., Gypsum, KS 67448
Phone: (785) 493-0790
Fax: (785) 493-0898

Topeka Federation of Labor
P.O. Box 8630, Topeka, KS 66608
Phone: (785) 276-9078
Fax: (785) 276-9077

**Tri-County Labor Council of Eastern
Kansas**
7540 Leavenworth Rd., Kansas City,
KS 66109
Phone: (913) 334-3505
Fax: (913) 334-6660

**Wichita/Hutchinson Labor Federation of
Central Kansas**
3219 W. Central Ave., Wichita, KS
67203
Phone: (316) 941-4061
Fax: (316) 942-9840
Web: www.ksworkbeat.org

Kentucky

Ashland Area Labor Council
P.O. Box 932, Ashland, KY 41105
Phone: (606) 324-8701
Fax: (606) 324-8701

Bluegrass Central Labor Council
P.O. Box 54728, Lexington, KY 40555
Phone: (859) 273-3791

Frankfort Central Labor Council
P.O. Box 4054, Frankfort, KY 40604
Phone: (502) 875-2273
Fax: (502) 875-3597

**Louisville Central Labor Council,
AFL-CIO (Greater)**
1244 S. Fourth St., Louisville, KY
40203
Phone: (502) 635-2867
Fax: (502) 635-2842

**Northern Kentucky, AFL-CIO Labor
Council**
9670 Mary Ingles Hwy., California,
KY 41007
Phone: (859) 635-7954

Owensboro Council of Labor
530 Yale Pl., Box 620, Owensboro, KY
42301
Phone: (270) 233-0615

Pennyrile Area Central Labor Council
433 Linda Dr., Hopkinsville, KY 42240
Phone: (270) 886-5756

Tri-County Council of Labor
230 S. Alvasia St., Henderson, KY 42420
Phone: (270) 827-2511
Fax: (270) 831-1768

Western Kentucky AFL-CIO Area Council
300 Hathaway Trail, Paducah, KY 42003
Phone: (270) 395-3155
Fax: (270) 443-2914

Louisiana

Acadian Central Labor Council
P.O. Box 804, Scott, LA 70583
Phone: (318) 235-4370
Fax: (318) 234-1030

Baton Rouge AFL-CIO (Greater)
P.O. Box 267, Baton Rouge, LA 70821
Phone: (225) 687-3691
Fax: (225) 687-3691

New Orleans AFL-CIO (Greater)
837 N. Carrollton Ave., New Orleans, LA 70119
Phone: (504) 488-6544
Fax: (504) 482-6958
Web: www.gnoaflcio.org

Ouachita Parish Central Trades and Labor Council
P.O. Box 555, West Monroe, LA 71294
Phone: (318) 322-1886

Ruston and Vicinity, AFL-CIO, Central Trades and Labor Council
P.O. Box 653, Ruston, LA 71273
Phone: (318) 257-2603
Fax: (318) 257-2562

Shreveport and Vicinity Central Trades and Labor Council
3924 Greenwood Rd., Shreveport, LA 71109
Phone: (318) 631-4254
Fax: (318) 631-4299

Southwest Louisiana Central Trades and Labor Council (Lake Charles)
223 Stagecoach Ln., Sulphur, LA 70663
Phone: (337) 528-2553

St. Tammany, Tangipahoa and Washington Parishes
P.O. Box 8428, Metairie, LA 70011
Phone: (504) 885-3054
Fax: (504) 454-2584

Thibodaux Central Labor Council
21030 Hwy. 20, Vacherie, LA 70090
Phone: (225) 869-2535
Fax: (225) 869-2172

Maine

Bangor Labor Council (Greater)
20 Ivers St., Brewer, ME 04412
Phone: (207) 989-4141
Web: www.gbaclc.org

Central Maine Labor Council
P.O. Box 561, Oakland, ME 04963
Phone: (207) 622-3151
Fax: (207) 465-8289

Katahdin Labor Council
695 Hudson Rd., Glenburn, ME 04401
Phone: (207) 947-4318
Fax: (207) 723-5746

Southern Maine Labor Council
P.O. Box 3472, Portland, ME 04104
Phone: (207) 773-5760
Fax: (207) 773-5760

Maryland

Central Maryland AFL-CIO Council
511 E. Franklin St., Hagerstown, MD 21740
Phone: (301) 739-9500
Fax: (301) 739-6936

Del-Mar-Va Peninsula Central Labor Council, AFL-CIO
106 W. Circle Dr., Salisbury, MD 21801
Phone: (410) 742-0234
Fax: (302) 934-7868

Metropolitan Baltimore Council of AFL-CIO Unions
2701 W. Patapsco Ave., Suite 110, Baltimore, MD 21230
Phone: (410) 242-1300
Fax: (410) 247-3197

Western Maryland Central Labor Council
152-154 N. Mechanic St., Cumberland, MD 21502
Phone: (301) 777-1820
Fax: (301) 777-0121

Massachusetts

Berkshire Central Labor Council
45 Hazelwood Terr., Pittsfield, MA 01201
Phone: (413) 448-8962
Fax: (413) 442-4892

Boston Labor Council (Greater)
8 Beacon St., Boston, MA 02108
Phone: (617) 723-2370
Fax: (617) 723-2480

Central Massachusetts AFL-CIO
400 Washington St., Auburn, MA 01501
Phone: (508) 832-4218
Fax: (508) 832-4219

Hampshire/Franklin Labor Council
P.O. Box 925, Northampton, MA 01061
Phone: (413) 732-5122
Fax: (413) 732-1035

Merrimack Valley Central Labor Council
169 Merrimack St., 4th Floor, Lowell, MA 01852
Phone: (978) 937-9039
Fax: (978) 937-9544

Norfolk County Labor Council
P.O. Box 690429, Quincy, MA 02269
Phone: (617) 288-5730
Fax: (617) 825-5128

North Shore Labor Council
112 Exchange St., Lynn, MA 01901
Phone: (781) 595-2538
Fax: (781) 595-8770

North Worcester County Central Labor Council
P.O. Box 1585, Leominster, MA 01453
Phone: (978) 343-6792

Pioneer Valley Labor Council
640 Page Blvd., Springfield, MA 01104
Phone: (413) 732-7970
Fax: (413) 732-1881
Web: www.pvaflcio.org

Plymouth-Bristol Central Labor Council
P.O. Box 1043, Lakeville, MA 02347
Phone: (508) 668-7997
Fax: (508) 668-7997

Southeastern Massachusetts Labor Council (Greater)
867 State Rd., North Dartmouth, MA 02747
Phone: (508) 992-5475
Fax: (508) 992-0340
Web: www.gsmlaborcouncil.org

Michigan

Bay County Labor Council
1300 W. Thomas St., Bay City, MI 48706
Phone: (989) 684-5480

Delta County Trades and Labor Council
P.O. Box 411, Gladstone, MI 49837
Phone: (906) 428-4865
Fax: (906) 329-7242

Detroit AFL-CIO, Metropolitan
600 W. Lafayette Blvd., Suite 200, Detroit, MI 48226
Phone: (313) 961-0800
Fax: (313) 961-9776

Dickinson-Iron Counties Labor Council
P.O. Box 863, Iron Mountain, MI 48801
Phone: (906) 774-6070
Fax: (906) 774-1199

Eastern Upper Peninsula Central Labor Council
79 Evergreen Dr., Kincheloe, MI 49788
Phone: (906) 495-2928

Flint AFL-CIO Council (Greater)
P.O. Box 245, Flint, MI 48501
Phone: (810) 232-5412
Fax: (810) 232-5412

Huron Valley Central Labor Council
1612 W. Cross St., Ypsilanti, MI 48197
Phone: (734) 482-1824
Fax: (734) 485-7255

Jackson/Hillsdale Counties Central Labor Council, AFL-CIO
P.O. Box 1092, Jackson, MI 49204
Phone: (517) 592-8823
Fax: (517) 582-8750

Kent-Ionia Labor Council
918 Benjamin Ave., N.E., Grand Rapids, MI 49503
Phone: (616) 742-5526
Fax: (616) 456-0574

Lansing Labor Council (Greater)
419 S. Washington Sq., Suite 302, Lansing, MI 48933
Phone: (517) 485-5169
Fax: (517) 485-5322

Marquette County Labor Council
710 Chippewa Sq., Marquette, MI 49855
Phone: (906) 225-1122
Fax: (906) 225-1530

Mid-Michigan Labor Council
3834 E. Station Rd., Sheridan, MI 48884
Phone: (989) 261-4233

Midland County Labor Council
5954 E. Isabella County Line, Coleman, MI 48618
Phone: (989) 465-6495
Fax: (989) 667-0923

Monroe/Lenawee County AFL-CIO Council
41 W. Front St., Monroe, MI 48161
Phone: (734) 242-2646
Fax: (734) 850-4217

Northwest Upper Peninsula Labor Council
410 Diamond St., Ontonagon, MI 49953
Phone: (906) 884-4798

Saginaw Labor Council
805 Bridgeview S., Saginaw, MI 48604
Phone: (989) 771-9000
Fax: (989) 771-9003

South Central Michigan AFL-CIO Labor Council
5906 E. Morgan Rd., Battle Creek, MI 49017
Phone: (269) 968-0993
Fax: (269) 968-0025

Southwestern Michigan Labor Council
2122 Rockyweed Rd., Berrien Springs, MI 49103
Phone: (574) 287-8655

St. Clair County Labor Council
2441 W. Water St., Port Huron, MI 48060
Phone: (810) 984-3982
Fax: (810) 984-3982

Thumb Area Michigan AFL-CIO Labor Council
1700 W. Atwater Rd., Bad Axe, MI 48413
Phone: (989) 375-2772

Thunder Bay AFL-CIO Council
P.O. Box 55, Alpena, MI 49707
Phone: (989) 356-4767

Traverse Bay Area Central Labor Council
P.O. Box 5547, Traverse City, MI 49696
Phone: (231) 922-9910
Fax: (231) 263-3870
Web: www.tbaclc.org

West Michigan Labor Council
490 W. Western Ave., Muskegon, MI 49440
Phone: (231) 722-6303
Fax: (231) 726-6764

Minnesota

Albert Lea Trades and Labor Assembly
404 E. Main St., Albert Lea, MN 56007
Phone: (507) 373-5938
Fax: (507) 373-4471

Austin Central Labor Union
316 Fourth Ave., N.E., Austin, MN 55912
Phone: (507) 437-8647
Fax: (507) 437-3767

Bemidji Central Labor Union
P.O. Box 1715, Bemidji, MN 56619
Phone: (218) 854-7550

Brainerd AFL-CIO Trades and Labor Assembly
15815 County Rd. 25, N.E., Brainerd, MN 56401
Phone: (218) 829-0222
Fax: (218) 455-0687

Carlton County Central Labor Body
1217 28th St., Cloquet, MN 55720
Phone: (218) 879-9242

Central Minnesota AFL-CIO Trades and Labor Assembly
1903 Fourth St., N., St. Cloud, MN 56303
Phone: (320) 252-4654
Fax: (320) 252-1002

Duluth AFL-CIO Central Body
2002 London Rd., Room 110, Duluth, MN 55812
Phone: (218) 724-1413
Fax: (218) 724-1413

Iron Range Labor Assembly
P.O. Box 211, Mount Iron, MN 55768
Phone: (218) 728-5174
Fax: (218) 735-1164

Mankato South Central Labor Union
310 McKenzie St., S., Mankato, MN
56001
Phone: (507) 387-2672

Minneapolis Central Labor Union Council
312 Central Ave., S.E., Room 542,
Minneapolis, MN 55414
Phone: (612) 379-4206
Fax: (612) 379-1307
Web: www.minneapolisunions.org

Red Wing Area AFL-CIO Council
319½ W. Third St., Red Wing, MN
55066
Phone: (651) 388-3785
Fax: (612) 388-9469

Southeast Central Labor Council
11 Fourth St., S.E., Rochester, MN
55904
Phone: (507) 252-0145
Fax: (507) 252-0145

Southern Dakota County Labor Council
P.O. Box 240477, Apple Valley, MN
55124
Phone: (651) 336-6248
Fax: (651) 480-1489

Southwest Central Labor Council
500 W. Hatting St., Luverne, MN
56156
Phone: (507) 283-2016

**St. Croix Valley AFL-CIO Central Labor
Union**
700 Olive St., St. Paul, MN 55101
Phone: (651) 379-0211
Fax: (651) 645-8318

**St. Paul AFL-CIO Trades and Labor
Assembly**
411 Main St., Suite 202, St. Paul, MN
55102
Phone: (651) 222-3787
Fax: (651) 293-1989

**Willmar AFL-CIO Trades and Labor
Assembly**
77579 Meadowbrook Rd., W.,
Ortonville, MN 56278
Phone: (320) 839-2192

Mississippi

Central Mississippi Central Labor Union
P.O. Box 20265, Jackson, MS 39289
Phone: (601) 948-0517
Fax: (601) 786-9258

**Columbus and Vicinity AFL-CIO, Central
Labor Union**
P.O. Box 561, West Point, MS 39773
Phone: (662) 494-6173
Fax: (662) 494-0275

**Jackson County AFL-CIO, Central Labor
Union of**
P.O. Box 1247, Pascagoula, MS 39568
Phone: (228) 762-2155
Fax: (228) 762-3642

**Mississippi Pine Belt Central Labor
Council**
990 Hardy St., Hattiesburg, MS 39401
Phone: (601) 543-0861

Natchez Central Labor Council
410 Gayosa Ave., Natchez, MS 39120
Phone: (601) 442-1773

South Central Labor Union
221 N. Lang Ave., Long Beach, MS
39560
Phone: (228) 214-9886
Fax: (228) 214-9828

Tupelo Central Labor Union
P.O. Box 234, Amory, MS 38821
Phone: (662) 257-6519
Fax: (662) 257-4007

Missouri

**Cape Girardeau Central Trades and
Labor Council**
P.O. Box 1242, Cape Girardeau, MO
63702
Phone: (573) 334-9987
Fax: (573) 334-9987

Central Missouri Labor Council
611 N. Garth Ave., Columbia, MO
65203
Phone: (573) 449-5723

Jefferson City Central Labor Union
230 W. Dunklin St., Suite 206,
Jefferson City, MO 65101
Phone: (573) 635-3160
Fax: (573) 635-0091

Kansas City Labor Council (Greater)
1021 Pennsylvania Ave., Kansas City,
MO 64105
Phone: (816) 221-6163
Fax: (816) 221-4518

**Northeast Missouri Trades and Labor
Council**
P.O. Box 735, Fulton, MO 65251
Phone: (573) 592-0201
Fax: (573) 592-0221

**Northwest Missouri Central Labor
Council**
1222 S. 10th St., St. Joseph, MO 64503
Phone: (816) 232-5213

Sedalia Federation of Labor
117 S. Osage Ave., Sedalia, MO 65301
Phone: (660) 826-4415

Springfield Labor Council
2902 E. Division St., Springfield, MO
65803
Phone: (417) 866-2236
Fax: (417) 869-1814

St. Louis Labor Council (Greater)
3301 Hollenberg Dr., Bridgeton, MO
63044
Phone: (314) 291-8666
Fax: (314) 291-8676

Montana

Big Sky Central Labor Council
P.O. Box 466, Helena, MT 59624
Phone: (406) 439-8543

Central Montana Central Labor Council
1112 Seventh St., S., Great Falls, MT
59405
Phone: (406) 453-3377

Eastern Montana Central Labor Council
P.O. Box 703, Sidney, MT 59270
Phone: (406) 482-2364

**Flathead Area County Central Trades and
Labor Council**
P.O. Box 1011, Kalispell, MT 59903
Phone: (406) 752-5895
Fax: (406) 755-2296

Missoula Area Central Labor Council
208 E. Main St., Missoula, MT 59802
Phone: (406) 549-5931
Fax: (406) 549-6346

Northwestern Montana Central Labor Council
653 Flower Creek Rd., Libby, MT 59923
Phone: (406) 293-9240

South Central Montana Central Labor Council
P.O. Box 4056, Bozeman, MT 59772
Phone: (406) 585-8979

Southeastern Montana Central Labor Council
P.O. Box 5024, Forsyth, MT 59327
Phone: (406) 356-2757

Southwestern Montana Central Labor Council
P.O. Box 3173, Butte, MT 59702
Phone: (406) 494-3051
Fax: (406) 494-5790

Yellowstone Central Labor Council (Greater)
1417 Cedar Canyon Rd., Billings, MT 59101
Phone: (406) 256-6316

Nebraska

Central Nebraska Central Labor Council
6715 46th Ave., Connie, NE 68805
Phone: (308) 382-1103

Lincoln Central Labor Union
4625 Y St., Lincoln, NE 68503
Phone: (402) 466-5444
Fax: (402) 466-5444

Midwest Nebraska Central Labor Council
306 S. Ash St., North Platte, NE 69101
Phone: (308) 534-3017

Northeast Nebraska Central Labor Council
2410 Colorado Ave., Fremont, NE 68025
Phone: (402) 721-4558

Omaha Federation of Labor
Twin Towers, Suite 5E, 3000 Farnum St., Omaha, NE 68131
Phone: (402) 346-4800
Fax: (402) 346-6669

Western Nebraska Central Labor Union
6562 Brown Rd., Hemingford, NE 69348
Phone: (308) 487-3400

Nevada

North Eastern Nevada Central Labor Council
2261 S. Redwood Rd., Suite E, Salt Lake City, UT 84119
Phone: (801) 972-5714
Fax: (801) 886-2127

Northern Nevada Central Labor Council
1819 Hymer Ave., Suite 105, Sparks, NV 89431
Phone: (775) 355-9200
Fax: (775) 355-9934

Southern Nevada Central Labor Council
1701 Whitney Mesa Dr., Suite 101, Henderson, NV 89014
Phone: (702) 452-8799
Fax: (702) 452-9537

New Hampshire

Manchester, Central Labor Council of
1671 Brown Ave., Manchester, NH 03103
Phone: (603) 623-3273
Fax: (603) 645-8594

Nashua Labor Council
124 Boutwell St., Manchester, NH 03102
Phone: (603) 623-7302

New Jersey

Atlantic and Cape May Counties Central Labor Council
P.O. Box 1118, Hammonton, NJ 08037
Phone: (609) 704-8351
Fax: (609) 704-0621

Bergen County Central Trades and Labor Council
205 Robin Rd., Suite 220, Paramus, NJ 07652
Phone: (201) 967-5953
Fax: (201) 967-1547
Web: www.bergenclc.org

Burlington County Central Labor Union
510 Eighth St., Riverside, NJ 08075
Phone: (732) 287-4011
Fax: (732) 248-0353

Essex-West Hudson Labor Council
11 Fairfield Pl., West Caldwell, NJ 07006
Phone: (973) 244-5801
Fax: (973) 227-1868

Hudson County Central Labor Council
P.O. Box 17328, Jersey City, NJ 07307
Phone: (201) 583-1300
Fax: (201) 653-7050
Web: www.laborcouncil.org

Mercer County Labor Union Council
2 Iron Ore Rd. at Rte. 33, Englishtown, NJ 07726
Phone: (732) 792-0999
Fax: (732) 792-1999

Middlesex County AFL-CIO Labor Council
15 Debonis Dr., Milltown, NJ 08850
Phone: (609) 989-8730
Fax: (732) 545-4481

Monmouth and Ocean Counties Central Labor Union
846 Paul Dr., Suite U, Toms River, NJ 08753
Phone: (732) 349-1779
Fax: (732) 349-1789

Passaic County Labor Council
1389 Broad St., Clifton, NJ 07013
Phone: (973) 777-3700
Fax: (973) 777-3430

Somerset County Central Labor Council
61 Woodhill St., Somerset, NJ 08873
Phone: (732) 418-3308
Fax: (732) 940-7096

Southern New Jersey Central Labor Council
4212 Beacon Ave., Pennsauken, NJ 08109
Phone: (856) 663-1555
Fax: (856) 663-1511
Web: www.snjaflcio.org

Union County AFL-CIO Council
35 Fadem Rd., Springfield, NJ 07081
Phone: (908) 400-2100
Fax: (973) 258-1240

Warren-Hunterdon Counties Central Labor Union
792 Chimney Rock Rd., Suite H, Martinsville, NJ 08836
Phone: (732) 748-2008
Fax: (732) 748-2016

New Mexico

Central New Mexico Central Labor Council
1209 Hall Ct., S.W., Albuquerque, NM 87105
Phone: (505) 877-5986

Four Corners Central Labor Council
P.O. Box 2567, Farmington, NM 87499
Phone: (505) 325-7012

Northern New Mexico Central Labor Council
510 San Pedro Dr., S.E., Albuquerque, NM 87108
Phone: (505) 265-1513

Southwestern New Mexico Central Labor Council, AFL-CIO
P.O. Box 1807, Las Cruces, NM 88004
Phone: (505) 266-5878
Fax: (505) 266-5879

New York

Albany Central Federation of Labor
890 Third St., Albany, NY 12206
Phone: (518) 489-5791
Fax: (518) 453-3588

Broome County Federation of Labor
2614 Grandview Pl., Endicott, NY 13760
Phone: (607) 658-9285
Fax: (607) 658-9283

Buffalo AFL-CIO Council
295 Main St., Room 832, Buffalo, NY 14203
Phone: (716) 852-0375
Fax: (716) 855-1802

Capital District Area Labor Federation
24 Fourth St., Troy, NY 12180
Phone: (518) 272-1000
Fax: (518) 272-3501
Web: www.cdalf.org

Cattaraugus-Allegany Counties Central Labor Council
67 Waverly St., Cattaraugus, NY 14719
Phone: (716) 257-3610

Cayuga County Labor Council
18 Asbury Rd., Lansing, NY 14882
Phone: (607) 256-9398
Fax: (315) 702-9791

Central New York Area Labor Federation
404 Oak St., Suite 130, Syracuse, NY 13203
Phone: (315) 422-3363
Fax: (315) 422-2260

Central New York Labor Council
270 Genesee St., Utica, NY 13502
Phone: (315) 735-6101
Fax: (315) 797-3329

Chemung County AFL-CIO Assembly
459 E. Church St., Elmira, NY 14901
Phone: (607) 734-8290
Fax: (607) 734-8219

Dunkirk Area Labor Council
133 S. Martin St., Dunkirk, NY 14048
Phone: (716) 366-1485
Fax: (716) 366-7360

Dutchess County Central Labor Council
157 Van Wagner Rd., Poughkeepsie, NY 12603
Phone: (845) 451-6065
Fax: (845) 485-6501

Glens Falls Central Labor Council (Greater)
P.O. Box 3294, Glens Falls, NY 12801
Phone: (518) 785-1900
Fax: (518) 785-1814

Hudson Valley Area Labor Federation
P.O. Box 10663, Newburgh, NY 12552
Phone: (845) 567-7760
Fax: (845) 567-7742

Hudson-Catskill Central Labor Council of New York
64 Stacey Lee Dr., Newburgh, NY 12550
Phone: (845) 627-4073
Fax: (845) 569-2257

Jamestown Area AFL-CIO
6460 Charlotte Center Rd., Sinclairville, NY 14782
Phone: (716) 962-5024
Fax: (716) 942-4747

Jefferson, Lewis and St. Lawrence Counties Central Trades and Labor Council
32 Andrews St., Massena, NY 13662
Phone: (315) 764-0271
Fax: (315) 769-5839

Long Island Federation of Labor
1111 Rte. 110, Suite 320, Farmingdale, NY 11735
Phone: (631) 396-1170
Fax: (631) 396-1174

Mid-State Central Labor Council
16 Dart Dr., Ithaca, NY 14850
Phone: (607) 257-7199
Fax: (607) 272-4111

New York City Central Labor Council
31 West 15th St., 3rd Floor, New York, NY 10011
Phone: (212) 604-9552
Fax: (212) 604-9550
Web: www.nycclc.org

Niagara-Orleans Labor Council
26 Oliver St., Lockport, NY 14094
Phone: (716) 433-3489

Northeast Central Labor Council
73 Lafayette St., Plattsburgh, NY 12901
Phone: (518) 561-6135
Fax: (518) 561-6135

Oswego County Labor Council
182 Creamery Rd., Oswego, NY 13126
Phone: (315) 349-7359

Rochester and Vicinity Labor Council
30 N. Union St., Suite 204, Rochester, NY 14607
Phone: (585) 427-8787
Fax: (585) 427-2002

Rochester-Genesee Valley Area Labor Federation
30 N. Union St., Suite 204, Rochester, NY 14607
Phone: (585) 263-2650
Fax: (585) 427-2002

Rockland County Central Labor Union
9 Johnsons Highway, New City, NY 10956
Phone: (914) 634-4601
Fax: (914) 634-4924

Saratoga County Central Labor Council
36 Briarhurst Dr., Gansevoort, NY 12831
Phone: (518) 581-3600

Schenectady Area Central Labor Council
10 Ted Dr., Johnstown, NY 12095
Phone: (518) 399-7970
Fax: (518) 862-0561

Steuben-Livingston Central Labor Council, AFL-CIO
29 Lyons St., Bath, NY 14810
Phone: (607) 734-8290
Fax: (607) 734-8219

Syracuse Labor Council (Greater)
404 Oak St., Lower Level, Syracuse, NY 13203
Phone: (315) 422-3363
Fax: (315) 422-2260

Tri-County Labor Council
P.O. Box 187, Mount Upton, NY 13809
Phone: (607) 843-3134
Fax: (607) 786-5749

Troy Area Labor Council
43 Madonna Lake Rd., Cropseyville, NY 12052
Phone: (518) 279-3749

Upper Hudson Valley Labor Council
11 Fieldstone Dr., New Paltz, NY 12561
Phone: (914) 204-0305
Fax: (845) 485-7290

Westchester-Putnam Counties AFL-CIO Central Labor Body
200 Bloomingdale Rd., White Plains, NY 10605
Phone: (914) 948-3800
Fax: (914) 948-1843

Western New York Area Labor Federation
585 Aero Dr., Buffalo, NY 14225
Phone: (716) 565-0303
Fax: (716) 565-0306

North Carolina

Eastern North Carolina Central Labor Council
2 Thornes Farm Rd., Newport, NC 28570
Phone: (252) 464-7427
Fax: (252) 464-7234

Eastern Piedmont Central Labor Body
P.O. Box 2, Seaboard, NC 27876
Phone: (252) 537-1009

Sandhills Central Labor Council, AFL-CIO (Greater)
P.O. Box 9577, Fayetteville, NC 28311
Phone: (910) 630-2118
Fax: (910) 485-7909

Southeastern North Carolina Central Labor Council
1707 Castle Hayne Rd., Wilmington, NC 28401
Phone: (910) 343-9408
Fax: (910) 253-6727

Southern Piedmont Central Labor Council
3100C Piper Ln., Charlotte, NC 28208
Phone: (704) 953-3033
Fax: (704) 357-0029

Tri-Ad Central Labor Body Union
325 W. JJ Dr., Suite 201, Greensboro, NC 27406
Phone: (336) 335-6600

Triangle Labor Council
1408 Hillsborough St., Raleigh, NC 27605
Phone: (919) 306-4169
Fax: (919) 828-2102

Western North Carolina Central Labor Council
210 Haywood Rd., Asheville, NC 28806
Phone: (828) 225-2909
Fax: (828) 251-9682

North Dakota

Missouri Slope Central Labor Council
1323 E. Front Ave., Bismarck, ND 58504
Phone: (701) 224-9503

Northern Plains United Labor Council, AFL-CIO
3002 First Ave., N., Fargo, ND 58102
Phone: (701) 232-7304
Fax: (701) 235-2341

Northern Valley Labor Council
1714½ N. Washington St., Grand Forks, ND 58203
Phone: (701) 772-7404
Fax: (701) 772-7404

Northwest Labor Council (Greater)
P.O. Box 1906, Minot, ND 58702
Phone: (701) 852-3025
Fax: (701) 852-3026

Ohio

Ashland County Ohio Central Labor Council
179 Holbrook Ave., Ashland, OH 44805
Phone: (419) 281-6456

Ashtabula County AFL-CIO Labor Council
587 State Rte. 534 S., Geneva, OH 44041
Phone: (440) 992-1420
Fax: (440) 992-1422

Bay Area Labor Council
P.O. Box 1365, Sandusky, OH 44871

Belmont and Monroe Counties AFL-CIO Trades and Labor Council
56080 Matt's Hwy., Shadyside, OH 43947
Phone: (740) 676-5650
Fax: (740) 676-5680

Butler-Warren-Clinton Counties AFL-CIO Labor Council
3043 MacIntosh Ln., Middletown, OH 45044
Phone: (513) 360-0405
Fax: (513) 360-0405

Central Ohio Labor Council, AFL-CIO
1545 Alum Creek Dr., 2nd Floor, Columbus, OH 43209
Phone: (614) 257-1920
Fax: (614) 257-1929

Cincinnati AFL-CIO Labor Council
1014 Vine St., Suite 2575, Cincinnati, OH 45202
Phone: (513) 421-1846
Fax: (513) 345-8833
Web: www.cincinnatiaflcio.org

Cleveland AFL-CIO Federation of Labor
3250 Euclid Ave., Room 250, Cleveland, OH 44115
Phone: (216) 881-7200
Fax: (216) 881-9025
Web: www.clevelandaflcio.org

Columbiana County AFL-CIO Labor Council (Upper)
P.O. Box 69, Salem, OH 44460
Phone: (330) 332-9032
Fax: (330) 332-0871

Crawford County AFL-CIO Council
P.O. Box 681, Galion, OH 44833
Phone: (419) 468-4766
Fax: (419) 468-3077

Dayton, Springfield, Sidney, Miami Valley AFL-CIO Regional Labor Council
4127 E. Second St., Dayton, OH 45403
Phone: (937) 259-9814
Fax: (937) 259-9815

Grand Lake Ohio Central Labor Council
625 E. Ervin Rd., Van Wert, OH 45891

Hancock County AFL-CIO Council
1130 Summit St., Findlay, OH 45840
Phone: (419) 422-4224

Jefferson County Trades and Labor Assembly
7037 Scio Rd., S.W., Carrollton, OH 44615
Phone: (740) 282-0971
Fax: (330) 627-7382

Knox County Labor Council
14180 Beckley Rd., Mount Vernon, OH 43050
Phone: (740) 397-7454
Fax: (740) 393-8929

Lake County AFL-CIO Central Labor Council
9437 Hamilton Dr., Mentor, OH 44060
Phone: (216) 881-4680
Fax: (216) 352-6664

Lancaster Federation of Labor, AFL-CIO
2149 Lendale Dr., Lancaster, OH 43130
Phone: (740) 654-7820
Fax: (740) 689-0601

Lima Regional AFL-CIO Federation of Labor
637 Ilata Ave., Lima, OH 45805
Phone: (419) 222-6803
Fax: (419) 222-4966

Lorain County AFL-CIO Federation of Labor
105 Cooper Foster Park Rd., W., Lorain, OH 44053
Phone: (440) 233-7156
Fax: (440) 277-9929

Mid-Ohio AFL-CIO Council
974 Woodrow Ave., Marion, OH 43302
Phone: (740) 387-8141
Fax: (740) 387-1914

Muskingum County AFL-CIO Central Labor Council
1016 Wabash Ave., Zanesville, OH 43701
Phone: (740) 453-3612
Fax: (740) 450-7947

Newark Area AFL-CIO Council
P.O. Box 977, Newark, OH 43058
Phone: (740) 345-1765

Richland County (Ohio) Council, AFL-CIO
67 S. Walnut St., Mansfield, OH 44902
Phone: (419) 526-4688
Fax: (419) 522-0705

Ross County AFL-CIO Council
330 Red Bud Rd., Chillicothe, OH 45601
Phone: (740) 352-3889
Fax: (740) 384-6951

Sandusky County Labor Council
3058 County Rd. 195, Clyde, OH 43410
Phone: (419) 547-8073

Shawnee District AFL-CIO Council
P.O. Box 577, Portsmouth, OH 45662
Phone: (740) 353-5810
Fax: (740) 353-5770

Southeastern Ohio AFL-CIO Council
P.O. Box 571, Marietta, OH 45750
Phone: (740) 374-8014

Stark County AFL-CIO Council (Greater)
618 High Ave., N.W., Room 4, Canton, OH 44703
Phone: (330) 453-3624
Fax: (330) 453-3688

Tiffin Central Labor Union
182 Melmore St., Tiffin, OH 44883
Phone: (419) 447-2171
Fax: (419) 447-2171

Toledo Area AFL-CIO Council
2300 Ashland Ave., Toledo, OH 43620
Phone: (419) 241-1851
Fax: (419) 241-1823
Web: www.toledoaflcio.com

Tri County Regional Labor Council, AFL-CIO
720 Wolf Ledges Pkwy., No. 207, Akron, OH 44311
Phone: (330) 253-2111
Fax: (330) 253-4447

Trumbull County Federation of Labor
1265 N. Main St., Niles, OH 44446
Phone: (330) 792-4500
Fax: (330) 792-5240

Tuscarawas County AFL-CIO Council
P.O. Box 2274, Dover, OH 44622
Phone: (330) 343-0378

Wayne-Holmes Labor Council, AFL-CIO
14771 Oak Grove Dr., Doylestown, OH 44230
Phone: (330) 465-0743

Williams County AFL-CIO Labor Council
15100 County Rd. 15, Pioneer, OH 43554
Phone: (419) 737-2267

Youngstown AFL-CIO Council (Greater)
25 N. Canfield-Niles Rd., Suite 80, Youngstown, OH 44515
Phone: (330) 792-0861
Fax: (330) 793-0611

Oklahoma

Central Oklahoma Federation of Labor, AFL-CIO
3400 S. Western Ave., Oklahoma City, OK 73109
Phone: (405) 634-4030
Fax: (405) 634-3732

Northeastern Oklahoma Labor Council
123 W. 11th St., Suite 102, Tulsa, OK 74119
Phone: (918) 832-8128
Fax: (918) 295-5933

Oregon

Central Oregon Labor Council
P.O. Box 384, Bend, OR 97709
Phone: (541) 420-2937
Fax: (541) 318-1737

Clatsop County Central Labor Council, AFL-CIO
P.O. Box 55, Astoria, OR 97103
Phone: (503) 325-7874

Eastern Oregon Central Labor Council
1902 Third St., No. 102, La Grande, OR 97850
Phone: (541) 963-3203

Lane County Labor Council
1116 S. A St., Springfield, OR 97477
Phone: (541) 915-3100

Linn-Benton-Lincoln Labor Council
14514 S.E. Helen St., Jefferson, OR 97352
Phone: (541) 327-3638
Fax: (541) 327-3638

Marion, Polk and Yamhill Counties Central Labor Council
P.O. Box 13940, Salem, OR 97309
Phone: (503) 390-9628

Mid-Columbia Labor Council
4700 Orchard Rd., The Dalles, OR
97058
Phone: (541) 296-6161

Northwest Oregon Labor Council,
AFL-CIO
1125 S.E. Madison St., Suite 100-D,
Portland, OR 97214
Phone: (503) 235-9444
Fax: (503) 233-8259

Southeastern Oregon Central Labor
Council
3836 Altamont Dr., Klamath Falls, OR
97603
Phone: (541) 884-8106

Southern Oregon Central Labor Council
4480 Rogue Valley Hwy., Suite 3,
Central Point, OR 97502
Phone: (541) 664-0800
Fax: (541) 664-0806

Southwestern Oregon Central Labor
Council
3427 Ash St., North Bend, OR 97459
Phone: (541) 756-2559
Fax: (541) 756-5612

Umatilla-Morrow Central Labor Council
P.O. Box 788, Pendleton, OR 97801
Phone: (541) 276-0762
Fax: (541) 276-2953

Pennsylvania

Allegheny County Labor Council
Arrott Bldg., Suite 501, 401 Wood St.,
Pittsburgh, PA 15222
Phone: (412) 281-7450
Fax: (412) 765-2673

Beaver-Lawrence Central Labor Council
P.O. Box A, Beaver, PA 15009
Phone: (724) 770-0606
Fax: (412) 922-5649
Web: www.beavercountyaflcio.org

Blair-Bedford Central Labor Council
302 E. Wopsononock Ave., Altoona,
PA 16601
Phone: (814) 944-4081
Fax: (814) 944-7809

Bucks County Federation of Trade and
Industrial Council of Pennsylvania
1811 Farragut Ave., Bristol, PA 19007
Phone: (215) 788-8155
Fax: (215) 785-3934

Butler County United Labor Council
P.O. Box 2148, Butler, PA 16003
Phone: (724) 287-2104
Fax: (724) 285-7745

Central Pennsylvania Area Labor
Federation, AFL-CIO
4031 Executive Park Dr., Harrisburg,
PA 17111
Phone: (717) 564-5123

Chester County AFL-CIO Council
151 S. Gay St., Parkersburg, PA 19365
Phone: (610) 384-9180
Fax: (610) 384-9187

Clearfield, Elk, Cameron and Jefferson
County Trades and Labor Council
1598 Chestnut Grove Hwy., Grampian,
PA 16838
Phone: (814) 236-3614

Delaware County AFL-CIO Council
400 N. Springfield Rd., Clifton
Heights, PA 19018
Phone: (610) 623-0555
Fax: (610) 623-8957

Erie-Crawford Central Labor Council,
AFL-CIO
1701 State St., Erie, PA 16501
Phone: (814) 455-4752
Fax: (814) 455-4340

Fayette County Central Labor Union
268 Duff Rd., McClellandtown, PA
15458
Phone: (724) 439-0582
Fax: (724) 439-0757

Five County United Labor Council
50 Country Rd., Lewisburg, PA 17837
Phone: (570) 524-7171
Fax: (570) 742-9654

Harrisburg Region Central Labor Council
522 S. 22nd St., Harrisburg, PA 17104
Phone: (717) 561-7830
Fax: (717) 561-7831

Indiana-Armstrong-Clarion Central
Labor Council, AFL-CIO
P.O. Box 104, Indiana, PA 15705
Phone: (724) 479-8692
Fax: (724) 479-4010

Johnstown Regional Central Labor
Council
519 Somerset St., Johnstown, PA
15901
Phone: (814) 535-7621
Fax: (814) 535-7624

Lancaster United Labor Council
675 Manor St., Lancaster, PA 17603
Phone: (717) 392-2518
Fax: (717) 392-7594

Lehigh Valley Labor Council, AFL-CIO
P.O. Box 20226, Lehigh Valley, PA
18002
Phone: (610) 226-0710
Fax: (610) 266-0834
Web: www.lehighvalleyclc.org

McKean and Potter Counties Federation
of Labor
10 N. Third St., Bradford, PA 16701
Phone: (814) 368-3622
Fax: (814) 368-3622

Mercer County Central Labor Council
1380 Hofius Ln., Hermitage, PA 16148
Phone: (724) 346-3537
Fax: (724) 346-1006

Montgomery County AFL-CIO Union
Council
5416 Rising Sun Ave., Philadelphia,
PA 19120
Phone: (215) 329-8833
Fax: (215) 329-8668

Northeast Pennsylvania Area Labor
Federation, AFL-CIO
1258 O'Neill Highway, Dunmore, PA
18512
Phone: (570) 961-5394
Fax: (570) 961-1706

Northern Tier Central Labor Council
250 Commerce Park Dr., New
Columbia, PA 17856
Fax: (570) 998-8609

Northwestern Pennsylvania Area Labor
Federation, AFL-CIO
1276 Liberty St., Franklin, PA 16323
Phone: (724) 346-3537
Fax: (724) 346-1006

Philadelphia Council of the AFL-CIO
22 S. 22nd St., 2nd Floor, Philadelphia,
PA 19103
Phone: (215) 665-9800
Fax: (215) 665-1973
Web: www.phillyunions.com/aflcio

Reading and Berks County, United Labor
Council of
116 N. Fifth St., Reading, PA 19601
Phone: (610) 374-2725
Fax: (610) 374-6521
Web: www.berkslabor.org

Pennsylvania (continued)

Schuylkill County, United Labor Council of
P.O. Box 475, Pottsville, PA 17901
Phone: (570) 544-8134

Scranton Central Labor Union, Greater
AFSCME Bldg., 1258 O'Neill Hwy.,
Dunmore, PA 18512
Phone: (570) 346-9440
Fax: (570) 961-1706

Southeastern Area Labor Federation of Pennsylvania, AFL-CIO
3031 Walton Rd., Bldg. C, Plymouth
Meeting, PA 19462
Phone: (610) 489-1185
Fax: (610) 489-6988

Southwestern Pennsylvania Area Labor Federation, AFL-CIO
401 Wood St., Arrott Bldg., Suite 50,
Pittsburgh, PA 15222
Phone: (412) 281-7450
Fax: (412) 765-2673

Venango County Labor Council
1276 Liberty St., Franklin, PA 16323
Phone: (814) 437-7654
Fax: (814) 432-8393

Warren County Central Labor Council
P.O. Box 832, Warren, PA 16365
Phone: (814) 723-0709
Fax: (814) 723-4759

Washington/Greene County Central Labor Council
746 Glenn St., Canonsburg, PA 15317
Phone: (724) 514-3228
Fax: (724) 514-3236

Westmoreland County Labor Union Council (Greater)
2428 State Rte. 381 Rd., Rector, PA
15677
Phone: (724) 238-7406
Fax: (724) 238-7416

Wilkes-Barre Labor Council (Greater)
501 E. Main St., Wilkes-Barre, PA
18702
Phone: (570) 823-6716
Fax: (570) 825-2219

York/Adams County Central Labor Council
1490 Hametown Rd., Glen Rock, PA
17327
Phone: (717) 235-1777
Fax: (717) 235-1777
Web: www.yorkadamslabor.org

Rhode Island

Pawtucket and Central Falls Central Labor Council
129 Rosemont Ave., Pawtucket, RI
02861
Phone: (401) 722-7181
Fax: (401) 728-5588

Providence Central Federated Council
514 Colwell Rd., Harrisville, RI 02830
Phone: (401) 467-3323
Fax: (401) 467-9480

Woonsocket Labor Council (Greater)
P.O. Box 1584, Woonsocket, RI 02895
Phone: (401) 769-7759
Fax: (401) 766-8860

South Carolina

Catawba Central Labor Union
1582 S. Hwy. 161, York, SC 29745
Phone: (704) 357-0027
Fax: (704) 357-0029

Charleston Labor Council (Greater)
P.O. Box 60850, Charleston, SC 29419
Phone: (843) 324-6384
Fax: (775) 871-2866
Web: www.charlestonlaborcouncil.org

Columbia Central Labor Union, Greater
116 Woodlands Village Dr., Columbia,
SC 29229
Phone: (803) 798-8300
Fax: (803) 798-2231

South Dakota

Aberdeen Central Labor Union
13552 39th Ave., Bath, SD 57427

Rapid City Central Labor Council
4702 Baldwin St., Rapid City, SD
57702
Phone: (605) 721-7097
Fax: (605) 343-4324

Sioux Falls Trades and Labor Assembly
101 S. Fairfax Ave., Sioux Falls, SD
57103
Phone: (605) 338-3091

Watertown AFL-CIO Trades and Labor Assembly
106 Second St., S.E., Watertown, SD
57201
Phone: (605) 882-0547

Tennessee

Chattanooga Area Labor Council
3922 Volunteer Dr., Suite 3,
Chattanooga, TN 37416
Phone: (423) 899-0134

Jackson Central Labor Council
P.O. Box 223, McLemoresville, TN
38235
Phone: (731) 986-5975

Knoxville-Oak Ridge Area Central Labor Council
311 Morgan St., Knoxville, TN 37917
Phone: (865) 523-9752
Fax: (865) 523-9478

Memphis AFL-CIO Labor Council
3035 Director Row, Bldg. B, Suite
1207, Memphis, TN 38131
Phone: (901) 332-3531
Fax: (901) 332-3532

Nashville and Middle Tennessee Central Labor Council
P.O. Box 290153, Nashville, TN 37229
Phone: (615) 780-2413
Fax: (615) 885-7776

Upper East Tennessee Central Labor Council
221 Trace Ct., Kingsport, TN 37664
Phone: (423) 416-2929

Texas

Abilene/Big Country Central Labor Council, AFL-CIO
P.O. Box 3161, Abilene, TX 79604
Phone: (915) 670-9001
Fax: (915) 672-4820

Amarillo Central Labor Council, AFL-CIO
P.O. Box 387, Amarillo, TX 79105
Phone: (803) 373-4574
Fax: (806) 374-4437

Anderson County Area Central Labor Council
P.O. Box 4174, Palestine, TX 75802
Phone: (903) 723-3020
Fax: (903) 723-3483

Austin Area AFL-CIO Council
P.O. Box 87, Austin, TX 78767
Phone: (512) 472-2850
Fax: (512) 472-1190

Bell County Central Labor Council
P.O. Box 10277, Killeen, TX 76547
Phone: (254) 200-4578

Brazos Valley Central Labor Council
P.O. Box 1355, Bryan, TX 77806
Phone: (979) 779-1028
Fax: (979) 775-8460

Central Texas Labor Council
702 Franklin Ave., Waco, TX 76701
Phone: (254) 755-7111
Fax: (254) 752-4491

Coastal Bend Labor Council
1210 S. Staples St., Corpus Christi, TX
78404
Phone: (361) 883-6137
Fax: (361) 883-6750

Dallas AFL-CIO Council
1408 N. Washington Ave., Suite 240,
Dallas, TX 75204
Phone: (214) 826-4808
Fax: (214) 826-0570
Web: www.dallasaflcio.org

Deep East Texas Council of Labor
1319 Whitehouse Dr., Lufkin, TX 75901
Phone: (936) 632-3958
Fax: (936) 824-3524

**East Texas Central Labor Council
(Greater)**
P.O. Box 1842, Longview, TX 75606
Phone: (903) 753-7646
Fax: (903) 758-7222

El Paso Central Labor Union
6967 Commerce St., P.O. Box 971365,
El Paso, TX 79997
Phone: (915) 781-0242
Fax: (915) 781-0540

Ellis County Labor Council
112 Auburn St., Waxahachie, TX
75165
Phone: (972) 937-2664

Galveston County AFL-CIO
7912 Larkspur Dr., Texas City, TX
77591
Phone: (409) 370-8423
Fax: (409) 938-3418

**Harris County Central Labor Council,
AFL-CIO**
2506 Sutherland St., Houston, TX
77023
Phone: (713) 923-9473
Fax: (713) 923-5010
Web: www.hcaflcio.org

**Henderson-Navarro Central Labor
Council**
6210 County Rd. 3925, Athens, TX
75752
Phone: (214) 215-5636

Lubbock Central Labor Union
405 50th St., Lubbock, TX 79404
Phone: (806) 747-5287
Fax: (806) 744-7852

Montgomery County AFL-CIO
P.O. Box 7694, The Woodlands, TX
77387
Phone: (713) 853-4911
Fax: (713) 853-4913

Paris Central Labor Council
2285 N.W. 19th St., Paris, TX 75460
Phone: (903) 785-3686

Permian Basin Central Labor Union
P.O. Box 60222, Midland, TX 79711
Phone: (432) 563-0583

Rio Grande Valley Central Labor Union
218 N. First St., Donna, TX 78537
Phone: (956) 464-5556
Fax: (956) 787-7085

Sabine Area Central Labor Council
1500 Jefferson Dr., Port Arthur, TX
77642
Phone: (409) 982-8180
Fax: (409) 985-3519

San Antonio AFL-CIO Council
311 S. St. Mary's St., No. 15E, San
Antonio, TX 78205
Phone: (210) 226-8447
Fax: (210) 226-6285

Smith County Central Labor Council
19968 F.M. 3079, Chandler, TX
75758
Phone: (903) 849-6667
Fax: (903) 595-3469

Tarrant County Central Labor Council
4025 Rufe Snow Dr., Fort Worth, TX
76180
Phone: (817) 284-1462
Fax: (817) 595-4894
Web: www.tcclc.org

Tideland Central Labor Council
8441 Gulf Fwy., Suite 305, Houston,
TX 77017
Phone: (713) 681-6786
Fax: (713) 681-8426

Victoria Area Central Labor Council
P.O. Box 4665, Victoria, TX 77903
Phone: (361) 576-6655

Wichita Falls Trades and Labor Council
507 N. Second St., Apt. B, Iowa Park,
TX 76367
Phone: (940) 676-2823
Fax: (940) 723-7169

Utah

Central Utah Federation of Labor
2261 S. Redwood Rd., Suite M, Salt
Lake City, UT 84119
Phone: (801) 608-3345
Fax: (801) 973-4830

Northern Utah Central Labor Council
900 N. 400 W., Suite 4, North Salt
Lake, UT 84054
Phone: (801) 295-6198

Vermont

Champlain Valley Labor Council
P.O. Box 5841, Burlington, VT
05402
Phone: (802) 860-4376

Northeast Kingdom Labor Council
P.O. Box 214, St. Johnsbury Center,
VT 05863
Phone: (802) 626-9995
Fax: (802) 626-3276

Rutland-Addison Central Labor Council
136 Oak St., Rutland, VT 05701
Phone: (802) 775-1803

**Washington and Orange Counties Labor
Council**
55 E. Bear Swamp Rd., 4th Floor,
Middlesex, VT 05602
Phone: (802) 223-4172
Fax: (802) 223-4172

Windham County Labor Council
619 Hucklehill Rd., Vernon, VT 05345

Virginia

Central Virginia Labor Council
P.O. Box 2853, Lynchburg, VA
24501
Phone: (434) 846-4204
Fax: (434) 239-0352

New River Valley Central Labor Council
270 White Pine Dr., Christiansburg, VA 24073
Phone: (540) 381-1575
Fax: (540) 674-2531

Northern Virginia Central Labor Council, AFL-CIO
P.O. Box 565, Annandale, VA 22003
Phone: (703) 750-3633
Fax: (703) 941-6210

Portsmouth Central Labor Council
P.O. Box 2440, Portsmouth, VA 23702
Phone: (757) 485-4144
Fax: (757) 485-4144

Richmond Regional Labor Council
231 E. Belt Blvd., Richmond, VA 23224
Phone: (804) 232-2955
Fax: (804) 233-2965

Roanoke United Central Labor Council
1202 Jamison Ave., S.E., Roanoke, VA 24013
Phone: (540) 345-4581
Fax: (540) 345-1300

Shenandoah Valley Central Labor Council
P.O. Box 871, Verona, VA 24482
Phone: (540) 886-4750
Fax: (540) 885-8380

Tidewater Central Labor Council (Greater)
3620 Tidewater Dr., Norfolk, VA 23509
Phone: (757) 623-1246
Fax: (757) 640-8467

Virginia Peninsula Central Labor Council
2013 Cunningham Dr., Suite 331, Hampton, VA 23666
Phone: (757) 825-8660
Fax: (757) 825-8783

Washington

Clark, Skamania and West Klickitat Counties, Central Labor Council of
P.O. Box 61929, Vancouver, WA 98666
Phone: (360) 921-7484

Cowlitz-Wahkiakum Counties Labor Council
P.O. Box 430, Longview, WA 98632
Phone: (360) 423-0950
Fax: (360) 423-5498

Grays Harbor County Labor Council
P.O. Box 1109, Aberdeen, WA 98520
Phone: (360) 532-2643
Fax: (360) 532-7596

King County Labor Council
2800 First Ave., Suite 206, Seattle, WA 98121
Phone: (206) 441-8510
Fax: (206) 441-7103
Web: www.kclc.org

Kitsap County Central Labor Council
632 Fifth St., Suite 5, Bremerton, WA 98337
Phone: (360) 373-5800
Fax: (360) 373-5800

North Central Washington Central Labor Council
27 N. Chelan Ave., Wenatchee, WA 98801
Phone: (509) 662-7912
Fax: (509) 886-1020

Northwest Washington Central Labor Council
1700 N. State St., Suite 202, Bellingham, WA 98225
Phone: (360) 676-0099
Fax: (360) 733-8840

Olympic Labor Council
P.O. Box 688, Port Angeles, WA 98362
Phone: (360) 417-8964
Fax: (360) 417-8964

Pacific County Labor Council
1610 Fowler St., Raymond, WA 98577
Phone: (360) 942-3316

Pierce County Central Labor Council
3049 S. 36th St., Suite 201, Tacoma, WA 98409
Phone: (253) 473-3810
Fax: (253) 472-6050

Snohomish County Labor Council
2812 Lombard Ave., Suite 207, Everett, WA 98201
Phone: (425) 259-7922
Fax: (425) 339-9173
Web: www.snolabor.org

Southeastern Washington Labor Council
P.O. Box 1324, Pasco, WA 99301
Phone: (509) 547-7553

Spokane Regional Labor Council, AFL-CIO
1226 N. Howard St., Suite 103, Spokane, WA 99201
Phone: (509) 327-7637
Fax: (509) 327-2331

Thurston-Lewis-Mason Counties Labor Council
P.O. Box 66, Olympia, WA 98507
Phone: (360) 520-9575

Yakima South Central Counties Central Labor Council
507 S. Third St., Yakima, WA 98901
Phone: (509) 248-3894
Fax: (509) 248-3894

West Virginia

Brooke-Hancock Labor Council
P.O. Box 307, Newell, WV 26050
Phone: (330) 853-0767

Kanawha Valley Labor Council
600 Leon Sullivan Way, Charleston, WV 25301
Phone: (304) 343-6952
Fax: (304) 343-3930

Marion County AFL-CIO
P.O. Box 96, Kingmont, WV 26578
Phone: (304) 367-0316
Fax: (304) 367-0195

Marshall, Wetzel, Tyler Central Labor Council
P.O. Box 416, New Martinsville, WV 26155
Phone: (304) 455-5500
Fax: (304) 455-5500

Mason-Jackson-Roane Labor Council
112 Hall St., Ripley, WV 25271
Phone: (304) 372-5361

Monongalia-Preston Labor Council
P.O. Box 551, Morgantown, WV 26507
Phone: (304) 864-5857
Fax: (304) 291-3849

North Central West Virginia Labor Council, AFL-CIO
518 Kuhl Ave., Clarksburg, WV 26301
Phone: (304) 622-6125
Fax: (304) 623-5997

Ohio Valley Trades and Labor Assembly of Wheeling
3822 Eoff St., Wheeling, WV 26003
Phone: (304) 232-4567

Parkersburg Area Labor Council
P.O. Box 1566, Parkersburg, WV 26102
Phone: (304) 489-9376
Fax: (304) 422-4597

South Central AFL-CIO
P.O. Box 718, Beckley, WV 25801
Phone: (304) 465-1072
Fax: (304) 465-1072

Southwestern District Labor Council
1201 7th Ave., Huntington, WV 25701
Phone: (304) 523-2353
Fax: (304) 523-0756

Tri-County Central Labor Council
82 Essie Ln., Martinsburg, WV 25401
Phone: (304) 267-5703

Wisconsin

Ashland Area Trades and Labor Council
46833 Benson Rd., Ashland, WI 54806
Phone: (715) 682-7089
Fax: (715) 682-2075

Chippewa County Central Labor Council
647 W. Canal St., Chippewa Falls, WI 54729
Phone: (715) 723-9613

Dodge County Central Labor Council
108 Winn Terr., Beaver Dam, WI 53916
Phone: (920) 887-8871
Fax: (920) 887-0105

Eau Claire Area Council
2233 Birch St., Eau Claire, WI 54703
Phone: (715) 832-3320

Fond du Lac County Labor Council
50 E. Bank St., Fond du Lac, WI 54935
Phone: (920) 921-9977
Fax: (920) 921-3199

Fox Valley Area Labor Council
P.O. Box 186, Menasha, WI 54952
Phone: (920) 727-1790
Fax: (920) 727-1794

Green Bay Labor Council (Greater)
1570 Elizabeth St., Green Bay, WI 54302
Phone: (920) 432-0053
Fax: (920) 437-6091

Jefferson County Central Labor Council
829 McCoy Park Rd., Fort Atkinson, WI 53538
Phone: (920) 563-6888
Fax: (902) 648-8000

Kenosha AFL-CIO Council
3030 39th Ave., Room 121, Kenosha, WI 53144
Phone: (262) 697-4681
Fax: (262) 657-5242

Lakes Regional Labor Council
5029 City U, Newton, WI 54220
Phone: (920) 726-4697
Fax: (920) 684-3150

Marathon County Labor Council
318 S. Third Ave., Wausau, WI 54401
Phone: (715) 848-3320

Marinette, Wisconsin and Menominee, Michigan Labor Council
71 Hosmer St., Marinette, WI 54143
Phone: (715) 789-2466

Marshfield Central Labor Council, AFL-CIO
P.O. Box 987, Marshfield, WI 54449
Phone: (715) 384-3591

Milwaukee County Labor Council
633 S. Hawley Rd., Suite 110, Milwaukee, WI 53214
Phone: (414) 771-7070
Fax: (414) 771-0509

Northern Area Wisconsin Labor Council
N-15873 State Hwy. 13 N., Park Falls, WI 54552
Phone: (715) 762-3764

Ozaukee County Trades and Labor Council
124 E. Pierron St., Port Washington, WI 53074
Phone: (262) 284-5838

Racine AFL-CIO Council
136 13th Ave., Union Grove, WI 53182
Phone: (262) 636-9126
Fax: (262) 878-3876

Rock County Central Labor Council, AFL-CIO
1620 Shore Dr., Beloit, WI 53511
Phone: (608) 362-2812
Fax: (608) 362-1028

Sheboygan County Labor Council
1104 Wisconsin Ave., Sheboygan, WI 53081
Phone: (920) 452-0321
Fax: (920) 452-0347

South Central Federation of Labor
1602 S. Park St., Suite 228, Madison, WI 53715
Phone: (608) 256-5111
Fax: (608) 256-6661
Web: www.scfl.org

Stevens Point, Portage County Central Labor Council
P.O. Box 995, Stevens Point, WI 54481
Phone: (715) 341-1413

Superior Federation of Labor
1415 Elm Ave., Superior, WI 54880
Phone: (715) 394-2896

Walworth County Central Labor Council
5102 Mound Rd., Elkhorn, WI 53121
Phone: (262) 723-4443
Fax: (262) 723-3430

Washington County Central Labor Council
8735 Hwy. 45, Kewaskum, WI 53040
Phone: (262) 626-4574
Fax: (262) 616-1419

Waukesha County Labor Council
6310 W. Appleton Ave., Milwaukee, WI 53210
Phone: (414) 873-4520
Fax: (414) 875-5155

Waupun Central Labor Council
635 Maxon St., Waupun, WI 53963
Phone: (920) 324-3379

West Central Wisconsin Labor Council
855 Hopwood Ave., Menomonie, WI 54751
Phone: (715) 235-4368

Western Wisconsin AFL-CIO
2020 Winnebago St., La Crosse, WI 54601
Phone: (608) 782-5851
Fax: (608) 782-8015

Winnebago County Labor Council
2211 Oregon St., Suite A3, Oshkosh, WI 54901
Phone: (866) 426-4707
Fax: (920) 688-3226

Wisconsin Rapids Central Labor Council
220 Johnson St., Wisconsin Rapids, WI 54495
Phone: (715) 423-4202
Fax: (715) 424-1407

Wyoming

Casper Area Trades and Labor Assembly
P.O. Box 369, Casper, WY 82602
Phone: (307) 237-9556

Northeast Wyoming Central Labor Council
P.O. Box 2668, Gillette, WY 82717
Phone: (307) 680-9395

Sheridan Area Central Labor Union
460 W. Loucks St., Sheridan, WY 82801
Phone: (307) 672-0894
Fax: (307) 672-9478

Southeast Wyoming Central Labor Union
P.O. Box 813, Cheyenne, WY 82003
Phone: (307) 683-3428

Southwest Wyoming Central Labor Council
P.O. Box 446, Rock Springs, WY 82902
Phone: (307) 362-4442
Fax: (307) 362-4156

PART V. Change to Win (CTW)

Change to Win

1900 L St., N.W.
Suite 900
Washington, DC 20036
Phone: (202) 721-0660
Fax: (202) 721-0661
Web: www.changetowin.org

Leadership Council

Chair: Anna Burger
    Secretary-Treasurer, Service
    Employees International Union

Secretary-Treasurer: Edgar Romney
    Executive Vice President, UNITE
    HERE

Joseph T. Hansen
    President, United Food and
    Commercial Workers International
    Union
James P. Hoffa
    President, International Brotherhood of
    Teamsters

Geralyn Lutty
    Vice President, United Food and
    Commercial Workers International
    Union
Douglas J. McCarron
    President, United Brotherhood of
    Carpenters and Joiners of America
Terence M. O'Sullivan
    President, Laborers' International
    Union of North America

Bruce S. Raynor
    President, UNITE HERE
Arturo S. Rodriguez
    President, United Farm Workers of
    America
Andrew L. Stern
    President, Service Employees
    International Union

Affiliated Unions

International Brotherhood of Teamsters
Laborers' International Union of North
    America
Service Employees International Union
United Brotherhood of Carpenters and
    Joiners of America
United Farm Workers
United Food and Commercial Workers
    International Union
UNITE HERE

Appendix A. BLS Union Membership and Earnings Data, 2004 and 2005

Table 1. Union affiliation of employed wage and salary workers by selected characteristics

(Numbers in thousands)

Characteristic	2004					2005				
	Total em-ployed	Members of unions[1]		Represented by unions[2]		Total em-ployed	Members of unions[1]		Represented by unions[2]	
		Total	Percent of em-ployed	Total	Percent of em-ployed		Total	Percent of em-ployed	Total	Percent of em-ployed
AGE AND SEX										
Total, 16 years and over	123,554	15,472	12.5	17,087	13.8	125,889	15,685	12.5	17,223	13.7
16 to 24 years	19,109	890	4.7	1,019	5.3	19,283	878	4.6	1,019	5.3
25 years and over	104,444	14,581	14.0	16,069	15.4	106,606	14,808	13.9	16,204	15.2
25 to 34 years	28,202	2,982	10.6	3,316	11.8	28,450	3,044	10.7	3,368	11.8
35 to 44 years	30,470	4,173	13.7	4,590	15.1	30,654	4,211	13.7	4,579	14.9
45 to 54 years	28,039	4,771	17.0	5,233	18.7	28,714	4,731	16.5	5,158	18.0
55 to 64 years	14,239	2,390	16.8	2,617	18.4	15,158	2,496	16.5	2,732	18.0
65 years and over	3,495	264	7.5	314	9.0	3,631	325	8.9	366	10.1
Men, 16 years and over	64,145	8,878	13.8	9,638	15.0	65,466	8,870	13.5	9,597	14.7
16 to 24 years	9,835	557	5.7	627	6.4	9,860	523	5.3	603	6.1
25 years and over	54,310	8,321	15.3	9,010	16.6	55,606	8,347	15.0	8,994	16.2
25 to 34 years	15,391	1,722	11.2	1,873	12.2	15,559	1,754	11.3	1,915	12.3
35 to 44 years	16,035	2,449	15.3	2,658	16.6	16,196	2,422	15.0	2,582	15.9
45 to 54 years	14,026	2,699	19.2	2,903	20.7	14,421	2,658	18.4	2,849	19.8
55 to 64 years	7,117	1,309	18.4	1,414	19.9	7,606	1,346	17.7	1,458	19.2
65 years and over	1,741	142	8.2	163	9.4	1,824	167	9.1	190	10.4
Women, 16 years and over	59,408	6,593	11.1	7,450	12.5	60,423	6,815	11.3	7,626	12.6
16 to 24 years	9,274	333	3.6	391	4.2	9,423	354	3.8	417	4.4
25 years and over	50,134	6,260	12.5	7,058	14.1	51,000	6,461	12.7	7,210	14.1
25 to 34 years	12,811	1,261	9.8	1,443	11.3	12,891	1,290	10.0	1,454	11.3
35 to 44 years	14,435	1,725	11.9	1,931	13.4	14,457	1,790	12.4	1,997	13.8
45 to 54 years	14,014	2,072	14.8	2,330	16.6	14,293	2,073	14.5	2,309	16.2
55 to 64 years	7,122	1,081	15.2	1,203	16.9	7,552	1,150	15.2	1,274	16.9
65 years and over	1,753	121	6.9	151	8.6	1,806	158	8.8	176	9.8
RACE, HISPANIC OR LATINO ETHNICITY, AND SEX										
White, 16 years and over	101,340	12,381	12.2	13,657	13.5	102,967	12,520	12.2	13,755	13.4
Men	53,432	7,260	13.6	7,854	14.7	54,462	7,275	13.4	7,858	14.4
Women	47,908	5,121	10.7	5,803	12.1	48,505	5,245	10.8	5,897	12.2
Black or African American, 16 years and over	14,090	2,130	15.1	2,355	16.7	14,459	2,178	15.1	2,391	16.5
Men	6,409	1,085	16.9	1,185	18.5	6,603	1,062	16.1	1,166	17.7
Women	7,681	1,045	13.6	1,170	15.2	7,857	1,115	14.2	1,225	15.6
Asian, 16 years and over	5,280	603	11.4	670	12.7	5,479	614	11.2	666	12.2
Men	2,815	328	11.7	371	13.2	2,881	314	10.9	337	11.7
Women	2,465	275	11.1	299	12.1	2,598	299	11.5	329	12.7
Hispanic or Latino, 16 years and over	16,533	1,676	10.1	1,888	11.4	17,191	1,793	10.4	1,981	11.5
Men	9,857	1,016	10.3	1,130	11.5	10,324	1,093	10.6	1,185	11.5
Women	6,676	661	9.9	758	11.4	6,866	700	10.2	796	11.6
FULL- OR PART-TIME STATUS[3]										
Full-time workers	101,224	14,029	13.9	15,463	15.3	103,560	14,207	13.7	15,551	15.0
Part-time workers	22,047	1,406	6.4	1,587	7.2	22,052	1,441	6.5	1,630	7.4

[1] Data refer to members of a labor union or an employee association similar to a union.
[2] Data refer to members of a labor union or an employee association similar to a union as well as workers who report no union affiliation but whose jobs are covered by a union or an employee association contract.
[3] The distinction between full- and part-time workers is based on hours usually worked. These data will not sum to totals because full- or part-time status on the principal job is not identifiable for a small number of multiple jobholders.

NOTE: Beginning in January 2005, data reflect revised population controls used in the household survey. Estimates for the above race groups (white, black or African American, and Asian) do not sum to totals because data are not presented for all races. In addition, persons whose ethnicity is identified as Hispanic or Latino may be of any race and, therefore, are classified by ethnicity as well as race. Data refer to the sole or principal job of full- and part-time workers. Excluded are all self-employed workers regardless of whether or not their businesses are incorporated.

Source: U.S. Department of Labor, Bureau of Labor Statistics, "Labor Force Statistics from the Current Population Survey," *available at* www.bls.gov/news.release/union2.toc.htm

Table 2. Median weekly earnings of full-time wage and salary workers by union affiliation and selected characteristics

Characteristic	2004				2005			
	Total	Members of unions[1]	Repre-sented by unions[2]	Non-union	Total	Members of unions[1]	Repre-sented by unions[2]	Non-union
AGE AND SEX								
Total, 16 years and over	$638	$781	$776	$612	$651	$801	$795	$622
16 to 24 years..................................	390	498	494	385	397	502	502	392
25 years and over............................	683	798	793	656	696	820	815	669
25 to 34 years..............................	604	724	717	590	610	735	729	595
35 to 44 years..............................	713	813	808	690	731	844	837	708
45 to 54 years..............................	743	834	831	718	748	854	851	722
55 to 64 years..............................	725	835	835	693	742	852	851	716
65 years and over.........................	560	728	744	520	569	679	683	551
Men, 16 years and over	713	829	828	685	722	857	855	692
16 to 24 years..................................	400	504	496	395	409	513	511	403
25 years and over............................	762	846	846	743	771	876	876	749
25 to 34 years..............................	639	751	748	620	644	763	760	624
35 to 44 years..............................	804	868	865	787	822	921	918	800
45 to 54 years..............................	857	878	881	847	853	911	912	831
55 to 64 years..............................	843	870	877	829	855	888	895	840
65 years and over.........................	641	753	776	620	644	758	768	625
Women, 16 years and over..................	573	723	719	541	585	731	726	559
16 to 24 years..................................	375	487	491	370	381	484	487	377
25 years and over............................	599	733	730	580	612	743	738	593
25 to 34 years..............................	561	678	665	541	573	693	682	548
35 to 44 years..............................	608	735	733	590	621	740	735	603
45 to 54 years..............................	625	758	755	604	644	760	758	619
55 to 64 years..............................	615	767	767	592	639	795	785	610
65 years and over.........................	478	687	733	455	492	610	599	480
RACE, HISPANIC OR LATINO ETHNICITY, AND SEX								
White, 16 years and over	657	808	802	626	672	830	824	641
Men...	732	855	854	704	743	884	884	714
Women	584	738	734	557	596	749	743	576
Black or African American, 16 years and over..	525	656	651	507	520	656	653	500
Men...	569	679	679	534	559	689	682	523
Women	505	629	621	490	499	632	630	478
Asian, 16 years and over	708	765	774	691	753	809	805	744
Men...	802	775	786	809	825	819	817	827
Women	613	756	762	594	665	789	785	643
Hispanic or Latino, 16 years and over .	456	679	670	428	471	673	661	449
Men...	480	697	690	455	489	713	704	473
Women	419	623	616	401	429	609	606	414

[1] Data refer to members of a labor union or an employee association similar to a union.
[2] Data refer to members of a labor union or an employee association similar to a union as well as workers who report no union affiliation but whose jobs are covered by a union or an employee association contract.

NOTE: Beginning in January 2005, data reflect revised population controls used in the household survey. Estimates for the above race groups (white, black or African American, and Asian) do not sum to totals because data are not presented for all races. In addition, persons whose ethnicity is identified as Hispanic or Latino may be of any race and, therefore, are classified by ethnicity as well as race. Data refer to the sole or principal job of full- and part-time workers. Excluded are all self-employed workers regardless of whether or not their businesses are incorporated.

Table 3. Union affiliation of employed wage and salary workers by occupation and industry

(Numbers in thousands)

Occupation and Industry	2004					2005				
	Total em-ployed	Members of unions[1]		Represented by unions[2]		Total em-ployed	Members of unions[1]		Represented by unions[2]	
		Total	Percent of em-ployed	Total	Percent of em-ployed		Total	Percent of em-ployed	Total	Percent of em-ployed
OCCUPATION										
Management, professional, and related occupations	41,451	5,418	13.1	6,256	15.1	42,226	5,639	13.4	6,385	15.1
Management, business, and financial operations occupations	15,758	732	4.6	895	5.7	15,955	793	5.0	939	5.9
Management occupations	10,796	441	4.1	553	5.1	10,921	485	4.4	585	5.4
Business and financial operations occupations	4,962	291	5.9	342	6.9	5,034	308	6.1	354	7.0
Professional and related occupations	25,693	4,686	18.2	5,361	20.9	26,271	4,845	18.4	5,447	20.7
Computer and mathematical occupations	2,962	128	4.3	171	5.8	3,067	142	4.6	172	5.6
Architecture and engineering occupations	2,597	209	8.0	246	9.5	2,593	221	8.5	259	10.0
Life, physical, and social science occupations	1,204	106	8.8	129	10.7	1,305	125	9.6	140	10.7
Community and social services occupations	2,132	370	17.4	422	19.8	2,100	346	16.5	376	17.9
Legal occupations	1,216	75	6.2	92	7.6	1,261	71	5.6	83	6.6
Education, training, and library occupations	7,636	2,874	37.6	3,235	42.4	7,813	3,006	38.5	3,354	42.9
Arts, design, entertainment, sports, and media occupations	1,894	162	8.6	184	9.7	1,957	152	7.8	171	8.8
Healthcare practitioner and technical occupations	6,052	762	12.6	882	14.6	6,175	782	12.7	892	14.4
Service occupations	20,724	2,371	11.4	2,552	12.3	21,074	2,446	11.6	2,659	12.6
Healthcare support occupations	2,791	290	10.4	315	11.3	2,971	286	9.6	317	10.7
Protective service occupations	2,840	1,059	37.3	1,118	39.4	2,843	1,051	37.0	1,109	39.0
Food preparation and serving related occupations	7,164	294	4.1	337	4.7	7,361	316	4.3	362	4.9
Building and grounds cleaning and maintenance occupations	4,597	490	10.7	529	11.5	4,525	504	11.1	553	12.2
Personal care and service occupations	3,331	238	7.1	254	7.6	3,373	288	8.5	317	9.4
Sales and office occupations	32,322	2,493	7.7	2,780	8.6	32,541	2,385	7.3	2,671	8.2
Sales and related occupations	13,527	488	3.6	548	4.1	13,630	451	3.3	519	3.8
Office and administrative support occupations	18,795	2,005	10.7	2,232	11.9	18,911	1,934	10.2	2,152	11.4
Natural resources, construction, and maintenance occupations	12,081	2,222	18.4	2,343	19.4	12,907	2,129	16.5	2,238	17.3
Farming, fishing, and forestry occupations	862	27	3.1	34	3.9	898	35	3.9	38	4.3
Construction and extraction occupations	6,680	1,312	19.6	1,370	20.5	7,296	1,283	17.6	1,348	18.5
Installation, maintenance, and repair occupations	4,540	883	19.4	939	20.7	4,713	811	17.2	851	18.1
Production, transportation, and material moving occupations	16,976	2,968	17.5	3,156	18.6	17,142	3,086	18.0	3,271	19.1
Production occupations	9,085	1,485	16.3	1,582	17.4	9,007	1,539	17.1	1,617	17.9
Transportation and material moving occupations	7,891	1,483	18.8	1,574	20.0	8,135	1,547	19.0	1,655	20.3

(Continued on next page)

Table 3. Union affiliation of employed wage and salary workers by occupation and industry (continued)

(Numbers in thousands)

Occupation and Industry	2004					2005				
	Total em-ployed	Members of unions[1]		Represented by unions[2]		Total em-ployed	Members of unions[1]		Represented by unions[2]	
		Total	Percent of em-ployed	Total	Percent of em-ployed		Total	Percent of em-ployed	Total	Percent of em-ployed
INDUSTRY										
Private sector	103,584	8,205	7.9	8,956	8.6	105,508	8,255	7.8	8,962	8.5
Agriculture and related industries	1,023	23	2.2	30	2.9	1,021	28	2.7	30	3.0
Nonagricultural industries	102,560	8,182	8.0	8,926	8.7	104,487	8,227	7.9	8,931	8.5
Mining	496	57	11.4	58	11.7	600	48	8.0	57	9.5
Construction	7,550	1,110	14.7	1,162	15.4	8,053	1,057	13.1	1,111	13.8
Manufacturing.................................	15,754	2,036	12.9	2,183	13.9	15,518	2,017	13.0	2,127	13.7
Durable goods............................	9,885	1,316	13.3	1,407	14.2	9,845	1,310	13.3	1,382	14.0
Nondurable goods......................	5,869	720	12.3	776	13.2	5,673	707	12.5	746	13.1
Wholesale and retail trade.............	18,754	1,028	5.5	1,107	5.9	18,989	1,021	5.4	1,122	5.9
Wholesale trade	4,083	189	4.6	214	5.2	4,017	236	5.9	259	6.4
Retail trade	14,671	839	5.7	893	6.1	14,973	785	5.2	864	5.8
Transportation and utilities	4,893	1,218	24.9	1,287	26.3	5,212	1,252	24.0	1,309	25.1
Transportation and warehousing.	4,043	976	24.2	1,031	25.5	4,379	1,024	23.4	1,071	24.4
Utilities..	850	241	28.4	256	30.1	833	228	27.4	239	28.6
Information[3]	3,058	433	14.2	470	15.4	2,934	398	13.6	422	14.4
Publishing, except Internet.........	778	52	6.7	59	7.6	765	68	8.8	74	9.7
Motion pictures and sound recording	329	52	15.7	54	16.4	277	42	15.0	43	15.5
Broadcasting, except Internet.....	502	47	9.3	53	10.5	534	46	8.6	48	9.0
Telecommunications	1,218	273	22.4	292	24.0	1,096	234	21.4	248	22.6
Financial activities	8,490	171	2.0	209	2.5	8,619	195	2.3	238	2.8
Finance and insurance...............	6,301	96	1.5	124	2.0	6,304	102	1.6	132	2.1
Finance	4,111	56	1.4	73	1.8	4,114	59	1.4	77	1.9
Insurance	2,191	40	1.8	51	2.3	2,190	44	2.0	54	2.5
Real estate and rental and leasing......................................	2,188	76	3.5	85	3.9	2,315	92	4.0	107	4.6
Professional and business services.	10,815	246	2.3	306	2.8	10,951	292	2.7	341	3.1
Professional and technical services	6,263	70	1.1	102	1.6	6,468	98	1.5	120	1.9
Management, administrative, and waste services............................	4,552	177	3.9	204	4.5	4,483	194	4.3	221	4.9
Education and health services.......	16,870	1,405	8.3	1,593	9.4	17,357	1,434	8.3	1,632	9.4
Educational services	3,243	421	13.0	475	14.6	3,312	435	13.1	511	15.4
Health care and social assistance	13,627	984	7.2	1,119	8.2	14,045	999	7.1	1,121	8.0
Leisure and hospitality...................	10,326	319	3.1	368	3.6	10,658	333	3.1	377	3.5
Arts, entertainment, and recreation	1,777	114	6.4	123	6.9	1,869	118	6.3	134	7.2
Accommodation and food services.	8,548	205	2.4	245	2.9	8,790	215	2.4	243	2.8
Accommodation	1,431	117	8.2	132	9.2	1,459	122	8.3	130	8.9
Food services and drinking places..	7,117	88	1.2	112	1.8	7,331	93	1.3	113	1.5
Other services[3]	5,556	158	2.8	183	3.3	5,596	181	3.2	194	3.5
Other services, except private households	4,782	148	3.1	172	3.6	4,799	175	3.7	188	3.9
Public sector	19,970	7,267	36.4	8,131	40.7	20,381	7,430	36.5	8,262	40.5
Federal government.........................	3,298	985	29.9	1,153	35.0	3,427	954	27.8	1,134	33.1
State government	5,712	1,751	30.7	1,961	34.3	5,874	1,838	31.3	2,056	35.0
Local government	10,961	4,532	41.3	5,017	45.8	11,080	4,638	41.9	5,071	45.8

[1] Data refer to members of a labor union or an employee association similar to a union.
[2] Data refer to members of a labor union or an employee association similar to a union as well as workers who report no union affiliation but whose jobs are covered by a union or an employee association contract.
[3] Includes other industries, not shown separately.

NOTE: Beginning in January 2005, data reflect revised population controls used in the household survey. Data refer to the sole or principal job of full- and part-time workers. Excluded are all self-employed workers regardless of whether or not their businesses are incorporated.

Table 4. Median weekly earnings of full-time wage and salary workers by union affiliation, occupation, and industry

Occupation and industry	2004				2005			
	Total	Members of unions[1]	Repre-sented by unions[2]	Non-union	Total	Members of unions[1]	Repre-sented by unions[2]	Non-union
OCCUPATION								
Management, professional, and related occupations..	$918	$921	$916	$918	$937	$942	$937	$937
Management, business, and financial operations occupations.....................	965	963	972	965	997	1,015	1,029	995
Management occupations	1,052	1,065	1,074	1,050	1,083	1,137	1,146	1,076
Business and financial operations occupations	847	880	881	844	871	854	866	872
Professional and related occupations......................................	883	915	907	875	902	932	924	894
Computer and mathematical occupations	1,114	1,000	983	1,124	1,132	1,009	1,029	1,141
Architecture and engineering occupations	1,098	1,080	1,090	1,100	1,105	1,133	1,133	1,101
Life, physical, and social science occupations	957	949	977	955	965	978	1,011	959
Community and social services occupations	707	827	817	666	725	880	865	693
Legal occupations.........................	1,070	1,174	1,155	1,058	1,052	1,147	1,155	1,042
Education, training, and library occupations	781	899	886	687	798	913	898	710
Arts, design, entertainment, sports, and media occupations.................	768	953	972	754	819	983	925	808
Healthcare practitioner and technical occupations	852	938	933	841	878	932	932	867
Service occupations.............................	411	655	647	389	413	643	629	392
Healthcare support occupations	407	458	462	401	410	466	462	405
Protective service occupations	700	907	897	567	678	896	886	568
Food preparation and serving related occupations.......................................	360	445	435	355	356	439	442	350
Building and grounds cleaning and maintenance occupations.................	385	515	513	368	394	528	518	378
Personal care and service occupations......................................	402	522	518	394	409	558	549	397
Sales and office occupations	558	662	658	545	575	681	675	562
Sales and related occupations	604	576	577	606	622	623	625	622
Office and administrative support occupations	535	676	671	519	550	689	682	528
Natural resources, construction, and maintenance occupations	621	867	858	581	623	910	903	585
Farming, fishing, and forestry occupations	356	(3)	(3)	352	372	(3)	(3)	369
Construction and extraction occupations	604	861	852	555	604	913	903	554
Installation, maintenance, and repair occupations	704	886	880	662	705	915	913	666
Production, transportation, and material moving occupations	523	687	681	498	540	709	704	510
Production occupations	526	681	674	503	538	698	693	511
Transportation and material moving occupations.......................	520	695	689	491	543	721	717	508

(Continued on next page)

Table 4. Median weekly earnings of full-time wage and salary workers by union affiliation, occupation, and industry (continued)

Occupation and industry	2004				2005			
	Total	Members of unions[1]	Repre-sented by unions[2]	Non-union	Total	Members of unions[1]	Repre-sented by unions[2]	Non-union
INDUSTRY								
Private sector	$615	$739	$734	$604	$625	$757	$752	$615
Agriculture and related industries	403	([3])	([3])	402	402	([3])	([3])	402
Nonagricultural industries	617	740	735	606	629	758	753	617
Mining	874	905	911	865	885	([3])	989	870
Construction	618	893	884	588	619	933	926	590
Manufacturing	662	694	692	654	676	722	719	667
Durable goods	691	707	706	687	704	751	747	695
Nondurable goods	611	670	662	602	624	676	672	618
Wholesale and retail trade	550	596	590	547	566	615	610	562
Wholesale trade	677	722	709	674	692	678	676	692
Retail trade	509	567	560	507	515	590	585	513
Transportation and utilities	711	854	850	662	726	864	860	676
Transportation and warehousing	668	819	814	619	688	829	827	640
Utilities	957	979	978	948	941	960	954	931
Information[4]	828	893	887	808	832	931	925	810
Publishing, except Internet	720	844	829	710	755	860	867	740
Motion pictures and sound recording	805	([3])	([3])	762	751	([3])	([3])	691
Broadcasting, except Internet	763	([3])	([3])	749	749	([3])	([3])	738
Telecommunications	918	910	897	929	927	937	935	923
Financial activities	706	657	649	708	741	698	696	743
Finance and insurance	738	630	629	740	765	692	696	767
Finance	735	606	616	737	765	650	667	768
Insurance	743	([3])	([3])	744	764	([3])	([3])	766
Real estate and rental and leasing	615	677	670	613	653	711	696	649
Professional and business services	709	679	694	710	739	663	673	743
Professional and technical services	927	940	937	927	961	770	858	963
Management, administrative, and waste services	478	607	606	470	488	586	578	485
Education and health services	613	717	728	603	627	731	736	617
Educational services	716	828	831	679	737	818	809	718
Health care and social assistance	595	656	671	588	607	684	692	601
Leisure and hospitality	407	518	508	402	409	513	510	405
Arts, entertainment, and recreation	523	677	662	513	521	652	618	515
Accommodation and food services	391	477	473	387	388	487	486	384
Accommodation	432	481	490	422	455	515	510	405
Food services and drinking places	378	467	422	377	372	400	406	372
Other services[4]	528	749	750	521	535	694	698	524
Other services, except private households	560	764	764	551	579	698	701	572
Public sector	751	832	827	683	758	850	842	692
Federal government	856	840	848	869	882	873	879	887
State government	725	788	781	681	733	802	798	684
Local government	731	844	834	627	738	858	844	633

[1] Data refer to members of a labor union or an employee association similar to a union.
[2] Data refer to members of a labor union or an employee association similar to a union as well as workers who report no union affiliation but whose jobs are covered by a union or an employee association contract.
[3] Data not shown where base is less than 50,000.
[4] Includes other industries, not shown separately.

NOTE: Beginning in January 2005, data reflect revised population controls used in the household survey. Data refer to the sole or principal job of full- and part-time workers. Excluded are all self-employed workers regardless of whether or not their businesses are incorporated.

Appendix B. BLS Union Membership Data by State, 2004 and 2005

Union affiliation of employed wage and salary workers by state

(Numbers in thousands)

State	2004					2005				
	Total employed	Members of unions[1]		Represented by unions[2]		Total employed	Members of unions[1]		Represented by unions[2]	
		Total	Percent of employed	Total	Percent of employed		Total	Percent of employed	Total	Percent of employed
Alabama	1,861	181	9.7	213	11.5	1,909	195	10.2	223	11.7
Alaska	268	54	20.1	60	22.4	275	63	22.8	66	24.1
Arizona	2,323	145	6.3	183	7.9	2,366	145	6.1	181	7.7
Arkansas	1,058	51	4.8	65	6.2	1,138	54	4.8	68	6.0
California	14,414	2,385	16.5	2,588	18.0	14,687	2,424	16.5	2,610	17.8
Colorado	2,050	172	8.4	191	9.3	2,052	170	8.3	193	9.4
Connecticut	1,539	235	15.3	256	16.6	1,550	247	15.9	263	17.0
Delaware	373	46	12.4	49	13.2	386	46	11.8	50	12.9
District of Columbia	258	33	12.7	38	14.5	259	29	11.3	33	12.8
Florida	6,943	414	6.0	533	7.7	7,389	401	5.4	532	7.2
Georgia	3,773	242	6.4	282	7.5	3,765	190	5.0	226	6.0
Hawaii	533	126	23.7	132	24.8	545	141	25.8	145	26.7
Idaho	561	33	5.8	44	7.9	606	31	5.2	38	6.3
Illinois	5,410	908	16.8	971	17.9	5,473	927	16.9	965	17.6
Indiana	2,717	311	11.4	338	12.4	2,789	346	12.4	368	13.2
Iowa	1,345	141	10.5	171	12.7	1,369	157	11.5	185	13.5
Kansas	1,223	103	8.4	132	10.8	1,210	85	7.0	115	9.5
Kentucky	1,699	164	9.6	197	11.6	1,696	164	9.7	184	10.8
Louisiana	1,697	129	7.6	157	9.3	1,778	114	6.4	132	7.4
Maine	564	64	11.3	74	13.2	582	69	11.9	79	13.6
Maryland	2,502	272	10.9	313	12.5	2,530	337	13.3	379	15.0
Massachusetts	2,920	393	13.5	430	14.7	2,886	402	13.9	431	14.9
Michigan	4,305	930	21.6	966	22.4	4,288	880	20.5	916	21.4
Minnesota	2,429	424	17.5	443	18.3	2,494	392	15.7	410	16.4
Mississippi	1,108	53	4.8	70	6.3	1,089	77	7.1	105	9.7
Missouri	2,546	315	12.4	357	14.0	2,532	290	11.5	319	12.6
Montana	366	43	11.7	46	12.6	391	42	10.7	48	12.2
Nebraska	831	69	8.3	83	10.0	830	69	8.3	79	9.5
Nevada	1,006	126	12.5	144	14.3	1,051	145	13.8	158	15.1
New Hampshire	618	61	9.9	68	11.0	627	65	10.4	72	11.5
New Jersey	3,769	745	19.8	813	21.6	3,868	791	20.5	838	21.7
New Mexico	734	49	6.7	65	8.9	777	63	8.1	83	10.7
New York	7,901	1,996	25.3	2,085	26.4	8,008	2,090	26.1	2,201	27.5
North Carolina	3,549	97	2.7	127	3.6	3,631	107	2.9	143	3.9
North Dakota	292	22	7.7	26	9.0	289	21	7.3	26	9.2
Ohio	4,998	759	15.2	820	16.4	5,039	804	16.0	866	17.2
Oklahoma	1,402	86	6.1	100	7.1	1,432	77	5.4	91	6.4
Oregon	1,471	224	15.2	243	16.5	1,470	213	14.5	231	15.7
Pennsylvania	5,298	793	15.0	842	15.9	5,456	753	13.8	818	15.0
Rhode Island	487	79	16.3	83	17.0	494	79	15.9	83	16.8
South Carolina	1,765	54	3.0	74	4.2	1,739	40	2.3	58	3.3
South Dakota	347	21	6.0	27	7.7	350	21	5.9	29	8.2
Tennessee	2,465	164	6.7	191	7.7	2,368	128	5.4	156	6.6
Texas	9,072	457	5.0	573	6.3	9,485	506	5.3	590	6.2
Utah	1,001	58	5.8	67	6.7	1,035	51	4.9	63	6.1
Vermont	291	29	9.8	33	11.4	287	31	10.8	37	13.0
Virginia	3,308	176	5.3	218	6.6	3,406	165	4.8	211	6.2
Washington	2,645	510	19.3	536	20.3	2,746	523	19.1	559	20.4
West Virginia	700	99	14.2	110	15.7	688	99	14.4	107	15.5
Wisconsin	2,597	414	16.0	439	16.9	2,551	410	16.1	438	17.2
Wyoming	222	18	8.0	22	9.8	228	18	7.9	22	9.5

[1] Data refer to members of a labor union or an employee association similar to a union.

[2] Data refer to members of a labor union or an employee association similar to a union as well as workers who report no union affiliation but whose jobs are covered by a union or an employee association contract.

NOTE: Beginning in January 2004, data reflect revised population controls used in the household survey. Data refer to the sole or principal job of full- and part-time workers. Excluded are all self-employed workers regardless of whether or not their businesses are incorporated.

Source: U.S. Department of Labor, Bureau of Labor Statistics, Current Population Survey, available at www.bls.gov/news.release/union2.toc.htm

Appendix C. AFL-CIO Membership Report

Schedule No. 1
Membership: National and International Unions and Directly Affiliated Local Unions

The following table shows the average two-year membership of the AFL-CIO for each two-year convention period. The totals do not include the membership numbers related to affiliates' associate members, for which the affiliates pay a reduced monthly per capita tax.

Period	Membership
1955	12,622,000
1956-1957	13,020,000
1958-1959	12,779,000
1960-1961	12,553,000
1962-1963	12,496,000
1964-1965	12,919,000
1966-1967	13,781,000
1968-1969	13,005,000
1970-1971	13,177,000
1972-1973	13,407,000
1974-1975	14,070,000
1976-1977	13,542,000
1978-1979	13,621,000
1980-1981	13,602,000
1982-1983	13,758,000
1984-1985	13,109,000
1986-1987	12,702,000
1988-1989	13,556,000
1990-1991	13,933,000
1992-1993	13,299,000
1994-1995	13,007,000
1996-1997	12,905,000
1998-1999	12,952,000
2000-2001	13,164,000
2004-2005	12,975,000

Schedule No. 2
Membership: National and International Union Affiliates

The average annual membership figures were computed by taking the total number of regular members on whom per capita tax payments were made to the AFL-CIO for the 12 months ending in June of "each year, and dividing that total by the number of months for which payments were made."

Membership reported at conventions and used as the basis for the determination of voting strength at conventions is determined by the average membership reported by affiliates during the 24-month period ending with the last calendar month occurring before the 90th day preceding the opening of the convention.

"Associate member payments are not included in the figures below, nor in computing average membership" for the purposes of determining voting strength at conventions.

The figures below incorporate all mergers that have occurred since the convention held in 2001.

Organization	FYE 6/30/03	FYE 6/30/04	FYE 6/30/05
Actors and Artistes	69,000	69,000	69,636
Air Line Pilots	52,132	49,290	49,120
Air Traffic Controllers	14,873	15,048	14,613
Asbestos Workers	17,928	18,311	18,311
Automobile, Aerospace and Agricultural Implement Workers	656,351	634,794	610,715
Bakery, Confectionery, Tobacco Workers and Grain Millers	96,926	90,538	87,428
Boilermakers	42,157	43,632	38,037
Bricklayers	93,761	93,761	93,761
Communications Workers	672,755	672,005	671,234
Electrical Workers	656,110	634,690	623,869
Elevator Constructors	24,297	23,671	23,310
Engineers, Operating	280,050	280,000	280,000
Farm Workers	16,000	16,000	16,000
Fire Fighters	220,667	227,500	230,000
Food and Commercial Workers	1,093,884	1,071,973	1,047,551
Glass, Molders, Pottery, Plastics and Allied Workers	46,687	42,645	40,410
Government Employees	200,085	204,354	210,133
Iron Workers	89,552	85,632	82,454
Laborers	337,884	363,533	382,730
Letter Carriers	210,000	210,000	210,000
Longshoremen	60,331	59,533	58,928
Longshore and Warehouse	35,611	33,899	33,069
Machinists and Aerospace Workers	379,156	349,974	326,967
Marine Engineers	20,384	20,384	20,384
Mine Workers	65,000	65,000	65,000
Musicians	7,200	7,200	7,200
Novelty and Production Workers	14,667	10,000	10,000
Nurses, United American	88,803	86,669	87,249
Office and Professional Employees	111,693	108,396	110,428
Painters and Allied Trades	101,075	90,895	86,366
Plasterers and Cement Masons	29,500	29,500	29,500
Plate Printers, Die Stampers and Engravers	200	200	200
Plumbing and Pipe Fitting	219,800	219,800	219,800
Police Associations	36,775	34,659	36,320
Postal Workers	244,900	232,561	233,390
Professional Athletes	1,700	1,705	1,710
Professional and Technical Engineers	51,414	50,694	50,000

Organization	FYE 6/30/03	FYE 6/30/04	FYE 6/30/05
Radio Association	100	100	100
Roofers, Waterproofers and Allied Workers	18,849	18,730	18,684
School Administrators	13,500	13,500	13,500
School Employees Association, California	129,000	129,000	129,000
Seafarers	80,250	82,898	84,790
Service Employees	1,350,000	1,400,000	1,308,197
Sheet Metal Workers	93,000	93,000	93,000
Signalmen, Railroad	8,695	8,602	8,447
Stage Employees and Moving Pictures Technicians	60,000	62,292	62,667
State, County and Municipal Employees	1,291,107	1,299,864	1,305,635
Steelworkers	625,646	579,993	564,377
Teachers	987,144	1,014,774	1,048,535
Teamsters	1,340,768	1,299,855	1,271,612
Train Dispatchers	2,100	2,100	2,100
Transit Union	119,384	120,191	118,951
Transport Workers	109,000	109,000	109,000
Transportation Communications	83,403	59,398	46,840
UNITE HERE	441,481	428,811	441,452
Utility Workers	42,520	48,025	50,558
Writers	4,000	4,100	4,000
Total	**13,159,255**	**13,021,679**	**12,857,268**

Schedule No. 3
Membership: National and International Union Affiliates

The following table shows the average per capita membership of current affiliates reported to the AFL-CIO for the year 1955; the two-year periods ending in 1965, 1975 and 1985; and the two-year periods ending June 30, 1995, 1997, 1999, 2001 and 2005. The totals are expressed in thousands of members.

Organizations	1955	1965	1975	1985	1995	1997	1999	2001	2005
Actors and Artistes of America, Associated	34	61	76	100	80	69	69	69	69
Air Line Pilots Association	9	18	47	33	35	37	40	45	49
Air Traffic Controllers Association, National							7	13	15
Asbestos Workers, International Association of Heat and Frost Insulators and	9	12	13	12	12	12	12	14	18
Automobile, Aerospace and Agricultural Implement Workers of America International Union, United	1260	1150	c	974	751	766	745	737	624
Bakery, Confectionery and Tobacco Workers International Union				115	96	95	p	p	p
Bakery, Confectionery, Tobacco Workers and Grain Millers International Union						110	p	106	89
Boilermakers, Iron Ship Builders, Blacksmiths, Forgers and Helpers, International Brotherhood of	151	108	123	110	42	43	40	39	41
Bricklayers and Allied Craftsworkers, International Union of	120	120	143	95	84	71	62	63	94
Communications Workers of America	249	288	476	524	478	480	508	626	665
Electronic, Electrical, Salaried, Machine and Furniture Workers, AFL-CIO, International Union of					135	130	119	u	u
Electrical Workers, International Brotherhood of	460	616	856	791	679	657	656	670	630
Elevator Constructors, International Union of	10	12	13	20	20	20	20	22	23
Engineers, International Union of Operating	200	270	300	330	298	295	291	281	280
Farm Workers of America, AFL-CIO, United		14	d	12	16	16	16	16	16
Fire Fighters, International Association of	72	87	123	142	151	155	166	184	229
Flight Attendants, Association of			17	f	31	34	38	42	x
Food and Commercial Workers International Union, United				989	983	986	1101	1135	1059
Glass, Molders, Pottery, Plastics and Allied Workers International Union		72	69	66	63	55	42		
Glass Workers Union, American Flint	28	31	35	24	20	18	18	18	z
Government Employees, American Federation of	47	132	255	199	153	167	179	194	207
Grain Millers, American Federation of	33	25	29	30	20	21	p	p	p
Graphic Communications International Union				141	94	93	87	80	ac
Health and Human Service Employees Union, National					57	n	n	n	n
Hotel Employees and Restaurant Employees International Union	300	300	421	327	241	223	228	238	aa
Iron Workers, International Association of Bridge, Structural, Ornamental and Reinforcing	133	132	160	140	82	80	81	88	84
Laborers' International Union of North America		403	475	383	352	298	298	306	372
Laundry and Dry Cleaning International Union, AFL-CIO	22	a	20	15	11	11	11	8	y
Letter Carriers, National Association of	100	130	151	186	210	210	210	210	210
Locomotive Engineers, Brotherhood of				19	i	19	21	26	ab
Longshoremen's Association, AFL-CIO, International		50	60	65	61	61	61	62	59
Longshore and Warehouse Union, International			36	j	32	j	35	37	34
Machinists and Aerospace Workers, International Association of	627	663	780	520	448	411	446	452	339
Maintenance of Way Employes, Brotherhood of	159	77	71	61	31	29	29	29	ac
Marine Engineers' Beneficial Association					27	27	26	28	20
Maritime Union, National				21	21	13	q	q	q
Mine Workers of America, United				75	k	75	75	73	65
Musicians of the United States and Canada, American Federation of	250	225	215	67	35	33	25	15	7
Newspaper Guild, The	21	23	26	24	20	22	r	r	r
Novelty and Production Workers, International Union of Allied				23	20	19	18	17	10
Nurses, United American							93	v	8
Office and Professional Employees International Union	44	52	74	90	86	82	90	101	10
Oil, Chemical and Atomic Workers International Union	160	140	145	108	83	81	s	s	s
Painters and Allied Trades of the United States and Canada, International Union of	182	160	160	133	95	80	92	102	89
Paper, Allied-Industrial, Chemical and Energy Workers International Union						293	s	273	ad
Paperworkers International Union, United			275	232	233	230	s	s	s

Organizations	1955	1965	1975	1985	1995	1997	1999	2001	2005
Plasterers' and Cement Masons' International Association of the United States and Canada, Operative	60	68	55	46	29	28	29	29	30
Plate Printers, Die Stampers and Engravers Union of North America, International	1	1	1	1	1	1	1	1	1
Plumbing and Pipe Fitting Industry of the United States and Canada, United Association of Journeymen and Apprentices of the	200	217	228	226	220	220	220	220	220
Police Associations, International Union of			14	g	26	25	27	38	35
Postal Workers Union, AFL-CIO, American			249	232	261	277	279	271	233
Professional Athletes, Federation of			2	h	2	2	2	2	2
Professional and Technical Engineers, International Federation of			14	19	22	23	25	34	50
Radio Association, American	2	2	1	1	1	1	1	1	1
Retail, Wholesale and Department Store Union	97	114	118	106	76	72	t	t	t
Roofers, Waterproofers and Allied Workers, United Union of				26	21	20	21	21	19
School Administrators, American Federation of		7	e	9	11	11	12	12	14
School Employees Association, California							125	w	129
Seafarers International Union of North America	42	80	80	80	80	80	79	80	84
Service Employees International Union, AFL-CIO			480	688	1027	1037	1104	1272	1363
Sheet Metal Workers International Association	50	100	120	108	106	96	93	93	93
Signalmen, Brotherhood of Railroad	15	11	10	11	10	10	10	9	9
Stage Employees and Moving Pictures Technicians, Artists and Allied Crafts of the United States and Canada, International Alliance of Theatrical	46	50	50	50	51	48	48	56	62
State, County and Municipal Employees, American Federation of	99	237	647	997	1183	1242	1242	1258	1302
Steel, Paper and Forestry, Rubber, Manufacturing, Energy, Allied Industrial and Service Workers, United	980	876	1062	572	403	503	479	445	ad
Teachers, American Federation of	40	97	396	470	613	682	759	858	1032
Teamsters, International Brotherhood of				1285	l	1276	1238	1222	1288
Train Dispatchers Department, American	3	b	3	3	2	2	2	2	2
Transit Union, Amalgamated		98	90	94	95	97	102	110	120
Transport Workers Union of America	80	80	95	85	75	75	75	82	109
Transportation Communications International Union					58	64	67	92	53
Utility Workers Union of America	53	50	52	52	46	46	42	39	49
UNITE						235	210	208	aa
UNITE HERE									435
Writers Guild of America, East, Inc.				3	m	3	4	4	4

a   Charter granted 5/12/58.
b   Charter granted 1/29/57.
c   Disaffiliated 7/1/68. Reaffiliated 7/1/81.
d   Charter granted 2/21/72.
e   Charter granted to School Administrators and Supervisors Organizing Committee 2/22/71; chartered under present title 2/21/76.
f   Charter granted 2/23/84.
g   Charter granted 2/19/79.
h   Charter granted 11/14/79.
i   Charter granted 4/1/89.
j   Charter granted 8/22/88. Exonerated from per capita taxes for calendar year 1995.
k   Affiliated 10/1/89.
l   International Brotherhood of Teamsters, Chauffeurs, Warehousemen and Helpers affiliated 11/1/87.
m   Affiliated 8/19/89.
n   National Health and Human Service Employees Union affiliated 2/20/96, then merged with Service Employees International Union effective 4/1/98.
o   Charter granted 3/20/98.
p   Bakery, Confectionery and Tobacco Workers International Union merged with American Federation of Grain Millers to form Bakery, Confectionery, Tobacco Workers and Grain Millers International Union effective 1/1/99.
q   National Maritime Union affiliated with Marine Engineers' Beneficial Association effective 3/27/98; disaffiliated from MEBA and affiliated with Seafarers International Union of North America effective 1/1/99. Average members reported for the two-year period ended 6/99 does not include NMU members for which payment was received from MEBA during the nine-month period of NMU's affiliation with MEBA. NMU fully merged with Seafarers International Union of North America effective 3/16/01.
r   The Newspaper Guild merged with Communications Workers of America effective 7/1/97.
s   United Paperworkers International Union merged with Oil, Chemical and Atomic Workers International Union to form Paper, Allied-Industrial, Chemical and Energy Workers International Union effective 1/4/99.
t   Retail, Wholesale and Department Store Union merger with United Food and Commercial Workers International Union completed 10/1/98.
u   International Union of Electronic, Electrical, Salaried, Machine and Furniture Workers merged with Communications Workers of America effective 10/1/00.
v   United American Nurses affiliated 7/1/01.
w   California School Employees Association affiliated 8/1/01.
x   merged with Communications Workers of America effective 12/31/03.
y   merged with UNITE 10/1/02.
z   merged with United Steelworkers of America 7/1/03.
aa   merged to form UNITE HERE 7/12/04.
ab   merged with International Brotherhood of Teamsters 1/1/04.
ac   merged with International Brotherhood of Teamsters 1/1/05.
ad   merged to form United Steel, Paper and Forestry, Rubber, Manufacturing, Energy, Allied Industrial and Service Workers International Union 4/12/05.

Schedule No. 4

The following table shows the average per capita membership paid to the AFL-CIO by former affiliates for the year 1955 and subsequent two-year periods ending in 1965, 1975, 1985 and 1995. The totals are expressed in thousands of members.

Organizations	1955	1965	1975	1985	1995	
Agricultural Workers Organizing Committee AFL-CIO		2				Charter granted to Farm Workers Organizing Committee 8/23/66, bringing together Agricultural Workers Organizing Committee, AFL-CIO and Independent National Farm Workers Association.
Agricultural Workers Union, National		4				Merged into Amalgamated Meat Cutters and Butcher Workmen, 8/16/60.
Air Line Dispatchers Association		1	1	1		Dissolved, 4/1/77.
Aluminum Workers International Union		20	22	27		Merged to form Aluminum, Brick and Clay Workers, 7/23/81.
Aluminum, Brick and Clay Workers International Union						Merged to form Aluminum, Brick and Glass Workers, 9/1/82.
Aluminum, Brick and Glass Workers, International Union of				49	37	Merged with United Steelworkers of America, 12/17/96.
Automobile Workers of America, International Union, United	73					Title changed to Allied Industrial Workers of America, 5/1/56.
Bakery and Confectionery Workers International Union, American			75			Merged to form Bakery and Confectionery Workers International Union of America, 12/4/69.
Bakery and Confectionery Workers International Union of America		136	123			Expelled by convention 12/12/57. Merged with American Bakery and Confectionery Workers 12/4/69 to form Bakery and Confectionery Workers International Union of America; then merged to form Bakery, Confectionery and Tobacco Workers, 8/17/78.
Barbers and Beauty Culturists Union of America		3				Reaffiliated with Barbers, Hairdressers and Cosmetologists', 5/1/56.
Barbers, Hairdressers and Cosmetologists' International Union of America, The Journeymen		65	73	42		Merged with United Food and Commercial Workers, 9/1/80.
Bill Posters, Billers and Distributors of the United States and Canada, International Alliance of		2	1			Charter surrendered, 10/31/71.
Bookbinders, International Brotherhood of		51	57			Merged to form Graphic Arts International Union, 9/4/72.
Boot Shoe Workers' Union		40	40	34		Merged with Retail Clerks, 9/1/77.
Brewery, Flour, Cereal, Soft Drink and Distillery Workers, International Union of, United		45	42			Certificate of affiliation revoked, AFL-CIO convention, 10/19/73.
Brick and Clay Workers of America, The United		23	21	16		Merged to form Aluminum, Brick and Clay Workers, 7/23/81.
Broadcast Employees and Technicians, National Association of	4	4	5	5		Merged with Communications Workers of America, 1/1/94.
Broom and Whisk Makers Union, International		1				Disbanded, 8/22/63.
Building Service Employees International Union		205	305			Title changed to Service Employees International Union, 2/19/68.
Carpenters and Joiners of America, United Brotherhood of	750	700	700	609	378	Disaffiliated effective 3/29/01.
Cement, Lime and Gypsum Workers International Union, United		35	30	29		Merged with Boilermakers, Iron Ship Builders, Blacksmiths, Forgers and Helpers, 4/1/84.
Chemical Workers Union, International		79	70	58	40	34	Merged with United Food and Commercial Workers International Union, 7/1/96.
Cigarmakers' International Union of America		9	4	2		Merged with Retail, Wholesale and Department Store Union, 8/6/74.
Clerks, National Federation of Post Office		97				Merged with National Postal Transport Association 12/6/61 to become United Federation of Postal Clerks.
Clothing and Textile Workers Union, Amalgamated				228	129	Merged with International Ladies' Garment Workers Union to form Union of Needletrades, Industrial and Textile Employees, 7/1/95.

Organizations	1955	1965	1975	1985	1995	
Clothing Workers of America, Amalgamated	210	288	232			Merged to form Amalgamated Clothing and Textile Workers Union, 6/2/76.
Commercial Telegraphers Union, The	29	22				Title changed to Telegraph Workers, 2/19/68.
Coopers International Union of North America	3	2	2	1		Merged with Glass, Molders, Pottery, Plastics and Allied Workers International Union, 9/1/92.
Distillery, Rectifying, Wine and Allied Workers International Union of America	26	24	18			Title changed to Distillery, Wine and Allied Workers International Union, 2/27/78.
Distillery, Wine and Allied Workers International Union, AFL-CIO/CLC				14	8	Merged with United Food and Commercial Workers International Union, 10/4/95.
Dolls, Toys, Playthings, Novelties and Allied Products of the United States and Canada, AFL-CIO, International Union of	14	22	30			Title changed to Novelty Production Workers, 2/27/78.
Electrical, Radio and Machine Workers, International Union of	271	265	255			Title changed to Electronic, Electrical, Technical, Salaried and Machine Workers, AFL-CIO, International Union of, 7/83.
Electronic, Electrical, Technical, Salaried and Machine Workers, AFL-CIO, International Union of				198		Title changed to Electronic, Electrical, Salaried, Machine and Furniture Workers, AFL-CIO, International Union, 1/1/87.
Engravers and Marking Device Workers Union, International Metal		1				Merged into International Association of Machinists, 9/1/56.
Firemen and Oilers, International Brotherhood of	57	44	40	25		Merged with Service Employees International Union, 2/1/95.
Flight Engineers' International Association	1	1	2	1	1	Disbanded effective 12/31/00.
Furniture Workers of America, United	34	32	28	21		Merged to form Electronic, Electrical, Salaried, Machine and Furniture Workers, AFL-CIO, International Union, 1/1/87.
Garment Workers of America, United	40	35	32	28		Merged with United Food and Commercial Workers International Union, 12/1/94.
Garment Workers Union, International Ladies'	383	363	363	210	123	Merged with Amalgamated Clothing and Textile Workers Union to form Needletrades, Industrial and Textile Employees, 7/1/95.
Glass and Ceramic Workers of North America, United	41	33	28			Merged to form Aluminum, Brick and Glass Workers, 9/1/82.
Glass Bottle Blowers' Association of the United States and Canada	47	65	75			Merged to form Glass, Pottery, Plastics and Allied Workers, 9/1/82.
Glass Cutters League of America, Window	2	1	1			Merged with Glass Bottle Blowers, 8/1/75.
Glove Workers Union of America, International	3					Merged into Amalgamated Clothing Workers, 12/6/61.
Government and Civic Employees Organizing Committee	27					Merged into State, County and Municipal Employees, 8/1/56.
Granite Cutters International Association of America, The	4	3	1			Merged with Tile, Marble, Terrazzo, Finishers and Shopmen, 5/23/83 (Retroactive to 1/7/80).
Graphic Arts International Union			93			Merged to form Graphic Communications International Union, 7/1/83.
Hatters, Cap and Millinery Workers International Union, United	32	32	15			Merged into Amalgamated Clothing and Textile Workers Union, 12/7/82.
Hod Carriers, Building and Common Laborers Union of America, International	372					Title changed to Laborers' International Union, 9/20/65.
Horseshoers of United States and Canada, International Union of Journeyman	1	1	1	1	1	Dissolved effective 11/03.
Hosiery Workers, American Federation of	15	5				Merged with Textile Workers Union of America, 4/28/65.
Hospital and Health Care Employees, National Union of				23		Charter granted 10/1/84; merged with Service Employees International Union and American Federation of State, County and Municipal Employees, 6/1/89.
Industrial Workers of America, International Union, Allied		71	93	63		Merged with United Paperworkers International, 1/1/94.
Insurance Agents International Union	13					Merged into Insurance Workers International Union, 5/18/59.

Organizations	1955	1965	1975	1985	1995	
Insurance Workers of America	9					Merged into Insurance Workers International Union, 5/18/59.
Insurance Workers International Union, AFL-CIO		21	22			Merged with United Food and Commercial Workers International Union, 10/1/83.
Jewelry Workers Union, International	20	14	10			Merged with Service Employees International Union, 7/1/80.
Lathers, International Union of Wood, Wire and Metal	16	16	12			Merged with United Brotherhood of Carpenters and Joiners, 8/16/79.
Leather Goods, Plastics and Novelty Workers Union, International	30	34	39	21	5	Merged with Service Employees International Union, 5/1/96.
Leather Workers International Union of North America	2	5	2	1		Suspended in accordance with Article XV, Section 5, of the AFL-CIO Constitution.
Lithographers and Photoengravers International Union			30*			*Affiliated for only part of period although membership shown is average for 24-month period. Merged to form Graphic Arts International Union, 9/24/72.
Lithographers of America, Amalgamated	28					Disaffiliated, 8/21/58.
Locomotive Firemen and Enginemen, Brotherhood of		41				Merged into United Transportation Union, 12/16/68.
Longshoremen, International Brotherhood of	8					Merged into Longshoremen's Association, 11/17/59.
Marble, Slate and Stone Polishers, Rubbers and Sawyers, Tile & Marble Setters Helpers and Terrazzo Helpers, International Association of	6	8	8			Title changed to Tile, Marble, Terrazzo, Finishers and Shopmen, 2/20/76.
Marine Engineers' Beneficial Association, National	9	9	20	22		At its 2/95 meeting, the AFL-CIO Executive Council agreed that henceforth the National Marine Engineers' Beneficial Association would become two separate entities: the Marine Engineers' Beneficial Association and the National Maritime Union.
Marine and Shipbuilding Workers of America, Industrial Union of	27	22	22	17		Merged into International Association of Machinists and Aerospace Workers, 10/17/88.
Maritime Union of America, National	37	45	35	17		Merged with National Marine Engineers' Beneficial Association, 3/29/88.
Masters, Mates and Pilots, International Organization of	9	9				Merged with Longshoremen's Association, 5/12/71.
Master Mechanics and Foremen of Navy Yards and Naval Stations, National Association of	1					Withdrew, 4/1/64.
Mechanics Educational Society of America	49	37	23	5	3	Merged with United Automobile, Aerospace & Agricultural Implement Workers International Union, 1/1/97.
Meat Cutters and Butcher Workmen of North America, Amalgamated	263	330	450			Merged to form United Food and Commercial Workers International Union, 8/8/79.
Metal Polishers, Buffers, Platers and Allied Workers International Union	15	11	9	5	3	Merged with International Brotherhood of Boilermakers, Iron Ship Builders, Blacksmiths, Forgers and Helpers, 12/1/96.
Molders and Allied Workers Union, AFL-CIO, International	67	50	50	32		Merged with Glass, Molders, Pottery, Plastics and Allied Workers International Union, 5/1/88.
Packinghouse, Food and Allied Workers, United	118	71				Merged with Meat Cutters and Butcher Workmen, 7/9/68.
Paper Makers, International Brotherhood of	60					Merged into Papermakers and Paperworkers, 3/6/57.
Paper Workers of America, United	40					Merged into Papermakers and Paperworkers, 3/6/57.
Papermakers and Paperworkers, United		121				Merged to form United Paperworkers International Union, 8/9/72.
Pattern Makers League of North America	11	10	10	8		Merged with International Association of Machinists and Aerospace Workers, 10/1/91.
Photo Engravers Union of North America, International	16					Merged into Lithographers and Photoengravers, 9/7/64.
Porters, Brotherhood of Sleeping Car	10	5	1			Merged with Brotherhood of Railway, Airline and Steamship Clerks, Freight Handlers, Express and Station Employees, 4/1/78.

Organizations	1955	1965	1975	1985	1995	
Post Office and General Service Maintenance Employees, National Association						Merged to form American Postal Workers Union, 7/1/71.
Post Office Mail Handlers, Watchmen, Messengers and Group Leaders, National Association of	1	1				Merged with Laborers, 4/20/68.
Post Office Motor Vehicle Employees, National Federation of	5					Merged to form American Postal Workers Union, 7/1/71.
Postal Transport Association, National	22					Merged with National Federation of Post Office Clerks, 12/6/61, to become United Federation of Postal Clerks.
Postal Clerks, United Federation of		117				Merged to form American Postal Workers Union, 7/1/71.
Pottery and Allied Workers, International Brotherhood of	23	19	17			Affiliated with Seafarers, 6/21/76; merged to form Glass, Pottery, Plastics and Allied Workers, 9/1/82.
Printing and Graphic Communications Union, International			105			Merged to form Graphic Communications International Union, 7/1/83.
Printing Pressmen's and Assistants' Union of North America, International	87	100				Merged to form Printing and Graphic Communications Union, 10/17/73.
Pulp, Sulphite and Paper Mill Workers of the United States and Canada, International Brotherhood of	154	135				Merged to form United Paperworkers International Union, 8/9/72.
Radio and Television Directors Guild	1					Disaffiliated, 1/1/60.
Railroad Telegraphers, The Order of	30					Title changed to Transportation-Communication Employees Union, 2/25/65.
Railroad Trainmen, Brotherhood of	98					Merged into United Transportation Union, 12/16/68.
Railway Carmen of the United States and Canada, Brotherhood of	116	84	56	33		Merged with Brotherhood of Railway, Airline and Steamship Clerks, Freight Handlers, Express and Station Employees, 8/6/86.
Railway, Airline and Steamship Clerks, Freight Handlers, Express and Station Employees, Brotherhood of	264	186	160	102		Title Changed to Transportation Communications Union, 9/1/87.
Railway Patrolmen's International Union	3	2				Merged with Brotherhood of Railway, Airline and Steamship Clerks, Freight Handlers, Express and Station Employees, 1/1/69.
Railway Supervisors Association, American	6	6				Merged with Brotherhood of Railway, Airline and Steamship Clerks, Freight Handlers, Express and Station Employees, 8/6/80.
Retail Clerks International Union	259	410	602			Merged to form United Food and Commercial Workers, 8/8/79.
Roofers, Damp and Waterproof Workers Association, United Slate, Tile and Composition	18	22	27			Title changed to Roofers, Waterproofers and Allied Workers, 8/7/78.
Rubber, Cork, Linoleum and Plastics Workers of America, United	163	153	173	106	79	Merged with International Brotherhood of Boilermakers, Iron Ship Builders, Blacksmiths, Forgers and Helpers, 12/1/96.
Shoe Workers of America, United	51	45	25			Merged with Amalgamated Clothing and Textile Workers Union, 3/5/79.
Siderographers, International Association of	1	1	1	1		Merged with International Association of Machinists and Aerospace Workers, 9/15/92.
Special Delivery Messengers, The National Association of	2	1				Merged to form American Postal Workers Union, 7/1/71.
Stereotypers', Electrotypers' and Platemakers' Union, International	12	11				Merged to form Printing and Graphic Communications Union, 10/17/73.
Stone and Allied Products Workers of America, United	11	11				Merged with Steelworkers, 11/1/72.
Stonecutters Association of North America, Journeymen	2	2				Merged with Laborers' International Union, 2/19/68.
Stove, Furnace and Allied Appliance Workers International Union of North America	10	9	3	3		Merged with International Brotherhood of Boilermakers, Iron Ship Builders, Blacksmiths, Forgers and Helpers, 10/1/94.
Street and Electric Railway Employees of America, Amalgamated Association of	139					Title changed to Amalgamated Transit Union, 2/5/61.

Organizations	1955	1965	1975	1985	1995	
Switchmen's Union of North America	11	9				Merged into United Transportation Union, 12/16/68.
Technical Engineers, American Federation of	10	11				Title changed to Professional and Technical Engineers, 5/73.
Telegraph Workers, United			12	9		Merged into Communications Workers of America, 10/17/86.
Textile Workers of America, United	49	36	36	23	15	Merged with United Food and Commercial Workers, International Union, 11/1/95.
Textile Workers Union of America	203	123	105			Merged to form Amalgamated Clothing and Textile Workers Union, 6/2/76.
Tile, Marble, Terrazzo, Finishers, Shop Workers and Granite Cutters International Union				7		Merged into United Brotherhood of Carpenters and Joiners, 11/10/88.
Tobacco Workers International Union	27	24	26			Merged to form Bakery, Confectionery and Tobacco Workers, 8/17/78.
Transport Service Employees of America, United	3	3				Merged with Brotherhood of Railway, Airline and Steamship Clerks, Freight Handlers, Express and Station Employees, 10/1/72.
Transportation-Communication Employees Union		29				Merged with Brotherhood of Railway, Airline and Steamship Clerks, Freight Handlers, Express and Station Employees, 2/21/69.
Typographic Union, International	78	87	73	38		Merged with Communications Workers of America, 1/1/87.
Upholsterers' International Union of North America	51	50	50	31		Merged with Steelworkers, 10/8/85.
Wallpaper Craftsmen and Workers of North America, United	1					Merged with Pulp, Sulphite and Paper Mill Workers, 4/28/58.
Weavers Protective Association, American Wire	1					Merged with Papermakers and Paperworkers, 2/16/58.
Woodworkers of America International	91	49	52	34		Merged with International Association of Machinists and Aerospace Workers, 5/1/94.
Yardmasters of America, Railroad	4	4	4	3		Merged with United Transportation Union, 10/1/85.

Appendix D. Reports Required Under the LMRDA and the CSRA

Union Reports

Form Number and Name	Report Required to be Filed by	Signatures Required	When Due
Form LM-1 (initial) Labor Organization Information Report	Each union subject to the LMRDA or CSRA	President and secretary or corresponding principal officers of the reporting union	Within 90 days after the union becomes subject to the LMRDA or CSRA
Form LM-1 (amended) Labor Organization Information Report	Each reporting union (except Federal employee unions) which made changes in practices and procedures listed in Item 18 of Form LM-1 which are not contained in the union's constitution and bylaws	President and treasurer or corresponding principal officers of the reporting union	With union's Form LM-2, LM-3, or LM-4 within 90 days after the end of the union's fiscal year during which the changes were made
Form LM-2* Labor Organization Annual Report	Each reporting union with total annual receipts of $250,000 or more ($200,000 or more for fiscal years beginning before July 1, 2004) and by the parent union for subordinate unions under trusteeship	President and treasurer or corresponding principal officers of the reporting union or, if under trusteeship at time of filing, by the president and treasurer or corresponding principal officers of the parent union, and trustees of the subordinate union	Within 90 days after the end of the union's fiscal year or, if the union loses its reporting identity through dissolution, merger, consolidation, or otherwise, within 30 days after date of termination
Form LM-3* Labor Organization Annual Report	Each reporting union with total annual receipts of less than $250,000 (less than $200,000 for fiscal years beginning before July 1, 2004) may use the simplified Form LM-3 if not in trusteeship	President and treasurer or corresponding principal officers of the reporting union	Within 90 days after the end of the union's fiscal year or, if the union loses its reporting identity through dissolution, merger, consolidation, or otherwise, within 30 days after date of termination

Ed. Note: Copies of reports for the years 2000 and later may be viewed at http://www.union-reports.dol.gov.

Source: U.S. Department of Labor, *available at* http://www.dol.gov/esa/regs/compliance/olms/rrlo/repreq.htm (last visited May 9, 2006).

Union Reports (continued)

Form LM-4* Labor Organization Annual Report	Each reporting union with total annual receipts of less than $10,000 may use the abbreviated Form LM-4 if not in trusteeship	President and treasurer or corresponding principal officers of the reporting union	Within 90 days after the end of the union's fiscal year or, if the union loses its reporting identity through dissolution, merger, consolidation, or otherwise, within 30 days after date of termination

Ed. Note: Copies of reports for the years 2000 and later may be viewed at http://www.union-reports.dol.gov.

Union Trusteeship Reports

Form Number and Name	Report Required to be Filed by	Signatures Required	When Due
Form LM-15 (initial) Trusteeship Report (including Statement of Assets and Liabilities)	Each parent union which imposes a trusteeship over a subordinate union	President and treasurer or corresponding principal officers of the parent union, and trustees of the subordinate union	Within 30 days after imposing the trusteeship
Form LM-15 (semiannual) Trusteeship Report (excluding Statement of Assets and Liabilities)	Each parent union which continues a trusteeship over a subordinate union for 6 months or more	President and treasurer or corresponding principal officers of the parent union, and trustees of the subordinate union	Within 30 days after the end of each 6-month period during the trusteeship
Form LM-15A Report on Selection of Delegates and Officers	Each parent union which imposes a trusteeship over a subordinate union if during the trusteeship the parent union held any convention or other policy-determining body to which the subordinate union sent delegates or would have sent delegates if not in trusteeship, or the parent union conducted an election of officers	President and treasurer or corresponding principal officers of the parent union, and trustees of the subordinate union	As required, with Form LM-15 within 30 days after the imposition of the trusteeship or end of each 6-month period, or with Form LM-16 within 90 days after the end of the trusteeship or the subordinate union's loss of reporting identity through dissolution, merger, consolidation, or otherwise
Form LM-16 Terminal Trusteeship Report	Each parent union which ends a trusteeship over a subordinate union or if the union in trusteeship loses its reporting identity	President and treasurer or corresponding principal officers of the parent union, and trustees of the subordinate union	Within 90 days after the end of the trusteeship or the subordinate union's loss of reporting identity through dissolution, merger, consolidation, or otherwise

Other Reports

Form Number and Name	Report Required to be Filed by	Signatures Required	When Due
Form LM-10 Employer Report	Each employer which engages in certain specified financial dealings with its employees, unions, union officers, or labor relations consultants or which makes expenditures for certain objects relating to employees' or unions' activities	President and treasurer or corresponding principal officers of the reporting employer	Within 90 days after the end of the employer's fiscal year
Form LM-20 Agreement and Activities Report	Each person who enters into an agreement or arrangement with an employer to persuade employees about exercising their rights to organize and bargain collectively, or to obtain information about employee or union activity in connection with a labor dispute involving the employer	President and treasurer or corresponding principal officers of the consultant firm or, if self-employed, the individual required to file the report	Within 30 days after entering into such agreement or arrangement
Form LM-21 Receipts and Disbursements Report	Each person who enters into an agreement or arrangement with an employer to persuade employees about exercising their rights to organize and bargain collectively, or to obtain information about employee or union activity in connection with a labor dispute involving the employer	President and treasurer or corresponding principal officers of the consultant firm or, if self-employed, the individual required to file the report	Within 90 days after the end of the consultant's fiscal year
Form LM-30 Labor Organization Officer and Employee Report	Each union officer (including trustees of subordinate unions under trusteeship) and employee (other than employees performing exclusively clerical or custodial services), if the officer/employee, or the officer/employee's spouse, or minor child directly or indirectly had certain economic interests during past fiscal year	Union officers and employees required to file such reports	Within 90 days after the end of the union officer's or employee's fiscal year
Form S-1 Surety Company Annual Report	Each surety company having a bond in force insuring a welfare or pension plan covered by ERISA, or insuring any union or trust in which a union covered by the LMRDA is interested	President and treasurer or corresponding principal officers of the surety company	Within 150 days after the end of the surety company's fiscal year

Web Sites Index

Abbreviations Index

Officers and Key Staff Index

Labor Organizations Index